PRIMULA

PRIMULA

JOHN RICHARDS

Illustrations by Brigid Edwards

Timber Press
Portland, Oregon

First published 1993
New edition published 2003

ISBN 0-88192-580-2

A CIP record for this book is available from the Library of Congress.

Printed in Singapore by Kyodo Printing Co.

First published in the UK by B T Batsford, London.

Published in North America in 2003 by
Timber Press, Inc.
The Haseltine Building
133 S.W. Second Avenue, Suite 450
Portland, Oregon 97204, U.S.A.

www.timberpress.com

Contents

Acknowledgements

I wish to thank the following people for their contributions, conscious or unwitting, which have helped in the writing of this book.

The first edition was originally commissioned for Christopher Helm by Graham Rice in 1988, and after the title had passed to B.T. Batsford, its publication was overseen by Tim Auger and expedited by Marion Boddy-Evans. I am grateful to Tina Persaud of Chrysalis Books for suggesting that a completely rewritten second edition, with some new plates, should be prepared, and for seeing this through to press.

Graham Rice particularly noted that of all the previous volumes on *Primula*, none had high-quality colour illustrations. Consequently, Brigid Edwards was commissioned to prepare a set of paintings of primula species from life. She undertook this at a relatively early stage in a meteorically successful career as a botanical artist, and once again I should like to thank her for her magnificent illustrations which subsequently formed the centre-piece of an Exhibition at Kew. Brigid's work was only made possible by the generous cooperation of many growers. Foremost amongst these was Tony Hall of Kew who took a close interest in Brigid's work throughout.

A number of colour photographs are published here with the generous permission of the photographers, who are individually acknowledged on the plates.

My interest in *Primula* was first kindled by Jack Crosby at the University of Durham, and was later renewed by Stan Woodell at the University of Oxford. In later years, I was fortunate to know several of the Scottish growers of fine primulas, such as Betty Sherriff, Bobby Masterton, David Livingstone and Alec Duguid, who helped me in many ways.

I should also like to express my gratitude to those research students at the University of Newcastle who, under my supervision, undertook research projects based on *Primula:* Halijah bt. Ibrahim, Fran Wedderburn, Hussen Al Wadi, Valsa Kurian, Juno McKee, Liz Arnold and Michelle Tremayne.

In recent years, I have benefited from discussions with other workers who have been concerned with the evolution of *Primula*, or of heterostyly and homostyly, notably Sylvia (Tass) Kelso, Ulla-Maj Hultgaard, Susan Mazer, Phil Gilmartin, Elena Conti, Austin Mast, Fabienne van Rossum, Pam Eveleigh, and David Winstanley, who painstakingly translated much of Ernst's classic works from the German for me.

I am coauthor with Tass, Elena and others in Austin's massive DNA study and I am grateful to Austin and the other authors for permission to publish diagrams from this.

During taxonomic investigations, I was greatly helped by the authorities at the Natural History Museum, the Royal Botanic Gardens at Kew and Edinburgh, and Gothenburg Botanic Garden, who have given me free access to their material.

A number of people have sent their thoughts, criticisms, additions or corrections to the first edition or to early drafts of the second edition, and in particular I would like to mention Chris Chadwell, David Rankin and Pam Eveleigh in this context. In addition a number of people, notably Anne Chambers, Tony Cox, the Miehes, David Rankin, Susan Maxwell, Henrik Zetterlund, Harry Jans, John and Hilary Birks, David Milward, Mike Hirst, Philip Cribb and Chris Grey-Wilson, but a number of others as well, have sent me records and/or photographic material to identify, usually from China.

Amongst the books published on *Primula* in

recent years, the present work owes a deep debt of gratitude to Fenderson (1986) and Smith *et al.* (1984). In particular, the latter work reviews the European species with such thoroughness that I have found it difficult to improve on the accounts there. The descriptions and Jarmila Haldova's inspirational illustrations in Josef Halda's *The Genus Primula in cultivation and the wild* (1992) have been a source of reference during the preparation of both editions, particularly for its access to Chinese material which became more readily available after the English version of the Chinese Flora was published.

Finally, it must be emphasized that the present work still depends heavily on Smith and Fletcher's great monograph. Over the intervening 60 years, many advances in the study of primulas have been made, and the present work differs from theirs in very many particulars. Nevertheless, their pioneering work had a great impact on studies on the genus. Without it, the present book could not have been written.

Introduction to the first edition

Primula is one of the three great garden genera. In terms of the number of varieties grown, the income generated by the horticultural industry, or its hold over the hearts and minds of the public, only *Rhododendron* and *Rosa* can compare with it.

Primulas are also familiar plants in the European countryside. In particular, the primrose and cowslip are delightful spring plants held in much affection by all visitors to the countryside, and greatly celebrated in prose and verse.

Primula is also one of the largest and most widespread of all genera. Approximately 430 species are distributed throughout the moister and cooler regions of the northern hemisphere. By far the greatest concentration of species is found in the great mountain chain of the Himalaya and western China. No less than 334 species are found in this region, some 78 per cent of the total. In China, more than 50 species grow on some mountains, an extraordinary concentration. The genus is classified into 37 sections, and of these, no less than 24 sections (65 per cent) are confined to the Sinohimalaya, while all except six sections (84 per cent) are found there. By way of contrast, Europe has only 34 species, classified into four sections, while north America has 20 species classified into five sections.

Primula is of equal fascination to the gardener and the botanist. Most species are beautiful, and although many are difficult to maintain in cultivation, some have proved to be very important as garden or house plants. To the horticultural trade, the primula industry is worth many millions of dollars annually.

For well over a century, evolutionists from Darwin to Darlington have been fascinated by the genetical and evolutionary implications of the pin and thrum flowered (heterostylous) mating system in *Primula*. This has resulted in hundreds of scientific publications, which continue to be produced as I write.

It is not surprising that such a charismatic genus has attracted previous authors. I am aware of at least 25 previous books devoted solely to *Primula*, and indeed I am responsible for one myself. The question must be asked 'why is another needed?'

In this book, there are several approaches, which I hope will prove new and valuable. I believed that a full account of all the species of *Primula* should be brought together in a single book. Previously, this has only been attempted by Smith and Fletcher's great monograph of the genus. This originally appeared over some seven years in ten scientific papers scattered through three journals. Although these were reprinted within a single volume in 1977, the monograph remains a scientific work rather inaccessible to non-botanists.

Sixty years have now elapsed since the monograph was published. In that time there have been major advances in the taxonomy, classification and cultivation of primulas. Most of the evolutionary and genetic studies in the genus have also appeared in the last 60 years.

Since Smith and Fletcher, important areas of the Himalaya, particularly Nepal, have become freely accessible for the first time. During these years, China effectively closed its gates to western travellers, and then opened them again. The last decade has witnessed a resurgence in the cultivation and understanding of the great wealth of western Chinese species. Much of this work has proceeded within China, and an account of *Primula* for the Flora of China by Professor Hu and the American Sylvia Kelso has appeared

In America, too, studies have advanced. Remarkably, no less than five new species have been described from there in the last 30 years.

Today, we have the benefit of new collections, modern insights into the nature of plant variation, and a wider experience of species in the wild and in cultivation. As a result, other workers and myself have made taxonomic and nomenclatural decisions, which, at times, vary widely from those of Smith and Fletcher. Consequently, it is hoped that this book can be considered as a modern taxonomic revision of the whole genus. Although Halda's (1992) recent book covers all the species and incorporates many taxonomic and classificatory changes, it does so in the absence of critical discussions or explanations.

This volume inevitably concentrates on the species. In recent years, several excellent books have appeared that concentrate on the cultivars of *Primula*. In the present work, some cultivars are mentioned under the sections of species accounts which discuss variation, but on the whole a greater emphasis is given to the species and varieties found in the wild.

In the systematic account, I have tried to dovetail evolutionary considerations into the taxonomy and classification. In *Primula*, we are fortunate that features of the breeding system, cytology and morphology are relatively informative with respect to the nature of some of the evolutionary mechanisms and pathways through which the genus has diversified.

In recent years there has been a surge in interest in the evolution and functioning of the curious pin and thrum flowered mating system in *Primula*. The breakdown of this system, giving rise to self-fertile homostyles, has also been intensively studied. We now know that both primary homostyles and secondary homostyles are found in *Primula,* and this information has resulted in several evolutionary insights.

Much of the cytological work in the genus had been completed by the time of Smith and Fletcher (chiefly in Bruun's great monograph published in 1932). However, those authors placed little stress on the cytological data, and modern insights into the interplay between the chromosomes and classification have radically altered some of our concepts, particularly at the sectional level.

Equally significant has been the role played by the use of the scanning electron microscope when applied to the study of pollen morphology. With respect to the classification of *Primula,* this new information has provided major new insights. Particularly when used in conjunction with cytological data, our ideas about the evolution and classification of the genus *Primula* have often been radically altered. The Norwegian Per Wendelbo and the German Otto Schwarz both deserve credit for their pioneer work in this field.

In attempting to write a book accessible to gardeners and botanists alike, I have tried to cross the gulf supposed to lie between them. By profession I am an evolutionary botanist, who has, together with six research students, worked on the *Primula* breeding system for some 25 years. By inclination, I am a gardener who has at various times grown (and usually lost!) about 160 species of *Primula* in the relatively amenable climate of northern England.

I have developed a great respect for the knowledge and expertise of the specialist gardener. In no way do I agree with the commonly held sentiment that gardeners are not interested in, and should not be exposed to, botanical information. Further, I believe that the botanist has a great deal to learn from the experiences and observations of the gardener. In this book I have tried to marry botanical and horticultural information in such a way that both camps may benefit.

To take one of many examples, information on the fertility of self-pollinations of pin flowers or of thrum flowers for a species mostly originates from scientific studies. Yet, this information is plainly of interest to the gardener. Furthermore, the gardener may acquire similar information which is new to the botanist.

There are other areas of equal interest to the botanist and the gardener, for instance hybridization, the history of introductions to cultivation, and ecological information.

We have tried to produce a book which will be attractive to own and use. A number of books on *Primula* contain some line drawings of the species. These are sometimes excellent, for instance the late Duncan Lowe's drawings in *Primulas of Europe and North America*, and Jarmila Haldova's drawings in Halda (1992). However, this is not always the case. Remarkably, although several books on *Primula* contain colour photographs, none have coloured illustrations. Brigid Edwards has produced for this volume an extremely beautiful set of paintings of most of the species most frequently seen in cultivation today. In my view, these will rank highly in the annals of botanical illustration, and they add immeasurably to the quality of this book.

We have also added a number of colour photographs. For these, I have concentrated on little-known species which have rarely been illustrated. Where possible, these photographs are taken in the wild and are selected to show the habitat. Most of these have never been published before. In many of the previous books on *Primula*, much of the book has been occupied by chapters on cultivation, hybridization, cultivars, and pests and diseases, with only a relatively short section being devoted to systematic accounts of a selection of the species.

For the present volume, I have written four relatively short introductory chapters on the history of the exploration and cultivation of *Primula,* on the cultivation of *Primula*, on the evolutionary history of *Primula* and some of its relatives, and on heterostyly and homostyly. However, much of the book is taken up with the systematic section, where many of these questions are addressed in more detail, as they apply to the various species.

However diverse the genus is, many features of the cultivation, biology or ecology of a species become more uniform when the species within a single section are considered. Characteristics which tend to be common to all the species within a section are given a detailed treatment in the sectional account. These features are only further mentioned in the species accounts where more detailed information is available, or when the species is in some way different from its relatives. It follows that if readers wish to refer to a particular topic in this book, it may pay them first to consult the sectional account before turning to the actual species concerned.

Readers should note that the systematic account is preceded by a guide to the structure and conventions used in each species account. Also, where unfamiliar terms are encountered, a glossary is provided (p.327).

Introduction to the second edition

As I write this, almost ten years have elapsed since I wrote the introduction to the first edition. If I queried then why yet another book on *Primula* was needed, it would be easy to support those who question the need of a further edition now. However, the first edition was on the whole well received and it sold well, so that it achieved a scarcity value a few years after it was first published, second-hand prices at times greatly exceeding the recommended shelf price. An ongoing demand caused kind friends to suggest to the publishers that the book should be reprinted. B.T. Batsford suggested to me in May 2001 that I might consider preparing a wholly new edition.

I was keen to undertake this revision for a number of reasons. Most importantly, great scientific advances in the study of *Primula* had been made during the intervening decade. First amongst these have been the intensive DNA studies, during which nearly a quarter of the species have been examined. In the first edition, I used deduction, intuition and guesswork as I attempted to elucidate evolutionary pathways and biological relationships between species and sections. Now these speculations have been completely superseded by incontrovertible evidence of these relationships. There are some weaknesses in this evidence; many key species are missing which might change the closeness (but not the direction) of some relationships. The evidence only informs us on maternally inherited relationships; and some of the conclusions are as yet tentative. Nevertheless, these studies provide us with a massive step forward, and I have depended heavily on this new evidence in the preparation of this new account.

Fortunately, few major taxonomic upheavals have resulted. The DNA evidence has largely agreed with our sectional concepts, and species affiliations, and in most cases it has also supported our previous conclusions about evolutionary pathways and higher order relationships between sections. This has been gratifying, so that on the few occasions when the evidence from the DNA completely disagreed with previous concepts, the new evidence has been accepted with acclamation (perhaps most strikingly in the discovery that the Dryadifolia should be placed in subgenus *Auganthus,* not *Aleuritia,* while the Pinnatae should be transferred in the reverse direction).

A good deal of progress has also been made in the study of heterostyly in *Primula*. Although the molecular structure of the heterostyly supergene remains as a challenge for future generations, work by Valsa Kurian, and a reworking of Ernst's original data by two doyens of population genetics, themselves almost of Ernst's generation, have revealed more of the complexity of this miracle of evolution.

We have also learnt much more about plants in the wild and in cultivation in the last ten years. Towards the end of the decade we received the astounding news that three new species of *Primula* had been described, not from some remote Asian fastness, but from Italy. The status of one of these, *P. grignensis*, requires confirmation, but I have included two of them here, and one, *P. albenensis*, is a remarkably distinct new discovery which has now settled into cultivation.

As I went to press in 1992, the initial results

of the first of the great Sino-European expeditions to western China, known by the acronym CLD, were becoming known. Since then we have had in rapid succession KGB, ACE, SQAE, ARGS and collections by a number of private individuals during the 1990s. Also, a number of organizations have organised tours to this extremely rich region, and even to south-east Tibet. I myself was able to visit north-west Yunnan in 1995, seeing 30 species, and this visit alone led to new insights on the status of *P. zambalensis, P. pulchelloides, P. nanobella* and others. Some herbarium material has come back, and some seed was introduced, some of which is still grown. But, especially, we have been flooded with high-quality colour photographs of plants, many of which were scarcely understood at the time and previously had seemed almost mythical. Even more importantly, we have been provided with a medium scarcely dreamt of a decade ago. Any traveller can now scan his photographs, or use a digital camera, and display his results to the world, on the web. A Canadian enthusiast, Pam Eveleigh, deserves great credit for dedicating her IT skills to the furtherance of our knowledge of *Primula* through her website www.primulaworld.com,which is a wonderful source of information on the genus. Her scholarship and research has resulted in the deserved success of this site and could be taken as an object lesson.

Another advantage of IT has been that I have been able to prepare this second edition using the original text already on disk. As a consequence, it has been relatively easy to incorporate changes of various magnitude throughout the book. Few passages of the original edition have survived unscathed, and much of the original edition has been completely rewritten, often including the plant descriptions. Another innovation has been the introduction of identification keys. Several reviewers, and a number of private individuals since, have commented that the usefulness of the first edition was limited by the absence of sectional keys. In many sections, I was originally disinclined to prepare identification keys because our state of knowledge at that time was inadequate. I have now written keys for all the sections except the still very poorly known Obconicolisteri. This discipline has also led to a better understanding of species descriptions, distinctions and limits, so that many diagnoses have benefited considerably.

I am delighted that Brigid Edwards' superb plates and her text drawings will continue to grace the present edition. This edition also contains the original 51 photographs by a number of photographers. Many of these are also superb, and I am glad that we are using them again. I would have liked to have replaced those few, mostly taken by the author, which are less than superb, but this would have involved a considerable increase in shelf price. Instead, I am delighted that I have been able to add more than 30 new images, mostly of species scarcely known in 1992, again by a variety of photographers. I hope that the result will be an attractive book which has been brought up to date, is mostly new, and in my view has been greatly improved, which I hope provides sufficient justification for its publication.

A Short History of the Exploration, Introduction and Cultivation of *Primula*

The origins of cultivated primulas are lost in the mists of time. From Elizabethan sources we know that complex hybrid derivatives of the primrose and cowslip, now called 'polyanthus', already formed an important component of many English knot gardens. Varieties of the primrose, some of them floral mutations such as 'Jack in the Green' and 'Hose in Hose' were also popular. Early primrose varieties are often known today as 'old-fashioned primroses'.

From the even earlier writings of Clusius, Gerard and others we know that central Europeans had by then also hybridized the yellow 'bear's ear', *P. auricula*, and the rose-coloured *P. hirsuta* from the Alps. These hybrids, the 'garden auricula', *P.* × *pubescens,* were popular plants for pots and parterres in the sixteenth century.

Garden Auriculas formed the subject of the next primula enthusiasm. As country folk mass-migrated into the new northern towns of the British Industrial Revolution, they found that the Auricula stood up to the sooty, acrid conditions better than many plants. Manure from the thousands of urban working horses was freely available, and formed the basis of complex, often secret composts and feeding rituals which fostered the cultivation of these remarkable plants. Many new, often startling varieties were bred, in which the paste-white foliage showed off the brilliantly or weirdly coloured flowers to great effect. Greenish flowers were as popular as the sealing-wax reds and velvetly blues, often set off by the mealy 'eye' of the flower.

The social life of the Lancashire mill-towns in the Victorian era often revolved around the many Auricula societies and their shows, where considerable sums of money could be won.

The modern Auricula is very much an invention of the English Working Class. Possibly, this is still reflected today in the archaic rules of some societies that Auriculas with 'paste' on the flowers are deemed unsuitable for exhibition, except sometimes in special classes. However, by the end of the nineteenth century, the big houses had often espoused the cause of the workers' Auricula, to the extent that elaborate 'theatres' with shelves and a matt-black background were specifically built to show them off in flower.

While the Europeans were breeding the hybrids of the primrose and the bears-ear, the Chinese and Japanese had equally developed a few of their own native species. When the horticultural riches of eastern Asia were first explored by Europeans in the early nineteenth century, they discovered that *P. sinensis* and *P. sieboldii* were being grown in a wide variety of forms, suggesting that they had been in cultivation for many centuries.

However, it fell to Europeans to introduce and breed the popular twentieth-century house-plants *P. obconica* and *P. malacoides.* Doubtless, those areas of western China where the great richness of primula species was later discovered by Europeans were as remote to the civilized, gardening eastern Asians as they were to the early European explorers.

The stage is now set for the great era of Sino-Himalayan exploration which revealed to the world the astonishingly rich primula flora of these regions.

The first botanical explorations were made into the western Himalaya, then part of 'British India', which was becoming a popular resort for the Raj in the early nineteenth century. The most important botanist there was not in fact British, but Austrian. Nathanial Wallich (1786–1854) became Superintendent of Calcutta Botanic Garden. Other botanists who discovered new primulas in the north-west Himalaya in the first half of the nineteenth century included J.F. Royle (1779–1858) and David Don (1799–1841).

By far the most important botanical explorer of the Himalaya in the nineteenth century was the younger of the 'Hookers of Kew', Sir Joseph (1817–1911). Sir Joseph was destined to become one of the most influential botanists of all time. At the age of 31, he already had a distinguished record of botanical exploration in the Southern Hemisphere, when, under the sponsorship of his father Sir William, he visited the central Himalaya. Based at Calcutta Botanic Garden, he made two expeditions into Sikkim, and a third to Assam (1848–51). Here he distinguished himself by reaching what was believed to be the highest point reached by man (5800 m, 19,000 ft), and was then incarcerated by Tibetans for 46 days after trespassing into that territory.

Hooker was the first botanist to demonstrate the great botanical riches of those regions, and in doing so he collected a number of new species of primula. Hooker also introduced several species of rhododendron, which formed the basis of extensive hybridization of that genus, transforming late nineteenth-century estates. It seems that the only primulas that he successfully introduced were *P. sikkimensis* and *P. capitata*.

At the turn of the twentieth century very few Primula species were yet in cultivation. *P. sinensis, P. sieboldii, P. obconica* and *P. cortusoides* had been introduced from China, *P. japonica* had been introduced via Hong Kong, and a few Himalayan species such as *P. denticulata, P. capitata, P. rosea, P. reidii, P. involucrata, P. prolifera, P. sikkimensis, P. floribunda* and *P. nana* were established. *P. verticillata* from Arabia, *P. luteola* from the Caucasus, and a few American species (*P. parryi, P. rusbyi* and *P. suffrutescens*) were also grown. Naturally, a number of European natives were firmly in cultivation, but it comes as a surprise to discover that such an accessible and familiar species as *P. allionii* was not in fact introduced until 1901. In the year 1900 it is probable that only some 30 species of primula were in cultivation.

In contrast, by the time of the fourth Primula conference of the RHS in 1928 it seems that at least another 60 species had become established in cultivation. At that date perhaps 100 species were being grown. The majority of these additions had recently arrived from the extremely rich regions of western China, which were being explored for the first time.

The first Western botanists in west China were French Catholic missionaries. In the last quarter of the nineteenth century, such familiar names as David, Delavay, Maire, Farges and Soulie were exploring virtually uncharted territory on the frontiers of China, Tibet and Burma. At that time this was a politically and religiously sensitive region (it still is today!), and more than one of them lost their life to religious fanatics (p. 10). Nevertheless, quantities of specimens were sent back to Paris, and the many specific epithets in *Primula* based on French names testify to the importance of these early collections.

The French missionaries were mostly working in forested zones, peopled with primitive tribes. Most of these forests have now been logged, and the peoples dispersed. Many of the forest primulas they found, for instance in sections Davidii, Chartacea, Carolinella, and Obconicolisteri have not been seen in recent years, and the fear is that they might now be extinct. What little seed the missionaries collected was poorly treated, so few introductions were effected. However, the Irishman Augustine Henry, who was also travelling in this area at this time, did make a few important introductions.

The introduction of the flora of Yunnan and Sichuan to Western gardens needed a further impetus, and this came from a rather unlikely source. Arthur Bulley was a Lancashire cotton millionaire who built a red sandstone house on the green hills of the Wirral, Cheshire, overlooking the Dee estuary. This is now the University of Liverpool Botanic Garden at

Ness. Bulley was an unusual magnate, perhaps, in that he was a socialist and a philanthropist. He started a seed firm, Bees seeds, maybe as a hobby, and was very keen that many of the plants discovered by the missionaries should be introduced into cultivation.

Bulley approached the Regius Keeper of the Royal Botanic Garden, Edinburgh, Sir Isaac Bayley Balfour, to recommend a man who could go to China as his collector. At this date (1904), Edinburgh already had a strong interest in the taxonomy and cultivation of primulas, resulting from the earlier work of G. Watt, W.G. Craib, and of Balfour himself. This has continued to the present day through Sir William Wright Smith, Harold Fletcher, Peter Davis, Jennifer Lamond and Andrew Grierson.

Balfour suggested George Forrest, a young man from Falkirk who had recently returned from Australia to take up a post as an assistant at the Botanic Garden. In this way, what was perhaps the most illustrious career in the history of plant collecting began (there is a good account of Forrest and his introductions in the Journal of the Scottish Rock Garden Club 13 (3) (1973)).

Forrest spent most of the rest of his life in China, supported by Bulley, and later by a syndicate of other growers. His first expedition (1904–6) was particularly adventurous. Having narrowly escaped a murderous attack on three missionaries by Tibetan lamas, and without clothing or boots, he was hunted in dense forest for eight days. When he finally reached a friendly village, he had lost all his collections and seeds. News of his supposed death had already reached Edinburgh and thence to Bulley, who was greatly upset. It is thus ironic that when Forrest did die at the end of his sixth Chinese expedition in 1932, it was of a heart attack while he was on a recreational duck-shooting trip.

Forrest was so superbly organized in the field that he was able to cover vast areas of uncharted country using hundreds of native collectors. Farrer, who was collecting in China at the time, wrote of 'Forrest's octopus tentacles'. There is no doubt that Forrest, a forthright and competitive man, deeply resented any activities from other collectors in what he regarded as 'his' territory.

In all, Forrest collected over 30,000 specimens, and introduced well over 1,000 species to European gardens. He is perhaps best known for his introductions of rhododendrons, but his influence on the cultivation of primulas was also considerable. In particular, *P. bulleyana*, *P. beesiana* and *P. aurantiaca* which play such a significant role in the drifts of 'candelabra' primulas, which form such a feature in many gardens today, were first collected by Forrest. Amongst other significant introductions he made were *P. vialii, P. chionantha, P. flaccida, P. malacoides,* and of course *P. forrestii* itself.

Later in his life, although untrained, Forrest became an expert botanist who took a special interest in the taxonomy of *Primula*. He described a number of species, and together with Smith prepared a systematic account of the whole genus in 1928.

Although Forrest carved out a special niche in the botanical exploration of western China, he was by no means alone in this field, although he refused to co-operate with the others. Working in similar areas at the same time were the Americans Ernest ('Chinese') Wilson and Joseph Rock, and the Englishmen Reginald Farrer and Frank Kingdon Ward, all resounding names in the annals of plant introduction.

Ernest Wilson was a professional plant collector who spent much of his career in China, specializing in the introduction of trees. Indeed, his first expedition was mounted especially to collect seed of the 'handkerchief tree', *Davidia*. He was subsidized by many sources, not least by Bulley, and the London nursery firm of Veitch, but he also worked for the Arnold Arboretum. He learned to speak many Chinese dialects, and often dressed as a Chinese. His many primula introductions included *P. secundiflora, P. polyneura, P. cockburniana* and *P. pulverulenta*.

Joseph Rock was originally Professor of Botany and Chinese in Hawaii. A well-known Chinese scholar, he lived in Yunnan for some years, and his Chinese collections spanned over 40 years. Sadly, he was forced to flee the country after the revolution in 1948. I have been fortunate enough to visit the house in which he lived in Lijiang (Lichiang) and which still contains many of his possessions. The occupant in 1995 was a great authority on local music who had known Rock personally, and who had spent a number of years in jail during the 'Cultural Revolution'. Rock's introductions of primulas included many species popular in the garden today, although none seem to have been collected by him first.

Reginald Farrer (1880–1920) was an extraordinary man; an aesthete, poet, novelist, playwright, poseur and *enfant terrible*, he was also an important botanical explorer who died from pneumonia while collecting in Burma. Almost incidentally, Farrer is generally regarded as the 'father of the modern rock garden', as a result of his imaginative and importunate garden books. The 'English Rock Garden', much of which was rewritten while he was in Gansu, is at the same time perhaps the most ambitious and the least accurate horticultural work ever published. Farrer's capacity for hyperbole never ceases to amaze, and this was also recognized by his contemporaries, for Forrest commented tersely 'all Farrer's sparrows are eagles'.

It seems that Farrer would dearly have liked to invade Forrest's regions, but Forrest's fierce territoriality drove Farrer firstly to Gansu with William Purdom as a paid companion (1914–15), and then to Upper Burma (1919–20), with Euan Cox as a companion for the first year. Particularly in Gansu, Farrer discovered a number of interesting new species in sections such as Crystallophlomis, Pulchella and Muscarioides, and several were introduced. Unfortunately, species from this area seem to be particularly difficult to grow, and none have survived.

Frank Kingdon Ward (1885–1958) was a unique character. A scholar by birth, and a traveller by inclination, he made a career as a kind of botanical travel writer, publishing no less than 700 articles and 25 books about his remarkable journeys. At times, his wanderings were subsidized by seed firms and syndicates (once again, Bulley was a sponsor), but Ward was a loner, travelling light, and both his botanical collections and gatherings of seed tended to be sparse. Ward's expeditions spanned over 40 years, from his first trip to Tatsienlu and Gansu in 1909, to his last to Manipur in 1953. Many of the regions he visited, for instance the Tsangpo valley in south-east Tibet, and the Mishmi hills in Assam, were then largely unexplored, and have been rarely visited by Western botanists since. As the only Westerner with experience of the Mishmis, Ward was employed by the USAF after the war as a guide to recover the bodies of American airmen lost on bombing raids from India to Japanese bases in south-east Asia. At this time he was already over 60 years old.

When Ward was 63, he married for the second time, Jean Macklin. They went on two further expeditions together, discovering the exquisite lily *Lilium. mackliniae*, and among many primulas *P. macklinae* which is described here for the first time. Some time after the first edition of 'Primula' was published, Kenneth Cox led a series of expeditions to Tsari and the Tsangpo bend, in which he largely retraced Ward's steps. This led to the reissue of a magnificent edition of Ward's 'The Riddle of the Tsangpo Gorges' (2001), edited in part by Cox and full of modern colour photographs. The preface was written by Jean Rasmussen, née Macklin and formerly Jean Ward. I was able to discover her address so that I could inform her that a primula now unofficially bore her maiden name, and received a gracious reply.

In *Primula*, Ward's botanical discoveries rate second only to those of Ludlow and Sherriff. His introductions of such magnificent species as *P. florindae, P. alpicola, P. burmanica, P. chungensis, P. concholoba, P. cawdoriana* and many others should enrich our gardens permanently.

Ward's journeyings into south-east Tibet, in the company of Lord Cawdor (1924–25), and again in 1935 introduced the world to a rich new ground for primulas, and set the scene for the most important primula expeditions ever made.

Frank Ludlow (1886–1972), originally a college-teacher in Biology and English at Karachi, was recruited after the First World War into the Indian Education Service, and later taught in Tibet. A keen bird-watcher, he was holidaying in Kashgar in 1929 (not a place to visit lightly, even today) where he met Major George Sherriff (1898–1967), originally of the Indian Army, who entered the consular service in 1928. Afterwards Ludlow undertook a major collecting expedition into Tien-Shan.

Ludlow's momentous meeting with Sherriff led to a discovery of shared interests in natural history and travel. Both men were keenly interested in the possibility of exploring the eastern Himalaya, particularly Bhutan and south-east Tibet, which were almost totally unknown to Westerners at the time. Their first expedition into this area was in 1933, and from then until the outbreak of war, and again from 1947 until 1949 they undertook seven major journeys together. On several of these they were accompanied by the medical men Lumsden, Elliott and Hicks, and by Sir George Taylor, later Director of Kew. The tale of these momentous journeys is well told in Harold Fletcher's book 'A Quest of Flowers' (1975). In his introduction to this book, Sir George told how these two great friends, who spent a good deal of their lives in each other's close company, often in perilous circumstances, could never bring themselves to address each other, except as 'Ludlow' and 'Sherriff'.

Sherriff married during the war, and took his bride to Lhasa where they replaced Ludlow as British Resident from 1943–45. Here they got to know the boy Dalai Lama very well, taking as a gift a Hornby toy train set. Betty Sherriff accompanied her husband on the post-war expeditions, breaking her arm on one occasion. On their retirement in 1950, George and Betty Sherriff built together a magnificent garden at Ascreavie, near Kirriemuir in Scotland, where they grew many of their Himalayan introductions. Some, such as *Primula kingii* and *Meconopsis sherriffii*, were only managed successfully by them.

George Sherriff was the organizing genius behind the expeditions. Often accompanied by 100 retainers, his staff work was immaculate, and his men and animals well cared for. Every night, it is said, Ludlow and Sherriff relaxed with a nip of whisky distilled at Sherriff's own family distillery.

Although both Ludlow and Sherriff were men of independent means, I have often wondered how it was that an ex-teacher and an ex-consular official were able to fund such ambitious expeditions during the prime of their careers. It seems probable that they were in fact part of what Kipling called 'the Great Game', and that their wanderings also served some tactical and political purposes.

However, whatever their primary motives, there is no doubt that the excitement and challenge of uncovering totally new botanical store-houses of great richness soon dominated their interests. Ludlow, a bird-watcher who seems initially to have been lukewarm about flowers, spent the later years of his life as a full-time plant taxonomist, while Sherriff became an authority on the taxonomy and cultivation of *Primula* and several other genera.

Bhutan had been visited previously by botanists such as W. Griffith (1838–39), Sir Claud White (1905–7) and R.E. Cooper (1914–15), while Ward had briefly explored the Tsangpo and Tsari in south-east Tibet. However, the thorough exploration of these areas by Ludlow and Sherriff first revealed fully the richness of these territories for a number of groups of *Primula*. For instance, Ludlow and Sherriff discovered no less than eight new species in section Minutissimae, six in section Petiolares, and four in section Soldanelloides. In all, they found no less than 26 species of *Primula* new to science.

On their early expeditions, Ludlow and Sherriff mostly collected herbarium material, and much of that from carefully selected genera. However, such was the interest that their expeditions generated that latterly they preserved all the plants they encountered (even dandelions!) Their herbarium specimens are amongst the best collected and most thoroughly annotated I have ever seen. Also, Sherriff took many superb photographs on a half plate camera.

Ludlow and Sherriff made second forays into selected areas for the purpose of collecting seed. They also pioneered the 'flown home' technique, often 'stashing' collected material in caches to be collected later and flown home to Edinburgh by aeroplane. In all they introduced at least 66 species of *Primula*, the majority of them new to cultivation. For many growers, their best introduction was, arguably the loveliest of all primulas, the ice-blue *P. bhutanica*.

Ludlow and Sherriff's activities in the eastern Himalaya ceased just as the next significant advance in the exploration of primulas was starting. For most of the previous 200 years, the Kingdom of Nepal had been closed to

Westerners, although Indian collectors from the Darjeeling herbarium and seed firms, and explorers such as Major Lal Dhjow, had introduced a few plants from this centrally placed region of the Himalaya.

Immediately Nepal became open, the British Museum sponsored a series of expeditions into Nepal. Adam Stainton, L.H.J. Williams, Oleg Polunin, a school-teacher from Charterhouse, and Lt. Col. Donald Lowndes were significant participants in these early explorations (1950–55). By 1956, it was possible for independent tourists like Marjorie Brough and S. Bowes-Lyon to visit new and remote districts which had not been explored botanically, discovering exciting species such as *P. aureata*.

This brief era links seamlessly with the present day when expertly arranged botanical 'holiday' tours to Nepal, and even to Bhutan and Tibet, are commonplace. During the 1970s and 1980s a host of enthusiasts introduced seed and living material of primulas from Nepal, notably George Smith, John Templar, Bernard Thompson, Edward Needham and Keith Rushforth. Professional botanists are still active in the area. Work centred on the Royal Botanic Garden, Edinburgh, led to the publication of a 'Flora of Bhutan'.

There was an initial period in the 1950s when several notable new species, such as *P. poluninii*, *P. megalocarpa* and *P. ramzanae* were discovered in the remoter parts of Nepal, while others such as *P. petiolaris* and *P. boothii* became much better understood. It now seems likely that few new discoveries remain to be made in this area.

There was a period of some 40 years when the botanical exploration of China by Westerners was not permitted. Notwithstanding, botanical work continued within that vast country, and a number of new species were published during the 1950s and until the 'Cultural Revolution', notably by Fang Yun-yi and Chen Feng-hwai. More recently, Professor Hu Chi-ming has revised the Chinese Primulaceae for 'Flora Republicae Popularis Sinicae' (1990) (Flora of China). In co-operation with the Missouri Botanic Garden, USA, and with Sylvia ('Tass') Kelso of the University College of Colorado Springs he collaborated in the preparation of an English translation of this fine work.

After 1981 a number of joint Sino-British expeditions revisited the hunting grounds of Forrest, Wilson and Rock in western China, such as the Cang Shan, Yulong Shan, the Zhongdian plateau, the Beima Shan, Da Xue Shan, Emei Shan, Wolong Shan, etc. In the early 1990s, several major expeditions made extensive seed collections from north-west Yunnan and south-west Sichuan available to the gardening public. The best known of these go under the acronyms CLD, KGB (Swedish) and ACE. A very large number of good new plants have successfully come into cultivation as a result, including such primulas as *P. dryadifolia*, *P. rupicola*, *P. yunnanensis*, *P. nanobella*, *P. deflexa*, *P. florida*, *P. brevicula* and others.

The purpose of these expeditions has been primarily scientific, the herbarium material gathered being split between Chinese and Western institutes. Most collection of living plants has rightly been discouraged, and since about 1995 it has been difficult to get permission even to gather seed. When Chinese authorities have discovered that seed has been furtively secreted away by botanical travellers, it has been confiscated and destroyed, and the miscreants have spent several worrying days in captivity.

Nevertheless, most of these districts are now on the tourist trail and can be visited on wild-flower holidays, in varying degrees of comfort. Hotels in Dali and Lijiang, which give easy access to amazingly rich floras, are now very good, although those who penetrate to Zhongdian or Deqen (Atuntse) can still sample the discomforts of 'old China'. Although some formerly remote areas are nowadays found to be heavily logged, many alpine localities have remained relatively undisturbed. Logging has allowed vehicular access into previously difficult country, and second growth often proves to be species-rich.

Undoubtedly, many good plants remain to be introduced from the fantastically rich regions of the 'Tibetan borderlands' of south-west China. At the turn of the Millennium, however, attention was directed towards Reginald Farrer's hunting grounds far to the north, in north Sichuan, Gansu and Qinghai. Although much less rich, these districts still have many interesting plants and it is hoped that these drier regions will yield plants more suited to many garden conditions (although this was not on the whole Farrer's experience). Participants (as in the SQAE expedition of 2000) have also experienced problems in persuading Chinese authorities to release seed outside the country. However, this trip, and a 'tourist' visit to the same districts in 2001, revealed many almost unknown species of great interest such as *P. limbata, P. optata, P. woodwardii, P. tangutica, P. maximowiczii, P.violacea* and *P. flava*.

Another previously remote region which became briefly accessible, if only under canvas, was the wonderfully rich districts of south-east Tibet. To the north of the Himalaya in rain-shadow, the Tibetan plateau is on the whole very dry. This huge, high region is drained eastwards by a single river, the Tsangpo, which turns very dramatically to the south-west as it penetrates the main chain and becomes the Brahmaputra. The gaps so created allow the monsoon to penetrate northwards across a few very wet passes into some limited wet and precipitous districts with a very rich, isolated and often endemic flora. The principal flower-rich districts of south-east Tibet are Tsari and Pemakochung, and even here the wet, plant-rich habitats are often localised and at a considerable altitude. It has been possible to drive to Tsari from Lhasa, and the best known of the recent expeditions have been organized during the 1990s by the Cox family, descendants of Euan who travelled to nearby regions of Burma with Farrer. The Cox expeditions have been chiefly organized to research and reintroduce the fantastically rich rhododendron flora of this district, and in this they have been phenomenally successful. However, they have also been able to visit many primulas which had only been seen once or twice previously, by Ludlow or Sherriff, or Ward, for instance *P. laeta, P. falcifolia, P. rhodochroa, P. genestieriana, P. jonardunii, P. advena* and others. South-east Tibet remains largely unexplored, and this is potentially the most rewarding region for future primula field work. Unfortunately, some of the richest passes such as the Doshong La have proved too close to the Indian border for the comfort of the relevant authorities and are closed again as I write (2002).

In the post-revolutionary years, vast areas of Siberia and central Asia became accessible to Soviet botanists. These areas are not rich in primula species, but the account by A. Federov in 'Flora SSSR' (1952) was a notable advance in our understanding of the species in this region. This work adopts an approach which 'splits' species too much for my taste. For instance, under the three species *P. veris, P. vulgaris* and *P. elatior*, Federov describes no less than 15 species, and of the 67 species listed there, I only accept 41 in the present account. Nevertheless, several striking new species were discovered in central Asia during this exploratory period, such as the Cortusoides species *P. eugeniae*, with yellow flowers.

In recent years, several Czechs, notably Josef Halda, have explored these regions thoroughly and have introduced a number of the little-known species from there into cultivation.

Central Asia forms the centre of diversity for a previously little-understood section, the Armerina. Schwarz (1972), in monographing this group, shows that no less than five species described after 1950 belong to this section and are confined to this area.

In recent years, our attention has been unexpectedly diverted from the treasure-house of Asia to the USA. Here there have been two important developments. Firstly, Tass Kelso very productively used her time at the University of Alaska to revise the north American species in sections Aleuritia, Armerina and Crystallophlomis. This has not only greatly increased our understanding of arctic-American species which were previous little known, but a new species, *P. anvilensis,* was described in 1987.

Secondly, the dry-land primulas of the western United States have become much better known. In the last 25 years, four new species have been described from this area, including two new localized segregates of *P. cusickiana, P. domensis* and *P. nevadensis*, treated in the present account as subspecies, the distinctive *P. capillaris*, and a local white-flowered relative of *P. modesta, P. alcalina*. These dry-land species have been well described by Jay Lunn (1991).

Primula gardens

Until the great era of Chinese exploration was under way, after 1904, there was little incentive for collectors to specialize in the growing of species primulas. Too few species were yet in cultivation. The cultivation of the many varieties to be found in *P. sinensis, P. sieboldii,* and the hybrid grexes derived from the primrose and the Auricula were popular nineteenth-century pastimes. However, these are of peripheral interest to this particular book.

The great wealth of species introduced from China, and later from the Himalaya, were on the whole found to thrive best in maritime climates with moderate, humid climates. Reports in the Fourth RHS Primula Conference (1928) make interesting reading. Several of the gardens which feature prominently there, the Royal Botanic Garden, Edinburgh, the University of Liverpool Garden at Ness, Wirral, and the RHS Garden at Wisley, Surrey, still figure prominently amongst important collections of primula species. However, it is perhaps significant that Bodnant in north Wales, still a magnificent garden well suited to the cultivation of primulas, nowadays seems unable to reconcile the interests of such short-lived (and portable?) plants as primulas with the pressures of its large numbers of visitors. At Edinburgh, Kew and Wisley, too, many of the more interesting species tend to be found 'behind the scenes'.

Unfortunately, some of these gardens have not survived the decease of their owners. Ascreavie, near Kirriemuir, was not maintained after Betty Sherriff's death in 1979, nor was the famous garden at Keillour Castle, Perth, after Mrs Knox-Finlay died. I continued to garden at Kilbryde near Corbridge in Northumberland for some seven years after Randall Cooke's death in 1973, but in the end the rarer plants were dispersed, many to other famous collections where some still survive. This has also been the case with respect to Gerry Mundey's hill-top garden at Tinney's Firs near Salisbury, after his death in 1989.

In other cases, famous gardens have 'gone public' after the death of their owners and, like Bodnant, have rarely been able to cope with the pressures of maintaining a collection of rare primula species. To various extents this is true of the garden of the Rentons at Branklyn, Perth, Inverewe in Wester Ross, Arduaine in Argyll, and Harlow Carr, the Northern Horticultural Society Garden near Harrogate, Yorkshire.

Cluny, near Aberfeldy, has proved to be an exception to this. Bobby Masterton, a vet who built up a superb collection of Asiatic species in magnificent mountain surroundings, has been succeeded by his son-in-law John Mattingley.

Over the last 50 years, some of the most interesting collections of primula species have been grown by specialist nurseries, and these sometimes survive the tenancy of their original owners. Jack Drake's nursery at Inshriach on Speyside continued to be been run by John Lawson for a number of years, when it still kept its proud record for succeeding with difficult species in sections Crystallophlomis and Soldanelloides which had proved short-lived elsewhere. Doubtless the reliable snow-cover and cool summers in that district helped to make this possible. These days, the reputation of north-east Scottish nurserymen as purveyors of fine and rare primulas is maintained by Ian Christie who lives near the Sherriffs' old home above Kirriemuir, Fred Carrie of the Tough Nursery, and Jim Sutherland and his son near Inverness.

Edrom, near Coldingham on the Berwickshire coast, was another well-known example. Originally started by two sisters, the Misses Logan-Hume before the Second World War, it was later owned by their gardener, Alec Duguid. On Alec's retirement, Jim Jermyn took over, since when this franchise has changed hands yet again, although this concern still offers a wide and interesting range of species. Edrom is a wooded site, and its proximity to the east coast ensures cool summers and mild winters. In the late 1990s, a master collector and grower of Sinohimalayan species, Ron McBeath, recognized these local qualities when he purchased a nursery high above the sea right on the Scottish border. He has rapidly established a most interesting collection of rare species, many of which he has introduced himself.

Most of the gardens listed above are best known for their collections of Asiatic species. Over the last 30 years there has been a resurgence of interest in the cultivation of the scarcer European species. This group in particular are grown superbly in the harsh climate of Askival, near Fort Augustus, where Michael and Polly Stone have created one of the finest private gardens in Scotland. Henry and Margaret Taylor of Invergowrie, and Brian Burrow in Lancashire are amongst other growers who have built up interesting collections of the European species.

Urban conditions do not always favour the cultivation of the scarcer primulas, as the warmer, drier conditions are not always to their liking. Nevertheless, many of the more interesting collections have always been found in the smaller private garden. In earlier years, names such as David Livingstone of Edinburgh, Dr McWatt of Duns, and Kenneth Corsair were amongst those especially associated with the cultivation of the rarer species. Today, it would perhaps be invidious to list names, but visits to the shows of the Alpine Garden Society, or the Scottish Rock Garden Club, demonstrate that a large number of growers maintain collections of the scarcer primulas.

This account is largely restricted to the British Isles, as this is the area with which I am most familiar. The north Pacific coast of the USA is another area with a long tradition of growing the less-common primula species. In the spring of 2001 I was fortunate enough to travel to this area and was able to visit a number of gardens and nurseries, many of whom have interesting collections of primulas. Many growers there struggle with the hot, dry, bright conditions experienced in their summers (northern Britain is so satisfactorily *gloomy*!) But Rick Lupp and Steve Doonan are amongst those able to supply a rich array of *Primula* species to an expanding market, and private growers such as Betty and Ned Lowry, Barbara Flynn and others are amongst those with very interesting collections in the Seattle area. I have discussed elsewhere the very recent trend to grow high alpines very satisfactorily in very cold districts (in winter) such as Alaska (Ed Burayaski) and Alberta (Pam Eveleigh). There is a Society in the US dedicated to the genus (the American Primula Society), just as there is in the UK (the National Primula and Auricula Society), while the more generic societies such as the Alpine Garden Society, American Rock Garden Society and the Scottish Rock Garden Society promote the cultivation of *Primula* as well as many other beautiful alpine genera.

This is perhaps the point to note the increasing influence of the internet in the dissemination of information, and of images, as I write in 2002. All the societies listed above possess websites which not only promote activities of the societies themseves, but are rich sources of links to many other types of information. There are chatlines, often owned by the Societies, but some managed independently. Alpine-L is one of the longest established. Many private individuals run rich websites with images and information about *Primula*, for instance John Lonsdale and Alan Grainger. For those particularly interested in species primula, by far the most rewarding is www.primulaworld.com run by Pam Eveleigh, which is a magnificent source of images of *Primula* species. Many other important databases can be accessed, for instance the *Primula* account in Flora of China, which contains a large number of images and drawings, and even individual specimens in major herbaria, for instance that at the New York Botanic Garden. It is possible to buy primulas on the internet, not only from conventional western sources, but also from China, where a dealer has been offering extremely interesting living collections by post. Although these are often not true to name, they are nevertheless frequently as interesting as those advertised, and the identity of most can be ascertained through previewed images available on the net. As yet the origin of this material has not been ascertained, and when mature specimens of difficult species are offered, it is hard to avoid the suspicion that many have been dug from the wild. Finally, I must acknowledge the power of the internet in allowing me to access photographs of plants from remote regions. Where formerly correspondents expensively and riskily had to pack up photographic images, or dried material, for my perusal, the judicious use of a scanner nowadays means that I rarely pass a morning without receiving an email containing one or more primula images for my pleasure, instruction or opinion.

The Cultivation of *Primula*

Species of *Primula* grow in a very wide range of habitats. *P. verticillata* is found on cliffs in the Arabian desert. We would not expect it to need the same conditions in cultivation as *P. buryana*, which is confined to glacial moraines in a Himalayan region subject to persistent monsoon rain. Equally, *P. egaliksensis*, a high arctic plant which grows in soggy hollows above permafrost, is likely to have very different requirements from *P. malacoides,* a bean-field weed in southern China.

It may at first sight seem remarkable that species from such diverse habitats can be grown in the same garden, where the conditions differ strikingly from those experienced in the wild. However, like most plants, primulas are, within essential parameters, highly adaptable to certain modified garden conditions. This chapter addresses how such modifications can be successfully made.

Of course, one would not expect every garden situation to grow all primulas equally well. Very few species can be grown in the subtropical conditions of Sydney, Australia, where *P. malacoides* is extensively used as a bedding plant, or in lowland California where *P. verticillata* can be grown outside. Neither of these species could be overwintered outside in the Highlands of Scotland, where *P. buryana* can succeed.

Even in a moderate temperate climate, such as that of central northern England where I garden, none of the aforementioned species can be grown without the provision of special conditions. I have grown *P. malacoides* as a house plant, or in the conservatory. *P. verticillata* thrives, self-sowing by the thousand, in glasshouses at the University of Newcastle Botanical Garden where humidity is kept high and the temperature minimum is 5°C. At home in a frost-free alpine-house where the humidity is lower, I struggle to keep it alive. Both *P. egaliksensis* and *P. buryana* were grown in a partially shaded frame where they received regular misting from an automatic watering system while in growth, but they were kept nearly dry (although unprotected from frost) when they were dormant. I have not grown either of these for many years now (2002), but the same frame has its new collection of novelties (*P. brevicula, P. stuartii, P. orbicularis* and others) as I write, most of which will doubtless prove equally impermanent!

Three lessons can be learnt from this short survey. Firstly, not every species will enjoy the same growing conditions in the garden. Consequently, I have dealt with the particular problems and preferences which each species presents under the species headings in the systematic section of this book. In many cases, related species respond in similar ways. More complete accounts of their cultural preferences may often be found under the sectional rather than the species headings.

Secondly, one must expect species to respond best in conditions which approximate to those that they experience in the wild. There are only a few primulas which thrive in the 'ordinary' garden conditions as may be found in the moist, temperate regions of the world where most primulas are grown (i.e. in north-west Europe; southern New Zealand; Victoria, Australia; the north Pacific coast of America and the Atlantic coasts north of New York; coastal regions of northern China and Japan).

Not surprisingly, in the wild these few 'everyday' primula species tend to grow in similar conditions to those found in the average unmodified garden. These species include the primrose, cowslip and oxlip, the drumstick primrose, *P. denticulata,* certain 'candelabra' primulas, notably *P. japonica, P. pulverulenta* and *P. bulleyana*, some species in section Sikkimensis, for instance *P. florindae* and *P. sikkimensis* itself, *P. rosea*, and *P. auricula* and its hybrids. For these species, and in some areas a few others, it is not usually necessary to prepare special composts and growing conditions; these plants will usually thrive in any fertile 'ordinary' garden soil. It is notable that many of the primulas most successful in unmodified garden conditions are hybrids, for instance the 'polyanthus' (*P.* × *polyantha*) and 'juliana' (*P.* × *pruhoniciana*) crosses of the primrose; complex hybrids in sections Proliferae and Sikkimensis; and the *P.* × *pubescens* hybrids in section Auricula.

The specialist grower, who wants to enjoy a wider range of species primula, must expect to have to provide a series of highly modified growing conditions. In a later section of this chapter I will describe a few of the more successful ways of providing such specialized growing conditions.

Thirdly, however strenuously (and expensively!) one may attempt to provide specialized conditions, there is no doubt that most species are grown more readily in some districts than others. Since the first edition of this book was published in 1993, it has become plain that climates most people would find marginal comfortwise (to put it mildly) suit many primulas very well. The current President of the American Primrose Society, Ed Burayaski, and several other leading members, garden in the vicinity of Juneau, Alaska. Ed and others mounted an expedition to Yunnan in 2000 which has allowed them to show that species classified in sections such as Crystallophlomis, Amethystina and Minutissimae (for instance), which most growers find very difficult, thrive in their conditions. Arctic Europe has also recently proved its worth. Finn Haugli, the Director of Tromso Botanic Garden, Norway, situated a long way north of the Arctic Circle at nearly 70°N, has recently demonstrated that the more difficult members of section Petiolares (*P. sonchifolia, P. calderiana* ssp. *strumosa, P. whitei*), difficult Crystallophlomis such as *P. nivalis* and *P. longipes*, tricky Auricula species such as *P. deorum* and north American Parryi species are amongst those which thrive unprotected and without special conditions in his environment.

Despite their arctic locations, both Juneau and Tromso enjoy relatively mild winters, due to their maritime positions. This is less true of Pam Eveleigh, custodian of the 'primulaworld' website, who gardens in Calgary, Alberta. Her ferociously difficult conditions can involve daily switches between –30°C and +10°C when the 'Chinook' blows in winter, so temperatures can be very low indeed when snow-cover is unreliable. But Pam is succeeding with many difficult species, so that I am tempted to conclude that conditions which allow high alpine species to go reliably dormant for five months or more are those in which they are most likely to succeed. For those of us living in more temperate climes, we may have much to learn from the judicious use of refrigerators, if not freezers.

Temperature and humidity

Nevertheless, many primulas dislike extremes of temperature. The majority of species live in regions where they are covered by snow during much of their resting period. Snow acts as a superb insulation, so that the temperature at the gently respiring leaf surface is usually at around 0°C (32°F), even though the ambient temperature might be –40°C (–40°F). Species which originate from mountain ranges which receive a deep and consistent covering of snow, for instance the Himalaya, or the Rocky Mountains of the USA, may never be subjected to very low temperatures in the wild. In these regions, the snow may only melt when warm, wet conditions, for instance the monsoon, stimulate the plants into rapid growth. Only a few species which grow on sites which remain free of snow, for instance rocky ridges and the crevices of cliffs, will have become adapted to resist a prolonged exposure to temperatures well below freezing in the absence of snow cover.

Ironically, it is sometimes found that the highest alpines from these regions are the least hardy. Such plants may rapidly succumb to the freeze/thaw cycles which characterize winters in the maritime temperate zones where they are usually grown. However, most high alpines will also fail in regions with a cold, continental-type winter where the snow cover is unreliable.

For pot-grown plants in cold regions, the answer is clearly to overwinter plants under glass in conditions with gentle heat, so that temperatures never fall below about –5°C (23°F). Less hardy species should be grown in frost-free conditions, but as will become clear from the systematic accounts, there are relatively few of these.

For species grown in the open ground, the effects of occasional cold spells in maritime climates can often be ameliorated by covering resting plants with fern fronds, sheets of newspaper or similar material. The worst effects of freeze/thaw cycles in wet winter conditions can frequently be overcome by the use of cloches or strategically placed panes of glass in the open garden. However, in many areas where winters are consistently very cold, it will have to be faced that many species of primula cannot be overwintered outside. This is rarely true in the British Isles, although it has been found in north-west Scotland, for instance, that some evergreen species perfectly hardy in much of the rest of the country tend to fail in cold winters.

Nearly all primulas also dislike conditions which are hot and dry when they are in growth. Most species have broad, flaccid leaves which are abundantly provided with stomata (the 'breathing' pores) on both sides. In many species it seems that these stomata have no mechanism whereby they can shut in hot, dry conditions, and thus they readily become dessicated. Only a few primulas have waxy coverings to the leaves, or a fleshy leaf structure, which could help them to resist dessication.

Species which come from mountain ranges or from woodlands usually enjoy cool and moist conditions when they are in growth. Even those species which originate from hotter, drier conditions are usually restricted to micro-habitats which remain cool and wet throughout the summer. Thus, the 'desert' primulas in section Sphondylia are always confined to the spray zone of the few waterfalls which run down the north side of cliffs in their western Asian fastnesses. Many of the species found in the hotter and drier regions of the Chinese and American mountains are restricted to cool, north-facing 'grottos' in limestone cliffs where water continually drips on them, and where they are totally shaded from the sun.

The very few primulas which have become adapted to a hot, dry summer microclimate have either evolved thick waxy leaves with few stomata (*P. auricula, P. suffrutescens*), or they escape from the summer drought by dying back in summer (*P. cusickiana, P. fedtschenkoi, P. palinuri*). Although these few species will tolerate some drying at the root (or in the case of *P. cusickiana* and *P. fedtschenkoi* positively demand it), as a general rule it can be stated that no primula should ever be allowed to become dry at the root.

It can be difficult to distinguish between the effects of heat and dryness in the summer. I well remember seeing a thriving specimen of *P. reptans*, a species which is notoriously susceptible to 'summer heat', growing in a polythene tunnel in which the temperature regularly exceeded 40°C (104°F). However, the whole tunnel was regularly hosed down, so that the humidity never dropped below saturation.

In most gardens, all primulas suffer when an unusually prolonged hot spell is experienced. However, it certainly helps if plants grow in, or can be moved to, a shady area, or if the location in which they grow can be artificially shaded and sprayed regularly with water.

One can conclude that most primula species tend to be intolerant of dry air with low humidity, as in these conditions, leaves will overheat and become dessicated. If possible, plants should be grown in humid locations, for instance by running water or a pond, or in soils where the soil surface of remains moist and open.

In summary, nearly all primulas enjoy conditions which are the most humid, and the most moderate that can be managed; if possible temperatures below freezing, and above 20°C (68°F), should be avoided at all times of year. The use of cloching, or greenhouse protection, in winter, and of shading and spraying in summer, will often allow the 'difficult' species to be grown.

Soil and composts

In common with many plants, most primulas need a constant supply of water and air at the root when they are in growth. This means that few species will enjoy an unmodified loam soil, as such soils tend to have a relatively high clay fraction which creates few air-spaces, and which impedes the free passage of water.

There are various ways of 'opening up' the soil so that water and oxygen are freely available to the root. Basically, these involve the addition of organic material, or grit, or both.

The organic material used can be of many different types. The most important point is that it should be fully broken down, as soil micro-organisms take a lot of nitrogen from the soil while they are still active. Many suitable composts are based on sphagnum peat. This is freely available from most suppliers, and is relatively cheap. However, in recent years, the use of horticultural peat has been thought by many to be environmentally unacceptable. In England at least, the digging of peat, mostly by one powerful and obdurate supplier, is destroying much valuable habitat. Some peat from elsewhere, for instance Ireland and Russia, is claimed to be environmentally 'friendly', coming from despoiled, or renewable, sources. These deserve consideration, not least in the support of beleaguered economies, so that an intelligent environmentalist might consider banning the use of garden peat in a targeted rather than an unselective way. A number of peat substitutes are now on the market, several made from rotted coconut fibre or pulverized bark, and these are said to be very acceptable, although I have not used them so far.

Peat, and its subsitutes, have the advantages of being light, relatively clean to handle, and sterile. Their major disadvantage is that they are virtually without nutrient, so that supplementary fertilizers or other food sources have to be added to peat-based composts.

Perhaps the ideal organic component is leaf-mould, made from the rotted leaves of broad-leaved trees. Many people lack the facility to collect leaves for this purpose, but it can be well worth taking the trouble to make trips into the countryside to collect leaf-mould from suitable areas (with the permission of the landowner!)

Some people make leaf compost from the rotted fronds of ferns (including bracken) or conifers. This material has to be very well broken down and weathered, so that the phenolics and terpenols found in these types of leaves have become completely dispersed.

Leaf-mould is not sterile, of course. Used in the open ground, this does not usually matter. Used in pots, the material should be sterilized. These days this is most often achieved by putting it in a microwave oven for about 30 minutes.

The third main source of organic material usually used is animal dung. I have used material from horses, cows and sheep equally successfully. Bird and pig manure should be avoided, because they contain uric acid or ammonia and are very acid. It is most important that the dung is very well rotted, and this usually means that it has been stacked for at least three years. Rotted dung is usually fairly sterile, although care should be taken that weed seeds have not fallen into the pile. Nearly all primulas are heavy feeders. With the exception of some high alpines, scree and cliff plants, most greatly enjoy a good measure of rotted dung, particularly if it is buried at some depth of 15 cm (6 in) or more.

In common with most gardeners I make a great deal of compost. I tend to use this to top-dress shrub borders and perennials. I find that the material I make tends to have too high a clay fraction (and to be too full of weed seed!) to be suitable for the culture of many primulas.

The inorganic component of primula composts should be a fine gravel, a grit, or a very coarse sand; material should pass through a 1 cm (⅜ in) sieve, but should be obstructed by a 0.2 cm (⅛ in) sieve. Granite grits are ideal, but quartzites, sandstones, flints and a variety of other materials are suitable, the sharper the better. Opinion differs as to the use of limestone. Some species of primula grow on lime-rich soils in the wild, and I have never seen definitive evidence of lime-chlorosis on any primula. At the same time it is probably best to avoid soft limestones, but in the absence of other material, hard limestones, especially magnesian limestones, are usually suitable. However, it is certain that there is no primula which positively requires free lime in the soil, except possibly when the natural materials are very acidic (pH less than 5.0). Most species of primula will thrive at pH levels between 5.0 and 7.0.

In recent years the use of artificially expanded inorganic materials based on pumice or clay (UK tradenames 'Perlite' and 'Vermiculite'; there are others) have become popular in compost mixes. These materials are very light with a huge water-storing capacity, so that they provide very good supplies of air and water to the root. Although at saturation equilibrium they provide for a steady release of water, it seems that this can be too much for dry-living primula species when dormant in winter. I have lost several important plants to rot this way, including my only *P. bracteata* at the time, and I have reverted once again to grit alone when growing alpine and crevice-dwelling species.

Given an organic component of peat, peat-subsitute, or leaf-mould, and an inorganic component of grit, two questions remain: the relative quantities of the two, and feeding.

The organic:inorganic ratio will depend on the plant, and the rainfall. Species from woodland or marshy sites, such as species in sections Petiolares, Reinii, Cortusoides and Sikkimensis, enjoy soils with a high organic component; perhaps 75 per cent organic. At the other extreme, high alpines from screes, such as species in sections Minutissimae, Soldanelloides, and some Crystallophlomis, Auricula, Parryi, etc., require composts with a high inorganic component, in which the grit might form 75 per cent or even more. Many species will fall between these limits. Growers will be able to judge from the species and sectional accounts what kind of mix might be the most suitable. However, in wet regions, it will normally be found necessary to increase the proportion of drainage in the compost, and this should be reduced in dry areas.

I like to make up special primula beds in the garden with a layer of well-rotted manure about 15 cm (6 in) down. This certainly gives the promise of relatively long-term feeding. In addition, I usually add a slow-release complete inorganic fertilizer in pellet form to the surface as the plants come into growth in the spring.

For plants in pots, I sometimes add some crumbled manure to the bottom of the pot; in any case I usually water with a half-strength complete liquid feed several times a year while they are in growth; and I avoid slow-release pellets which I find tends to burn the tender foliage.

Also for these, I top-dress the compost with at least 2 cm (¾ in) of the grit; this avoids soil splash, modifies water loss, inhibits moss, liverwort and weed growth, and looks good!

In the open ground, I top-dress areas such as troughs, raised beds and rock gardens with very gritty composts with 5 cm (2 in) of grit; this gives conditions very suitable for the cultivation of most members of sections Auricula, Aleuritia and others. Cooler, often less sharply drained areas with composts containing a high organic fraction are top-dressed with 3–4 cm (1–2 in) of the organic material (but not manure). In the open garden, most top-dressings need replacing or 'topping up' at least every two years.

In summary, most primula species are heavy feeders which also require very good supplies of oxygen and free (not stagnant) water at the root. Apart from the few species which thrive in 'ordinary' garden soils (p. 18), most are best grown in made-up composts, both in pots and in the garden. These composts should consist entirely of well-rotted organic matter, and inorganic grit in various proportions.

Propagation

A past President of the Royal Horticultural Society once said '... seed raising is the royal road to success in the cultivation of Asiatic Primulas'. Undoubtedly, this is as true today as it was 75 years ago, and not only for the Asiatic species. There are several reasons why seed-grown primulas are more satisfactory than those raised vegetatively:

- many primulas are short-lived;
- many species seem to flower more freely when young;
- many clones suffer from a build-up of virus, but seedlings are usually virus-free.

However, there are a number of problems involved with the raising of primulas from seed.

Firstly, seedlings rarely come true to type, so that a good form may be lost. (But, then again, if you raise enough seedlings you may get a better one!)

Secondly, many species rarely set seed in the garden. Indeed, if only one clone of a species is grown (a pin, or a thrum), seedlings raised may be hybrid, and very possibly sterile. However, if legitimate (pin × thrum) pollinations are made with a distantly related species, it is sometimes found that this stimulates the mother to self-fertilize, and seedlings can come true to type. This is known as 'certation'. Such selfed seedlings may often be weak (see p. 63), and it is usually more satisfactory to raise seedlings from crosses between pins and thrums. For homostyle species as well (p. 62), seedlings resulting from crosses, which need to be made by the grower, are more satisfactory than those from selfs, although self-fertilization otherwise takes place automatically. Even when pins and thrums are grown together in the garden, it may be necessary to undertake an intentional crossing programme between the two, if seed is to be obtained. I have shown that not only do seedlings arising from crosses survive and flower better than those from selfs, in both heterostyles and in homostyle species like *P. scotica,* but that seedlings resulting from crosses between pins and thrums are much better 'doers' than crosses between different pins, in *P.* × *polyantha* (Richards, 2002, copied here in the heterostyly chapter).

Thirdly, the seed of many primulas may be viable for only a short time. Most primulas do not have a primary seed dormancy, and if seed is sown immediately it is ripe, it will usually germinate rapidly. However, if it is not sown immediately, seed usually assumes a secondary dormancy, and this can be difficult to break (for instance in section Petiolares). Considerable success has been obtained in germinating such obdurately secondarily dormant seed (of e.g. *P. calderiana*) by germinating it in a solution of gibberellic acid (GA3). Incidentally this is not water-soluble, but must first be dissolved in a spirit-based solvent.

I usually sow seed on to a loose mixture of two parts finely sieved peat to one part fine grit. The seed is then covered with about 1 cm (½ in) of the grit. I try to sow seed thinly, usually in a plastic pot, which is then stood in water for 15 minutes, before it is plunged in sand in a frame. In summer the frame is covered with netting as a partial shading, and to keep out birds and cats. In winter it is covered with a plastic light, so that excessive soaking, splash, and cold is avoided. However, if it snows heavily, I sometimes shovel snow into the frame before closing it again. This gives some protection from extreme cold and helps to stop the pots from becoming too dry in winter.

I usually sow short-lived primula seed as soon as it is available, except during periods of heavy frost. However, in summer it is most important that the pan is shaded from direct sunlight, and is never allowed to dry out. For species with a longer viability, I sow the seed together with most other species, in December.

Seed received more than about three weeks after ripening often benefits from stratification. Seed is soaked in a wet tissue for 24 hours, and then in this condition it is placed in a refrigerator for two to three weeks at about 4°C (39°F). After this it is sown, and if it can be given gentle bottom heat in a greenhouse or in a propagator it will probably germinate and grow faster. This process breaks the secondary dormancy of the seed, mimicking the onset of spring in the wild. Alternatively, the seed can be sown and placed outside in a frame in the normal way, where it will probably not germinate until the following spring.

Once seedlings have developed two true leaves, I usually prick them out individually, or if there are many sometimes in pairs, into 8 cm (3 in) diameter plastic pots. I use the same compost and top dressing as for the seeds. For vigorous plants, like some Sikkimensis and Proliferae primulas, I sometimes line them out in boxes. The young plants are then plunged into frames once again and treated much as the seed-pans. However, every two weeks in the growing season they are given a dilute liquid feed. At this stage plants appreciate gentle bottom heat, as long as the conditions are kept moist and humid.

Plants destined for the open garden are usually transplanted the April or May after they have germinated, while they are in active growth.

Pot plants are repotted into larger pots while in active growth when roots emerge into the plunge material. Pot plants are invariably plunged in sand, which is kept moist. For species which like moist conditions, I use plastic pots, and a compost largely composed of organic material. For species which require good drainage, I use crock pots, and a compost with about 50 per cent grit in addition to the organic material. It is important that the soil is not compressed or 'firmed down' too much; primulas like a very fluffy medium.

Primulas can be propagated vegetatively. Indeed, for vigorous species it is necessary to divide up congested clumps every two to three years if they are to give of their best. Large clumps harbour diseases and pests, and rosettes tend to die off in the centre of the clump where water and air cannot penetrate. Division also allows offsets to be planted in fresh soil, which is important as so many primulas are greedy feeders. I have found that for some petiolarid clones such as *P.* × 'Arduane' annual division into single crowns after flowering (early April) is essential, as multicrowned plants rot. This technique seems not to be appreciated by show judges who view large pans of 30 crowns or more disparagingly, noting that 'there is more than one plant'. No indeed, it is only a single individual, properly managed, which takes as much time and skill as a large cushion of another genus! Nevertheless, repeated division can weaken a clone, and it is always a good plan to have fresh seedlings growing on.

In a few groups, other forms of vegetative propagation are possible. In a few species, leafy buds can form at the top of the stem below the flowers, and these should be pegged down to form new plants. It has also been suggested that leaf-cuttings can be used in section Petiolares, although it is my experience that the species most suitable for this technique respond more readily to simple division.

Pests and diseases

Primulas suffer from a wide range of pests and diseases. Undoubtedly, the effects of many of these can be minimized by suitable cultivation. Young seed-grown plants grown in cool, humid conditions in an open nutritious compost often remain unscathed while older divisions, or plants grown in poor conditions nearby, struggle with a variety of predators and pathogens. Nevertheless, it is a wise precaution to take some prophylactic precautions against attacks by certain invertebrates and diseases.

It is also important to be tidy. Plant diseases often overwinter on dead foliage, while many pests use debris to hide away during the day. Hygienic gardeners clear away dead leaves, twigs and foliage from their gardens, frames and alpine houses, and their plants suffer relatively little as a result.

Unfortunately, primulas suffer from two serious problems, one of which is essentially incurable, and each of which can effectively destroy a collection. However, good cultivation and a good hygienic routine will minimize the effects of both virus and vine weevil.

It has been known for many years that all primulas suffer to some extent from cucumber mosaic virus. Work by David Walkey, formerly a professional plant virologist at Horticulture International, Wellesbourne, UK, who is a keen grower of primulas, suggested that several viruses are in fact implicated in primula infection. Some diseased clones apparently carry more than one.

The symptoms of viral disease are various. Typically, leaves are distorted, stunted and are sometimes yellowish around the margin and between the veins. Flowers are distorted and streaked, stocks woody, while roots may be stubby and poorly developed. In all cases, plants grow slowly. Resistance to viral attack appears to differ markedly between clones. For instance, *P.* × 'scapeosa' appears to have died out rapidly once virus became fully established, while *P.* × 'Soup-plate' survived relatively unscathed for some years with a considerable viral load, although it is rarely seen in 2002.

Clearly, it is the surviving clones which are more dangerous in a collection. Growers who succeed in keeping collections largely free from aphids (a Herculean and probably unrealistic task) will minimize the effects of viral disease. The more seedlings raised, the fewer will be the problems. David Winstanley used to maintain a seed-grown stock of 'polyanthus' which he knew showed early symptoms of virus. He regularly cross-injected sap from plants in his collection into these, and if the test plants indicated that a plant was infected, he destroyed, or at least isolated, the infected plant. He claimed that it was easy accidentally to cross-infect plants merely by handling them.

It is a brave and ruthless grower who will burn an expensive and perhaps rare plant because it is infected with virus, particularly if, like 'Soup-plate', it appeared to be fairly healthy. It is important to remember that virus is more usually spread by aphids which inject their styli right into the phloem sap. Infected plants can be placed into an 'isolation ward', sufficiently far from the main collection that cross-infection becomes unlikely. Here the infected plant can hopefully be induced to set seed, for this will be the ultimate salvation of that line.

For some reason which seems not to be fully understood, virus rarely if ever passes through the seed. Perhaps the main reason why primula seedlings tend to be so much more vigorous than divisions is that they are free of a viral load. Even when a clone shows no outward symptoms, the chances are that a loss of vigour can be attributed to viral infection, and the vigour will be restored when seedlings are raised. It is also found that plants raised by micropropagation from meristem culture are also usually virus-free. *P. aureata* is one of several species rarely setting seed that have been 'cleaned-up' by this technology. 'Micropropping' can have other hazards, however. Modern (2002) micropropagated *P. aureata* is a poor wizened charade of the glorious plant originally grown in the 1970s. It appears not to have virus, but looks 'wrong', perhaps because chromosomal mutations have resulted from the micropropagation process.

The other main disease which can affect some primulas is botrytis. This is usually associated with stagnant air. Often the fruiting bodies ('grey mould') are not seen, but leaves rot rapidly and basally from the same condition. I have found a few species particularly susceptible to this condition, notably *P. drummondiana*. It is possible that the 'basal rot' which affects some Himalayan primulas in sections Petiolares and Crystallophlomis in hot weather is also caused by botrytis.

If caught early enough, botrytis is often curable. All rotten parts should be scraped from the plant, which should then be submerged in a fungicide. The plant should then be repotted into a fresh mix and given 'intensive care' in a cool, humid but well-aerated frame. In well-aerated, cool conditions, the disease should rarely be seen.

Of the pests from which primulas suffer, by far the most important is vine-weevil. This evil insect is particularly associated with peat-based soils, and is very difficult to eradicate. The adults are like slightly larger black woodworm beetles, with the same protuding snout, and are nocturnal, rapidly scuttling to cover. Their presence is readily detected, for in summer they take characteristic notches out of the margin of the young leaves of evergreen shrubs such as rhododendron and pieris, rather like those made by a leaf-cutting ant.

Adult vine-weevils are, I regret to say, all female, and each lays about 200 eggs as carbon copies of their wicked selves. The grubs are stout, comma-shaped, and off-white with an orange head. They live under the crown of primulas, often gouging out a lair in the stock, and they eat through the roots. Like foxes with chickens, they are not content with one root, but wantonly snap each in turn until, as the last one is severed, the plant rapidly wilts and dies, by then beyond resuscitation.

When I wrote in 1993, there was no environmentally friendly and effective answer to the vine-weevil. Noxious and persistent systemic organochlorides such as aldrin and dieldrin controlled it well, but these have been banned for many years. The biological control, 'nemesis', based on a nematode pathogen of the weevil, is now readily available and can be very successful when used under heated glass in a confined space. However, it is only successful when the soil is warm. Fortunately, an excellent systemic control is now (2002) available which has a very short half-life in soil, and it is claimed, low human toxicity. In the UK this is marketed as 'Provado', and it provides very good control of aphids as well.

There are as well a number of prophylactic measures that can be undertaken which together help to limit weevil infestations. Weevils seem particularly to enjoy living in peat-based composts in plastic pots, and the more composts based on leaf-mould and manure are used in crock pots, the less happy weevils will be. If these composts have 'bromophos' powder or similar mixed in, weevils seem to be further deterred, although the powder seems not to kill them. Hygienic practices which limit the hiding places which the adult weevils seek, under dry leaves, cardboard boxes, etc., will also limit levels of infection. Hunting for the adults with a torch amongst the plants and pots on a warm, dry night can also be effective. If a plant is found in a collapsed state, it should be dug up and the weevil grubs killed. It is worth examining the roots of nearby primulas, which may also be infected. For pot plants, an examination of the root systems and crowns during an annual repotting in August to September will help to control larval numbers.

Compared to the vine-weevil, few other primula pests need mentioning, and most are easily controlled. Aphids can be easily kept at bay by the regular use of a systemic insecticide while plants are in growth, although they will never be eradicated. Root-aphis, found as fluffy white growths on primula roots, are rarely a major problem in my experience. They will respond to some systemic insecticides, or the roots can be dunked into a contact insecticide mixed with a dilute detergent. No primula should be grown in conditions dry enough to encourage red spider; should the diagnostic yellow punctate spotting and fine 'web' on the leaves appear in a hot spell, the plants (even *P. allionii!*) should be regularly sprayed with water, or put outside in a cool, humid place, where the problem should soon disappear. Slugs are an ever-present garden menace, and the regular use of a slug-bait can be recommended. Unfortunately, this can also result in the demise of the hedgehog, which eats large numbers of slugs including poisoned ones.

Several large garden inhabitants can be a menace. I know gardens whose primulas are savaged by deer, hares, rabbits or even sheep. Expensively erected wire netting can be an answer, as can a taste for venison and jugged hare (only in very isolated localities!) Voles and moles can undermine plants with lethal results. Our personal answer to these problems are domestic cats; incidentally they rarely use our garden for toilet purposes, neither do they allow any other cats to do so.

In our suburban setting, the main vertebrate pest is the blackbird, which often uproots woodland species while scratching. This is a close relative of the American Robin which has similar habits transatlantically. These birds laugh at our cats, and the only answer is vigilance, for a plant can usually be successfully rerooted if not left for too long. I know growers who are forced to cover their woodland beds with netting in response to this problem, but we have not yet been driven to this unsightly remedy. There are gardens, particularly public gardens, which suffer from very knowledgeable, two-legged predators, but this is another sort of problem.

Special conditions

Specialist growers are by nature experimenters, and each will use different techniques to allow the less-easy primula species to adapt to the particular conditions found in their own garden. I know a grower in Scotland who is lucky enough to have a waterfall alongside which he can plant *P. sonchifolia* (less successfully than formerly he claims in post-Millennial conditions of Climate Change). Most of us are not fortunate enough to have garden conditions which so closely match those found in the wild. In this short section I shall describe briefly a few special sites I have prepared in my own garden, and how they are managed.

Woodland conditions

My site of 0.2 ha in the north of England slopes gently to the north, and is bounded by 25 m (80 ft) lime trees on the south boundary. To the north of these, just outside the direct effect of the canopy and roots I have built raised beds surrounded by railway sleepers. These have good but unmodified top soil 30 cm (1 ft) down, but above this they are made up with a mix of two parts peat to two parts leaf-mould and one part rotted horse manure and sawdust. This is topdressed annually in early spring with about 5 cm (2 in) of leaf-mould above a scattering of a pelleted slow-release general fertilizer. In this bed are grown a variety of dwarf ericaceous shrubs. In between these a number of primulas in sections Petiolares, Cortusoides, Denticulata, Capitatae, Cordifoliae, Crystallophlomis, Oreophlomis and Muscarioides, *P. megasaeifolia* and *P. juliae* grow quite well. Delicate species, particularly those requiring very cool summer conditions are tucked under the north side of rhododendrons. A few, notably petiolarid and nivalid species are covered by a frame-light from late October to the end of March.

I rarely if ever need to water this bed, but on hot nights I sometimes spray plants briefly with a hose to cool them down and increase local humidity.

Bog conditions

I inherited a sunken 'patio' paved with flags on a heavy clay soil in full sun. I have removed groups of pavers, dug out the soil to about 35 cm (14 in), and have filled in with a mixture of one part leaf-mould to one part well-rotted cow manure and straw. Most of the rain falling on to the terrace drains into these areas which remain soggy but open throughout the year. They grow a wide variety of Proliferae and Sikkimensis species well.

Scree conditions

Also in full sun is a 30 degree east-facing slope. This has been dug out to about 70 cm (2 ft) depth. The bottom 40 cm (16 in) is filled with pure leaf mould, and above this is 30 cm (1 ft) depth of pure sandstone ⅜ in gravel. The slope ensures that all water drains out at the bottom: there is no 'sump'. This area lies directly below the alpine house which is automatically watered, so a continuous supply of water trickles through this scree during the summer months. European Auricula species in particular seem to appreciate these conditions.

Alpine house and frame

The 4 m (12 ft) aluminium-alloy alpine house stands in full sun in summer. It is well provided with vents and louvres. Pots are plunged to the rim in coarse sand and the plunge is automatically watered by a drip system, although this is usually switched off in winter. Crock pots absorb water through the side, but plastic pots only through the drainage, and it is important that a good contact is maintained between the compost and the sand. A thermostatically controlled fan heater is used to circulate air, and to keep winter temperatures at or just below freezing. Plants are regularly repotted when roots appear at the drainage holes, usually in spring.

Very few primulas enjoy the dry conditions of the alpine house in summer, where the temperature can reach 40°C. These include *P. allionii, P. fedtschenkoi, P. forrestii,* and the various species in section Sphondylia. Most other pot plants are removed to a sand plunge outside in summer where they are regularly misted in hot weather. This frame is covered with glass in winter. Various Muscarioides, Soldanelloides, Cortusoides and Armerina species are amongst those which have enjoyed a permanent position in the misted frame in full sun, covered in winter.

In summary, primulas tend to be greedy feeders which grow best in open, fluffy, humus-rich soils in moderate temperatures and high humidity. Good hygiene, and regular prophylactic measures will help to protect them from their main enemies in the garden, virus, and vine-weevil.

The Evolutionary History of *Primula* and its Relatives

This chapter has three sections. After an introduction, I shall describe briefly the geographical distribution of the genus, and discuss what information this can give us about the time and place of the evolutionary origin and subsequent migrations of *Primula* and its relatives. Secondly, I shall examine certain 'biological' characteristics of *Primula* with a high 'information content' to see what the distribution of these throughout the genus tells us about how species of *Primula* evolved. Thirdly, I shall use evidence from the DNA to deduce evolutionary relationships amongst the 95 species examined.

Introduction

An evolutionary study is set in four dimensions. For many animals with a good fossil record, one can see how evolution has progressed through geological time. It is also possible to use biochemical studies of large molecules such as haemoglobin, cytochrome c and the DNA as 'molecular clocks'. It is known that such molecules tend to evolve at relatively constant rates, so that if the differences in these molecules is calculated for two species, the point in time when these species diverged can be estimated. Since the first edition of this volume was published in 1993, two groups of workers have acquired a great deal of information about DNA sequence variation between many species of *Primula* and their relatives for two nuclear genes and one chloroplast gene. These studies have added immeasurably to our understanding of the relationships of *Primula* species, and have led to a number of reclassifications in the present account.

Similarities between living things can be measured in many other ways, for instance by their interfertility, or their morphological resemblance. Similarities between any two individuals (for interfertility, morphological resemblance, the DNA or any other measure) can be measured on a single dimension. As soon as another individual is included, the number of dimensions involved becomes two. Thus, estimates of similarity within a group of species are multidimensional, the number of dimensions involved being one less than the number of species being considered. It is difficult for the human brain to contemplate the interrelationships between more than four units, although a computer may be programmed to do so.

Without a knowledge of the time dimension, one has to be very careful how measurements of resemblance between living species are interpreted in the context of their evolutionary history. It may be tempting to consider that *P. verticillata*, for instance, is the ancestor of *P. boveana*. However, *P. verticillata* and *P. boveana* are in reality equally descendants of an unknown common parent. Nevertheless, it is possible that *P. verticillata* has diverged from that common ancestor less far than has *P. boveana*. Thus, the difficult words 'primitive' and 'advanced' must be interpreted solely in terms of supposed degrees of divergence from a hypothetical point of common origin. When I suggest that an ancestor of *P. boveana* may be 'represented' today by *P. verticillata*, I am in reality suggesting that *P. verticillata* is the extant species which may be closest to their (unknown or hypothetical) common ancestor.

On examining relationships between living species, it often seems that chains of evolutionary relationships survive in apparently linear sequences. The effects of natural selection, and chance, may have produced patterns of relationships which are less complex than might have been the case. On examining morphological resemblance, geographical distributions and the evolution of the pin/thrum system, it appears that one example of an apparently linear progression leads from *P. simensis* to *P. verticillata, P. boveana, P. gaubeana,* and *P. davisii* and possibly *P. edelbergii*. It is less clear where *P. floribunda*, which superficially resembles *P. edelbergii*, stands in this array. Nevertheless, one must be cautious in making such suggestions for three reasons.

Firstly, in one sense, all living things are equally advanced. Thus, one can only be saying that here is a graduated range of separate evolutionary divergences from a common ancestor. In fact, if one takes another sort of character, the chemical products called flavonoids, this becomes more clear.

	hesperidin	**malvidin**	**kaempferol**	**aurometin**
P. simensis	+		+	
P. verticillata	+		+	
P. boveana	+	+		
P. gaubeana		+	+	
P. edelbergii	+			+
P. floribunda		+	+	

If one takes the evidence of the flavonoids by itself, it now appears that *P. verticillata, P. simensis* and *P. boveana* are all equally divergent from *P. floribunda*, for they each share only one flavonoid in common. Also, *P. edelbergii* and *P. floribunda*, which superficially appear to be closely related, are now seen to have evolved by separate pathways.

Second, however tempting it may be to consider one end of the morphological sequence (*P. simensis* and *P. verticillata*) 'advanced' and the other (*P. floribunda*) 'primitive', it is difficult to be sure which end of an evolutionary sequence has diverged least (i.e. is 'primitive') from their hypothetical common ancestor. Recent evidence from the DNA now suggests that *P. floribunda* might in fact represent the less advanced end.

Third, such considerations assume that a particular character has only evolved once, and can therefore be used as a marker for a particular evolutionary line. However, it is possible that certain characters may have evolved more than once, in parallel.

In *Primula*, the 'petiolarid' capsule with its membranous dehiscence appears to be a good example of this last phenonemon (p. 165). It is found in section Crystallophlomis subsection Agleniana, in section Petiolares, and in sections Obconicolisteri, Davidii and Chartacea. Wendelbo (1961b) weighted this character highly, and so placed the Petiolares, Davidii and Chartacea together in one, highly diverse, subgenus which he called Craibia. However, it seems to me that this distinctive character may have arisen on at least two separate occasions.

Characters which are stable within groups and show a coordinated variation between groups are considered to have a high information content, and are 'weighted' highly. An example in *Primula* is the relationship between plants with multicellular hairs and the base chromosome number. As far as is known, all primulas with x = 12 and x = 10 have multicellular hairs, while this character is very rare for plants with x = 9 and x = 8 chromosomes. Consequently, one tends to value the information provided by these characters highly.

Equally, characters which do not show stability and coordinated variation have a low information content. A good example is flower colour. A number of species have individuals with either purple flowers or with yellow flowers. Such characters should not be used for phyletic studies.

Geographical distribution

The Russian agronomist Vavilov first suggested that the geographical origin of a group of plants is most likely to coincide with the region of its greatest diversity. Later he conceded that in some genera there have been secondary 'evolutionary hot-spots'. A good example are the cats-ears, *Hypochaeris*. This genus almost certainly originated in western Eurasia, although its greatest diversity today is to be found in South America.

There can be no doubt today as to the region where *Primula* shows its greatest diversity. In the eastern Sinohimalaya, between 90° and 100° E and 25° to 30° N, a relatively small mountainous region encompassing Sichuan, Yunnan, Upper Burma, Assam and south-east Tibet, over half of all *Primula* species are to be found, and most are restricted to this region.

Region	**Number of species**	**%**
Eastern Sinohimalaya	225	52
Central Himalaya (80–90°E)	63	15
Western Himalaya (70–80°E)	29	6.7
Rest of China	26	6
Central Asia	17	3.9
Greater Caucasus	14	3.2
Siberia	14	3.2
Japan	13	3
Europe	34	7.9
North America	20	4.6
South-east Asia	5	1.2
Arabia	4	0.9
South America	1	0.2

(**Note**: the total of 465 is greater than the number of *Primula* species (430) because some species are found in more than one region.)

The only other region of the world which musters more than 10 per cent of species is the adjacent region of the central Himalaya. The total Sinohimalayan range, together with the adjacent ranges in Central Asia, account for some 78 per cent of all *Primula* species.

From this central concentration of species, densities drop rapidly in surrounding areas, so that Japan, the rest of China, Siberia, south-east Asia (south of the Burmese and Chinese borders) and the Caucasian complex of mountains do not individually have more than six per cent of the species. In this context, it is evident that two areas show small secondary concentrations of species. The completely European section Auricula has 23 species, while diversification in the related section Parryi and in the Aleuritia results in 20 species being recorded from the north American continent. One can be fairly sure that these represent secondary centres of diversification because the species in these areas belong to only a few taxonomic groups in the genus *Primula*, and because these regions are a long way from the main concentration of species.

Following Vavilov, it seems very likely that *Primula* arose in the mountains of the eastern Sinohimalaya. Not only is by far the greatest concentration of species found here, but no less than 26 of the 38 sections of the genus (68 per cent) occur in this region.

Most primulas are mountain plants. If *Primula* did evolve, or at least underwent its first diversification, in the eastern Sino-himalaya, it seems probable that it did so in, and possibly in response to the circumstances of, a mountainous region. The eastern Sino-hamalaya is a very recent mountain system. It is still being uplifted as the Indian tectonic plate moves northwards, diving underneath the Tibetan plateau. This uplift is thought to have started only about 40 million years ago, and high mountains have been characteristic of this region for less than 20 million years. We can deduce that most of the diversification in *Primula* has taken place over the last 25 million years or so.

There are a few other geographical pointers as to the time and place of origin of *Primula*. *Primula* is absent from Australasia, from south-east Asia south of the 'Wallace line', and from central and southern Africa. One can conclude from this that *Primula* seems not to have been represented on the southern continent Gondwanaland at the time of its split from Laurasia some 60 million years ago, so that it might not have evolved by then.

The occurrence of *Primula* in South America (by one species) is likely to be of much more recent origin. Colonization of this area through Central America and down the Andes will have occurred during cooler, wetter climatic phases associated with the Ice Ages. During those times, the drop in sea-level also allowed land bridges to form between Asia and North America, between Asia and Japan, and across the north Atlantic. Isolated mountain systems such as the Caucasus and the Alps could also have been colonized during the Ice Ages, when much of the intervening ground would have been more suitable for *Primulas* than is the case today.

So it seems possible that most regions away from the Himalaya, such as North America, Arabia, and even the European mountains, could have been colonized by primulas as recently as the Glacial Periods. If this was the case, one must presume that much of the evolution of *Primula* has occurred within the last one million years.

Primula may have arisen in the Sinohimalaya, less than 30 million years ago. What evidence exists as to the nature of this original 'archaeprimula'?

High Information Biological Characters

In *Primula*, several 'high information' characters (p. 41) tend to vary between groups in a co-ordinated way. For each of these there seems to be a linear progression. For instance:

	?'primitive'		?'advanced'
inflorescence	'candelabroid'	single whorl	single flower
leaf hairs	multicellular	unicellular	gland
bracts	leaf-like	narrower	tiny
section	Proliferae	Denticulata	Minutissimae

Ideally, such evolutionary sequences for characters can be given 'polarity' by using 'biological markers', characteristics for which one can be sure which is the least derived end.

In *Primula*, it is fortunate that three different types of biological marker can be used, and that on the whole these give a consistent picture.

1. Chromosome number

The number of chromosomes, on which the genetic information is carried in each cell, varies in two main ways in plants.

In a diploid plant, each type of chromosome is present twice. In a polyploid plant it is present more than twice (in a 'tetraploid' = 4×, four times; in a 'hexaploid' = 6×, six times, etc.). The 'chromosome base number' is the number of chromosomes in each set. Thus, in section Aleuritia where the chromosome numbers 18, 36, 54, 72 and 126 are found, 2×, 4×, 6×, 8× and 14× polyploid races occur and the chromosome base number is 9.

The 'chromosome base number' should be relatively stable for a group like *Primula* where most reproduction is by seed. However, on rare occasions the chromosomes can become reorganized by breaking and rejoining. When this happens, it is very much more common for the number of chromosomes to become reduced, than for it to increase.

In *Primula,* the base numbers 12, 11, 10, 9 and 8 are found. It follows that plants with the base numbers 12 and 11 are likely to be the least derived, and those with 9 and 8 the most derived from a hypothetical ancestor. Of the numbers 11 and 12, $x = 11$ is the more widespread in both the tribe Primuleae, and in *Primula* itself, and there is a case for regarding this as the base number primitive to *Primula*.

Fortunately in *Primula* the chromosome base number varies so much, yet appears to be exceptionally stable within groups. In fact, the classification in this book is constructed so that the chromosome base number hardly varies at all within a section. This was also the case for most of the sections used by Smith and Fletcher in their monograph.

The notable exception to this consistency was Smith and Fletcher's use of the section Farinosae, which in their interpretation contained species with x = 11, 10, 9, and 8. This section (of over 80 species) included species with all the pollen types known in the genus, and was heterogenous in other ways as well. Consequently, I have subdivided it into no less than 6 sections, the Oreophlomis (x = 11), Armerina (x = 11, 10), Yunnanensis (x = 11), Aleuritia (x = 9) Pulchella (x = 8) and Glabra (x = 8).

The level of polyploidy can also be used as a biological marker in evolutionary work. The development of a polyploid series is essentially 'one way'; it is extremely unlikely that a polyploid species could develop into a diploid. In general, it can be considered that polyploids are evolutionarily derived with respect to diploid relatives. For instance, *P. halleri* (4×) and *P. scotica* (6×) can be regarded as derived with respect to their diploid relative *P. farinosa* (2×). It follows that the two sections which are entirely polyploid, the Parryi (4×) and the Auricula (6×) can be considered derived with respect to their closest relative with involute vernation, the Cuneifolia, which has one diploid and one tetraploid species.

2. Pollen type

The nomenclature of pollen types is complex. Pollen may be spherical in shape, or prolate (longer from pole to pole than wide) or oblate (shorter from pole to pole than wide). Pollen grains germinate through points of weakness in their wall (exine). These may be furrows (colpae), pores, or pores in furrows (colporae). If a grain has points of weakness in colpae which are not fully developed as pores, it is known as colporoidate. Where furrows join at the poles, the grain is syncolpate, and if the furrows are many, but do not join it is called stephanocolpate (stephanus is a garland in Latin). The number of furrows/pores is denoted by a number-prefix.

Three main types of pollen are known in *Primula* (Wendelbo, 1961c, Spanowsky, 1962):

- *3-(4) colpor(oid)ate* (Fig. 1). The spherical to (usually) prolate grain has three equally spaced longitudinal furrows which do not meet and at the centre of each of which is a pore (colporate) or at least a point of weakness (colporoidate). Variants include species in which one or both morphs have grains with one or two furrows (section Sphondylia, Al Wadi & Richards, 1992), or four furrows (chiefly in section Pulchella). Occasional cases are also known in these two sections in which the furrow is almost absent (3–4-porate).

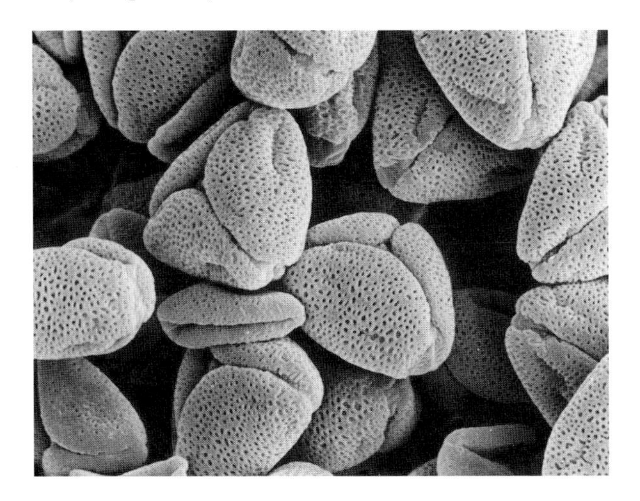

- *3(–5) (para)syncolpate* (Fig. 2). The (usually) oblate grain has three to five equally spaced longitudinal furrows which meet the poles (syncolpate) or fuse to form a wider triangular to pentangular area at the poles (parasyncolpate). Kelso (1991b) shows that the number of colpae tend to increase with 'ploidy level in section Aleuritia, so that 2× and 4× species are 3-syncolpate, 6× and 8× species 4-syncolpate, and the 14× *P. stricta* is 5-syncolpate. In section Armerina, the 4× species *P. egaliksensis* has an unique pollen type best described as 5-stephanosyncolpate which presumably has resulted from a hybrid origin between species in sections Aleuritia (3-syncolpate pollen) and Armerina (6-stephanocolpate pollen).

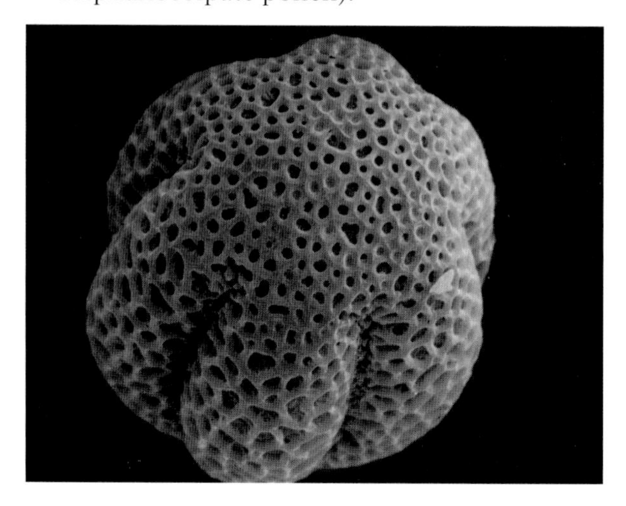

- *(5)-6-(7)-stephanocolpate* (Fig. 3). The spheroid to slightly oblate grain has a number of regular lateral furrows without obvious pores. In *Primula*, these seem to be fairly regular in number, but in *Dionysia* there is a tendency for the larger thrum grain to have more furrows (Al Wadi and Richards, 1992).

Viewing the Primulaceae as a whole, Wendelbo (1961c) concludes that the 3-colporate grain represents the ancestral type. From this, he identifies two main evolutionary trends:

- Loss of pore, and fusion of colpae, resulting in syncolpate grains.
- Loss of pore, and increase in colpa number, resulting in stephanocolpate grains.

I am fully in agreement with this, and thus one must consider the 3-colpor(oid)ate pollen type the least derived in *Primula*.

3. Primary homostyly

Heterostyly and homostyly are more fully discussed on pp. 42–63. From crossing relationships with related heterostyles, it is concluded that homostylous self-fertile primulas are either

- primary non-recombinational homostyles (diploid), which appear to represent the condition in the genus before the evolution of heterostyly, or
- secondary recombinational homostyles (usually polyploid) which have evolved from heterostylous species.

It follows that primary homostyles can be considered the least derived breeding systems in the genus, while secondary homostyles are highly derived.

The primitive primula

Of course, a plant cannot be considered to be of a 'primitive' type, close to the hypothetical 'archaeprimula' root, merely because it possesses biological markers of an underived nature. It may have undergone considerable adaptive radiation in morphological characteristics while maintaining its original chromosome number, pollen type and breeding system.

Nevertheless, underived states of other, morphological characters are more likely to be associated with primitive biological characters than with derived ones. In a search for an 'archaeotype', primary homostyles with 3-colporoidate pollen and 22 chromosomes (x = 11) growing in the eastern Himalaya would merit a close examination. Such characteristics are found together today only in certain species in section Proliferae. (The only other candidates for 'the most primitive living primulas' occur in section Cortusoides with x = 11 or 12, and in section Sphondylia which, however, has x = 9 chromosomes and an Arabian to western Himalayan distribution).

On the basis of biological marker characteristics, the least derived of present-day primulas seem to be the Proliferae species *P. cockburniana*, *P. chungensis*, *P. prolifera*, and *P. miyabeana*. The Proliferae, a widespread and diverse section from temperate forests, are centred around the eastern Sinohimalaya, and not only have primary homostyle species, but at least two species which have both homostyle and heterostyle races. In many ways, they make excellent candidates for the living primulas which most resemble the 'archaeprimula', linking as they do to a number of other Sinohimalayan sections of a more derived type such as the Crystallophlomis, Sikkimensis and Monocarpicae. Together with the primitive Cortusoides, the Proliferae share a number of characters which, as they rarely vary within sections, tend to be highly 'weighted':

- Multicellular hairs on the leaves.
- No meal.
- Leaf-like, unpouched bracts.
- Inflorescences of superimposed whorls.
- Globose, valvate capsules with small seeds.

Thus, a case can be made for considering these characters, together with primary homostyly, a chromosome base number of x = 11, and 3-colporoidate pollen, to be typical of the most primitive primulas, and as such, closest to the original 'archaeprimula' (p. 41).

Interestingly, of all the characters which have been thought to be 'primitive' in earlier phylogenetic speculations about *Primula,* (e.g. Bruun, 1932; Wendelbo, 1961b,c; Spanowsky, 1962; Cain, 1965) only leaf vernation is missing here. This character deserves further discussion.

Leaf vernation

If, when young leaves appear, they are inrolled, the vernation is said to be involute. If however, the margins are reflexed, the vernation is said to be revolute. This character was first noticed by R.E. Cooper and was used by Smith to show that the involute American section Parryi, superficially so similar to the revolute Asian Crystallophlomis, was in fact more closely related to the involute European Auricula and Asian-American Cuneifolia and Suffrutescens. In *Primula,* involute vernation is otherwise found only in sections Amethystina and some Armerina. It was long thought to be a characteristic of subgenus Sphondylia as well, but Austin Mast has recently convincingly shown (Mast *et al.*, 2001) that the vernation in that group is better interpreted as conduplicate (folded together), a characteristic which could well have evolved from the common condition of revolute (recoiled) vernation.

However, although involute vernation is only found in six sections of *Primula*, it is nevertheless the sole condition known in all other Primulaceae (except *Cortusa* and *Dionysia* which evolved from within *Primula,* p. 38). This suggests that involute leaf vernation may have been the original condition in *Primula.* However, none of the 'primitive' primulas identified here (for instance in section Proliferae) have involute vernation. There are three hypotheses which might explain this anomaly:

- revolution vernation was a characteristic of the earliest primulas, reverting to involute vernation in some later developments of the genus;
- the Proliferae do not represent the earliest primulas;
- *Primula* is not monophyletic, but evolved from more than one evolutionary 'stem', one of which was involute and the other revolute.

It seems quite likely that the third hypothesis provides the explanation. Arguments for and against the monophyly of *Primula* will be discussed at the end of the next section.

Relationships in *Primula* according to DNA

In the first edition of this book (1993), I used a cladistic analysis, based on high information biological characters, to assess likely relationships between sections of *Primula*, and their evolutionary pathways. Since then, this analysis has been superseded by two major studies which compare sequence variation for particular genes in the chloroplast DNA between relatively large numbers of species. The first, by Ida Trift (2001) working with Arne Anderberg and Mari Kallersjo at Stockholm, was based on the chloroplast DNA gene *rbc*L. This examined 39 primula samples classified in 32 species in the context of a total 90 samples within the Primulales. The second study was undertaken by Austin Mast and co-workers working with Elena Conti at the University of Zurich. This examined sequence variation in two chloroplast genes, the *trn*L and *rpl*16 introns for 119 samples which included no less than 95 *Primula* species (Mast *et al.*, 2001). Information from these two sequences shared a high degree of correspondence, and the final analysis (cladogram) is based on both sequences. This analysis, in particular, has been used extensively in the consideration of relationships and classifications in the systematic part of this book, although both studies agree with respect to several important conclusions (pp. 39–40).

As a consequence of these studies, we now have a much clearer idea of relationships within the genus, and many problems have been resolved, or partly so. In general, the clusters derived from DNA sequences (cladogram) closely follow traditional classifications based on morphology and high information biological characters, and expounded by Bruun (1932), Wendelbo (1961), Spanowsky (1962), Rosvik (1968), Schwarz (1968) and Richards (1993). I have needed to make few major changes to the classification published in the latter work. Consequently, in the few cases where the DNA results do depart from these classifications, I am inclined to give a great deal of credence to the previously unsuspected relationships that they reveal.

Nevertheless, when these clusters are used to provide interpretations of evolutionary pathways, it is very important to remember that all our DNA information is based only on maternally inherited characteristics, and so only the asexual, seed-germplasm evolutionary lines are revealed. The male component to evolutionary pathways remains obscure. This limitation may be particularly important for allopolyploids in which half or more of the parentage of a species is not maternal. A good example is *P. egaliksensis* which appears from the chloroplast DNA to be embedded deeply within the Aleuritia species and closely related to *P. mistassinica*. However, Kelso (1991) clearly shows that this Armerina-like plant is in fact an allotetraploid derivative between an Aleuritia species and an Armerina species. Because the Aleuritia parent was presumably the female parent to this cross, the maternal DNA reveals no trace of the Armerina parentage so clearly shown by the pollen morphology and other features.

When interpreting relationships revealed by differences in DNA sequence patterns, it is also important to remember that more than three-quarters of all *Primula* species are missing from this analysis, so that many sections are unrepresented, or are represented by very few samples, which may be untypical of the section as a whole. When information from missing species becomes available, it could change our concept of relationships. For instance, a new sample could prove to be more closely related to one of a pair of species currently regarded as 'sister' than the other member of this pair. It should also be noted that all species are only represented by a single sample. Conceivably, two or more DNA lines could coexist in the maternal germplasm of a single species. However, one of the chief sources of error in studies of this kind, incorrect taxonomic identification, is hopefully minimized here, as the greatest care was taken to check and document species identity with several authorities, including the present author. Nevertheless, there are a very few possible problems of identity which are discussed below.

Confirmation of possibly controversial classifications

The DNA has confirmed the following possibly controversial changes to the classification of *Primula* which were introduced in Richards (1993).

- Species classified within sections Souliei, Yunnanensis, Oreophlomis, Armerina and Pulchella are not strongly identified with section Aleuritia (all were originally classified within section Farinosae).
- *P. megaseifolia* and *P. juliae* are embedded within section Primula.
- *P. secundiflora* is a Proliferae, not a Sikkimensis species.

New insights within *Primula*

The main new findings from the DNA, some of which have led to taxonomic conclusions which contradict earlier classifications (e.g. Richards 1993) follow in systematic order: this basically follows the cladogram (pp.39–40) from the bottom upwards.

- *P. dryadifolia* is related to members of subgenus *Auganthus*, rather than to the Minutissimae in subgenus *Aleuritia* as originally thought (both studies show this). I have moved this section (Dryadifolia) to subgenus *Auganthus* within which morphological features suggest that it is presumably most closely related to section Bullatae.
- *P. suffrutescens* is sister to *Dodecatheon pulchellum* rather than to other Cuneifolia, suggesting that it should be placed within a separate section in *Primula*.
- Members of section Petiolares are perhaps rather more closely related to section Proliferae rather than to section Crystallophlomis as originally thought.
- *P. cicutariifolia* in section Pinnatae has no close relatives, but is clearly placed in a subgenus *Aleuritia* rather than in a subgenus *Auganthus* clade.
- *Sredinskya grandis* may be embedded within section Primula, suggesting that it should be classified within subgenus *Primula* of *Primula* (as *P. grandis*) and placed close to section Primula.
- *P. pulchella* is sister to *P. concinna*, which was originally of uncertain affinity and should now be classified within section Pulchella.
- The American Aleuritia species *P. alcalina*, *P. specuicola* and *P. borealis* are sisters of the Japanese *P. modesta* rather than the north American *P. mistassinica*. Rather surprisingly *P. capitellata* is also placed here: the identity of this plant is suspect.
- The central Asian Aleuritia species *P. algida*, *P. daraliaca* and *P. longiscapa* are sister to one another but are probably less related to other Aleuritia species, and are more closely allied to two Oreophlomis species. Conceivably, they arose from Oreophlomis (mother) × Aleuritia intersectional hybridization. Consequently, this group of species is placed in a separate subsection Algida.
- *P. zambalensis* is sister to *P. nutans* in section Armerina. The *P. gemmifera* group to which *P. zambalensis* belongs has long been of uncertain affinity, but we can now safely regard them as members of section Armerina.
- *P. glomerata* is sister to *P. capitata* rather than *P. denticulata*. This finding provides welcome confirmation to a recent chromosome count which suggested that *P. glomerata* should be classified in section Capitatae rather than Denticulata.
- *P. erratica* is sister to *P. denticulata*. The affinity of the related pair of stoloniferous species *P. erratica* and *P. caldaria* has long been uncertain, but we can now safely regard them as members of section Denticulata.
- *P. flaccida* is sister to *P. vialii*. There have long been geographical, ecological, morphological and cultural reasons for regarding *P. flaccida* and its relatives as more related to Muscarioides than Soldanelloides. This finding confirms that view.
- *P. reidii* is embedded within section Muscarioides. This confirms the close relationship between sections Muscarioides and Soldanelloides, but until more Soldanelloides species are included in the analysis, I have chosen to keep the sections apart.
- *P. yunnanensis* and *P. membranifolia* are sisters. This tends to confirm the close relationship between species previously classified within sections Yunnanensis and Souliei, and for this and a number of other reasons these sections have now been fused.

Subgeneric classification within *Primula*

The subgenera employed within the first edition of this book (Richards 1993) were largely based on those in Wendelbo (1961b), but differed in that I abandoned his subgenus *Craibia*, assigning the section Petiolares to subgenus *Aleuritia*, and leaving the subgeneric placing of sections Davidii and Chartacea open. I commented that this classification was largely supported by the cladistic analysis I undertook then, so it is worth considering to what extent this classification has withstood a later and more rigorous examination by the DNA (cladogram). This new analysis clearly identifies six major groups ('clades') in the genus, of roughly equal standing. These are listed below, with their subgeneric status (unfortunately no members of subgenus *Carolinella* were available for testing).

- Clade 1. *Primula* subgenus *Sphondylia* (and *Dionysia*).
- Clade II. *Primula* subgenus *Aleuritia* (in part).
- Clade III. *Primula* subgenus *Primula*.
- Clade IV. *Primula* subgenus *Aleuritia* (in part) (including sections Pinnatae and Davidii).
- Clade V. *Primula* subgenus *Auriculastrum* (including *Dodecatheon*).
- Clade VI. *Primula* subgenus *Auganthus* (including *Cortusa*).

We can conclude that the DNA provides strong justification for all of Wendelbo's subgenera (except for *Craibia*), but that the largest subgenus, *Aleuritia*, comprises two clear clades. It might be thought that a good case could be made for the description of a new subgenus, based on Clade IV (Clade II contains section Aleuritia and so is validly entitled subgenus *Aleuritia*). The subgenus encompassing Clade IV would include sections Pinnatae, Davidii, Petiolares, Proliferae, Crystallophlomis, Cordifoliae and Fedtschenkoana. It is of particular interest, as it includes some of the most 'primitive' species in the genus (p. 32), a conclusion not unsupported by the cladogram. As this clade contains the components of Wendelbo's subgenus *Craibia*, a suitable prior name also exists for this grouping.

Unfortunately, both Austin Mast and I have independently come to the conclusion that no morphological characteristics uniquely define the component members of Clade IV, so that the morphological diagnosis of any subgenus based on this Clade would fail. At present, we are limited to a morphologically-based classification which fails to separate two DNA-based clades.

New insights within the Primulaceae

Both DNA studies also include a number of other representatives from within the Primulaceae. Some of the conclusions from these studies are far-reaching, showing for instance that a number of genera traditionally placed within the Primulaceae, such as *Cyclamen*, are better classified elsewhere, for instance in the Myrsinaceae (Anderberg *et al.* 2000). Those conclusions which directly affect our understanding of relationships within *Primula* are detailed below.

- *Dionysia* is sister to subgenus *Sphondylia* (both studies show this unambiguously). Although it differs from members of that section in pollen type (stephanocolpate), leaf vernation (revolute), base chromosome number ($x = 10$) and woolly rather than powdery farina, it seems nevertheless to have evolved from forerunners of the Sphondylia. This conclusion agrees with Wendelbo (1961a,b) and disagrees with Al Wadi and Richards (1992) and Richards (1993) who had suggested that it might have been derived from the Armerina.
- *Cortusa* is embedded within subgenus *Auganthus* and presumably evolved from forerunners of present representatives in this group (also an unambiguous finding of both studies).
- *Dodecatheon pulchellum* is sister to *P. suffrutescens* and well included within the subgenus *Auriculastrum* clade. This is a slightly surprising result. I had argued (Richards 1993) that the American genus of 'shooting stars', *Dodecatheon,* had indeed evolved from forerunners of modern members placed in subgenus Auriculastrum, but I had expected that modern section Parryi species were the most likely closest relatives of *Dodecatheon*. If *Dodecatheon* is in fact more related to Suffrutescens relatives, we must suppose that the similarity in vegetative features and fruit of, for instance, *D. pulchellum* to *P. parryi*, which often grows with it, must be assigned to earlier evolutionary links.
- *Omphalogramma*, *Soldanella* and *Hottonia* are sisters. It is no surprise to find a close relationship between *Omphalogramma* and *Soldanella* which are linked by the untested monotypic genus *Bryocarpum* (Plate 20). It would also be interesting to discover where

members of *Primula* subgenus *Carolinella* lie in this relationship, as they share the circumscissile capsule type of *Soldanella* and *Bryocarpum* (although Anderberg & El-Ghazaly 2000 point out that the *Carolinella* have several pollen types and may be polyphyletic). It is much more surprising to discover that the aquatic, filigree-leaved *Hottonia* is placed here, too. Not only is the candelabroid inflorescence of this genus very primula-like, but it has exactly the same type of heterostyly as *Primula*, and we must now consider the possibility that *Hottonia* may have evolved heterostyly quite independently from *Primula*, an unlikely outcome.

The polyphyletic evolution of *Primula*

I have pointed out that the phyletic analysis of *Primula*, whether based on the DNA or high information biological characters, has some awkward features. Principal amongst these, perhaps, is the distribution of species with involute, revolute and conduplicate vernation, as these seem to be the most stable, highly weighted, features in the genus. Apart from genera derivative from *Primula* (p. 37), the rest of the family has involute vernation, but I have argued that the most primitive primulas today have revolute vernation. This raises the question as to whether *Primula* might be polyphyletic, that it might have arisen from more than one evolutionary stem. It seems unlikely that early developments of the genus having evolved revolute vernation, should have reverted once again to involute vernation. It is possible that two or more basal lines, at least one of which was revolute and one involute in vernation, independently developed into what we know today as *Primula*. In this context, it is interesting to ask whether the DNA analysis can give us new information.

Although the smaller cladogram of Ida Trift and the larger one produced by Austin Mast differ in particulars, which is not surprising as they were based on different gene sequences, it is noteworthy that the major relationships they demonstrate are very similar. Both studies conclude that the genus *Primula* is composed of three clades, represented by subgenus *Auriculastrum*, subgenus *Auganthus*, and the rest. It is noteworthy that both studies agree that the conduplicate subgenus *Sphondylia*, so often considered to represent the most primitive primula (for instance in Wendelbo 1961b), is firmly embedded within the third clade. The subgenus *Auriculastrum* clade includes all the involute *Primula* species (with the exception of a few Armerina species; it is possible that the Armerina could originally have been part of an involute or revolute clade, some branches of which formed new hybridogenous species by crossing with revolute species).

At an early stage three lines had evolved which would all develop into plants we call *Primula* today. Two of these had developed from a newly arisen revolute line, while the third remained involute like its ancestors. The involute line, which became subgenus *Auriculastrum*, and one of the revolute lines which possibly resembled present-day Proliferae, had x = 11, tricolporoidate pollen and unicellular hairs or glands. However, the other revolute line had x = 12, trisyncolpate pollen and multicellular hairs and this became subgenus *Auganthus*. The subsequent evolution of the other four subgenera developed from the Proliferae line, in which a reduction in chromosome base number (p. 30), and development of other pollen types (p. 31), were striking developments.

It is interesting that heterostyly is widespread in representatives of all three lines, but that what I deduce to be primary homostyly is still found in both the revolute lines (p. 32). It is possible that heterostyly evolved independently in all three lines. Some credence is given to this model by the suggestion that various lines with independently evolved heterostylous features might have hybridized to give a more efficient, 'highly evolved' system (p. 53). Alternatively, the basic features of heterostyly in *Primula* might have evolved only once, at a very early evolutionary stage, so that *Hottonia*, which branched off before the genus showed much diversification, already possessed these features. In this case we have to explain the persistence of primary homostyly to the present day in several parts of the genus. However, homostyly, apparently of a primary type, undoubtedly does still coexist with heterostyly in a number of species. Studies on the primrose, *P. vulgaris*, explained in detail elsewhere (p. 55), show that balancing selection for heterostyly and homostyly might allow both systems to persist side by side over considerable lengths of time. Whether heterostyly evolved once or several times, homostyly has apparently been able to survive over considerable periods of time on occasions.

Derivative genera

As has already been pointed out, the DNA makes it quite clear that three currently recognized genera evolved from within *Primula* long after the genus had started to diversify. It had already been recognized in Richards (1993) that these genera had probably been derived from within *Primula*, but the DNA makes this certain.

- *Dodecatheon* is an entirely American genus with purplish reflexed petals, involute vernation, 3-colporoidate pollen and a chromosome base number of x = 11. Vegetatively, and in capsule type, species closely resemble members of *Primula* section Parryi. It has been frequently suggested that *Dodecatheon* evolved from forerunners of section Parryi, by developing reflexed petals on homostyle flowers. However, the DNA suggests that another American Auriculastrum line, which led to *P. suffrutescens,* may have been more closely involved.
- *Cortusa* is a widespread Eurasiatic genus with anthers fused into a ring, revolute vernation, 3-syncolpate pollen, and a chromosome base number of x = 12. The few species (some classifications have only one) closely resemble contemporary members of *Primula* section Cortusoides, for instance *P. geranifolia*. From these, *Cortusa* only really differs by the fused anther-ring, and by being homostylous (as are some Cortusoides). Doubtless, *Cortusa* evolved from forerunners of this section in the fairly recent past, although it is interesting that this genus now has a far wider distribution than the Cortusoides, occurring as far west as France. There is a good case for including *Cortusa* within *Primula*, perhaps as a separate section within subgenus *Auganthus*. However, until *Cortusa* is thoroughly revised, no easy matter, it is more easily omitted!
- *Dionysia* is a genus of some 50 species restricted to desert cliffs in the Middle East, from Turkey to Pakistan. Many species form dense cushions, unlike any *Primula,* but these grade into tall, woody, yellow-flowered plants which closely resemble members of *Primula* section Sphondylia occurring in the same region, and have apparently been derived from them. All except one of the dionysias are heterostylous, in exactly the same way as is *Primula*, and it is reasonable to suggest that this beautiful genus represents a specialized evolutionary relative of *Primula* section Sphondylia, despite the possession of revolute vernation of the leaves, a chromosome base number of x = 11, stephanocolpate pollen, and a woolly type of meal quite different to that in the Sphondylia.

The more 'aggressive' brand of Cladist might be strongly tempted on the basis of this evidence to include these three genera within *Primula.* I have already done so for the genus *Sredinskya*, which, however, had frequently been regarded as a *Primula* in earlier classifications. However, with the possible exception of *Cortusa,* I believe it would be a mistake to do so for the other genera. *Dodecatheon, Dionysia* and *Cortusa* are each distinctive, well-defined, and very probably monophyletic, and *Primula* is quite large enough a genus already!

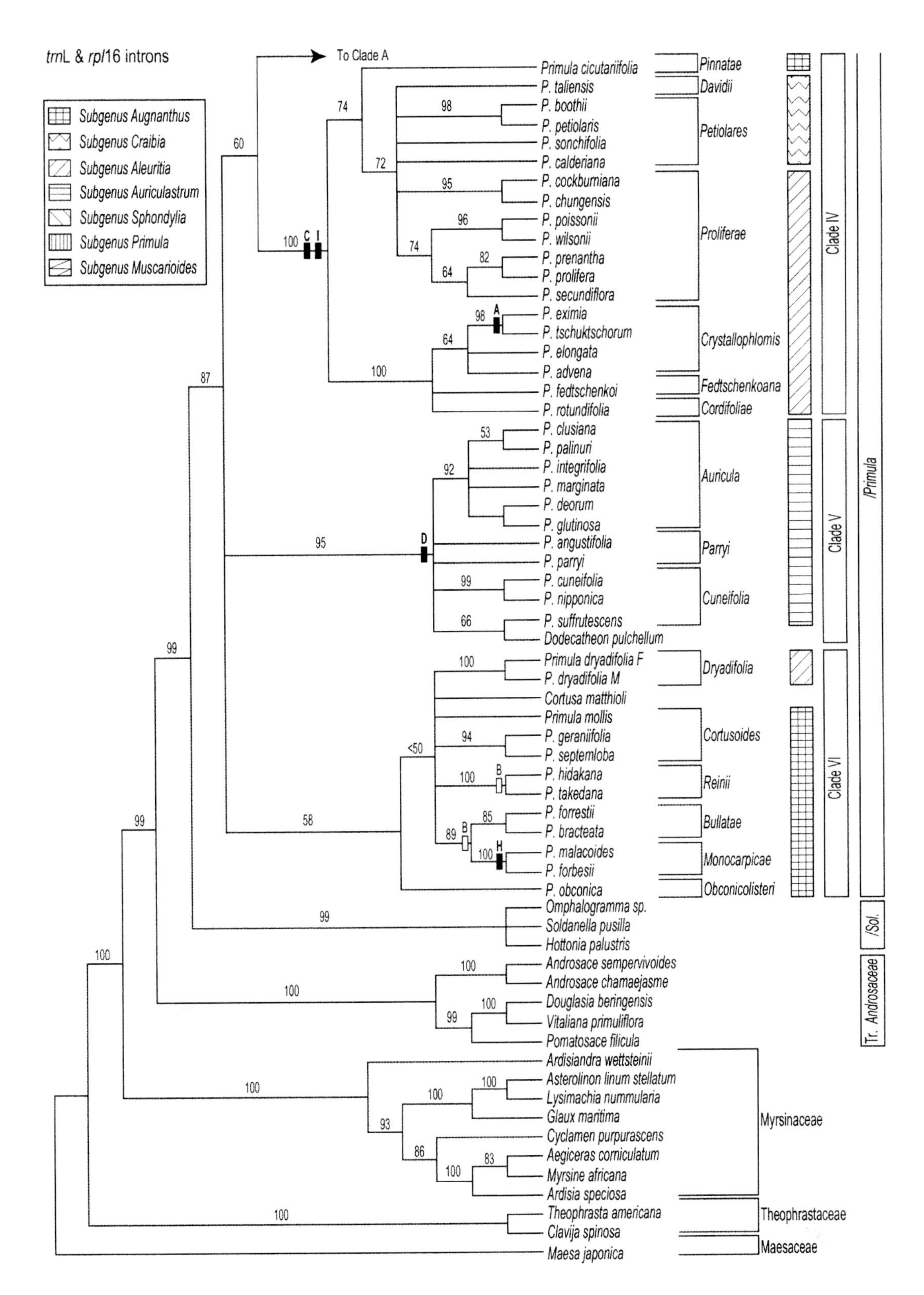

Cladogram from Mast et al (2001) based on relationships in two chloroplast DNA sequences *trn*L and *rpl*16 between 95 *Primula* species and 24 related species. At the top of the diagram, the link to the other half of the cladogram on p. 40 is shown. Subgeneric classifications are those of Wendelbo (1961b). Numbers show bootstrap confidence estimates.

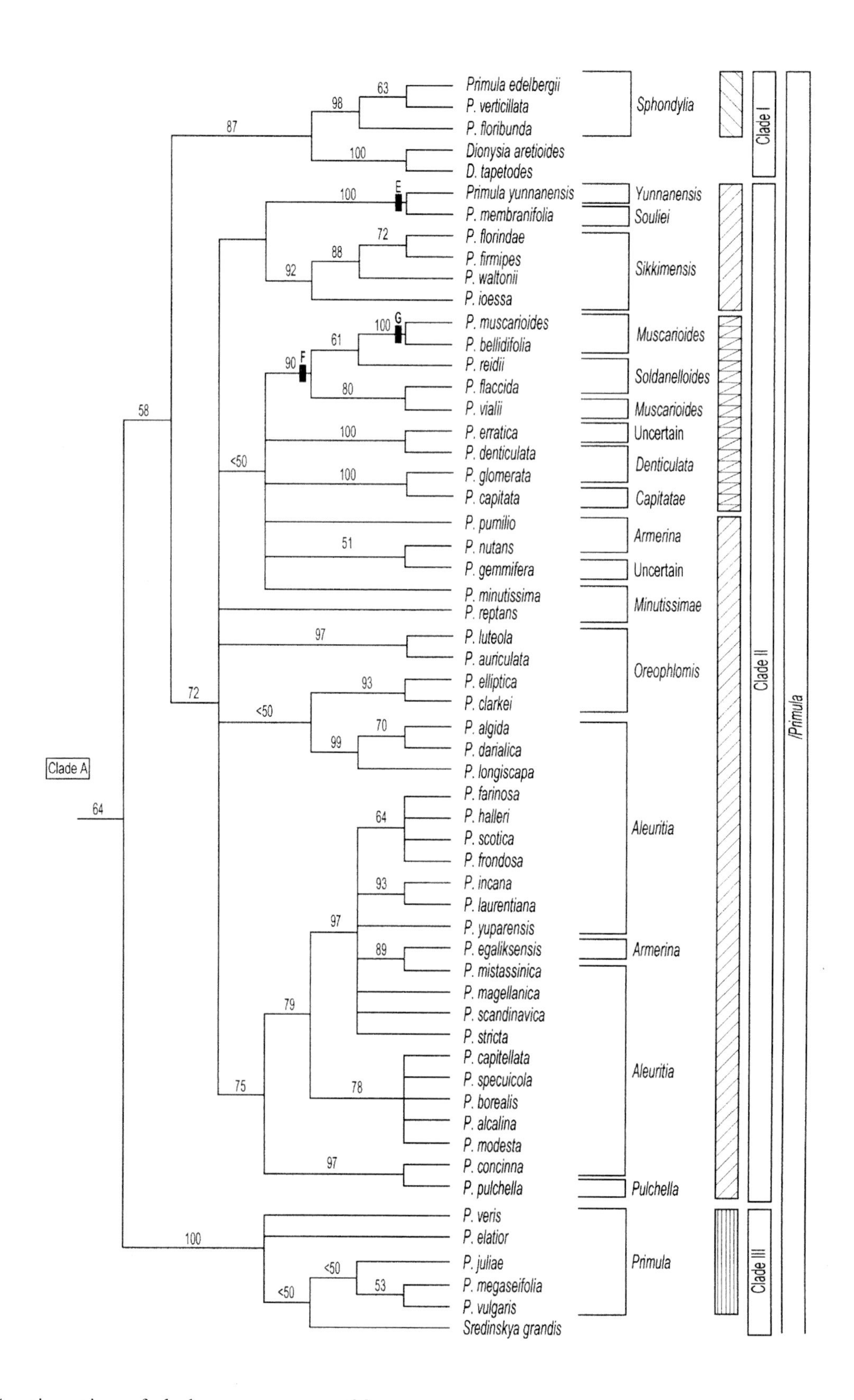

Continuation of cladogram on page 39.

The Most Important Biological Characters used in Sectional Classification in *Primula*

Section	Primary homo-styly	Leaves involute	Pollen type	Chromosome base no.	Multi-cellular hairs	Meal	Whorls super-imposed
Proliferae	+-	-	3-c	11	-	+-	+-
Cortusoides	+-	-	3-s	11,12	+	-	+-
Sphondylia	+-	+	1–3-c	9	+-	+-	+-
Cuneifolia	-	+	3-s	11	-	-	-
Suffrutescens	-	+	3-s	11	-	-	-
Amethystina	-	+	3-c	11	-	-	-
Parryi	-	+	3-s	22	-	+-	+-
Auricula	-	+	3-c	33	-	+-	-
Primula	-	-	st	11	+	-	-(+)
Sredinskya	+	-	st	11	+	+	-
Auganthus	-	-	3-s/st	12	+	-	+-
Monocarpicae	-	-	3-c/s	9	+	+	+
Obconicolisteri	-	-	3-c/s	12	+	-	-
Malvacea	-	-	3-s	12	+	-	sp
Pycnoloba	-	-	3-s	12	+	-	-
Pinnatae	-	-	st	12	+	-	-
Reinii	-	-	3-s	12	+	-	-
Bullatae	-	-	3-c	12	+	+-	-
Dryadifolia	-	-	3-s	?	-	+	-
Carolinella	-	-	?	?	+	-	sp
Chartacea	-	-	?	?	-	-	-
Davidii	-	-	3-s	?	+	-	-
Petiolares	-	-	3-s	11	-	+-	-
Crystallophlomis	-	-	3-s	11	-	+	+-
Cordifoliae	-	-	3-s	11	-	+	-
Sikkimensis	-	-	3-s	11	-	+	+-
Oreophlomis	-	-	3-s	11	-	-	-
Fedtschenkoana	-	-	3-s	11	-	-	-
Armerina	-	-	st	11,10	-	-	-
Glabra	-	-	3-s	8	-	-	-
Yunnanensis	-	-	3–4-c	8 (11)	-	+	-
Aleuritia	-	-	3–5-s	9	-	+	-
Pulchella	-	-	3–4-c	8	-	+	-
Minutissimae	-	-	3-c/s	11	-	+-	-
Denticulata	-	-	3-s	11	-	+-	-
Capitatae	-	-	3-s	9	-	+	-
Muscarioides	-	-	3-s	10	+-	+-	-sp
Soldanelloides	-	-	3-s	10	+-	+-	-sp

Notes:

3-c	pollen 3-colporoidate	3-s	pollen 3-syncolpate
st	pollen stephanocolpate	sp	flowers arranged in a spike (in the remainder, flowers borne in whorls, or solitary)

Heterostyly and Homostyly

Evolution of heterostyly in *Primula*

Heterostyly is perhaps the most distinctive feature of *Primula*. In most species (91 per cent), all the flowers on a plant either have a long style ('pin morph'), so that the stigma sits at the mouth of the corolla like a pin, or a short style ('thrum morph') where the stigma is buried deep in the corolla tube. The anthers of the pin lie deep in the corolla tube, and the anthers of the thrum are attached near the mouth of the corolla (the word 'thrum' derives from the supposed resemblance of these to the end of a weaving spindle). Thus, in the two morphs, the sites of pollen issue (anthers) and pollen receipt (stigma) take reciprocal positions (Plate 21).

In *Primula*, mating types seem almost always to be associated with these two flower morphs. In general, viable seed is only set when pollination occurs between the pin and the thrum, or the thrum and the pin. Such crosses are termed 'legitimate'. As a result, heterostyly is of great interest to gardeners and botanists alike. Nevertheless, in many species illegitimate pollinations (selfs, or crosses between plants of the same morph) will result in some seed-set, although fertility is never as great as for legitimate crosses (Table 1). For illegitimate pollinations, selfs and crosses seem not to differ in their fertility, but there is some evidence that the offspring of illegitimate crosses are more viable than those of selfs (Table 3).

When pins can be selfed, only pin seedlings result. However, when thrums are selfed, about two thrum seedlings are found for every pin seedling. True breeding thrums have rarely been reported, although Mather & de Winton (1941) report the occurrence of rather inviable true-breeding *SS* thrums in *P. sinensis*. Thus, one can be sure that the thrum is usually a heterozygote *Ss* with the thrum features *S* dominant, while the pin is a homozygote *ss*. It follows that the offspring of a legitimate cross *Ss* × *ss* should be half thrum *Ss* and half pin *ss*, and this does usually seem to be the case. Another consequence is that pin and thrum individuals should occur in the wild at a roughly equal frequency, and this is also usually found. (Excesses of pins would indicate that significant proportions of illegitimate fertilizations were occurring.)

As a result, for a species where illegitimate pollinations are inviable, only about half the individuals in the population (or the garden) are available for crossing. Evolutionarily, this is wasteful, and later in this chapter I will discuss the circumstances by which this apparently inefficient mechanism may have evolved.

From a garden point of view, the lesson is that several different individuals (seedlings) including pins and thrums need to be grown together if seed is to be obtained.

Heterostyly is a fairly widespread phenomenon, being known in 155 genera distributed through 24 flowering plant families (Ganders, 1979). In the Primulaceae, heterostyly is found in three other genera. *Vitaliana* will be discussed later. In *Hottonia* and *Dionysia,* it appears to operate exactly as in Primula. This strongly suggests that *Dionysia* at least evolved from *Primula* after heterostyly had developed (p. 38).

It is a quite extraordinary happenstance that a number of different features which at first sight seem unrelated coincide in most heterostylous plants, not just in *Primula*.

Morph	Pin	Thrum
Mating type	'pin'	'thrum'
Genetic control	recessive *ss*	dominant *Ss*
Style	long	short
Style cells	long	short
Stigma papillae	long	short
Pollen	small	large

Plants with heterostylous flowers tend to have a similar flower shape, with fused petals that form a tube or trumpet, and they are usually visited by large specialist pollinators such as bees. Nevertheless, they occur in many diverse groups. Some examples familiar to the gardener include *Forsythia* (Oleaceae), *Linum* (Linaceae), *Pulmonaria* (Boraginaceae), *Plumbago* (Plumbaginaceae) and *Houstonia* (Rubiaceae). Some garden *Oxalis* (Oxalidaceae), *Lythrum* (Lythraceae) and the water hyacinth *Eichhornia* (Pontederiaceae) are tristylous, with three morphs and three mating-types. In these, the long-styled morph is once again genetically homozygous and tends to have the smaller pollen.

It will be evident that these various plants are quite unrelated to one another, and to *Primula*, yet for all these, similar sets of shared characteristics differ between pins and thrums. This strongly suggests that similar selection pressures have accompanied the development of heterostyly in all these diverse groups. If one can understand the role played by each of these features, one should gain a clearer picture of the evolution and function of this complex and fascinating mechanism.

Style length and anther position

Intuitively, it seems likely that the reciprocal positioning of the sites of pollen issue and pollen receipt in pins and thrums would increase the efficiency of legitimate pollen flow between the two mating types, in insect-pollinated flowers. They should also decrease illegitimate pollination and selfing. Although this was suggested for *Primula* by Darwin (1877), no hard evidence for such a mating pattern (known as 'dissortative') was published until over a century later.

Studies of this kind are readily made for most heterostylous genera, including *Primula*. Due to the difference in pollen size between the pins and thrums, it is easy to see which pollen grains on a stigma have come from plants of the same morph, and which from a different morph. However, it was not realized for many years that selection for heterostyly could only have occurred with respect to pollen incoming to the flower. When a flower is visited by an insect, it will cause a good deal of within-flower pollination to occur, but this is unlikely to result in fertilization. It is also irrelevant with respect to the role played by the insect in transporting legitimate rather than illegitimate pollen between flowers. If pollen loads are studied on the stigmas of intact flowers, selfed pollen is likely to mask the patterns of pollen travel between flowers.

However, if the intact anthers are removed from a flower as it opens ('emasculated'), pollen loads on stigmas will all result from other flowers. The Canadian, Fred Ganders (1974) seems to have been the first person to do this, for *Jepsonia* (Saxifragaceae). He duly reported dissortative pollination, finding that relatively more thrum pollen arrived on pin stigmas, and more pin pollen on thrum stigmas. Latterly, similar observations have been made for the primrose, *P. vulgaris*, with similar results (Piper & Charlesworth, 1986). John Piper found that roughly twice as many legitimate grains as illegitimate were found on the stigmas of emasculated primrose flowers, proving that Darwin was correct in his assumption that the heterostyly encourages pollen to travel between the two mating types.

Darwin looked at the distribution of pollen grains on the bodies of bees that were visiting cowslips, and reported that pin grains were concentrated on the head of the bee, while thrum grains were mostly found on the body. In 1958, two Russians, Rosov and Screbtsova convincingly showed that similar distribution patterns of grains occur on the bodies of hive bees visiting the heterostylous buckwheat (*Fagopyrum*).

There is no doubt that the reciprocal positioning of the stigma and anthers between the pin and thrum mating types increases sexual efficiency in an inherently inefficient system.

Style cell length and papilla length

In most heterostylous species, the long styled pin also has longer stigma papillae and longer style cells. These are potentially important features, for the pollen grains germinate on the papillae, and the pollen tube penetrates them near the base, while the pollen tube later travels down the style cells on its journey to the ovary.

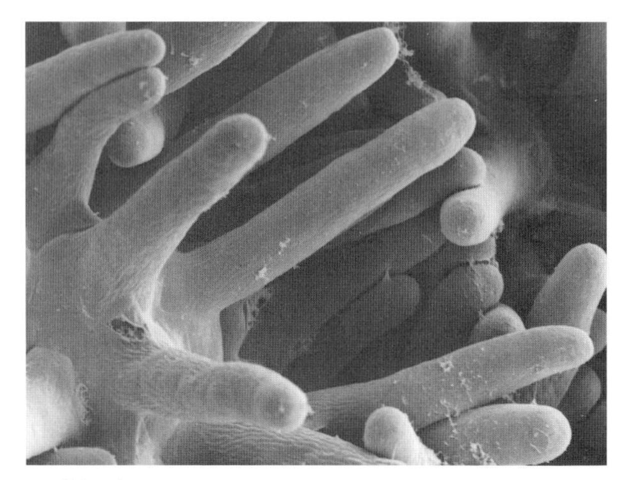

Fig 4. Long stigma papillae of a pin flower

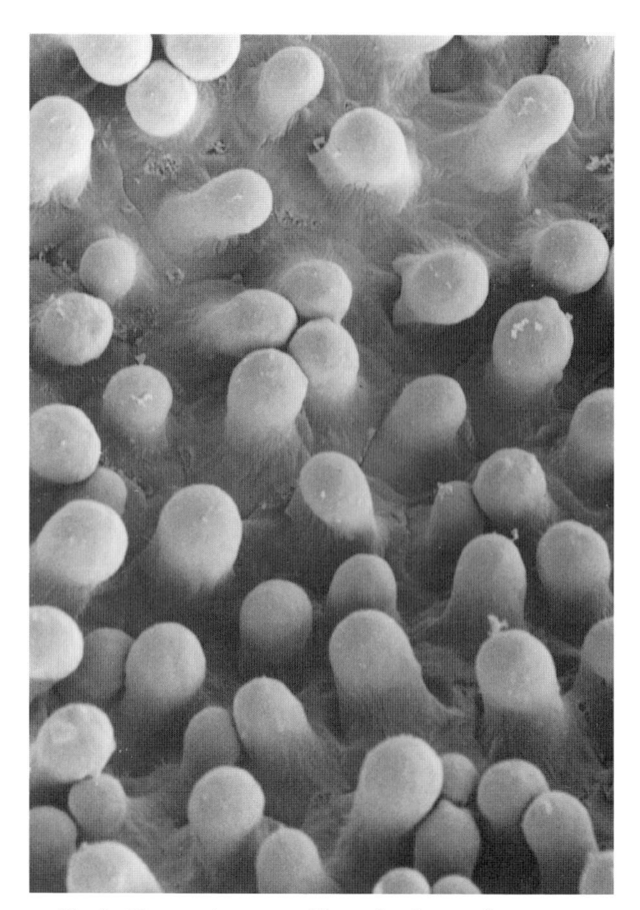

Fig 5. Short stigma papillae of a thrum flower

Evidence that these features may play a direct, although minor, role in the functioning of the mating types in primula comes from the primrose. Shivanna *et al.* (1983) have shown that previously desiccated thrum pollen grains germinate better in a humid environment. It seems likely that the the long stigma papillae of the pin provides a microclimate at the stigma surface which is moister than that at the thrum stigma surface (Figs 4, 5), and this might therefore encourage legitimate pollen germination. Additional evidence comes from the work of Mather (1950) on *P. sinensis*. In this species, a gene a shortens the pin stigma and stigma papillae and these plants become somewhat less receptive to thrum pollen.

In fact, as Mather found, long stigma papillae in long styled plants are also nearly always associated with long style cells. It might be reasonably suggested that pin and thrum styles have the same number of cells, and that the difference in length between them is controlled solely by cell elongation. If this was the case, one would expect pins to have longer style cells, and as stigma papillae are merely the terminal extension of the style, longer papillae as well. One would also expect that the difference in style cell and papilla sizes between pins and thrums to be of the same order of magnitude as the difference in style length between the two morphs, and this does seem to be the case.

A good test is to look at style cell lengths and papilla lengths in a homostylous primula which nevertheless has a good deal of casual variation in style length. *P. verticillata* and its relative *P. simensis* are such plants. Hussen Al Wadi and I found strong correlations between style length, and each of style cell length and papilla length in these species. We have concluded that differences in style cell length and papilla length are developmental correlates of style length. If they have an adaptive significance, for instance by the promotion of thrum pollen germination on a long-papilla pin style, such adaptations probably arose secondarily.

This conclusion agrees well with the findings of Mather (1950) in *P. sinensis*, where the 'Primrose Queen' mutant *a*, which shortens style length, also shortens stigmatic papilla length and discourages legitimate thrum pollen germination.

Pollen size

In almost all heterostylous plants, pins have smaller pollen than thrums. Despite early suggestions to the contrary, it is quite clear that this is nothing to do with the distance that the pollen tube has to grow. In *Primula*, pollen varies in volume between pin grains and thrum grains by a factor of approximately three. Yet, within the genus, pollen varies in volume between species by a factor of at least 500, and some of the smallest grains have to grow down the longest styles!

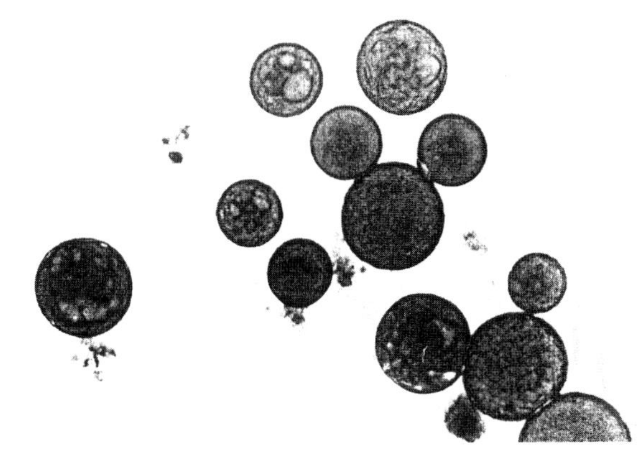

Fig 6. A mixture of pin (small) and thrum (large) pollen

Pollen size also has no direct relationship with anther position. Mather (1950) shows that the 'fertile double' gene *m* which also raises anthers in pins to the thrum position affects neither pollen size nor male mating behaviour, while Ernst (1955) shows that pollen size and anther position are genetically recombinable (p. 54).

Perhaps the most significant finding with respect to the difference in pollen grain size between pins and thrums was reported by John Piper for primroses in 1986. He discovered that anthers of pin plants produce on average more than twice as many grains as those of thrum plants (36,620 against 17,165). However, the numbers of grains removed by insects showed no significant difference between the two morphs, suggesting that pin pollen is less easily removed from the anthers of pin plants, sunk deep in the corolla tube. When pollen loads were studied on the stigmas of emasculated flowers, it was found that 18 per cent more pin grains than thrum grains were discovered on stigmas, but this difference was statistically unimportant. The total number of pollen grains found was exactly the same on emasculated pin and thrum stigmas.

Comparable results have been found for other heterostylous genera. Ganders (1979) reviews relative pollen numbers of pins and thrums for 12 heterostylous taxa (data for *Amsinckia* which is not typically heterostylous is omitted). For each of these, pin pollen is invariably more numerous, by factors from 1.34 to 3.12. These ratios are closely related to the ratios of pollen volumes. As anther size rarely differs between pins and thrums (it seems never to do so in *Primula*), it seems likely that selection occurs for differences in pollen number between pins and thrums, and this is achieved by differences in pollen size.

From John Piper's work, it seems likely that greater pollen grain numbers are favoured in pins because pin pollen, and its legitimate thrum stigma, are both less accessible to visiting insects than thrum pollen and pin stigmas. Thus, the smaller pin pollen, and its consequently greater number, allows the male fitness of pins to equal that of thrums. If the anther position drops from the homostyle position in the mouth of the corolla tube down to the pin position, this will increase levels of outcrossing of pin pollen onto the thrum stigma. However, unless this change in position is also accompanied by a decrease in pollen size and an increase in pollen number, pin pollen will lose its overall fitness in a self-fertile primula.

Genetic control and evolution of heterostyly

In almost all heterostylous plants, the pin is homozygous *ss* and the thrum heterozygous *Ss*. In fact, the genetic control is a good deal more complex than this, but for the time being we will suppose that heterostyly is controlled by a single gene *S*/*s*. It would seem that the correspondence of genetic dominance with the thrum condition in so many unrelated plants is more than coincidental, suggesting that heterostyly arose in a similar way in each.

Lloyd & Webb (1992) assumed that heterostyly first evolved from a self-fertile 'approach herkogamous' ancestor, that is one with stigma and anthers in the 'pin' position. Such a plant would be moderately outcrossed, and so its offspring would be liable to inbreeding depression when selfing occurred. They argue that a mutation which shortened the stigma into the 'thrum' position would be favoured by chiefly receiving outcrossed pollen from the pin morphs; this would also increase the fitness of pin pollen. It follows that the thrum configuration arose later than the pin morph, so that it would only become established in conditions of thrum dominance. We can deduce from this that the thrum condition evolved after the pin syndrome in most heterostylous genera, with thrum dominance.

I have no objection to this model which seems a valid and plausible hypothesis for many heterostylous genera, but it fails to explain two features peculiar to *Primula*. As mentioned earlier, it is rarely possible to obtain pure-breeding thrum lines in *Primula*. Mather & de Winton (1941) found that some thrum homozygotes *SS* do occur in *P. sinensis*, but these are less viable than thrum heterozygotes, only about 70 per cent of those expected occurring (p. 56). In other species, genetic segregations which had suggested that *SS* homozygotes are inviable were proved beyond reasonable doubt by Kurian & Richards (1997) for *P.* × *polyantha*. Consequently, Richards (1998) was able to deduce that a recessive lethal or sublethal was linked on the thrum chromosome, and suggested that this could have been instrumental in the evolution of heterostyly.

The other noteworthy feature of *Primula* is the array of isolated species in section Sphondylia which taken together appear to provide a graphic demonstration of the evolution of heterostyly (Al Wadi & Richards, 1993). Amongst these, the primitive condition today appears to be represented by self-fertile diploid long homostyles in which the anthers and stigma lie together at the mouth of the flower (*P. verticillata* and *P. simensis*). These may represent the genus before heterostyly evolved, but of course, homostyly may have evolved from approach herkogamy in these species during the intervening millennia.

Nevertheless, I have suggested an alternative route by which heterostyly may have evolved in *Primula* (Richards, 1998). Lloyd & Webb (1992) note that a problem exists with a hypothetical long homostyle selfing ancestor. A newly evolving thrum with a lowered stigma position would avoid inbreeding depression by being outcrossed, and consequently it would be so successful in comparison to its selfing homostyle ancestor that it would rapidly proceed to fixation; a homostyle/thrum balance could not equilibriate. However, if a lethal recessive became linked to the thrum chromosome in conditions of restricted recombination, the thrum chromosome could not proceed to fixation (*SS* homozygotes would be inviable), so that a thrum/homostyle equilibrium could establish. This would provide the conditions in which a recessive mutation which promoted the lowering of the homostyle anthers into the pin position would be favoured. The main argument in favour of this alternative scheme is that it appears exactly to describe the observed shift in thrum stigma position between *P. verticillata* and *P. boveana*, and then the shift in pin anther position between *P. boveana* and *P. gaubeana* (p. 60).

Mating type

Outside section Sphondylia, all heterostylous primulas have a two-factor mating system, so that like recognizes like and this tends to result in reproductive failure. Only when unlike morphs mate (P × T or T × P) is seed usually set. There are a number of heterostylous plants which do not have a two-factor mating system. Some of these, like *Amsinckia, Narcissus triandrus*, and *Primula floribunda* and its relatives, are self-fertile. Others, like *Narcissus tazetta, N. assoanus* and *Anchusa* species, are self-sterile, but have a multi-factor mating system. This means that they can set seed with most other partners whether pin or thrum, but not with themselves.

No plant is known which has a two-factor mating system but no heterostyly. Therefore, it seems extremely likely that heterostyly arose before the mating type, not afterwards.

Our knowledge of patterns of pollination in homostyle and heterostyle primroses (Piper & Charlesworth, 1986) shows that the pin is just as much self-pollinated as the homostyle, but the thrum receives about five times less self pollen than pins or homostyles. Thus, in a self-fertile heterostyle, the pin will benefit more from a self-sterility gene than will a thrum. The self-sterility gene would only be likely to succeed if recessive and linked to the pin chromosome.

As is discussed later in this chapter, it is known that the male and female functions of the mating type occur separately on the chromosome, for they can be recombined. Therefore, it seems likely that the same gene is duplicated (occurs twice), once with a male operator function, and once with a female operator function.

As the gene would not work until both operators were functioning, the various parts of the gene could accumulate on a chromosome without having an effect, until a final recessive mutation caused a pin plant carrying both copies to be self-sterile. If this gene was advantageous, as we would expect, it would spread until all copies of the pin (*s*) chromosome carried it.

At this evolutionary stage, pins would be self-sterile, and could only be fertilized by thrums. Thrums on the other hand would be self-fertile, although evidence from primrose suggests that about half their seed would be outcrossed. Because thrum homozygotes *SS* would have been lethal, so that all thrums were heterozygotes *Ss*, between one-third and a half of all thrum offspring would be self-sterile pins.

Selfing plants usually carry an automatic advantage over outcrossing plants, for they can self and outcross, while outcrossers can only outcross. Thus, selfing plants should donate more selfing genes to the next generation. However, this is not true of selfing thrums, for the more they outcross, the more outcrossing pins they leave in the next generation. Selfing thrums have no advantage over outcrossing pins, unless by the production of more seeds, and they have the disadvantage that about half of their offspring are selfed, and may suffer from inbreeding depression.

Thus, once a self-sterility gene is fully established in pins, but not before, a self-sterility gene arising in thrums would also be favoured. Naturally, this would have to be linked to the thrum (*S*) chromosome if it were not to spread through all the population. It would also have to be dominant, for if it were recessive, it could only be expressed in the (lethal) homozygote. As in the pin, the expression of thrum self-sterility on the male and female sides are separated, being recombinable. Although the recognition factor for thrum self-sterility would have to be quite different from that of pin self-sterility, it is possible that the thrum incompatibility male and female operators might be the same as the pin operators. The operators could have been recombined onto the thrum (*S*) chromosome from the pin (*s*) chromosome. This would explain why male and female self-sterility functions are closely linked to pollen size and style characters respectively on both the pin and thrum chromosomes.

Thus, the current model for the evolution of heterostyly and two-factor self-incompatibility in *Primula* can be summarised as follows:

- Heterostyly evolved from a self-compatible long-homostyle such as *P. verticillata* or *P. chungensis*. We call these 'primary homostyles'. (It could also have evolved from a self-fertile approach-herkogamous ancestor).
- A dominant mutation *G* for the short thrum style became linked to a recessive lethal gene. Plants with thrum stigmas were favoured as they would have been more outcrossed, and their offspring would have been more fit. However, they could only exist as heterozygotes, so that thrums gave rise to some long homostyles which remained in the population.
- A recessive mutation for (lower) pin anther position *a* became linked to the *g* (homostyle) chromosome. Plants with pin position anthers were favoured, as their pollen outnumbered pollen from homostyle anthers on thrum stigmas, and their pollen selfed pin stigmas less than homostyle pollen selfed homostyle stigmas. This mutation *a* would only succeed if recessive and in linkage with *g*. The *ga* pin chromosome thus established would out-compete the *gA* homostyle chromosome, until a stable equilibrium of *GA*/*ga* thrums and

ga/ga pins was established.

- A recessive mutation for decreased pollen size/increased pollen number *p* became linked to the *ga* (pin) chromosome. Plants with anthers in the pin position with more numerous pollen would outcompete pin plants with less numerous pollen. Pins with large pollen have their male fitness limited by relative unavailability of pollen produced in the included anther position. Thus, the pin linkage group became *gap* (long style, small pollen, low anther) and the thrum linkage group became *GAP* (short style, large pollen, high anther).

(In fact, either of the mutations *a* (pin anther position) or *p* (reduced pollen size) could have successfully established linkage with the *g* chromosome first, by increasing male fitness in pins. In section Sphondylia it seems that the pollen size mutation *p* evolved first, as *P. boveana* shows pollen size dimorphy, but only one anther position (p. 60). Male fitness in pins would have been further enhanced by the establishment of the other feature secondarily. This is shown by reference to *Linum*, in which the pins have smaller pollen, but all anthers are in the same position, and by *Vitaliana*, in which all plants have pollen of the same size, but pins have anthers in the lowered pin position.)

- A recessive self-sterility recognition factor *s* was duplicated in linkage on the pin chromosome. One duplicate, closely linked to *p*, became associated with a male operator *sm*, while the other, closely linked to *g*, became associated with a female operator *sf*. The pin linkage group would now read *g sf a sm p*. Self-sterility would be favoured on the highly self-pollinated pin, as outcrossed individuals would produce fitter offspring than would selfers, and this advantage would outweigh the poorer seed-set and automatic disadvantage of outcrossing. The outcrossing pin chromosome should have outcompeted the somewhat selfing thrum chromosome, and become more common to a point where thrum rarity made the pin chromosome, which depends on thrums for reproduction, less successful.
- A dominant self-sterility recognition factor *S*, quite different to *s*, was duplicated in linkage to the thrum chromosome. Once they became associated with the male and female operators recombined from the pin chromosome, thrums would also become self-sterile. The thrum linkage group would now read *G Sf A Sm P*. An outcrossing gene associated with thrums would not carry an automatic disadvantage, as selfed thrums also gave rise to a proportion of outcrossing pins. Thus, an outcrossing gene in thrums should rapidly succeed, leading to the full (thrum) *G Sf A Sm P/g sf a sm p:* (pin) *g sf a smpa/g sf a sm p* heterostyly with two mating factor incompatibility that we see today.

Although this process seems complex, there is a certain inevitability about its evolutionary progress once the initial thrum mutation has become linked to a recessive lethal. Presumably, this explains why so many unrelated heterostylous plants show the same suite of characters. Nevertheless, there are certain examples which have apparently only proceeded so far along the evolutionary development of full heterostyly with incompatibility, and some of these are noted in the above account.

How does the *Primula* mating system work?

Until 1990, there were a number of confused and conflicting reports as to how self fertilizations failed to set seed in *Primula*. Many of these problems were resolved by Wedderburn & Richards (1990), who examined 52 species of *Primula*, and showed that a great variation occurred between species in the operation of the incompatibility.

In order to describe this variation, it is first necessary to give a brief description of the sexual process in *Primula*, and its inhibition by self-incompatibility.

Pollen grains will only usually germinate successfully when attached to the stigma papillae.

(Eisikowitch & Woodell (1975) describe how pollen grains do in fact germinate in water if the corolla-tube fills with rain water, although in primrose, which has erect flowers, this is partially inhibited by the presence of the anthers. In the oxlip, *P. elatior*, which has drooping flowers, no such inhibition occurs. These water-germinated grains will be unavailable for fertilization, and they may be one of the reasons why short homostyles, where the anthers are sunk in the pin position, are rarely found. I have also once observed that at temperatures in excess of 30°C (86°F), the pollen grains of cowslip, *P. veris*, will germinate in the nectary, and pollen tubes can penetrate the ovary from this position, although there is no evidence that this can result in fertilization.)

Primula pollen grains are rather dry, but the anther plasters the outside with a sticky substance. This may cause the pollen grain to adhere to the cuticle of the stigma papilla. Once stuck, the grain becomes hydrated, and this hydration is controlled by the sticky substance, although the hydration may depend as much on local humidity as any effect from the (rather dry) papilla itself. Once hydrated, a pollen tube may pass out through a pore or slit in the pollen grain wall.

In pin primroses, the tubes of thrum grains bore a hole in the papilla cuticle near the thick walled apex, but the tubes of pin grains grow down the outside of the short thrum papilla and penetrate the stigma cell walls near the papilla base.

Pollen tubes then grow through the stigmatic tissue, aiming for the central conducting tissue of the narrow style, which they then pass down (Fig. 7). They pass round the ovary wall, burrow out of the wall near an ovule, enter free space within the ovary, and penetrate the ovule through the micropile (Fig. 8). Immediately afterwards, fertilization of the egg cell and the polar nucleus by the two generative nuclei takes place to form an embryo, and its nurse tissue, the endosperm. Seed development then proceeds.

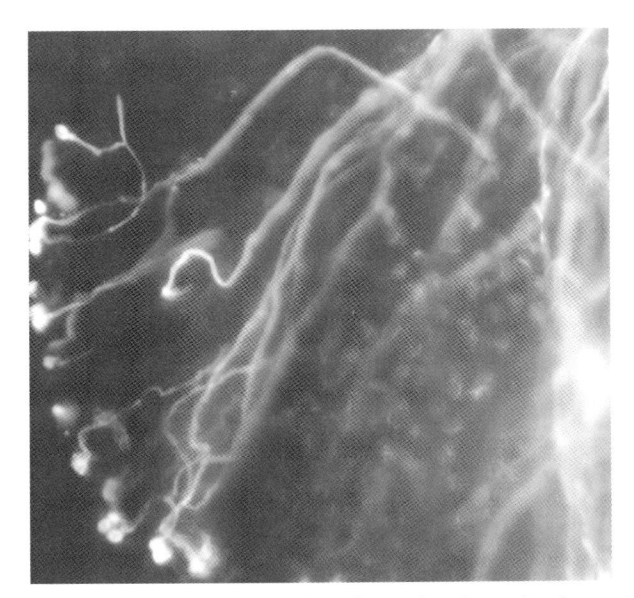

Fig 7. Pollen tubes growing through stigmatic tissue after a legitimate cross

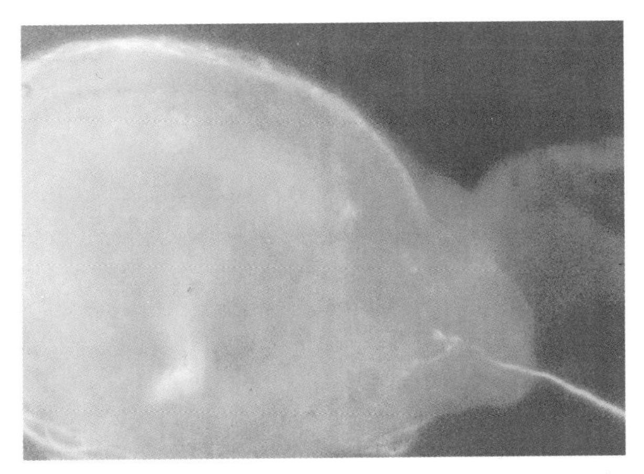

Fig. 8 A pollen tube enterting the ovule via the micropile (right) prior to fertilisation

It seems that incompatibility causes this process to fail at one or more of the following stages:

- Illegitimate pollen grains fail to germinate on the stigma, presumably because they fail to hydrate (it is also possible that pin and thrum grains show a differential adhesion to legitimate and illegitimate stigmas; however, any such effect, if it occurs, is not great).

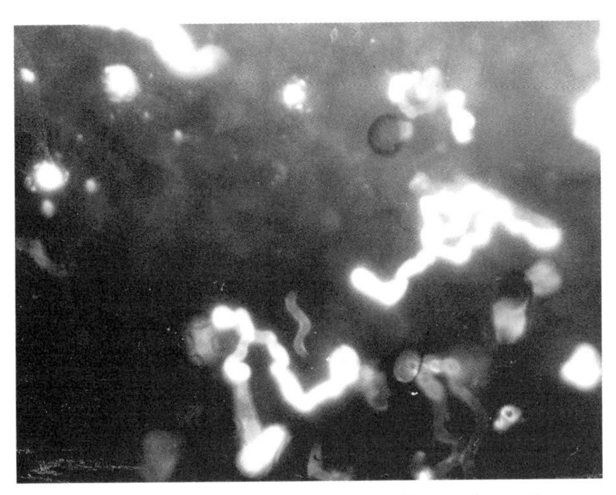

Fig. 9 Abnormal thick sinuous pollen tubes after an illegitimate T x T cross

- Illegitimate pollen tubes fail to penetrate the stigma. When this occurs, it is because the pollen tubes are often abnormal and characteristically thick and sinuous (Fig. 9). Both these reactions, classed together as 'stigma surface reactions', are usually associated with the production of callose on the stigma surface in the area of the illegitimate grain; callose is a complex carbohydrate usually produced as a 'wounding response' in plants.
- Illegitimate pollen tubes cease growing in the stigma tissue.
- Illegitimate pollen tubes cease growing in the style.

(The latter two reactions are classed together as 'internal reactions', and are probably controlled in the same way. Typically, the tip of the inhibited pollen tube swells slightly, and may once again be associated with the production of callose, (Fig. 10).)

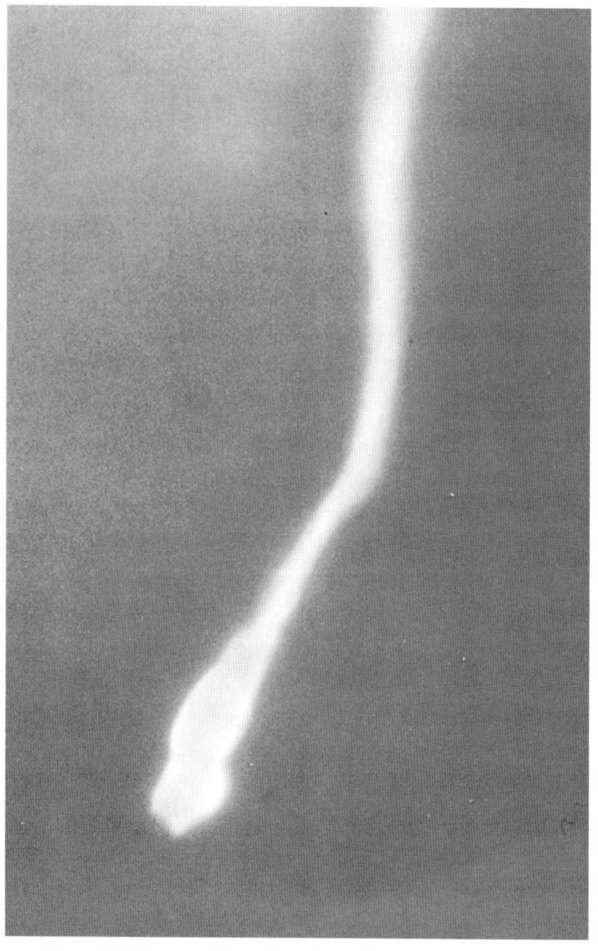

Fig. 10 The swollen tip of an illegitimate P x P pollen tube

Quite a lot is now understood about the biochemistry of the incompatibility reaction in *Primula*. A fuller account can be found in Richards (1997), or Wedderburn & Richards (1990). These findings can be summarized as follows:

- For the pollen grain at the stigma surface, the recognition chemical is contained in the sticky substance plastered onto the grain by the anther. It follows that all pollen grains from a given father will behave in the same way. Thus, the pollen grains from the heterozygous thrum *Ss* may have the individual genotypes *S* or *s*, but all will act as *S* (thrum). The recognition chemical is known to be a glycoprotein, and it is known to differ substantially between pin and thrum pollen. It is not known what controls the male side of the inhibition of the illegitimate pollen tube within the stigma and style.
- At least two recognition proteins seem to be involved on the female side. One is bound to the cuticle of the stigma papilla and is involved with the inhibition of pollen grain hydration, and its subsequent germination. It seems to be relatively small. The other stigma protein may be bound to the papilla cuticle and to internal membranes. It is relatively large in size, and it may inhibit both pollen tube penetration, and pollen tube growth after penetration. It is possible, however, that these two functions are under separate control.
- It is possible that self recognition results from the same chemical being produced on the pollen grain (and pollen tube), and on and in the stigma. When these meet they might fuse to form a larger chemical which then plays an inhibitory role. As we know that the pollen chemical and each of the two stigmatic chemicals differ in size and nature, the recognition factor probably only forms part of the recognition chemical (male and female operators might form the remainder).
- Within a species of *Primula*, the illegitimate inhibition of pollen tubes invariably takes a quite different course in pins and thrums. Furthermore, from what one can guess about the evolution of this inhibition (p. 47), it

seems likely that the pin recognition factor is quite different from the thrum inhibition factor. Thus, within a species, one would not expect the self recognition chemical to be the same between pins and thrums, even if the male and female operators were the same for both morphs. The evidence available bears this out. For instance, it seems that in *P. obconica*, the stigmatic recognition protein is chemically quite different between pins and thrums.

- One can conclude that the incompatibility reaction in *Primula* is complex, often operating at more than one site, and it always differs between pin selfs and thrum selfs, both in its operation and its control. However, the incompatibility reaction is always oppositional in nature. It invariably involves something stopping the process of fertilization, rather than something encouraging this process.

How does the mating system vary between *Primula* species?

Wedderburn & Richards (1990) showed that a great variation occurs between *Primula* species in the efficiency of the incompatibility, and how the incompatibility inhibition operates. This information is of considerable interest to gardeners. For many species one can predict how much self seed-set will occur after self-pollination. Where this information is known, it is given in the systematic account under each species. This self seed-set will, of course, partly depend on how much self-pollination occurs. In many species, particularly in pins, flowers are automatically self-pollinated.

For others in the open garden, insect visits will usually result in adequate self-pollination, but there are some species with narrow corolla tubes (e.g. section Muscarioides) in which artificial self-pollination with a paint brush is needed before pollination occurs. Presumably these have a specialist pollinator in the wild which is usually missing in gardens. Under glass, of course, it is necessary to pollinate artificially (p. 22).

There are very few species of *Primula* which, given adequate self-pollination, fail to set any seed at all. However, many more will fail to set any self seed as a pin, or as a thrum, but are relatively self-fertile in the other morph. There is no consistent pattern as to pin and thrum self-fertility. Over 35 species, for the percentage of ovules that set viable seed after selfing, pins average seven per cent (range 0–62 per cent, the highest figure being in the primrose, *P. vulgaris*), while for 37 species, the same figure for thrums is eight per cent (range 0–87 per cent, the highest figure being for *P. muscarioides*) (Table 1).

However, self seed-set is always poorer than seed set after legitimate crosses, and the quality of seedlings will also be higher after crossing (Tables 2, 3, p. 63). Thus, for short-lived species which require replacement from seed, gardeners should always aim to grow several individuals including pins and thrums close together if they are to maximize the quantity and quality of their seedlings.

As a general rule, there is a relationship between the position where incompatibility inhibition occurs, and the efficency of the incompatibility as assessed by self seed-set. Those selfs where much of the inhibition takes place in the stigma and style tend to be more self-compatible than those where much of the inhibition takes place on the stigma surface, resulting in about twice as much seed-set. Not surprisingly perhaps, the most efficient incompatibility occurs when inhibition occurs in all three areas, for these inhibitions presumably reinforce each other.

There is a difference in patterns of inhibition between pins and thrums. In the thrums investigated, 28 of the species (76 per cent) had most of the inhibition restricted to the stigma surface, while in the pins only 14 species (40 per cent) were so inhibited.

It will be seen that although there is no real systematic pattern to this data, a few generalizations can be made. In section Aleuritia, it seems clear that for the heterostylous species there is always total thrum self incompatibility. This results from an almost total lack of thrum pollen germination on thrum stigmas. In contrast, relatively high levels of self seed-set seems to be typical of both pins and thrums in sections Armerina and Oreophlomis (which were originally classified with the Aleuritia).

Table 1. Average seed sets after legitimate crosses and illegitimate selfs in *Primula*. For blank cells there is no information.

Species	**legitimate** %	**P × P** %	**T × T** %	**Species**	**legitimate** %	**P × P** %	**T × T** %
auricula	49.4	0.1	2.9	pulverulenta	60.1	0	0
marginata	57.5	0.8		secundiflora	67.4	3.4	0.7
elatior	67.8	0	1.1	alpicola	38.5	0.8	24.3
veris	75.7	14.5	0.6	florindae	18.4	0.6	0
vulgaris	70.1	61.8	0	sikkimensis	61.2	0.5	0
× polyantha	56.3	9.1	8.2	chionantha	47.3	0	3.9
sinensis		2.7		rosea	74.4	44.2	26.1
malacoides	40.7	15.5	0.2	luteola	28.6	2.7	3.1
cortusoides	40.9	1.2	0	involucrata	63	7.3	3.2
geranifolia	35.8	2.4	4.5	farinosa	57.8	0.4	0
polyneura	76.1	0	0	frondosa	56.2	10.5	0
obconica	60.1	4.6	3	modesta	26.3	0	0
sinolisteri			21.4	fauriae	37.9	4.3	0
anisodora	67.9	6.1	2.7	atrodentata	47.4	20	60
wilsonii	62.5	8.3	4.8	denticulata	67.4	14.1	0
aurantiaca	80.3	0	2.9	muscarioides			86.6
burmanica	86.7	2.8	0	vialii	63.4	0	0.5
prolifera	66.5	1.2	26	flaccida	54.4	1.1	0
poissonii	56.1	2.3	9.6	erythrocarpa*	92.5	0	46.6
tanneri*		2		clusiana*			4.5
calderiana*	95	0	0	deorum*			0
sonchifolia*	93	0	0	parryi*		33.5	
bracteosa*		0		rusbyi*		0	
irregularis*			5	nutans*		0	
deuteronana		0		sharmae*			0
nana*			4				
drummondiana*			14	**mean**	**56.5**	**6.9**	**8.5**
*							

* predicted from pollen-tubes

homostyle species seed sets

floribunda	62.6	halleri	47.8	
verticillata	75.3	laurentiana	79.2	
mollis	87.8	magellanica	24.5	
chungensis	83.4	scotica	71.1 74.3	
cockburniana	79.8	scandinavica	57.1	
japonica	71.2	stricta	81.2	79.8
		mean	**69.70%**	

Other sections are notable for their lack of consistency. In section Primula, the primrose, *P. vulgaris*, and the cowslip, *P. veris*, are totally thrum self-sterile, but are quite self-fertile in pins, although this is more true of the primrose. In total contrast, in the related oxlip, *P. elatior*, pins are totally self-sterile, but a small amount of self seed-set is recorded in thrums.

In section Proliferae, an interesting progression can be seen from relatively self-fertile and apparently more primitive species *P. prolifera* (of which there are also primary homostyle forms), and its relatives *P. poissonii, P. wilsonii* and *P. secundiflora*, through to the derived species *P. pulverulenta* which is fully self-sterile. Interestingly, *P. aurantiaca* and *P. burmanica*, which take an intermediate position in the section, are pin self-sterile and thrum self-sterile respectively. This suggests that two different routes to full self-sterility may have evolved in this relatively primitive section. Possibly, fully self-sterile species such as *P. pulverulenta* have arisen as the result of hybridization between the pin self-sterile and the thrum self-sterile lines.

By far the commonest incompatibility mechanism is failure of pollen germination, which is responsible for more than a quarter of total inhibition in more than 80 per cent of species. It is reasonable to suggest that failure of pollen germination was in fact the original incompatibility mechanism, and that inhibitions of pollen tube penetration and growth evolved later as 'back-up' mechanisms.

However, only four species are known today in which the principal inhibition is restricted to failure of pollen grain germination in both pins and thrums. These are *P. geranifolia* and *P. polyneura* (section Cortusoides), *P. chionantha* (section Crystallophlomis) and *P. involucrata* (section Armerina). None of these species are very self-fertile, but only *P. polyneura* is fully self-incompatible. Arguably, these four species represent incompatibility today in its 'original', simplest form.

Presumably, after the two-factor mating type first evolved in *Primula*, controlling illegitimate pollen germination, at least one other gene became linked to each of the *s* and *S* chromosomes. These additional genes, which were probably different for pins and thrums, would have coded for proteins which were expressed within the stigma and style and differed from those expressed at the papilla surface. Independent evolutionary lines for this more complex and efficient incompatibility in the pin, and in the thrum, could have come together by hybridization.

The result would have been a plant with multisite inhibition and full self-incompatibility in both pins and thrums. Amongst contemporary species which have been investigated, *P. pulverulenta* is the best example of this.

The structure of the *Primula* heterostyly/mating system linkage group

One of the features of heterostyly in *Primula* is that several different characteristics occur together in each of the pin and thrum. Characters usually vary independently (consider hair colour and eye colour in humans), but in this case they are normally associated, so that, for instance, pins almost always have smaller pollen than thrums. These associations are because the various genes concerned are 'linked' together on the same chromosome, so that they cannot 'sort' (segregate) independently on different chromosomes.

Linked genes can in fact be 'sorted' , but only between chromosomes of the same type by chiasmata which 'swap' (recombine) chromosome segments at meiosis. It will pay a plant to position genes which work in concert close together on the same chromosome, so that they are rarely 'mixed-up' by either segregation or recombination.

It may even pay the plant to ensure that no chiasmata ever successfully occur within the chromosome segment on which the 'coadapted' genes are linked, so that they are never swapped (recombined). The usual way this is achieved is for that part of the chromosome on which the linkage group occurs to be turned round ('inverted') with respect to other chromosome. The best example of this is in the control of gender, where those parts of the X chromosome which determine primary and secondary female characteristics are often inverted with respect to the part of the Y chromosome which controls male characteristics. In this way, intersex chromosomes rarely occur.

As yet, the only suggestion that the heterostyly genes in *Primula* are protected from recombination by an inversion comes from section Muscarioides (Bruun, 1932). Bruun shows that several species in this section have one pair of chromosomes visibly different from each other in thrums, but not in pins. These form a loop when they associate at meiosis in the heterozygous thrum. Such a loop is typical of an inversion, and it is reasonable to suggest that this chromosome, with two types in thrums, is the chromosome which carries the heterostyly genes (p. 308).

Heterostyly in *Primula* is famous amongst geneticists as the best example of a 'coadapted linkage group' or 'supergene' in plants. As such, one will find it in almost any genetics textbook, and it has been assiduously learnt by generations of students. However, only one person has closely studied this linkage group, the Swiss Ernst, who published a series of papers from 1933 to 1958. His results were reanalysed by Lewis & Jones (1992).

One of the problems involved in this work is that the various genes which make up the *S Primula* linkage group are closely linked together, so that they are only rarely 'swapped'. The study of such a system is based on the detection of plants in which the genes have been swapped (recombined), for instance a pin plant which has large rather than the usual small pollen. This involved Ernst in the painstaking screening of thousands of seedlings.

Ernst worked with *P.* × *pubescens* (which he called 'P. hortensis') and, rather surprisingly, *P. latifolia* (which he called 'P. viscosa'). David Winstanley has shown that most of Ernst's cultivations were undertaken at a small experimental station next to a rack and pinion railway high above Zurich at Diavolezza, well above 2000 m, where the rather tricky *P. latifolia* thrives nearby as a native plant. No trace of this garden remains today.

Eventually, Ernst was able to report six variants to the normal pin and thrum mode of reproduction. Ernst did not at first realize the significance of these results. He believed that he was looking at mutants to a single *S* gene which controlled all the various attributes of the heterostyly. It fell to Dowrick (1956) to suggest that these results did in fact show that there were three recombinable elements, or distinct genes on the *S* chromosome, namely:

- *G/g* style length, stigma papilla length, stylar cell length, female mating type.
- *A/a* anther position.
- *P/p* male mating type, pollen size.

The six variants Ernst reported were as follows (Dowrick's proposed genotypes in brackets):

1. Self-fertile long homostyles (*gAP*).
2. Self-fertile short homostyles (*Gap*).
3. Self-fertile pins (*gaP*).
4. Self-fertile thrums (*GAp*).
5. Self-sterile long homostyles (*gAp*).
6. Self-sterile short homostyles (*GaP*).

In long homostyles, the anthers are in the thrum position and the stigma in the pin position, so that both appear side by side at the mouth of the flower (Plate 22). In short homostyles, the anthers are in the pin position, and the stigma in the thrum position, so that both appear side by side deep in the tube of the flower .

Male mating type and pollen size usually go together, so that self-fertile long homostyles, which have 'thrum' mating behaviour on the male side, always have large, thrum type pollen, while self-sterile long homostyles, which have 'pin' mating behaviour on the male side, have small, pin type pollen. However, we now know of a recombinant in which male mating type had been recombined with the dominance control for pollen size. Half of its pollen was pin sized and half thrum sized (so that the individual pollen grain genotype for pollen size was expressed), but all the grains had the thrum mating type (Kurian & Richards 1997). Clearly, mating type is not a function of pollen size, so we must assume that the genes which control pollen size and male mating type are different but closely linked to one another.

In the same way, the female mating type seems to be linked to the female characteristics, so that long styled plants always have long stigma papillae, and have a 'pin' mating type, whether they are heterostyle or homostyle. However, Mather (1950) found plants with a pin mating type in which modifier genes had caused the style to become short, and similar plants were reported by Kurian & Richards (1997). Once again, the female mating type is not a direct function of style length, but the genes which control style length and female mating type must be closely linked as these features are rarely recombined.

As a result of Valsa Kurian's work, we have been able to show that another four recombinable loci at least are seemingly linked to the *S* chromosome in addition to those proposed by Dowrick, making seven in total. These control:

- pollen size dominance (*Mpm/mpm*)
- style length (in part, additive to *G/g*) (*Gm/gm*)
- male compatibility (*Pm/pm*)
- thrum-linked recessive lethality (*L/l*)

Consequently, our suggestion for the structure of the *S/s* supergene is:

<u>*G A P Pm Mpm l Gm*</u>
g a p pm mpm L gm

In Richards (1997, I have added hypothetical male (*Sm*) and female (*Sf*) operators for incompatibility recognition to this model, as discussed on p. 48), so that it now reads:

<u>*G Sf A Sm P Pm Mpm l Gm*</u>
g sf a sm p pm mpm L gm

i.e. the *S* gene may consist of no less than nine linked and probably recombinable factors.

Other genes also linked to the heterostyly chromosome are known. In *P.* × *polyantha*, Valsa Kurian has shown that two recessive genes *mg* ('magenta') and *ma* ('maroon') control red and purple flower colours. These are both linked to the heterostyly chromosome, apparently at different ends and at a considerable distance from the heterostyly *S* linkage group, although *ma* seems to be closer to it than *mg*. De Winton & Mather (1935) give an account of flower colour gene linkage in *P. sinensis*. Although this species is only distantly related to *P.* × *polyantha*, they also show a red/magenta gene is linked to the heterostyly supergene *S*, and in addition show that four other characters have this linkage. *Ma/ma* and *Mg/mg* seem to be the genes termed 'R' and 'D' by Chittenden (1928) and Marsden-Jones & Turrill (1944), although neither of these authors noted the S-linkage of these colour variants.

Casual secondary homostyly

The various recombinant types within the heterostyly linkage group occur only rarely in Ernst's studies. One can assume that they sometimes occur in the wild, but are usually evolutionarily unsuccessful, and disappear. The exception to this seems to be the self-fertile long homostyle recombinant (*gAP* to use Dowrick's terminology) in the primrose, *P. vulgaris*, which has been subjected to close scrutiny.

Populations of primroses in Somerset and in the English Chilterns containing self-fertile long homostyle primroses were first recognized in 1940 and were investigated by Jack Crosby (1949). Homostyles were found in nearly all populations within these two discrete regions, each of which have a diameter of about 30 km (18 m), but they seem to occur rarely, if ever, away from these zones. Within these areas, Crosby examined over 100 populations. He found a very consistent pattern, so that when homostyles were scarce, pins and thrums occurred in roughly equal proportions. However, when homostyles were common, pins usually persisted, but thrums tended to disappear completely.

Crosby explained this by suggesting that as long homostyles have effectively 'thrum type' pollen, they will compete with the pollen of thrums on pin stigmas, and will have the additional advantage of being able to self-fertilize, which thrums cannot. As a result, when homostyles are successful, thrums should disappear from the population.

As homozygous thrums (*GAP/GAP*) seem to be inviable because of lethal recessive linkage (p. 46), the question arises as to whether homozygous (true-breeding) homostyles (*gAP/gAP*) are viable. This would of course depend on whether the lethal gene(s) was linked more closely to *G* or *AP*. If it was linked to *G*, *gAP*/*gAP* long homostyle homozygotes which do not contain *G* should be viable. The answer to this is not unambiguous. It seems that homostyle homozygotes do occur in primrose, but Crosby (1949) suggests that they may be less viable than heterozygous homozygotes *gAP*/*gap*. His interpretation of Catcheside's (unpublished) results suggests that only about two-thirds of the expected proportion of homozygous homostyles actually occurs. (It is possible that more than one recessive sublethal gene is linked to the thrum chromosome, and when these are both present on homozygous chromosomes the effect is lethal, or virtually so. Maybe only one of these sublethals is closely linked to *AP*, so that the *gAP* long homostyle has reduced viability, but is not fully lethal. This might also explain why thrum homozygote *P. sinensis* has a reduced viability, but is not fully lethal (p. 246)).

In any case, it seems that the low viability of homostyle homozygotes will ensure a high proportion of homostyles will be heterozygous for the pin chromosome, and on selfing these will, of course, give rise to more than a quarter pins. Thus, it is not surprising that pins remain in many homostyle populations.

Were homostyle homozygotes as viable as heterozygotes, one would expect that the automatic reproductive and genetic advantage of homostyles should cause them to outcompete thrums and pins. Crosby (1949) calculated that if homostyle homozygotes were more than 81.5 per cent as successful as pins, pins as well as thrums should disappear from the population. In fact, Crosby estimates that homostyle homozygotes are in fact only about 65 per cent as successful as pins, and that such populations should 'settle down' to an equilibrium of about 80 per cent homostyles and 20 per cent pins. However, most homostyle populations have a lower proportion of homostyles than this.

Crosby's prediction caused Curtis & Curtis (1985) to resurvey Crosby's populations some 30 years after his original counts (in Somerset). Contrary to Crosby's expectation, only minor changes in the frequencies of homostyles, pins and thrums had taken place in the intervening time. However, the Curtises discovered that the frequency of homostyles had tended to increase slightly where they had originally been scarce, but where they were very common, their frequency had, if anything, become less.

The Curtises found that only a narrow range of fitnesses for homostyles as a whole, and for homozygous homostyles would match their finding that changes in homostyle frequency differed with the commoness of homostyles. If Crosby's suggestion that homostyle homozygotes are 65 per cent as successful as pins is adhered to, homostyles as a whole must be only about 71 per cent as successful as pins (and thus homostyle heterozygotes about 80 per cent as successful as pins).

The question then arises as to why homostyles are in general less fit than heterostyles in these primrose populations. The answer to this question would tell one why few populations reach the 80 per cent equilibrium frequency of homostyles predicted by Crosby on the basis of homostyle homozygote disadvantage. This question, and indeed the whole study of primrose homostyles, is not so esoteric as might initially be thought. The key to the success of the remarkable phenonemon of heterostyly in most primulas, and in many other genera, may be discovered through this work. Indeed, homostyle primroses may tell us a good deal about selection for outcrossing, or for selfing, in plants generally. Years after his published work, Jack Crosby made a television film for the first BBC series 'Bellamy on Botany' entitled 'The Wars of the Primroses'. In this, he highlighted the ongoing competition between the original heterostyles and the recombinant long homostyles in the woods of Somerset as a classic example of mating system evolution in progress. And so it is.

The pollination patterns and reproductive successes of homostyle, pin and thrum primroses in Somerset have been studied in detail by both John Piper (Piper & Charlesworth, 1986; Piper *et al*., 1986) and by Mark Boyd (Boyd *et al*., 1990). This work showed that homostyles on the whole produce more seed than do pins and thrums (about 65 per cent more on average), while thrums produce the least, although these figures varied greatly from site to site and year to year. It was also shown that homostyles are about 10 per cent outcrossed (estimates from population genetics suggested 8 per cent outcrossed, and observations of pollen on emasculated stigmas suggested about 14 per cent outcrossed). The amount of outcrossed pollen they receive differs little from that received by pins, although pins are somewhat self-sterile. In contrast, thrums receive about five times as little selfed pollen as pins, and are completely self-sterile.

As Crosby had predicted, homostyles have a reproductive advantage over pins and thrums, as well as a genetic one. Nevertheless, it seems that they are less fit than pins and thrums and several explanations have been produced as to why this should be, so that they never take over completely. These include the possibility that slug grazing removes both the stigma and the anthers in a homostyle, but either the anthers or the stigma is protected within the corolla tube in a heterostyle. Another theory is that the fatter capsules of homostyles are more attractive to rodents. It is also very possible that selfed homostyles suffer from more inbreeding depression than do outcrossed pins and thrums. These possibilities are more fully discussed in Richards (1997).

Boyd's work shows that none of these ideas seem to be true. Homostyle heterozygotes have if anything a longer life-span than pins and thrums, and seem not to suffer from undue predation of the flowers or the fruits. Boyd does, however, show that there is an inverse relationship between seed number and seed size, so that when homostyles set more seed than pins and thrums, the seed is smaller. This, he suggests, may cause homostyle seed to be less fit. Tremayne & Richards (2000) show that seedlings resulting from lighter seeds are indeed less fit in another primula species (*P. farinosa*).

In summary, it looks as if the relative lack of success of primrose homostyles may have two explanations, one of which has a general applicability, and the other of which is specific to primulas:

- It may pay perennial outcrossers to set fewer seeds per capsule than selfers, as these seeds will be heavier and more fit.
- The origin of heterostyly, through the linkage of thrumness to recessive lethality, may cause homostyle homozygotes to be less fit than pins and thrums.

It is worth considering briefly why short homostyles, *Gap* (or *GaP*), rarely become established, as they presumably arise at the same frequency as do long homostyles (I have found a short homostyle in a large garden population of *P. vulgaris*). Such plants would suffer from having the anthers and stigma buried deep in the corolla tube, so that both pollen issue and pollen receipt would be impeded. Although *Gap* homostyles would automatically self, they would suffer genetically from reduced outcrossing rates, making them more inbred. They would also be less able to disseminate the homostyle 'gene', because when short homostyle pollen crosses with thrums, only half the offspring are short homostyle. However, there is a little-known short-homostyle subspecies of *P. septemloba*.

It would also be interesting to know whether casual secondary homostyly occurs in other heterostyle primula species apart from the primrose, and *P. latifolia*. I have found occasional isolated long homostyle individuals in populations of cowslip *P. veris*, and in recent years Washitani and co-workers have undertaken intensive studies of *P. sieboldii*, finding both short and long homostyle recombinants (see under that species for a more detailed account). It is probable that recombination homostyles occur in all heterostyle primulas, but few if any display populations polymorphic for homostyles and heterostyles, as is the case in the primrose.

An alternative form of long homostyly

Mather (1950) has shown for *P. sinensis* that long homostyly can arise in a quite different way in this species. Two mutants are known which also affect style length and anther position. These are unlinked to the heterostyly chromosome, and so have no relationship to the primary heterostyly, but seem rather to act as later-evolving modifiers:

- 'Primrose Queen' reduces the size of the

orange 'eye' of the flower in this species. This is a recessive allele *a* which has the additional effect of shortening the pin style towards the thrum position. The stigma papillae also become shorter, and the stigma becomes less receptive to thrum pollen.

- 'Fertile double' in pin flowers carries anthers on double petals in a 'high' (i.e. nearly thrum) position. It has no effect on the mating system. It is controlled by a recessive allele *m*.

Thus plants which are phenotypically *aM* are effectively short homostyles, while those which are phenotypically *Am* are effectively long homostyles. Pins with the genotype *aamm* look like thrums and are called 'pseudothrums' although their mating system is more like pins. Thrums can also exhibit these characteristics, and those with the genotype *aamm* are called 'superthrums'.

Such plants are not encountered in the wild, and probably result from many years of highly selective breeding of *P. sinensis* in cultivation. This supposition is supported by Mather's additional finding that inbred lines of *P. sinensis* show much greater developmental variability in the expression of 'pinness' and 'thrumness' in flowers than do outcrossed lines.

However, there is no doubt that genetic modifiers also exist in wild populations which alter degrees of the manifestation of 'pinness' and 'thrumness'. Working with cowslip, *P. veris*, Fran Wedderburn (1988) showed that considerable variation occurred in the length of the style, particularly in pins, and this was not only consistent between individuals, but tended to be inherited after pin selfs. Crosses between relatively long and short styled pin individuals, and between these and thrums, showed that the control of the inheritance of pin style length was complex and not linked to the heterostyly linkage group. There was no indication that variations in pin style length had any detectable effect on the mating system, nor did any plants approach homostyly. However, it is likely that variations in pin style length might well effect levels of self-pollination that occur in pin flowers.

It is also worth recalling that Mather & de Winton (1941) showed that pin selfs in *P. sinensis* showed 70.6 per cent of the seed-set of pin crosses with thrums, whereas Hildebrand (1864) and Darwin (1877) showed comparable figures of 18.2 per cent and 12.5 per cent respectively. These calculations (which are not the same as Mather's, but seem more relevant) clearly support his claim that repeated selfing of pins had selected for greater pin self-fertility in the intervening 70 years or so. In contrast, thrums, which were already 67.9 per cent (Darwin) or 34.6 per cent (Hildebrand) self-fertile in the nineteenth century when compared with legitimate crosses onto thrums, were found to be 46.9 per cent self-fertile by Mather.

One can conclude that various modifying genes, unlinked to the heterostyly linkage group, occur in *Primula* which will influence both levels of self-pollination and of self-fertilization. Recombinational long homostyly can be viewed as an 'instant escape' from the reproductive straitjacket of outcrossing, but there are also more subtle evolutionary mechanisms by which primulas can influence the amount of out-crossing and selfing that they receive.

Fixed secondary homostyly

Of the 430 species of *Primula*, 40 (nine per cent) are partly or completely long homostyle. In all of these, the anthers and the stigma occur together at the mouth of the flower, so that automatic self-pollination occurs, and all are fully self-fertile. As a result, these species are mostly selfed, although some outcrossing may also occur in the wild. From the garden point of view, these species usually set seed well, even when isolated and not artificially pollinated, although it is often found that seedlings from homostyles artificially outcrossed are more vigorous.

Homostyle primulas seem to fall into two main groups: 'primary' homostyles, and 'secondary' homostyles of recombinational origin. There is only one certain way of determining which group a homostyle species falls into. Secondary long homostyles have arisen in the same way as the casual homostyles in the primrose (p. 56), by crossing over (recombination) within the heterostyly linkage group. Thus, they are effectively thrum males and pin females, which explains why they are self-fertile; a self is effectively a 'legitimate' cross. If secondary homostyles are crossed with related heterostylous species, it is found that for a given gender they behave as if they were heterostyles. Thus homostyle female × thrum male crosses are fertile, or at least show good pollen germination and growth. Thus, homostyles behave as if they were pins when female. Equally, pin female × homostyle male crosses are fertile, because homostyles behave as if they were thrum when male.

This effect was first recorded by Ernst (1955) for crosses between the homostyle tetraploid *P. japonica* and the heterostyles *P. pulverulenta* and *P. burmanica*. It demonstrates quite convincingly that secondary homostyles have arisen by recombination within the heterostyly linkage group. Recently, similar experiments have been undertaken with the homostyle Aleuritia species *P. halleri, P. scotica, P. stricta, P. laurentiana* and *P. magellanica*, crossed with their heterostyle relatives *P. farinosa, P. frondosa* and *P. modesta* (Wedderburn & Richards, 1992). These crosses clearly show that these five homostyle species have also evolved from heterostyle ancestors by recombination. The crosses also show that 'illegitimate' crosses between homostyles and heterostyles of different species fail in the same way as illegitimate crosses fail within heterostylous species.

However, 'legitimate' crosses between homostyles and heterostyles fail, if they do so, in a quite different way from 'illegitimate' crosses. Such 'barriers to hybridization' between species are caused by pollen tubes ceasing to grow at the bottom of the style, in the ovary, or by fertilized seeds failing to develop. Similar effects are noted when legitimate crosses are made between two heterostyle species. Thus, in *Primula* one can distinguish quite clearly between pollen incompatibility as expressed in the mating system, and interspecific incompatibility as part of a 'speciation' mechanism.

In contrast, 'primary' homostyles are thought to represent survivors from a time before heterostyly evolved in *Primula*. If this is so, they should not exhibit any 'remnants' of the heterostyly systems. If they are crossed with heterostyles, one would not expect crosses with pins or with thrums to differ in their behaviour or fertility. One might, however, expect crosses to differ in their fertility depending on whether the homostyle was the mother or father to the cross, but only because this type of reciprocal cross difference is commonly found in interspecific crosses.

Ernst (1955) crossed the heterostyles *P. pulverulenta* and *P. burmanica* with the diploid homostyles *P. chungensis* and *P. cockburniana*. These latter two species are closely related to one another, and *P. chungensis* is one of only a few species (*P. prolifera* and *P. floribunda* are others) in which both homostyle and heterostyle races are reported. Ernst found no evidence of any meaningful differences in the behaviour of crosses between the homostyles and pins or thrums, and came to the conclusion that these homostyles might be of a primary kind, as they showed no evidence of 'remnants' of the heterostyly system. As I shall show, it is apparently significant that they are diploid, while *P. japonica*, and the Aleuritia homostyles, are polyploid.

Features of primary and secondary homostyle species

The only certain way of showing whether a species is a primary or secondary homostyle is to make crosses with heterostyle relatives. However, there are certain features which tend to be associated with primitive and secondary homostyly, which can be used as additional indicators:

	Primary homostyly	Secondary homostyly
Chromosome number	diploid	polyploid
Heterostyles also present	yes	homostyle only
Sectional affiliations	'primitive'	'derived' (p. 32)
Geographical distribution	warm temperate	arctic or alpine

One might expect that 'primary' homostyles, representing as they appear to do an early condition in the evolution of the genus, would be more likely to be diploid, and would be more likely to occur in sections considered 'primitive', i.e. those that have changed relatively little from the ancestors of the genus. One might also expect that in a few cases (for instance *P. chungensis* or *P. floribunda*) one might also be able to observe conditions representing the early development of heterostyly, always supposing that conditions which favoured each mating system continued to exist.

It is less immediately clear why secondary homostyly should be associated with polyploidy, and with extreme arctic or alpine conditions.

Primary homostyly and the development of heterostyly

In an earlier section (p. 46) I have discussed how heterostyly is thought to have evolved in *Primula*. One of the main reasons it is thought likely that the morphological heterostyly (pins and thrums) arose before the mating system is that several species or groups of *Primula* species show both primary homostyly and self-fertile heterostyly. It seems likely that these represent intermediate stages in the evolution of 'full' heterostyly, 'frozen' in evolutionary time.

Although *P. chungensis* and *P. prolifera* have both homostyle and self-fertile heterostyle races, the best studied examples of this situation are found in section Sphondylia. The species in this section are nowadays isolated and scattered in the mountains of western and central Asia, presumably relict from cooler and wetter eras when their ancestors were more widespread in the intervening desert. All appear to be self-fertile. Amongst these eight species, heterostyly appears to have evolved at least twice as demonstrated by the following five groups of species:

- *P. simensis* and *P. verticillata*. Homostyles from the mountains of Ethiopia, the Yemen and Arabia. Considerable variation occurs with respect to style length, but there is no true heterostyly or change in anther position.
- *P. boveana*. This species, isolated and nowadays very rare on Mt. Sinai, shows development of pin and thrum style lengths, together with some difference in pollen size between the two, but only one 'thrum' anther height position is known. This suggests that heteromorphy for style length, and pollen size, evolved before that for anther position in this group. *P. boveana* is geographically, morphologically, and with respect to its heterostyly, intermediate between *P. verticillata* and *P. gaubeana*.
- *P. floribunda*. This species, from the western Himalaya, is particularly interesting as it is heterostyle but self-fertile at low altitudes, but at higher elevations it becomes increasingly homostyle (Richards, 1997). Heterostyly may have arisen in this species independently from that in *P. boveana* and *P. gaubeana*.
- *P. davisii, P. gaubeana*. These two species, from the mountains of south-east Turkey and western Iran respectively, show a full heterostyly although they are self-fertile. They have apparently evolved from *P. verticillata* and *P. boveana*.
- *P. edelbergii* and *P. afghanica,* from east Afghanistan, are also fully heterostyle, and self-fertile, but are morphologically and geographically related to *P. floribunda*.

Within this group there is a variety in pollen morphology, described more fully in the systematic section. As is discussed more fully in Al Wadi & Richards (1992), this strongly suggests that heterostyly arose at least twice and possibly three times in this section alone. There seem to have been two clear evolutionary trends, one northwards from Arabia, and one westwards from the Himalaya.

Secondary homostyly and polyploidy

Of the 29 homostyle species for which the chromosome number is known, 16 (55 per cent) are polyploid. These include tetraploids (four sets of chromosomes = 4×), hexaploids (6×), octoploids (8×) and a 14-'ploid. In contrast, only five heterostyle species are polyploid (4 per cent), apart from the sections Parryi and Auricula where all the species are tetraploid and hexaploid respectively. These heterostyle polyploids are *P. suffrutescens, P. borealis, P. luteola,* and *P. auriculata*.

Of the 13 homostyle diploid species, it seems certain or very likely for reasons given above that the following are primary homostyles:

P. chungensis, P. cockburniana, P. prolifera, P. miyabeanum, P. morsheadiana, P. floribunda, P. verticillata, P. simensis.

It is also very possible that the Cortusoides diploid homostyle *P. mollis* may also represent primary homostyly, as this section also takes a rather primitive position. However, it seems likely that the Alaskan diploid homostyles *P. eximia* and *P. cuneifolia* subsp. *saxifragifolia* are secondary and recombinational in origin, as *P. filipes* and *P. septemloba* probably are, although this has yet to be tested.

Thus, it is probable that 16/20 secondary homostyles for which the chromosome number is known are polyploid. Why should this be the case, when polyploidy is so unusual amongst heterostyles?

Four possible explanations for this relationship can be suggested:

- The genetic control of the pin/thrum system does not usually work in polyploids.
- Most polyploids, and most secondary homostyles, are found in the Arctic, i.e. it is an indirect relationship.
- Polyploidy is more likely to establish in a self-fertile plant which can mate with itself.
- Polyploids are more likely to resist the inbreeding effects resulting from selfing homostyles.

All of these explanations could be true in part. However, from the Auricula species, and other examples, it is known that the control of heterostyly can work perfectly well in some polyploids. Also, there are a number of apparently secondary homostyles, or polyploids, which live in temperate (section Muscarioides, *P. japonica*) or even subtropical (*P. sherriffae*) climates. One may suppose that the most likely explanations arise from the genetic interactions between polyploidy and selfing; in plants generally it is more commonly found that polyploids are self-fertile.

Species	Distribution	Latitude °N	hetero-/homostyle	2n =
modesta	Japan	33–43	heterostyle	18
specuicola	SW USA	36	heterostyle	18
algida	W Asia	36–40	heterostyle	18
exigua	Bulgaria	42	heterostyle	18
frondosa	Bulgaria	43	heterostyle	18
daraliaca	Caucasus	43	heterostyle	18
alcalina	Idaho	45	heterostyle	18
longiscapa	C Asia	39–46	heterostyle	18
mistassinica	N America	42–60	heterostyle	18
farinosa	Europe	43–63	heterostyle	18
anvilensis	Alaska	65	heterostyle	18
borealis	Alaska	52–70	heterostyle	36
halleri	Alps, Bulgaria	42–47	homostyle	36
yuparensis	Hokkaido	43	homostyle	36
scotica	N Scotland	59	homostyle	54
incana	N America	38–61	homostyle	54
scandinavica	Scandinavia	59–70	homostyle	72
laurentiana	N America	45–55	homostyle	72
magellanica	S America	43–55	homostyle	72
stricta	high arctic	62–73	homostyle	ca.126

Secondary homostyly and arctic alpine conditions

Many of the northernmost primulas are homostyles, and this is also true of some alpine species. This is well illustrated by the Aleuritia species (p. 61):

In other sections as well, a tendency can be noted for high arctic species to be homostyles. Thus, the Alaskan species *P. eximia* (section Crystallophlomis) and *P. cuneifolia* subsp. *saxifragifolia* (section Cuneifolia) are homostyle, as is the Armerina species *P. egaliksensis*.

The corresponding relationship between homostyly and high alpine conditions is much less well marked. However, I could not help but be struck by the way that the polyploid homostyles *P. incana* and *P. egaliksensis* grew side by side in the marshes of South Park, Colorado, at an altitude of some 3400 m. (11,000 ft). Here, the snow disappears for four short months of the year, and in the short summer it rains almost every day.

Polyploid homostyles also occur on the tops of the mountains of Japan (*P. yuparensis* and *P. macrocarpa*), and in the Himalayas. Some of the highest occurring of all plants are polyploid homostyle primulas, for instance *P. clutterbuckii, P. hookeri*, and three species in section Muscarioides. However, other very high altitude species, for instance *P. caveana* and *P. concinna*, are heterostyle. There is a tendency for lowland homostyles in the Himalaya to be winter flowering (*P. filipes, P. floribunda*), although several other winter-flowering species are heterostyle.

Overall, there is tendency for homostyle species to inhabit areas where the climate is very unreliable at flowering time, so that the plant cannot rely on insect visits to mediate pollen transfer from pins to thrums. In these circumstances, a self-pollinating, self-fertilizing homostyle recombinant may well be favoured. In a few cases, notably *P. sherriffae*, over-specialization on a single pollinator may have favoured the evolution of secondary homostyly.

However, many *Primula* species which grow in conditions where reproductive assurance must be poor are nevertheless heterostylous. This suggests that selfing homostyly carries a sanction imposed by inbreeding depression, so that this system is only adopted as a 'necessary evil' in extreme circumstances. Work by Bullard *et al.* (1987) on the homostylous *Primula scotica* illustrates this well.

P. scotica is restricted to the north coast of Scotland and the Orkney Islands, areas which tend to have cold and wet early summers when this species flowers. It was shown that most plants are short-lived and flower poorly, but after occasional good summers, robust, long-lived, free-flowering individuals arise. It is suggested that these result from bouts of outcrossing, these individuals showing 'hybrid vigour' relative to the 'inbreeding depression' typical of the majority which arise from selfing. We tested this (Tremayne & Richards 1997) by transplanting back into natural populations

Table 2: Germination rate, seedling parameters, survival and flowering one year after the offspring of crosses and selfs of the selfing homostyle *P. scotica* were transplanted into wild populations.

	after crosses	after selfs	*P*
Days to germination +/- standard error	8.02 +/- 0.29	9.09 +/- 0.33	<0.05*
mean leaf number at transplantation	20.2 +/- 1.1	15.3 +/- 0.2	<0.001***
mean leaf number one year later	14.2 +/- 0.8	11.8 +/- 0.7	<0.01**
mean rosette diameter at transplantation mm	44.8 +/- 1.5	37.9 +/- 0.5	<0.001***
mean rosette diameter one year later mm	28.0 +/- 0.9	24.5 +/- 0.2	<0.001***
proportion of transplants surviving one year	45/50	41/50	ns
proportion of transplants flowering at one year	8/45	0/41	<0.01**

Table 3: Performance of P × P illegitimate crosses and P selfs in *Primula* × *polyantha* relative to average performance of legitimate crosses which score 1

Generation	P × P or self	relative seed-set	relative seed germination	relative survival to flowering
	1 P × P	0.656	0.435	0.902
	1 self	0.411	0.326	0.423
	2 P × P	0.651	0.584	0.896
	2 self	0.367	0.348	0.355
	3 P × P	0.622	0.583	0.712
	3 self	0.421	0.311	0.307
	4 P × P	0.625	not	not
	4 self	0.332	tested	tested

seedlings which had been raised after controlled selfs, and crosses. Although differences were not huge, the offspring of crosses did better than those of selfs for every measure. Perhaps the most striking finding was that none of the offspring of selfs flowered in their first year, whereas one-fifth of the offspring of crosses were able to do so (Table 2).

Although Boyd *et al.* (1990) failed to find inbreeding depression in homostylous primroses (p. 57) it should be noted that homostyle primroses are about 10 per cent outcrossed and it may be that this degree of outcrossing in a homostyle is sufficient to overcome the worst effects of repeated selfing. However, when Valsa Kurian selfed a line of *P.* × *polyantha* over four generations, she obtained very clear evidence of inbreeding depression. The unexpected feature of these results is the finding that crosses made between pins also resulted in inbreeding depression, compared to legitimate crosses (Table 3).

The lesson to the gardener is clear. For any *Primula*, such as a homostyle, which is prone to selfing, artificial cross-pollination is likely to give rise to strains of seedlings which should prove to be much better garden plants.

A Key to the Sections of the Genus *Primula*

With 430 species, the genus *Primula* is unfortunately far too unwieldy for a single successful identification key to be written for all the species (although this has been attempted on at least two occasions!) Instead, for this edition I have written dichotomous identification keys for each of the sections of the genus which I hope will allow an unknown species to be correctly identified. Nevertheless, it is difficult to write, or use, such keys in a completely foolproof fashion, and it is important that a tentative diagnosis is checked against the text, and illustrations if available. If the identification is geographically implausible, or the characters don't fit, it is probably wrong!

One major potential source of error is sectional identity. Although a few sections are unmistakable, nevertheless it is easy to be confused as to the section affinity of many specimens. The key provided here is designed to direct you to the correct section as far as possible, but it may at times fail, so that the specific diagnosis you reach proves to be implausible. In this case, your first recourse should be a reconsideration of sectional identity.

Species within a section often differ considerably, and so it has sometimes proved necessary to use rather 'botanical' characters. Some of these require a careful examination, for instance with a lens. Where necessary, I have tried to explain these characters in the key. Explanations for some of the characters can be found in the glossary (p. 327). However, wherever possible I have tried to confine myself to quite simple characters.

This is a dichotomous key, which works in a logical manner. Having decided which of two alternatives is correct for a plant, proceed to the point in the key indicated by the number following the alternative chosen. It is very important to read the choices in the key carefully, and to take the meanings of the choice given literally. Some sections key out on more than one occasion.

Having decided which section a plant belongs to, read the description at the head of each section to see if it answers to this.

I have assumed that the user grows the plant, and is therefore familiar with its behaviour over a period of time.

1. Young leaves conduplicate (i.e. emerging with the margins folded together; flowers yellow, often in superimposed whorls; W Asia and N Africa. .... **Sphondylia**
1. Young leaves involute (i.e. emerging 'rolled-up' onto upper surface). 2
1. Young leaves revolute (i.e. emerging with the margins recoiled onto lower surface) 7

2. Flowers narrowly bell-shaped; leaves without hairs, with a usually toothed thickened border and pits (Sinohimalaya) .... **Amethystina**
2. If flowers bell-shaped, then leaves hairy and/or lacking pits (mostly absent in Himalaya) 3

3. Flowers annulate (the mouth constricted by a ring); leaves usually widest near the apex 4
3. Flowers usually exannulate; leaves usually widest about halfway down (except *P. minima*) 5

4. Plants herbaceous, tufted (Pacific Rim)..**Cuneifolia**
4. Stems subshrubby, trailing (California)..**Suffrutescens**

5. Plants lacking meal or hairs; bracts with downward-pointing saccate appendages..................**Armerina**
5. Plants usually either mealy or hairy; saccate appendages absent..6

6. European; bracts usually shorter than flower-stalks; plants sometimes mealy; leaves sometimes toothed, flowers glabrous ....**Auricula**
6. American; bracts usually longer than flower-stalks; leaves never mealy; leaves rarely toothed, flowers glabrous ....**Parryi**
6. Himalayan; face of flower hairy...*P. dickieana* (N.B. There is no simple way of telling members of the Auriculastrum from the Parryi for certain; however, they have different distributions, pollen and different chromosome numbers.)

7. Leaf-blade more or less orbicular, not more than 1.5 times as long as wide 8
7. Leaf-blade more than 1.5 times as long as wide...23

8. Leaves bluntly lobed to at least 1/10 of radius, usually hairy..9
8. Leaves entire or sharply and often deeply toothed, but not lobed, often without hairs 16

9. Flowers forming a dense spiky globular head ....**Pycnoloba**
9. Flowers not borne in a head 10

10. Japanese; flowers rarely more than 3 on a stem; flower stalk usually longer than stem ....**Reinii**
10. Flowers generally more than 3 on a stem, the flower stalk shorter than the stem...............................11

11. Calyx with a flattened base..12
11. Calyx with a narrow or rounded base...13

12. Calyx flattened, disc-like...**Malvacea**
12. Calyx inflated like a balloon ....**Auganthus**

13. Capsule dehiscing by 5 apical teeth; calyx narrow and ribbed 14
13. Capsule dehiscing by means of a crumbling membrane; calyx bell-shaped, not noticeably ribbed...15

14. Flowers in superimposed whorls or spikes; calyx mealy ....**Monocarpicae**
14. Flowers usually in a single umbel; calyx never mealy ....**Cortusoides**

15. Leaves very thin in texture, lacking hairs...**Chartacea**
15. Leaves thicker in texture, hairy ....**Obconicolisteri**

16. Plant creeping; leaves lacking hairs, the blade not more than 3 cm; flowers borne singly......17
16. Plant not creeping, usually hairy, the blade usually more than 3 cm; flowers several on a stem...18

17. Flowers purple with a white eye, exannulate..*P. reptans*
17. Flowers purple with a yellow eye, annulate ....*P. juliae*
17. Flowers pink, exannulate..*P. clarkei*

18. Flowers in superimposed whorls or spikes, the calyx mealy ....**Monocarpicae**
18. Flowers in a single whorl, or if in a spike, the calyx not mealy 19

19. Plant mealy, at least on the resting bud, lacking hairs...**Cordifoliae**
19. Plant lacking meal, usually hairy 20

20. Flowers in spikes; capsule dehiscing by a lid ....**Carolinella**
20. Flowers in an umbel; capsule dehiscing by a membrane or by teeth 21

21. Leaves very thin in texture, lacking hairs ....**Chartacea**
21. Leaves thicker in texture, hairy 22

22. Bracts leaf-like; capsule top-shaped, dehiscing by a membrane.................................**Obconicolisteri**

22. Bracts narrow; capsule elongate, dehiscing by teeth ....*P. megaseifolia, P. renifolia*

23. Flowers arranged in a spike 24
23. Flowers arranged in whorls, or borne singly 27

24. Calyx disk-like ....**Malvacea**
24. Calyx tubular to bell-shaped 25

25. Leaves leathery with sharp teeth; calyx regular ....**Carolinella**
25. Leaves soft, without sharp teeth; calyx larger on one side 26

26. Corolla-tube usually shorter than the petal-lobes; flowers fewer than 5 ....**Soldanelloides**
26. Corolla-tube usually longer than the petal-lobes; flowers more than 5 ....**Muscarioides**

27. Plant with multicellular hairs 28
27. Plant without multicellular hairs, although unicellular glands sometimes present (use a lens) 35

28. Calyx bell-shaped, larger on one side, often purplish 29
28. Calyx regular, not larger on one side 30

29. Corolla-tube shorter than the petal-lobes; flowers fewer than 5 ....**Soldanelloides**
29. Corolla-tube longer than the petal-lobes; flowers more than 5 ....**Muscarioides**

30. Leaf-blades dissected almost to the mid-rib; delicate plants with filmy leaves ....**Pinnatae**
30. Leaf-blades entire to shallowly lobed; leaves not very thin 31

31. Capsule dehiscing by means of a crumbling membrane; flowers blue to pink; not yellow 32
31. Capsule dehiscing by apical teeth; flowers yellow, pink or purple 33

32 Stem usually shorter than leaves, or absent; leaf-stalk usually shorter than blade, or absent ....**Davidii**
32. Stem usually longer than leaves; leaf-stalk usually longer than blade ....**Obconicolisteri**

33. Plants sticky, sometimes mealy underneath the leaves, somewhat woody at the base; flowers exannulate ....**Bullatae**
33. Plants not sticky, mealy or woody; flowers usually annulate 34

34. Leaves with small regular teeth; flowers yellow, less commonly pink, purple or white ....**Primula**
34. Leaves with large, irregular teeth; flowers pink or purple, rarely white or yellow ....**Cortusoides**

35. Flowers borne in a tight head, the stalks absent or not more than half the length of the calyx 36
35 . Flowers borne singly, or in a lax head with longer stalks 43

36. Only 1–3 flowers usually borne on each stem 37
36. More than 10 flowers generally borne on each stem 39

37. Leaves leathery, evergreen, the old leaves persistent on woody mats ....**Dryadifolia**
37. Leaves deciduous, not persistent; plants without woody bases 38

38. Corolla-tube short and broad, not exceeding the calyx; meal absent ....**Glabra**
38. Corolla-tube narrow, exceeding the calyx, meal often present ....**Minutissimae**

39. Central flowers in head sterile, never opening ....**Capitatae**
39. All flowers opening, fertile. 40

40. Bracts conspicuous, pouch-shaped at the base; flowers usually rose-pink; leaves without meal ....*P. auriculata*
40. Bracts small, not pouch-shaped; flowers usually lilac; leaves often mealy 41

41. Leaves strongly mealy, at least below, not exceeding 10 cm ....**Aleuritia**
41. Mature leaves rarely mealy; if so, more than 15 cm 42

42. Leaves spoon-shaped, not exceeding 10 cm when mature ....**Glabra**
42. Leaves oblong, exceeding 15 cm when mature ....**Denticulata**

43. Plant disappearing in summer; flowers pink to violet 44
43. Plant disappearing in winter, or evergreen; flowers various colours 45

44. Corolla lobes entire .... **Fedtschenkoana**
44. Corolla lobes notched .... *P. specuicola*
(N.B. *P. cusickiana* with involute vernation also aestivates.)

45. Flowers bell-shaped, nodding on long stalks which usually exceed the flower 46
45. Flowers not usually bell-shaped, or if so, not nodding 49

46. Face of flower mealy; leaf-stalks usually exceeding blade, leaves without meal .... **Sikkimensis**
46. Face of flower not mealy; if leaf stalks longer than blade, then leaves mealy beneath 47

47. Plant without meal; leaves with thickened toothed margins .... **Amethystina**
47. Plant mealy, at least on the resting bud and on the leaves beneath; leaf margins not thickened 48

48. Robust plants arising from bulb-like bases .... **Crystallophlomis** subsect. **Agleniana**
48. Small plants; bases not bulb-like .... **Yunnanensis**

49. Evergreen plants with pink (rarely yellow) flowers which are apparently basal (stemless) at flowering .... **Petiolares** subsect. **Petiolares**
49. Deciduous plants; flowers stemless at flowering or nearly so, bright blue (rarely yellow) .... **Petiolares** subsect. **Sonchifolia**
49. Deciduous plants; flowers borne on a stem at flowering, rarely bright blue 50

50 Flowers borne in several superimposed whorls 51
50. Flowers borne in a single whorl 52

51. Leaves usually bullate; resting buds inconspicuous; capsules orbicular .... **Proliferae**
51. Leaves smooth; resting buds conspicuous, usually mealy; capsules elongate .... **Crystallophlomis** subsect. **Crystallophlomis**

52. Bracts conspicuous, pouched at the base; plants usually lacking meal; flowers commonly pinkish, yellow in *P. luteola* 53
52. Bracts not pouched at the base; plants frequently mealy; flowers various colours 54

53. Resting buds above ground, rooted; capsules short, not exceeding the calyx .... **Oreophlomis**
53. Resting buds below ground, small and spherical, more or less rootless; capsules exceeding the calyx .... **Armerina**

54. Petal-lobes narrow, usually reflexed .... **Crystallophlomis** subsect. **Maximowiczii**
54 Petal-lobes contiguous to overlapping, not reflexed 54

55. Corolla-tube narrow, not more than 2 mm in diameter; mature leaves mealy beneath; bud scales not persistent, and leaves not noticeably sheathing at base 56
55. Corolla-tube broader, more than 2 mm in diameter; if mature leaves mealy beneath, then bud scales persistent and leaves sheathing at base 57

56. Leaves narrowly spear-shaped, thickly mealy beneath but usually without meal above; flowers few, long-stalked, usually exannulate .... **Pulchella**
56. Leaves usually spoon-shaped, usually mealy on both surfaces; flowers usually more than 6 borne on a stem, usually annulate .... **Aleuritia**

57. Petals notched; flowers strongly annulate; capsule orbicular, dehiscing by teeth .... **Crystallophlomis** subsect. **Calliantha**
57. Petals entire or notched, flowers annulate; capsule orbicular, dehiscing by a crumbling membrane .... **Petiolares** subsect. **Griffithii**
57. Petals entire, flowers usually exannulate; capsule elongate, dehiscing by teeth .... **Crystallophlomis** subsect. **Crystallophlomis**

Notes on the Systematic Account

The ordering of the sections in this systematic account roughly follows that of Windelbo (1961b) and of Fenderson (1986). Within the sections, the species order is my own, following my own concepts of species relationships within the sections; in both the Smith and Fletcher monograph, and in Fenderson, species orders within the sections are alphabetical.

Each sectional and species account follows a set order, which in full is as follows:

- Valid name and place of publication
- Synonymy
- Description (in which characters also follow a set order)
- Chromosome number, breeding behaviour and flowering time
- Illustration
- Distribution
- Habitat, including altitudinal range
- Taxonomic and other general notes
- Variation
- Cultivation
- Hybridization
- Literature.

However, where information is missing, or is not relevant, sections may be missed out, or fused. Where species closely resemble a species already described in full, only those characters which differentiate them are cited, often in the order of their importance.

For a less well-known species, accounts are truncated, often greatly so, and are only partially sectionalized, or are not sectionalized, although information usually follows the same set order.

In descriptions, technical terms have been kept to a minimum, to the extent that non-botanical terms such as 'meal' are used in place of farina, or 'stem' in place of scape. However, it was felt necessary to use a minimum of technical terms, and these are defined in the glossary.

Place names In the Himalayas and China, I have had great difficulty in deciding which names for political divisions and place names to use. Finally, I have been guided by those names that I considered would be most familiar to a Western audience, and this has resulted in inconsistencies. Thus, in the Indian Subcontinent I have persisted with the name Assam, which has long been superseded, and with other political divisions such as Burma, Tibet, Kashmir and Sikkim which are today either known by other names, or are of disputed political status. When much of the exploration of these areas was at its peak, these names and divisions were current, and they are mostly unambiguously understood by a Western audience.

In China, the inconsistencies of usage are if anything even greater. For place names, I have usually employed those names and transliterations used by the Western collectors in these areas, such as Forrest, Farrer, Rock, Wilson and Ward, and these do not usually differ from those given by Smith and Fletcher. However, for major political divisions such as provinces, I have usually given post-revolutionary spellings, for instance Sichuan for Szechwan, Gansu for Kansu, Beijing for Peking. However, I have persisted with the usage of Tibet instead of Xijang.

In the former USSR, I have mostly used place names in accordance with the transliteration in Federov (1952).

Illustrations Where I am aware of good, usually coloured, published photographs of little-known species not illustrated in this volume, I have often referred to these. In particular, I have used the Bulletin of the Alpine Garden Society (later the Alpine Gardener); the Journal of the Scottish Rock Garden Club (later 'the Rock Garden'); the Journal of the Royal Horticultural Society 54 (1929); Polunin and Stainton (1984); Stainton (1988); Fletcher (1975); Smith *et al.* (1984); and Halda (1992) as sources for these. These references are *not* designed to be comprehensive, but merely to act as a helpful guide.

Plant awards All awards given to plants by the Joint Rock Garden Committee of the Royal Horticultural Society and the Scottish Rock Garden Club after 1960 are listed. **PC** = Preliminary Commendation; **AM** = Award of Merit; **FCC** = First Class Certificate.

Some awards given to plants by the Royal Horticultural Society prior to that date are also listed, but prior to 1960 the coverage is not comprehensive.

Habitat descriptions At times these are quoted verbatim. For Chinese species these quotes usually come from Handel-Mazzetti (1929), and for eastern Himalayan species from Fletcher (1975). Other quotes usually originate from articles in the Bulletin of the Alpine Garden Society, and references are usually given to these.

SYNOPSIS OF THE GENUS *PRIMULA*

Primula L. Gen. Pl. ed. 5: 70 (1754).
Type species: *P. veris* L.

Subgenus **Sphondylia** (Duby) Rupr.,

Bull. Acad. Imp. Sci. St. Pet. 6: 218 (1863).
Type species *P. verticillata* Forssk.

Section **Sphondylia**

(Section Floribundae Pax (1889))

DESCRIPTION Perennial evergreen plants; leaves with a winged stalk, toothed, green and sticky-hairy or whitish-mealy, with *conduplicate* vernation. Stem with *leafy* bracts and 1–6 *superimposed* umbels of *yellow* homostyle to heterostyle exannulate flowers. Calyx narrowly bell-shaped. Pollen grains spherical to prolate, commonly 3-colporoidate, but from 1–3 colpate to colporoidate. Capsules globose, *persistent,* opening by 5–10 valves. x = 9. All species seem to be potentially self-fertile, but *P. edelbergii*, some *P. floribunda* and probably *P. gaubeana* and *P. davisii* fail to set seed in the absence of pollination. Flowering throughout the year in the wild, although principally during the winter. In cultivation, most flowering occurs from December to April.

DISTRIBUTION South-east Turkey, Sinai and Ethiopia to northern India. Wet shaded usually calcareous cliffs, more rarely wet meadows and stream banks, in arid areas.

This is an unmistakable group of plants. With superimposed whorls of yellow flowers and leafy bracts, the Sphondylia could only be mistaken for members of section Proliferae, which however have leaves with revolute vernation. Species in section Sphondylia come from regions where few other primulas grow. They have a superficial resemblance to members of *Dionysia* section Anacamptophyllum growing in some of the same areas, and recent DNA studies have shown these two groups to be closely related. Dionysias are best distinguished from *Primula* section Sphondylia by having revolute leaf vernation and stephanocolpate pollen. It is not the case, as stated by Al Wadi & Richards (1992) and Richards (1993) that all Dionysias have woolly meal. It is powdery in some sections of that genus.

It was originally thought that the *Sphondylia* shared with the otherwise apparently unrelated *Primula* subgenus *Auriculastrum,* and most other Primulaceae but no other primula, involute vernation. This suggested that involute vernation had re-evolved secondarily in the genus, a problematic concept. However, Mast *et al.* (2001) point out that the vernation of the Sphondylia is perhaps better interpreted as conduplicate, which could, they suggest, have evolved secondarily from the revolute type more readily than could involute vernation.

The Sphondylia were considered by Wendelbo (1961b) to be amongst the most primitive of all primulas, but DNA studies do not support this suggestion, although the Sphondylia seem to have few close relatives. Species occur in isolated mountain localities over a large area of dry country. They seem to form a morphological and geographical series from the white-mealy homostyles *P. simensis* and *P. verticillata* in the south-west to the green glandular heterostyles *P. floribunda, P. edelbergii* and *P. afghanica* in the north-east. *P. boveana, P. gaubeana* and *P. davisii* seem to take intermediate positions. However, hybrids can be formed between the two morphological extremes, *P.*

verticillata and *P. floribunda*, so these species are apparently still closely related.

Evidence from pollen morphology (Al Wadi and Richards, 1992) and the flavonoid pigments (p. 28) suggest that the relationships between the species are more complex than they first appear. It seems that a westwards migration from the homostylous forerunners of *P. floribunda* in the Himalaya led to the evolution of plants possessing meal and lacking hairs, which are today represented by *P. verticillata* and *P. simensis*. These gained the flavonoid hesperidin, while losing another (malvidin). Predecessors of the homostyle *P. simensis* and *P. verticillata* then migrated northwards, leaving behind the partial heterostyle *P. boveana*, which has the same pollen type and flavonoids, on Mt. Sinai as a witness to this development. Further north, this line is now represented by heterostyles *P. gaubeana* and *P. davisii* which have lost one flavonoid (hesperidin) and gained another (aurometin). The pollen became much smaller, so that the particularly small pin pollen of these two species now only has one pore, and the thrum pollen two.

The final species, *P. edelbergii*, from east Afghanistan, is an interesting case. Although it appears superficially to be related to *P. floribunda* and *P. afghanica*, with the same heterostyly, it has lost kaempferol, and has acquired aurometin, otherwise only known in *P. gaubeana*, and hesperidin. It has also lost two pores in its thrum, not its pin pollen (which remains 3-coloporidate). Its origins are not clear, but it does not seem to have evolved directly from *P. floribunda*.

Wendelbo suggests that the present disjunct distribution of the section is relictic from earlier cooler and wetter periods when precursors were more widespread. Its disjunction in north-east Africa is paralleled by the recent discovery of *Cyclamen somalense* in Somalia, indicating the presence of ancient migration routes down the mountains bordering the western edge of the Red Sea, which are today very dry.

It is clear that some Sphondylia are primary homostyles (p. 60). Interestingly, they are potentially self-fertile, although several species are fully heterostyle. *P. boveana* is particularly significant, as it is geographically and morphologically intermediate between the homostyle *P. verticillata* and the heterostyle *P. gaubeana*, and also demonstrates an imperfect development of heterostyly. It is difficult to escape the view that the Sphondylia represent stages in the development of heterostyly, 'frozen' in time, before incompatibility evolved. As such, they are of particular interest, a sort of living laboratory.

P. floribunda is one of the few primula species having both primary homostyles and heterostyles in the same species.

CULTIVATION Six species are still in cultivation, although *P. edelbergii*, *P. gaubeana* and *P. boveana* are very scarce. None are hardy outside in normal UK conditions; under glass they will tolerate light frosts. They grow well in cool greenhouses in peat-based composts in plastic pots; kept rather dry and in full light in the winter, but wetter and lightly shaded in summer. In these conditions, all the species except *P. gaubeana* and probably *P. davisii* grow vigorously, and often self-sow with abandon.

HYBRIDIZATION Sterile hybrids are recorded between *P. verticillata* and *P. floribunda* (*P.* × *kewensis* Wats.), and between *P. verticillata* and *P. edelbergii* (*P.* × *jenensis* Schwarz).

LITERATURE. Wendelbo (1961b); Al Wadi and Richards (1992).

KEY TO SPECIES

1. Plant mealy, at least on calyx 2
1. Plant lacking meal 5

2. Leaves with some meal, especially when young; corolla tube exceeding 15 mm 3
2. Leaves lacking meal; corolla tube not exceeding 14 mm .... *P. gaubeana*

3. Corolla tube not exceeding 22 mm; leaves coarsely toothed .... *P. boveana*
3. Corolla tube exceeding 20 mm; leaves finely toothed 4

4. Leaves toothed to one-third length, lateral veins about 7; calyx divided to one half .... *P. simensis*
4. Leaves toothed to one-half length; lateral veins about 12; calyx divided to two-thirds .... *P. verticillata*

5. Leaves and stems with multicellular hairs, not sticky .... *P. floribunda*
5. Plant glabrous, or with unicellular sticky glands 6

6. Leaf blades as wide as long, not sticky .... *P. afghanica*
6. Leaf blades at least twice as long as wide, sticky 7

7. Plant robust, exceeding 10 cm; flowers in several superimposed whorls .... *P. edelbergii*
7. Plant small, not exceeding 6 cm; flowers in a single whorl .... *P. davisii*

Primula verticillata Forsskal, Fl. Aegypt.-Arab. 42 (1775)

DESCRIPTION Rather robust plants to 80 cm, sparsely covered throughout in *white meal*, so that leaves are usually grey-green, lacking hairs. *Leaves* broadly spear-shaped, to 30 × 8 cm, finely and somewhat doubly-toothed in the upper half, with about 12 lateral veins, the broadly winged entire stalk about one-third of leaf length. *Stems* bearing up to 4 whorls each bearing up to 18 golden yellow flowers; bracts large and leaf-like, to 10 cm. *Calyx* narrowly bell-shaped, 9–12 mm, divided to at least two-thirds of the length. *Corolla* 15–25 mm in diameter, flat-faced, *homostylous*, the anthers inserted just inside the tube; style of varying lengths, sometimes exserted; corolla-tube 28–38 mm in length, very slender; petal-lobes entire or shallowly notched; the prolate 3-colporoidate pollen is the largest in this group (diameter 26 μm). 2n = 18. (Plates 1, 23).

DISTRIBUTION On the east side of the southern Red Sea in the Asir mountains, Saudi Arabia, and in Yemen, from Jebel Sawdah southwards to the Dhala Highlands.

Very wet north-facing limestone cliffs, 1700–4200 m. Occasionally in irrigation ditches as a weed.

In a complex of similar species (*P. simensis, P. boveana, P. gaubeana*), *P. verticillata* has the largest flowers with the longest corolla-tube, and the most dissected calyx. The leaf-shape is subtly different from its relatives. Although self-fertile, varieties with longer styles are more outcrossed than those with shorter styles.

CULTIVATION Probably in cultivation for many years, although early records are confused with *P. simensis*. Recently reintroduced by David Walkey from Yemen (about 1985) and by Hussen Al Wadi from the Asir (1990). An easy, vigorous and long-lived plant in suitable conditions, often self-sowing in the greenhouse.

HYBRIDIZATION In 1899, a seedling of *P. floribunda* at Kew Gardens was found to resemble '*P. verticillata*', although with the leaf-shape of its mother. Later intentional crosses with '*P. verticillata*' onto *P. floribunda* proved the parentage of this cross (in fact it seems very possible that the pollen parent was not *P. verticillata,* but the closely related *P. simensis*). These hybrids were sterile, having poor chromosome pairing at meiosis (2n = 18). However, they were vigorous growers, and offsets were distributed. These formed fertile, true-breeding lines on three separate occasions, in 1905 (Messer Veitch), 1923 (Kew) and 1926 (John Innes Institute). From the first of these, Digby obtained the chromosome count 2n = 36 in 1912.

Newton and Pellew (J. Gen. 20: 405) interpreted this as allotetraploidy, where a diploid hybrid, rendered sterile by poor chromosome pairing at meiosis, becomes fertile and true-breeding, effectively a 'new species', after chromosome doubling. This is now known to be an important mechanism in plant evolution, and is extensively used in plant breeding. However, this hybrid, *P.* × *kewensis* W. Wats., was the first case in which allotetraploidy had been shown to occur in cultivation.

P. × *kewensis* is a vigorous grower in cultivation and tends to be more popular than its parents. Over the last 90 years, some variants have appeared, including dwarf and non-mealy strains.

Hybrids have also been raised between *P. verticillata* and *P. edelbergii* by Schwarz (Bull. AGS, 32: 283–290, 1964). These were sterile and lacked meal, or had meal on the stem only.

Primula simensis Hochst., Iter Abyss. 2: 662 (1843)

P. verticillata Forssk. subsp. *simensis* (Hochst.) Smith and Fletcher (1928)

DESCRIPTION Differs from *P. verticillata* as follows: heavily mealy so that leaves generally appear *white*; leaves usually neatly and *regularly* toothed to a *third* the length of the leaf, lateral veins about 7; calyx divided to about half way; corolla tube 20–30 mm in length. In general a neater and more attractive plant than *P. verticillata,* to which is undoubtedly closely related. 2n = 18.

DISTRIBUTION Only one of two primulas native to Africa, occurring through much of the Ethiopian Highlands from 39°E 14° N to 42° E 9° N. Plants from a single locality in Somalia are little known and of uncertain affinity.

Pollen and flavonoids of this species are indistinguishable from those of *P. verticillata*. However, there seem to be some crossability barriers between the two, and in view of minor morphological differences, and geographical disjunction, I have decided to treat them as separate species.

CULTIVATION It seems likely that the plants originally grown at Kew, which gave rise to *P.* × *kewensis*, were not *P. verticillata,* but *P. simensis*. Some forms of *P.* × *kewensis* are much more mealy than is usually found in *P. verticillata*. Certainly, some of the 'older' strains of '*P. verticillata*' in cultivation today match *P. simensis,* but the history of introduction is confused between the two species. Does as well as *P. verticillata*.

Primula boveana Decne. ex Duby in DC, Prodr. 8: 34 (1844)

P. verticillata Forssk. subsp. *boveana* (Duby) W.W. Smith and Forrest (1928)
P. involucrata Sweet (1844) non Wallich

DESCRIPTION Differs from *P. verticillata* as follows: less robust plants to 30 cm, the leaves not exceeding 20 cm; leaves obovate, *bluntly* pointed, *coarsely* double-toothed to more than half-way, *lightly* mealy, with a broadly winged stalk; whorls of flowers not exceeding 10 in number; bracts not exceeding 7 cm, rather *narrow* and acute; calyx 9–16 mm, cut over half-way into narrow sharp sepal-lobes; corolla 8–12 mm in diameter, the tube 15–22 mm; distylous, but anthers always in thrum position. Pollen 3-colporoidate, 18 μm in diameter, slightly larger in thrums, less prolate in shape and with deeper colpi than in *P. verticillata*. (Plate 1.)

DISTRIBUTION Endemic to St. Catharine's Mount (Jebel Katarina), Mt. Sinai, Egypt at 2600 m. The original locality was given as 'low down by springs, but also on rocks in the area of the place Raphidium, where it is said that Moses caused the water to flow forth from a rock by striking it with his staff'.

Geographically very isolated from its nearest relatives, *P. verticillata* and *P. simensis* 1400 km to the south and *P. gaubaeana* 1400 km to the east, the presence of *P. boveana* on the isolated massif of St. Catharine is very unexpected. Morphologically, *P. boveana* also takes an intermediate position. The flowers are longer than those of *P. gaubeana*, but shorter than in either *P. verticillata* or *P. simensis*. The flowers are distylous, but the anthers monomorphic, thus also taking an intermediate position between the heterostyle *P. gaubeana* and the homostyle *P. verticillata*.

When discovered by Bove in 1835, *P. boveana* seems to have been quite common on Jebel Katarina, occurring all the way to the base of the north side of the mountain. It has been rarely seen since; until 1991 the most recent collection was in 1945.

In March 1991, after an exhaustive exploration lasting several days, Hussen Al Wadi was able to locate only one population of this species just below the summit of Jebel Katarina. Here, below a spring where no other plants grow, some 2000 individuals were restricted to an area a few metres across. The site lies directly beneath the position where what were believed to be the relicts of St. Catharine herself were discovered early in the 1980s, and her remains conceivably contributed to the well-being of the population.

This area is at present in the grip of a very dry period; it is possible that during wetter cycles the population is more widespread on the mountain. However, at the moment *P. boveana* must count amongst the rarest and most threatened plants in the world. There is an article on this subject in Bull. AGS 61: 68–70.

CULTIVATION *P. boveana* is not common in cultivation. It has survived for many years at the Gothenburg Botanic Gardens, and was reintroduced from a German source by Ron Beeston in 1991. This introduction was offered through the trade on several occasions in the late 1990s. Seedlings from Al Wadi's collections originally grew vigorously, but later sowings lost vigour, perhaps as the result of selfing, and this introduction disappeared in 2000. Although of great botanical interest, it is not so attractive as *P. simensis* and *P. verticillata*.

Primula gaubeana Bornm., Mitt. Thuring. Bot. Ver. N.F. 47: 132–7 (1941)

DESCRIPTION A less robust plant than the previous three species, to 15 cm. Hairless, or with sparse glands, not sticky, and *leaves* lacking meal or very sparsely mealy, with a narrowly winged to unwinged stalk 1–3 times the length of the blade; *stems* with 1–3 whorls of about 6 flowers; calyx *white-mealy*, to 8 mm; *corolla* to 10 mm in diameter, the tube not exceeding 14 mm; heterostylous. Pollen prolate, very small, 12 µm in diameter and with one pore in pins, 16 µm and with two pores in thrums. 2n = 18. (Fig. Halda: 7.)

DISTRIBUTION Luristan, west Iran. Known from five sites, 600–1500 m.

Intermediate between *P. boveana* and *P. davisii*, distinct from both, but fully heterostylous as in *P. davisii*, and with similar pollen and the same flavonoids.

CULTIVATION Discovered by Gauba in 1936 near Khorrambad together with *Dionysia gaubeana*. Introduced by Trott from Pol-e-Doktar in 1947. Now very rare in cultivation, although still grown at Gothenburg. An insignificant species, which however posses a graceful charm. Magnificent plants grown under this name are forms of *P.* × *kewensis*.

Primula davisii W.W. Smith. Not. Roy. Bot. Gdn. Edinb. 22: 45 (1955)

DESCRIPTION Much *smaller* than its relatives (to 6 cm), densely glandular, but *lacking* hairs or *meal*; stem with *one* whorl of (1)–3 heterostylous flowers. Pin pollen with only one pore, thrum pollen with two, pollen spheroidal, very small, 12 µm in diameter in pins, 18 µm in thrums. 2n = 18.

DISTRIBUTION Endemic to the Hakkari and Mardin provinces of extreme south-east Turkey at Cilo Da, (Diz Derezi, Zab gorge), and Cudi Da, 1200–2000 m. 'More or less shady and moist crevices of nearly vertical limestone (dolomitic) rocks'.

In two of its known sites, *P. davisii* is associated with *Dionysia* species in their only Turkish sites, namely *D. bornmuelleri* (Pax) Melchior at Cudi Da, and *D. teucrioides* Davis and Wendelbo at Cilo Da.

CULTIVATION First discovered and introduced in 1954 by Peter Davis and Oleg Polunin, but lost before 1966. Reintroduced by Ron Cain, Jo Darrah and John Watson in 1966 from the Zab Gorge. Exhibited at AGS Shows in 1968 and 1969, and still in cultivation in 1976. No seed was set by this entirely pin-eyed collection, so this species may be self-sterile. Seed recollected by Jim Archibald in 1989 germinated at the Royal Botanic Garden, Edinburgh, but the seedlings were lost. Apparently always rare and difficult, and now extinct in cultivation.

Primula edelbergii O.Schwarz. Feddes Rep. 64: 85–87 (1961)

P. floribunda Wall. subsp. *occidentalis* Wendelbo. Biol. Skr. Dan. Vid. Selsk. 10: 66 (1958)

DESCRIPTION Similar to the more familiar *P. floribunda,* but *sticky* with short (0.2 mm) glandular hairs; leaves *not* mealy, *bright* olive-green, strongly rugose, the blade *oval* and abruptly *cuneate* into the stalk at the base, finely toothed; stems with 1–3 whorls each of about 7 flowers; flower stalks 13–30 mm; *calyx* 7–9 mm with narrow, sharp sepal-lobes. *Flowers* heterostylous, golden, about 13 mm in diameter, the tube more than 1.5× the calyx. Pollen 3-colporoidate in pins, but 1–colporate and larger in thrums. 2n = 18. (Plate 6.)

DISTRIBUTION Known from two sites in eastern Afghanistan, where it was first discovered in 1948; near Kabul (Tang-e-Gharu, or Tankikana gorge); and Vama, Nuristan, 600–2100 m.

A little-known species of rather mysterious affinity, superficially resembling *P. floribunda* and *P. afghanica*, but with different pollen and flavonoids. Interfertile with *P. verticillata*. The texture, shape, scent, colour, and resinous stickiness of the leaves are remarkably reminiscent of *P. forrestii*.

CULTIVATION Introduced, probably by Mrs Priemer from near Kabul, in about 1958. Still in cultivation in a few specialist collections in 2001.

Primula afghanica Wendelbo, Biol. Skr. 10: 63 (1958)

DESCRIPTION Plant lacking meal, hairs or sticky glands. *Leaf* blades membranous, *orbicular*, 2–4 cm in diameter, heart-shaped at the base with large irregular teeth; leaf stalks *unwinged*, somewhat exceeding the blade. *Stems* slender, somewhat exceeding leaves, bearing a single whorl of 2–5 flowers on suberect stalks. *Bracts* linear, to 6 mm, channeled at the base, forming a weak involucre. *Calyx* tubular, to 6 mm, cut to three-quarters. *Corolla* yellow, heterostylous, flat-faced, 11–20 mm in diameter, the tube 1–5–2.5× the calyx. Pollen 3-colporoidate.

DISTRIBUTION Afghanistan, Nuristan, Nishei, and at Vama where it grows with *P. edelbergii*, but at higher altitudes. Wet north-facing localities beneath limestone overhangs, 1400–2700 m.

Only known from three herbarium specimens, all collected by Edelberg in 1948. The single plant from Nishei has larger flowers and longer flower-stalks, but seems to be of the same species.

P. afghanica was placed by Wendelbo (1961) in its own section Troglydyta. It has several individual characteristics not typical of the Sphondylia, notably the very thin-textured leaves and narrow bracts; Wendelbo also claims that it lacks a rhizome and has basal bud scales (suggesting that it is deciduous), but these features are not clear on the specimens, and it is in full growth and flower in April.

P. afghanica has conduplicate vernation, and the inflorescence strongly resembles that of *P. edelbergii*, although the leaf-shape is very different. I do not hesitate in placing it in the Sphondylia, although it might be considered the most derived member of the group.

Primula floribunda Wallich. Tentamen florae napalensis illustratae: 43 (1826)

Androsace obovata Wall. ex Duby in DC, Prodr. 8: 35 (1844)

DESCRIPTION Delicate to subrobust, to 25 cm, with *multicellular* hairs of about 1 mm throughout, lacking meal, *not* sticky. *Leaves* to 10 × 4 cm, dull olive-green, weakly rugose, spoon-shaped, rounded at the end, coarsely and irregularly toothed, gradually narrowing to a slender almost unwinged stalk about half the length of the leaf. *Stems* rather weak with (1)–6 whorls of 3–6 flowers; lowest *bracts* to 25 × 12 mm, similar to the leaves, the upper smaller. *Flower-stalks* to 15 mm, elongating further in fruit. Calyx 5–6 mm, cut to half-way into ovate rather blunt sepal-lobes which reflex later. Corolla golden to cream (var. *isabellina* Hort.), to 14 mm in diameter, heterostyle at altitudes below 1500 m, but homostyle above 2000 m, tube 10–13 mm, petal-lobes 5–6 mm, entire to shallowly notched. Pollen 3-colporoidate, about 14 μm in diameter in pins, about 18 μm in thrums. Heterostyles said to be self-sterile. 2n = 18. (Plate 1.)

DISTRIBUTION North-west Himalaya, from the Khyber Pass (71° E, 34° N) to extreme south-west Nepal (81° E, 28° N) in a linear band, 500–2700 m. Humid shady places by rivers and waterfalls.

As noted by Wendelbo (1961), *P. floribunda* forms a very interesting morphological and geographical link between the south-western mealy Sphondylia and the Sinohimalayan section Proliferae, although the multicellular hairs are typical of neither. The pollen type, flavonoids, chromosome number and crossability all suggest that it is more closely related to *P. verticillata* than superficially seems to be the case. If the Sphondylia migrated westwards from a Sinohimalyan origin close to the Proliferae, *P. floribunda* might today represent that link.

In the west of its range. *P. floribunda* is not far disjunct from *P. edelbergii* and *P. afghanica*, but today these species seem to be only distantly related to it.

P. floribunda is of special interest in having heterostyle and homostyle races which tend to be altitudinally separated.

CULTIVATION *P. floribunda* has been widespread in cultivation for at least 100 years, and is vigorous when protected from excess damp and cold, under glass in the UK, but grown outside in California. Several variants have been noted including var. *isabellina* Hort. (flowers cream) and var. *grandiflora* Pax (large flowers). Recently reintroduced by Blaise and Dupey 451 (1985). For *P.* × *kewensis*, see under *P. verticillata*.

Subgenus **Auriculastrum** Schott,

Sippen Osterr. Primeln: 11(1851).

Type species *P. auricula* L.

Section **Auricula** Duby, Bot.Gall. 1: 384 (1828).

(Section Auriculastrum Wendelbo (1961) nom.superfl.)

(Section Arthritica Duby (1844) p.p.)

DESCRIPTION *Leaves* leathery, smooth, with *involute* vernation, farinose or glandular. *Stems* bear rudimentary bracts and a single umbel of pink, red or purple (less commonly yellow or white) exannulate (annulate in *P. palinuri*) heterostylous flowers. Pollen prolate, 3-colporoidate. *Capsules* globose, persistent, opening by 5 valves. x = 31, 33, with some aneuploids and tetraploids. Self-incompatible. Flowering March–July (January to May in cultivation).

DISTRIBUTION Confined to the mountains of central and southern Europe, including the Pyrenees (3 species), Carpathians (4 species), Apennines (3 species), Cordillera Cantabrica (1 species), Velebit mountains (1 species) and Alps (20 species), showing a high degree of local endemism. Only 4 of the 22 species in the section are at all widespread.

Most closely allied to the other sections with involute vernation, the Cuneifolia (x = 11), Amethystina (x = 11) and the Parryi (x = 22). Forerunners of Auricula may have migrated into the alpine regions of Europe from the west across Atlantic bridges during Glacial Periods, thus colonizing from the Asiatic heartland of primula in a clockwise direction. Alternatively, they may have colonized in an anti-clockwise direction, with the Amethystina serving witness to their passage through the Sinohimalaya. Once in the Alps, repeated emigration and reimmigration into high regions after later glacial episodes doubtless encouraged the high level of localized species diversification we find today. Remarkably, two distinctive new species *P. albenensis* and *P. recubariensis* have been described from well-frequented regions of Italy during the late 1990s, and the possibility of yet another, third, new local endemic (P. 'grignensis') has been discussed (p.89). Recent opinion (Kress (1981)) suggests that *P. apennina* is best treated as a subspecies of *P. pedemontana*.

Rock detritus, cliffs, alpine meadows. (*P. palinuri* on sea-cliffs). While this edition was in proof, I became aware of the as-yet unpublished work of Zhang & Kadereit (MS, 2002). This study used DNA techniques (ITS sequence, and AFLPs) to investigate relationships among 52 accessions of *Primula* section Auricula. Although most of the known taxa were examined in this study, many of the critical groups were only represented by a sigle sample, so it was not possible to be sure that minor differences observed in the DNA between samples were representative of the taxon as a whole. Consequently, I have for the present ignored many of Zhang and Kadereit's findings.

However, two major findings are beyond doubt. The DNA showed to major phylogenetic groupings (clades) within the section, which Zhang and Kadereit characterise as subsetions Euauricula Pax (1889) (including *P. auricula*, *P. balbisii*, *P. palinuri*, *P. latifolia*, *P. marginata*, *P. carniolica*, *P. albenensis*, *P. allionii*, *P. hirsuta*, *P. recubariensis*, *P. daonensis*, *P. pedemontana* and *P. villosa*); and subsection Cuanopsis (Schott) Pax (1889), comprising the remaining species.

The second incontrovertible finding is that *P. auricula* as conceived here is composed of two clades, *P. auricula* from Germany, the Tatra and the northern Alps, and *P. balbisii* Lehm. (1817) from the southern Alps, Balkans, Hungary and south-west Carpathians. These taxa are separated by *P. auricula,* having glabrous, entire leaf margins and pale yellow flowers, while *P. balbisii* is said to have dentate leaves with a glandular-hairy margin and flowers of a deeper yellow.

However, it is certainly the case that many individuals of *P. balbisii* have entire leaves, while flower colour is very variable in both taxa. Thus it may be that only the hairiness of the leaf margin will separate these taxa, which may be more distinct in the DNA and in distribution than they are morpholocially.

CULTIVATION Most species are fully hardy in UK conditions, and will grow outside in cool, well-drained situations, although many are very slow, and flower poorly, particularly after the first flowering. Some cliff species (notably *P. allionii* and *P. tyrolensis*) are intolerant of winter wet, and must be grown under glass. The high alpine turf species *P. glutinosa* and *P. minima* are difficult to flower successfully.

Remarkably few species are regularly cultivated (about 7). The poor flowering, and superficial similarity of many of the 22 species has not encouraged growers, although cultivation of the scarcer species is straightforward in a climate with cool summers and cold winters and has been lately espoused by Scottish growers Henry and Margaret Taylor and Mike and Polly Stone, and by European growers Dieter Schimmel and Fritz Kummert.

However, *P. marginata, P. auricula,* and *P. hirsuta* are excellent garden plants, while *P. allionii* is one of the great alpine house subjects. Some species, notably *P. marginata* and *P. latifolia* are slow to germinate from seed, often taking three or four years.

HYBRIDIZATION In the mountains, species often occur singly, and it is uncommon to find more than two species coexisting. When species occur together, hybridization frequently occurs, and 24 different hybrids have been recorded between 17 of the species. It is unlikely that any barriers to primary hybridization occur within the section, so such apparently unlikely crosses as *P. auricula* × *allionii* have been raised in cultivation.

Hybrids between *P. auricula* and *P. hirsuta* have been bred since the 16th century, and are known correctly as *P.* × *pubescens* Jacq. Horticulturally, those clones lacking farina (from the *P. auricula* parent) are known as 'alpine auriculas', and those with farina ('paste'), particularly on the flowers and stems, are termed 'show auriculas'.

Many hybrids are at least partially fertile, and very many hybrid clones are known in cultivation, involving various combinations of at least 12 of the species (see Smith *et al.*, p.178). *P. auricula, P. hirsuta* and *P. marginata* have been the most successful parents, but hybrids of for instance *P. minima* and *P. allionii* prove much more free-flowering and/or suitable for outdoor cultivation than their parents. In general, the section Auricula hybrids are more vigorous and more suitable as garden plants than their parents. *P. marginata* is perhaps the only exception to this rule.

LITERATURE. Smith, Burrows and Lowe (1984).

KEY TO SPECIES

1. Flowers yellow 2
1. Flowers pink or blue, rarely white 3

2. Leaves without meal; bracts large, leaf-like, to 25 mm; flowers funnel-shaped .... *P. palinuri*
2. Leaves usually mealy, at least at edge; bracts small; flowers with a spreading limb .... *P. auricula*

3. Leaves smooth, not hairy, rough or sticky 4
3. Leaves downy, at least on margin, rough, or glandular-sticky 12

4. Leaf edge mealy, often with few large teeth. Flowers often bluish 5
4. Leaf edge not mealy, usually entire. Flowers usually pink or purple 6

5. Plant aromatic; leaves not more than 2× as long as wide .... *P. albenensis*
5. Plant scentless; leaves more than 3× as long as wide .... *P. marginata*

6. Plant dwarf, not exceeding 1 cm, leaves deeply dissected with apical teeth .... *P. minima*
6. Stems exceeding 2 cm; leaves entire 7

7. Stems exceeding 10 cm; leaves not pointed, lacking pale edge 8
7. Stems less than 12 cm; leaves often pointed, with a pale edge 9

8. Corolla with mealy ring in throat .... *P. carniolica*
8. Corolla throat lacking mealy ring .... *P. deorum*

9. Calyx divided to two-thirds; corolla-tube scarcely exceeding calyx .... *P. glaucescens*
9. Calyx divided to less than half; corolla tube usually 2× calyx 10

10. Leaves not pointed, finely pitted on top surface .... *P. spectabilis*
10. Leaves usually pointed, smooth 11

11. Calyx-lobes rounded; corolla-lobe divisions rounded .... *P. clusiana*
11. Calyx-lobes obtuse but not rounded; corolla-lobe divisions narrow, strap-shaped .... *P. wulfeniana*

12. Stems exceeding 12 cm; flowers borne on one side, lacking a white eye .... *P. latifolia*
12. Stems less than 12 cm; flowers usually borne round the stem, often with a white eye 13

13. Cushion forming; flowers usually borne singly .... *P. allionii*
13. Individual rosettes obvious; flowers usually with two or more on a stem 14

14. Leaves more than 4× as long as wide, suberect 15
14. Leaves less than 4× as long as wide, prostrate to erect 16

15. Leaves sticky throughout; flowers blue to violet .... *P. glutinosa*
15. Leaves slightly sticky at edge only; flowers pink .... *P. integrifolia*

16. Flower-stems to 2 cm, flowers pink, not more than two per stem .... *P. tyrolensis*
16. If flowers stems less than 2 cm, then flowers violet, or more than two per stem 17

17. Flowers usually 1–2 per stem, borne on one side .... *P. kitaibeliana*
17. Flowers usually more than 2 per stem, borne around the stem 18

18. Stem not exceeding leaves at flowering; leaf glands usually not reddish 19
18. Stem exceeding leaves at flowering; leaf glands usually reddish 20

19. Flowers violet; plant aromatic .... *P. recubariensis*
19. Flowers pink; plant not aromatic .... *P. hirsuta*

20. Leaves glabrous and shiny on top, with red glands at edge only .... *P. pedemontana*
20. Leaves red-glandular throughout 21

21. Leaf hairs to 0.4 mm with a round coloured terminal gland (use a lens!) .... *P. daonensis*
21. Leaf hairs usually exceeding 0.5 mm with an oval coloured terminal gland .... *P. villosa*

Subsection **Auricula**

Plants mealy, flowers yellow.

Primula auricula L. Sp. Pl.: 143 (1753) non Vill. 'BEARS-EAR'

P. lutea Vill. (1787)
P. alpina Salisb. (1796)
P. crenata Fuss. (1886)
P. balbisii Lehm. (1817)
P. ciliata Moretti (?1815)
P. nivalis Don ex Reichenb. (1830) non Pallas
P. bellunensis Venzo (1890)
P. similis Stein (1886)

DESCRIPTION *Leaves* circular to bluntly spear-shaped, 1.5–12 × 1–6 mm, spreading, rounded to bluntly pointed, entire to sharply toothed, green to white-mealy with a thick green to white margin which can be smooth, glandular, or glandular-ciliate. *Stems* to 16 cm, stiff, green to white, bearing 2–30 flowers. *Flower-stalks* 2–20 mm, stiff to drooping. *Calyx* 3–7.5 mm, bell-shaped, cut to about half-way into bluntly triangular lobes. *Corolla* pale lemon to deep golden yellow, usually with a mealy white eye, funnel-shaped to flat-faced, 15–25 mm in diameter, corolla-tube 7–13 mm, about 3× the calyx, rather broad, petal lobes usually overlapping, notched. 2n = 62, 63, 64, 65, 66. Pins fully self-sterile; thrums 3 per cent self-fertile. (Plate 2.)

DISTRIBUTION Northern Alps from the Dauphine eastwards to Vienna, south-east Alps from Lake Como eastwards to Slovenia, the Tatra and Fatra of Poland and Czechoslovakia, and the Apennines from La Spezia southwards almost to Naples. Absent from much of the western Alps, Switzerland, the Tyrol and the eastern Alps, but with a few isolated stations in this central band. Also away from the high mountains in several isolated localities where it is almost certainly a late-glacial relict: Jura, Black Forest (e.g. Hollental gorge at only 600 m), north of Munich, and near the Danube Iron Gates on the Yugoslav/Romanian border.

Usually confined to rock crevices on limestone, typically on large boulders and pillars facing N and E, but also in boulder scree, rather local, 250–2900 m, flowering May–July depending on altitude.

VARIATION Not surprisingly for such a widespread and disjunct species, *P. auricula* is exceptionally variable. A number of local races have been given varietal or subspecific status, and are grown under these names in the garden, but variation is so complex in the field, and individual populations are so variable, that these names have more horticultural than botanical value.

- Subsp. *auricula* has smooth or shortly glandular leaf margins, and lemon-coloured flowers.
- Var. *albocincta* Widmer has grey-green leaves with a white margin, and is common in the Dolomites (the only type found there).
- Var. *monacensis* Widmer refers to the long-leaved plants of the Munich area.
- Var. *widmerae* Pax has narrow, thin leaves (Black Forest).
- Var. *serratifolia* (Roch.) Ludi with sharply toothed leaves comes from the Danube Gates.
- Subsp. *ciliata* (Moretti) Ludi, (syn. subsp. *balbisii*) is without farina and has long marginal cilia on rounded leaves with golden flowers, and is typical of the south-eastern regions, although in fact many types and intermediates can be found there. However, Zhang & Kadereit (2002, unpublished) suggest that *P. balbisii* Lehm. is recognised a specific rank (p. 77).

CULTIVATION *P. auricula* has been a popular garden plant for at least five centuries, and indeed was one of the first decorative plants to be cultivated in Europe. Although often supplanted by its many *P.* × *pubescens* hybrids, very few of which have yellow flowers, the 'bears-ear' can still be found in various forms as popular bedding or edging plants. It is encountered especially in old towns and villages, where it persists and flowers very well, often in 'ordinary garden soil'. Some of the smaller and more decorative forms (e.g. 'Blairside Yellow') are popular pot plants with alpine gardeners, but it can be surprisingly difficult to obtain true *P. auricula* through the trade.

HYBRIDIZATION As well as the manifold hybrids with *P. hirsuta* (*P.* × *pubescens*), hybrids in the wild have also been reported with *P. carniolica* (*P.* × *venusta* Host.), *P. daonensis* (*P.* × *discolor* Leyb.), *P. clusiana* (*P.* × *lempergii* F. Buxb.), *P. integrifolia* (*P.* × *escheri* Brugg) and *P. tyrolensis* (*P.* × *obovata* Huter). Of these, only *P.* × *venusta* is at all important in cultivation.

In cultivation, *P. auricula* has also been successfully hybridized with *P. marginata* (e.g. *P.* 'Rhenaniana'), *P. kitaibeliana, P. pedemontana* (*P.* × *sendtneri*), *P. latifolia, P. villosa* and *P. allionii* (*P.* × *loiseleurii*). The latter, which was originally raised by Brian Burrow includes the clone 'Lismore Yellow' (**PC** 1982) which promises to introduce yellow colour breaks into the range of *P. allionii* hybrids. Later developments by Peter Lister involved white forms of *P. allionii* crossed with *P. auricula* 'Blairside Yellow' and are excellent dwarf whites ('Aire Mist' and 'Aire Waves' both **PC** 1999). *P. auricula* has hybridized with 12 of the 22 other species in the section, more than any other species.

Primula palinuri Petagna, Inst. Bot. 2: 332 (1787)

DESCRIPTION Superficially very like some of the larger forms of *P. auricula*, but even *larger*, with *leaves* to 20 × 7 cm, and stems to 25 cm. The leaves are always *without* meal, are sometimes shortly glandular-hairy, and are irregularly *toothed*. Distinctively, the bracts are relatively large, to 25 × 10 mm and leaf-like, the flowers are *funnel*-shaped, *annulate*, and *nod* one-sidedly. Flowering stems and calyces are white-mealy. 2n = 66. (Plate 2.)

DISTRIBUTION Confined to maritime cliffs in south-west Italy (Calabria), around the Gulf of Poliocastro, from Cape Palinuro to Scalea. Grows only high up on sea-cliffs on ledges and crevices in sand or sandy tufa. A rare plant in the wild, which had the distinction of being one of two European plants in the first IUCN Red Data Book. It is still the only primula in the world Red Data list.

Although *P. palinuri* occurs only 200 km south of the southernmost mountain localities of its nearest relative, *P. auricula*, it is the only maritime primula, the only primula occurring in a Mediterranean climate anywhere, and it shares with only *P. fedtschenkoi, P. cusickiana* and *P. specuicola* a summer-dormant (aestivating) habit in the wild.

P. palinuri probably developed from *P. auricula* during a cool wet episode, and later evolved to resist the hot dry summers currently experienced in its southern locality.

CULTIVATION *P. palinuri* is unexpectedly hardy in colder, wetter climates, growing well without protection in any well-drained site, where it is usually summer green. However, it became dormant during the hot summer of 1989 in northern England. In cultivation it flowers rather unreliably (in May) in the open, although better after a hot summer; under glass it flowers reliably, and over a long period. It rarely sets seed in cultivation, but is easily propagated by division. It remains rather scarce in cultivation, perhaps because the flowers are somewhat insignificant, and the foliage is rather 'cabbagy'.

Subsection **Arthritica** Schott., Sippen Osterr. Primeln 11: (1851)

Leaves leathery, with a thick nearly entire margin, often pointed, without meal, hairless except sometimes on the margin, or with scattered short glandular hairs. Flowers pink, rose or red, usually flowering in May in the wild.

Primula clusiana Tausch., Flora (Regensb.) 4: 364 (1821)

P. spectabilis Mertens and Koch (1826) non Tratt. (1814) and var. *ciliata* Koch
P. integrifolia L. non L. (1753)
P. churchillii Gusmus (1890)

DESCRIPTION Forms hemispherical clumps of tight rosettes of many dark green, ovate to spear-shaped shiny *leaves*, prostrate below, erect above, up to 6 × 2.5 mm, rounded to pointed, fringed with short colourless glandular hairs, otherwise hairless. *Stem* to 8 cm in flower, covered in glandular hairs, green, with from 1–4 flowers borne on stiff erect *stalks* up to 12 mm; *bracts* usually longer than the flower-stalks, up to 18 mm, often purplish. *Calyx* tubular egg-shaped, swollen in the middle, 8–17 mm, often reddish, cut from a third to a half into ovate, subrounded, erect sepal lobes. *Corolla* bright rose, fading bluer, with a white eye, widely funnel-shaped, 1.5–4 cm in diameter; corolla-tube about 2× the calyx; petal-lobes broad, dissected to half-way into two broadly divergent blunt segments. 2n = ca. 198. (Plate 3.)

DISTRIBUTION North-eastern Alps of Austria, west to 13° E, from the German/Austrian frontier in the Berchtesgarden salient eastwards mostly to the north of Liezen, Leoben and Murzzuschlag to the Wiener Schneeberg, just west of Vienna. Its northern limit is confined by the limit of alpine high ground. Invariably on limestone, usually from 1800–2500 m, above the tree-line, although occasionally dropping to 600 m on cliffs.

Grows in a variety of open habitats, from turf, where it can form dense colonies, to stabilized scree and crevices in cliffs.

Very closely related to the three following species, which, however, all occur in quite distinct geographical regions. *P. clusiana* and *P. wulfeniana* are distinguished from the others by the egg-shaped calyx with blunt broad sepal-lobes (except subsp. *baumgarteniana*); *P. clusiana* can also be safely differentiated from *P. glaucescens* and *P. spectabilis* by the fringe of glandular hairs to the leaves (use a lens to be sure). It tends to be a more robust plant with longer stems and more flowers per stem than *P. wulfeniana*.

VARIATION *P. clusiana* is most commonly grown as the large-flowered, vigorous and free-flowering clone 'Murray-Lyon', named after the Late Major-General D. Murray-Lyon, who found it in his collection and distributed it. Although he was never sure of its origin, the late David Livingstone thought he may have given it to Murray-Lyon. It has been suggested by Henry Taylor that 'Murray-Lyon' may in fact be a form of *P.* × *intermedia* Porta (*P. clusiana* × *minima*), a cross formerly grown by Farrer and Ingwersen, and rated highly by them. Certainly, 'Murray-Lyon' seems to be sterile, but it otherwise shows very little influence of the other putative parent.

CULTIVATION These four slow-growing small species all require careful culture in a rich scree mix, either in pots, troughs or raised beds in full light, but kept as cool and humid as possible in summer. They can grow well inserted into holes in lumps of tufa. They appreciate regular foliar feeding, and like many primulas seem to flower best as young plants from seed. Some clones and strains are noticeably more free-flowering than others. They seem particularly vigorous and free-flowering in the north of Scotland.

HYBRIDIZATION No hybrids are otherwise reported today in cultivation, but hybridization with *P. minima* is known in the wild, and hybridization with *P. auricula* has also been rather doubtfully claimed.

Primula glaucescens Moretti non Reichb., Gior. Fis. (Brugnat.) ser.2, 5: 249 (1822)

P. calycina Duby (1828)
P. laevigata Duby ex Reichb. (1831)
P. longobarda Porta (1882)

DESCRIPTION Very similar to *P. clusiana*, but with the leaf margin *hairless*, and finely crenulate-*toothed* (examine with a lens), and with the leaves always sharply pointed. The calyx is more cylindrical, and is cut to two-thirds into narrow sharp sepal-lobes. Flowers more pinky-lilac, the corolla-tube only just exceeding the calyx. 2n = 66. (Plate 2.)

DISTRIBUTION Limited to a small area of northern Italy north of Bergamo, from Lake Como in the west to the Valli Giudicarie, just west of Lake Garda in the east, only on the southern slopes of the range. Invariably on limestone in rather shady situations often under trees, or on shady cliffs and banks, growing in crevices, scree or soil, 450–2400 m.

VARIATION Two subspecies are sometimes recognized:

- Subsp. *glaucescens* (subsp. *calycina* (Duby) Pax) is relatively robust, with the calyx to 20 mm and the flower to 30 mm diameter; throughout the range.
- Subsp. *longobarda* (Porta) Widmer (*P. longobarda* Porta in Huter, Cat. Pl. Exsicc. (1882)) is more delicate, calyx to 10 mm, corolla diameter to 20 mm; east of the Oglio valley.

Unusual in cultivation, but often vigorous, although except for occasional clones shy flowering.

HYBRIDIZATION Where it overlaps with *P. spectabilis*, in a tiny area near Bagolino at the south end of the western flank of the Valli Giudicaire, hybrids (*P.* × *carueli* Porta) are found. A hybrid with *P. minima* has been raised in cultivation.

Primula spectabilis Tratt., Ausgem. Taf. Arch. Gewachsk. 4: 34 (1814) non Mertens and Koch (1826) nec Josch. (1853)

P. glaucescens Reichb. (1830) non Moretti. p.p.
P. calycina Sprengel (1823) non Duby.
P. carniolica Pollini (1822) non Jacq.
P. integrifolia Jacq. (1778) non L.
P. integrifolia Tausch (1821) non L.
P. polliniana Moretti (1831)
P. baldensis Goiran ex Parl. (1889)
P. parletorii Porta (1889)
P. weldeniana Reichb. (1911)

DESCRIPTION Very similar to *P. clusiana*, and *P. glaucescens*, but larger, with *leaves* to 10 cm, stems to 12 cm, and corolla to 4 cm diameter; leaves usually blunt, wavy, untidy and nearly prostrate apart from the young leaves which hug the stem. *Calyx* cylindrical, as in *P. glaucescens*, but cut to only one-third. *Corolla* pink to rose, occasionally white, the tube 1–3× the calyx. Diagnostically, the upper leaf surface is microscopically pitted, and bears minute glandular hairs; both characters need a lens for certain examination. This species has a distinctive facies, the shape of the looser rosette differing from that of the other species. 2n = 66.

DISTRIBUTION In a small area of northern Italy, immediately to the east of, and in part running parallel with the distribution of, *P. glaucescens*. From the mountains surrounding Lake Garda, Cima Tombea and Monte Baldo, west to Valli Guidicarie, north to the Brenta Dolomites, and south and west of the Val Sugano from Trento to Bassano and Monte Grappa.

Confined to limestone, where it is often locally abundant and even dominant in grassland and on rocky ridges from 500–2500 m, staining whole hillsides pink in May.

Generally disappointing in cultivation, flowering uncertainly and weakly, a pale reflection of its glory in the wild. However, a vigorous form gained a **PC** in 1989.

VARIATION A very variable species in the wild, varying markedly in size, vigour, leaf-shape, flower colour, and the presence of an 'eye' to the flower. This variation shows no geographical trends, but may arise from past episodes of hybridization in some localities.

HYBRIDIZATION Hybridizes with *P. glaucescens* in the wild where the two species meet to the north of Brescia. Hybrids are very variable and often difficult to tell from the two similar and related parents. In the same area (west slopes of Valli Guidicaire) and further north to Brenta hybrids with *P. minima* (*P.* × *facchinii* Schott) are also frequently encountered, especially at Alpe Magiassone. In cultivation single hybrid individuals crossed with *P. minima* var. *alba*, and with *P. pedemontana* have been raised by Henry and Margaret Taylor.

Primula wulfeniana Schott, Wilde Blendl. Osterr. Primeln 17 (1852)

P. spectabilis Josch. non Tratt. (1853) p.p.
P. glaucescens Reichb. (1830) non Moretti p.p.
P. carniolica Wulfen (1858) non Jacq. (1778)
P. baumgarteniana Degen and Moesz (1908)

DESCRIPTION Differs from *P. clusiana*, *P. glaucescens* and *P. spectabilis* by being the smallest member of the group, with leaves to 4 cm, and stems to 7 cm. Similar to *P. clusiana* in having *leaves* hairless apart from marginal glands, an egg-shaped *calyx* with blunt sepal lobes, and the *corolla*-tube twice the length of the calyx, but differs in the calyx being cut to one third only into blunt but not rounded sepal-lobes, and by the rather strap-shaped petal-lobes being narrowly notched, and a pinky-violet, a colour with more blue in it and darker in hue than any of the other species in this group. 2n = 66. (Plate 2).

DISTRIBUTION There are four disjunct areas of distribution, three in the extreme south-east Alps around the borders of Italy, Yugoslavia and Austria, and one in central Transylvania (subsp. *baumgarteniana*). The main alpine localities are throughout the length of the Karawanken, encompassing the Julian and Kamnicka Alps in Yugoslavia. There are also isolated localities to the west of this area near Cimolais, just north-east of Belluno, and to the north in the Gailtal Alps on the Italian/Austrian frontier.

Limestone grassland, rocks and scree, mostly 1800–2100 m, but occasionally much lower.

Grows well in cultivation, and successful in tufa, but rarely flowers for more than one season unless a good form is hit upon.

VARIATION

- Subsp. *baumgarteniana* (Degen and Moesz) A.J. Richards **stat. et comb. nov.** (*P. baumgarteniana* Degen and Moesz, Mag. Bot. Lap. 7: 92 (1908)). Differs in possessing the deeply dissected calyx with narrow sepal lobes and glabrous leaf margins of *P. glaucescens*, but superficially much more resembling the dwarf *P. wulfeniana*. Restricted to the Piatra Craiului of central Transylvania (Koenigstein). Halda (1992) has seen this species in the wild and considers this to be a distinct species. The isolated locality would support this view, but plants I currently (2001) grow from Halda's seed are close to *P. wulfeniana*.

HYBRIDIZATION No hybrids of *P. wulfeniana* have been made in cultivation, but, unexpectedly as the habitats are very different, hybrids with *P. tyrolensis* (*P.* × *venzoides* Huter) have occasionally been reported where the two species overlap west of Cimolais. This hybrid has been in cultivation where it is reported to be shy flowering. Hybrids with *P. minima* (*P.* × *vochinensis* Gusmus) are quite common in the wild where the two species overlap in the western part of the range of *P. wulfeniana*, and at least one clone is available in the trade. In my experience it is persistent, but very shy flowering.

Subsection **Brevibracteata** Widmer, Europ. Art. Primul. 138 (1891)

Relatively tall plants with fleshy but scarcely leathery deciduous leaves, covered with colourless glands, mealy, at least on the blue, pink or purple corolla. Bracts very short, to 4 mm, ovate, usually membranous.

Primula latifolia Lapeyr., Hist. Abr. Pyr. 97 (1813)

P. viscosa All. (1785) non Villars (1787)
P. glutinosa Lapeyr. (1813) non Wulfen (1778)
P. hirsuta Vill. (1787) non All. (1773)
P. alpina Lois. 1828 non Salisb. (1796)
P. graveolens Hegetsch. and Heer (1840)

DESCRIPTION *Stems* erect, woody, leaves dying back to narrow green resting buds in winter. *Leaves* rather erect, bluntly and broadly spear-shaped, to 18 × 5 cm, dull green, without meal but sticky-glandular, entire, wavy or coarsely toothed, gradually narrowing to a winged stalk about the length of the blade, fragrant. *Stem* to 20 cm, green, sticky, slender but firm, with from 2 to 25 flowers carried one-sidedly on rather drooping stalks of different lengths, to 20 mm. *Calyx* short, to 6 mm, bell-shaped, green, sticky, cut to half way into triangular sepal-lobes. *Corolla* violet to reddish-purple, occasionally white, most usually an intense violet-purple, sometimes slightly farinose in the throat, narrowly funnel-shaped, up to 20 mm in diameter, the long cylindrical tube up to 14 mm long and 4× the length of the calyx; petal-lobes oblong, not overlapping, narrowly notched to one-third. 2n = 64, 65, 66, 67. (Photo: Bull. AGS 67: 329.) (Plate 2.)

DISTRIBUTION In four disjunct areas: the east Pyrenees from Andorra eastwards (f. *pyrenaica* Pax); the Maritime Alps, west of the Col di Tenda around Monte Argentera and Mont Clapier on the Italian/French frontier; the Dauphine, Vanoise, Graian, north Cottian and Pennine Alps, from the Col de Lautaret in France to the Col de la Croix in Switzerland and the Col di Turlo in Italy (f. *cynoglossifolia* Widmer); and the central Alps of northern Italy and east Switzerland, from the north of Lake Como northwards to Klosters, and eastwards almost as far as the Austrian frontier (f. *graveolens* (Hegetsch. & Heer) Pax).

Shaded and damp ledges and vertical crevices, invariably on mineral-rich volcanic rocks, 1900–2700 m, usually flowering in June.

Although variable, particularly between the disjunct areas, *P. latifolia* is unmistakable. Most confusion has resulted from the use of the name *P. viscosa*, which has also been applied to the very different *P. hirsuta*. Together with forms of *P. marginata* and *P. auricula* the largest of the Auricula primulas, and at best a plant with a stately dignified beauty. The narrow, dark purplish flowers borne one-sidedly on tall stems are distinctive.

VARIATION Pyrenean plants tend to have the most toothed leaves, while the eastern plants tend to be the smallest, but there is some overlap in form.

CULTIVATION Surprisingly infrequently met in cultivation, although available through the trade.

Grows well in the open garden, especially in a well-drained but water-retentive soil in full light, and an excellent and long-lived subject for pot culture. Flowers freely, but tends to become drawn in poor light. Propagates well by division while in growth, or by seed; it is worth selecting a really good colour form (a good white received a **PC** in 1978). One of the very few really distinct and worthwhile plants in the group.

HYBRIDIZATION Hybrids occur in the wild with *P. marginata* in the Maritimes (*P.* × *crucis* Bowles); with *P. integrifolia* in the Upper Engadine (*P.* × *muretiana* Muritzi, sometimes met with in cultivation, and its reciprocal cross *P.* × *thomasii*); and with the closely related group of species *P. hirsuta* (*P.* × *berninae* Kerner), *P. daonensis* (*P.* × *kolbiana* Widm.) and *P. pedemontana* (*P.* × *bowlesiana* Farrer).

Most of these hybrids have been repeated in cultivation, including a white *P.* × *berninae*. The latter hybrid has also provided the deservedly popular clone 'Windrush' in cultivation, which combines the best features of its beautiful parents. *P.* × *crucis* once provided Farrer with a beautiful clone 'Blue Bowl' which seems to have been lost, but other hybrids of this parentage have recently been raised. Although frequently occurring in company with other species, *P. latifolia* flowers later than most of the other species, which may account for the scarcity of hybrids, although in the Upper Engadine, *P.* × *berninae* and *P.* × *muretiana* can be common.

In cultivation, hybrids have also been produced with *P. auricula* and *P. villosa*, but these seem to be little known.

Primula marginata Curtis, Bot. Mag. 6, t. 191 (1792)

P. auricula Vill. (1787) non L. (1753) nec Hill (1765)
P. crenata Lam. (1793)
P. microcalyx Lehm. (1817)

DESCRIPTION *Plant* erect to sprawling, woody, leaves dying back to ovate farinose resting buds in winter. *Leaves* fleshy, firm, mealy, becoming grey-green, oblong with a blunt end, with regular jagged white-bordered teeth, to 10 × 4 cm, tapering to a broad short stalk. *Stems* to 12 cm, mealy, bearing up to 20 symmetrically arranged flowers on stiff erect stalks of up to 20 mm. *Calyx* bell-shaped, to 5 mm, cut to about a half into rounded or obtuse sepal-lobes, very mealy. *Corolla* from royal blue through lilac to pinkish, occasionally white, usually lilac-blue, with a mealy eye-ring, shallowly funnel-shaped, to 30 mm in diameter, the tube up to 4× the length of the calyx; petal-lobes broad, blunt, sometimes overlapping, cut to one-quarter into two lobes, the notch relatively broad. 2n = 62, 63, 124, 126, 127, 128. Pins about one per cent self-fertile. (Plate 2.)

DISTRIBUTION The Maritime and Cottian Alps of Provence, France and extreme north-west Italy, north to the Col de la Croix, north of Monte Viso, east of Queyras; the eastern and southern limits are set by high ground; the western limit runs from Grasse to Digne and up the Durance valley as far as Guillestre.

Local but often abundant, confined to shady, usually north-facing cliffs and steep slopes on limestone and dolomite, 500–3000 m, flowering March–June.

VARIATION There is no obvious morphological difference between diploids and tetraploids, but tetraploids are confined to the south-east area of the range, and diploids further to the west and north.

Variable in the wild and in cultivation, in flower colour, size, leaf-shape, degree of mealiness, etc., but not taxonomically subdivided, and always totally distinct with the bluish to pinkish flowers and white-edged jagged leaves. Some populations (e.g. Val de Cairos) seem to have uniformly poor forms with small lilac flowers; others (e.g. above La Brigue) are much finer.

Many clones are available in commerce (25 are listed in Smith *et al.* (1984)). Amongst the most distinct are 'Boothman's variety', very large and vigorous with wavy, lilac-blue flowers; 'Holden's variety' (= 'Holden Clough'), small and compact with narrow whitish leaves and dark blue flowers; 'Pritchard's variety' (**AM**), with purple flowers and large grey leaves; 'Barbara Clough' with pink flowers and yellowish meal; and 'Beatrice Lascario' (= 'Beatrice Lascaris'), a tiny form with good blue flowers. 'Caerulea' (**AM**) is another good blue form. There is also a poor whitish form.

CULTIVATION A deservedly popular and absolutely first-rate garden plant, in cultivation since 1777, and growing and flowering well in any well-drained position. Very suitable for growing in walls, and also makes an excellent subject for pot culture, for both flowers and foliage, the meal of the latter best protected from the weather under glass. Easily propagated by division and cuttings; occasional propagation is recommended to prevent the plant becoming too leggy and to restore vigour. Many clones are very old, but do not seem to suffer from virus.

HYBRIDIZATION In the wild, hybridizes with *P. latifolia*, and with *P. allionii*. The latter hybrid, *P.* × *meridionalis* A.J.Richards, has been found amongst *P. allionii* on only three occasions. The first discovery, by C.C. Mountfort in 1927, remains in cultivation ('Miniera', **AM** 1979), as do both the others. 'Violet Chambers' and 'Sunrise' are clones which have arisen in cultivation.

Hybrids in cultivation with the following species have also been raised: *P. auricula, P. pedemontana* and *P. villosa*. Of these, only the first, *P.* 'Rhenaniana', is at all important.

There are also several outstanding hybrid clones in cultivation, where the other parent is itself hybrid, or is uncertain. 'Linda Pope' (**FCC** 1967) with large rounded pale mauve-blue white-eyed flowers, and its equally outstanding seedling 'White Lady', formerly and confusingly known as 'White Linda Pope' (**FCC** 1996, photo: Bull. AGS 64: 412), 'Marven' (× *P.* × *venusta*) (**AM** 1965) with dark violet flowers, 'Hyacinthia' (**AM** 1945) with mid-blue flowers and entire leaves, are amongst the best known; all are at least 50 years old.

Primula albenensis Banfi & Ferlinghetti, Webbia 47: 203–212 (1993)

DESCRIPTION Whole plant strongly and sweetly *aromatic*, shortly pubescent and often strongly *mealy* throughout. Shoots short, erect, woody at base, semi-deciduous. Leaves *round* to oblong, to 7 × 3.5 cm, narrowing to a poorly marked petiole, rather thick and *leathery*, with a few large blunt *teeth* at the rounded apex, or entire, enlarging considerably in summer. Stems to 5 cm, single, often angled, mealy, bearing 2–12 (–18) symmetrically arranged flowers borne on apically mealy stalks 6–10 mm, just above the leaves. Calyx bell-shaped, 4–8 mm, teeth blunt or slightly toothed, *white-mealy*. Corolla pale violet to *lilac-blue* with a large white-mealy *eye*, to 22 mm in diameter, petal-lobes usually weakly bilobed, the lobes rounded; corolla tube about twice length of calyx (Plate 71).

DISTRIBUTION Restricted to the western, eastern and south-eastern areas of Monte Alben in the Bergamasque Prealps of Lombardy, Italy.

'More or less shady fissures, sometimes even under overhangs, of the main dolomite in the typical black soil derived from the decomposing of this rock, at between 1150–2000 m', accompanied by *Saxifraga vandelii* and *Ranunculus bilobus,* flowering late April to late May. Very local, but not endangered.

It is extraordinary that this very beautiful and distinct species escaped notice until the 1990s. However, its localities are rather remote and difficult of access, although not far from well-frequented footpaths. Although the authors compare this species with *P. hirsuta*, I have little doubt that its closest relative is *P. marginata,* or possibly *P. auricula*. The combination of rounded, bluntly toothed leathery leaves which can be so mealy in cultivation as to appear pure white, a velvety texture, and large bluish, white-eyed flowers is very distinctive, while the strong, sweetly resinous scent suggests that it may not have any very close living relatives. No hybrids have yet been reported with the other primula to occur nearby, *P. glaucescens*.

CULTIVATION Seed was introduced shortly after its discovery by Filippo Prosser, and introductions were also made by Margaret and Henry Taylor, Fritz Kummert and Vojtek Holubec. As yet uncommon, but has appeared in Alpine Garden Society Shows since 1999, although it appears to be somewhat shy to flower in cultivation. Seems not to require winter cover. As seen at the Taylors in 2002, very variable in leaf shape and colour.

Primula carniolica Jacq., Misc. Austr. 1: 160 (1778) non Pollini (1822)

P. integrifolia Scop. (1771) non L. (1753)
P. freyeri Hoppe (1844)
P. jellenkiana Freyer (1881)

DESCRIPTION Differs from *P. latifolia* and *P. marginata* by lacking a woody stem, by the entire, hooded, rather pale green leaves which lack meal or (usually) hairs, and the pink flowers (rarely white), which are held one-sidedly as in *P. latifolia*, but have a mealy ring on the throat as in *P. marginata*. A much taller plant than *P. albenensis*, and with non-mealy leaves. 2n = 62, c.68.

DISTRIBUTION Endemic to a small area of the Slovenian Alps (Yugoslavia) around the town of Idria (Tarnovski Gozd).

Shady sites on limestone in light woodland or open grassland, often on shaded cliffs, 900–1000 m.

An entirely distinct species which is however little known in the wild or in cultivation. The relatively large entire hooded leaves are distinctive, while the long flowering stem (to 25 cm), and the short blunt papery bracts typical of this group will immediately distinguish it from any other pink flowered species.

CULTIVATION Said to be moderately easy to grow in a rich moisture retentive soil, for instance a peat bed, in partial shade, or in pots shaded in summer. Propagated by division. Appreciates much water in summer. Offered by Susan Tindall in 2002.

HYBRIDIZATION Hybridizes with *P. auricula* (*P.* × *venusta*) in the wild, the only species with which it grows. This hybrid was once grown in many forms, but has not been seen in recent years, although its offspring *P.* 'Marven' is very popular. Hybrids with *P. allionii* (*P.* 'Ivanel') and *P. pedemontana* have been made in cultivation.

Subsection **Chamaecallis** Schott, Sippen Osterr. Primeln 13 (1851)

Very dwarf, lacking meal, evergreen; leaves broadest and toothed only at the tip; bracts leaf-like; flowers 1–(2), petal-lobes divided almost to the base, pink.

Primula minima L. Sp. Pl. 1: 143 (1753) non Mertens (1830)

DESCRIPTION Shortly creeping, with rosettes of about 2 cm diameter hugging the ground. *Leaves* v-shaped, with a broad jagged tip, to 2× 1 cm, dark shining green. Stem less than 1 cm, flowers lacking stalks at flowering. Bracts green, narrow, to 6 mm. *Calyx* narrowly bell-shaped, to 7 mm, cut to one-third into broad blunt sepal lobes. *Corolla* rose-purple to pale lilac-pink with a broad white eye, occasionally all white (var. *alba* Hort), the limb flat or nearly so, disproportionately large for the plant, to 3 cm in diameter; corolla tube white, about 2× the calyx; petal-lobes Y-shaped, broadest at the tip and dissected to three-quarters or more into two strap-shaped lobes. 2n = 66, 67, 68, 69, 70, 73. (Plate 3.)

DISTRIBUTION Very widespread and scattered. Eastern Alps from the Otztal (10°30'E) in the west eastwards to Vienna. Also in the Krknose (Czech Republic), the High Tatra, the Rodna Alps and north of Bucharest, Romania, Moldovia, the Balkan mountains in southern Yugoslavia (Shar in Montenegro), and Bulgaria (Stara Planina, Rila and Pirin) almost to the Greek border.

Always a high alpine, occurring above the tree-line, invariably on acidic soils, except in Bulgaria where it can occur on limestone. Dropping to 1200 m in Poland, but from 1700 to 3000 m elsewhere. Typically growing in very thin wet turf or bare soil, often in areas of late snow-lie, typically without associates, sharing this habitat only with *P. glutinosa* of the European species; more rarely in scree or cliffs.

P. minima is a very distinctive species without close relatives, which shows no important variation between its disjunct areas of distribution. However, it often forms considerable hybrid swarms with *P. glutinosa*, and locally with *P. wulfeniana* and *P. spectabilis*, in the wild, and great difficulty can be experienced in distinguishing between hybrids and natural variation.

CULTIVATION Although *P. minima* survives in a gritty compost in a trough, raised bed or pot so long as it is not allowed to dry out, it almost invariably flowers poorly. It has been suggested that it performs best when grown in root association with other species. Most of the successful clones are suspected of hybridity, and a number of popular hybrid clones, superficially very similar to *P. minima*, are much better garden plants, so that most growers prefer these to the true species. However, a white clone of the species currently in cultivation seems to be more free with its flowers.

HYBRIDIZATION Despite being very distinct morphologically, *P. minima* hybridizes in the wild with *P. daonensis* (*P.* × *pumila* Kerner), *P. hirsuta*

(*P.* × *forsteri* Stein), *P. villosa* (*P.* × *truncata* Lehm.), *P. clusiana, P. spectabilis, P. wulfeniana, P. tyrolensis* (*P.* × *juribella* Sunderm.) and *P. glutinosa* (*P.* × *floerkiana* Schrad.). *P. minima* occurs in different habitats from most of these, and crosses with *P. hirsuta, P. villosa, P. daonensis, P. clusiana* and *P. tyrolensis* are probably sterile, so that hybrids are invariable and are encountered only infrequently.

P. minima commonly hybridizes with *P. glutinosa* and hybrids are fully fertile, so that much back-crossing occurs. In some localities it can be difficult to find typical plants of either species. Such a hybrid swarm occurs on Timmelsjoch, Otztaler Alp, where in early July 1969 I found thousands of *P. minima* and a full range of *P.* × *floerkiana,* but only two *P. glutinosa*. On the same date in 1986, *P. glutinosa* coloured the hillside blue and a handful of *P.* × *floerkiana* were discovered. A close hands-and-knees search revealed that the abundant *P. minima* had failed to flower that year.

Hybrids approaching *P. minima* are called f. *biflora* (in cultivation) and specimens approaching *P. glutinosa* are termed f. *huteri*.

P. × *forsteri* is popular in cultivation, and has virtually supplanted *P. minima*. Plants resembling *P. minima* (sometimes virtually indistinguishable except by sterility) are termed f. *bilekii*, and intermediate plants are termed f. *steinii*. *P.* × *forsteri* f. *kellereri,* resembling *P. hirsuta*, is less commonly encountered. All these flower with a much greater freedom than *P. minima* in cultivation. The other wild hybrids of *P. minima* are rarely met with in cultivation, although a form of *P.* × *juribella* is grown.

Additional hybrids have been made in cultivation with *P. allionii* and *P. kitaibeliana*.

Subsection **Cyanopsis** Schott, Sippen Osterr. Primeln 14 (1851)

Plants lacking meal or hairs. Leaves evergreen, often sticky, pitted, narrow, erect, fleshy, entire or finely toothed; bracts leaf-like; flowers blue or purple, borne one-sidedly, several on a stem.

Primula glutinosa Wulfen in Jacq., Fl. Aust. 5: 41 (1778) non All. (1789) nec Lapeyr. (1813)

DESCRIPTION *Leaves* dull olive-green, to 6 × 0.8 cm, bluntly pointed, usually minutely toothed on the border, sticky from sunken dot-glands, leaf-stalk not apparent. *Stem* exceeding leaves, to 9 cm, stout, green, sticky. *Bracts* enveloping the calyces in a green or purple bell-shaped involucre, blunt. Flowers 1–8 per stem, stalkless at flowering. *Calyx* to 8 mm, narrowly bell-shaped, sticky, purple, cut to one-third into blunt sepal-lobes. *Corolla* blue-violet fading to violet (other colours are hybrids), the limb cup-shaped, to 18 mm in diameter; corolla-tube paler, slightly exceeding the calyx; corolla-lobes broad, narrowly notched to about half-way. 2n = 66, 67. (Plate 24.)

DISTRIBUTION Eastern Alps, from the Otztal (Austria), and just within Switzerland in the Lower Engadine (and two localities above Arosa to the west) eastwards to the Koralpe, west of Graz. Absent from most of the limestone Dolomites, but on the volcanic series from the Rolle Pass to Val Sugano in an isolated area. Otherwise within this area the northern and southern limits are set by suitable habitat on high ground. Also in a small disjunct area, 400 km to the south-east, in the Vranjica mountains in Bosnia.

Heavy acidic soils, sometimes turfy, but often open and very wet on volcanic or shaly series above the tree-line, especially on north-facing slopes with late snow-lie. Occurs abundantly in habitats otherwise species-poor and botanically uninteresting. 2000–3100 m.

P. glutinosa is, discounting widespread hybridization with *P. minima*, morphologically remarkably uniform throughout its distribution. It is an exceptionally beautiful plant which takes an isolated position amongst the European species, superficially more closely resembling species in sections Oreophlomis, Amethystina and Soldanelloides from the Himalaya.

CULTIVATION In cultivation, *P. glutinosa* is one of the more intractable species in the section, and although it can be grown for some years, it rarely flowers. It needs cool, wet, but not waterlogged conditions in acidic, peaty soils, and most success has been obtained in Scotland. It abhors lime. It can be propagated by careful division, but is very susceptible to aphid attack. *P. glutinosa*-like forms (f. *huteri*) of *P.* × *floerkiana* are easier in cultivation. Unfortunately, many tend to have flowers of a dull amethyst colour, miserable in contrast to the exciting deep blue of the parent.

No other hybrids are known.

Primula deorum Velen., Sitzungsber. Konigl. Bohm. Ges. Wiss. Prag., Math.-Naturwiss. Cl 1: 55 (1890)

P. bulgarica Georgieff (1937)

DESCRIPTION The largest member of the section, with erect to incurved, glabrous, smooth leaves to 20 × 2.5 cm., and stems to 25 cm which bear a loose, somewhat one-sided umbel of funnel-shaped flowers of a rich purple-red, to 18 mm in diameter. Resembles no other European species, but in habit and habitat strongly resembles the American *P. parryi*. Various members of section Crystallophlomis are also similar but have revolute vernation. 2n = 66. Thrums fully self-sterile, pins not tested. (Plate 25).

DISTRIBUTION Endemic to about 63 km sq. in the Rila mountains, Bulgaria. Streamsides and very wet boggy ground, often growing in running water, bare peat, etc. in acidic areas above the tree-line, 2000–2600 m, commonest at about 2200 m. Grows in intimate association with *P. exigua*, and often with *Gentiana pyrenaica* and *Pinguicula balcanica*. Above Malyovitsa astonishingly abundant for such a localized plant, often completely dominant for hundreds of square metres on suitable ground; less common around Musala ('mountain of God', hence 'deorum') to the east.

Remarkably this conspicuously beautiful and locally abundant plant has only been known to science for 110 years. Its sites are highly disjunct from those of other members of the section, and it seems to be only distantly related to its supposed relatives. *P. deorum* is apparently a 'palaeoendemic' that may have survived on the Rila in isolation for hundreds of thousands of years. As such, it may be the species closest to the original Auricula founder (Parryi relative) that colonized the European mountains from the west.

CULTIVATION Intermittently offered through the trade, but uncommonly met with and usually shy-flowering. Has been grown and flowered successfully in a trough full of sphagnum, and in mixtures of sphagnum moss and chippings. Very wet acidic conditions with good aeration and water-flow mimic its wild habitat and are most likely to meet with success.

Subsection **Erythrodosum** Schott, Sippen Osterr. Primeln. 12 (1851)

Plants evergreen, lacking meal, covered with coloured glands. Leaves broad, usually toothed. Bracts ovate, usually membranous. Flowers pink or red, several on a short stem.

Primula hirsuta All., Auct. Synop. Meth. Stirp. Hort. Reg. Taurin. 10 (1773) non All. (1785) nec Adr. Juss (1829) nec Vill. (1787)

P. rubra J. Gmelin (1775)
P. viscosa Vill. (1787) non All. (1785)
P. ciliata Schrank (1792) non Moretti (1815)
P. confinis Schott (1855)
P. decora Sims (1922)
P. decipiens Stein ex Pax (1915) non Duby (1844) = *P. magellanica*.
P. exscapa Hegetsch. and Heer
P. pallida Schott (1852)
P. grignensis D.M. Moser, Candollea 53: 387–393 (1998)

DESCRIPTION *Leaves* rounded, broadly and bluntly toothed, to 6 × 2 cm, tapering to broadly winged stalk, sticky due to a covering of three-celled hairs about 0.2 mm in length, with small colourless to yellow (rarely red) orbicular glands. *Stem* to 7 cm, usually shorter than the leaves, often almost absent, sticky hairy. *Flowers* symmetrically arranged on stiff sticky stalks to 10 mm, 1–10 in number. *Bracts* 1–3 mm, papery. *Calyx* bell-shaped, green, sticky, to 7 mm, cut to about a half into spreading, triangular sepal-lobes. *Corolla* usually bright rose-pink, varying from purple-pink to lilac-pink, occasionally white, usually with a white eye, the limb flat-faced to slightly cupped, to 25 mm in diameter; corolla-tube paler, up to 3× the length of the calyx; petal-lobes ovate, broadly notched to a half into two rounded segments. Mature fruiting capsule not more than 0.8× length of calyx. 2n = 62, 63, 64, 67. (Plate 3.)

DISTRIBUTION Most of the Alps and Pyrenees. Alps, excluding the Maritimes and the southern Cottians in the south, and eastwards to the Grossgluckner in Austria, but excluding the eastern Dolomites and regions to the east of there. Commonest in the volcanic regions of the Dauphine, Switzerland and the Tyrol. Scarcer in the Pyrenees, commonest in the central section, not found west of Jaca, and very scarce in the east.

Almost invariably on acidic rocks, normally of volcanic origin, usually in crevices of cliffs and boulders facing north, often very common. 220 m to 3600 m, commonest at about 1600 m. Some populations from limestones in the southern Italian Alps have recently been given specific rank (see below), but Kummert (The Alpine Gardener 69: 305, 2001) has noted that some variable populations from these regions are nevertheless apparently *P. hirsuta*.

P. hirsuta is the correct name for the widespread primula familar in the wild and cultivation, but often known as *P. rubra*, or *P. viscosa*. It stands in the centre of a confusing group of no less than 11 taxa, most of which are very localized, and much less well known. From most of these it is diagnosed by a combination of the stem being shorter than the leaves, the fruiting capsule shorter than the calyx and the leaf-glands most commonly yellowish, and rather small.

VARIATION Very variable in the wild in the Alps, even within a single population, every plant differing in flower colour, shape, size of eye, stature, leaf-shape, etc. Much less variable in the Pyrenees, where the normal form is rather large and multi-flowered. A number of names have been given to variants, but these have no geographical distinction. The most distinct forms are var. *exscapa* (Hegetsch. and Heer) Pax, from altitudes above 2800 m, with virtually stemless flowers, and var. *nivea* Hort. **AM**, a compact white form which bears many small flowers clustered in a tight head.

In the 1990s, two new species closely related to *P. hirsuta* were described from limestone rocks in the southern Italian Alps. As *P. hirsuta* is so variable, and apparently can occur on limestone in this region, and in a group with so many rather trivial taxa, it has been exceptionally difficult to know how to evaluate these. My interim solution has been to treat *P. recubariensis* at specific rank, as its distinctive violet flowers are quite different from those of all forms of *P. hirsuta*. However, for the present I am inclined to treat *P. grignensis* as a form of *P. hirsuta*. It differs in its very dwarf stature (leaves not exceeding 2 cm with a very marked petiole) and large coloured glands and erect sepals. In the last two features it resembles *P. daonensis,* and it seems to take an intermediate position between these closely related species.

CULTIVATION Usually the best of this subsection in cultivation, easily grown in a well-drained but moisture-retentive site in partial shade. Very suitable for troughs, especially if planted on the north side of a rock, or planted vertically in a wall. Also responds well to cultivation under glass if grown sufficiently cool. Propagated by division, and often long-lived. One clone has been in my possession for 33 years, and it is still reasonably vigorous. It is well worth selecting a good form, as some clones in cultivation are weak, poor flowering or unattractive. At its best, a most beautiful plant.

HYBRIDIZATION As one parent (with *P. auricula*) of the manifold *P. ×pubescens* hybrids, *P. hirsuta* has presumably been in cultivation for more than 400 years. Some of the *P.* × *pubescens* clones closely resemble larger and more vigorous forms of *P. hirsuta*, and may be more suitable for the open garden in some climates, for instance 'Boothman's Variety' and 'Faldonside'. Of many other clones, 'Harlow Carr' (**AM**) and 'Beverley White' are good whites; 'Mrs J.H. Wilson' is an old and excellent variety with luminous violet flowers; 'The General' and 'Rufus' are good reds, the former being particularly vigorous; and 'Freedom', which might also have *P. marginata* blood in it, is perhaps the most vigorous of all, dwarf, with lilac-pink flowers. Similar plants are often found in the wild where the limestone (*P. auricula*) and acidic rocks (*P. hirsuta*) meet. Hybrids can have mixed and weird colours; pink-flowered hybrids can often be detected by the presence of meal, or a more entire leaf than is found on *P. hirsuta*.

Wild hybrids have also been found with *P. latifolia, P. minima, P. daonensis* (*P.* × *seriana* Widm.), and *P. integrifolia* (*P.* × *heerii* Brugg). *P.* × *seriana* is difficult to detect as the parents are so similar. *P.* × *heerii* is known from scattered localities in the Alps and Pyrenees, for instance the Bernina Pass. Clones bearing this name are occasionally met with in cultivation. Formerly they seem to have been more popular.

In cultivation, hybrids of *P. hirsuta* have also been raised with *P. villosa, P. pedemontana* and *P. allionii*. *P.* × 'Ice Cap' (**AM** 1997) was raised by Henry and Margaret Taylor who crossed white forms of *P. pedemontana* and *P. hirsuta*. A number of first-rate dwarf hybrids have been raised with *P. allionii* in recent years, which make excellent pot plants for the alpine house, while some such as 'Gloria Johnstone' flourish in a trough without cover. The oldest and best known of these is 'Ethel Barker'. *P.* × 'Snow Cap' is a white-flowered form of this hybrid raised by Brian Burrow.

Primula recubariensis Prosser & Scortegagna, Willdenowia 28: 27–45 (1998)

DESCRIPTION A dwarf plant, usually smaller than other members of the group, and like *P. hirsuta* with a stem which does not exceed the short broad leaves. Distinguished from *P. hirsuta* by the *lilac-violet* flowers borne in groups of 2–5, a strong resinous scent (as in *P. albenensis*), and by microscopic details of the leaf hairs which are mostly *four*-celled (three in *P. hirsuta*) and with a narrowly *oval* (not orbicular) terminal gland (Plate 72).

DISTRIBUTION SE side of the Carega massif (SE Italian Prealps) where the districts of Trento, Verona and Vicenza meet. Most records are restricted to two mountain chains above Recoaro named Il Fumanto and Tre Croci.

Crevices in north-facing shaded dolomitic limestone cliffs between 1400 and 2030 m in a very wet region, growing with *Physoplexis comosa, Paedorata bonarata, Rhodothamnus chamaecistus*, etc.

Another most unexpected recent discovery (cf. *P. albenensis*) of a new species of primula growing on limestone in the Italian Prealps, but in this case from much further east in the 'Piccole Dolomiti'. The mountain chain on which it grows is rather severe and difficult of access, but the remarkable flower colour of this most attractive small plant renders it the most distinctive member of this subsection, and it is perhaps surprising that it was not described before.

CULTIVATION Seed was introduced shortly after its discovery by Filippo Prosser, and introductions have also been made by Margaret and Henry Taylor, Fritz Kummert and Vojtek Holubec. As yet uncommon and may prove to be slow growing and rather difficult, perhaps requiring winter cover.

HYBRIDIZATION Hybridizes in the wild with *P. auricula* which grows nearby. Hybrids have violet or yellow, violet-rimmed flowers with a yellow throat and have been described as *P.* × *vallarsae* Prosser & Scortegagna.

Primula pedemontana E.Thomas ex Gaudin, Cat. Pl. Suisses 24 (1818)

P. villosa Wulfen var. *glandulosa* Duby (1844)
P. bonjeani Hugenin (1882)
P. apennina Widmer, Europ. Art. Primul. 45 (1891)

DESCRIPTION In the type subspecies, differing from *P. hirsuta* by the wedge-shaped, rather square-ended leaf with usually entire margins (occasionally very shallowly wavy-toothed), and by the *very short* (0.1 mm) *dark red glands* being confined to the leaf margin, giving the leaf a *conspicuous reddish edge*. The remainder of the leaf, being hairless, is *shiny*. However, subsp. *apennina* is less distinct from *P. hirsuta*, differing chiefly by the narrower, more entire leaves, which are at best very shallowly scalloped. In both subspecies, the scape *exceeds* the leaves, forming a more clustered head of flowers with a hint of *blue* in the pink to red perianth. Usually lacks the conspicuous angled white eye of *P. daoensis*. 2n = 62 (both subspecies).

DISTRIBUTION Extraordinarily disjunct. Two small areas in the Alps, along the French/Italian border from Mt. Cenis in the south to the Petit St. Bernard in the north the French Alps; the Cantabrian Mountains of western Spain on the Curavacas, between Oviedo and Santander some 1000 km to the west; and the north-western Italian Etruscan Apennines in a small area between Parma and Florence, centred on Monte Orsaro.

More often found in acidic grassland, in stabilized scree or peaty turf, than its relatives, but also on shaded volcanic cliffs. 1400–3000 m. Subsp. *apennina* in north-facing sandstone cliffs between 1400 m and 2000 m.

VARIATION

- Subsp. *apennina* (Widmer) Kress. Primulaceen studien (D) 2: 1–4 (1981). Leaf less shiny on top surface, tending to be narrower and with a more rounded end than subsp. *pedemontana* but features overlap. Apennines.

A white form of subsp. *pedemontana*, known as 'alba' is popular in cultivation in 2001. Spanish plants have been separated as subsp. *iberica* Losa and P. Monts., Anal. Inst. Bot. Cavanilles 10 (2): 482 (1952), but they seem even more dubiously distinct than subsp. *apennina*.

CULTIVATION Uncommon in cultivation, and less vigorous than *P. hirsuta*, but generally not so difficult as *P. daonensis*.

HYBRIDIZATION Known to hybridize with *P. latifolia* in the wild, especially in the vicinity of Petit Mt. Cenis where hybrids are abundant and apparently fertile, but flower at a different time from *P. pedemontana*. This hybrid has been raised in cultivation recently. Hybridizes with *P. villosa* near Turin (Fenestrelle) (*P.* × *boni-auxilii* Kress).

Hybrids of *P. pedemontana* with *P. auricula, P. carniolica, P. marginata, P. hirsuta, P. spectabilis* and *P. allionii* have also been raised in cultivation.

Primula daonensis (Leyb.) Leyb., Flora 38: 345 (1855)

P. villosa Wulfen var. *daonensis* Leyb. (1854)
P. oenensis E.Thomas ex Gremli (1867)
P. plantae Brugg (1880)

DESCRIPTION Very similar to *P. hirsuta,* which it replaces in granitic areas of the south-central Alps. Differs by the hairs of up to 0.4 mm carrying relatively *large, reddish nearly orbicular glands* which can be seen by close examination with the naked eye, and which give the usually *narrower* and more *entire* leaf a rather *ferruginous* hue all over; by the stem equalling or *exceeding* the leaves; and by the fruiting capsule equalling or *exceeding* the calyx. The flowers often present a large, strongly demarcated and angled *white eye*. This is distinctive, but not diagnostic. 2n = 62, 63, 64.

DISTRIBUTION Almost confined to a small area of the Italian Alps north-west of Lake Garda, from Val Seriano in the west, north to Bormio and south-east to the Val Guidicaire, just entering Switzerland at the Stelvio Pass north of Bormio. There is also an isolated occurrence a little to the north in the western Otztaler Alps on the frontiers of Italy, Austria and Switzerland, and another to the east of Trento.

Confined to acidic rocks, usually granite; shady rock crevices and stabilized scree, 1500–3000 m.

VARIATION Not as variable as *P. hirsuta* in the wild, but varying in leaf-shape. Some forms have narrower, more entire leaves than is ever found in *P. hirsuta*.

CULTIVATION Unusual in cultivation. Slow growing, temperamental, and sometimes difficult to flower, but magnificent forms have been produced by growers in northern England and Scotland.

HYBRIDIZATION Hybrids are known in the wild with *P. auricula, P. latifolia, P. hirsuta* (from the Val Seriano, where both species just overlap), and *P. minima*. None are important in cultivation. No further hybrids have yet been raised in cultivation.

Primula villosa Wulfen in Jacq., Fl. Austr. 5: 41 (1778)

P. hirsuta All.(1785) p.p. non All. (1773)
P. hirsuta Adr. Juss.(1829) non All. (1773)
P. cottia Widmer (1889)
P. commutata Schott (1852)
P. simsii Sweet (1827)

DESCRIPTION Usually the *largest* in this group, but closely allied to *P. daonensis* and especially *P. pedemontana* which is sometimes included within it. Differs from these species and *P. hirsuta* by the leaves up to *15* × *3.5* cm, and the rather *stout* stem up to *15* cm, usually exceeding the leaves; the entire plant is covered with dark reddish *oval* glands, giving it a rusty sheen, as in *P. daonensis*, but these are borne on *longer* hairs, from 0.3 to 1 mm in length (in the type subspecies only; confusingly the hairs are shorter in other subspecies); the leaves are relatively narrow, as in *P. daonensis* and *P. pedemontana*, and they are usually toothed as is usual for the former, but are occasionally entire as is more typical for the latter. The seed capsule *exceeds* the calyx. The pinkish corolla has a blue cast in comparison with *P. hirsuta*. 2n = 62, 63, 64. (Plate 3).

DISTRIBUTION Another species with an extraordinarily disjunct distribution, which does not overlap with the other species in this group. The main occurrences are in six small areas of the eastern Alps of Austria and Yugoslavia, from the Gurktal Alps north of Klagenfurt, eastwards along the Mur to Bruck, and then south-east to Weiz. The Yugoslav site lies just over the border south-east of Klagenfurt on Kameni. There are also two isolated stations in the western Italian Alps, some 600 km to the west, the Valle Germanasca near Perrero, west of Turin (Cottian Alps), and Monte Mars, Biella, west of Milan (south Pennine Alps) ('P. cottia', which like 'P. commutata' is robust).

Confined to acidic regions, mostly on volcanic series, on shaded cliff ledges and stabilized screes, never in turf. 350–2950 m.

VARIATION It is often suggested that the robust western Italian populations should be distinguished as *P. cottia* (most recently by Zhang and Kadereit (2002, unpublished)), and with their large size and toothed leaves they often appear distinct in cultivation. To confuse issues.

- Subsp. *infecta* Kress, Primulaceen studien (D) 2: 1–4 (1981) was also described from this region (Santuaria d'Oropa, Alpi di Biella, 950–1500 m). This differs in technicalities of gland shape, and has tightly globose flowering heads.

Kress also described a subspecies from the eastern distribution:

- Subsp. *irmingardis* Kress, Primulaceen studien (D) 2: 1–4 (1981) which occurs on the Rappoltkogel in Austrian Styria (about 1800 m) in which the leaf hairs are less than 0.3 mm in length. Unlike *P. pedemontana*, hairs occur throughout the leaf.

Also in Austria grows a distinct large var. *commutata* (Schott) Ludi at only 375 m at the Schloss Herberstein, and this is sometimes cultivated.

CULTIVATION Uncommon in cultivation, but can grow and flower well, and may be the easiest of the taller species in this group to keep. Cultivation as for *P. hirsuta*, but enjoying more humid, shady sites.

HYBRIDIZATION Sterile hybrids with *P. minima* are reported from Austria. In cultivation hybrids have been raised with *P. auricula, P. marginata, P. latifolia, P. hirsuta,* and *P. allionii*. None have yet proved to be significant horticulturally.

Subsection **Rhopsidium** Schott, Sippen Osterr. Primelm 13 (1851)

Dwarf evergreen or deciduous creeping or sometimes cushion-forming plants lacking meal but covered with colourless glandular hairs; leaves fleshy and more or less entire; bracts leaf-like (except in *P. allionii*); flowers rose to violet borne on one or few-flowered stems.

Primula allionii Lois., J.Bot. (Desvaux) 2: 262 (1809)

P. glutinosa All. (1789) non Wulfen (1778)

DESCRIPTION *Plants* forming dense evergreen cushions formed of persistent leaf-remains, up to 25 cm across. *Leaves* rhomboid-rounded to spoon-shaped, grey-green and sticky, blunt, up to 5 × 1.5 cm, entire or less commonly toothed, forming a short wide paler stalk. *Stem* absent or very short, but elongating to 0.8 cm in fruit; bracts small, to 2 mm, rounded, papery; *flower-stalks* short, to 4 mm, flower*s* usually borne singly on the cushion, but sometimes up to five are joined to a single stem. *Calyx* bell-shaped, very glandular-hairy, to 6 mm, divided to half into blunt sepal-lobes. *Corolla* often pure pink, but varying from white to magenta with a white eye, flat-faced, up to 3 cm in diameter; corolla-tube up to 3× calyx, whitish; corolla-lobes broadest at the tip, widely and usually shallowly notched. Fruit takes six months to ripen. 2n = 66. (Plate 3.)

DISTRIBUTION Endemic to a tiny area of the Maritime Alps on the French/Italian border north of Menton, to the north (Italy, 15 km sq) and south (France, 200 km sq within the drainage of the Roya) of the Col de Tende. Very local within this area, and confined to moist and shaded cliffs of tufaceous limestone conglomerate (brecchia), where it grows vertically, or even upside-down, and usually inaccessibly, 700–1900 m. Flowers from March to April in the wild. Some clones flower as early as January in cultivation.

A most exciting and individual species, resembling only the much less well-known *P. tyrolensis*. Despite its very localized distribution, this is perhaps the most popular of all alpine house plants and it is possible that more plants are in cultivation than survive in the wild. There is a very thorough illustrated account of this species in the wild by Jules Fouarge in Bull. AGS 64: 313–321.

VARIATION Quite extraordinarily variable for such a local plant in the wild, particularly in flower shape, size and colour. In some localities, every plant is quite distinct. Not surprisingly, a very wide range of cultivars have been bred from this natural variation. Some of the most distinct and best known are 'Anna Griffith' **FCC,** very dwarf and slow with frilled petal-lobes lacking an eye; 'Avalanche' (**AM**), perhaps the best of the whites; 'Crowsley Variety' (**AM**), with deep crimson flowers; 'Margaret Earle' (**AM**) and its parent 'Superba', with huge wavy pink flowers; and 'Pinkie' (**AM**), tiny and slow with baby-pink flowers. 'Mary Berry' is arguably the finest of all, very large and vigorous with large well-formed flowers of a bright purple, but it may be hybrid.

Over the last 50 years, very many new varieties and hybrids of *P. allionii* have been raised, particularly by Ken Wooster who produced over 900 new seedlings, and George Berry. These developments are continuing as I write, although in the last decade growers have tended to concentrate on relatively few good clones. The results are far too complex to report here but good accounts can be found in the Bulletin of the Alpine Garden Society by Margaret Earle (53: 276–294, 1985) and Tony Marcham (69: 255, 1992).

CULTIVATION Very difficult to grow outside, although plants will survive for some years if grown vertically or upside-down in tufa, but they do not increase or flower well. An easy and vigorous pot-plant under glass, totally hardy as long as water is never allowed on the foliage. First collected in 1901. Individual plants of more than 30 years age are known, while clones seem to be immortal, and do not suffer from virus. The major enemies in cultivation are botrytis and aphids. Good ventilation, careful watering, the removal of all dead flowers and leaves, and the use of systemic insecticides promotes good cultivation, but plants under glass survive surprising amounts of neglect. Propagation by cuttings, which root easily in early summer, or by seed.

HYBRIDIZATION Hybrids in the wild are known with *P. marginata*, (*P.* × *meridionalis* A.J. Richards) the only species which grows in the same region. A very popular parent for hybridization in cultivation, as hybridizers attempt to increase the outdoors potential and colour range of plants with the appealing dwarf cushion aspect of *P. allionii*. Hybrids have been raised with *P. auricula, P. carniolica, P. marginata, P. hirsuta, P. pedemontana, P. villosa* and *P. minima*. These have already been discussed under the other parents.

However, most of the horticulturally significant *P. allionii* hybrids have been made by crosses with other hybrids, or where the other parent is known. Perhaps the finest of all is *P.* 'Clarence Elliott' which forms vigorous cushions with large lilac-blue flowers. Until recently 'Beatrice Wooster' (× 'Linda Pope') (**FCC**), a vigorous plant raised in 1947, was a strong contender, but in the twenty-first century most stocks seem finally to have acquired virus. *P.* 'Fairy Rose' **AM**, *P.* 'Joan Hughes' **AM** and *P.* 'Purple Emperor' have the same parentage. The latter two have purple flowers. Some successful hybrids have also been made by crossing *P. allionii* with various *P.* × *pubescens* clones, for instance 'Margaret'.

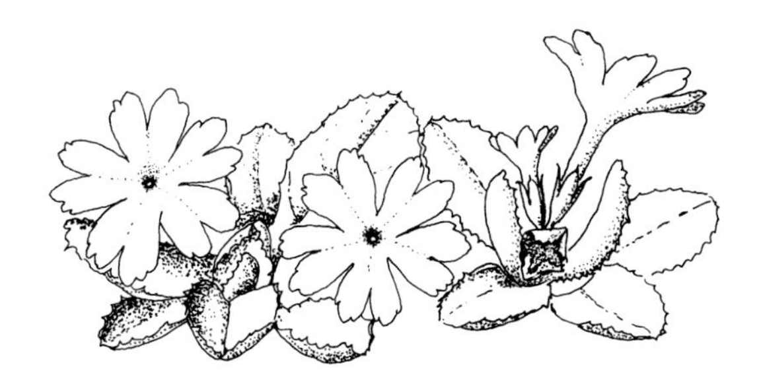

Fig. 11. *P. tyrolensis*

Primula tyrolensis Schott, Sippen Osterr. Primeln 13 (1851)

P. allionii Hausm. (1852) non Lois. (1809)

DESCRIPTION Differs from *P. allionii* by growing

as more or less individual rosettes, rather than in cushions, and by dying back to a resting bud. Leaves finely denticulate. Flowering stems up to 2 cm, frequently bearing two flowers. Bracts narrow, leaf-like. Flower stalks not more than 2 mm, calyx up to 8 mm. Flowers most commonly rose-coloured, translucent. 2n = 66. (Fig. 11).

DISTRIBUTION Endemic to the south-eastern Dolomites (Italy) to a small area about 40 km in radius from the Biois valley, south of the Marmolada in the north, west to the Rolle Pass, and south-eastwards to the river Piave at Belluno, westwards to Feltre. An outlying station occurs 30 km to the south-west to the east of Trento in the Val Caldiera. I was shown a small colony unexpectedly discovered in 1990 above the Pordoi Pass, north of the Marmolada (still there in 2001).

Damp shaded earthy fissures and ledges in limestone cliffs and boulders, occasionally in stabilized scree below cliffs, as on the Rolle and Pordoi Passes. 1000–2300 m.

According to Zhang and Kadereit (2002, unpublished), not related to *P. allionii*, being classified by them in their subsection Cyanopsis.

CULTIVATION Much less variable than *P. allionii* in the wild and in cultivation. A charming and delicate species in the wild, but not so vigorous or free-flowering in cultivation as *P. allionii*, although it will survive more readily in the open garden without protection. Reputed to flower more freely in Scotland, but rarely makes a good show in the wild or in cultivation. Grows best in a rich gritty compost, lightly shaded in summer.

HYBRIDIZATION Hybrids are known with *P. auricula*, *P. minima* and *P. wulfeniana* in the wild, the former two in the Val Venegia, near the Rolle. No other hybrids are known in cultivation.

Primula integrifolia L. Sp. Pl. 1: 144 (1753) p.p. non Oeder. (= *P. nutans* Georgi)

P. candolleana Agardh in Reichb. (1828)
P. incisa Lam. (1778) non Franchet (1886) = *P. florida*

DESCRIPTION Forms scattered colonies of small partially deciduous rosettes tight against the ground. *Leaves* erect, still developing at flowering, to 5 × 1.2 cm, spear-shaped, effectively stalkless, entire, blunt, fleshy, slightly sticky, with sparse hairs, fringed with glandular hairs. *Stem* to 7 cm at fruiting, much shorter at flowering, hairy, 1–3 flowered. *Bracts* leaf-like, to 10 mm, often reddish. Flower-stalks absent or very short at flowering. *Calyx* subcylindrical, hairy, often reddish, to 11 mm, cut to one-third into bluntly trianular sepal-lobes. *Corolla* rose to purple, usually lacking an eye, cup-shaped, to 25 mm in diameter; corolla tube dark, up to 2× calyx; petal-lobes triangular, broadest at the apex, deeply v-notched. 2n = 66, ca 68, ca 70. (Plate 3.)

DISTRIBUTION Widely distributed and locally common throughout the Pyrenees. In the Alps, localized in the central Alps from the north end of Lake Como (Italy), through the Austrian and Swiss Tyrol to Lichtenstein and west to Interlaken.

Usually in acidic areas, characteristically the primula of late snow-lie patches, often growing with soldanellas and *Crocus vernus*. Wet peaty turf and stabilized scree, often growing in running snow-melt water, 1500–3000 m. A very beautiful plant when encountered en masse in the Pyrenees. In many ways resembles the American *P. angustifolia*.

VARIATION Rather invariable in the wild and in cultivation, although it is said that Pyrenean plants are a better colour. Very distinctive, the creeping habit, tiny entire rosettes and few-flowered stems making it difficult to confuse with other species.

CULTIVATION Grows vigorously in cultivation in peaty screes, particularly if kept moist while in growth, but often poor flowering, and generally disappointing and unpopular in cultivation. A relatively free flowering clone was however offered in 1992.

HYBRIDIZATION Wild hybrids have been encountered with *P. auricula*, *P. latifolia*, and *P. hirsuta*. All are probably sterile.

Primula kitaibeliana Schott, Osterr. Bot. Wochenbl. 2: 268 (1852)

P. integrifolia Vis. (1847) non L. (1753)

DESCRIPTION Much like a larger version of *P. integrifolia*, but fully deciduous, and less creeping, with leaves to 9 × 4 cm, pale green and erect when young, slightly toothed, narrowing to a distinct stalk, aromatic. Stem to 5 cm at flowering, elongating afterwards, bearing 1–2 (–5) flowers rather one-sidedly on stalks to 4 mm; flowers with a distinct, often star-shaped, white eye. 2n = 66.

DISTRIBUTION Confined to mountains along the Adriatic coast of Yugoslavia, from Mt. Klek in Croatia in the north south-eastwards to southern Herzegovina. The distribution is scattered, and highly localized, but is as yet still imperfectly known. Overlaps only with *P. glutinosa*, which however occurs higher on acidic ground. Restricted to north-facing sites on limestone, in cool moist sites in stabilized scree or in turf. 350–2000 m.

An isolated and fairly distinct species little known in the wild or in cultivation. It could possibly be confused in cultivation with the longer-stemmed members of subsection Erythrodosum, from which it can be distinguished by the deciduous habit, leaf-like bracts, the colourless glands on the leaf, and the few-flowered stems. Apparently rather invariable in the wild.

CULTIVATION Rarely tried in cultivation, but apparently difficult, resenting root-disturbance. Said to be easier outside in a partially shaded rich scree than under glass. Flowers readily if established, but difficult to propagate.

HYBRIDIZATION Not surprisingly, no wild hybrids have been reported. In cultivation, hybrids have been raised with *P. auricula* and *P. minima* by Franz Kummert in Austria.

Section **Cuneifolia** Balf. f., J. Roy. Hort. Soc. 39: 178 (1913). Type species *P. cuneifolia*

DESCRIPTION Leaves with involute vernation, deciduous or evergreen, hairless but sticky-glandular, lacking meal, v-shaped (widest at the cut-off, toothed apex). Stems with small bracts and a single umbel of few annulate, heterostyle or homostyle rose or white flowers. Pollen oblate, 3-syncolpate. Capsule globose, rather large, with large winged seeds, opening by 5 valves. x = 11. Two species from Japan and north-western America. Flowering June–July in the wild, May in cultivation.

DISTRIBUTION Pacific coasts. One species in Japan, and one ranging from northern Japan to British Columbia.

The two species in section Cuneifolia form an interesting morphological and geographical link between section Auricula from Europe, section Parryi in north America, and the Asian 'heartland' of the genus where its closest relatives are found in section Amethystina. In leaf-shape and growth habit they resemble such Auricula species as the widespread *P. minima,* but in common with section Parryi species they lack hairs, and have annulate flowers and a similar pollen type. DNA studies (p. 39) show that they are related to these sections, and that *P. cuneifolia* and *P. nipponica* are sister species. The Californian *P. suffrutescens* was formerly placed here too, but it is less closely related, and seems to be sister to the American genus *Dodecatheon*. From cytological evidence, it seems that the diploid (x = 11) Asiatic Cuneifolia are primitive to both the tetraploid (x = 22) Parryi and *P. suffrutescens,* and to the hexaploid (x = 33-based) Auricula.

CULTIVATION Both species can be occasionally found in cultivation today, although they tend to be rather impermanent, and need to be kept going from seed (which germinates best after chilling). They are attractive, although sometimes shy-flowering little plants, most suitable for cultivation in partial shade in a pot or trough in a well-drained, peaty compost. They are fully hardy, but often survive better outside with some protection from winter wet in the UK. No hybrids are known.

LITERATURE. Kelso (1991a), Smith *et al.* (1984).

Primula cuneifolia Ledeb., Mem. Acad. Imp. Sci. St.Petersb. Hist. Acad. 5: 522 (1815)

P. minima Mertens non L.(1830)
P. hakusanensis Franch. (1886)
P. heterodonta Franch. (1886)
P. saxifragifolia Lehm. (1817)
P. hypoborea Spreng. (1825)
P. macrocarpa Tanaka (1874) non Maxim. (1868)

DESCRIPTION Dwarf, rather fleshy deciduous plants with pale green or purple few-leaved rosettes hugging the ground, very reminiscent of *Saxifraga nivalis*. *Leaves* to 8 × 2.5 cm, often smaller, widest near the rounded tip which bears 6–8 large rounded to acute teeth, the rest of the leaf entire, narrowed gradually into a wide stalk about half the length of the leaf. *Stem* varying from almost stemless (some forms of subsp. *saxifragifolia*) to 30 cm in fruit, rather slender, bearing 1–9 flowers on inclined stalks up to 2 cm long; bracts narrow, to 5 mm. *Calyx* broadly bell-shaped, green to reddish, to 6 mm, cut to two-thirds into rather narrow blunt sepal-lobes. *Corolla* heterostyle or (subsp. *saxifragifolia*) homostyle, pink, rose, red, magenta or white with a yellow, sometimes white-rimmed eye, flat-faced, to 2 cm in diameter; corolla-tube slightly exceeding the calyx, sometimes (subsp. *heterodonta*) longer; petal-lobes y-shaped, widest at the tip, deeply and widely bilobed. 2n = 22. (Photo: Bull. AGS 57: 228 (1989).)

DISTRIBUTION Japan: central Honshu, Mt. Hakusan, Mt. Shirouma (subsp. *hakusanensis*); extreme north-western Honshu, Mt. Iwaki (subsp. *heterodonta*); Hokkaido, Rishiri, Mt. Yoichi. Kuriles and west Aleutians. Sakhalin. Kamtchatka, east Siberian coast in Ochotsk Sea area and the Lena delta (subsp. *cuneifolia*). Aleutian Islands, western and southern coasts of Alaska, and inland north to the Alaska range, with a disjunct area in the Canadian coastal range south to the north end of Vancouver Island (subsp. *saxifragifolia*).

An alpine plant from damp shaded rocks and wet alpine slopes above the tree-line in Japan and southern Alaska, but becoming a submaritime plant from wet meadows further north. '... abundant on wet alpine slopes in Hokkaido ... widespread in this (Daisetsu Range in the north of Hokkaido) range of volcanic mountains ... while more shallowly-rooting than the European counterparts, a rich soil that is never likely to dry out and the provision of maximum light should suit it well.'

VARIATION An extremely variable species from throughout its wide range in the northern Pacific.

- Subsp. *saxifragifolia* (Lehm.) Smith & Forrest, Notes Roy. Bot. Gdn. Edinb. 41: 20 (1928) is relatively dwarf, the stems rarely exceeding 5 cm and often virtually stemless, with blunt-toothed often purplish leaves and large homostylous flowers. The most attractive race, often grown in a white-flowered form, although this is apparently rare in the wild. One of the few diploid homostyles; self-fertile.

Subsp. *heterodonta* (Franch.) Smith & Forrest (loc. cit.) and subsp. *hakusanensis* (Franch.) Smith & Forrest (loc. cit.) are very closely related to subsp. *cuneifolia* from which they may be inseparable.

- Subsp. *heterodonta* is a larger plant with more flowers and longer flower-stalks, relatively larger leaf-teeth which may themselves be finely toothed, and the corolla-tube up to twice the length of the calyx.
- Subsp. *hakusanensis* has shallow sharp leaf-teeth, and the corolla-tube exceeds the calyx.

CULTIVATION Probably first introduced from Japan in 1933; in the late 1980s, subsp. *saxifragifolia* was successfully introduced from Alaska and persisted for some years, but it is rarely seen in 2001. I have found subsp. *heterodonta* a vigorous and easy, but short-lived plant in pots under glass and in a raised bed, flowering in nine months from seed, but never surviving a second flowering.

Primula nipponica Yatabe, Bot. Mag. (Tokyo) (1890) non Yatabe in Pflanzenr. (1905)

DESCRIPTION Differs from *P. cuneifolia*, to which it is very closely related, chiefly by its slender habit and smaller size, and by its invariably white flowers. In the pin form, the stigma is held well clear of the flower (in *P. cuneifolia* it only reaches the annulus). 2n = 22. (Plate 4.)

DISTRIBUTION Endemic to the mountains of northern Honshu, Japan, where it is widespread and locally abundant in suitable habitats within a limited area from Sakata and Miyako northwards to Mutsu on the northern tip; chiefly recorded from Mt. Chokaisan and Mt. Iwatesan. Not apparently found in company with *P. cuneifolia* subsp. *heterodonta* at its only locality on Iwaki.

Wet alpine slopes, well below 1000 m on the Mutsui mountains. 'A wide open area created by the levelling out of a modest water course had formed a marshy community. Some areas had been allowed partially to dry out by the side of streams, rich in volcanic material of a fine particle size. Throughout the area, both in the boggy turf amongst *Drosera, Parnassia* and the dainty *Gentiana nipponica* and along the course of the dried up stream bed grew our minature *Primula nipponica* in plenty.'

P. nipponica is a pretty little plant, the only one of its relatives which normally has white flowers. It appears to vary little except in stature, but differs little from the variable *P. cuneifolia* complex except for flower colour, and might be best considered as a subspecies.

CULTIVATION First introduced in 1916, but little known or absent until about 1985 when introduced from wild Japanese seed and grown for instance by Henrik Zetterlund at Gothenburg. Seed was also collected from Mt. Hakkoda by the AGSJ expedition in 1988 (162). In 2001 it is still to be found in cultivation, short-lived, but growing strongly from seed in the same conditions as for *P. cuneifolia.*

Section **Suffrutescens** A.J. Richards **Sectio Nova** Type species *P. suffrutescens* A. Gray

Planta perennis, subfruticosa, sempervirens, decumbens. Folia involuta, glabra, viscida, efarinosa, cuneatotruncata. Caules bracteae parvae flores pauci rosei heterostyli ferentes. Fructus globosus submagnus seminis alatis continens.

DESCRIPTION Perennial with trailing *subwoody* stems. Leaves with *involute* vernation, *evergreen,* hairless but *sticky-glandular,* lacking meal, *v-shaped* (widest at the cut-off, toothed apex). Stems with small bracts and a single umbel of few annulate, heterostyle rose flowers. Pollen oblate, 3-syncolpate. Capsule *globose,* rather large, with large winged seeds, opening by 5 valves. x = 22.

DISTRIBUTION The single species is endemic to the Sierra Nevada, California. Flowering June–July in the wild, May in cultivation.

Primula suffrutescens A. Gray, Proc. Amer. Acad. 7: 371 (1868)

DESCRIPTION Together with *P. forrestii* and *P. marginata,* the closest approximation to a shrub in the genus, with often long, trailing subwoody growth clothed with persistent dead foliage and terminating in living evergreen leathery rosettes, covered with stalkless sticky glands. At times can form very attractive loose hemispherical cushions in the wild, but never seems to do so in cultivation. *Leaves* to 4 × 1 cm, widest at the rounded or even 'sawn-off' bluntly toothed tip, entire elsewhere, dark green above, rather yellowish beneath, narrowing to a winged stalk. *Stems* about 5 cm, elongating to 12 cm in fruit, stiff, slender, erect, bearing 1–9 rather erect flowers on short (to 12 mm) stalks; bracts narrow, to 6 mm. *Calyx* bell-shaped, green, to 8 mm, cut to half-way into sharp sepal-lobes. *Corolla* pink, rose, red or purple with a yellow eye, heterostylous, flat-faced, to 20 mm diameter; corolla-tube yellow, about 2× calyx; petal-lobes broad, shallowly notched. 2n = 44. (Photo: Bull. AGS 67: 353.) (Plate 4.)

DISTRIBUTION Limited to the Sierra Nevada, California, east of San Francisco, where it is found in three distinct areas over some 250 km: Ellis Peak near Lake Tahoe in the north; around Yosemite; and around Mt. Whitney in the south.

Crevices and boulder scree on granite, flowering close to the snow-line near mountain summits, 3300–4000 m.

A distinctive and isolated species, the only primula in California, occurring today 2000 km to the south of *P. cuneifolia.* Cytologically and geographically, *P. suffrutescens* might be considered more related to species placed in section Parryi. However, DNA studies show it to be more closely related to *Dodecatheon,* with which it might share an extinct ancestor. The subwoody and evergreen habit is not otherwise known in *Dodecatheon,* or the Parryi and Cuneifolia sections of primula, so I have decided to create a section for this species alone.

CULTIVATION Introduced in 1884, and probably continuously in cultivation since that time, although never common, perhaps because it tends to be shy-flowering. Often long-lived in the open, as on the rock garden of the Royal Botanic Garden, Edinburgh. Shows little variability except in flower colour. Easily propagated vegetatively by cuttings or division.

Section **Amethystina** Balf. f., J. Roy. Hort. Soc. 39: 153 (1913). Type species *P. amethystina* Franchet.

DESCRIPTION Perennial *deciduous* plants with *involute vernation* forming a small resting bud at soil level, lacking meal or hairs, developing firm smooth fleshy leaves with a *horny margin*, remote teeth and pitted glands; the leaf-stalk is poorly demarcated. *Stems* generally exceeding leaves, slender but firm, bearing a single few-flowered umbel of usually nodding flowers. *Bracts* small, very narrow. *Calyx* broadly bell-shaped, short. *Corolla* usually narrowly bell-shaped, usually exannulate, heterostylous, violet, blue, purple, red, yellow or white. *Pollen* prolate, 3-colporoidate. *Capsule* ovoid, about equalling the calyx, dehiscing by 5 valves; seeds small, nearly round, dark. 2n = 22. Flowering late spring-early summer.

DISTRIBUTION From easternmost Nepal through Sikkim, Bhutan, south-east Tibet to East Yunnan, Sichuan and northern Burma.

Ecologically very distinct, all species growing in very wet, peaty meadows above the tree-line, mostly in high rainfall areas, 2500–5000 m. Locally distributed, but often abundant or even dominant where they occur.

The Amethystina forms a small but very distinct and natural assemblage with excellent ecological and morphological coherence. The species have all proved difficult to grow and were poorly understood, so that for many years, relationships outside the section were rather obscure. In 2001, Tass Kelso recognized that several, probably all, species classified here have involute rather than revolute vernation as had been supposed (although this suggestion had in fact already been made by Smith & Fletcher (1942) but later ignored).

As discussed on page 33, leaf vernation appears to be a highly conserved character in the family, so that this observation has caused me completely to re-evaluate the position of this section. Taken together with the chromosome base number of x = 11, and the prolate, 3-colporoidate pollen, it now seems that the Amethystina are in fact most closely related to the Cuneifolia. This raises the fascinating possibility that a westerly extension through Asia, rather than an easterly migration through America, caused Europe to be invaded by the forerunners of the Auricula.

Nevertheless, it is possible that the Amethystina also link to Asian sections with revolute vernation, and I noted a resemblance of some Amethystina species to the familiar *P. secundiflora* (1993).

CULTIVATION Unfortunately, the Amethystina have proved to be very difficult to maintain in cultivation. The only species which proved at all permanent was *P. kingii*, which thrived in a few gardens in the Scottish Highlands, notably the Sherriffs' garden at Ascreavie, for 30 years. It only set seed sporadically, which probably caused its eventual downfall. *P. dickieana* has been introduced on a number of occasions, while *P. amethystina*, *P. odontica* and *P. faberi* have all been flowered in cultivation, but they invariably proved short-lived and failed to set seed.

P. kingii was grown in a slightly raised border in a gritty humus-rich mix, north-facing but with good light in a very summer-cool garden with reliable winter snow cover. It is likely that these conditions, perhaps accompanied by cloching in winter, could suit other species. Later introductions of *P. dickieana* tend to have been confined to the alpine house or frame, and these conditions are likely to prove too dry in summer. In the wild, plants grow in extremely wet conditions, with intricate root associations with grasses and sedges while in growth, and are protected by deep snow for more than six months. These conditions are very difficult to simulate in the garden

No hybrids have been reported.

KEY TO SPECIES

1. Flowers with a flat, hairy face .... *P. dickieana*
1. Flowers bell-shaped 2

2. Flowers yellow .... *P. faberi*
2. Flowers blue, purple or red 3

3. Leaves more than 4× as long as wide, sharp 4
3. Leaves less than 4× as long as wide, rounded 6

4.	Corolla and calyx dark blue	*P. virginis*
4.	Corolla and calyx dark red to blackish	5
5.	Corolla-tube equalling calyx, lacking hairs	*P. kingii*
5.	Corolla-tube almost absent, corolla hairy inside	*P. valentiniana*
6.	Leaves with large, distant teeth; flowers deep red	*P. odontica*
6.	Leaves entire or teeth small; flowers deep blue	7
7.	Leaves oblong; flower bell at least 12 mm long	*P. amethystina*
7.	Leaves orbicular; flower bell less than 10 mm long	*P. silaensis*

Primula amethystina Franchet, Bull. Soc. Bot. Fr. 32: 268 (1885)

P. brevifolia Forrest (1908)
P. argutidens Franchet (1895)
P. riae Pax & Hoffm. (1921)
?*P. sikangensis* Chen (1939)

DESCRIPTION *Leaves* obovate, to 5 × 2 cm, the margin finely toothed. *Corolla* violet, or purple-blue, or deep blue, not amethyst, very rarely white, bell-shaped, to 15 mm long, the lobes entire, with a short tooth or fringed. (Fig. Halda: 219. Plate 49.)

DISTRIBUTION Widespread in west and north-west Yunnan, south-west Sichuan, and just over the border into Tibet. Locally common around the Zhongdian plateau at frequently visited sites such as Tianchi Lake, on the Beima Shan, Da Xue Shan, Yulong Shan and these days familiar to most botanical visitors to this region.

Typically in very wet turfy ground, where the ground has become too wet for cassiopes and rhododendrons, often abundant. 3500–5000 m. By Tianchi associates with *Lilium souliei* and *Mandragora caulescens*. A very beautiful plant. Poorly dried material appears to be pink flowered, hence the name, and this can be true of colour photos, but the actual colour is usually a deep violet-blue.

VARIATION

- Var. *amethystina*. Confined to the Cang Shan, west Yunnan.
- Var. *argutidens* (Franchet) Smith & Fletcher, Trans. Bot. Soc. Edinb. 33: 213 (1942). A very small delicate plant with deeply toothed leaves reminiscent of *P. sappharina*. South-west Sichuan.
- Var. *brevifolia* (Forrest) Smith & Fletcher, Notes Roy. Bot. Gdn. Edinb. 16: 13 (1928). The usual form. Frequently more robust than var. *amethystina*, with up to 20 flowers borne on stems to 25 cm. Corolla narrowly bell-shaped and fringed. Widespread throughout the range.

CULTIVATION Forrest 28366 was flowered by R.B. Cooke at Kilbryde, probably in 1933; colour photos still exist. Reintroduced mostly as subsp. *brevifolia* by CLD 821 (subsp. *amethystina*), KGB (60, and 821 which was v. *argutidens*) in 1993 and ACE (1178, 2153) in 1994, and on a number of other occasions, most recently ARGS 699, 780 from Tianchi, Zhongdian and Hong Shan respectively (2000) but did not thrive. However, Peter Cox had a large planting in 2002.

Primula virginis Levl., Le Monde des Plantes 92: 1 (1915)

P. leimonophila Balf. f. (1915)
?*P. petrophyes* Balf. f. (1915)

DESCRIPTION A little-known relative of *P. amethystina*, but with narrow sharp leaves, a cylindrical dark blue calyx and a dark blue bell-shaped corolla with rather narrow lobes. Only collected once from the Io-Chan plateau in E. Yunnan, wet meadows at 3300 m. (Fig. Halda: 225.)

Primula silaensis Petitm., Bull. Herb. Boiss. ser.II, 7: 524 (1907)

DESCRIPTION A tiny fragile relative of *P. amethystina* var. *argutidens*, but with rounded leaves with minute teeth and a small flower less than 10 mm long. Widespread on the borders of Yunnan, Assam, south-east Tibet and Burma, from Tsarong in the west, south to the Delei valley along the Salween gorge country. 'A subalpine swamp plant on mica slate, more rarely on steep alpine lawns on limestone', 4000–4800 m. (Fig. Halda: 224.)

Primula odontica Smith, Notes Roy. Bot. Gdn. Edinb. 19: 199 (1937)

DESCRIPTION A relative of *P. amethystina* and *P. valentiniana*, but with deeply and irregularly toothed leaves and deep claret-red annulate flowers with an orange eye, and a very short tube; the calyx is divided to half-way into narrow acute lobes; although the flower colour is similar to *P. kingii*, the flower and leaf structure is quite different. Said to be strikingly beautiful. (Fig. Halda: 223.)

DISTRIBUTION Endemic to Tsari, south-east Tibet; Chickchar and Takar La. Wet hillsides and avalanche slopes, 4300–5000 m. Flowered by R.B. Cooke in 1938 from 1936 Ludlow and Sherriff seed, lost after 1942. Seen by Tony Cox and others to the south of Tsari Valley above the tree-line on the Yarap Cha La in 2000.

Primula faberi Oliver, Hook. Ic. Pl. 58: t.1789 (1888)

P. lecomtei Petitm. (1907)
P. cylindriflora Hand.-Mazz. (1920)

DESCRIPTION Very distinct with *yellow* bell-shaped flowers forming a tight head surrounded by long bracts forming an involucre, but otherwise closely resembles *P. amethystina* of which it is essentially a yellow variety. Central Sichuan to east Yunnan, best known on the Emei Shan; wet places and along rivulets in meadows on sandstone in relatively dry regions, 2700–3500 m. (Fig. Halda: 221). Collected by Steve Hootman (SEH 215) in 1995, and flowered by Ian Scott in 2000, still in cultivation in 2002 for Peter Cox.

Primula kingii Watt, J. Linn. Soc. Bot. 20: 9 (1882)

P. gageana Balf. f. & Smith (1915)

DESCRIPTION *Leaves* suberect, dark green and rather shiny, spear-shaped, to 6 × 1 cm. *Stem* to 20 cm, usually about 10 cm at flowering, bearing a somewhat one-sided umbel of 2–10 semipendant flowers on stalks to 15 mm. *Calyx* bell-shaped, to 8 mm, pale green to blackish, divided to one-third into blunt triangular lobes. *Corolla* a deep velvety blackish claret, usually with a narrow golden eye, exannulate, bell-shaped, to 18 mm long, the tube equalling the calyx, the limb to 15 mm in diameter (unexpanded); corolla-lobes oblong with a slightly indented tip. (Photo: A Quest of Flowers: 10 (the colour photo in this book opposite p.179 is of *P. secundiflora*). (Fig. Halda: 222.)

DISTRIBUTION Very disjunct, although locally abundant, with several localities in north-eastern Sikkim close to Chumbi, and in the neighbouring Ha valley, Bhutan, and then again 600 km to the east on the main range on the Tsari Sama pass, and south of here on the Dirang Dzong, Assam. Open wet meadows and swampy ground in fir forest, 3500–4300 m.

P. kingii is in general the most robust Amethystina, and it has a resemblance to small forms of *P. secundiflora*. However, the flower colour is of a very deep and intense red, with no blue tones, and has a velvety texture not found in the latter. *P. secundiflora* also has a quite different calyx, silver with meal and with very narrow sepal-lobes. The flowers of *P. kingii* are disproportionately large, making this a most desirable plant.

CULTIVATION Introduced as seed from Ha by Ludlow and Sherriff in 1934, (survived until 1939, **AM** 1936), and then again, probably as flown-home plants from Ha, in 1949. The latter introduction succeeded spectacularly for the Sherriffs themselves in their new garden Ascreavie near Kirriemuir, and by the early 1970s Betty Sherriff had a planting of over 100, a most wonderful sight. It was also grown successfully for a time at Cluny, Keillour, Kilbryde and elsewhere.

On Betty Sherriff's death in 1979 the plants were dispersed, and a few survived for a while at Cluny. In 1989, seed was offered from New Zealand, giving rise to the hope that one of Betty Sherriff's many correspondents there still grew it then, but not heard of since.

Primula valentiniana Hand.-Mazz., Anz. Akad. Wiss. Wien Math.-Nat. 59: 249 (1922)

DESCRIPTION Closely related to *P. kingii* and with similar leaves, but with a short (5 mm) cup-shaped calyx and the wine-crimson to cherry-red corolla almost lacking a tube, hairy inside. The border region between Yunnan and south-east Tibet to both sides of the Tsangpo bend gorge, and north Burma. Extends west in Tibet to Tsari at 94° E. Wet meadows, 4000–5000 m. It has never been successfully grown. (Fig. Halda: 224.)

Primula dickieana Watt, J. Linn. Soc. Bot. 20: 9 (1882)

P. pantlingii King (1886)
P. aureostellata Balf. f. & Cooper 1915)

DESCRIPTION *Leaves* narrowly oblong, to 7 × 1 cm, spreading, strongly tufted. *Stem* slender, to 20 cm, but about 7 cm in flower, bearing 1–6 flowers held horizontally on short stout stalks to 7 mm in flower. *Corolla* almost flat-faced, the broad eye and inside the tube velvety hairy, violet, purple, magenta, yellow or white, often with an orange eye, to 30 mm in diameter; tube narrow, 2× calyx; corolla-lobes broad, blunt, broadly notched. (Photo: A Quest of Flowers: 196; Riddle of the Tsangpo Gorge: 150.) (Fig. Halda: 221.)

DISTRIBUTION Widespread in the Sinohimalaya, from the Everest region of east Nepal through Sikkim, Bhutan, south-east Tibet to just within Yunnan and north-east Burma on the Salween divides. Common and locally abundant, found in most suitable localities where exposed ridges on the south side of the main range meet the full brunt of the monsoon.

Very wet alpine meadows, often growing in running water, 4000–5000 m. '(Damp) grassy turf on mica slate, particularly along avalanche tracks, together with *Pogonia yunnanensis, Pleione scopulorum, Leontopodium jacotianum, Utricularia salwinensis, Vaccinium modestum* and gentians, not long after the snow has melted.'

This very distinctive species is aberrant amongst the Amethystina in having a flat and hairy-faced flower. However, the leaf is exactly of the Amethystina type, and there is no doubt as to its affinities.

VARIATION In common with many other primulas as diverse as the primrose, *P. calderiana, P. hookeri* and *P. alpicola, P. dickieana* is extremely variable in flower colour. Interestingly, a cline in flower colour comparable to that in the petiolarids *P. calderiana* and *P. tanneri* seems to occur. Populations in Nepal and Sikkim east to central Bhutan (e.g. Rudo La) are yellow. In the Me La region of north-east Bhutan, mixed populations with white, yellow and purple flowers are found, while in the Tsari and Tsangpo bend areas of south-east Tibet, most populations are purplish or white, although the Doshong La (95° E) also has a few yellow plants.

Flower colour is however associated with other characters, and this has led to the naming of the following varieties:

- Var. *chlorops* Smith & Forrest, Notes Roy. Bot. Gdn. Edinb. 14: 39 (1923). Very dwarf; flowers deep purple-blue with a green eye, Tsarong near the Tibet-Yunnan border, growing with var. *dickieana*.
- Var. *aureostellata* (Balf. f. & Cooper) Fletcher, Trans. Bot. Soc. Edinb. 33: 218 (1942). Robust, to 40 cm, flowers white or yellow with an orange eye. Central Bhutan.
- Var. *gouldii* Fletcher, Trans. Bot. Soc. Edinb. 33: 218 (1942). Similar to the last, but flowers wine-coloured with unnotched petal-lobes. Ra La, Bhutan.

CULTIVATION Introduced on several occasions by Ludlow & Sherriff, but did not survive for long. An introduction of seed by George Smith in 1976 flowered for Ray Johnstone in 1977 and 1978 and was exhibited, but did not set seed. Introduced by KEKE in 1990, and by Ron McBeath from the Upper Barun Khola in 1991, but again did not establish. Anne Chambers, Kenneth Cox and companions regularly saw this species in south-east Tibet in 1995, 1997 and 1998, for instance on the Doshong La.

Section **Parryi** W.W. Smith ex Wendelbo, Aarbok Univ. Bergen, Mat.-Nat. 11: 34 (1961).
Type species *P. parryi* A. Gray.

(Section Nivales Pax (1905) p. min.p.)
(Section Parryi W.W. Smith in W.W. Smith and Fletcher (1948) sin. diag. lat.)

DESCRIPTION Robust to small deciduous plants forming clumps of involute, glabrous but sometimes glandular, smooth and fleshy or leathery, rather narrow, entire or shallowly toothed leaves, lacking meal. *Stems* bearing a single whorl of flowers (rarely two), and narrow conspicuous bracts. *Calyx* mealy or lacking meal. *Corolla* rose to purple, occasionally white, heterostylous, exannulate or annulate. *Pollen* oblate, 3-syncolpate. *Capsule* globose to oblong, shorter than the calyx, opening by five valves. x = 22. Flowering May–August in the wild, May in cultivation.

DISTRIBUTION Western north America. Mostly local endemics, ranging from Montana and Wyoming (*P. parryi*), Oregon and Idaho (*P. cusickiana*) to southern Arizona (*P. rusbyi*). Chiefly plants from wet places (at the time of growth) in the mountains.

The species in section Parryi bear a superficial resemblance to Asiatic species placed in section Crystallophlomis. They were originally placed there until R.E. Cooper of the Royal Botanic Garden, Edinburgh drew the attention of Sir William Wright Smith to the fact that members of sections Parryi and Cuneifolia had leaves with involute rather than revolute vernation. Smith concluded these American species were unrelated to the Crystallophlomis, but were rather related to the European section Auricula. This has since been confirmed by DNA studies (p. 39).

Cytologically, as well, this relationship is well supported, and the sections Parryi and Auricula can in fact only be safely separated by microscopical details of the pollen, and by the more frequent occurrence of annulate flowers in the former. Some pairs of species in these two sections resemble each other very closely, for instance *P. integrifolia* and *P. angustifolia*, or *P. deorum* and *P. parryi*.

Out of flower, some Parryi also resemble some *Dodecatheon*, for instance at Zion Canyon where *P. parryi* and *D. zionense* are readily confused in fruit, but DNA studies suggest that *Dodecatheon* may in fact be closer to *P. suffrutescens*.

Modern thinking in the USA after 1993 suggests that *P. ellisiae* is best treated as a subspecies of *P. rusbyi*, and that the localized segregates of *P. cusickiana*, *P. maguirei*, *P. nevadensis* and *P. domensis* are best treated at subspecific rank, although Holmgren and Kelso (2001) have treated them as varieties.

CULTIVATION A section of diverse habit and habitat. Species from summer-wet sites survive well in the open garden although they tend not to flower as they age. Aestivating species from summer-dry sites (*P. cusickiana* group) are however very tricky to grow. All species are probably fully hardy.

Wild hybridization has recently been reported between *P. parryi* and *P. angustifolia*. Miller *et al.* (1994). Holmgren NH, Kelso, S. (2001).

LITERATURE. J. Lunn (1991)
Smith *et al.* (1984).
Holmgren NH, Kelso, S. (2001)

KEY TO SPECIES

1. Calyx without meal 2
1. Calyx with mealy stripes 3

2. Plant robust, 8–40 cm, strongly scented; flowers 5–20 per stem .... *P. parryi*
2. Plant dwarf, to 5 cm, unscented; flowers 1–(4) per stem .... *P. angustifolia*

3. Plant fairly robust, to 20 cm; calyx exceeding 10 mm .... *P. rusbyi*
3. Plant not exceeding 10 cm; calyx less than 10 mm 4

4. Leaves less than 5 mm wide, flowers less than 10 mm in diameter .... *P. capillaris*
4. Leaves more than 5 mm wide; flowers more than 10 mm diameter 5

5. Flowers violet-blue, 1–8 together on a stem 6
5. Flowers rose to lavender, 1–3 together on a stem 7

6. Leaves to 5 cm; flowers with a spreading limb .... *P. cusickiana* ssp. *cusickiana*
6. Leaves to 10 cm; flowers funnel-shaped .... *P. cusickiana* ssp.*nevadensis*

7. Corolla-tube 2× calyx; stem scarcely exceeding leaves .... *P. cusickiana* ssp. *maguirei*
7. Corolla-tube scarcely exceeding calyx; stem exceeding leaves .... *P. cusickiana* ssp. *domensis*

Primula parryi A. Gray, Amer. J. Sci. Arts, 2nd. ser. 34: 257 (1862)

P. mucronata Greene (1897)

DESCRIPTION A robust plant, when well grown amongst the largest of primulas, with a persistent and disgusting sickly resinous scent, lacking meal. *Leaves* slightly sticky, to 33 × 6 cm, entire or slightly toothed, bluntly spear-shaped, graduating into a short winged stalk. *Stems* stout, to 40 cm, bearing up to 20 flowers one-sidedly in one or occasionally two umbels on rather long (to 10 cm) slightly nodding stalks of varying length. *Bracts* narrow, to 15 mm. *Calyx* sticky and usually purplish, tubular, to 15 mm, cut to half into narrow sharp sepal-lobes. *Corolla* magenta to purple with a golden eye, exannulate, the limb saucer-shaped, to 30 mm in diameter; corolla-tube yellowish, slightly longer than the calyx; corolla lobes broad, often overlapping, rounded or slightly and shallowly notched. 2n = 44. (Plates 4, 26.)

DISTRIBUTION Widespread and scattered in the Rocky Mountains of the USA from south-western Montana in the Bitterroot Range through Wyoming, Colorado and New Mexico (Bighorns to Alberquerque); the mountains of the Grand Canyon National Park in Arizona (Humphrey's Peak), Utah above Cedar Breaks, and the mountains of north-eastern Nevada (East Humboldt mountains).

Wet places on mountains, usually above the tree-line; running snow-melt, stream-banks, lake margins and especially on seepage-lines at the base of cliffs, also in boulder-fields; very local but sometimes abundant. 2700–4200 m, not above 3000 m in Montana. Frequently associated with *Caltha leptosepala*.

Miller *et al.* (1994) have investigated the reproductive biology of this species in detail. It is visited by a wide variety of pollinators, including nine *Bombus* species, although predominantly by *B. balteatus*, and even hummingbirds. It usually sets a high proportion of its seed and is abundantly fertile. In its best forms a fine showy primula, distinguished from the other relatively large species in this section, *P. rusbyi,* by the absence of farina and exannulate flowers.

VARIATION Extremely variable in size and vigour both in the wild and cultivation. Plants from exposed snow-melt areas may have leaves to 6 cm and stems to 8 cm, and remain relatively dwarf in cultivation. A gradation of forms is seen in the wild, and they have been given no formal recognition.

Hybrids with *P. angustifolia* were recognized on Mt. Evans at 3700 m in company with both parents by Michael and Polly Stone in 1989.

CULTIVATION Often long-lived in the open garden, particularly when grown in a partially shaded site in peat, but flowers intermittently, and sometimes dies without apparent cause. Easily propagated by division or from seed. Best kept on the dry side in the winter, and very wet in the summer. In cultivation by 1865 (**FCC**), only four years after its discovery by Dr Parry in Colorado.

Primula angustifolia Torrey, Ann. Lyc. New York 1: 34 (1823)

? *P. brodheadae* Jones, Zoe 3: 306 (1892)
P. parryi Pax (1905) and Balf. f. (1913) p.p. non A. Gray

DESCRIPTION A *dwarf* plant, lacking meal, much smaller than the foregoing, and with a superficial resemblance to *P. integrifolia. Leaves* entire, boat-shaped, up to 7 × 1 cm. *Stems* with 1 (–4) flowers, rarely exceeding 1 cm at flowering but elongating in fruit, flower-stalks and bracts slender, to 8 mm. *Calyx* to 8 mm. *Corolla* exannulate, lilac, rose or purple, rarely white, with a yellow eye surrounded by a white zone, flat-faced, up to 20 mm in diameter, sometimes appearing disproportionately large for the plant; corolla lobes shallowly notched and slightly keeled. 2n = 44. (Photo: Bull. Amer. Rock Gdn. Soc. 49: 120–1.) (Plate 4. Fig. 12.)

DISTRIBUTION Rocky Mountains of Colorado and northern New Mexico, overlapping with *P. parryi*. From the Rocky Mountain National Park north of Boulder, southwards to Santa Fe. Intermediate forms with *P. cusickiana* also occur in north Utah and south Idaho (see below).

Above the tree-line in rather wet sites in tundra habitats, e.g. under boulders or in snow-melt hollows; very locally abundant. 2400–4350 m.

According to Miller *et al.* (1994), *P. angustifolia* is visited by a smaller suite of pollinators than *P. parryi,* and sets less seed, doubtless reflecting its adaptation to the extreme tundra habitat.

VARIATION Very variable in stature, flower number and colour. There are some good forms of a rich purple. Plants from New Mexico are generally white-flowered (var. *helenae* Pollard and Cockerell (1902)). Larger plants intermediate with *P. cusickiana*, but lacking meal, and with up to 4 flowers per stem are sometimes separated as *P. brodheadae* Jones; these occur in the mountains north of Salt Lake City, in north Utah and south Idaho, thus forming a geographical as well as a morphological link with *P. cusickiana*. *P. brodheadae* links imperceptibly with *P. angustifolia* southwards, in forms sometimes known as *P. brodheadae* var. *minor* Jones (1892).

CULTIVATION Sometimes long-lived and fairly free-flowering in cultivation, but rarely sets seed; 'plants raised from seed at Edinburgh in 1932 are represented in 1945 by one lone survivor'. It has been reintroduced on several occasions in the 1980s and 1990s. Mostly grown in pots under glass, in a rich gritty mix, nearly dry in winter, but well-watered and never allowed to dry out in summer. Has grown well in troughs, covered in winter, in western Scotland.

Primula rusbyi Greene, Bull. Torrey Bot. Club 8: 122 (1881)

P. serra Small (1898)
P. ellisiae Pollard & Cockerell (1902)

DESCRIPTION Forming modest clumps which disappear completely below ground in winter, and arise rapidly very late in mid-May, to flower within two weeks. *Leaves* to 15 × 3 cm, finely toothed, sticky. *Stems* to 20 cm, mealy above, bearing a one-sided umbel of up to 8 flowers. *Bracts*, to 9 mm and flower-stalks to 4 cm, white-mealy and unequal. *Calyx* cylindrical, to 13 mm, cut to half-way into very narrow sharp brownish sepal-lobes, fringed with meal, and in the lower half forming 10 ridges, alternately brownish and white-mealy. *Corolla* magenta to violet-blue with a yellow eye, annulate, flat-faced, to 30 mm in diameter; corolla-tube equalling the calyx, often yellowish; corolla-lobes broad and overlapping, shallowly to deeply and broadly notched, slightly folded down a centre line. 2n = 44. (Plate 4.)

DISTRIBUTION Subspecies *rusbyi* occurs through the high mountains of south-western New Mexico and south-eastern Arizona, further south than *P. parryi*. From Mt. Wrightson and Chiricahua Peak north-east to the south of the Black Range at Whitewater Baldy. Just to the north at Eagle Peak subsp. *ellisiae* replaces it. Also in Mexico around Flechas, Durango Province, some 800 km to the south, where it seems to be very little-known, and has recently been reported from Guatemala; the only primula occurring in central America.

Above the tree-line in crevices and seepage-lines in shade, particularly at the base of cliffs. 2400–3300 m.

A distinctive medium-sized Parryi species with a white-farinose calyx beautifully tipped by dark calyx-teeth.

VARIATION

● subsp. *ellisiae* (Pollard & Cockerell) Halda (1992) (*Primula ellisiae* Pollard & Cockerell, Proc. Biol. Soc. Washington 15: 178 (1902))

Corolla-tube short, equalling the long calyx, whereas subsp. *rusbyi* has a calyx not exceeding 8 mm, with the corolla-tube 2–3× this length. The flowers of ssp. *ellisiae* are more commonly bluish and larger in diameter with more overlapping petals, but flower colour varies in both subspecies, as does the relative length of the flower tube. Endemic to central New Mexico, apparently restricted to Sandia Peak and the Eagle Peak-Horse Mountain complex.

CULTIVATION Although described only in 1881, by 1884 Dean of Ealing had imported plants into Britain, which were immediately, and perhaps in retrospect rather precipitously, awarded the **FCC**. Although still relatively uncommon in cultivation, the easiest member of the section under glass but has survived more than 10 years for me in the open garden as both subspecies. Initially free-flowering, but often languishing in a vegetative state when older. Needs plenty of water with good drainage in summer, but may be best kept only just moist in winter, although it survives much wetter conditions. Variable from seed, and it is worth selecting a good form which can be an exceptionally beautiful plant, one of the finest of all primulas, particularly as subsp. *ellisiae*.

Primula cusickiana (A. Gray) A. Gray, Synopt. Fl. N. Amer. 2: 399 (1886)

P. angustifolia Torrey var. *cusickiana* A. Gray, Synopt. Fl. N. Amer. 1: 393 (1878)

DESCRIPTION Vegetatively resembles a dwarf *P. parryi,* but with leaves not exceeding 5 × 1 cm, broader and flatter than *P. angustifolia* and sometimes slightly toothed above. The calyx, with alternating purple ridges forming narrow sharp sepal-teeth, and white-mealy sinuses, is similar to *P. ellisiae*, although not exceeding 9 mm. The exannulate flowers are usually a lustrous deep violet with a yellow eye, quite different in colour to the preceding species (a white form is also known), with an elusive violet-like scent. Up to four flowers are borne together on a short stem to 10 cm. Flowering April into early May. (Photo: Bull. Amer. Rock Gdn. Soc. 49: 122–124; Bull. AGS 60: 385.)

DISTRIBUTION Wallowa Mountains, in north-eastern Oregon, and across the Snake River Canyon in adjacent Idaho; north-east and western Utah and north-east Nevada.

South-facing subalpine rocky slopes in saturated glutinous clay or gypsum as the snow melts; further east amongst sagebrush. These sites are later baked brick-hard, and *P. cusickiana* completely disappears (aestivates) until the following spring. 1000–2600 m. However, the subspecies are races from alpine limestone localities at higher altitudes

Geographically and ecologically distinct, *P. cusickiana* nevertheless forms a morphological link between the larger Parryi species, and *P. angustifolia* which is more alpine in character. Although the calyx resembles *P. ellisiae*, the flowers are exannulate, and a most beautiful colour.

CULTIVATION Unfortunately, for it is a most attractive little plant, *P. cusickiana* is one of the most intractable of all species in cultivation. Although success has been reported in western America, it has never been properly established elsewhere. It requires abundant moisture during its short growing season, but must be dried out (but not completely?) when dormant from the early summer to the early spring. 'The main problem is keeping the seedlings growing long enough before they go dormant'; 'mainly a disappearing plant'. It has been suggested that conditions suiting *Dionysia* might be worth trying. However, some of the cliff-dwelling subspecies are less intractable and are dealt with below.

VARIATION

- subsp. *maguirei* (L.O. Williams) Richards (1993) (*Primula maguirei* L.O. Williams, American Midland Naturalist 17: 747 (1936))

Differs from *P. cusickiana* by the corolla rose to lavender with a darker ring surrounding the yellow eye; corolla tube 2× calyx. Ledges and crevices of limestone boulders on the north-facing wall of Logan Canyon, Wasatch Mountains, north-east Utah, 1200–1800 m over 19 km. Genetic studies (Wolf & Sinclair, 1997) have shown that upper-canyon plants have diverged considerably from lower-canyon plants, presumably as a result of genetic isolation and drift in post-glacial times. However, populations and subpopulations show no effects of isolation or inbreeding within themselves. Seed offered through the AGS (1985) resulted in a few plants in cultivation, but not seen after about 1995.

- Subsp. *nevadensis* (N. Holmgren) Richards (1993) (*Primula nevadensis* N. Holmgren, Madrono 19: 27 (1967))

Differs from *P. cusickiana* by the leaves to 10 cm; stems bearing up to 8 rather funnel-shaped violet flowers. Limestone outcrops and scree above 3100 m in the Snake and Grant ranges on the Nevada–Utah border, e.g Mt. Washington, often under *Pinus longaeva*. Flowers late June to early July in the wild. Grown at Kew in 1991 from ARJJ 2609, and persisting in cultivation in very small numbers until at least 2001 in the UK and Oregon.

- Subsp. *domensis* (Kass & Welsh) Halda (1992) (*Primula domensis* R.J. Kass & S.L. Welsh, Great Basin Nat. 45, 3 (1985))

Differs from *P. cusickiana* by the inflorescence overtopping foliage, flowers rose to lavender, the tubes scarcely exceeding the larger calyx; leaves somewhat toothed. House range, western Utah; along limestone rocks and under trees on east-facing slopes, 2450–3000 m. Flowering mid-May to early June in the wild, April in cultivation. Grown at Kew in 1991 from ARJJ 2608, and still fairly widespread in cultivation and occasionally offered in the trade in the UK and western USA, 2001. Apparently the most tractable of the relatives of *P. cusickiana* in cultivation.

Primula capillaris N. & A. Holmgren, Brittonia 26: 313 (1974)

DESCRIPTION Also related to *P. cusickiana*, but tiny, with very narrow upright leaves, not exceeding 5 mm in width and smaller flowers to 8 mm in diameter. Endemic to the Ruby Mountains of east-central Nevada, within the range of *P. parryi*. Turf and mats of *Selaginella* on north-facing slopes in a single locality between 2800 and 3000 m. Not known in cultivation.

Subgenus **Primula**

(Subgenus *Primulastrum* (Duby) Schott (1851))

Section **Primula**

(Section Primulastrum Duby (1844))
(Section Euprimula Schott (1851))
(Section Verbasculum Ruprecht (1863))
(Section Vernales Pax (1889))

DESCRIPTION *Leaves* reticulate and rough, usually hairy, not leathery or fleshy, lacking meal, usually evergreen, toothed, with revolute vernation. *Calyx* ribbed, hairy, sometimes inflated. *Flowers* stemless, or stems bearing small linear bracts and a single umbel of yellow, or more rarely white, pink or purple flowers with a yellow eye, heterostylous, annulate. *Pollen* subglobose to oblate, stephanocolpate (with 6–10 furrows). *Capsules* included in the calyx, opening by 5 valves x = 11. Self-incompatible. Flowering from January to June in the wild, from November to May in cultivation.

DISTRIBUTION Western Eurasia, and Siberia from Norway to the Atlas Mountains, eastwards to the Amur on the Siberian/Manchurian border. Woodlands, grasslands and mountain habitats in temperate and boreal zones.

This section is composed of three very familiar species, the primrose, cowslip and the oxlip, and three purple-flowered Caucasian species. Although most authors place *P. juliae* in a section Julia, and *P. megaseifolia* and *P. renifolia* in a section Megaseifolia, five of these species have been shown to be interfertile, and they share an unusual pollen type, so I have placed them in the same section, and this is supported by the DNA. DNA studies have also shown that highly divergent *P. grandis* (*Sredinskya grandis*) which is mealy and bears tube-shaped flowers with long-exserted stigmas (but the same unusual pollen type) is embedded within this section. However, it is not known to hybridize with the other species and is so divergent in a number of morphological features, that I have placed it in its own section.

The primrose, cowslip and oxlip all have vast distributional ranges, are exceedingly variable, and have been split into a number of subspecies, which are treated as species by Flora SSSR.

Traditionally, these plants have been called the 'Vernales' primulas, but under current nomenclatural law, the type species of *Primula*, which is the cowslip, *P. veris* L., should form the type of a section which bears the same name as the genus.

The section takes a rather isolated position in the genus. It seems likely that the ancestors of section Primula had an Asiatic origin, migrating westwards into Europe. Although the pollen type is distinctive, most of the other features are shared by members of such sections as Auganthus and Davidii.

CULTIVATION Cowslips and primroses were amongst the earliest of all decorative garden plants;

by the sixteenth century they were very familiar, and much developed and hybridized. Both species and their hybrids are vigorous, free-flowering and long-lived, although preferring fertile, moisture-retentive soils which are not too acidic, and relatively cool conditions. Clones are prone to cucumber mosaic virus, while in some areas vine weevil and root aphis can be severe pests.

HYBRIDIZATION Extensive observations on hybridization in the wild, and experimental investigations of hybridization in cultivation have been carried out, particularly by the late David Valentine and his students such as Stan Woodell, H.T. Clifford, Christine Maxwell, Judy Burrows and myself. Much of the work has concerned British populations of the primrose, cowslip and oxlip.

It has been shown that species tend to be separated by a seed incompatibility. This is controlled by the innate growth rates of the embryo and the endosperm in the seed. Because the endosperm has two maternal sets of chromosomes, but only one paternal set, it tends to adopt maternal characteristics more than the embryo which has one set from each parent. Of these three species, the oxlip seeds develop the most slowly and those of the cowslip the most quickly. In hybrid seed, where the oxlip is the mother, the embryo outgrows the endosperm and dies of starvation. Where the cowslip is the mother, the endosperm smothers the embryo (Woodell, 1960).

Each of the three species is also separated at least in part by flowering time and/or ecology ('ecospecies'). However, where habitat preferences overlap, usually as the result of disturbance by man, widespread hybridization can occur. Primroses and cowslips can only cross with the cowslip as the female parent. Hybridization is especially prevalent in northern Britain, where differences in flowering time and habitat are minimized. Hybrids are vigorous and fertile, but backcrossing is limited in most localities, and seems to occur more in the direction of the cowslip.

Primroses and oxlips flower at the same time, but are usually separated by habitat. Coppicing has brought the species together in eastern England, and hybridization is locally abundant where the populations meet (*P.* × *digenea*). Hybrids are fairly fertile, and extensive backcrossing and even introgression in the absence of one parent is frequently detected.

Cowslips and oxlips rarely occur together, flower at different times, and cross with great difficulty, so that hybrids (*P.* × *media*) are extremely rare. The few that have been discovered proved to be triploid.

Most garden hybrids in this group are based on *P.* × *polyantha* (so-called 'polyanthus' primulas), the cross between the primrose and the cowslip. These hybrids were already extensively grown in the sixteenth century, by which time pink, red and purple colours had been introduced, presumably from the pink-flowered *P. vulgaris* subsp. *sibthorpii* and subsp. *heterochroma* from Greece eastwards. Hybrids between stemmed species such as the cowslip and oxlip, and stemless species such as the primrose are mostly stemmed, but tend to throw some basal flowers, indicating that the genetic control for this feature shows incomplete dominance.

Following the discovery of *P. juliae* in 1900, extensive hybridization was carried out with *P. vulgaris* and *P.* × *polyantha* to give rise to the 'juliana' primulas (*P.* × *pruhoniciana*).

Hybrids have also been raised between *P. megaseifolia* and *P. vulgaris*, and between *P. juliae* and *P. elatior*. The latter cross, which tends to resemble *P. elatior* subsp. *meyeri*, is currently quite popular as the clone 'David Valentine'.

It is probable that some hybrid clones of a 'polyanthus' type, for instance 'Lady Greer' and 'McWatt's Cream' also have *P. elatior* as a parent.

Although well over 120 named hybrid clones are known in this group, many are now rare or extinct as a result of virus. Plants in this group are best replenished from seed from time to time, and these days popular strains have largely replaced the clones. Some of these strains, such the popular 'Pacific Giant' strains, developed in western north America, are spectacular, vigorous plants with a dwarf habit, and very large flowers with a magnificent range of good blue, red and pink colours. They are extremely popular for bedding schemes, and as pot plants, and form the basis of a large industry.

Other well-known strains include the Garryard strains and clones, developed in Eire, all of which have bronzed foliage and red stems, and the Barnhaven strain, originating from Florence Bellis's work on the Canadian Cowichan polyanthus in the USA and developed in Lancashire, which tend to have velvety eyeless flowers. There is a good account of primrose hybrids and varieties in Robinson (1990).

LITERATURE. Smith *et al.* (1984).
Richards (1989)
Woodell (1960)

KEY TO SPECIES

1. Flowers borne basally 2
1. Flowers borne on stems 4

2. Stems creeping; leaves glabrous, waxy; flowers deep purple .... *P. juliae*
2. Rosette-forming; leaves hairy, at least on edges; flowers not usually deep purple 3

3. Leaf-blades truncate at base, white-woolly beneath; flowers blue-violet .... *P. renifolia*
3. Leaf-blades graduating to stalk, rarely white-woolly beneath; flowers rarely blue-violet .... *P. vulgaris*

4. Leaf-blades not more than 1.5 times as long as wide; flowers purple .... *P. megaseifolia*
4. Leaf-blades more than 1.5 times as long as wide; flowers yellow, blue or purple 5

5. Flowers nodding to one side; plant covered with short crisped hairs (use a lens) .... *P. elatior*
5. Flowers not noticeably one-sided; hairs not crisped 6

6. Flowers yellow; calyx baggy .... *P. veris*
6. Flowers blue-violet; calyx narrowly cylindrical .... *P. renifolia*

Primula veris L., Sp. Pl. 1: 142 (1753) "Cowslip"

P. columnae Ten. (1811)
P. cordifolia Rupr. (1863) non Schur.
P. cordifolia Schur. (1886) non Rupr.
P. coronaria Salisb. (1796)
P. discolor Schur. (1886) non Leyb.
P. domestica Hoffm.
P. inflata Duby (1844) non Lehm.
P. inflata Lehm. (1817) non Duby
P. legionensis Willmot (1929)
P. macrocalyx Bunge (1829)
P. montana Reuter (1881) non Opiz
P. officinalis (L.) Hill (1764)
P. pannonica Kerner (1886)
P. praticola Fritsch. (1922) non Craib
P. pyrenaica Miegev. (1868)
P. suaveolens Bertol. (1813)
P. uralensis Fischer
P. velenowskyi (Domin) Fritsch. (1922)

DESCRIPTION *Leaves* prostrate to suberect, to 20 × 6 cm, leaf-blade rounded, coarsely and irregularly toothed, abruptly or gradually contracted to form a narrowly winged stalk about one-third the length of the leaf. *Stem* firm, minutely greyish-hairy, to 30 cm, bearing up to 16 slightly drooping flowers on unequal stalks up to 20 mm. *Calyx* broadly bell-shaped, baggy, pale-green, shortly hairy, cut to $^1/_3$ into triangular sepal-lobes. *Corolla* golden-yellow with an orange to reddish spot at the base of each lobe, the limb cup-shaped to flat-faced, up to 30 mm in diameter; corolla-tube equalling or exceeding the calyx; petal-lobes broad, overlapping, shallowly notched. 2n = 22. Pins 14% self-fertile, but thrums only 0.6% self-fertile. (Plate 5.)

DISTRIBUTION One of the most widespread of all primulas, occurring from Norway and Ireland to south-east Spain, northern Greece, Turkey, the Caucasus and Iran eastwards through Siberia to the Amur north of Manchuria, and not far from the Pacific coast, a total range of 9000 km. Absent from Africa, the extreme south of Europe and the Mediterranean islands, Iceland, northern Siberia and much of the drier areas of central Asia.

Well-drained neutral to basic grasslands or scrub, more rarely in light woodland, from sea-level to about 3000 m.

The cowslip is amongst the most familiar of all European plants, beloved of poets such as Shakespeare who likened the reddish spots at the petal-bases to rubies, and who correctly identified the main pollinator as bees ('where the bee sucks, there suck I/ In a cowslips' bell I lie'). Flowering chiefly in May, cowslips are usually efficiently visited, and in most areas, seed-set is good despite the requirement for cross-pollination.

Formerly common in old meadows and pastures in much of England (except the south-west; it is also much more local in Wales, Scotland and Ireland), it became scarcer during the twentieth century through grassland 'improvement' and habitat destruction. Cowslips also suffered from heavy picking, not least for an excellent wine which is made from the flowers. After the 1980s the species has made a notable comeback, largely because its seeds are usually included in 'amenity seed-mixes'. As a result, it is nowadays often seen on road and motorway verges, and urban conservation areas, often in large, dense stands.

The cowslip is unlikely to be confused with any other primula with the possible exception of the oxlip. The latter species has pale yellow flowers with diffuse orange markings, a narrow calyx, and the hairs throughout are crisped, rather than straight as in the cowslip (this character requires a lens).

VARIATION

- Subsp. *veris*. Leaf-blade abruptly contracted into the stalk, usually shortly hairy beneath; calyx not exceeding 15 mm; corolla cup-shaped, to 12 mm diameter; corolla-tube equalling the calyx. Throughout the range of the species, excepting the mountains of central and southern Europe, Turkey, the Caucasus and south-central Asia.
- Subsp. *canescens* (Opiz) Hayek in Hegi, Fl. Mitt.-Eur. 5: 1752 (1927). Leaf-blade gradually narrowed into the stalk, grey-hairy beneath; calyx 16–20 mm; corolla shallowly bowl-shaped, 8–20 mm in diameter; corolla-tube equalling the calyx. Alps, Pyrenees and mountains of northern Spain.
- Subsp. *columnae* (Ten.) Ludi in Hegi, loc. cit. (including subsp. *suaveolens* (Bertol.) Gutermk. & Ehrend (1973)). Leaf-blade abruptly contracted into the stalk, plastered white-hairy beneath; calyx 16–20 mm; corolla flat-faced, 10–22 mm in diameter; corolla-tube exceeding the calyx. Mountains of central Spain, central Italy, northern Greece and north-east Turkey.
- Subsp. *macrocalyx* (Bunge) Ludi in Hegi, loc. cit.. Leaf-blade gradually narrowed into the stalk, grey-hairy to hairless beneath; calyx conical, 15–20 mm, very hairy; corolla flat-faced, 18–28 mm in diameter; corolla-tube exceeding the calyx. South-east Russia, Caucasus and south-central Asia, extending to east Siberia.

CULTIVATION All four subspecies are sometimes found in gardens. Subsp. *veris* is perhaps the least spectacular, but is very suitable for naturalizing in rough grass, etc. Subsp. *columnae* is perhaps the most attractive race for culture in specialized conditions, and it is a suitable and easy subject for the rock garden, or even as a pot plant for exhibition purposes. It is worth selecting a good form as seed of garden origin often has a mixed parentage. Subsp. *macrocalyx*, despite having the largest flowers, lacks the charm of the others, and often resembles a poor form of 'polyanthus'.

HYBRIDIZATION See under the sectional heading. Strains with red flowers, otherwise resembling subsp. *veris*, are sometimes grown, often known as 'Canadian cowslips'. As reddish colours are not known in wild cowslips, these presumably originate from backcrossing to red forms of the primrose.

The garden cross with *P. vulgaris*, *P.* × *polyantha* Miller, the 'polyanthus' primula shows pin self-fertility of 9% and thrum self-fertility of 8%, thus falling between its parents for this characteristic.

Primula elatior (L.) Hill, Veg. Syst. 8: 25 (1764) OXLIP

P. alpestris Schur (1852)
P. amoena M.Bieb. (1808)
P. amoena Bieb. subsp. *lazica* Schwarz (1968)
P. amoena Bieb. var. *meyeri* (Rupr.) Boiss.(1879)
P. amoena Bieb. subsp. *meyeri* (Rupr.) Smith & Forrest (1928)
P. ambigua Salisb. (1796)
P. carpathica Fuss. (1831)
P. columnae Schur. non Ten.
P. cordifolia Rupr. (1863) non Schur.
P. crenata Salzer (1860) non Fuss nec Lam.
P. danubialis Richter (1888)
P. fluggeana Lehm. (1808)
P. hispanica Willmot (1929)
P. intricata Gren. & Godr. (1853)
P. kusnetsovii Federov (1952)
P. leucophylla Pax (1897)
P. lofthousei Heslop-Harrison (1929)
P. meyeri Rupr. (1863)
P. montana Opiz (1825) non Reuter
P. oblongifolia Schur (1866)
P. pallasii Lehm. (1817)
P. poloninensis (Domin.) Federov (1952)
P. pseudoelatior Kusn. (1900)
P. rhododendricola Sennen (1936)
P. ruprechtii Kusn. (1899)
P. veris L. var. *elatior* L. (1753)

DESCRIPTION The whole plant is usually covered with very short, crisped hairs. *Leaves* up to 20 × 7 cm, usually abruptly contracted to a virtually unwinged stalk, sometimes gradually narrowed, rounded at the tip, finely toothed. *Stem* to 30 cm, stiff, bearing up to 12 flowers in a one-sided drooping umbel on flower-stalks of varying lengths, to 20 mm. *Calyx* tubular, to 15 mm, yellowish with five green ridges, cut to a half into pointed sepal-lobes. *Corolla* pale to bright (but never golden) yellow, or purple in subspecies *meyeri,* with diffuse greenish to orange throat markings, saucer-shaped to flat-faced, to 25 mm in diameter; corolla-tube exceeding calyx; corolla-lobes broad, overlapping, shallowly and widely v-notched. The mature fruit exceeds the calyx, unlike the cowslip and primrose. 2n = 22. Pins fully self-sterile; thrums 1% self-fertile. (Plate 5.)

DISTRIBUTION From south Sweden (one locality), eastern England, and central Spain eastwards to the Ukraine, eastern Turkey, northern Iran, the Altai and Siberia, with isolated ocurrences in southern Spain, the Italian Apennines, and the Urals. Absent from northern Europe, the Mediterranean islands and Greece.

In north-west Europe restricted to wet, shaded woodland, but elsewhere found in a variety of habitats from alpine grassland and late snow-lie patches to scrub by rivers and steppic grassland. Survives hotter drier summers than its relatives. Sea-level to 4000 m.

The oxlip is a much less familiar British plant than its relatives, being highly localized to broad-leaved woodland, usually oak standard with coppice hazel understorey, on wet chalky boulder clay in East Anglia, centred on the borders of Cambridgeshire, Suffolk and Essex. Although rarely found elsewhere in the UK, it is probably always a garden escape there. Plants called 'oxlips' in other areas usually prove to be *P.* × *polyantha* (primrose × cowslip hybrids) which can superficially resemble the true oxlip. The latter is always known by the short crisped hairs throughout (use a lens), by the strictly one-sided inflorescence, and by the exserted seed-pod.

Within the restricted British range, oxlips became scarcer during the twentieth century due to habitat destruction. Originally they seem to have rarely coexisted with primroses, preferring wetter, more shaded habitats. However, perhaps as a result of coppicing, mixed populations now occur in some areas, where there is a danger of primroses 'hybridizing oxlips out of existence'. Many hybrids but few true oxlips can be found today in these areas. However, the oxlip remains pure and locally abundant in some areas, and it has been suggested that there was something of a comeback during the 1980s.

Like the cowslip, oxlips are largely visited by hive bees and long-tongued bumble-bees. Despite the early flowering period (usually April in England) and the requirement for cross-pollination, seed-set is usually good.

Oxlips are locally abundant in the Alps and Pyrenees, where they flower very early, often as the snow melts. However, they are mostly confined to limestone districts, and are frequently absent from apparently suitable habitat.

VARIATION

- Subsp. *elatior*. Leaves hairy, the blade abruptly narrowed, toothed. Flowers usually many on a stem, sulphur yellow, to 25 mm in diameter. Throughout much of the range, except where replaced by the following.
- Subsp. *intricata* (Gren. & Godr.) Ludi in Hegi, Fl. Mitt.-Eur. 3: 1748 (1927) (includes subsp. *carpathica* (Fuss) Smith & Forrest, 1928). Leaves hairy, the blade gradually narrowed into the stalk, almost entire. Flowers few to a stem (up to 7), bright yellow, flat-faced, to 20 mm in diameter. Mountains of southern Europe, including the Pyrenees, southern Carpathians, Apennines and Dolomites, but excluding the rest of the Alps and the Sierra Nevada.
- Subsp. *leucophylla* (Pax) Heslop-Harrison. Trans. North. Nat. Union 1:49 (1931). (subsp. *ruprechtii* (Kusn.) Heslop-Harrison (loc. cit)). Leaves deciduous, appearing with the flowers, initially grey-hairy, gradually narrowed into a stalk, minutely rounded-toothed to entire. Flowers few to a stem, pale yellow, funnel-shaped, to 16 mm in diameter. Eastern Carpathians of Roumania and the Caucasus region.
- Subsp. *lofthousei* (J. Heslop-Harrison) Smith & Fletcher, Trans. Bot. Soc. Edin. 34: 423 (1948). Differs from subsp. *intricata* by the many-flowered heads of smaller flowers of a deep butter yellow. Endemic to the Sierra Nevada of southern Spain.
- Subsp. *meyeri* (Rupr.) Valentine & Lamond, Notes Roy. Bot. Gdn. Ednb. 36: 42 (1978). (*P. amoena* M. Bieb. (1808)). Very variable, encompassing much of the variability of the species, and sometimes divided into the three species *P.*

amoena, *P. meyeri* and *P. kusnetsovii* (Federov, 1952) or into six varieties (Smith *et al.*, 1984: 17), but always blue to purple flowered. Pontus of north-eastern Turkey, and the entire Caucasus range, always in the mountains. Valentine & Lamond (1978) show that 'P. amoena' is interfertile with the other subspecies of oxlip, but not with other relatives, and it differs from the oxlip in little except flower colour. When including it in *P. elatior*, they chose the epithet 'meyeri' rather than the more familiar 'amoena', as *meyeri* had previously been used at subspecific rank.

- Subsp. *pallasii* (Lehm.) Smith & Forrest 16: 42 (1928). Leaves hairless or nearly so, gradually contracted into the stalk, coarsely toothed. Flowers few to a stem, to 25 mm in diameter, pale yellow. The eastern part of the range of the species, from Turkey (Anatolia) and northern Iran to the Urals, the Altai, and east Siberia.
- Subsp. *cordifolia* (Rupr.) Smith & Forrest loc.cit.. A neat plant with relatively smooth, bronze-green, hairless leaves abruptly contracted to a long narrow stalk. Stems dark, contrasting beautifully with the luminous lemon yellow flowers. Caucasus and Armenia, usually at lower levels from subsp. *meyeri* and completely distinct from it.
- Subsp. *pseudoelatior* (Kusn.) Smith & Forrest loc. cit.. Differs from subsp. *elatior* chiefly by the heart-shaped leaf-blades and hairier leaves. North-eastern Turkey and the Caucasus.

CULTIVATION All oxlips make splendid rock garden plants, although they are less suitable than cowslips or primroses for naturalizing, being less vigorous in most garden conditions. Subsp. *elatior* and *pseudoelatior* (**AM** 1994) are perhaps the best choice.

However, several of the subspecies are well worth growing on their own account, having distinctive personalities and considerable charm. Some are choice and difficult to obtain, and may be best treated as specimen plants in pots. The initially dwarf subsp. *leucophylla*, flowering as it emerges from the ground in the early spring like a bulb, the slow and fascinating subsp. *cordifolia* with its delightful colour combinations, and the superb purple subsp. *meyeri* are amongst the most distinguished of all primulas, and should be grown much more often.

HYBRIDIZATION See sectional account. Hybridizes frequently with the primrose where the two meet in the wild, and some gardens now boast impressive hybrid swarms between these species, especially in Scotland. A hybrid with *P. juliae* has been obtained more than once (Bot. Mag. 171: 302 (1956–57)). A magnificent clone resulting from this cross was raised by David Valentine in about 1968 and was maintained by his ex-student Judy Burrows who named it after the raiser. This is an extremely vigorous and robust plant with plum-purple flowers. **AM** 2001. Hybrids have also been raised with *P. megaseifolia*.

Primula vulgaris Hudson, Fl. Anglica: 70 (1762) PRIMROSE

P. abschasica Sosn. (1938)
P. acaulis (L.) Hill (1764)
P. bicolor Rafinesque (1810)
P. grandiflora Lam. (1778)
P. heterochroma Stapf (1885)
P. hybrida Schrank (1789)
P. komarovii Losink. (1933)
P. officinalis L. var. *acaulis* L. (1753)
P. sibthorpii Hoffm. (1824)
P. uniflora Gmelin (1805)
P. veris L. var. *acaulis* L. (1753)
P. woronovii Losink. (1933)

DESCRIPTION *Leaves* to 25 × 6 cm, shorter at flowering, oblong, rounded at the tip, gradually narrowing to the short, broadly winged stalk, irregularly toothed, hairless above, shortly hairy beneath on veins. *Stem* absent; flowers borne basally on shaggy stalks to 20 cm, erect to nodding, up to 25 together. *Calyx* tubular, strongly 5-ribbed, often pinkish with green ribs, long-hairy, cut to a half into narrow pointed sepal-lobes. *Corolla* primrose-yellow (!), with dull diffuse orange marks at the base, less commonly white, pink, red or purple; heterostylous or rarely homostylous, flat-faced, to 40 mm in diameter; corolla-tube equalling calyx; corolla-lobes broad, overlapping, shallowly and widely notched. *Fruit* shorter than the calyx. 2n = 22. Pins 62% self-fertile, thrums completely self-sterile. (Plate 5.)

DISTRIBUTION Southern Norway, Denmark, the British Isles, France, northern and western Iberia,

Italy, Yugoslavia, Greece, south-west and northern Turkey, south-west Ukraine, the Crimea, Caucasus and southern shores of the Caspian Sea. Most of the larger Mediterranean islands, but absent from Sardinia and Cyprus. North Africa from Gibraltar to Tunisia (only one of two primulas native to Africa), Syria, Lebanon and Israel.

Prefers habitats which are cool and humid in summer, and relatively mild in winter, thus showing a largely Atlantic and Mediterranean distribution, and often submaritime in marginal areas. Usually in open woodland, often on banks, but in more northerly areas also in north-facing grasslands. Avoids light or very acidic soils, and heavy waterlogging. Sea-level to 2400 m, but not usually exceeding 1500 m in Europe.

The primrose is one of the best-known and loved plants within its native areas. Often known as a harbinger of spring, it is so familiar that it is used to describe the colour of paint and sunsets, and as a Christian name.

Curiously, its scientific name is much less settled. Linnaeus' epithet *acaulis* first appears in a list without diagnosis or rank in *Flora Anglica*. This publication predates Hudson's *vulgaris* by nine years, but there is a considerable dispute as to which rank Linnaeus considered it took. As Linnaeus subsequently used *acaulis* only at varietal rank, current opinion suggests that it should not be considered to form the basionym for this species. Although this decision is now enshrined in *Flora Europaea*, this species is still usually called *P. acaulis* in non-English-speaking areas.

Primroses are still locally abundant in many parts of the British Isles, but in many other parts of the large range they are local and scarce. In Britain, they were dug up for sale in street markets for centuries, and this deprivation, together with habitat loss, rendered them scarce, particularly in urban areas where they often only survived on railway embankments. Since 1975, the uprooting of primroses (or any other plant) became illegal in Britain, and after some prosecutions, street trading virtually ceased. As a result, primroses became noticeably more common again during the 1980s.

Unlike its relatives, primrose seed is provided with a gelatinous outgrowth ('elaiosome') which is attractive to ants which scavenge the seeds, and carry them to their nests. Consequently, seedlings are frequently found clustered around old ant nests.

Unlike cowslips and oxlips which are mostly cross-pollinated by bees, primroses are visited by a wide range of long-tongued insects such as syrphids, bee-flies and even butterflies and moths, although successful visits are also made by long-tongued bumble-bees. Flowering early in the season, from March to May (June in the far north), visiting can be spasmodic, and in some seasons primroses set very little seed.

VARIATION The primrose shows remarkably little variation through much of its considerable range. However, in the south and east of its distribution, three subspecies are delimited.

- Subsp. *vulgaris*. Leaves green beneath, stalk short. Flowers yellow. Throughout the range of the species, excepting the regions listed below.
- Subsp. *balearica* (Willk.) Smith & Forrest, Notes Roy. Bot. Gdn. Edinb. 16: 42 (1928). Leaves green beneath, stalk long, exceeding the blade. Flowers white. Mountains of Mallorca, chiefly on the north side of Puig Major above 1000 m. Similar plants can be found in north Africa.
- Subsp. *heterochroma* (Stapf) Smith & Forrest loc. cit. Leaves whitish-hairy beneath. Flowers violet, purple, red, pink, white or yellow. South shore of the Caspian Sea (Elburz Mountains), Iran and Azerbaijan, in a disjunct area.
- Subsp. *sibthorpii* (Hoffm.) Smith & Forrest loc. cit. (subsp. *ingwerseniana* Heslop-Harrison 1930). Leaves grey-green beneath, often contracted to a distinct stalk almost as long as the blade. Flowers purple, lilac, red, pink or white, only very rarely yellow. Northern and central Greece (but not the Peloponnese or Crete), Turkey, Crimea, Caucasus and Armenia. In Turkey, grows at lower levels than subsp. *vulgaris*. On the Black Sea coast of the Caucasus, there is an abrupt change from yellow-flowered to red flowered plants near Sochi. Plants from the eastern shore of the Mediterranean are nearly always white in colour.

Unlike its relatives, the primrose has given rise to a vast range of variants in cultivation, quite apart from its hybrids. Floral mutants such as doubles (*flore pleno*) and semi-doubles, 'Hose-in-hose' (petaloid calyx), 'Jack in the green' (leaf-like calyx), and colour breaks such as gold and silver-laced petals were popular in Elizabethan times, and persist to today in a large range of strains and clones. The genetics of some of the calyx mutants are discussed in Webster & Grant, Heredity 64: 121–4 (1990).

These so-called 'old-fashioned primroses' became increasingly popular towards the end of the twentieth century, and a number of commercial outlets, and at least two specialist societies, are dedicated to their culture. Lists of some of the many cultivars presently available will be found in Smith *et al.* (1984: 192–197) and Robinson (1990).

The wild plant varies in vigour, and in flower size. Where plants self-sow it is well-worth weeding out poor forms. In this way spectacular large-flowered strains can be perpetuated.

CULTIVATION An easy, even invasive plant in many gardens, but recalcitrant or even impossible in others. It seems to respond to fertile, heavy soils of a neutral or basic reaction in cultivation, especially when grown in dappled light, and will often do well in almost pure clay. In these circumstances it will tolerate a good deal of drought and desiccation in summer, the leaves becoming very limp, and often disappearing entirely in a hot spell. In parts of its Mediterranean range it can aestivate for up to three months. However, in light soils, very acidic soils, or when provided with too much drainage, exposure or direct sunshine, it will die. Most successful where it seeds around, and also responds well to frequent division. Old plants are susceptible to virus, root-aphis and weevils, and clones can prove difficult to keep.

Subsp. *sibthorpii* is an easy and vigorous plant very suitable for the woodland garden, which however rarely seeds around. White forms from the eastern Mediterranean (Syria and Lebanon) seem often to be vigorous in British conditions, multiplying rapidly. Subsp. *balearica* is rare in cultivation, but appears to be slow growing and temperamental. It may be resentful of winter damp and excessive cold, and is best grown in a shady frame or cold house. There seems to be little news of subsp. *heterochroma* in cultivation.

HYBRIDIZATION See sectional account. Sometimes hybridizes extensively with cowslips, and with oxlips in the wild (rarely overlaps with oxlips except in eastern England). In cultivation, perhaps the most significant parent in primula, having spawned a major horticultural industry through its hybrids with cowslips and *P. juliae*.

The Caucasian 'species' *P. abchasica*, *P. komarovii* and *P. woronowii* are considered to represent hybrid segregates between subsp. *vulgaris* and subsp. *sibthorpii*.

Primula megaseifolia Boiss. & Bal., Fl. Orient. 4: 26 (1875)

DESCRIPTION Forms stout, horizontally creeping stocks from which arise clusters of thickish purplish bud-scales and suberect young leaves borne once a year in early spring shortly after flowering which later lie horizontally on the ground and persist for 12 months. *Leaf*-blades initially lime-green and soft, later dark green and leathery, kidney-shaped, to 15 × 12 cm, margins entire or with regular short rounded teeth, hairless and rather smooth above, shortly hairy below; leaf-stalks reddish, sheathing, clothed with long black hairs, to 10 cm. *Stems* stout, green, hairy below, to 20 cm , bearing 1 (–3) whorls of up to 9 flowers on very short stalks. *Calyx* tubular, 5-ridged, purple, to 15 mm, cut to one-third into sharp sepal-lobes. *Corolla* pink to purple with a cream eye deepening to yellow in the centre, rather funnel-shaped, to 25 mm in diameter; corolla-tube exceeding the calyx, yellowish; petal-lobes not overlapping, widest near the tip, with a deep and broad v-shaped notch. 2n = 22. (Plate 5.)

DISTRIBUTION Endemic to the south-eastern corner of the Black Sea on the Turkish/Georgian border between Trabzon (Trebizond) and Batumi, over some 130 km, confined to regions close to the coast.

Mossy humid gullies in full shade associated with *Rhododendron ponticum* under species-rich beech forest in an extremely wet region which also receives heavy snow-falls in winter. 50–1100 m. Apparently local and scarce in the wild.

P. megaseifolia is a most distinctive and unusual species. Although the flowers are unexceptionable, and in some forms not very attractive, the foliage and growth habit is quite unlike any other species, having the appearence of some saxifrages (section Geum), Geums, or indeed *Bergenia* (formerly known as Megasea). Although not the easiest species to grow, nor the most attractive, it is an interesting addition to a specialist collection.

VARIATION Variable in the size and colour of the flowers in cultivation. There are presently some good forms, especially in Scottish gardens, with large well-formed flowers of a clear pink and an almost flat face which are preferable to the commoner magenta forms and are worth seeking.

CULTIVATION Relatively uncommon in cultivation, although in some gardens, notably the Saville Garden, Windsor Great Park, it is grown in quantity. Long-lived in shaded, rich, moisture-retentive but well-drained sites, but rarely sets seed, probably because only one clone is usually grown. Unlike most primulas it seems to resent disturbance, and takes some time to settle down and flower after replanting. Foliage is damaged by slugs and heavy frost, and as leaves are only produced annually, the plant tends to look very untidy at flowering time.

HYBRIDIZATION Experiments by D. H. Valentine, Christine Maxwell and Jackie Langton in the mid-1960s showed that sterile hybrids with primroses and fertile hybrids with oxlips can be raised with difficulty. Similar hybrids with primroses have since been raised by Lawrence Wigley, the late Gerry Mundey, and Edward Needham. They are pink-flowered and retain the early-flowering habit. Although they are well spoken-of, those I grew were disappointing and lacking in vigour.

Valentine and co-workers also raised *P. megaseifolia* × *P. juliae*. A similar hybrid, *P.* × 'John Fielding' (**PC** 1990) has been backcrossed to *P. juliae* to give *P.* × 'Barbara Midwinter' (**PC** 1992) and both are still seen in 2001. No wild hybrids have been reported.

Primula renifolia Volg., Bot. Mat. Gerb. Bot. Inst. Kom. Akad. Nauk. SSSR 8: 111 (1940)

DESCRIPTION Probably closely related to *P. megaseifolia*, but presenting a quite different appearance. Differs by being very much smaller, the leaf-blades not exceeding 5 cm, strongly wrinkled above and densely white-woolly beneath. Often virtually stemless at flowering, the stem elongates in fruit but does not exceed the leaves, bearing 1–3 flowers on slender flower-stalks of about 2 cm. Corolla blue-violet with a yellow eye, flat-faced and disproportionately large, up to 30 mm in diameter; corolla-tube at least 2× the calyx; corolla-lobes broad, overlapping, shallowly and quite narrowly notched. 2n = 22. Colour photo in Burrow *et al.* (1984: plate 57). (Plate 5.)

DISTRIBUTION Endemic to the north-western Caucasus, Dombai mountains, around the Teberda valley in the Cherkessk province south of Stavropol, 200 km north of *P. megaseifolia*.

Wet mossy forest, north-facing alpine banks, around waterfalls, etc., in mixed beech or pine forest, 1200–2100 m. Locally abundant.

P. renifolia is a quite delightful dwarf species with a character all of its own. Although frequently stated to be very close to, or even a dwarf form of *P. megaseifolia*, and not accepted by Smith and Fletcher (1948), we can now state firmly that it is totally distinct, and indeed takes a rather isolated morphological position. Horticulturally, it is a far finer species than *P. megaseifolia*. Unfortunately, however, the single introduction to date is nearly lost to cultivation, and a new incursion is badly needed. Being very dwarf and slow, and with very large virtually stemless flowers of a luminous lilac-blue, it is an ideal subject for the alpine specialist.

CULTIVATION Introduced into the UK in 1982 from Leningrad Botanical Garden. **PC** 1986. Only one thrum clone is presently cultivated in the UK, and so propagation has been by division which proved very slow. Initially it presented few problems grown in pots in the alpine house in a well-drained but water-retentive compost, but plants have latterly lost vigour and in 2002 one plant remains. It is fully hardy and flowers freely in late March. No hybrids are known.

Primula juliae Kusnetsow, Trady Bot. Sada Imp. Jur'evsk Univ. 1: 67 (1899)

DESCRIPTION A dwarf *deciduous* rather waxy creeping plant lacking meal and hairs and forming mats of small pinkish resting buds at the soil surface, from which arise leaves before flowering, as early as January. Leaf-blade broadly *kidney*-shaped, slightly wider than long, up to about 3 cm, rather shiny dark green and thin in texture, coarsely and regularly toothed; leaf-stalk narrow, pink, longer than the blade. Stems absent; flowers borne laterally to the rosette directly from a fork in the creeping stock in groups of 1–5 on erect pink stalks which exceed the leaf-stalks. *Calyx* narrowly tubular, pink to purple, 5-ribbed, cut to about one-third into narrow sharp sepal-lobes. *Corolla* bright magenta-purple with a yellow eye, funnel-shaped, exannulate, heterostylous, to 30 mm in diameter; corolla-tube narrow, whitish-yellow, twice the length of the calyx; corolla-lobes narrow, not overlapping, with a rather deep v-shaped notch. *Pollen* oblate, stephanocolpate. Capsules narrow, exceeding the calyx, opening by 5 valves. 2n = 22. ?Fully self-incompatible. Flowering March–April in cultivation. (Plate 5.)

DISTRIBUTION Fairly widespread in the eastern half of the Caucasus, in Georgia from Osetia eastwards, including parts of Dagestan (Pala-Kata gorge) and Azerbaijan (Nukha district, e.g. Damir-Aporon-Chai gorge).

Wet mossy rocks, often near rivers, in montane forests. 700–1800 m.

The Caucasus were amongst the last mountain ranges of the world to be explored botanically. Thus it was not until 1897 that this relatively widespread, accessible and conspicuous primula was discovered by the eponymous Professor Julia Mlokossjewicz (or Mlokosewitch) in the region of what is today the Lagodekh Gorge National Park. On the same expedition, two other notable garden plants, *Paeonia mlokosewitchii* and *Gentiana lagodechiana*, were discovered and introduced to cultivation.

P. juliae is a distinctive and delightful little primula which is very suitable for open-ground cultivation. Curiously, it is seldom grown, although it is long lived and not difficult in suitable conditions, and is easily propagated by division. Nevertheless, it has become extensively naturalized on the banks above a reservoir not far from Glasgow, Scotland (Peter MacPherson *pers. comm.*).

The very vigorous and showy offspring of the 'Juliana' grex (*P.* × *pruhoniciana*) which resulted from its hybridization with coloured primroses shortly after its introduction, have largely supplanted it in gardens. Some, such as the very well-known clone 'Wanda', resemble it quite closely, but none have the delicate charm of the parent; unlike *P. juliae*, all are rosette-forming.

P. juliae takes an isolated morphological position, being the only member of this section to be hairless, to have a creeping mode of growth, to have laterally borne flowering stems (i.e. not arising from the centre of the rosette), and apart from the primrose, to be stemless. Nevertheless, it hybridizes readily with the primrose and oxlip, and hybrids have also been raised with *P. megaseifolia*, while the pollen type also strongly suggests that it has a common origin with these other species in section Primula.

No significant variation or hybridization is reported in the wild.

CULTIVATION Introduced by Kusnetsow of Dorpat to Kew and Oxford in 1911. Grows and flowers freely in damp shaded conditions, in rich but reasonably well-drained sites, and also makes a good pot-plant for a shady frame. Perfectly hardy in UK conditions, persisting well in the open ground, but vulnerable to vine-weevil attacks. Enjoys frequent division and replanting in early spring.

Section **Sredinskya** Stein
Samenkat. Bot. Gart. Bresl. (1881).
Type species *P. grandis* Trautv.

(*Sredinskya* (Stein) Federov (1951))

DESCRIPTION Robust, glabrous, tufted, deciduous plants bearing rugose leaves with revolute vernation and *mealy stems*. Corolla exannulate, the lobes yellow, *linear*, erect, forming *no limb*. Stigma *long-exserted*, flowers *homostylous*. Pollen stephanocolpate. Capsules narrow, exceeding calyx, opening by 5 valves. x = 11.

DISTRIBUTION The single species is endemic to the W and N Caucasus; wet meadows and streamsides.

Primula grandis Trautv. Bull. Acad. Sci. Petersb. 10: 395

Sredinskya grandis (Trautv.) Fed.

DESCRIPTION A robust, *deciduous, glabrous* plant, bearing *meal* on the upper part of the stems and calyx. *Leaves* erect, to 30 cm, the leaf-blade bluntly triangular, to 20 × 15 cm, rounded at the tip and truncate at the base with a stout but unwinged green petiole to 15 cm; leaf margin coarsely crenate toothed. *Stems* to 40 cm, mealy above, bearing a *large drooping cluster* of up to 30 flowers. *Flower* *stalks* to 10 cm, wiry, mealy. *Calyx mealy*, narrowly bell-shaped, to 6 mm, cut to 1/3 into rather blunt lobes. Corolla yellow, corolla-lobes narrow to *linear*, fused only near the base, forming a tube about 2 × the calyx but *without a limb*. Homostylous, stigma *exserted* from the corolla-tube by 5 mm, anthers included within the tube. *Pollen* oblate, stephano-colpate. Capsules narrow, exceeding the calyx, opening by 5 valves. 2n = 22. Flowering April in cultivation, June–July in the wild. (Plate 73.)

DISTRIBUTION Western end of the main Caucasian chain, Abkhazia and Svanetiya (Georgia). Also recorded from further north in the cis-Caucasian chain (Kabardia).

Wet alpine meadows and banks of mountain streams, often growing in shallow running water, 1200–3200 m.

This extraordinary plant is, in floral features, so unlike other primulas that it has usually been placed in a separate genus, *Sredinskya*, and it was so treated in the first edition of this monograph. Since then, DNA studies have proved conclusively that not only is it undoubtedly best placed in the genus *Primula*, but that it is in fact nested well within the other species of section Primula, with which it also shares the same chromosome number and pollen type (p.35). However, it seems not to be interfertile with these species, and it is remarkable how far it has diverged from its close relatives in a number of significant features. It is the only primula with tube-shaped flowers which lack a limb and are divided nearly to the base, and with long-exserted stigmas, while all its relatives in section Primula lack meal. It seems likely that the remarkable floral features have arisen rather recently in response to the particular requirements of a pollinator (a moth?); in many other aspects *P. grandis* is evidently a relative of the cowslip and oxlip. No significant variation has been recorded.

CULTIVATION Was fairly widespread in cultivation in the early 1970s, but nowadays rarely seen, although offered by at least one nurseryman in the UK in 2001. Not to everyone's taste, and probably kept in cultivation by botanic gardens. Several Tours have visited its localities near Elbrus in the 1990s and it may have been reintroduced.

Germinates freely and grows on well to flower in 18 months if planted out in a rich moist soil which remains wet throughout the year (e.g. accompanying members of sections Proliferae and Sikkimensis). In my experience, not long-lived. Self-fertile, but does not often set seed in the garden unless hand-pollinated.

Subgenus **Auganthus** (Link)

Wendelbo, Aarbok Univ. Bergen, Mat.-Nat. 11: 34 (1961).

Type species *P. sinensis* Sabine.

Section **Auganthus** (Link) Pax ex Balf. f.,

J. Roy. Hort. Soc. 39: 139 (1913)

(Section Sinenses Pax (1889))

(*Auganthus* Link (1829))

(*Oscaria* Lilja (1839))

(*Primulidium* Spach (1840))

DESCRIPTION Rhizomatous evergreen perennials. Leaves soft and fleshy, smooth to pleated, with long hairs, glandular on the stem and inflorescence, lacking meal, shallowly to deeply lobed, the blade circular in outline, heart-shaped at the base with a long narrow stalk, showing revolute vernation. *Flowers* borne in one to several superimposed umbels on long stalks. Bracts small, but leaf-like. *Calyx* inflated, with a broad, flattened base. *Corolla* red to white (in the wild) usually with a yellow eye, heterostylous, exannulate. *Pollen* subglobose, 3-syncolpate (also reported as stephanocolpate). *Capsules* persistent, globose, opening by five short valves. x = 12. Weakly self-incompatible, but some cultivated forms fully self-compatible at least in pins. Flowering in the winter in the wild, but also sporadically throughout the year in cultivation.

DISTRIBUTION North-central China, on the borders of north-east Sichuan, Shaanxi and Hubei.

Within subgenus *Auganthus*, the various sections are, with the exception of section Bullatae, quite closely related to one another. They bear rounded, lobed, hairy leaves on long stalks, and usually pink to purple flowers borne in umbels with persistent and sometimes curiously shaped calyces. Species have an eastern Asiatic distribution, and are further distinguished by all except section Monocarpicae and a few subsection Geranioides having the chromosome number 2n = 24 (x = 12), which is otherwise unknown in the genus. However, some cultivated polyploids are known.

Little can be deduced about the origins of members of subgenus *Auganthus*, which seem to be derived from a common ancestor. They are considered to be rather primitive primulas which may have migrated north-eastwards into China during the late Tertiary and may be derived from forerunners of the present section Proliferae.

The two species in section Auganthus can be separated from their many Chinese relatives by their distinctively broad and flat-bottomed calyx. Halda (1992) follows Chen & Hu (1990) in mysteriously placing *P. filchnerae* in this section. I agree with Smith & Fletcher that it is a rather clear member of section Pinnatae.

CULTIVATION Neither *P. sinensis* nor *P. rupestris* can be considered at all hardy in UK conditions, although they make excellent winter bedding plants in areas such as the south of France, Australia, New Zealand and California. However, they are intolerant of both drought and humid heat, and so they rarely survive summers in these areas, needing to be replaced from seed annually. In the UK, *P. sinensis* is a well-known subject for cool greenhouse or conservatory culture, but has been overtaken in popularity by *P. malacoides,* and especially *P. obconica*.

P. sinensis is invariably grown from seed, which is usually sown in the late summer. If kept frost-free under maximum light and ventilation in cool humid conditions during the autumn and winter, seedlings develop rapidly in a standard loam-based potting compost, to flower in midwinter and on into the spring. Plants are best kept in shaded conditions under glass until seed has been saved, and then discarded. Although they are short-lived perennials which can flower more than once, they are difficult to oversummer successfully, and they rarely perform so well at a second flowering.

P. rupestris may no longer be in cultivation.

LITERATURE. De Winton & Haldane (1935), Mather & de Winton (1941), Mather (1950).

Primula sinensis Sabine ex Lindley, Coll. Bot.: 7 (1821)

P. praenitens Ker-Gawl. (1821)
P. sertulosa Kickx (1826)
P. mandarina Hoffmans. (1835)
P. semperflorens Loisl. (1841)
Auganthus praenitens Link. (1829)
Oscaria chinensis Lilja (1839)
Primulidium sinense Spach (1840)

Note: *P. praenitens* was published a few months earlier than *P. sinensis* Sabine, which is in any case a later homonym of the illegitimate *P. sinensis* Lour. (1790). However, *P. sinensis* Sabine is a conserved name.

DESCRIPTION *Leaf*-blade darkish green above, paler and slightly stained purplish below, with sparse long hairs mostly confined to the veins, deeply 7–9 lobed, each lobe toothed, and subdivided into three shallow lobes, from 3–13 cm in diameter; leaf-stalks to 20 cm, purplish, sheathing at the base, fleshy and non-persistent. *Stem* to 30 cm, fleshy, stout, green and hairy, bearing 1–3 umbels of from 3–12 flowers on stiff somewhat erect fleshy stalks to 7 cm. Bracts to 3× 1 cm, leaf-like. *Calyx* resembling that of *Abutilon*, with a broad flat or even concave inflated base up to 2 cm in diameter, the lobes strongly flexed inwards to meet the corolla tube, strongly ribbed, cut to one-third into 5 broadly triangular lobes, or 10 narrower lobes, or irregularly cut or frilled. *Corolla* white, pink, rose or purple with a yellow eye, flat-faced, to 4 cm in diameter; corolla-tube not exceeding the calyx, short and broad; corolla-lobes broad, overlapping, notched, toothed or frilled. 2n = 24, 36, 48. (Plate 6.)

DISTRIBUTION There is a long-standing mystery and debate as to the origin of *P. sinensis*, which is admirably summarized by Smith and Fletcher (Trans. Roy. Soc. Edinb. 61: 433–435 (1946)).

After several efforts, a single plant was successfully brought home in 1821 from 'gardens in Canton'. We know that *P. sinensis* had been cultivated through much of China, possibly for many centuries, but this single individual seems to have been the parent of all cultivated plants elsewhere.

Similar, but smaller and less spectacular plants, differing largely by their wiry and persistent leaf-stalks, were found in limestone gorges in the Yangtse basin in north-central China by Delavay (1882), and subsequently by Pratt, Henry, Wilson and Farrer. These plants, best known from the Yangtse gorge at Ichang, were for 30 years considered to be the wild progenitor of *P. sinensis*, but were subsequently named *P. rupestris* after the well-known geneticist Bateson showed in 1914 that the wild plants were totally intersterile with cultivated *P. sinensis*. However, Halda (1992) unites *P. rupestris* with *P. sinensis*.

HYBRIDIZATION Repeated attempts to make the hybrid between *P. rupestris* and *P. sinensis* have since failed, but no more convincing wild candidate for the parentage of *P. sinensis* has been discovered. Gregory, De Winton and Bateson (J. Genet. 13: 219 (1923)) suggested that the variability in cultivated *P. sinensis* might be of hybrid origin, but confess that its fertility argues otherwise. They hypothesize that centuries of cultivation in China may have led to the selection of *P. sinensis* stock so genetically distinct from its wild progenitor that it had become intersterile with it.

A related hypothesis is that the single individual from which all non-Chinese stocks of *P. sinensis* were derived, carried a chromosome mutant, such as a translocation or an inversion, which rendered it intersterile with all non-mutants, including the original wild *P. rupestris*, while remaining fertile within its own line.

VARIATION Within a few years of its introduction, the progeny of the single ancestor of all the non-Chinese cultivated stock had shown a quite fantastic capability for variation. This variability aroused the interests of the first geneticists, and from 1900 to 1930, *Primula sinensis* was the subject of intensive experimentation, chiefly at the John Innes Institute. At one stage it was amongst the best understood of all plants, genetically, and it played a major part in the development of early theoretical genetics, and of plant breeding.

Another result of this variability was that *P. sinensis* became a 'cult' plant with amateur growers, interest peaking during the latter half of the nineteenth century, when many shows, particularly in the north of England, were devoted to this species alone.

A curious byproduct of this intense enthusiasm was that only pin-flowered plants were acceptable by fanciers, and true-breeding self-fertile pin strains developed (see p.).

Amongst the many variable features which have been bred into strains of *P. sinensis* are: flower colour, which varies from blue and purple, through magenta, crimson, red, salmon, pink and white to yellow; semi-double and double flowers; toothed and frilled petals; white petal-edge; zonal petal colour; green and brown flower eye colour, and eyeless flowers; narrow petals forming 'star-like' flowers; calyces with 10 segments, or with frilled edges; highly cut foliage; crested foliage; dwarf habit; and 'giant' forms, which are spontaneously arising autotetraploids thought to have arisen independently on several occasions (Darlington, J. Genet. 24: 65–96 (1931)). See also discussion concerning homostyly (pp. 57–58).

The wild species *Primula rupestris* appears to be rather invariable in the wild, but it may be that early Chinese horticulturists unconsciously selected strains with high mutation rates when developing *P. sinensis*.

Smith and Fletcher (1946) list 64 strains of *P. sinensis*, of which 23 had been given an **AM** by that date. The number obtainable today is probably much fewer, and it is now quite unusual to see *P. sinensis* offered through the trade. One possible explanation of this decline in popularity is that *P. sinensis* is perhaps the most allergenic of all species, certainly more so than *P. obconica*. Also, *P. sinensis* seems to be less suited to modern centrally-heated houses than is *P. obconica*.

Primula rupestris Balf. f. & Farrer, Trans. Bot. Soc. Edinb. 27: 240 (1918)

P. calciphila Hutchinson (1923)

DESCRIPTION Differs from *P. sinensis* by being a smaller, neater, less fleshy plant with persistent wiry leaf-stalks, and the corolla-tube at least 2× the calyx. The corolla varies from white to rose in colour, and the notched petal-lobes are non-overlapping forming a flower not exceeding 25 mm in diameter. 2n = 24. (Photo: RHS Primula Conference Report, t. 8 (1928).)

DISTRIBUTION The best-known sites are the gorges of the Yangtse at Ichang (Hubei), and Ta-Pa-Shan (where the Yangtse forms the border between

Sichuan and Shaanxi), but it also occurs on Emei Shan in Sichuan where it was recollected by Edward Needham in 1989. Limestone ledges, 2000–3000 m.

CULTIVATION Introduced from Ichang by Pratt (1891) and by Farrer from Ta-Pa-Shan in 1915 (flowered, Royal Botanic Garden, Edinburgh, 1916). It was still in cultivation in the 1920s when it was used experimentally at the John Innes Institute, but seems to have disappeared by about 1935.

Section **Monocarpicae** Franchet ex Pax,

Bot. Jahr. Syst. 10: 171 (1889).
Type species: *P. malacoides* Franchet.
(Section Malacoides Balf. f. (1913))

DESCRIPTION *Annuals*, winter annuals, biennials, or short-lived perennials, often monocarpic (flowering only once). *Leaves* thin with glandular and/or non-glandular hairs and revolute vernation, forming a basal rosette, or in one species distributed up the stem and not rosette-forming. *Leaf*-blades short and broad, lobed and toothed; leaf-stalks long and slender. *Stems* often mealy with several (up to 7) whorls of flowers, or in two species with flowers in a spike. *Calyx* slender and often mealy, joined to the fruit. *Corolla* purple, pink or white, exannulate, heterostylous. *Pollen* subglobose, 3-syncolpate or (uniquely in this subgenus) 3-colporoidate. *Capsules* globose, persistent, opening by five short valves. x = 9 (uniquely in this subgenus). Self-incompatible. Flowering in the winter or early spring.

DISTRIBUTION Western China; south-west Sichuan, Yunnan, Kweichow; north-east Burma and Thailand. Most species are very localized, and some are only known from a single locality. Several species may have become extinct during the last 50 years due to deforestation or through other pressures on the very specialized and localized 'grotto' habitats. However, in recent years four new species have been described, three from one area. Most are represented by very few specimens and are poorly understood taxonomically, and there may well be more species described than distinct taxonomic entities; this section needs revision.

Seasonally damp open ground; weedy fields and paddy margins and path edges, canal banks, seasonally flooded marshes, flushed areas by streams, moist ground in caves and damp shady cliffs, often on limestone. 1500–2500 m.

Many species in section Monocarpicae are very unusual within *Primula*, being monocarpic (dying after flowering). Also, they are often both mealy, and have glandular and long non-glandular hairs. This, together with the 'candelabroid' habit of the inflorescence in many species, marks them out in subgenus *Auganthus*. The botanical characters of the 3-colporoidate pollen of some species, and the chromosome number, are also unique in the subgenus. *P. aromatica* and *P. runcinata* are also anomalous in this subgenus in having flowers arranged in spikes rather than in whorls or umbels. *P. caulifera* is an extraordinary plant, the only primula not to have its leaves forming a basal rosette. Morphologically, section Monocarpicae seems to lie between section Obconicolisteri and section Proliferae. However, DNA studies reveal that *P. malacoides* and *P. forbesii* clearly belong to subgenus *Auganthus* and are very closely related sister species which are more closely related to members of section Bullatae than to other members of the subgenus.

CULTIVATION None of the 'grotto' species have been in cultivation. Two annuals, *P. forbesii* and *P. malacoides* seed regularly and grow vigorously under glass. Although *P. forbesii* appears to have been easily grown initially, and was still regularly grown in 1946, it is not often seen today.

No hybrids have been reported.

(Note: *Primula umbellata* (Lour.) Bentv. (Fl. Malesiana 6: 191–2, 1962) from India to New Guinea, is placed in section Monocarpicae by Fenderson (1986), while Halda (1992) gives it a subgenus (*Umbellatae*) of its own. In my view it clearly belongs to *Androsace* (*A. umbellata* (Lour.) Merr. 1919.)

(Note: *P. wangii* Chen & Hu (1990) from the Guangnan Shan, south-east Yunnan was originally placed in section Carolinella, but shares none of the distinctive features of that section and should apparently be placed in section Monocarpicae. I have not seen herbarium material and it is difficult to be sure from published descriptions whether it is distinct from other species of this region, especially *P. duclouxii*.)

KEY TO SPECIES

1. Leaves in a basal rosette 2
1. Leaves arranged alternately up stem .... *P. caulifera*

2. Flowers arranged in a spike.......... *P. aromatica*
2. Flowers borne in one or more whorls 3

3. Annual; stems and calyx mealy, usually glabrous 4
3. Short-lived perennial; plant often lacking meal, calyx often hairy 8

4. Lowest whorl of flowers overtopping the leaves .... *P. forbesii*
4. Stem below lowest whorl of flowers not exceeding the leaves.......... 5

5. Plant not more than 6 cm high, usually less 6
5. Stem usually exceeding 10 cm.......... 7

6. Fruits strongly deflexed, flowers 10 mm diameter .... *P. duclouxii*
6. Fruit patent, flowers to 30 mm diameter.......... *P. epilithica*

7. Calyx-lobes triangular; corolla-tube white to pink .... *P. malacoides*
7. Calyx-lobes finely drawn-out; corolla-tube yellow to orange.......... *P. effusa*

8. Plant not more than 5 cm high, usually less 9
8. Stem usually exceeding 10 cm, at least in fruit 10

9. Flower-stalks 6–13 mm; calyx 2–3 mm long.......... *P. divaricata*
9. Flower-stalks 3–6 mm; calyx 3.5–6 mm long .... *P. petrocallis*

10. Calyx teeth recurved.......... *P. pellucida*
10. Calyx teeth erect to patent 11

11. Flowers pink to rose, 20 mm in diameter or more .... *P. interjacens*
11. Flowers rose to purple, not exceeding 15 mm in diameter 12

12. Plant covered in rusty hairs, not sticky.......... *P. cavaleriei*
12. Plant slightly glandular, lacking rusty hairs.......... *P. lithophila*

Primula malacoides Franchet, Bull. Soc. Bot. Fr. 33:64 (1886)

P. pseudomalacoides Stewart (1915)
P. delicata Petitm. (1908)

DESCRIPTION *Annual*, with hairy leaves which are sometimes mealy beneath, and usually with mealy stems and flowers. *Leaf*-blade to 10 × 8 cm, very variable in shape but usually with 6–8 shallow toothed lobes, heart-shaped or rounded at the base; leaf-stalk to 15 cm, fleshy and long-hairy. *Stem* to 40 cm, with up to 6 whorls each with up to 20 flowers. Flower-stalks slender, set at right-angles to the stem, to 4 cm. *Calyx* to 7 mm, narrowly bell-shaped, cut to 1/2 into triangular lobes which later hug the fruit. *Corolla* purple, rose, lavender, pink or white, usually with a yellow eye, flat-faced, to 30 mm in diameter (in cultivation; rarely exceeds 15 mm in the wild); corolla tube widely cylindrical, up to 2× the calyx; corolla lobes rounded, notched (frilled in some cultivated forms). 2n = 18, 36, 72. Pins 15% self-fertile, thrums almost completely self-sterile. (Plate 6.)

DISTRIBUTION From just inside Burma on the Yunnan border near the Salween, throughout Yunnan to western Kweichow.

A weed of cultivated fields at around 2000 m. Forrest used to relate that in his experience it had become very much more widespread owing to the cultivation of beans, for bundles of these were carried into villages with fruiting sprays of the primula intermixed.

From 1900 to 1930, *P. malacoides* was clearly an abundant field weed in such well-botanised localities as the neighbourhoods of Dali (Tali), Lichiang, Tengyueh, Yunnanfu and Yunnansen. Many Sino-British Expeditions and holiday tours have visited these localities since the 1980s without reporting any trace of the primula. As with so many arable weeds of western Europe, modern cultivation methods may have rendered this man-dependent species very rare in the wild. However it is possible that all traces of this winter-flowering plant have disappeared before most tourists arrive.

Closely related to the two other weed species, *P. forbesii* and *P. effusa*.

VARIATION In the wild, a number of variants were collected, for instance a dwarf form (*P. delicata*) from Yunnanfu, very hairy forms, almost hairless forms, and forms lacking meal. *P. pseudomalacoides* is described from cultivated material, but probably just refers to robust forms of *P. malacoides*.

All cultivated material outside China probably originated from a single seed gathering from Dali (Forrest 1802), flowering in 1908. *P. malacoides* was rapidly adopted by commercial seed firms under whose selection it underwent a spectacular transformation. Within 10 years, it was reported that increases in vigour, overall size, flower size, fragrance, and range of colour had been achieved. Later developments included the so-called 'gracilis' strains, which showed rapid crown multiplication, and the 'gigantea' strains, with further increased size and vigour, which were tetraploid. In cultivation, *P. malacoides* apparently shows a marked tendency towards autopolyploidy, tetraploids arising in as many as one in 200 seedlings. These formed, for instance, the 'Dwarf Eclipse' strain of Suttons, and the 'Peter Pan' strain of Carters. *P. malacoides* is frequently cited in text-books as a good example of how polyploidy can be used to 'improve' garden plants.

Many named strains were raised by competing seed firms, and some lasted only a few years, being superseded in popularity. New strains were raised in France, Germany and the USA, while the most significant developments were made at Wadenswil, near Zurich. Smith and Fletcher (1946) limit themselves to 22 strains they consider to be horticulturally significant, 16 of which had been awarded the **AM** by that date, and one ('Mauve Queen') the equivalent of the modern **FCC**. Most modern strains are now octoploid (8×).

CULTIVATION *P. malacoides* is today still a popular plant for heated glasshouse and conservatory culture. It is less suitable than *P. obconica* as a house plant, being shorter-lived, less tolerant of modern central heating and very allergenic. Some years ago, a friend grew many magnificent plants which he presented to his colleagues for Christmas. One lady was immediately smitten by a severe rash, headaches and nausea, and was forced to spend a miserable Christmas in bed. It was only when, on a friend's suggestion, the gift-wrapped *P. malacoides* was removed from beside her sick-bed, that she made a speedy recovery! Fortunately, relatively few people suffer such severe reactions.

P. malacoides is best sown into loam-based composts and kept at between 10 and 15°C until germination has occurred. Under glass, at temperatures between 15 and 20°C it develops rapidly, to flower within 4 months if kept at less than 15 hour days. It appreciates a buoyant, humid atmosphere in good light, but should be kept away from direct sunshine. It benefits from regular foliar feeding, and should not allowed to be dried out. It is rather susceptible to botrytis in stagnant air, can be plagued by aphids, and is instantly killed by frost. If cross-pollinated, it sets abundant seed.

I have seen it grown in large quantities as a municipal bedding plant in Sydney, Auckland, Christchurch and Singapore, and it is sometimes used for this purpose in the south of England, although it should not be put out until early June.

Primula forbesii Franchet, Bull. Soc. Bot. Fr. 33: 64 (1886)

P. barbeyana Petitm. (1907)
P. willmottiae Petitm. (1907)
P. androsacea Pax (1905)
P. multicaulis Petitm. (1907)
P. hypoleuca Hand.-Mazz. (1920)
P. meiantha Balf. f. & Smith (1915)

DESCRIPTION Annual, similar to *P. malacoides*, but with much less divided leaves with fine teeth, and short leaf-stalks, so that the bottommost flowers greatly exceed the leaves, which are arranged in more compact rosettes; the flower-stalks and calyx are relatively shorter and the stems relatively longer than in *P. malacoides*. 2n = 18. (Photo: RHS Primula Conference Report, t. 21 (1928).)

DISTRIBUTION Yunnan, south Sichuan, and the Shan States, Burma (subsp. *meiantha*). Also occurs by temples near Kathmandu, Nepal, where it is presumably an escape from cultivation.

Open ground in marshes, canal edges and uncultivated rice paddy, 2000–3300 m. Subsp. *androsacea* occurs on 'alluvial soil, the mud of which is suited to the growth of rice ... found often in big masses on the ridges of rice fields, or more accurately bean fields, for it flowers before the rice is planted; in the same masses on abandoned fields of the same kind; and on the grass patches, green all the year round, alongside the canals of water between them, and along natural streams. It flowers together with (broad bean) in February, but also in November, and occasionally during the whole winter, seeds quickly, and soon disappears ... *P. forbesii* (i.e. subsp. *forbesii*) was observed by me in a small spring at the head of a patch of meadow covering very decomposing granite soil ... *P. hypoleuca* (i.e. subsp. *hypoleuca*) ... grows in the very shallow part of Yunnanfu lake on islets of common reed ... and flowers somewhat later in the spring' (Handel-Mazzetti, 1928).

VARIATION A confusing and variable species, linking with *P. malacoides* on one hand, and *P. pellucida* and *P. duclouxii* on the other. Smith and Fletcher (1946: 449) considered that *P. barbeyana* and *P. willmottiae* were probably not distinct, and treated *P. androsacea, P. hypoleuca* and *P. meiantha* as subspecies of *P. forbesii,* although they admit that the situation was still fluid. No further progress on the taxonomy of this complex has been made. It may be that many of the forms are today very rare as a result of agricultural improvement and habitat loss.

- Subsp. *androsacea* (Pax) Smith & Forrest (*P. androsacea* Pax in Engler, Pflzenr.: 34 (1905)) is a short stout form with simple umbels.
- Subsp. *hypoleuca* (Hand.-Mazz.) Smith & Forrest (*P. hypoleuca* Hand.-Mazz., Anz. Akad. Wiss. Wien 58: 238 (1920)) is hairless with leaves plastered white below.
- Subsp. *meiantha* (Balf. f. & Smith) Smith & Forrest (*P. meiantha* Balf. f. & Smith, Notes Roy. Bot. Gdn. Edinb. 9: 28 (1915) is a form with tiny flowers restricted to the Shan States, Burma.

CULTIVATION Introduced by Vilmorin of Paris in 1891, and grown for 60 years, apparently thriving in the same conditions as *P. malacoides*. It persists today and I grew several generations of a pale pink form in the late 1990s. They flowered from November to February and some formed spectacular mounds of winter colour in the conservatory.

Primula effusa Smith & Forrest, Notes Roy. Bot. Gdn. Edinb. 14: 40 (1923)

DESCRIPTION Annual, differing from *P. malacoides* by the more entire leaves which lose meal and hairs early, the finely drawn-out calyx teeth, and and longer corolla-tube. 2n = 18. Wet thickets and stream-banks, also wet niches under overhanging conglomerate rocks, in north-west Yunnan, 1400–2600 m. In cultivation at Edinburgh, 1924–30, but did not seed, and apparently difficult. Seed collected by Yu under this name in 1939 proved to be a new Muscarioides species *P. inopinata*.

Primula duclouxii Petitm., Le Monde des Plantes 7: (1908)

P. forbesii Franchet subsp. *duclouxii* (Petitm.) Smith & Forrest (1928)
P. forbesii Franchet var. *brevipes* Bonati (1909)
P. refracta Hand.-Mazz. (1920)

DESCRIPTION An annual plant, very close to *P. malacoides*, but much smaller, to 6 cm and with distinctive down-pointed fruits, and flowers to 10 mm diameter, growing in a quite different habitat. Endemic to shaded limestone crevices at 2250 m near 'Long Men' ('Dragon Gate') in the West Hills (Hsi-shan) on the western shore of Lake Kun-yang-hay, near Kunming, south-east Yunnan, flowering in January and February. Being close to the normal point of arrival for travellers to Yunnan, this popular tourist locality has frequently been visited by Westerners in recent years, although rarely in mid-winter when this species flowers. (Photo: Bull. AGS 51: 59 (1983).)

See also sectional note concerning *P. wangii*.

Primula epilithica Chen & Hu, Fl. Rep. Pop. Sin. 2: 289 (1990)

DESCRIPTION A new discovery from the Jingdong Shan, Yunnan, an annual with large pink flowers to 30 mm in diameter hanging on long flower stalks to 2.5 cm; the stems are only 2.5 cm tall and the leaves lack meal. Wet rock surfaces, 2300–3000 m.

Primula lithophila Chen & Hu, Fl. Rep. Pop. Sin. 2: 290 (1990)

DESCRIPTION Very similar to *P. malacoides*, but perennial, and with shorter flower stalks (to 15 mm) and small flowers to 8 mm in diameter. Kweichow,

Guanduo district, Changling; wet rock surfaces near valley floors, 1800–2900 m.

Primula petrocallis Chen & Hu, Fl. Rep. Pop. Sin. 2: 289 (1990)

DESCRIPTION Perennial; leaves with a rounded, irregularly lobed blade which is white-mealy on both sides. Dwarf plants with a single umbel of 2–10 flowers hanging from filiform stalks to 6 mm. Corolla purple red, 10–15 mm in diameter, the tube 20 mm long. Wet rocks in mixed forest, 2200–3000 m.; Yunnan, Jingdong Shan.

Primula divaricata Chen & Hu, Fl. Rep. Pop. Sin. 2: 289 (1990)

DESCRIPTION A dwarf perennial relative of *P. malacoides* with the small leaves mealy on both surfaces, and stems to only 3.5 cm. Flower stalks to 13 mm. Wet rocky slopes above roads, 1800–2700 m. Yunnan; Jingdong Shan.

Primula cavaleriei Petitm., Bull. Acad. Geog. Bot. 18: 256 (1908)

DESCRIPTION Another probably perennial fragile plant covered with rusty hairs, and lacking sticky hairs or meal; flowers in superimposed umbels. Only known from limestone caves at Lin-tchouan, south of Tin-fan, Kweichow, and at Mengtze, Yunnan.

Primula interjacens Chen, Acta Phytotax. Sin. 1: 175 (1951)

DESCRIPTION A dwarf perennial with a hairy calyx; closely related to *P. pellucida* and especially *P. cavaleriei,* but mealy, and with larger flowers. Apparently very attractive. Endemic to limestone crevices on Wu-Liang-Shan, near Chung-Ting, 2200 m, on the Red River–Mekong divide in west Yunnan.

Curiously, Halda (1992) gives both this species, and, in section Malvacea, its homonym, *P. interjacens* Smith & Forrest (1923: 32). However, I can find no trace of the latter in the literature.

Primula pellucida Franchet, Bull. Soc. Bot. Fr. 35: 428 (1888)

P. speluncicola Petitm. (1908)
P. debilis Bonati (1909)

DESCRIPTION A perennial related to *P. forbesii* and *P. cavaleriei,* but lacking meal, with very thin textured leaves, a long-exserted corolla-tube and slender, recurved calyx-teeth. Limestone caves at Tchen-fon-Chan, Chao-tung, and Yunnansen, north-east Yunnan; about 2000 m.

Primula caulifera C.M. Hu, Notes Roy. Bot. Gdn. Edinb. 41: 327 (1983)

DESCRIPTION A quite extraordinary annual primula with no basal rosette of leaves, and long-stalked leaves with rounded blades arranged *alternately* up the stem. The small rose flowers are in several superimposed umbels. From moist savannah at 800 m at Tunkamang, Chaiyaphum District, Thailand (16° 20' N, 101° 45' E). Although placed in section Monocarpicae by Hu, this, one of only three primulas found in Thailand, seems to be related to no other primula, and probably deserves its own section.

Primula aromatica Smith & Forrest, Notes Roy. Bot. Gdn. Edinb. 14: 32 (1923)

P. runcinata Smith & Fletcher ex Hu (1983)

DESCRIPTION A perennial, fragile plant with aromatic hairy foliage, sticky stems, no meal, and flowers arranged in a *spike*. Apparently intermediate with members of section Obconicolisteri, but little known or understood. Halda (1992) following Chen & Hu (1990) places this species in section Malvacea under the later synonym *P. runcinata*. Damp limestone caves, Zhongdian plateau, Yunnan-Sichuan border, 3000–3300 m. Has never been cultivated.

Section **Obconicolisteri** Balf. f., J. Roy. Hort. Soc. 39: 141 (1913). Type species *P. obconica* Hance. (Section Obconica Smith & Forrest 1928)

DESCRIPTION *Rhizomatous* evergreen perennials, lacking meal, with long hairs and sticky hairs. *Leaf*-blades rounded, entire to shallowly lobed, usually heart-shaped at the base with a long stalk, with revolute vernation. *Stems* with a single umbel of not more than 12 flowers, usually exceeding the leaves; bracts small but leaf-like. *Calyx* cup-shaped, usually scarcely lobed, attached to the fruit. *Corolla* rose to white, sometimes with a yellow eye, heterostylous or homostylous, annulate or exannulate; *pollen* subglobular, 3-syncolpate or 3-colporoidate. *Capsule* persistent, top-shaped (i.e. widest at the flattened top), without valves, crumbling at maturity. x = 12. Flowering from the winter to late spring.

DISTRIBUTION South-east Asia from Nepal through Bhutan, Assam, Burma and Manipur to south-east Tibet, and the provinces of Yunnan, Sichuan, Kweichow, Hubei and Kwangtung. Wet rocks and shaded woodland from 2000–3000 m (*P. filipes* to 4000 m.).

Section Obconicolisteri has been composed of 16 species centred around *P. obconica*, most of which are little known, very poorly represented in herbaria, and are of dubious status. Essentially these fall into one of two categories: (i) local variants of *P. obconica* from near Dali, Yunnan, and (ii) segregates on the geographical cline westwards from typical Chinese *P. obconica* through *P. sinolisteri*, *P. listeri* to the Himalayan *P. filipes*. It is doubtful whether more than about nine distinct taxa can be distinguished in this section, but until the segregates are better known and have been treated to a serious monographic treatment, I am leaving them in their traditional classification. In our present state of knowledge it is impossible to write a key for their successful identification.

The section occupies a rather central position in subgenus *Auganthus* morphologically, but is diagnosed by the cup-shaped calyx, and most importantly by the top-shaped capsule, and its mode of dehiscence. Plants always lack meal and have a single whorl of flowers. DNA studies place it within subgenus *Auganthus*, but in a rather isolated position without any close relatives. The distinctive mode of capsule dehiscence might suggest a link to section Davidii, but scanty DNA evidence presently suggests otherwise.

P. kwantungensis and *P. kweichouensis* were transferred to section Carolinella by Hu (1990).

CULTIVATION With the possible exception of *P. filipes*, none of the species are hardy in UK conditions. *P. sinolisteri* can tolerate unheated greenhouses, and in these conditions has survived a –6°C frost with me.

P. obconica is an extremely popular subject for heated glasshouses, and is by far the most successful primula as a house plant, being sold in great quantity throughout the world. It is remarkably tolerant of modern central heating, but is relatively short-lived, needing replacement from seed.

In tropical and Mediterranean climates *P. obconica* is sometimes used for decorative bedding schemes, but is less popular than *P. malacoides* or *P. sinensis*, being slower to flower. *P. obconica* is also very successful in windowboxes and hanging baskets. Seed is best sown at about 20°C. and seedlings should be grown on in a fertile compost. Plants are tolerant of dry air, and detest over-watering, which often leads to 'damping off'. They can be trimmed and repotted after flowering, and when so treated may last several years, although they rarely flower so well on subsequent occasions. Plants showing signs of virus should be burnt. *P. obconica* is a martyr to whitefly, but responds well to occasional sprays with a systemic insecticide.

Generally, *P. obconica* seems to be less allergenic than *P. malacoides* or *P. sinensis*, but nevertheless some people do react severely to it; a non-allergenic strain was introduced in 1990.

No hybrids have been reported.

Primula obconica Hance, J. Bot. 18: 234 (1880)

P. begoniiformis Petitm. (1907)
P. bonatii Knuth (1910)
P. poculiformis Hook. f. (1881)
P. werringtonensis Forrest (1924)

DESCRIPTION *Leaf*-blades to 17 × 11 cm, entire, slightly toothed, wavy, or shallowly lobed; leaf-stalk fleshy, to 10 cm, white or tawny-hairy. *Stem* to 25 cm, stout, hairy, carrying up to 13 flowers, usually in a single umbel on hairy stalks to 25 mm. *Calyx* bell-shaped, hairy, to 10 mm, scarcely cut in most plants, but occasionally divided to one-third into broadly triangular lobes. *Corolla* heterostylous or homostylous, exannulate to weakly annulate, rose, lavender, pink or white, flat-faced, to 2.5 cm diameter in the wild, but up to 5 cm in cultivation; the tube about 2× the calyx; petal-lobes broad, rounded, notched; *capsule* globose to top-shaped. 2n = 24, 48. Pin flowers 4% self-fertile, thrum flowers 3% self-fertile. (Plate 6.)

DISTRIBUTION Widespread in Yunnan and Sichuan, apparently less so in Hubei, Kweichow, Kwangtung and south-east Tibet (Tsarong); subsp. *intanoensis* in northern Thailand.

'Thickets of deciduous shrubs, often along rivulets, preferring soil somewhat covered by leaves, on limestone, sandstone and clay-slate, which indeed may all hold lime, occurring up to (3200 m).' In 1995 I found this species (var. *werringtonensis*) at about 2600 m in the Cang Shan above Dali, growing in the partial shade of shrubs on limestone outcrops. In late May, plants were just going over flower.

VARIATION An exceptionally variable species in the wild, contrasting with its behaviour in cultivation. It has been suggested that most horticultural variants found today were already present amongst the seedlings of Maries' initial introduction. Most horticultural variation is restricted to the colour and form of the flowers, types with double, fimbriated and wavy flowers being known. The vigour and large flower size found in modern flowers is probably associated with tetraploidy.

P. obconica, so variable in the wild, and throwing so few sports in cultivation, has been compared with *P. sinensis*, which is so invariable (as *P. rupestris*) in the wild, but presents such an infinity of variation in cultivation.

In fact, it has been found difficult to determine the limits of variation of *P. obconica* in the wild, as *P. barbicalyx*, *P. filipes*, *P. listeri*, *P. obconica*, *P. parva*, *P. petitmengini* and *P. sinolisteri* tend to form a morphological continuum.

Smith and Fletcher (1946: 426) recognize three varieties within *P. obconica* in the narrow sense, but admit that further work might result in more species being included in *P. obconica*. A modern revision would be valuable.

- Var. *nigroglandulosa* Smith & Fletcher (1946) (subsp. *nigroglandulosa* (Smith & Fletcher) Hu (1990)), covered with black glands (Yunnan).
- Var. *rotundifolia* Franchet (1886) (=*P. begoniiformis*) with small round dissected leaves (Yunnan).
- Var. *werringtonensis* (Forrest) Smith & Fletcher (1946), delicate hairless forms with a long corolla tube (Yunnan).
- Subsp. *intanoensis* (Yamazaki) Halda (1992) (*P. intanoensis* Yamazaki, J. Jap. Bot. 63: 211 (1988)) has a small white corolla with a long tube. It is restricted to northern Thailand.

Quite apart from these named variants, wild populations vary widely in size, leaf-shape and hairiness, and flower colour and form.

Smith and Fletcher list only 10 horticultural variants, of which 7 had gained the **AM** by 1946.

New strains, claimed to lack the allergen 'primine' were introduced onto the market in 1990, under the names 'Freedom' and 'Beauty'.

CULTIVATION See sectional comments. The type plant was introduced by Maries from Ichang, west Hubei (where it grows with *P. rupestris*) in 1879 for Messers.Veitch. Var. *werringtonensis* was introduced by Forrest from the Lichiang Range, and perhaps from elsewhere, probably on several occasions (11 Forrest numbers refer to this plant). This neat variety is intermediate with *P. sinolisteri*. It is still in cultivation. A recent introduction was made by Needham (EN 991) from Lijiang (Wei Bi Shan).

Primula petitmengini Bonati, Bull. Soc. Bot. Fr. 9: 466 (1909)

P. obconica subsp. *petitmengini* (Bonati) Smith & Forrest (1928)

DESCRIPTION A dubiously valid species, very little known, with a short scape and large membranous leaves; from caves east of Er-Hai lake, Dali, Yunnan. Probably a modification of *P. obconica*.

Primula vilmoriana Petitm., Bull. Herb. Boiss. 8: 365 (1908)

P. obconica subsp. *vilmoriana* (Petitm.) Smith & Forrest (1928)
P. subtropica Hand.-Mazz. (1925)

DESCRIPTION A relative of *P. obconica* with leaves honeycombed below, and with a tight cluster of very small flowers. Shaded thickets on a limey shale, 1600–2600 m. East of Er-Hai Lake, Dali, Yunnan, and possibly also on the Burma-Yunnan frontier. Probably a modification of *P. obconica*.

Primula barbicalyx Wright, Kew Bull. 109: 24 (1896)

DESCRIPTION A dubiously distinct, short-stemmed form of *P. obconica* from limestone crags at 2900 m, Mengtse, Yunnan. Has not been in cultivation.

Primula parva Balf. f., Trans. Bot. Soc. Edinb. 26: 321 (1915)

P. obconica subsp. *parva* (Balf. f.) Smith & Forrest (1928)

DESCRIPTION Like *P. barbicalyx*, a dwarf limestone cliff relative of *P. obconica;* it is dubiously distinguished from the former by thicker, less lobed leaves, and from the latter chiefly by size (leaf blade not exceeding 4 cm). From Kunming, Yunnan, and Yuyuen, Kwangtung province. Has never been cultivated.

Primula sinolisteri Balf. f., Trans. Bot. Soc. Edinb. 26: 330 (1915)

P. listeri var. *glabrescens* Franchet (1886)

DESCRIPTION Differs from *P. obconica* by being a much smaller and more delicate plant with pale green velvety, ivy-shaped leaves with about 7 lobes showing very marked veins on the lower surface, and white or very pale pink flowers. 2n = 24. Thrum flowers 21% self-fertile (pins not known).

DISTRIBUTION North-west Yunnan, from the Dali range to the Tibetan border; dry rocky pasture, 2300–3000 m.

P. sinolisteri is part of a geographical and morphological continuum between the Chinese *P. obconica*, especially var. *werringtonensis,* and the Himalayan *P. listeri*. At various times it has been associated with both these very different species, and future study may well decide to place them together into one very widespread and variable species. However, for horticultural purposes, *P. sinolisteri* is very distinct. In cultivation it has a grace and charm quite lacking in its gross and popular relative, and it deserves to be grown far more often.

VARIATION From the Shweli–Salween divide, var. *aspera* Smith & Fletcher (1946) has been described. This has homostylous flowers, a larger calyx to 10 mm, and longer hairs, and in many ways is close to *P. obconica* var. *werringtonensis*.

CULTIVATION Introduced by Forrest from the Cang Shan range in 1906. It has remained in cultivation to the present time as a plant for the cool greenhouse, although rarely seen today. Rarely if ever setting seed, it easily comes from cuttings from the fragile multicrowned stock. Rather slow growing, suspectible to aphid attack, and damping off from overwatering, but reasonably hardy and long-lived, and persisting well under glass. A modest plant which will rarely outgrow a 15 cm pot.

Primula listeri King ex Hook. f., Fl. Brit. India 3: 485 (1882)

DESCRIPTION Similar to the Chinese *P. sinolisteri*, but with the stem shorter than the leaves and homomorphic flowers; the Himalayan relative *P. filipes* has more entire leaves and much longer flower-stalks. Smells strongly of herb robert. Bamboo jungles from east Nepal through Sikkim and Bhutan to Assam and Manipur, 2400–3800 m. Despite several introductions of seed, has never been cultivated successfully.

Primula filipes Watt, J. Linn. Soc. 20: 5 (1882)

P. wallichiana O. Ktze (1891)
Androsace cordifolia Wall. (1820)

DESCRIPTION A delicate minature relative of *P. obconica* from the Himalayas, with little spoon-shaped leaves, to 10 cm, bearing reddish hairs below, slender stems and flower stalks each rarely exceeding 2 cm, and white or mauve exannulate homostylous flowers with a greenish eye. 2n = 24. Flowering in February, when sites are usually bone-dry.

DISTRIBUTION Cliffs and rocks from warm-temperate forests of the eastern Himalaya from east Nepal to Assam, and possibly in Burma, 2000–2700 m. Although based on *A. cordifolia*, the epithet cordifolia could not be used by Watt, as it was already taken by *P. cordifolia* Rupr. (1863).

CULTIVATION Introduced by Ward (11400) from Assam, and still in cultivation in 1946. Not apparently seen recently. Smith and Fletcher say 'of no horticulural merit', but in fact it seems to have been a delightful little plant.

Primula densa Balf. f., Notes Roy. Bot. Gdn. Edinb. 13: 9 (1920)

DESCRIPTION Similar to *P. filipes*, but with longer stems, and annulate heterostylous flowers. Hpimaw region of Upper Burma, damp moss on limestone ledges in deep shade, 2300–2700 m. Introduced by Ward in 1914, Ward and Farrer in 1919 and Ward in 1939. Did not persist.

Primula dictyophylla Smith, Notes Roy. Bot. Gdn. Edinb. 19: 168 (1936)

DESCRIPTION A robust rusty-hairy plant with congested umbels or heads of heterostylous white, orange-eyed flowers, and leaves covered with black glands below. Shaly slopes in forest, 2000–2800 m, Upper Burma. Introduced by Ward in 1938, but only persisting for four years.

Primula ambita Balf. f., Trans. Bot. Soc. Edinb.,26: 325 (1915)

P. flavicans Hand.-Mazz. (1924)

DESCRIPTION Similar to *P. dictyophylla*, but *yellow* flowered and lacking black glands. Between Dali and Kunming, Yunnan. 'Sandstone rocks under the shrubs of a cut wayside', 2400–2700 m. Has not been in cultivation.

Primula tsiangii Smith, Notes Roy. Bot. Gdn. Edinb. 18: 63 (1933)

DESCRIPTION A dwarf plant from damp limestone cliffs at only 450 m. Totally covered in a rusty 'fur' which pulls out in tufts. Flowers lilac. Endemic to the Tung-tze region of northern Kweichow. Has never been cultivated. Treated as a subspecies of *P. oreodoxa* by Halda (1992) although his combination is illegitimate.

Primula rubrifolia Hu, Acta Phytotax. Sin. 26: 307 (1988)

DESCRIPTION Another close relative of *P. obconica* with rose flowers, but leaves covered with brown hairs, and the leaf blade equally long as wide. Jingdong Shan, Yunnan, rocks in woods, 1600–3000 m.

Primula asarifolia Fletcher, J. Linn. Soc. 52: 336 (1942)

DESCRIPTION An undistinguished plant with small round hairless leaves and very small purple flowers from Chen Kang Hsien, south-west Yunnan, 2600 m. Has not been in cultivation.

Primula dumicola Smith & Forrest, Notes Roy. Bot. Gdn. Edinb. 14: 40 (1923)

DESCRIPTION A *robust* plant with hairy narrowly-oblong, *many-lobed* leaves, and rose-coloured, exannulate, homostylous flowers. Wet cold-temperate forests along rivulets on granite rocks, 2000–2700 m. Tsarong (Tibet), north-west Yunnan, and Upper Burma. Has not been in cultivation.

Primula oreodoxa Franchet, Bull. Soc. Bot. Fr. 23: 66 (1886)

DESCRIPTION Similar to *P. dumicola* with narrowly oblong multilobed leaves, but with larger, heteromorphic flowers to 2 cm in diameter and toothed calyx lobes. West Sichuan, in the Moupine district, including Mt. Omei and Mt. Wu, 1200–2500 m. Little known and has never been cultivated.

Section **Malvacea** Balf. f., Notes Roy. Bot. Gdn. Edinb. 9: 9 (1915). (J. Roy. Hort. Soc. 39: 145 (1913) sin. diag.). Type species *P. malvacea* Franchet.

DESCRIPTION Erect probably deciduous *perennials* covered with long soft hairs, and with glandular hairs on the stems, lacking meal. *Leaves* smooth to wrinkled, soft and rather fleshy with a rounded, lobed or toothed blade, heart-shaped, and with a long narrow hairy stalk, with revolute vernation. *Stems tall*, hairy and sticky with long-stalked flowers in long *spikes*, or flowers in whorls (*P. malvacea*), bracts small but leaf-like. *Calyx* large, open or even flat-faced, forming a distinctive and conspicuous disc-like organ in fruit. Flowers blue, violet, purple, rose, white, yellow or orange, large and showy, annulate, heteromorphic. *Pollen* subglobose, 3-syncolpate. *Capsule* globose, dehiscing by 5 (–10) longitudinal valves. Chromosome number and breeding behaviour unknown. Apparently growing and flowering in late summer during the monsoon.

DISTRIBUTION China, confined to Yunnan and south-west Sichuan. Sheltered areas, shaded by boulders, cliffs or open scrub in dry steppic limestone regions which receive limited rain, and then only during the monsoon. Probably dormant for the dry 10 months of the year. 2000–4000 m.

The five species in section Malvacea form a natural and homogenous group of tall fleshy perennials. They present a very distinctive aspect, in some species like red campion, and in others like a mullein, while the distinctive plate-like calyces are reminscent of mallows.

Although they are restricted to the 'home of primula' in Yunnan and Sichuan, these species mostly inhabit dry steppic regions where few other primulas occur. These areas are not otherwise very species-rich, and have rarely been visited during the monsoon, so these plants have been very little studied.

Apart from the distinctive calyx, these species are rather typical of subgenus *Auganthus,* although in the absence of cytological and DNA evidence, it is not possible to be more positive about their origins. Halda (1992) includes *P. runcinata* (Smith & Fletcher) Hu (= *P. aromatica*) and *P. interjacens* Smith & Forrest non Chen in this section, apparently by mistake.

CULTIVATION Although three of the five species have been in cultivation, none have persisted to the present day. Seed was rarely set in cultivation, although propagation from root-cuttings was successful. Now that their natural habitat is more fully understood, it is possible that the provision of a long dry rest from September to May, such as might be given to a *Calochortus* or an Oncocyclus *Iris* could succeed where earlier regimes failed. No hybrids are recorded.

KEY TO SPECIES

1. Flowers yellow or orange 2
1. Flowers pink to purple, rarely white 3

2. Leaf blades exceeding stalk, rounded at base .... *P. saturata*
2. Leaf blades shorter than stalk, heart-shaped (cordate) at base .... *P. bathangensis*

3. Leaf blade at least 1.5 × as long as wide; flowers in spikes 4
3. Leaf blade no longer than wide; flowers usually borne in whorls .... *P. malvacea*

4. Leaf blades exceeding stalk; flowers pink to purple .... *P. blattariformis*
4. Leaf blades shorter than stalk; flowers violet .... *P. celsiaeformis*

Primula bathangensis Petitm., Bull. Herb. Boiss. 8: 365 (1908)

P. pintchouanensis Petitm. (1908)
P. racemosa Bonati (1909)
P. stephanocalyx Hand.-Mazz. (1923)

DESCRIPTION *Leaf-blades* kidney-shaped, with a wavy margin, shorter than the stalk. *Stems* tall, to 70 cm, bearing a long spike of up to 40 yellow flowers, looking superficially like a *Verbascum*. Widespread in the Lichiang and Yangtse bend regions of north-west Yunnan, extending into south-west Sichuan around Muli and Tatsienlu, thus approaching the border with Tibet. Introduced by Forrest on at least seven occasions from 1913 to 1934, still in cultivation at Edinburgh in 1944, but apparently lost soon after. (Photo: J. Roy. Hort. Soc. 54 t.10 (1928); APS Quarterly 25 (1967).)

Primula blattariformis Franchet, Gard. Chron. 1: 575 (1887)

P. microstachys Balf. f & Forrest (1923)

DESCRIPTION *Leaf-blades* oval with a rounded end and base, bluntly toothed to wavy margined, longer than the stalk. *Stems* tall and robust, to 55 cm, bearing a one-sided spike of pink, rose or purple sweet-scented, yellow-eyed flowers. Widespread in north-west Yunnan, from Dali almost to the Tibetan border, and around Muli in south-west Sichuan, thus largely overlapping the previous species. Introduced by Forrest in 1913–14, and still sparingly in cultivation at Edinburgh in 1944. (Photo: APS Quarterly 25 (1967).)

P. blattariformis subsp. *tenana* (Bonati ex Balf. f.) Smith & Forrest, Notes Roy. Bot. Gdn. Edinb. 16: 27 (1928) is a dwarf form which may come from further east in Yunnan. It is very little understood.

Primula celsiaeformis Balf. f., Notes Roy. Bot. Gdn. Edinb. 9: 7 (1915)

P. racemosa Levl. (1915) non Bonati

DESCRIPTION Similar to *P. blattariformis*, but with the leaf-stalk equalling or exceeding the blade, and the blade base heart-shaped; the violet flowers are arranged in a long spike. Only known from a single site, Ta-tchai in north-east Yunnan, quite remote from the other species. Has never been in cultivation.

Primula malvacea Franchet, Bull. Soc. Bot. Fr. 23: 65 (1886)

P. neurocalyx Franchet (1895)
P. rosthornii Diels (1900)
P. langkongensis Forrest (1908)
P. barybotrys Hand.-Mazz. (1923)
P. atrotubata Smith & Forrest (1923)
P. baokongensis Chen & Hu (1983)

DESCRIPTION A very variable species having kidney-shaped leaf-blades with wavy margins, exceeded by the leaf-stalks, and inflorescences which can vary from whorls to spikes in structure, the flowers being purple, rose, pink, or less commonly bluish or white; in some forms the calyx lobes are toothed. The leaf is similar to *P. bathangensis*, with which it sometimes grows, but which has spikes of yellow flowers. It is possible that the two species intergrade. *P. blattariformis* and *P. celsiaeformis* have oval, not kidney-shaped, leaf-blades.

DISTRIBUTION Widespread in north-west Yunnan and south-west Sichuan, especially in the regions of the Yangtse bend, and Muli. 'A steppe plant on clay-slate and limestone, in situations where rarely some drops of rain fall, and never snow, and certainly the thermometer never drops to 32°F'. Halda (1992) separates out *P. neurocalyx* (including *P. rosthornii*) and treats it as a species in section Cortusoides, but without comment. Until more evidence is available, I am following Smith & Fletcher.

CULTIVATION Introduced to Edinburgh by Forrest (1908), who also introduced a white form (1922); both persisted for a few years, the white form until at least 1944, but both are now lost. (Photo: J. Roy. Hort. Soc. 54 t.9 (1928).)

Primula saturata Smith & Fletcher, Trans. Bot. Soc. Edinb. 34: 129–131 (1944)

DESCRIPTION Leaf-blades oval, bluntly toothed, rounded at the top and base, exceeding the stalk.

The large deep orange flowers are arranged in a spike. Similar to *P. blattariformis* in general aspect, of which it might be regarded as a form, but with flowers of a quite different, startling colour. The other yellow-flowered relative, *P. bathangensis*, has quite different kidney-shaped leaves.

Mixed forest at 4000 m on the Muti Konka snow range east of the Yalung, Muli, Sichuan. Inhabits rather different situations from the other species, and might be expected to be more amenable to culture in the UK, but it has never been introduced.

Section **Pycnoloba** Balf. f., J. Roy. Hort. Soc. 39: 141. Type species *P. pycnoloba* Bureau & Franchet.

Primula pycnoloba Bureau & Franchet, Jour. de Bot. 5: 99 (1891)

DESCRIPTION A rather robust probably *deciduous* rhizomatous perennial capable of some vegetative spread. Leaves very similar to *P. malvacea,* thus soft, fleshy, wrinkled and with long hairs, lacking meal and with revolute vernation. The *leaf-blade* is kidney-shaped and slightly wavy on the margin, to 15 cm; the *leaf-stalk* is very hairy and about as long as the blade. Flowering *stems* are shorter than the leaves, to 20 cm, and like the leaf-stalks are densely clothed with white hairs; they are erect, but recoil at the top; the bracts are small (to 2 cm) and leaf-like. The remarkable *inflorescence* of about 20 flowers is contracted into a head, forming a more or less orbicular ball of spiky flowers. *Calyx* pale green and hairy, very large and bell-shaped, 25 mm long and up to 30 mm wide at the top, cut to about two-thirds into long sharp narrow lobes. *Corolla* with a violet to dark red limb, but a yellowish-green tube and eye, narrowly cylindrical, to 15 mm and thus included within the large calyx, the limb almost erect, small and rounded, the diameter of the tube-like flower thus rarely exceeding 8 mm, exannulate, heterostylous. *Pollen* subglobose, 3-syncolpate. *Capsules* apparently unknown. x = 12. Apparently fully self-incompatible. Flowering time not recorded, ? early summer. (Photo: J. Roy. Hort. Soc. 54 t.58 (1928).)

DISTRIBUTION Western Sichuan, apparently endemic to the Tatsienlu area; the only detailed locality seems to be meadows at between 1900–2000 m at Hualinpin.

Within the subgenus *Auganthus*, the extraordinary ball of pale green spiky calyces within which are included the insignificant tube-like flowers is quite unique, and no obvious links with related sections can be discerned.

P. pycnoloba seems to be rare in the wild, having been discovered on only three occasions, by Prince Henri d'Orleans in 1890, by Ernest ('Chinese') Wilson in 1906 (introduced into cultivation), and by the Swede Harry Smith in 1934.

CULTIVATION After Wilson's introduction, *P. pycnoloba* persisted as a curiosity in cultivation for at least 30 years, although it was certainly extinct by the early 1970s. Said to thrive well under ordinary alpine treatment in a shaded portion of the rock garden, but never set seed in cultivation, and propagation depended on the detachment of new rosettes formed from the rhizome. It is unexpected that this bizarre plant should have proved hardy, coming as it does from a relatively low altitude. No hybrids were reported.

Section **Reinii** Balf. f., J. Roy. Hort. Soc. 39: 177. Type species *P. reinii* Franchet & Savat. (Section Fallaces Pax (1889) p.p.)

DESCRIPTION *Dwarf deciduous* hairy perennials forming an above-ground scaly resting bud in winter, the leaves lacking meal and with revolute vernation. Leaves emerging with the flowers, often reddish and like half-opened umbrellas when young, later becoming flat or with down-turned margins and green. *Leaf-blades* usually orbicular, toothed or shallowly lobed, with a long narrow stalk. *Stems* relatively short, slender and few-flowered, with narrow bracts of about 5 mm. *Calyx* rather small, narrowly bell-shaped. *Corolla* often disproportionately large, usually held horizontally, flat-faced and annulate, but bell-shaped and exannulate in *P. takedana*, purple, lilac, rose or white, heterostylous. *Pollen* subglobose, 3-syncolpate. *Capsule* narrow, sometimes curved, often exserted from the calyx, dehiscing by five narrow valves. x = 12. Self-incompatible. Flowering in the spring (usually April in cultivation, May in the wild).

DISTRIBUTION Confined to the mountains of Japan, where the four species are all very localized, two on Hokkaido, and two on Honshu, one of which also occurs on Shikoku and Kyushu. Shady wet rocks.

For most key features, for instance the 3-syncolpate pollen and the chromosome number x = 12, section Reinii is typical for subgenus *Auganthus*. It has been noted, however, that the chromosomes are quite distinct in shape and size from those in section Cortusoides and most other related *Auganthus*, from which the narrow exserted capsule and above-ground resting bud also distingishes section Reinii. DNA studies show that *P. takedana* and *P. hidakana* are sister species which form a distinct grouping about equally closely related to section Cortusoides and section Bullatae.

All the Reinii species are very localized and rare in the wild, and are threatened species. Although little known in the days of Smith and Fletcher (1946), the Reinii are now better studied in the wild, and all species are grown in small quantities.

CULTIVATION Being slow-growing, shallowly rooted, dwarf plants, very susceptible to heat and desiccation, and still rather unusual in cultivation, the Reinii species are usually grown in pots, kept almost dry in winter. In a rich water-retentive but well-drained compost plunged in a cool shaded frame with good ventilation, the species usually prove reliable and long-lived. It has been suggested that repotting both before and after flowering is beneficial. Propagation is possible from freshly harvested seed, or by division, best done in the early spring as growth starts. Most forms are reasonably free-flowering. No hybrids seem to be known.

LITERATURE. Oogaki *et al.* (1992).
Also in Bull. AGS 60: 366–369.

KEY TO SPECIES

1. Stems creeping; flowers usually solitary .... *P. takedana*
1. Rosette-forming; 1–6 flowers borne on a stem 2

2. Flowers white, funnel-shaped, exannulate .... *P. hidakana*
2. Flowers pink, flat-faced, annulate 3

3. Corolla-tube about 3× calyx, corolla lobes shallow notched .... *P. tosaensis*
3. Corolla-tube scarcely exceeding calyx; corolla lobes divided to half-way .... *P. reinii*

Primula reinii Franchet & Savat., Enum. Pl. Japan 2: 428 (1879)

P. okamotoi Koidz. (1923)
P. kitadakensis Hara (1936)
P. hisauchii Miyabe & Tatew. (1940)
P. hakonensis Nakai (1950)

DESCRIPTION *Rosettes* growing from small resting buds covered with brown scales. *Leaf-blade* kidney-shaped, usually somewhat wider than long, to 7 × 9 cm and flat when mature, but much smaller and umbrella-shaped at flowering, dark green and scarcely hairy above, paler and more hairy beneath, the margin wavy, forming 7–9 shallow lobes each bluntly to sharply toothed, pairs of veins arising from a mid-vein; leaf-stalk long and stout, to 20 cm, thickly covered with white to pink hairs. *Stem* shorter than leaves at maturity, to 10 cm, sparsely hairy, carrying 1–2 (–6) large flowers on rather long (to 3 cm) slender stalks. *Calyx* to 9 mm, hairless, cut to half-way into sharp, hard-tipped lobes. *Corolla* rose to purple with a white-rimmed yellow eye, flat-faced, up to 35 mm in diameter, the tube just exceeding the calyx, petal-lobes deeply notched to half-way. 2n = 24. (Photo: Bull. AGS 53: 56) (Plate 7.)

DISTRIBUTION Mountains of central Honshu in the provinces of Kanto, Chubu and Yamato, to the west of Tokyo; 'Mt. Miogison, Mt. Bukkyogatake, Mt. Yoshinogori, Mt. Omine'. Wet shaded rocky cliffs in the mountains, to 2500 m. Apparently very rare.

Closely related to *P. tosaensis,* from which it can be distinguished by the more lobed leaf, the larger corolla, the lobes of which are more deeply notched, and the shorter corolla tube. The most attractive of the group, which often presents a few relatively huge flowers just above the very dwarf emerging foliage.

VARIATION A variable species in the wild, with several synonyms. Most of these are trivial variants, although var. *kitadakensis* (Hara) Ohwi (1953) (= *P. kitadakensis* Hara), a high-altitude form from Kai province, is said to have thinner, more deeply and sharply lobed leaves, and very hairy flower-stalks. There is also considerable variation in the wild in the size and colour of the flowers, and it is worth selecting good forms for cultivation. In the south of its range, *P. reinii* may merge into the more southerly *P. tosaensis*, as discussed under that species.

CULTIVATION First flowering in the UK in 1909, and probably introduced by seed from Japanese gardens on several subsequent occasions. *P. reinii* has been maintained in cultivation in the UK since then, although it has never been common. Var. *kitadensis* was introduced from wild seed by Robert Rolfe in about 1985 (Bull. AGS 60: 367).

Primula tosaensis Yatabe, Tokyo Bot. Mag. 4: 1 (1890)

P. senanensis Koidz. (1923)
P. reinii var. *ovatifolia* Ohwi

DESCRIPTION Most closely related to *P. reinii* from which it differs by having purple bud scales, more entire leaf-blades which are almost hairless above and hairy only on the veins beneath, rather more numerous but smaller flowers, frequently up to 6 on a stem, but only up to 25 mm in diameter. These have a much longer corolla tube, about 3× the shorter (to 7 mm) calyx; the pale purple corolla-lobes are only shallowly notched. (Photo Bull. AGS 31: 51.)(Fig. 14.)

DISTRIBUTION Southern Japan, on the islands of Shikoku (Tosa Province) and Kyushu; and on southern Honshu (Mino Province and Kinko District, to the north of Hiroshima).

Fig. 14 *P. tosaensis*

Wet shaded rocks in mountains; high woodlands. Altitude not specified. Apparently very local and rare.

P. tosaensis apparently represents a southerly variant of its relative from central Honshu, *P. reinii*. It is distinct in the south of its range, but further north, as far as Kanto, it intergrades with *P. reinii* through var. *brachycarpa* (Hara) Ohwi (1965), which has shorter corolla-tubes, and through var. *rhodotricha* (Nakai & Maek.) Ohwi (1965) with more divided leaves.

CULTIVATION Introduced to the Royal Botanic Gardens, Edinburgh in 1933, and flowering and setting good seed there in 1937. 'With careful cultivation plants may survive for a considerable number of years.' A cool shaded position in a soil rich in leaf-mould is suggested, and a susceptibility to spring frosts is noted. Survives outside in north-west Scotland, but does not flower if the early growths are frosted. Still unusual in cultivation, although the RBG Edinburgh have a stock which appears to have been in continuous cultivation for nearly 60 years.

Primula takedana Tatew., J. Jap. Bot. 5: 29–32 (1928)

DESCRIPTION *Rosettes* growing from small pointed pinkish resting buds. *Leaves* hairy when young, but becoming hairless; *leaf-blades* dark green above, paler and more hairy beneath, kidney-shaped, to 5 cm when mature, with 5–8 shallowly triangular lobes, each usually shallowly and bluntly toothed; leaf-stalk to 12 cm, exceeding the blade, silky hairy, the hairs later turning brown. *Stems* to 15 cm, exceeding the leaves, slender, hairy at first, carrying 2–3 (–5) flowers on slender erect stalks of about 10 mm. *Calyx* to 7 mm, scarcely hairy, cut to two-thirds into narrow sharp sepal-lobes, each spiny-tipped. *Corolla* sweetly fragrant, exannulate, white with a rose eye, bell-shaped, about 15 mm in diameter, the tube funnel-shaped and usually exceeding the calyx; petal-lobes broadest at the tip, shallowly and widely notched. (Photo: Bull. AGS 56: 65.)

DISTRIBUTION Endemic to the Nupuromapporo valley gorge, a side branch of the Teshio river, Teshio province, Hokkaido. 'Steep embankment of fine soap stone (serpentine) scree just above the river ...' 'At a very disturbed site next to a stream ... growing in what appeared to be a mixture of grey clay and sharp grit. The soil in this area has very variable levels of minerals, and this undoubtedly affects the distribution of the plants.' Altitude not recorded.

Apparently a very rare and localized species in the wild, better known in cultivation. A distinctive and rather pretty little species, immediately known by its bell-shaped white flowers with an open (exannulate) mouth.

CULTIVATION Young plants were sent from Japan to Edinburgh in 1933, first flowering in 1936. Although seed is sparingly set, the species has persisted until the present day, when it is not uncommonly met with and is sometimes offered.

'This primula needs full exposure and an abundance of moisture, but accord it acute drainage.'

Primula hidakana Miyabe & Kudo in Nakai, Icon. Pl. Asiae Orient. 1: 16 (1935)

P. kamuiana Miyabe & Tatew. (1939)

DESCRIPTION Related to *P. reinii*, but with a quite different mode of growth, single leaves, or occasionally pairs, arising from along a creeping rhizome at or just below soil surface; the rhizome is covered with brown scales, and with the persistent bases of leaf-stalks. Leaves similar to *P. reinii*, although with veins radiating from a common origin, and lobes rather sharper in outline, copper-red when young, becoming dark green. Stem hairless, or hairy in var. *kamuiana*, and usually only carrying one large rose flower with a narrow yellow eye, arising from a hairy calyx. (Photo: Bull. AGS 37: 342; 53: 348; 60: 367) (Plate 7, Fig. 13.)

Fig. 13. *P. hidakana*

DISTRIBUTION Hidaka and Ishikari (Tokachi) provinces, south Hokkaido, including Mt. Apoi, Mt. Rakko and Mt. Kamuiekuushikanshi.

Above the tree-line, 700–1470 m. 'The steep slope would periodically flatten out into terraces where there was a greater depth of soil with an increase in vegetation ... in wet patches on these terraces were a number of primula species' (*P. modesta* and *P. hidakana*). From the summit of Mt. Apoi; 'truly saxatile ... in all its tight seams and crevices.' This relatively low region is subject to heavy fogs in the summer so that the tree-line is low. Another very pretty little plant which is rare and little known in the field. Both *P. hidakana* and *P. takedana* replace the 'mainland' *P. reinii* on the northern island of Hokkaido. One of the few primulas with a truly creeping mode of growth.

CULTIVATION Not cultivated in the UK in 1946, distributed by Mrs C. Greenfield and probably first shown by S.V. Horton in 1969; not rare at the present time. **AM** 1985. Reintroduced from wild seed in about 1986 by Robert Rolfe who gives a detailed account of cultivation (Bull. AGS 60: 366–9).

Section **Cortusoides** Balf. f., J. Roy. Hort. Soc. 39: 140 (1913). Type species *P. cortusoides* L. (Section Sinenses Pax (1889) p.p.) (Section Geranioides Balf. f. (1913)) (Section Mollis Balf. f. (1913))

DESCRIPTION *Deciduous*, or rarely evergreen perennials, lacking meal, arising from below-ground stocks. *Leaves* soft and usually hairy, often pleated; leaf-blades more or less rounded at the tip, circular to ovate in outline, heart-shaped at the base, toothed, and usually shallowly to deeply lobed, rarely unlobed, with revolute vernation; leaf-stalks long, narrow and usually hairy. *Stems* long, usually exceeding the leaves, bearing one or rarely several superimposed whorls of flowers, and narrow bracts. *Calyx* narrow, tubular, rigid and usually ribbed, with erect sepal-lobes. *Corolla* violet, purple, pink, white or rarely yellow, usually with a yellow eye, annulate, or occasionally exannulate, usually flat-faced with a narrow tube, heterostylous, but homostylous in *P. mollis* and *P. septemloba*. *Pollen* subglobose, 3-syncolpate. *Capsules* rarely exserted from the calyx, dehiscing by five short valves. x = 11, 12. Self-sterile, or self-compatible in homostylous species. Flowering May–June.

DISTRIBUTION Central and eastern Asia, from the Urals, Tien Shan, Pamir and eastern Afghanistan eastwards to Eastern Siberia, China and Japan. Chiefly montane woodlands, but also alpine rock-crevices, mostly from 1000–4000 m.

Section Cortusoides is a large group of species, including some easy and familiar garden plants, which are sometimes known as the 'woodland primulas'. They lack the distinctive calyx forms found in several of the other sections in this group. They are most closely related to the Japanese Reinii, from which they most obviously differ by the longer flower-stem, bearing more flowers, and by the usually shorter capsule. Also, they lack winter resting-buds on the soil surface.

The section is much more widely distributed than any other in subgenus *Auganthus*, and some species have a wide distribution in the mountains of Soviet Asia.

As the name suggests, Cortusoides species are closely related to the genus *Cortusa*, a genus of some eight species distributed from France to Japan. *Cortusa* is very similar in most features, but has an open, bell-shaped corolla which lacks a limb (unlike the similar *P. geraniifolia*), and a ring within the flower formed by the filament bases. DNA studies have suggested that *Cortusa* is embedded within *Primula* subgenus *Auganthus* but may be distinct from section Cortusoides, although it will be necessary to study more species of both groups before a definitive answer is reached. In this account I have decided to omit *Cortusa* until this information is forthcoming. I have been encouraged to reach this decision by the knowledge that *Cortusa* is in serious need of a complete revision which would be best undertaken by Russian or Asian taxonomists.

CULTIVATION *P. polyneura, P. cortusoides, P. sieboldii* and *P. kisoana* are long-lived, free-flowering and undemanding plants for a cool, sheltered, moisture-retentive but well-drained site in a peaty or 'woodsy' soil. Some are very attractive plants which are well worth a place in any garden, and deserve to be better known. They are readily grown from seed, and can be propagated by division, especially those species such as *P. sieboldii* which are creeping. Several other species such as *P. palmata, P. latisecta, P. minkwitzae* and *P. septemloba* have been introduced in recent years and seem to be established at present (2001).

Some other species come from lower forest zones, and seem not to be very hardy in most British conditions, especially *P. geranifolia, P. mollis* and probably *P. vaginata*.

A further group, notably *P. eucyclia, P. pauliana* and *P. alsophila* persisted for some years in cultivation, but proved slow to increase and difficult to propagate, and were eventually lost, although *P. heucherifolia* still persists. No hybrids seem to have been reported.

KEY TO SPECIES

1. Leaf-veins branching from the mid-rib. Calyx many-nerved 2
1. Leaf-veins radiating from the base (i.e. leaf palmate), calyx few-nerved 12

2. Flowers yellow or white, rosette-forming or tufted 3
2. Flowers pink to purple, or if flowers white then plant of creeping habit 4

3. Flowers yellow, tube concolorous .... *P. eugeniae*
3. Flowers white with a violet tube .... *P. lactiflora*

4. Habit creeping; flowers more than 25 mm in diameter .... *P. sieboldii*
4. Rosette-forming or tufted; flowers not exceeding 30 mm in diameter, usually smaller 5

5. Flowers borne in whorls; calyx reddish, flowers not exceeding 15 mm in diameter 6
5. Flowers borne in an umbel, rarely with 2–3 whorls; calyx usually green; flowers usually exceeding 15 mm diameter.... 8

6. Leaf-blades softly hairy, scarcely lobed 7
6. Leaf-blades almost lacking hairs, obviously lobed .... *P. violaris*

7. Leaf-blades longer than wide; calyx not exceeding 9 mm .... *P. cinerascens*
7. Leaf blades wider than long; calyx to 12 mm .... *P. mollis*

8. Flowers violet; calyx glabrous .... *P. kaufmanniana*
8. Flowers pink to purple; calyx usually hairy, at least on veins 9

9. Flowers in a single whorl, usually not overtopping the leaves .... *P. minkwitziae*
9. Flowers often in two or more whorls, the top flowers easily overtopping the leaves 10

10. Leaf-blade scarcely longer than wide; calyx 8–12 mm long .... *P. polyneura*
10. Leaf-blade about 1.5× as long as wide; calyx not exceeding 7 mm 11

11. Leaf-blades lobed to more than half-way to mid-rib .... *P. dueckelmanii*
11. Leaf-blades lobed to less than half-way to mid-rib .... *P. cortusoides*

12. Flowers yellow, forming a spike; capsule long, narrow and curved .... *P. pauliana*
12. Flowers usually pinkish, in whorls or umbels; capsule not long and curved 13

13. Forming above-ground stolons ('runners') like a strawberry 14
13. Above-ground stolons absent, creeping underground by rhizomes or clump-forming 15

14. Leaves divided to one-third; flower-stalks exceeding 1 cm .... *P. alsophila*
14. Leaves divided to more than one-half; flower stalks less than 1 cm .... *P. eucyclia*

15. Leaf-stalks with small scattered hairs, or hairless 16
15. Leaf-stalks thickly furnished with long hairs 17

16. Plant exceeding 12 cm, usually with several superimposed umbels .... *P. jesoana*
16. Plant less than 12 cm, flowers forming a single umbel .... *P. vaginata*

17. Leaves dissected to half-way or beyond 18
17. Leaves dissected to less than half-way 21

18. Flowers borne at the level of the leaves, flat-faced with a whitish eye 19
18. Stem below lowest flowers usually exceeding the leaves; flowers cup-shaped without an eye 20

19. Sinus between leaf-lobes acute; calyx not exceeding 7 mm .... *P. palmata*
19. Sinus between leaf-lobes acute; calyx exceeding 7 mm .... *P. latisecta*

20. Stems to 50 cm, usually bearing more than one whorl of homostylous flowers .... *P. septemloba*
20. Stems not exceeding 25 cm, flowers heterostylous, borne in a single whorl .... *P. geraniifolia*

21. Flowers narrowly bell-shaped, borne to one side .... *P. heucherifolia*
21. Flowers flat-faced, borne around the stem 22

22. Shortly creeping by rhizomes; lowest flowers not overtopping leaves .... *P. kisoana*
22. Clump-forming; stem below lowest flowers exceeding leaves .... *P. jesoana*

Subsection **Cortusoides**

Leaf-veins branching from the mid-rib. Calyx many-nerved.

Primula cortusoides L. Sp. Pl. 1: 144 (1753)

P. dentiflora Andrews (1804)
P. dentata Donn (1819)
P. saxatilis Komarov (1901)
Androsace primuloides Moench. (1802)
Aleuritia cortusoides Spach (1840)

DESCRIPTION *Leaves* clumped, deciduous, arising from a short stout rhizome. *Leaf-blade* sparsely hairy on both sides, rather thin in texture, narrowly oval, to 9 × 6 cm, corrugated, with 4–6 shallow and blunt irregular lobes on each side between veins, the lobes toothed; leaf-stalks usually longer than the blade, thickly hairy. *Stem* up to 50 cm, usually less, disproportionately slender, hairy, at least below, bearing one or occasionally more umbels of 2–15 slightly pendulous flowers on stalks from 1 to 3 cm. *Calyx* to 7 mm, softly hairy or rarely hairless, cut to half-way into erect narrow sharp lobes. *Corolla* rose, red or purplish-red, rarely white, usually with a yellow eye, flat-faced, to 20 mm in diameter, the tube exceeding the calyx, heterostylous; petal-lobes rounded and variably notched. *Capsule* oblong, exceeding the calyx. 2n = 24. Pins 1% self-fertile, thrums fully self-sterile. (Plate 7.)

DISTRIBUTION Very widespread, from the western (European) slope of the Urals, through the Irtusk region of western Siberia, the Altai and the Tomsk region of eastern Siberia to Mongolia (Ala Shan), Manchuria, north Korea and northern China in the provinces of Gansu, Shaanxi and possibly north Sichuan. It is thus broadly distributed between the latitudes 40° N and 55° N and between the longitudes 57° E and 130° E, a distance of some 4800 km.

P. cortusoides has been reported from a wide variety of habitats: cliffs of an elevated basaltic plateau; rock fissures filled with humus; sparse mountain woods; rocky slopes; birch woods on the plains. Low and middle altitudes.

There is a long-standing dispute as to whether the Linnean *P. cortusoides*, described from western Siberia, is the same species as Komarov's *P. saxatilis*, described from much further east on the boundaries of Manchuria and northern Korea. Federov (1952) and Smith & Fletcher (1944) admit that few if any reliable characters separate these widely disjunct types. It had generally been considered that *P. saxatilis* has longer flower-stalks, resulting in umbels with a more open and drooping aspect, but *P. cortusoides* appears to be variable for this character, and in particular, the flower-stalks in this species tend to lengthen with maturity. We have shown at Newcastle that plants from these different areas are fully interfertile, and I am including *P. saxatilis* within *P. cortusoides*.

A further confusion has resulted from the use of the illegitimate name *P. patens* Turcz. (1838), described from Dahuria, i.e. from the Manchurian–Korean frontier close to Vladivostock. This is an area close to where '*P. saxatilis*' occurs, but further to the north. Thus, 'P. patens' has at times been considered to be the correct and prior name for the latter. However, Smith & Fletcher (1944) included *P. patens* within the eastern Asiatic *P. sieboldii*, a species differing in many characters from *P. cortusoides*. *P. sieboldii* was originally described from Japan, but is recognized today as having a wider distributional range on the Asiatic mainland, to the north of the eastern fringe of the range of *P. cortusoides*.

VARIATION A moderately variable species as seen in cultivation; little is recorded of its variation in the wild. Some cultivated strains are of a poor lilac-pink with small flowers on very long spindly stems. It is worth selecting relatively compact forms of a good colour. A white form has been recorded from the wild under the name var. *albiflora* Theod. & Fed. from the Sayan foothills. Plants seen in 1998 and 2000 (SBQE 754, 760, 796) in Gansu included many large-flowered compact individuals which seemed intermediate with *P. polyneura*.

CULTIVATION In cultivation since 1794, when Pallas sent seeds from Siberia to the Hammersmith firm of Lee & Kennedy, while it was also grown in Berlin in 1806. It has probably been in cultivation since that time. It has never been particularly popular, being rather overshadowed as a garden plant by the next two species. However, in a cool, shaded but well-drained site it is a good doer, multiplying well, and is readily replaced from seed.

Recent introductions from Gansu under SBQE numbers are well worth seeking out.

Primula polyneura Franchet, Journ. de Bot. 9: 448 (1895)

P. veitchii Duthie (1905)
P. lichiangensis Forrest (1911)
P. hymenophylla Balf. f. & Forrest (1920)
P. sataniensis Balf. f. & Farrer (1920)
P. sikuensis Balf. f. & Farrer (1920)
P. saxatilis Kom. var. *pubescens* Pax & Hoffm. (1921)

DESCRIPTION *Leaves* clumped, deciduous, arising from a stout stock, sparsely hairy to hairless above, usually thickly covered with whitish, or more rarely reddish bristly or cottony hairs beneath, especially on the veins, but occasionally nearly hairless. *Leaf-blades* thicker in texture than *P. cortusoides*, scarcely longer than wide, to about 10 cm, divided to one-third into between 7 and 11 rather regular, somewhat blunt triangular lobes which are distinctly longer and more regular than those in *P. cortusoides*. Leaf-stalk to 20 cm, rather stout, usually very white-hairy. *Stem* to 50 cm, usually much less but exceeding the leaves, usually rather stout and very hairy, bearing 1–(3) whorls of between 2 and 12 flowers. Flower stalks rather stiff, usually suberect, to 25 mm. *Calyx* to 12 mm, narrowly tubular, usually hairy, cut to about half-way into narrow sharp sepal-lobes. *Corolla* pale pink to purple, including good reds, with a greenish-yellow to orange eye, flat-faced, to 25 mm in diameter, the tube exceeding the calyx, heterostylous; petal-lobes with widely notched, or rarely toothed end. Capsule about equalling the calyx. 2n = 24. Totally self-sterile. (Plate 7.)

DISTRIBUTION Widespread in north-west China from south-eastern Gansu (south of *P. cortusoides*) southwards through western and central Sichuan to the Tibetan–Yunnan frontier area on the divides between the Salween, Mekong and Yangtse rivers. Frequently reported from such well-known primula localities as the Tatsienlu area, the Muli area, Moupine, the Zhongdian plateau, the Lichiang snow range and the Yangtse bend area. Widespread and locally frequent, 2300–4300 m.

'Open and stony lime soil' in the upper zone of fir forests, 'moist, shaded wooded areas', flowering in June in the wild. In my experience it is most commonly found on steep but vegetated banks above paths on the edge of mixed woodland at about 3500 m.

Of the Cortusoides primulas that the gardener is likely to encounter, *P. polyneura* is readily distinguished by its robust tufted habit, and its rather thick, bristly-hairy and rounded, not elongate, leaf-blades with regular fairly deep lobes.

VARIATION An extremely variable plant in the wild and in the garden; the synonyms listed above refer to distinct geographical forms which have since been placed within one species. *P. veitchii* refers to robust white-hairy plants which often have flowers of a deep rose-crimson. *P. lichiangensis* was a name given to relatively hairless forms, although var. *hapala* Balf. f. & Forrest referred to much hairier forms indistinguishable from less robust forms of *P. polyneura*. Plants from the Lichiang range often seem to have pale pink flowers with a darker eye. *P. hymenophylla* is even less hairy, with thinner leaves, while *P. sataniensis* from Kansu is a generally smaller plant with hairless leaves, but very hairy stems and flower-stalks. *P. sikuensis* also refers to small plants from Kansu. These latter two taxa refer to gradations towards *P. cortusoides* which occur at the northern edge of the range of *P. polyneura*.

CULTIVATION First introduced by Ernest Wilson in 1905 from west Sichuan as *P. veitchii*, and subsequently on several occasions by Farrer and Forrest under a variety of names. In recent years, several introductions were made from north-west Yunnan under KGB numbers in 1993 (377, 398, 613) and ACE numbers in 1994 (1429, 2431). Long-lived, easily raised from seed, and grows well in suitable cool, well-drained situations in the garden. Perhaps the best general garden plant in the group, and in its best forms very attractive. Most garden plants fall under the *P. veitchii* heading, being robust large-flowered bristly-hairy plants, with flowers varying in colour from a soft baby-pink to a strident magenta-crimson.

Primula sieboldii E. Morren, Belg. Hort. 23: 97 (1873)

P. cortusoides Thunb. (1784) non L. (1753)
P. patens Trautv. (1884)

P. saxatilis Pax (1905) p.p. non Komarov (1952)
P. gracilis Stein (1881)

DESCRIPTION A *creeping* deciduous plant with one or a few leaves arising at intervals from a slender rhizome, but eventually making large clumps. *Leaves* erect, pale-green, with long scattered hairs on both surfaces. *Leaf-blades* oblong or narrowly oval, corrugated and convex, turned down at the margin, to 10 × 6 cm, with many regular blunt large-teeth/short lobules; leaf-stalk to 12 cm, narrow and hairy. *Stems* to 30 cm, usually shorter, hairy below but more or less hairless above, rather slender, bearing 1–(2) whorls of 2–15 flowers on suberect more or less hairless and slender stalks up to 4 cm in length. *Calyx* bell-shaped, to 12 mm, hairless or nearly so, often red-lined, cut to two-thirds into widely spreading narrow sharp sepal-lobes. *Corolla* purple, magenta, red, pink or white, usually with a white eye of varying size, flat-faced, to 35 mm in diameter, the tube about 2× the calyx, heterostylous; petal-lobes broadly dissected into two large lobes, which are sometimes strongly toothed or even lacerate. *Capsule* shorter than the calyx. 2n = 24, also 36 (cultivars). Pins partly self-fertile; thrums self-sterile. (Plate 7.)

DISTRIBUTION From eastern Siberia (Nertschinsk, just north of the Mongolian–Manchurian frontier), south-eastwards through northern Manchuria, the northern extremity of Korea, Amurland, north of Vladivostock to Japan (southern Hokkaido, Honshu and Kyushu), thus having a range of about 1600 km in north-east Asia. Grows to the north of *P. polyneura*, and to the east and north of *P. cortusoides*. 'Wet grassy places in lowlands along rivers' (Japan); 'meadows and scrub' (Siberia), 'in light woods'. Altitudinal range, to 2000 m?. As a boreal or even subarctic species, occurring to the north of its relatives, *P. sieboldii* is less of an alpine, but coming from these localities is certainly fully hardy.

The type of *P. patens* shows the spreading or even reflexed sepal-lobes characteristic of *P. sieboldii*. In Fl. SSSR, *P. patens* Turcz. (1838) is the name given to *P. sieboldii*, but this publication is invalid, and the first valid publication (Trautv. 1884) postdates the correct name *P. sieboldii*. *P. sieboldii* is readily distinguished from *P. cortusoides* and *P. polyneura* by the spreading sepal lobes, and the creeping habit. Also, the flower never has a yellow eye.

Pollinated chiefly by queen *Bombus*. I. Washitani and co-workers have investigated intensively the reproductive biology of small threatened remnant populations in populated regions of Japan. Seed-set tended to be very low or zero in small populations, but higher in large populations, and thrum seed-set was favoured by a high stigma position, but pins merely by size of plant. Seed-set relied entirely on pollinator activity. Seed-set often failed due to predation by *Eusphalerum* beetles and disease by *Orocystis* smuts. At least one recombinant self-fertile short homostyle was discovered by these studies, which, it was predicted, should succeed in conditions of pollinator shortage brought about by anthropogenic disturbance.

VARIATION Little is recorded of the variability of this species in the wild, but *P. sieboldii* is an exceptionally variable species in cultivation. It appears to have been popular as a decorative plant in Japan long before its introduction into western gardens, and most of the variants grown today seem to have been selected there, and bear Japanese names. Indeed, it is said that a specialist society still exists in Japan devoted entirely to this species, and more than 100 named varieties have been known there (a similar society devoted to the culture of dandelions is also said to have once flourished there!)

Few of these variants seem to be available in the UK today, although they were more common formerly. An excellent white form, sometimes known as 'Snowflake', is widely grown, and a large-flowered pink form with lacerated petals called 'Geisha Girl' is also sometimes seen. Most plants currently seen in UK gardens have magenta-purple flowers with a large diffuse white eye, and probably closely resemble wild forms. 'Madam Butterfly', **PC** 1963.

CULTIVATION *P. sieboldii* was first introduced from Japanese gardens by von Siebold to his garden at Leiden, and from there to Messrs Veitch, London, in 1862. It is readily grown in the open garden without protection. It thrives best in a peaty, partially shaded site where it has plenty of room to run about undisturbed. Compared to its relatives, it seems to set seed rarely in cultivation, perhaps because only one clone is usually grown in a given place, but it is very readily propagated by division as it comes into growth.

P. sieboldii remains underground in a dormant condition from early August to mid-May. In my experience, the main threat to its well-being results from the gardener forgetting its position! As it is shallowly rooted, it also suffers from the activities of birds such as blackbirds, and some growers place it under chicken netting.

LITERATURE (All by authors I. Washitani and co-workers)

Plant Species Biology 6: 27–37
Plant Species Biology 9: 169–176
Journal of Ecology 82: 571–579
Conservation Biology 10: 59–64
Researches on Population Ecology 38: 249–256
Functional Ecology 14: 502–512
Ecological Research 15: 307–322

Primula kaufmanniana Regel, Acta Hort. Petrop. 3: 131 (1874)

DESCRIPTION The most widespread of this group of five closely related central Asiatic species which morphologically lie near *P. polyneura* and *P. cortusoides*. From the former this species is best diagnosed as having *violet* flowers (rarely white), thinner leaves, and a hairless calyx; from the latter also by having round, not oblong-oval leaf-blades. There is usually only one whorl of flowers with 3–6 small (to 15 mm in diameter) flowers per whorl. (Fig. Halda: 76.)

DISTRIBUTION Confined to the mountains of Soviet central Asia, where it is fairly widespread, from the Pamirs (adjacent to *P. dueckelmanii*) north-westwards through the Alai Range (Ala-Tau) in Tadzhikstan to Bokhara in Uzbekistan, and then north-eastwards through the Kirghizhian mountains (Tass Alau and Altau) (near *P. minkwitziae* and *P. eugeniae*) to the Alma Altai and the eastern Tien Shan, thus encompassing the more limited ranges of *P. lactiflora*, *P. eugeniae* and *P. minkwitziae*.

'Rocks in the subalpine and upper forest zone of mountains', 1000–3700 m. In cultivation at Edinburgh from 1905 to about 1927. Seems not to have been in cultivation, at least in the west, since then. Compared with its relatives, it seems not to be a particularly desirable species.

Primula dueckelmanii Gilli, Feddes Rep. 62: 22 (1959)

DESCRIPTION A close relative of *P. kaufmanniana*, from which it may not be distinct, but with reddish flowers and with more (2–4) superimposed whorls of flowers. Leaf-blades dissected to more than half-way to mid-rib. Wakhan corridor, east Afghanistan, 'sunny slope in small stream valley'. Although this species has probably not been in cultivation, several Western expeditions to Afghanistan in the 1960s and 1970s visited the Wakhan corridor and saw '*P. kaufmanniana*', which was probably this species.

Primula minkwitziae Smith, Notes Roy. Bot. Gdn. Edinb. 18: 181 (1935)

DESCRIPTION Another relative of *P. kaufmanniana*, but an alpine which is therefore dwarfer, with large (to 25 mm diameter) bright *pinky-lilac* flowers in a single whorl at the level of the leaves, and leaves with a thick covering of soft hairs. The orbicular, even kidney-shaped leaf-blades were said to have palmate venation, which would place this species in subsection Geranioides, but in Halda's superb photos (Bull. ARGS, 49: 144) they are clearly seen to have pinnate venation. Potentially a most attractive species.

DISTRIBUTION Mt. Dschebogli, southern Kazakhstan; Talassian Alatau; Ala Archa valley, Kyrgyzhian Altau. Limestone crevices and high screes to 3000 m, descending to 1000 m in north-facing crevices just south of Bisket in the Ala-Archa National Park.

In cultivation in 1991, perhaps from Halda's (1989) seed, and recollected by him in 1994. Some of these seedlings proved to be a *Cortusa*, but others are correctly named and have persisted in cultivation, although they have proved shy to flower.

Primula eugeniae Federov, Bot. Zhurn. SSSR 33: 31 (1948)

DESCRIPTION Another close relative of *P. kaufmanniana*, and of *P. lactiflora*, but immediately distinct as the only member of this section with *sulphur-yellow* flowers. Crevices of marble rocks in the upper alpine zone between 3700 and 4000 m, Mt. Baubash-Ata, Fergana Range, Altau mountains of Kirghizhia. This little-known endemic was first discovered in 1945, and has unfortunately not been in cultivation. It sounds very desirable. Very rare, described in the Red Data book for the USSR. (Fig. Halda: 76.)

Primula lactiflora S. Turk., Bot. Mat. Gerb. Glavn. Bot. Sada RSFSR 2: 13 (1921)

DESCRIPTION A more refined relative of *P. kaufmanniana*, more delicate and slender throughout, and distinguished by the *white* petal-lobes and narrow violet tube to the corolla, a prominently ribbed calyx, and broad bracts. Said to have a poor root system, which is fragrant, and a tiny winter bud.

DISTRIBUTION Endemic to the Zeravschan in the Pamir-Altai range of Tadzhikstan and south Kirghizia, north to Fergana. Cold rock ledges, walls and islands of tiny shrubs in screes, 2800–3500 m, but descending to 1800 m around streams. Wet dolomite walls and between large mossy boulders in deep, soil-rich scree.

Apparently introduced by Halda in about 1990 (no details given in Bull. American Rock Garden Society 50: 176), where he says it was easily raised from seed and propagated by division, and that it failed to flower in heavy shade. Fig. Halda: 77. There seems to have been no further news.

Var. *lactocortusoides* Schipczinsky (1921) is smaller and more hairy.

P. geranophylla Koval., Izv. Akad. Nauk. Uzbek. SSR ser. Biol. 15: 14 (1959), is structurally very similar to *P. lactiflora*, but has purple flowers. It comes from lower altitudes in Tadzhikstan and Usbekistan (1000–2400 m, dry open woodland), and it may be best regarded as an aestivating, altitudinal subspecies of it. Fig. Halda: 83. Also discussed by Halda, Bull. ARGS 50: 176.

Primula mollis Nutt., Bot. Mag. t.4798 (1854)

P. seclusa Balf. f. & Forrest (1915)

DESCRIPTION A *clump* forming, or somewhat creeping *evergreen* plant, densely covered throughout with short soft hairs. The *leaf-blades* are formed like a half-opened umbrella, round to kidney-shaped, to 18cm across, smaller in winter, pale green, with a shallowly wavy and obscurely toothed margin; the leaf-stalk is densely woolly, to 20 cm. *Stems* to 60 cm, but usually shorter in cultivation, very hairy, with 2–10 (usually about 5 in cultivation) whorls of between 4 to 9 flowers borne on stout, very hairy stalks to 3 cm. *Calyx* bell-shaped, to 12 mm, deep red, softly hairy, cut to half-way into rather blunt 5-veined lobes. *Corolla* dull pink to crimson, with a yellow eye, usually homostylous, rather funnel-shaped, about 15 mm in diameter, the tube 2× the calyx, with rounded shallowly notched petal-lobes. Capsule equalling the calyx. 2n = 24. Self-fertile.

DISTRIBUTION Widespread but apparently scattered in the eastern Sinohimalaya, from Bhutan through Assam to upper Burma and the Yunnan salient around Zhongdian, on both sides of the Salween, thus distributed for some 800 km around the headwaters of the Brahmaputra and Irrawaddy.

'Shady situations on the margins of thickets and big streams, 2100–3300 m'.

A very distinctive species with its soft round umbrella leaves and its candelabras of rather unattractive small rosy flowers. *P. seclusa* from Yunnan was originally thought to have a larger calyx, but no other significant variants have been described.

P. mollis is very probably a homostyle relative of *P. cinerascens*. It is interesting that, as in the other homostyle Cortusoides, *P. septemloba*, homostyly occurs at the diploid level (p.61). DNA studies show that *P. mollis* is not sister to the two other species in this section tested, but is nevertheless embedded within the relevant part of subgenus *Auganthus*. More species need to be studied before firm conclusions can be made as to its exact affinities.

CULTIVATION Introduced by Booth from Bhutan in 1852–3, and by Forrest from Yunnan in 1913. It has persisted in cultivation since that time, but is not often met with. However, it has persisted at Glasgow Botanic Garden for many years under glass and is currently (2001) being distributed from that source. The young growth is tender, so that it is readily lost to spring frosts. Nevertheless, its scarcity may rather reflect its rather unattractive flowers, although it has interesting foliage. Being homostylous it sets abundant seed regularly and this germinates well, so that the species sometimes self-sows modestly in a cool damp situation although most permanent colonies have been kept under shady, humid glass, just frost-free.

Primula cinerascens Franchet, Journ. de Bot. 9: 448 (1895)

P. violodora Dunn (1902)
P. riparia Balf. f. & Forrest (1915)
P. sinomollis Balf. f. & Forrest (1915)
P. sylvicola Hutchinson (1918)

DESCRIPTION A close relative of *P. mollis*, but with the leaf-blade usually longer than wide, a shorter calyx (rarely exceeding 9 mm) and heterostylous flowers. From further east, south-east Gansu, extreme north-east Sichuan and west Hubei (subsp. *cinerascens*), and north-west Yunnan (subsp. *sinomollis*). Woods, mountain cliffs, 1300–2300 m. Cultivated at Edinburgh 1913–18, but soon lost. *P.c.* subsp. *sinomollis* is a larger plant with more numerous whorls to the inflorescence and a hairier calyx.

Primula violaris Smith & Fletcher, Trans. Bot. Soc. Edinb. 34: 85 (1944)

DESCRIPTION Another relative of *P. mollis*, but with even larger and much more lobed leaves which are almost hairless except for the shaggily hairy leaf-stalks. Chienshi and Tzu Kwei, Hsien, west Hubei, overlapping with *P. cinerascens*.

Subsection **Geranioides** (Balf. f.) Smith & Fletcher, Trans. Bot. Soc. Edinb. 33: 57 (1944) (section Geranioides Balf. f. (1913))

Leaf-veins radiating from the base (i.e. leaf palmate), calyx few-nerved. Some species with x = 11.

Primula kisoana Miq., Ann. Mus. Bot. Lugd. Bot. 3: 119 (1867)

DESCRIPTION A rather robust clumped but also shortly creeping (stoloniferous) deciduous plant. *Leaf-blades* kidney-shaped, to 7 cm, rather thick and covered with long white hairs, thinly above, but more thickly below; margins wavy to shallowly and bluntly lobed; leaf-stalk stout and fleshy, pinkish, to 10 cm, covered with pinkish hairs. *Stem* to 20 cm, scarcely exceeding the leaves, stout and hairy with (1)–4 superimposed umbels of 2–8 flowers borne on hairy stalks to 30 mm. *Calyx* narrowly bell-shaped, to 12 mm, covered with pinkish hairs, cut to two-thirds into narrow sharp spreading lobes. *Corolla* pink, rose-violet with a darker eye and tube, or white with a greenish-yellow eye; flat-faced, to 30 mm in diameter; tube 2× the calyx, hairy on the outside, and at the mouth; petal-lobes widest near the apex and narrowly and deeply notched. *Capsule* equalling the calyx. 2n = 24. (Plate .7)

DISTRIBUTION Southern Japan, Kanto and the south-central district on Honshu, and on the island of Shikoku.

'Damp shaded sites in the alpine zone.' This species, which has become increasingly familiar and popular in cultivation in recent years, appears to be extremely rare in the wild, being only known from a few scattered sites where it usually survives in very small quantity.

P. kisoana comes closest to its Japanese relative *P. jesoana,* but has relatively shorter stems and less lobed leaves. As seen in cultivation it can be a spectacular plant, one of the most attractive of all primulas, especially in its fine white form.

VARIATION This seems to be largely restricted to flower colour. At present we have in cultivation a superb snow-white form, and forms ranging from a clear pink with a greenish eye to a deep rose-crimson with a darker eye.

CULTIVATION Cultivated in Japan by 1733. Grown at Edinburgh, 1916–18, and again 1934–43 (**AM** 1934 for a rose form). Well established in the USA in 1948, and the rose-coloured form has probably persisted until the present day.

At the International Rock Garden Conference at Nottingham in 1981 (**AM**), a veritable sensation was caused by an extremely beautiful exhibit of the white form in a rustic wooden box which had been brought directly from Japan.

This form is markedly rhizomatous, and is easily propagated, and has now become widespread. A baby-pink form is currently in circulation.

Grows well in large pots sunk in a shady position in a very open compost, or in the shade of dwarf shrubs in a 'woodsy' soil in the open garden. Grows magnificently at Kew.

LITERATURE

Deno, N.C. (1992). *Bull. American Rock Garden Society* 50: 211–213.

Primula jesoana Miq., Ann. Mus. Bot. Lugd.-Bat. 3: 119 (1867)

P. yesomontana Nakai & Kitag. (1936)
P. hondoensis Nakai & Kitag. (1936)
P. yedoensis Franchet & Savat. (1879)
P. yesoana Petitm. (1907)
P. loeseneri Kitag. (1936)
P. paxiana Gilg (1904) non Kuntze
P. tyoseniana Nakai ex Kitag. (1936)
P. maclarenii Balf. f. (1919)
P. hallaisanensis Nakai ex Kitag. (1936)

DESCRIPTION Differs from *P. kisoana* by the more slender, non-creeping habit with more slender stems, a more elongate inflorescence which easily tops the leaves, and the smaller flowers (to 20 mm in diameter), which are hairless. The leaves are also less hairy than in *P. kisoana* and more deeply lobed and the leaf-stalks are less hairy. 2n = 24, 26.

DISTRIBUTION Japan; widespread but rare and scattered through the mountains of western Hokkaido and the northern half of Honshu. The dubiously distinct *P. loeseneri* occurs in Korea including Cheju island, to the Manchurian border. 'High mountains.'

VARIATION Variable both within and between the scarce and local scattered populations, thus accounting for the large number of (mostly Japanese) synonyms created. Varies in size, leaf-shape, hairiness and in flower colour from soft pink to rose-purple, and occasionally white, although no white forms seem to be currently cultivated. Var. *pubescens* (Takeda) Takeda & Hara (= *P. yesomontana*) from Hokkaido differs by the more shallowly lobed leaves, and long spreading hairs on the leaf-stalks and veins beneath. Korean material (= *P. loeseneri*) is said usually to have less deeply heart-shaped leaves, and a longer corolla tube more than 2× the calyx.

In flower, *P. jesoana* differs from all its relatives (with radiating leaf-veins), except for *P. kisoana*, in almost always having a 'candelabra' type of inflorescence with superimposed whorls of flowers.

CULTIVATION First introduced into the West as dormant plants sent from Japan to the Royal Botanic Garden, Edinburgh in 1932. It was still grown there in 1943, and was apparently familiar in the USA in the 1960s. Seed and occasionally plants are still offered today, but in my experience these usually prove to be *P. polyneura* or *P. cortusoides*.

However, correctly named plants can be found at Kew and Branklyn, and with a few specialist gardeners, and these seem to represent recent introductions from seed.

P. jesoana is likely to thrive in the same situations as suit *P. kisoana*, although it may not be so long lived.

Primula heucherifolia Franchet, Bull. Soc. Bot. Fr. 33: 65 (1886) (ut *P. heucheraefolia* sic.).

P. gagnepainii Petitm. (1907)
P. lanata Pax & Hoffm. (1921)
P. oculata Duthie ex Balf. f. (1913)

DESCRIPTION Rhizomatous and *shortly creeping*, plantlets occurring near the parent, deciduous. *Leaf-blades* round, 7 × 6 cm, deeply heart-shaped at the base, with 7–11 rounded lobes, the lobes themselves blunt-toothed, sparsely hairy above; leaf-stalks about equalling the blade, thickly whitish to tawny-hairy. *Stem* to 30 cm, slender, softly hairy, bearing a single umbel of 3–10 unidirectionally nodding flowers on slender stalks to 3 cm in length. *Calyx* bell-shaped, to 7 mm, cut to half-way into somewhat rounded or shortly pointed three-veined lobes, shortly hairy. *Corolla* limb lilac-mauve to deep rich purple, narrowly bell-shaped, nodding, to 25 mm in diameter, exannulate, the tube cylindrical and exceeding the calyx; petal-lobes rounded and shortly notched. *Capsule* rounded and shorter than the calyx. Flowering in April in cultivation, about one month earlier than most relatives. 2n = 22. (Plate 28.)

DISTRIBUTION West Sichuan; Moupine, Wa-shan, Pao-hsien Hsien, Emei Shan and Tatsienlu, 2000–3200 m, shady humid places under rocks, in grass and occasionally under trees. Apparently scarce; it seems to have been collected on only five occasions.

This handsome primula is immediately known from its relatives by its deeply coloured narrow bells, hanging in one direction, and by its rounded leaf-lobes. Although seed and plants under this name are frequently offered today, these usually prove to be the very different *P. polyneura*, with its pinnately veined leaves and pink, flat-faced flowers.

CULTIVATION Introduced by Wilson (4054) from Tatsienlu and flowered in 1906 by Ellen Willmott (as *P. gagnepainii*) and by Messers Veitch (named by Duthie *P. oculata*). It survived for R.B. Cooke and Wisley until the 1930s, for Edinburgh until 1940, and at Barnhaven, Oregon until at least that date. Appeared at an Alpine Garden Society Show in 1996, the property of John Forrest, who had obtained it from the late Reginald Kaye some 20 years previously. Has now been propagated and is grown successfully by several enthusiasts (2001). Seems straightforward plunged in a cool frame, potted annually and kept nearly dry in winter; hardy to at least –10°C. Recollected by Needham from a cliff edge under rhododendrons at Lei Deng Ping, 2430 m, in 1991, but it is not known if this introduction survived.

Primula geraniifolia Hook. f., Fl. Brit. India 3: 484 (1882)

P. humicola Balf. f. & Forrest (1920)

DESCRIPTION A shortly creeping plant forming rosettes of deciduous kidney-shaped leaves, somewhat resembling those of *P. reinii* and *P. vaginata*, the blade up to 8 cm in diameter, markedly heart-shaped at the base, with 7–9 sharp lobes, often very shallow but sometimes more deeply incised, and subdivided, each bluntly and rather regularly toothed, dark green or tinged purplish and somewhat shiny above with sparse long hairs; leaf-stalk about equalling the blade, thickly covered with tawny hairs. *Stem* exceeding the leaves, dark and covered with spreading hairs, bearing 1–(2) umbels of 3–12 spreading or drooping flowers on slender hairy stalks which become erect in fruit. *Calyx* 5–10 mm, bell-shaped, usually reddish, cut to half-way into sharp and narrow usually three-nerved lobes. *Corolla* limb rose to purple, cup-shaped, with or without a cream eye, to 20 mm in diameter but usually smaller, exannulate or slightly annulate, the rather narrow cylindrical tube exceeding the calyx; petal-lobes broadest near the tip, entire, notched, or divided into two rounded lobes; stigma two-lobed. *Capsule* usually slightly exceeding the calyx. 2n = 22. Pins 2% self-fertile, thrums 4% self-fertile. (Photo: Fls. Himalaya: fig. 851.)

DISTRIBUTION Widespread in the eastern Himalaya, from Pokhara in central Nepal though Sikkim, Bhutan and south-east Tibet to just within the Yunnan border on the Salweed–Mekong divide. Shady forest areas amongst boulders, usually growing in thick moss, in areas of high monsoon rainfall, 2700–4500 m.

An attractive, delicate plant which vegetatively resembles *Cortusa matthioli* closely, differing mostly in flower structure. It is often confused with it in the trade; the exserted stigmas of the latter are the best guide. Also closely allied to the Chinese *P. septemloba*, as shown by the DNA, which differs in being more robust and by having homostylous flowers. *P. kisoana* and *P. jesoana* have paler non-shiny leaves, and whitish hairs. Superficially resembles *P. vaginata* from the same area, but with non-channelled hairy-glandular leaf-stalks.

CULTIVATION There seems to be no record of the introduction of *P. geraniifolia* into cultivation, but it was grown in Edinburgh and elsewhere in 1928, 1932, 1943 and in the 1960s. Latterly, most plants or seed offered under this name have proved to be the ubiquitous *P. polyneura*, and this may be why one account states that it is coarse and hardy, for it seems to be neither.

J. Forrest of Blackpool raised seedlings from wild-collected Nepalese seed in 1989. These are best kept in a cool shaded site in summer, and protected in a frame from severe frost in winter. Plants still persist in 2001, but are not often seen. The KEKE introduction in 1989 is *P. vaginata*.

Primula septemloba Franchet, Bull. Soc. Bot. Fr. 32: 265 (1885)

DESCRIPTION A close relative of *P. geraniifolia,* from which it mostly differs by being larger, and *long homostylous.* The leaf-blades can be up to 15 cm in diameter and the scapes to 50 cm, often bearing several superimposed whorls of flowers. The rose-purple flowers also differ in being funnel-shaped, annulate and smaller (to 15 mm in diameter). Flowers long-homostyle and presumably self-fertile. 2n = 24.

DISTRIBUTION North west Yunnan and south west Sichuan. Locally common and widespread in well-known localities such as the Lichiang, Dali, Litang and Muli ranges. Moist shady situations in mixed forest, 3000–4300 m. 'On limestone . . . in most luxuriant mixed forest, where hardly any other primulas grow, especially under dwarf bamboo, which are nowhere absent, on deep soil certainly rich in foodstuffs.' I saw it growing at about 3600 m on the west side of the Beima Shan, in leaf soil under quite dense shade.

- Var. *minor* Ward, Ann. Bot. 44: 123 (1930) from the Mishmi hills, Assam, differs by its smaller stature, and even more narrowly tubular flowers which are short homostyle, the only primula species known regularly to possess this condition. This is the only Cortusoides species with funnel-shaped, annulate, homostyle flowers.

As in *P. mollis*, the homostyle *P. septemloba* and its var. *minor* are diploids. As *P. septemloba* is a long homostyle, and var. *minor* is a short homostyle, they are presumably secondary homostyles, being derived from a heterostyle species by recombination (p. 57). Most related species for which we know the chromosome number have 2n = 22, while *P. septemloba*, in common with most of the subgenus, has 2n = 24. Despite this, a sister species to *P. geraniifolia* according to the DNA analysis.

CULTIVATION Introduced by Forrest from Lichiang (1906), and lost some time between 1943 and 1977. Although in cultivation for at least 40 years, it seems to have given rise to little comment. Plants are occasionally seen under this name today, but are usually *P. polyneura*. However, the true plant was grown at Cluny gardens in 1992, received from Edinburgh. Not introduced by either KGB in 1993 or ACE in 1994 although seen in flower by both.

Primula vaginata Watt, J. Linn. Soc. 20: 4 (1882)

P. normaniana Ward (1930)

DESCRIPTION Similar to *P. geraniifolia*, but with wide channelled purple almost hairless leaf-bases and with usually smaller flowers, the calyx not exceeding 5 mm. More robust than *P. eucyclia*, with leaves to 5 cm in diameter, and stems held above the leaves with up to 9 often lacerate flowers, each not exceeding 10 cm in diameter. Limited to shady woodland banks and rocks between 3000 and 3500 m, east Sikkim (Laghep, Karponang, Kanglasa) and the nearby Chumbi valley (Tibet).

- Subsp. *normaniana* (Ward) Chen & Hu (1990) (Fig. 15) differs chiefly by the brilliant pinkish flowers with highly lacerate petal-lobes which are rather larger (to 15 mm in diameter) with a longer calyx (more than 5 mm). It is vegetatively similar to *P. geraniifolia*, but with the reddish leaf-stalk deeply channelled and only sparsely hairy. The robust purplish stem carries the dense flower head well above the leaves and carries leaf-like bracts which can be pinned down to form a new plant. The flower head closely resembles the unrelated *P. lacerata* in section Petiolares with which it sometimes grows. Eastern Himalaya, east of subsp. *vaginata*; four sites on the south side of the main divide in a high monsoon region; the Rip La, Me La, Pang La, and Lo La passes, north-central Bhutan; Tsari, south-east Tibet; and the Mishmi valley, Assam; steep shady stream banks in bamboo, rhododendron and mixed forest, 2200–4000 m.

CULTIVATION Several introductions by seed claimed as *P. vaginata* proved to be *P. geraniifolia*, for instance that figured in Bull. AGS September 1951: 277 which is said to have 'glistening ruby-red hairs on the petioles' (the leaf-stalks of *P. vaginata* are almost glabrous). Subsp. *vaginata* was introduced apparently for the first time in 1989 (KEKE) as *P. geraniifolia*, but may not have persisted. Subsp. *normaniana* was introduced from Mishmi by Ward

(8295) (flowered 1931) and from the Me La by Hicks, working with Ludlow and Sherriff (21038) in 1949. Plants from the later introduction flourished for a time at Branklyn, Keillour and Kilbryde (**AM** 1962), but seem never to have set seed, and had largely disappeared by about 1965.

Two years after R.B. Cooke's death in 1973, I discovered two clumps of leaves resembling a small geranium or geum saxifrage on a shady spring-fed north-facing bed at Kilbryde, Corbridge in company with *Primula griffithii* and *Omphalogramma souliei*. They were much overgrown, and when cleared-out and fed, they flowered and proved to be vigorous plants of subsp. *normaniana*. These two plants were very hardy and permanent, surviving –28°C in 1979. However, when the garden was sold and the plants divided and moved in 1980, the plants proved extremely difficult to establish, and it is now extinct in cultivation.

Primula eucyclia Smith & Forrest, Notes Roy. Bot. Gdn. Edinb. 14: 41 (1923)

DESCRIPTION A delicate dwarf creeping high alpine relative of *P. vaginata* with a channelled leaf-stalk, 'forming a tiny plant like a seedling geranium'. 'Coral-red runners radiate from the plant and throw up sprigs of chubby leaves which take root.' The round sharply lobed and subdissected leaf-blades do not exceed 3 cm in diameter, and the flower-stalk, 'crimson threads', usually carrying two flowers, does not exceed 6 cm. The flat-faced pink to purple yellow-eyed flowers with fringed petal-lobes are about 15 mm in diameter.

DISTRIBUTION Confined to high mountains on both sides of the upper Salween, in Tibet and the Yunnan border (Tsarong, Kenichunpo, Champutong), and in Burma (Seinghku Wang). 'Crowded colonies forming mats many yards in extent sheeted with bloom, on stony alpine meadows and cliffs'; 'limestone crags'; 'bamboo undergrowth of the fir forests on very loose soil covered with leaves and needles.' 3900–4600 m.

Introduced by Ward from Burma (1926, **AM** 1930). In 1928, Wisley (who grew it under glass in a cold house) considered it did not look robust enough ever to become common, but it seems to have persisted there until the 1960s, although it disappeared before 1977.

Primula alsophila Balf. f. & Farrer, Notes Roy. Bot. Gdn. Edinb. 9: 4 (1915)

DESCRIPTION A slender creeping delicate plant with long frail runners. Distinguished from its relatives by having thin-textured leaves with only 5(–7) lobes, and frail stems with only 2–3 flowers (*P. eucyclia* is a dwarfer alpine plant). A rather charmless plant from deep moss in coniferous forests from 3300–4000 m in north Sichuan, Gansu and nearby Tibet. After Farrer and Purdom's introduction in 1914, persisted until 1923, but attracted little attention. Found by SQAE 472 at 3400 m between Juizhaigou and Songpan in 2000 but not introduced. (Fig. Halda: 81.)

Primula latisecta Smith, Notes Roy. Bot. Gdn. Edinb. 15: 74 (1926)

DESCRIPTION Leaves arising in small tufts from a *long-creeping* rhizome, deciduous. Leaf-blades wider than long, thick in texture, to 6 × 8 cm, divided to two-thirds into narrow trilobate lobes, the sinuses between the lobes rounded, and the lobules narrow, blunt and bluntly toothed, slightly hairy above; leaf-stalks equalling the leaf, very thickly covered with very long pale tawny hairs. Flowers borne 1–3 together at the level of the leaves, differing from *P. geraniifolia* by having annulate flowers with a white eye. 2n = 22. (Photo J. Roy. Hort. Soc. 44: fig 57.)

DISTRIBUTION To the north of the divide in south-east Tibet, from the Nyima La, and from the Pangkar region (Drukla Chu, Tongyuk river east of the Nambu La). Forest in heavy shade, 4000 m.

In its creeping mode of growth, and beautiful deeply dissected and narrowly but bluntly lobed foliage, *P. latisecta* is only likely to be confused with *P. palmata*, which has sharply lobed foliage.

CULTIVATION Introduced by Ward on the discovery of the species on the Nyima La in 1924, and flowered in 1927. Setting seed regularly, and easily propagated by its creeping growth, this delicate-looking species has persisted well. Reintroduced by George Smith in 1986 to Edinburgh, and offered in the trade by 1990. Now (2001) quite readily available. I grow two distinct clones, both pin, which have formed considerable patches in well-drained cool positions. Flowers regularly, but not profusely, in late May. Hardy to at least –15°C, not requiring winter cover.

Primula palmata Hand.-Mazz., Anz. Akad. Wiss. Wien Math.-Nat. 61: 132 (1925)

DESCRIPTION Differs from *P. latisecta* by its even more deeply divided leaves (to three-quarters), the lobes of which are sharply pointed, and the sinuses of which are also sharp; and by the shorter calyx (not exceeding 7 mm). Apparently limited to the vicinity of Songpan, north-west Sichuan, woodlands, 2300–2700 m. Overlaps *P. alsophila* which is a much more delicate plant with narrow petioles from high altitudes. Introduced into cultivation for the first time by Peter Cox in 1987. Has remained in cultivation in the trade (2001) and easily propagated through its creeping habit. Now commonly met in many Highland gardens in Scotland.

Primula pauliana Smith & Forrest, Notes Roy. Bot, Gdn. Edinb. 14: 51 (1923)

DESCRIPTION Totally distinct from all its supposed relatives in forming a long spike of yellow flowers, and superificially resembling *P. bathangensis* (section Malvacea). However, it lacks the distinctive calyx of the Malvacea, while the long curved capsule is unlike any other primula. Probably deserves a section of its own. 2n = 24. Meadows and the edges of thickets, south-east of Yungning, south-west Sichuan, 3700–4000 m. Introduced by Forrest to Edinburgh (1923); lost after 1932. (Photo: J. Roy. Hort. Soc. 54 fig.2 (1928).)

Section **Bullatae** Pax, Bot. Jahrb. Syst. 10: 176 (1889). Type species *P. bullata* Franchet. (Section Suffruticosae Balf. f. 1913)

DESCRIPTION Rhizomatous to cushion-forming woody-based long-lived *evergreen* perennials. Leaves *leathery*, persistent, strongly rough-reticulate (*rugose*), entire or finely toothed, with a narrowly oval somewhat convex blade and a well-marked stalk, *sticky*-glandular and often sweetly *fragrant*, often also with multicellular hairs, with or without meal, with revolute vernation. *Stems* sticky, with an umbel of flowers (or rarely single flowers); bracts small but leaf-like. *Calyx* bell-shaped. *Corolla* yellow, white or pink, exannulate, heterostylous. *Pollen* globose, 3-colporoidate. *Capsule* globose, shorter than the calyx, dehiscing by 5 longitudinal valves; seeds large, few, angular, usually dark brown. x = 12. Strongly self-incompatible. Flowering April–May.

DISTRIBUTION Yunnan, Sichuan and adjoining parts of Tibet, Shaanxi, centred on the limestone ranges either side of the upper Salween. Limestone rocks and cliffs in dry sunny locations, usually chasmophytic, 2600–4500 m.

Section Bullatae is composed of eight closely related species which form a very natural group, and which show few obvious connections with other species, except for section Dryadifolia. Superficially they resemble some members of section Primula, particularly through the form and rugosity of the leaves, and in the flowers, but the leathery persistent leaves, woody growth, capsule type, pollen type, and the number and form of the chromosomes suggest a quite different relationship. Bruun (1930, 1932) showed that both the number and form of the chromosomes in the Bullatae (which are rather large and regular in shape) show a close correspondence to those of various sections in subgenus *Auganthus,* notably sections Auganthus, Malacoides and Cortusoides. Although this link seems at first surprising for such 'primrose-like' plants, apparently far removed from the 'woodland primulas', it is supported by the DNA which shows that two members of this section are firmly embedded within the subgenus *Auganthus*, lying between the sections Cortusoides and Monocarpicae, as was originally suggested by Wendelbo (1961). Nevertheless, the 3-colporoidate pollen differs from all subgenus *Auganthus* except some species in sections Obconicolisteri and Monocarpicae.

CULTIVATION Of the four species introduced into cultivation, only *P. forrestii* has persisted for any length of time. All species are adapted to survive long periods of drought during the Chinese autumn, winter and spring while dormant in their exposed and dry limestone crevices. In cultivation they seem to be intolerant of winter wet. Pot culture in alpine house conditions with very careful winter watering which avoids the foliage and vulnerable neck of the plant is indicated for all species, or they can be planted out in tufa under glass.

In the open garden, some success has been met with by planting *P. forrestii* (and formerly *P. rockii*) in vertical cervices under overhangs in the rock garden, preferably in a site with partial sun. In the mild conditions at Bodnant, north Wales for instance, massive plants of *P. forrestii* decades old grew and self-sowed in these conditions, although they have now disappeared. However, I have found that *P. forrestii* tended to die after severe frosts in these circumstances in the north of England.

Propagation is best by seed, which is set fairly freely. Although division or cuttings seem to be potential methods of increase, I can find no report of their effectiveness.

No hybrids have been recorded.

KEY TO SPECIES

1. Stem equalling or exceeding the leaves; flowers usually more than 5 together 2
1. Stem shorter than leaves, or 0. Flowers 1–5 together 3

2. Leaves with some long hairs above (use lens); base of leaf-blade heart-shaped .... *P. forrestii*
2. Leaves glabrous above, or hairs very short; base of leaf-blade attenuate .... *P. bullata*

3. Plant with at least some meal 4
3. Plant lacking meal 5

4. Flowers pinkish; meal yellow .... *P. dubernardiana*
4. Flowers yellow or white; meal white .... *P. henrici*

5. Flowers yellow or orange; leaves spoon-shaped .... *P. rockii*
5. Flowers pink or purple; leaves attenuate at base 6

6. Plant sticky-glandular; flowers solitary .... *P. bracteata*
6. Plant softly hairy, not sticky; flowers 2–5 together .... *P. huashanensis*

Primula forrestii Balf. f., Notes Roy. Bot. Gdn. Edinb. 4: 215 (1908)

P. redolens Balf. f. & Ward (1916)

DESCRIPTION A *robust* subshrubby long-lived plant forming large long-stemmed tussocks encrusted with leaf scars and marcescent foliage. *Leaf-blades* olive green with golden glands and yellow-mealy below when young, narrowly oval with regular small rounded teeth and revolute margins, to 8 × 5 cm at flowering, larger in fruit; leaf-stalks equalling the blade, broad and slightly flattened especially at the base, long-hairy and often mealy when young, becoming persistent and tough. *Stems* to 15 cm, stout, erect, long-hairy and sticky, bearing an umbel of 5–25 flowers borne on stiff upright hairy and sticky stalks to 4 cm. *Calyx* narrowly bell-shaped, to 15 mm, cut to one-third into broad blunt lobes, green and glandular-sticky. *Corolla* sweetly scented, golden-yellow with an orange eye, flat-faced, to 25 mm in diameter, the tube broad and somewhat exceeding the calyx, the rounded petal-lobes deeply notched. 2n = 24. (Plate 6.)

DISTRIBUTION North-west Yunnan, especially the Yulong Shan, but extending to the south-west around Langkong (overlapping with *P. bullata*), and to the north and north-east of the Yangtse bend which circumscribes the Yulong Shan snow range.

'Crevices and ledges of limestone rock ... on drier places.... their long lignescent rhizomes enable them to expand over barren rock.' Locally abundant in a variety of dry limestone habitats ranging from grassy plateaux to rock-ledges, 2800–3200 m (possibly to 4500 m). Even occurs beside the road on the plain leading north from Lijiang towards the Yulong Shan on low outcrops. At flowering time in May, the habitat and the plant are dust-dry, and have received little precipitation for 8 months, although within weeks they will be deluged in a torrential and ceaseless monsoon. *P. forrestii* may be very long-lived. Halda (1992) suggests that he found an individual photographed by Forrest 80 years previously, and I saw what is very probably the same plant in 1995.

P. forrestii is by far the most familiar member of this section. The only robust yellow-flowered relative, *P. bullata,* has leaves lacking a distinct stalk. The general effect of *P. forrestii* is of a robust, woody, golden, spectacular cowslip. When well-grown it is amongst the most effective of all primulas in cultivation. In many ways it is very similar to *P. edelbergii,* although quite unrelated to it. They are both plants of dry limestone cliffs.

VARIATION

- Var. *redolens* (Balf. f. & Ward) Richards **stat. et comb. nov**. (*P. redolens* Balf. f. & Ward, Notes Roy. Bot. Gdn. Edinb. 9: 196 (1916).) Flowers opening pink to lilac with a yellow eye, turning cream later, or rarely opening milk-white and turning pale lilac. 2n = 24. Only a single pink-flowered clump has ever been discovered, by Ward in 1911 on dry limestone rocks in the Mekong gorge west of Lichiang and near Weisi. However, some cream-coloured *P. forrestii* have recently been discovered in the Yulong Shan and these might also be best placed here. Interfertile with subsp. *forrestii,* and hybridizing with it freely in cultivation, so that later versions named *P. redolens* had cream-coloured flowers. Fairly frequently grown in cool greenhouses in the 1920s and 1930s.

CULTIVATION First introduced by Forrest (2117) by seed from Lichiang in 1906, and has probably been continuously in cultivation since. Although it had become very scarce by 1980, reintroduced by seed by Roy Lancaster (1688) in 1986, and by Beckett and Lancaster (12220), and by later expeditions in the 1990s such as KGB, ACE and ARGS and is now quite commonly propagated by seed and readily obtained through the trade. Not difficult in the alpine house, kept almost dry in winter, protected from severe frosts, given adequate water as the flower buds form, and repotted regularly after flowering. It is important to cut rather than to pull off decaying foliage.

Primula bullata Franchet. Bull. Soc. Bot. Fr. 32: 265 (1885)

DESCRIPTION Related to *P. forrestii*, but smaller, less robust, lacking long hairs, and with leaf-blades tapering into the stalk. Apparently limited to the Langkong-Hoching divide in the vicinity of Hee-chan-men, half-way between Dali and Lijiang. Dubiously distinct from *P. forrestii*, and *P. rufa* Balf. f. (1913) is intermediate between the two. Although *P. bullata* has not apparently been in cultivation, it seems that this locality has been visited frequently by Western visitors in recent years, and it is possible that some recent collections referred to *P. forrestii* may be better placed here.

Primula rockii Smith, Notes Roy. Bot. Gdn. Edinb. 16: 224 (1932)

DESCRIPTION A dwarf almost cushion-forming plant, lacking meal, with small spoon-shaped leaves with long narrow stalks and round blades about 2.5 cm across. The yellow or orange flowers, about 15 mm in diameter, are borne singly, or in groups of up to 5 on a very short stalk, at the level of the cushion.

DISTRIBUTION Mountains of Kulu and Muli, south-west Sichuan, in crevices in limestone cliffs and boulders, 3000–4425 m.

Immediately distinguished from dwarf cushion-forming relatives such as *P. dubernardiana* and *P. bracteata* by the spoon-shaped leaves and yellow or orange flowers.

CULTIVATION Introduced by Rock (16451, 17401–2, 17885) in 1928 and flowered in 1935 (**AM**). This appears to have been the most delightful dwarf subject for pan culture '... a perfectly adorable plant, very small with orange flowers ... some very keen gardeners in BC have been flowering it for four or five years ... it has a woody stock and is hard to divide'. Grown successfully in the 1930s at Wisley, Edinburgh and Kilbryde, but apparently lost by the 1960s.

Primula dubernardiana Forrest, Notes Roy. Bot. Gdn. Edinb. 4: 221 (1908)

P. monbeigii Balf. f. (1913)

DESCRIPTION Similar to *P. rockii*, but copiously covered with yellow meal, and with the long narrow leaf-blades tapering to the stalk. Corolla rose with an orange eye, or whitish, flushed rose. (Photo: J. Roy. Hort. Soc. 54: fig.24 (1929), Bot. Mag. t.9266 (1931).)

DISTRIBUTION North-west Yunnan, Thrana (a local landmark meaning 'black nose') near Tsekou, Mekong valley. Dense cushions on dry shady limestone cliffs at 3000 m. Apparently almost confined to this single locality, although there is a record from nearby Tsarong in south-east Tibet.

P. dubernardiana was named by George Forrest after his friend, companion and fellow botanist Pere Dubernard who was killed in horrific circumstances (p. 10). One of the most spectacularly beautiful of all primulas, the relatively large rosy flowers nestling in yellow-mealy cushions.

CULTIVATION Introduced by Forrest in 1917 (16180, 16392), and flowered at Kew and elsewhere in 1919. 'Responds to cultivation with a fair amount of success if planted in a good calcareous loam in a retaining wall facing west with a stone placed overhead, or in a cleft between rocks where it joins up to the soil behind. The chief requirements are to have sufficient moisture at the roots, and the foliage kept more or less dry.' 'Managed successfully in frames, but never flourished in the open.' Grown at Kew, Wisley, Edinburgh and elsewhere in the 1930s, but seems to have departed by about 1950.

Primula henrici Bur. & Franchet, Journ. de Bot. 5: 98 (1891)

P. pseudobracteata Petitm. (1908)
P. tapeina Balf. f. & Forrest (1923)
P. articulata var. *sublinearis* Smith (1938)

DESCRIPTION Similar to *P. dubernardiana*, but yellow or white flowered and with copious *white* meal. A variable species, which has never been in cultivation in the West. Dry limestone cliffs at about 4000 m; scattered localities in Tibet on the Yunnan border (Tsarong, Yirong Gorge, Chiangka river, Lho Dzong; south-west Sichuan (east of Yalung river); and north-west Yunnan (Shiku, west of Yangtse bend).

Primula bracteata Franchet, Bull. Soc. Bot. Fr. 32: 266 (1885)

P. pulvinata Balf. f. & Forrest (1916)
P. ulophylla Hand.-Mazz. (1925)

DESCRIPTION Similar to *P. dubernardiana* and *P. henrici,* forming a loose cushion, but lacking meal and glandular, with narrow sticky acutely pointed leaves with acute teeth; flowers solitary and usually rose-pink with a darker centre and yellow eye, but white- and even yellow-flowered forms have been reported. (Photo: Proceedings 7th Int. Rock Garden Conf. plate 4.5. (Plate 74.)

DISTRIBUTION Said to be locally common on limestone or sandstone cliffs in extreme north-west Yunnan, from Dali, Lichiang, Langkong to Shiku; and north-east of Muli in south-west Sichuan, 2600–3700 m. In recent years the only record has been for ACE 1671, 'fine vertical cracks ... in ... a sheer limestone cliff in open woodland, north side of 'Little Snow Mountain' (between Geza and Wengsui) at 3560 m' (almost on the Yunnan-Sichuan border).

CULTIVATION ACE 1671 has proved one of the outstanding introductions of recent years (1994) and has been acknowledged with a PC (1999) and a Farrer medal of the Alpine Garden Society. It is grown in the alpine house in identical circumstances to *P. allionii,* with overhead water avoided at all costs, and repotted after flowering. In these conditions it forms a most attractive loose cushion, covered with glowing pink flowers at cushion level at the end of March. It has been successfully propagated by cuttings taken as for *Dionysia* (it somewhat resembles a giant *D. freitagii*) and by seed, after pin and thrum plants have been introduced to one another at shows. Seed ripens in late October. I lost what was then my only plant by repotting into a mix containing considerable quantities of 'perlite' (expanded silica) which has considerable water-holding properties. The compost should be not only acutely drained, but on the dry side especially in winter. Although it is best somewhat 'underpotted', plants have now been shown in 25 cm pans.

Primula huashanensis Chen & Hu, Fl. Rep. Pop. Sin. 2: 294 (1990)

DESCRIPTION A little-known species, related to *P. henrici* and *P. bracteata,* but flowers purple with a golden eye, and leaves with soft hairs, edged with acute teeth. Shaanxi; Hua Shan, Nanfeng; stony slopes and open woods, 3000–3800 m. Despite its purple flowers, *P. huashanensis* seems a rather typical member of the Bullatae. Surprisingly it was classified by Halda in section Aleuritia, however.

Section **Dryadifolia** Balf. f., J. Roy. Hort. Soc. 39: 165 (1913). Type species *P. dryadifolia* Franchet

DESCRIPTION *Evergreen* long-lived perennial plants forming *cushion*-like mats of foliage arising from prostrate branching *subwoody* rhizomes which are clothed in withered leaves. *Leaves leathery*, often shiny with the nerves sunken, *without hairs*, mealy beneath, or not, rather small, usually oval and deeply and regularly toothed, with short stalks and revolute vernation, often remaining *revolute* at the margin. *Stem* very short, 1–few flowered, with a pair of conspicuous hooded bracts and relatively large, usually nodding virtually stalkless flowers. *Calyx* bell-shaped, rather loose and baggy, often mealy, often stained purple. *Corolla* rose, magenta or yellow, often with a yellow or white eye, bowl-shaped to flat-faced, 10–25 mm in diameter, usually annulate, heterostylous, the broad tube somewhat exceeding the calyx and usually somewhat hairy within; corolla lobes deeply notched. *Pollen* 3-syncolpate. *Capsule* oblong to cylindrical, equalling the calyx and dehiscing by apical teeth or valves; seed usually about 1 mm, rounded to quadrate, covered throughout with conspicuous blisters. Chromosome number unknown. Pins and thrums both strongly self-incompatible. Flowering June in the wild, shortly before the monsoon.

DISTRIBUTION From Bhutan eastwards through south-east Tibet to west Yunnan, northern Burma and south-west Sichuan.

High alpine habitats; peaty pastures, screes, rocky hillsides, cliff-ledges and crevices, mossy boulders, 4000–5500 m.

This small section of five species is centred around the distinctive and splendid *P. dryadifolia*. The name of this species derives from the similarity of the growth habit and foliage to the mountain avens, *Dryas octopetala*. *P. dryadifolia* usually has pink flowers, but the resemblance to *Dryas* is taken still further by the creamy and more often solitary flowers of var. *chlorodryas*. The other three species are much smaller plants with single flowers buried in the foliage, and these, especially *P. tsongpenii*, more closely resemble members of section Minutissimae, in which *P. triloba* forms an obvious bridging species.

Perhaps the most remarkable conclusion reached by DNA studies was that *P. dryadifolia* was related, not to subgenus *Aleuritia* as has previously been supposed, but to subgenus *Auganthus,* in which we must suppose that the Bullatae are their closest relatives. This result is quite unambiguous and beyond doubt, and with the benefit of hindsight easily supported by such features shared with the Bullatae as a woody, evergreen marcescent cushion-forming habit, leathery leaves and well-formed bracts. Thus, it seems that the Dryadifolia represent highly reduced high alpine derivatives of the Bullatae. To ape an illustrious forebear, 'how stupid not to have thought of that'. Nevertheless, the pollen and capsule type differ strongly between the two sections.

This relationship now raises issues as to the affinities of some Minutissimae, to which the Dryadifolia are apparently related. Although the DNA clearly shows that *P. reptans* and *P. minutissima* are quite unrelated to the Dryadifolia, it seems that *P. triloba* (which Halda follows Chen & Hu, 1990, in placing in the Dryadifolia) may well be derivative from Dryadifolia-like *Auganthus*.

CULTIVATION Attempts have been made to introduce three of the species. Two failed immediately. More success has been met with *P. dryadifolia*. Initially, it never stayed in cultivation for very long, possibly because its growth habit suggested a dry sunny location. Repeated introductions allowed this species to be tested extensively, and post-war introductions by Ludlow and Sherriff lasted for at least two decades in some gardens in Scotland and the north of England. Here it seems to have grown best in a cool north-facing raised bed in good light and with good drainage, but with abundant moisture in summer. In recent years it has been grown with the greatest success in cool, partly shaded troughs with winter cover, and I grew subsp. *congestifolia* for some years in tufa in a trough, where it finally succumbed to lime-chlorosis. Some growers have achieved very good results in pots, plunged in a shaded frame in summer and kept nearly dry and well-lit in winter. It can be propagated vegetatively, by division or cuttings, and sets fertile seed well when pins and thrums are crossed. A difficult but not impossible plant.

No hybrids have been reported in the section.

KEY TO SPECIES

1. Flowers held well above the foliage .... *P. dryadifolia*
1. Flowers immersed in or held at the level of the foliage 2

2. Leaf-stalk long and narrow; corolla-tube without hairs .... *P. mystrophylla*
2. Leaf-stalk short and broad; corolla-tube hairy within 3

3. Leaf margins almost entire; corolla-tube sparsely hairy .... *P. jonardunii*
3. Leaf-margins strongly crenate; corolla tube plugged with a cottony pom-pom .... *P. tsongpenii*

Primula dryadifolia Franchet, Bull. Soc. Bot. Fr. 32: 270 (1885)

P. congestifolia Forrest (1908)
P. chlorodryas Smith
P. chrysophylla Balf. f. & Forrest (1920)
P. cycliophylla Balf. f. & Farrer (1920)
P. philoresia Balf. f. (1915)

DESCRIPTION *Leaf-blades to 2*× 1.3 cm, crenately toothed, tightly inrolled at the margin, thickly white or yellow-mealy beneath. *Stems* to 10 cm, shorter in flower, bearing 1–5 flowers. *Calyx* purplish, to 12 mm. *Corolla* rose-crimson with a darker, or yellowish eye, saucer-shaped, to 25 mm in diameter, the tube nearly hairless. Pollen 3-syncolpate. (Photo: Bull. AGS 56: 237; Halda: 118 seq.; fig: 299.) (Plate 65.)

DISTRIBUTION Very widespread in the high mountains of Yunnan and western Sichuan, extending a short distance into Burma, and in south-east Tibet mostly just inside the Tsangpo bend near the Yunnan frontier, but disjunct in the west near the Bhutan frontier at Mago and Tsona, and just into Bhutan on the Cho La (92° E).

Forming patches and carpets on screes, stony pastures on 'snow-ground', cliff faces, rock crevices and ledges, and the shelter of boulders, facing north or north-west, apparently usually on limestone, but also on gneiss and granite. 3000–5500 m.

A beautiful and very variable species, varying in size, height of stem, leaf-shape, colour of meal, etc. Totally unmistakable.

CULTIVATION Introduced by Forrest in 1911, and on several subsequent occasions. The most successful early introduction was made by Hicks (Ludlow and Sherriff 21185) in 1949, which the Rentons, Randall Cooke, Jack Drake and Bobby Masterton, among others, suceeded with for some years (see sectional account). Still sparingly in cultivation from the Yulong Shan introduction in 1987, and from CLD 1091 in 1990 (flowered at Edinburgh in 1991). Reintroduced by KGB (122, 304, 709, and as subsp. *congestifolia*, 512) and by ACE (1326, 1733, 1781, 2159), mostly from Da Xue Shan ('Big Snow Mountain') and Beima Shan, 1993 and 1994. Also ARGS s.n. from Da Xue Shan in 2000. **PC** 2000. Well established but difficult in 2001, with both the type subspecies and subsp. *congestifolia* established. See sectional account for growing conditions.

VARIATION

- Var. *chlorodryas* (Smith) Richards **stat. et comb. nov.** (*P. chlorodryas* Smith, Notes Roy. Bot. Gdn. Edinb. 16: 223 (1932). Flowers creamy-yellow, hairy within the tube. Only known from Fuchuan Shan, south-west of Wei-Hsi on the Mekong–Salween divide. Limestone boulders at 4450 m. Introduced in 1932 (F30232), flowered in 1934, and at Kilbryde in 1937, but soon lost. Fig. Halda: 300, 304. Said to have been introduced by Halda in 1999.
- Subsp. *cycliophylla* (Balf. f. & Forrest) Smith & Forrest (1928) (*P. cycliophylla* Balf. f.& Forrest, Notes Roy. Bot. Gdn. Edinb. 16: 22 (1920)). Has

a shorter, broader calyx than subsp. *dryadifolia*. Fig. Halda: 300.

- Subsp. *congestifolia* (Forrest) Smith & Forrest (1928) (*P. congestifolia* Forrest, Notes Roy. Bot. Gdn. Edinb. 4: 226 (1908)). Flowers solitary, upward facing.
- Subsp. *philoresia* (Balf. f.) Halda (1992) (*P. philoresia* Balf. f., Notes Roy. Bot. Gdn. Edinb. 9: 34 (1915)). Calyx and leaves narrower than subsp. *dryadifolia*. Fig. Halda: 301.

Primula jonardunii Smith, Rec. Bot. Surv. India 4: 269 (1911)

P. oreina Balf. f. & Cooper (1916)

DESCRIPTION A much more dwarf species than the preceding, with the *rounded* leaves not exceeding 1 cm with reflexed marginal crenulations, the leaf-stalk short and broad and the usually one-flowered stem only 5 mm, the flowers being sunk amongst the leaves. Flowers rose-crimson, to 25 mm in diameter, hairy within the tube. (Fig. Halda: 300, 304.). (Plate 76.)

Widespread in the very wet zones of north-east Bhutan and south-east Tibet, including such rich primula localities as the Me La, Bimbi La, Mipa and east to the Doshong La (94° E), 3900–4700 m. Although Fletcher latterly seemed to regard this species as no more than a reduced state of *P. dryadifolia*, it is very distinct, as confirmed by Anne Chambers when she saw this species on the Doshong La in 1995.

Primula mystrophylla Balf. f. & Forrest, Notes Roy. Bot. Gdn. Edinb. 13: 14 (1920)

DESCRIPTION Much dwarfer than *P. dryadifolia*, and less woody than *P. jonardunii*, the rhizomes being persistent, but thin. The spoon-shaped, long-stalked leaves are thickly yellow-mealy beneath. Flowers hidden in the foliage on a very short stalk, similar to *P. jonardunii*, but without hairs in the tube.

Yunnan/Tibet border in the Tsarong area, on the divides each side of the Salween. Moist rocks, cliff crevices and screes, 4600–5000 m. Seed collected in 1918 did not succeed in cultivation. Fig. Halda: 301, 304.

Primula tsongpenii Fletcher, J. Linn. Soc. 52: 340 (1942)

DESCRIPTION Very similar in structure to *P. mystrophylla*, but virtually lacking meal, with leaves more similar to *P. jonardunii* in shape, and with the single sugar-pink flowers having the throat blocked by a pom-pom of white hairs, as in *P. bella* and *P. primulina*.

Only known from four very wet passes at about 94° E in south-east Tibet, between Pachakshiri and the Tsangpo, the Lo La, Kucha La, Deyang La and Tsanang La. Bare open rocky hillsides, often growing in company with *P. jonardunii*, 4600–5000 m. Seed collected in 1938 did not succeed in cultivation. (Photo: A Quest of Flowers: 293. Fig. Halda: 303, 304.)

P. tsongpenii was named for the Lepcha collector Tsongpen who was a close associate and friend of Sherriff during his Himalayan explorations. It falls between the Dryadifolia and Minutissimae such as *P. bella* and *P. primulina* which share the corolla 'pom-pom'. The best reason for maintaining this intermediate species in the Dryadifolia is the pair of oval, cup-shaped bracts.

Subgenus **Carolinella** (Helmsley) Wendelbo, Aarb. Univ. Bergen 11: 36 (1961)

Type species *P. partschiana* (Helmsley) Pax

Section **Carolinella** (Helmsley) Pax, Pflanzenreich 4: 237, 45 (1905) (*Carolinella* Helmsley, Icon. Pl. t.2726,2775 (1902–3))

DESCRIPTION Deciduous (?) perennials, with revolute vernation, bearing *very few* (usually 1–3) large often leathery entire rough-reticulate (*rugose*) sometimes *spiny-edged* heart-shaped leaves with long narrow stalks arising from stout rhizomes bearing old leaf-scar pegs and *rusty hairs*; lacking meal and with long multicellular hairs. *Stems* bearing few flowered spikes or whorls of flowers on hairy stalks, bracts small, narrow, sometimes forming a ruff below the inflorescence. *Calyx* narrowly bell-shaped, with sharp sepal-lobes. *Corolla* rose, violet or white, annulate, rarely exannulate, heterostylous or homostylous. *Pollen* tricolpate, tricolporoidate, trisyncolpate or polycolpate. *Capsules* pear-shaped, dehiscing uniquely in *Primula* by means of an operculate lid with a persistent style (looking and functioning like a moss capsule), after which the mouth develops a ring of hairs or membranous teeth ('fimbriate'), many-seeded. Chromosome number and breeding behaviour not known. Flowering in the spring.

DISTRIBUTION South-east Yunnan and just over the border into Vietnam ('Tonkin'), an area with few if any other primulas; one species recently described from Thailand. Steep slopes and cliffs, usually under trees in low-lying humid, warm-temperate (to subtropical) regions, 1500–2600 m.

The Carolinella are the most enigmatic of all primulas. Each of the nine species has been collected on only a single occasion, three of them by the Irishman Dr Augustine Henry between 1896–7. None have ever been in cultivation, so we are ignorant about most facets of their biology. Most species are probably very rare, if not now extinct, although it is good to see that at least two survived, undiscovered, until 1988. A recent study has suggested that this may be a heterogenous group of species (Anderberg & El-Ghazaly, 2000). Although the remarkable capsule type is only found in this section of the genus, all the pollen types known in the genus occur, suggesting that this capsule type may have evolved more than once.

Superficially, the species resemble the Obconicolisteri, from which they are best distinguished by the capsules, and the narrowly bell-shaped calyx. The capsules are unique in the genus. Indeed, the 'circumscissile' capsule, dehiscing by a lid, is an unusual type amongst all flowering plants, and is found in the Primulaceae only in the pimpernels (*Anagallis*), in the European *Soldanella*, and in the monotypic east Himalayan *Bryocarpum*. The last genus is of real interest, being morphologically allied to *Soldanella*, and to the Sinohimalayan *Omphalogramma*, which however has valvate capsules. The leaves of *Omphalogramma* and *Bryocarpum* are not dissimilar to those of the *Carolinella*, although with involute vernation. It seems that the Carolinella may represent an evolutionary link between *Primula* section Obconicolisteri on one hand, and *Bryocarpum*, leading ultimately to *Omphalogramma* and *Soldanella*, on the other. Unfortunately, no species have been available for DNA testing. Although Trift (2001) claims that I classified *P. veitchiana*, which she had examined, in subgenus *Carolinella*, this is not the case as it is placed in section Chartacea which I did not assign to a subgenus in 1993.

There is a recent account of the section by Hu (1990) in which he describes a new species and transfers *P. kwangtungensis* and *P. kweichouensis* to this section.

LITERATURE Anderberg, A. A. & El-Ghazaly, G. (2000).
Hu C. M. (1990).

KEY TO SPECIES

1. Leaf tip pointed; flowers numerous on a stalk 2
1. Leaf tip rounded; flowers usually fewer, sometimes solitary 3

2. Leaf stalks lacking hairs; flowers in a spike .... *P. henryi*
2. Leaf stalks with long rusty hairs; flowers in an umbel or very short spike .... *P. chapaensis*

3. Leaf blades more than twice as long as wide, rounded at the base .... *P. rugosa*
3. Leaf-blades less than twice as long as wide, heart-shaped at base 4

4. Flowers to 8 mm in diameter, white, homostylous .... *P. larsenii*
4. Flowers usually larger, usually pink, heterostylous 5

5. Calyx exceeding 5 mm; corolla more than 10 mm in diameter 6
5. Calyx not exceeding 5 mm; corolla less than 10 mm in diameter 7

6. Leaf-stalk exceeding 10 cm .... *P. partschiana*
6. Leaf-stalk less than 1 cm .... *P. kwantungensis*

7. Flowers more than 6 in an umbel .... *P. cardioeides*
7. Flowers less than 6 in an umbel 8

8. Calyx and flower stalks hairy .... *P. kweichouensis*
8. Calyx and flower stalks lacking hairs .... *P. laevicalyx*

Primula cardioeides Smith & Fletcher, Trans. Bot. Soc. Edinb. 61: 464–5 (1946)

P. cordata Merrill (1939) non Balf. f. (1928)

DESCRIPTION Leaves 6–8, rounded at the apex, the blade to 6 × 5 cm, heart-shaped at the base, the stalk shorter. Stems to 10 cm, carrying 6–10 rose-coloured flowers, the calyx about 2.5 mm and the corolla about 8 mm in diameter. Chapa, North Vietnam, near the Yunnan border, clayey humid talus slopes, 1800 m.

Primula partschiana Pax, Pflanzenreich Primulaceae: 45 (1905)

P. cyclaminifolia Franch. ex Petitm. (1907)
Carolinella cordifolia Helmsley (1903) non *P. cordifolia* Rupr. (1863)

DESCRIPTION Leaves usually 2, rounded at the apex, the blade to 20 × 15 cm, heart-shaped, about equalling the stalk. Stem to 20 cm, carrying up to 15 rose-coloured flowers, the calyx about 5 mm, and the corolla diameter about 15 mm. South-east Yunnan, south-west of Mengtze, south of the Red River on the watershed with the Black River, in densely forested virgin country, shaded banks under trees. (Fig. Halda: 124.)

Primula rugosa Balakr., J. Bombay Nat. Hist. Soc. 62: 63 (1973)

P. obovata (Helmsley) Pax (1905) non Duby (1844) nec Huter (1873)
Carolinella obovata Helmsley (1903)

DESCRIPTION Leaves 1–6, the blade rounded, to 14 × 5 cm, longer than the stalk, not heart-shaped at the base. Stem to 14 cm, carrying up to 12 flowers on a short umbellate spike, the flowers pink to purple, to 12 mm in diameter, the calyx to 4 mm. Yunnan, cliffs in forests to the south-east and south-west of Mengtze, 1700 m. (Photo: J. Roy. Hort. Soc. 54: 20 (1929).)

Primula henryi (Helmsley) Pax, Pflanzenreich Primulaceae: 47 (1905)

Carolinella henryi Helmsley (1903)

DESCRIPTION Leaves 2–3, the blade pointed, to 18 × 8 cm with an attenuate base, shorter than the hairless stalk. Stem to 20 cm, hairless, carrying up to 20 flowers in a very short spike, the calyx to 4 mm. South-east Yunnan; mountain forests to the south-east of Mengtze at 1650 m. (Fig. Halda: 122.)

Primula chapaensis Gagnep., Bull. Soc. Bot. Fr. 76: 139 (1929)

P. huana Smith (1936)

DESCRIPTION Leaves 1–2, the blade pointed, to 22 × 17 cm with a heart-shaped base, rather shorter than the stalk which bears reddish hairs at the base. Stem hairy, to 35 cm, with a short or umbellate spike of up to 30 violet flowers, each 12 mm in diameter, the calyx about 11 mm long. Vietnam; Mt. Chapa, 1500 m, where it grows with the much smaller *P. cardioeides;* Yunnan; Ma-Kwan Hsien, 1700 m. (Fig. Halda: 121.)

Primula kwangtungensis Smith, Sunyatsenia 3: 244 (1937)

DESCRIPTION A robust plant with long reddish hairs throughout and oblong leaves to 12 × 7 cm, including a very short stalk of 1 cm. The exannulate heterostylous flowers are bluish. A little-known species endemic to the district of Yuyuen, Kwangtung province, not far from Hong Kong. Has not been in cultivation.

Primula kweichouensis Smith, Notes Roy. Bot. Gdn. Edinb. 16: 225 (1931)

DESCRIPTION Similar to *P. kwangtungensis*, but much smaller and more delicate, with the leaf stalk half the length of the blade, the calyx deeply cut to two-thirds, and the corolla rose in colour. Another little-known species which has not been in cultivation from the province of Kweichow near the Yunnan border in the region of Yunnansen. (Fig. Halda: 123.)

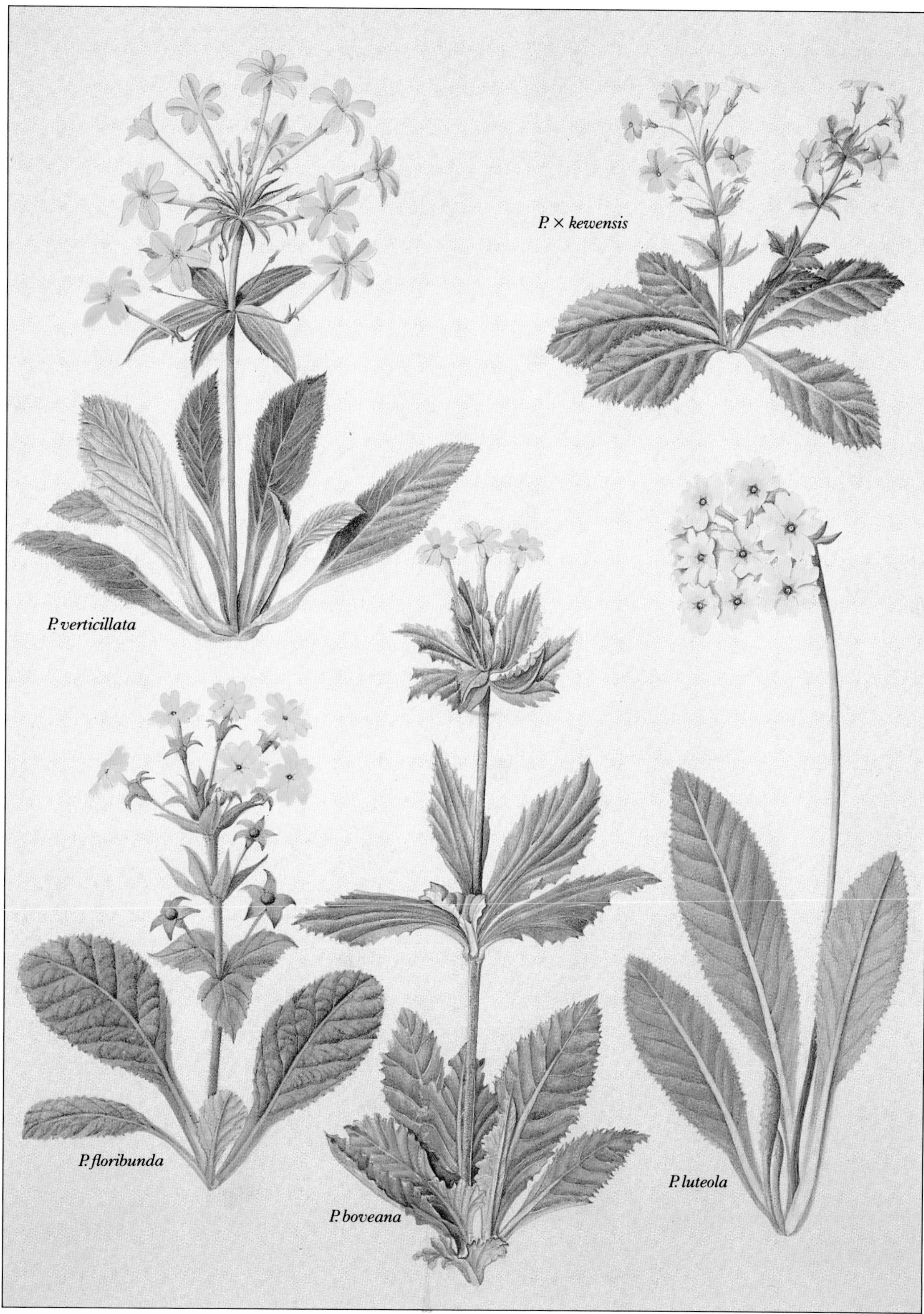

Plate 1

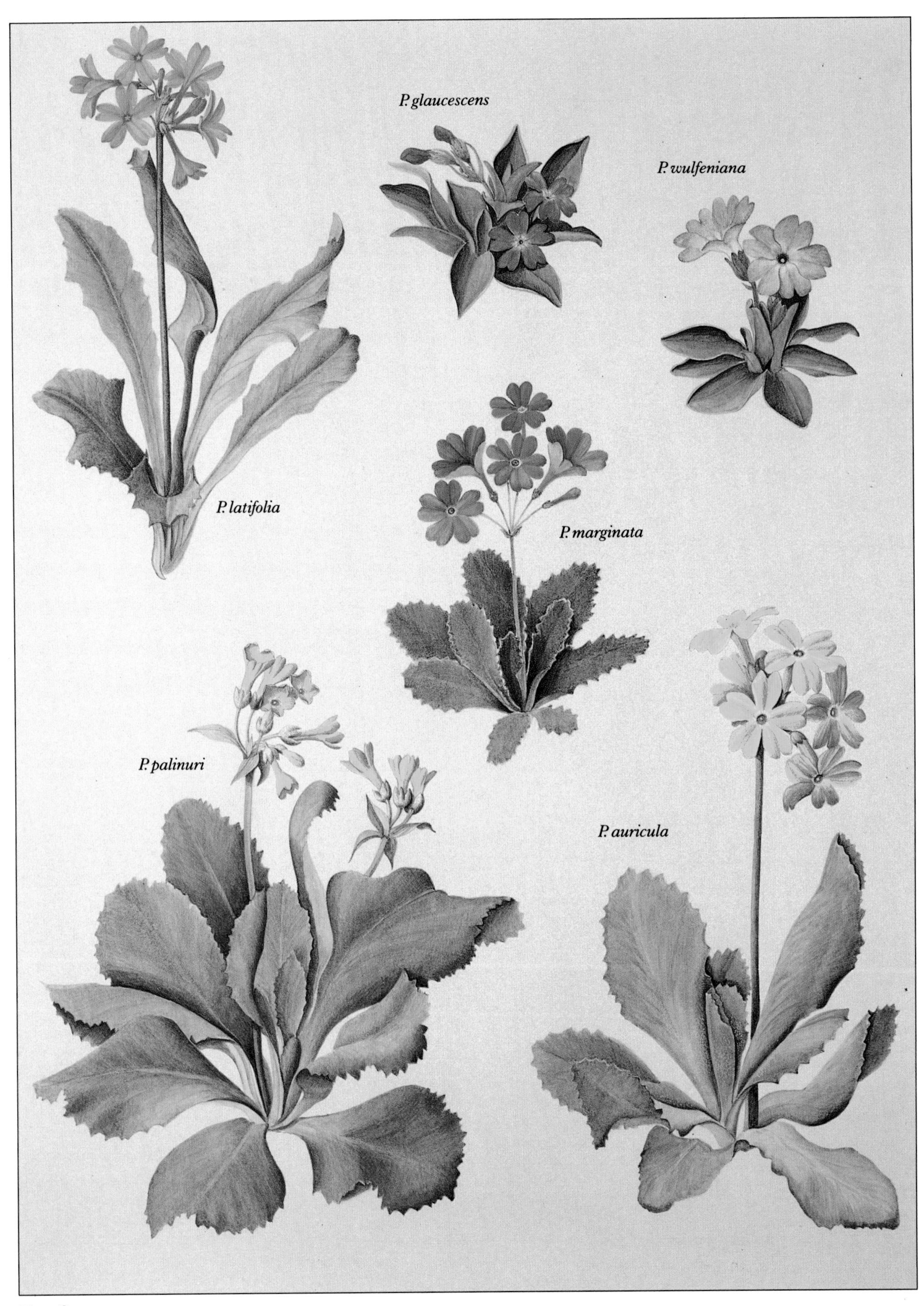
P. glaucescens
P. wulfeniana
P. latifolia
P. marginata
P. palinuri
P. auricula

Plate 2

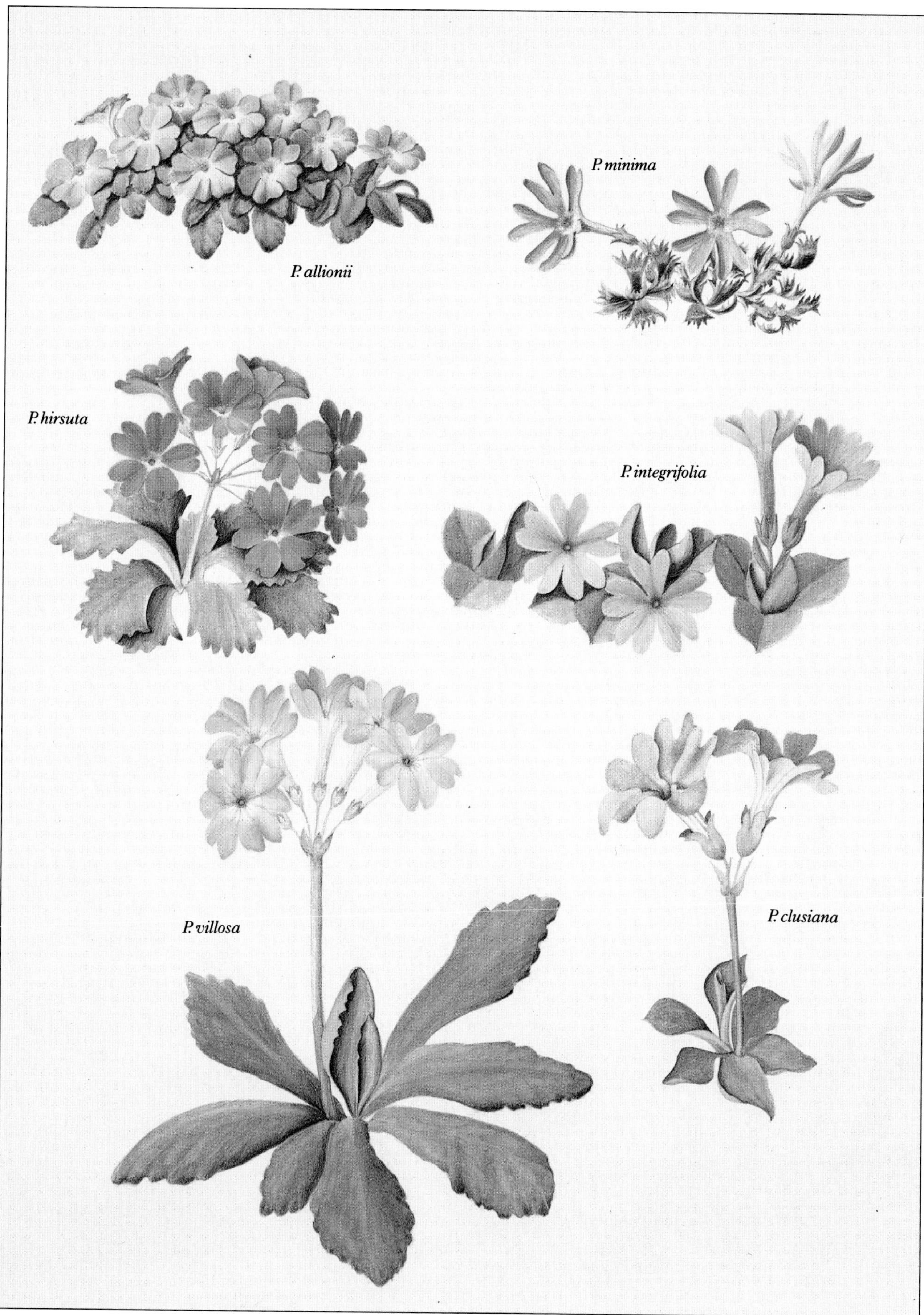
P. allionii
P. minima
P. hirsuta
P. integrifolia
P. villosa
P. clusiana

Plate 3

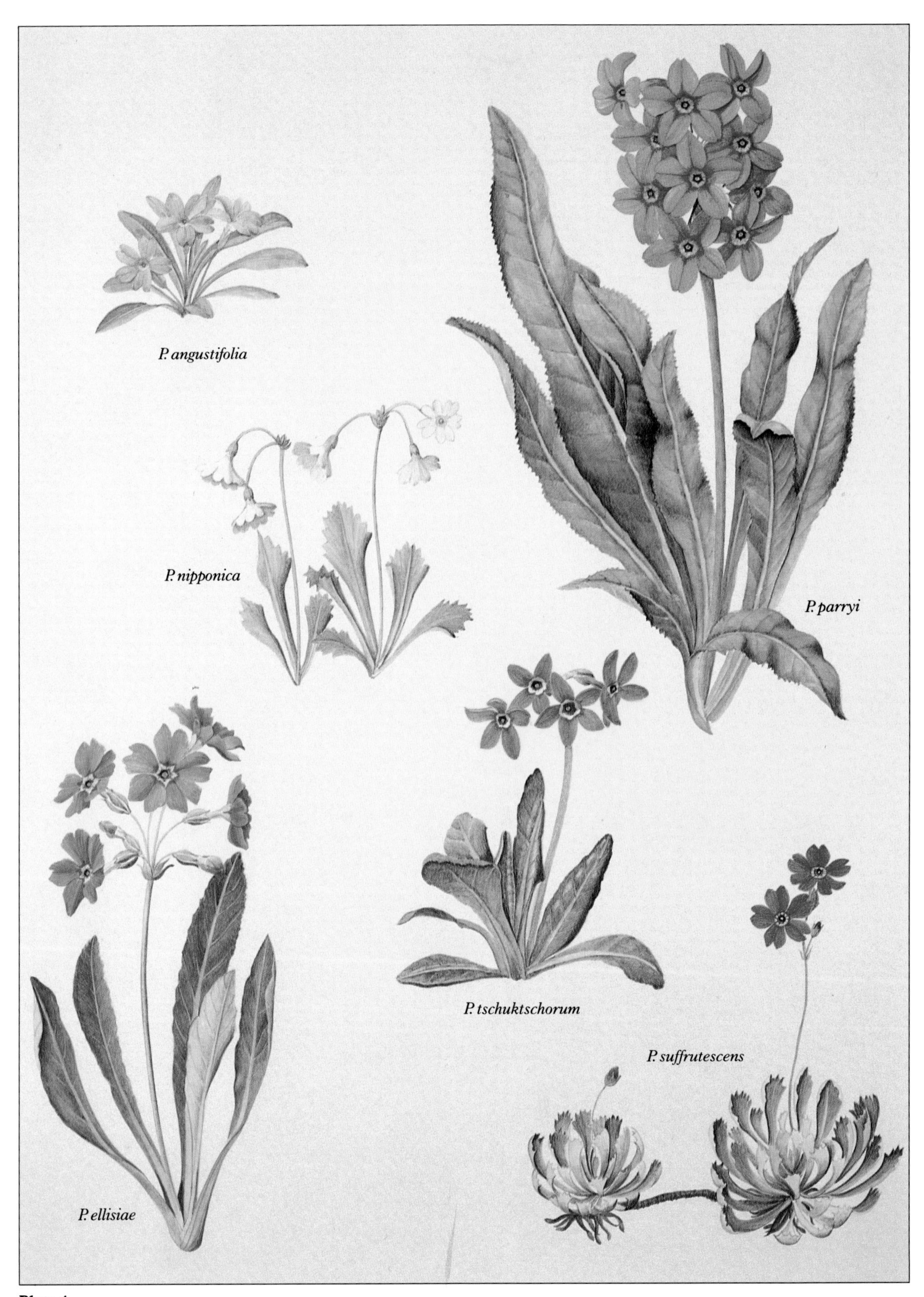
P. angustifolia
P. nipponica
P. parryi
P. tschuktschorum
P. suffrutescens
P. ellisiae

Plate 4

P. megaseifolia
P. veris
P. juliae
P. elatior
P. renifolia
P. vulgaris

Plate 5

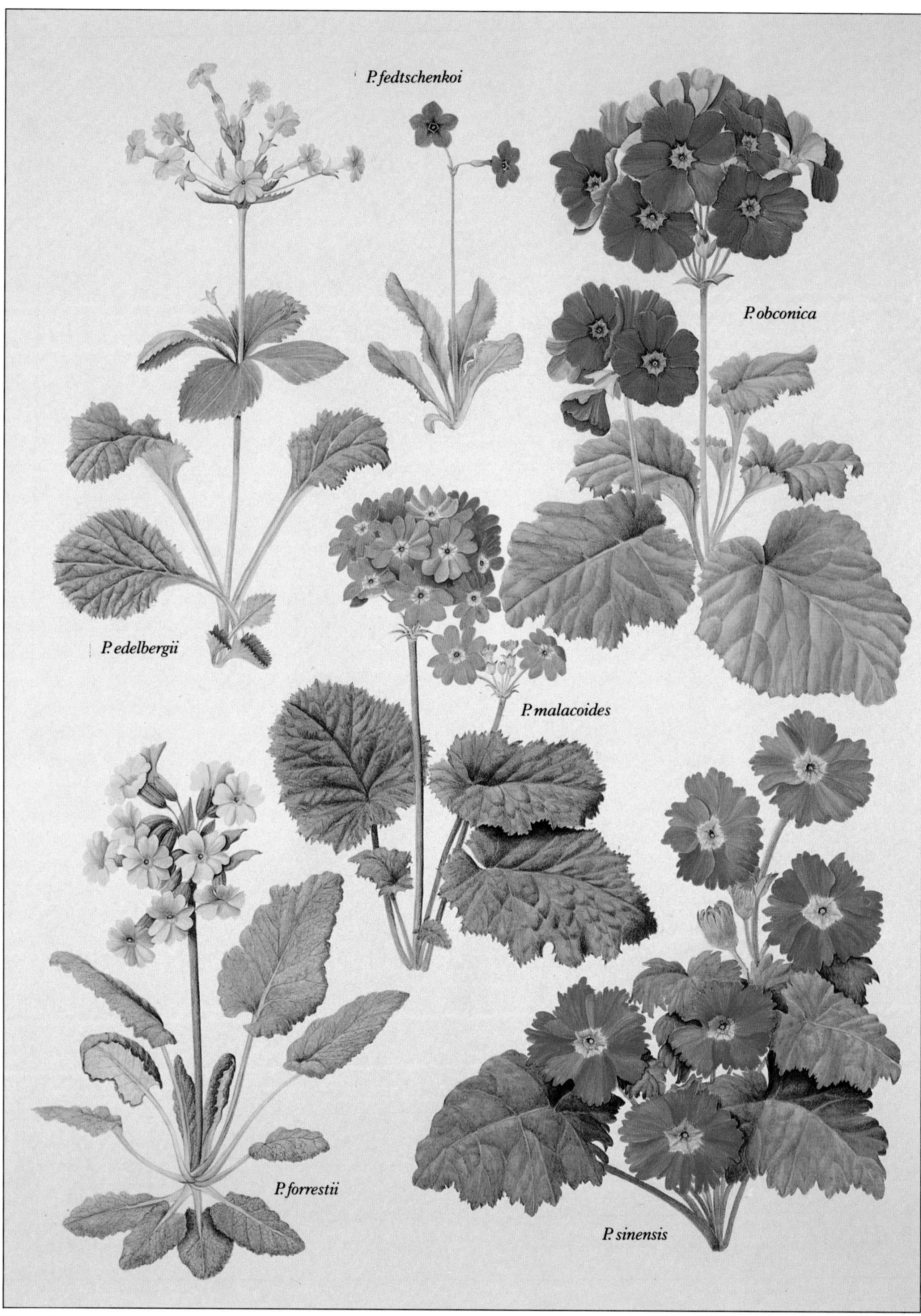
P. fedtschenkoi
P. obconica
P. edelbergii
P. malacoides
P. forrestii
P. sinensis

Plate 6

P. cortusoides
P. hidakana
P. polyneura
P. reinii
P. sieboldii
P. kisoana

Plate 7

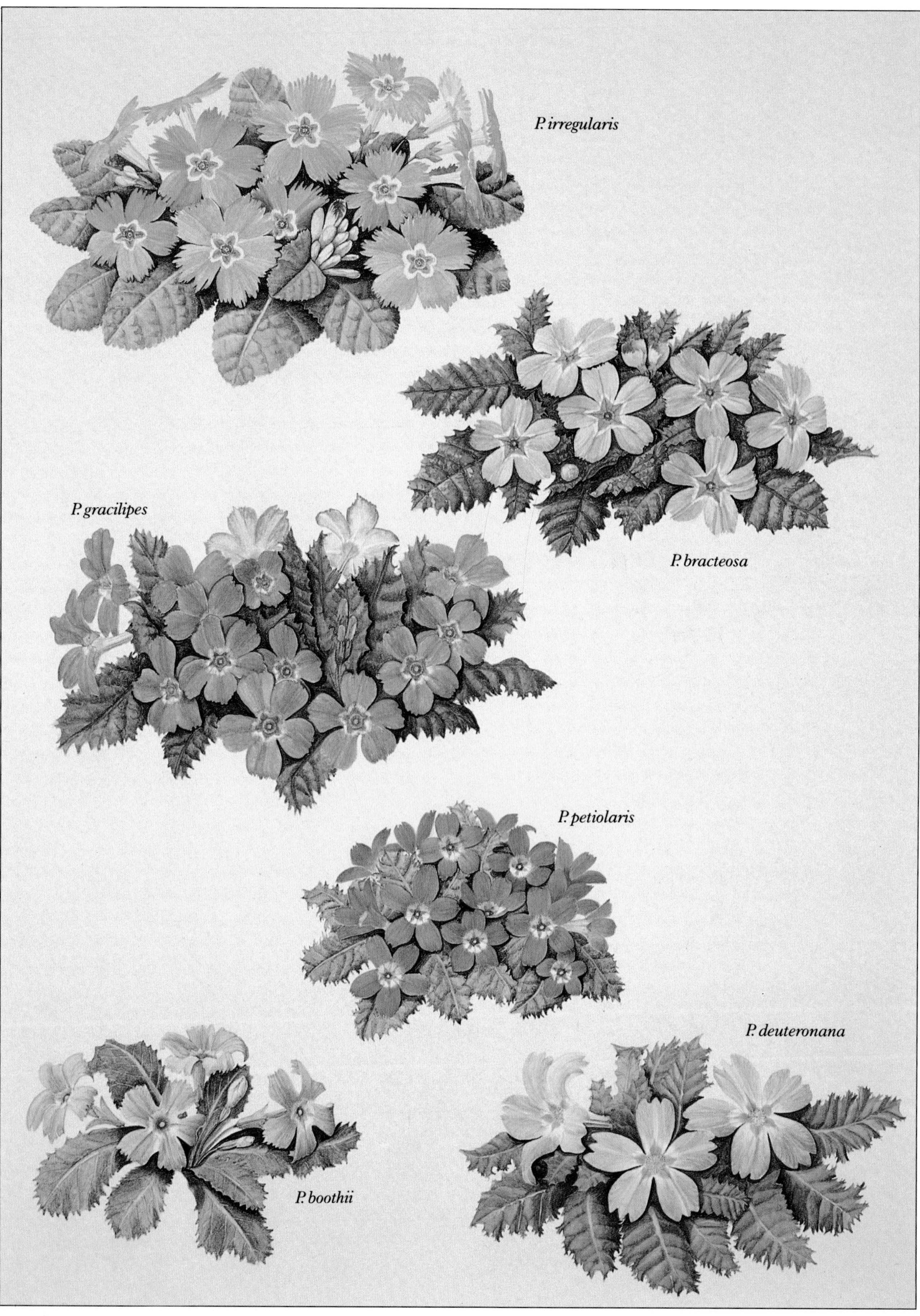
P. irregularis
P. bracteosa
P. gracilipes
P. petiolaris
P. deuteronana
P. boothii

Plate 8

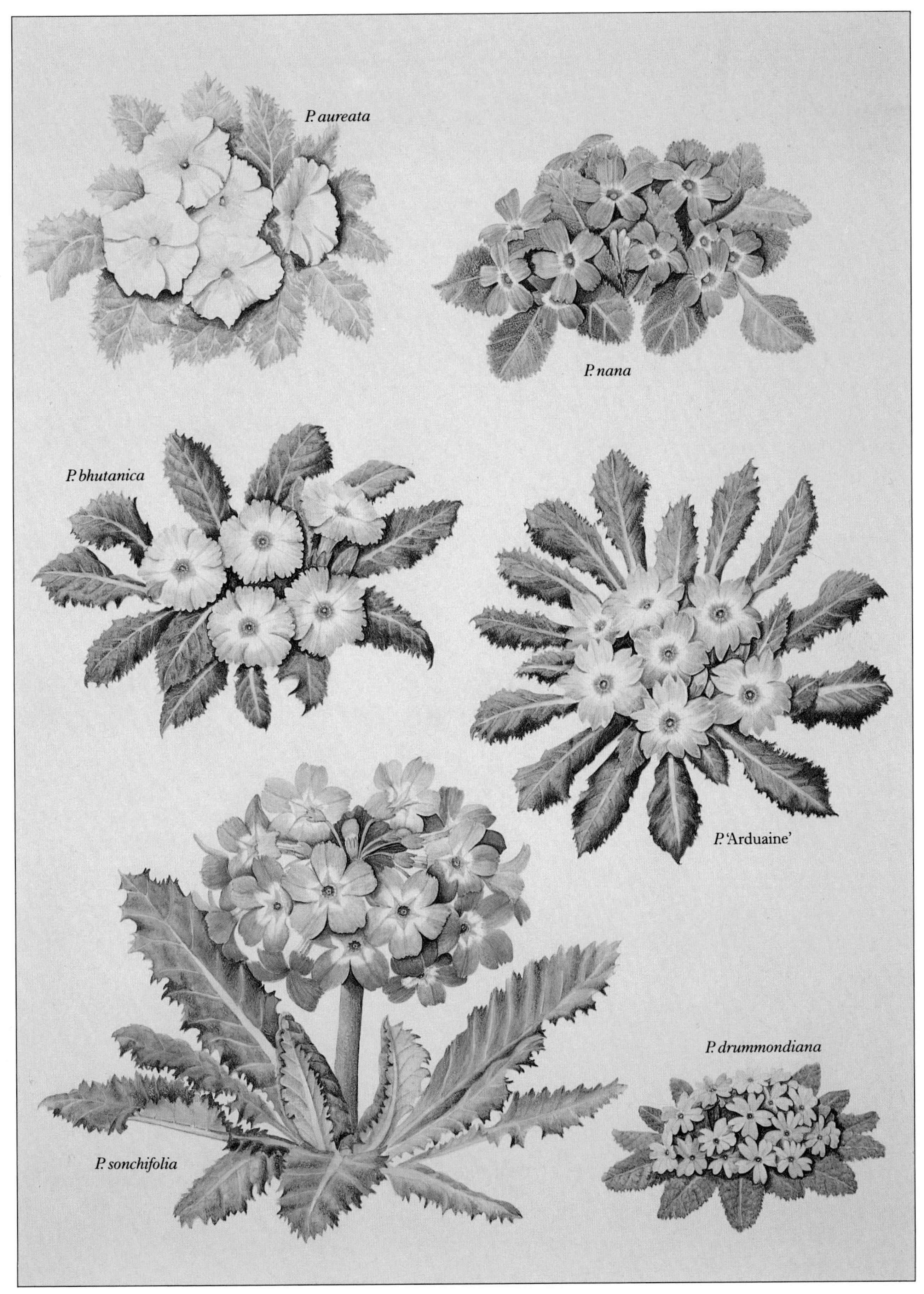
P. aureata
P. nana
P. bhutanica
P. 'Arduaine'
P. sonchifolia
P. drummondiana

Plate 9

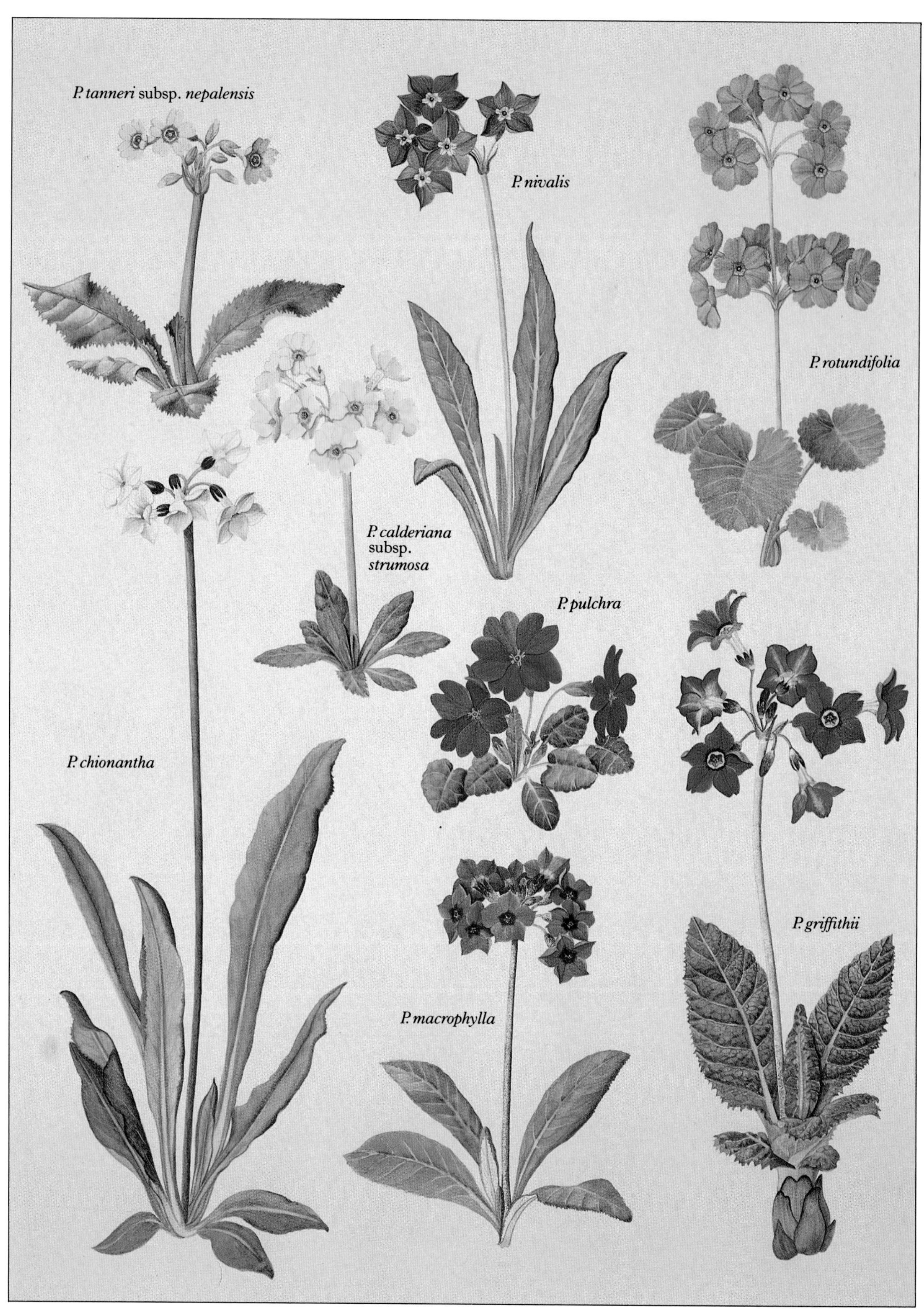
P. tanneri subsp. nepalensis
P. nivalis
P. rotundifolia
P. calderiana subsp. strumosa
P. pulchra
P. chionantha
P. griffithii
P. macrophylla
Plate 10

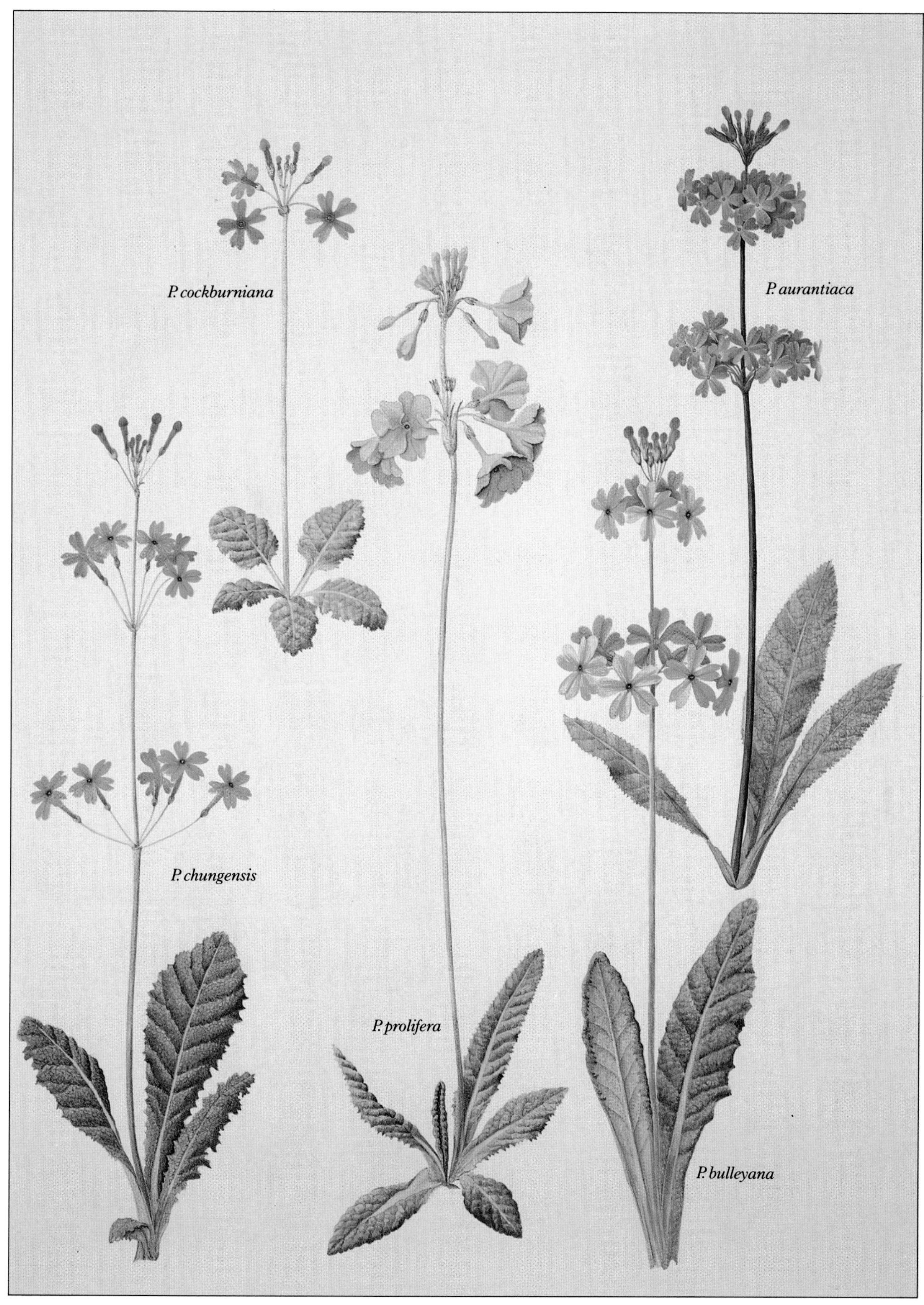
P. cockburniana
P. aurantiaca
P. chungensis
P. prolifera
P. bulleyana

Plate 11

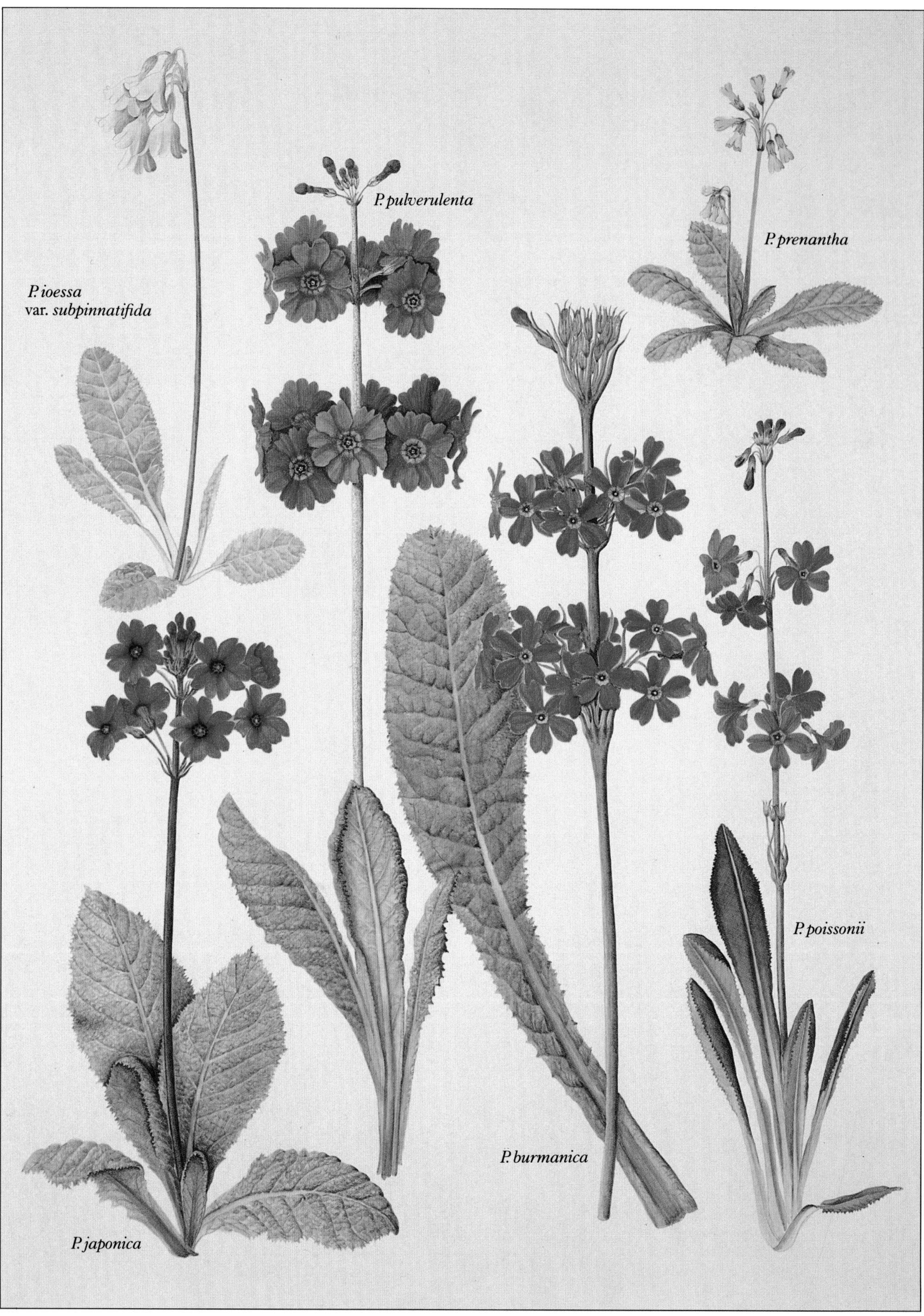
P. ioessa
var. subpinnatifida
P. pulverulenta
P. prenantha
P. burmanica
P. poissonii
P. japonica

Plate 12

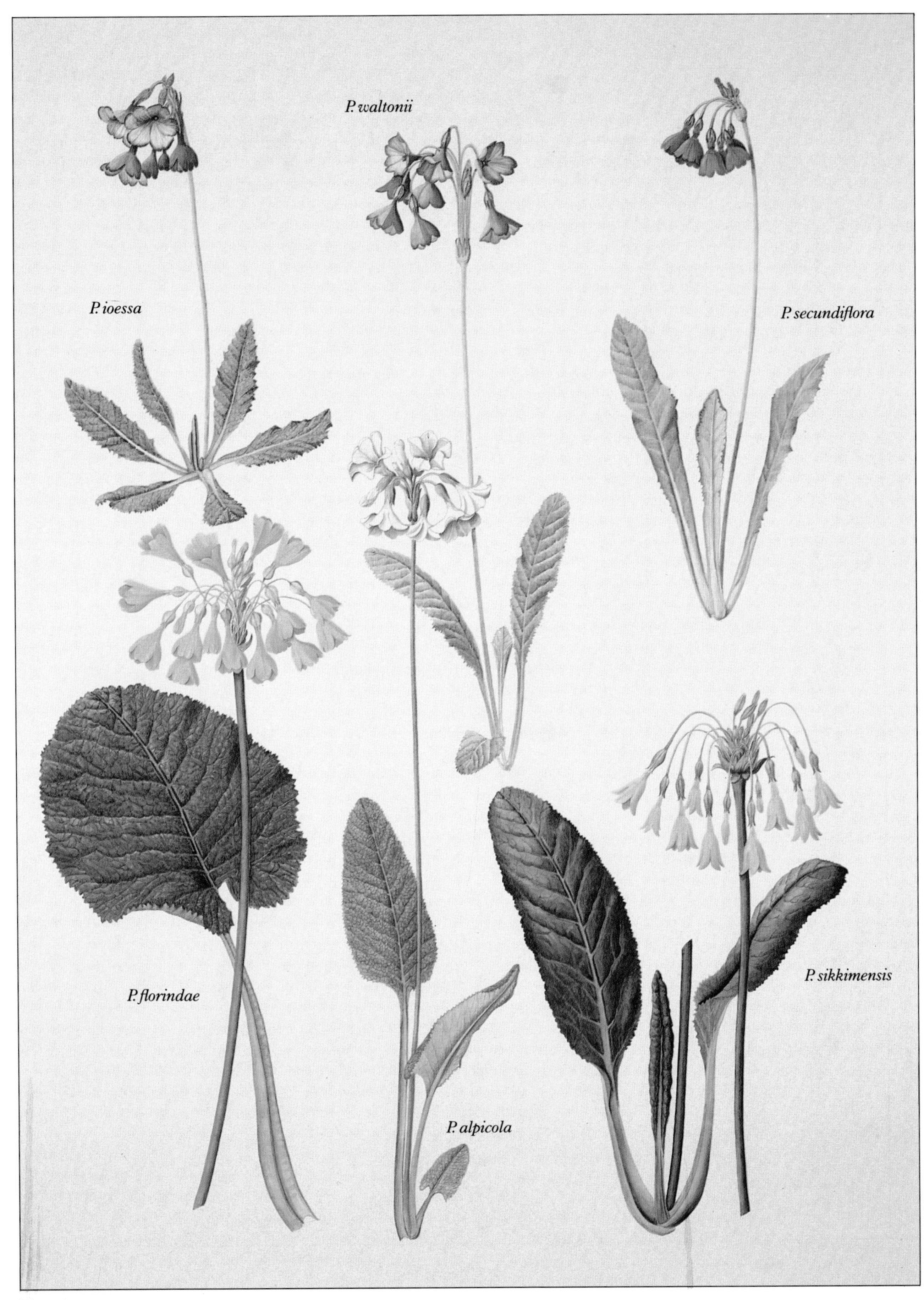
P. waltonii
P. ioessa
P. secundiflora
P. florindae
P. sikkimensis
P. alpicola

Plate 13

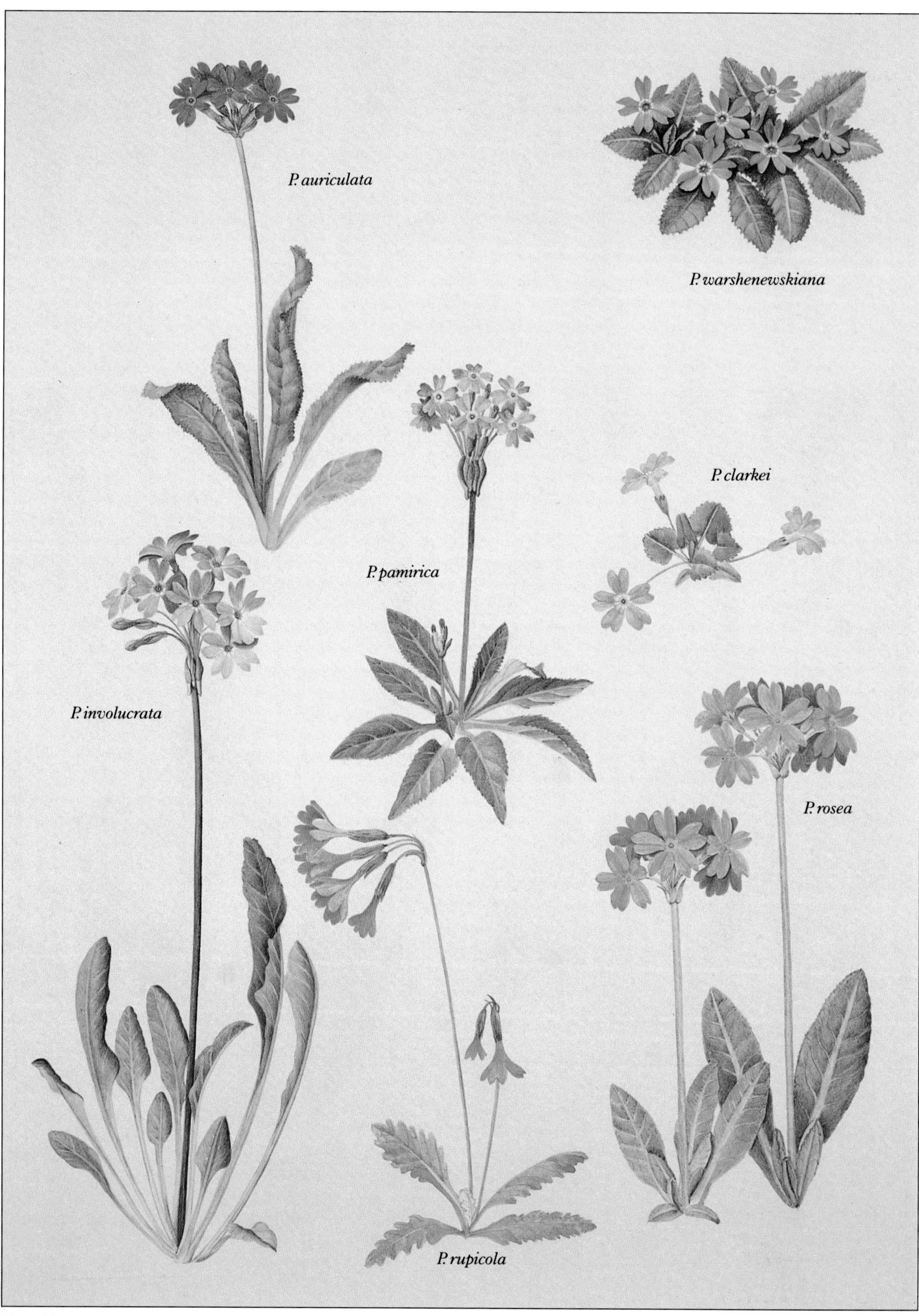
P. auriculata
P. warshenewskiana
P. clarkei
P. pamirica
P. involucrata
P. rosea
P. rupicola

Plate 14

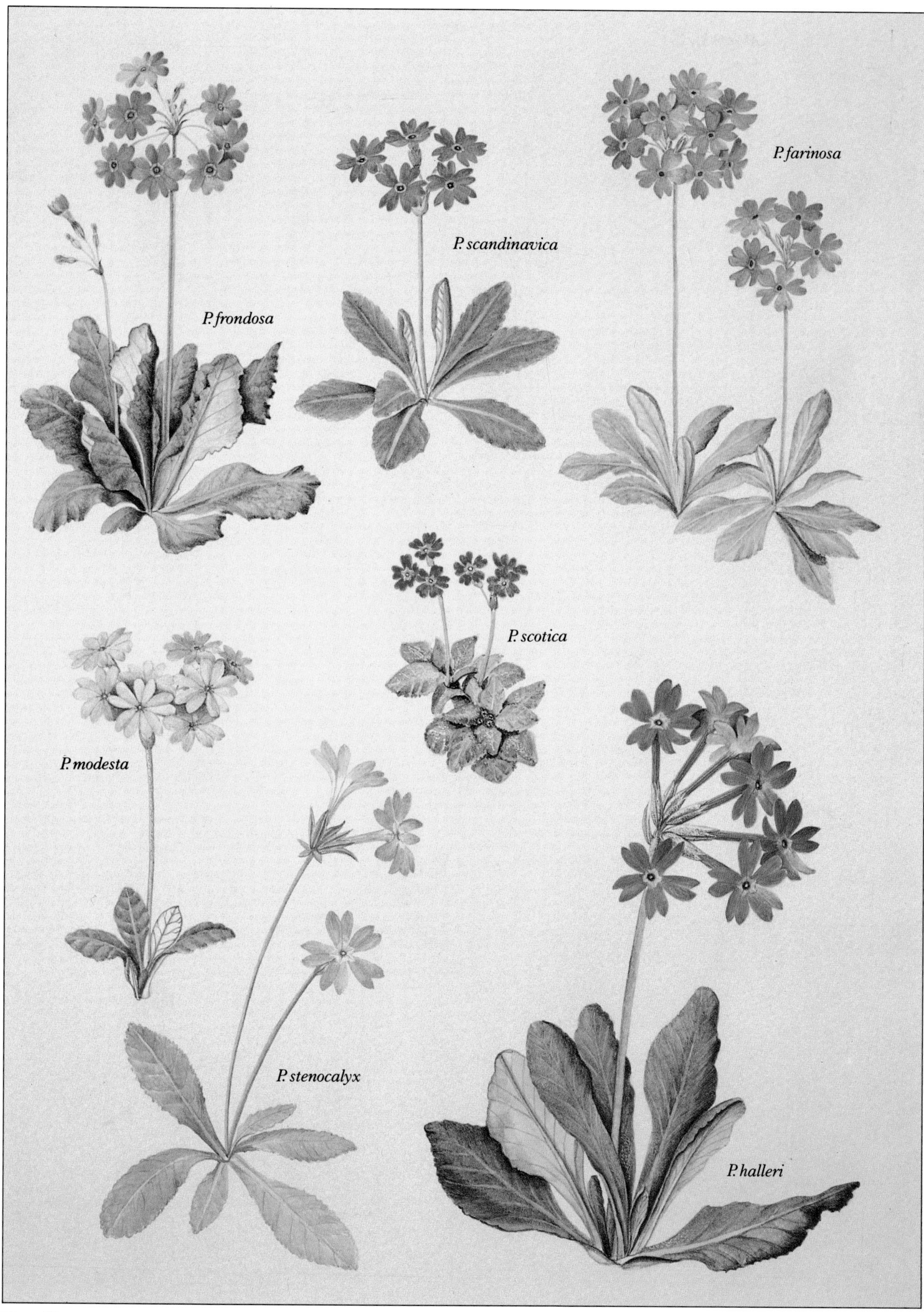
P. frondosa
P. scandinavica
P. farinosa
P. scotica
P. modesta
P. stenocalyx
P. halleri

Plate 15

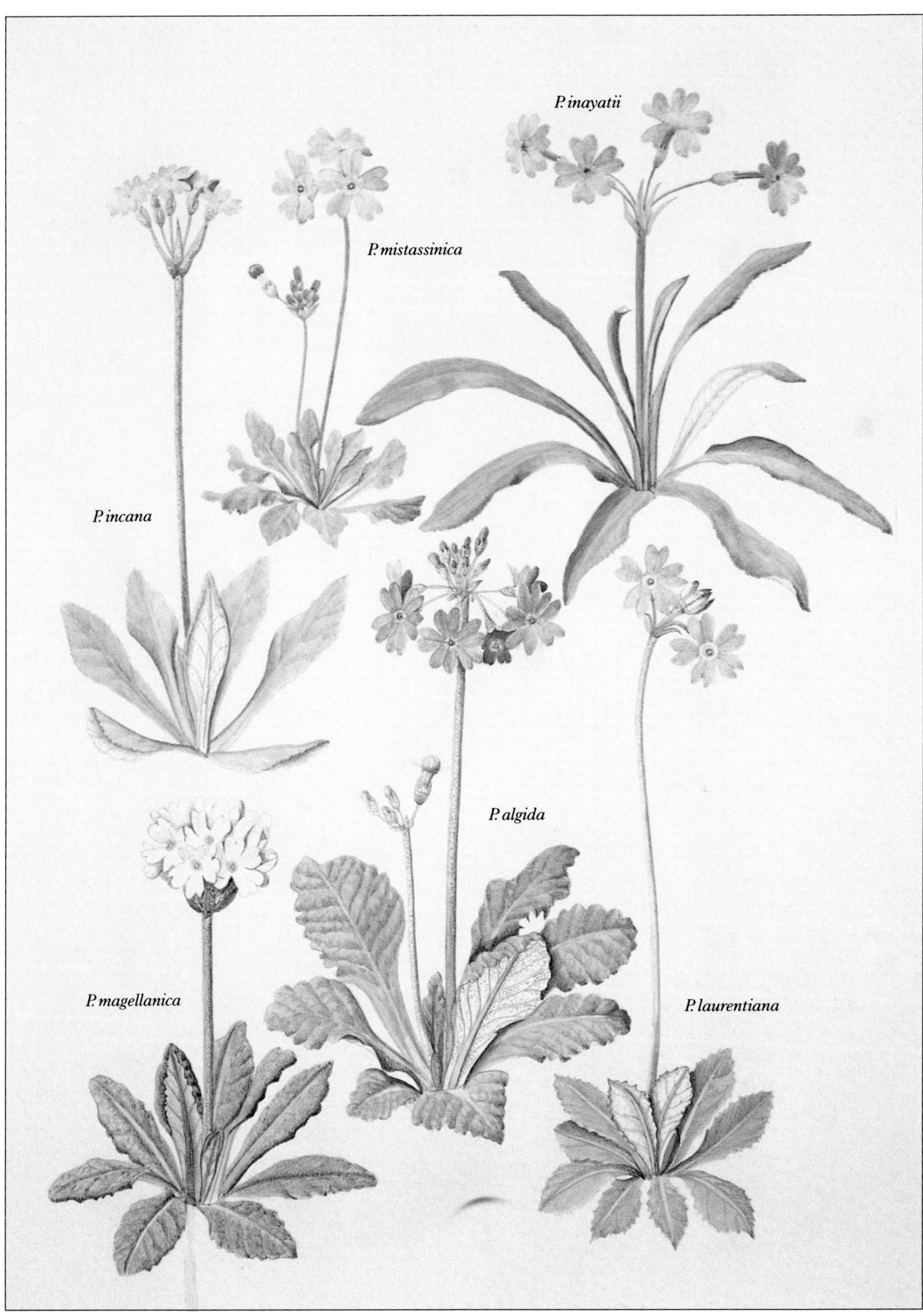
P. inayatii
P. mistassinica
P. incana
P. algida
P. magellanica
P. laurentiana

Plate 16

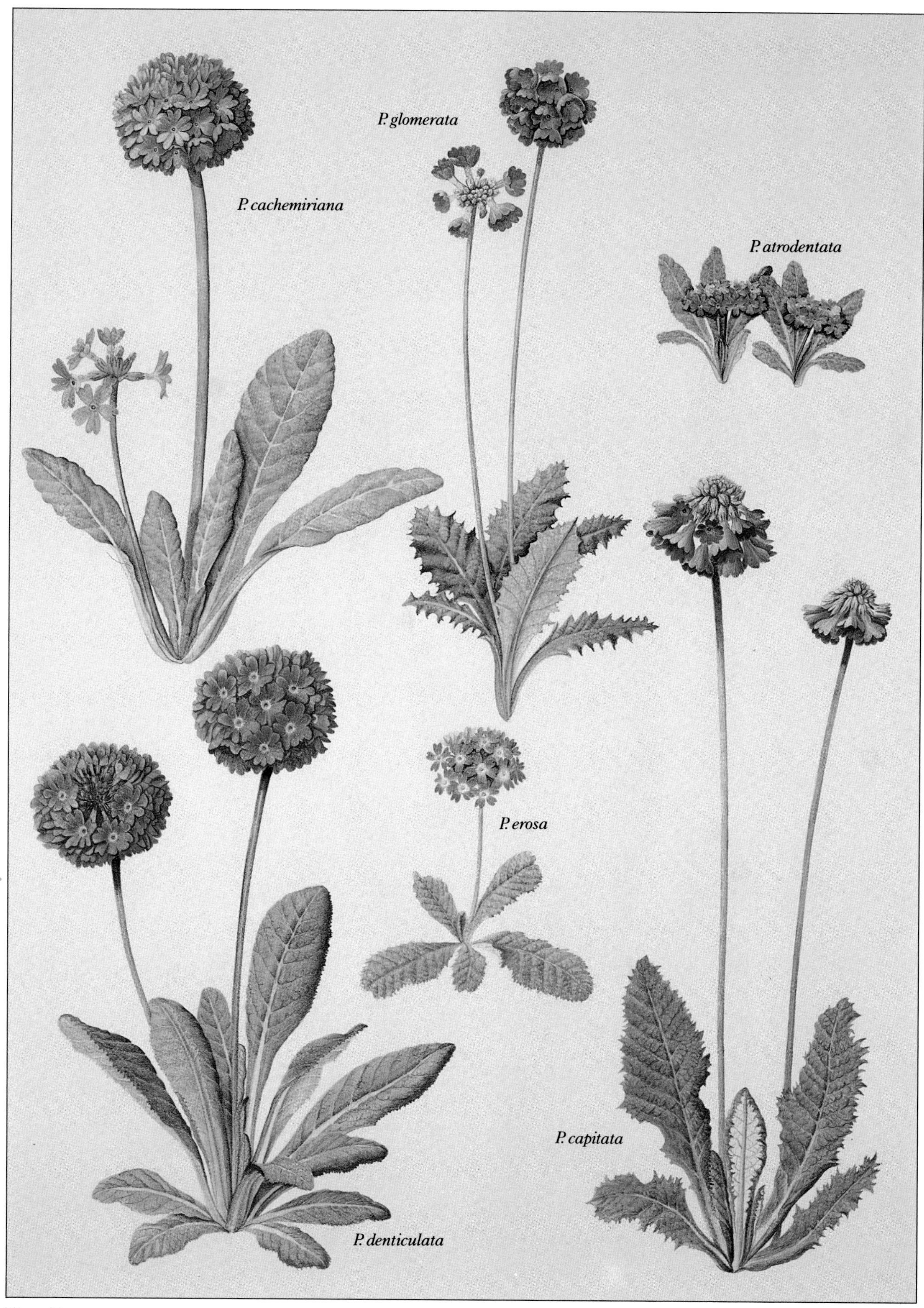
P. glomerata
P. cachemiriana
P. atrodentata
P. erosa
P. capitata
P. denticulata

Plate 17

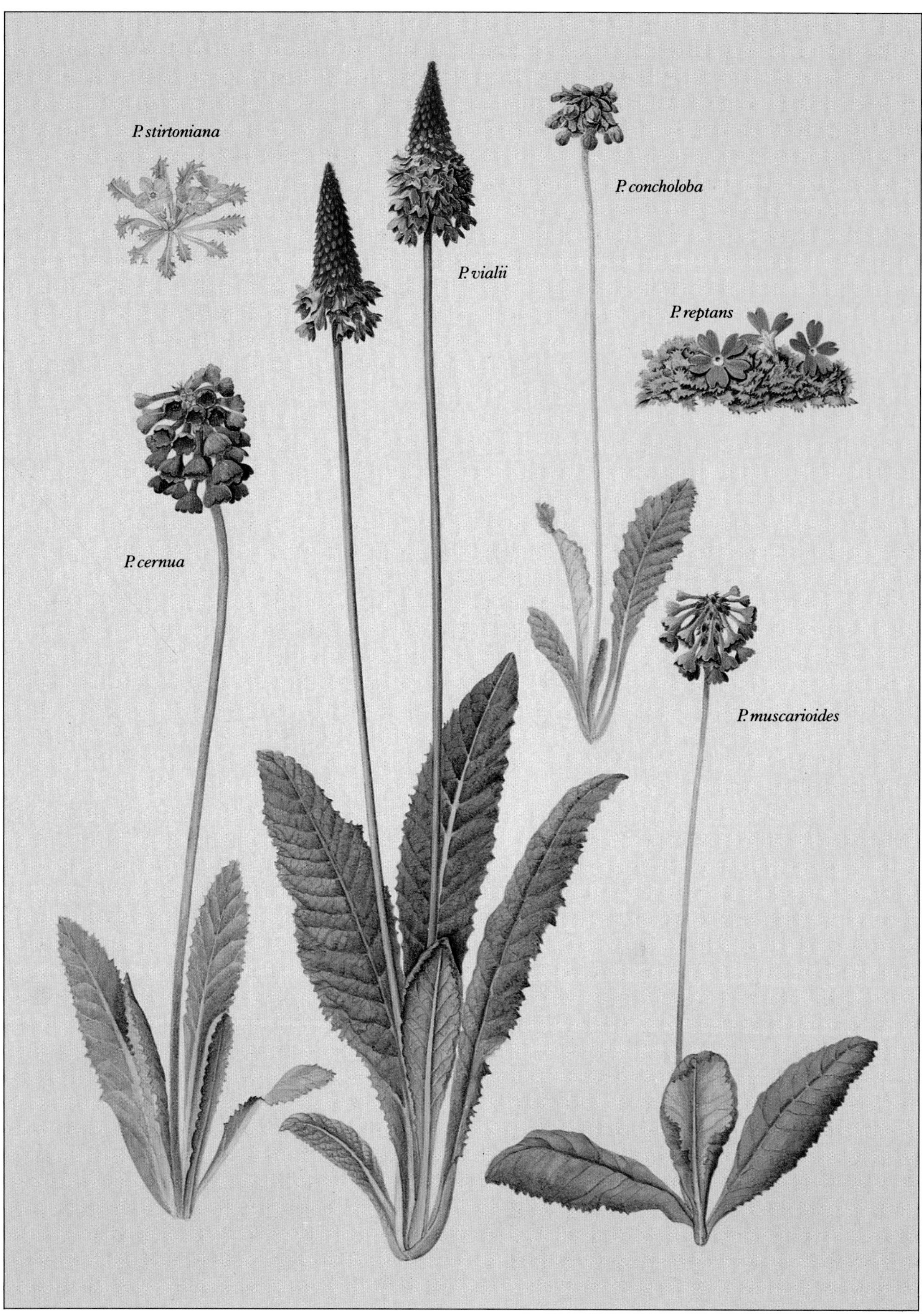
P. stirtoniana
P. concholoba
P. vialii
P. reptans
P. cernua
P. muscarioides

Plate 18

P. sherriffae
P. cawdoriana
P. pinnatifida
P. buryana
P. reidii
P. flaccida

Plate 19

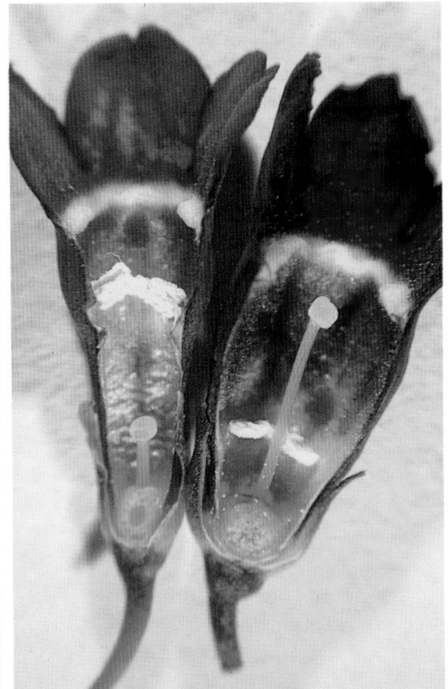

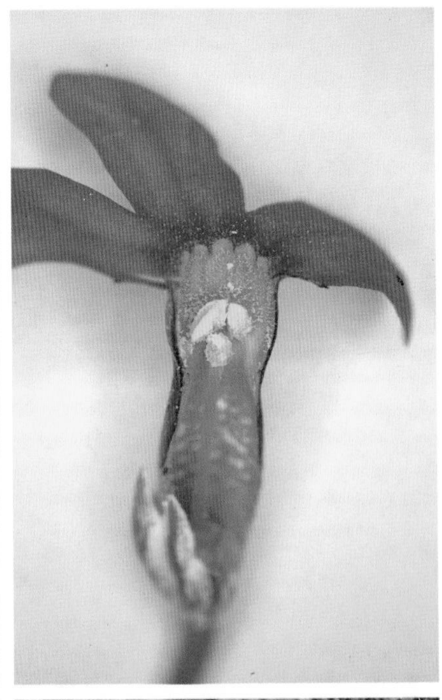

Plate 20. (Top left) *Bryocarpum himalaicum,* Bhutan. (Photo: D. Milward)
Plate 21. (Top centre) Heterostylous flowers in *P. wilsonii.* Thrum flower left, pin flower right. (Photo: F.M. Wedderburn)
Plate 22. (Top right) The homostyle flower of *P. cockburniana.*
(Photo: F.M. Wedderburn)
Plate 23. (Left) *P. verticillata* at Tanumah, Saudi Arabia. (Photo: A.J. Richards)
Plate 24. (Above) *P. glutinosa,* Timmelsjoch, Austria.
(Photo: A.J. Richards)

Plate 25. (Left) *P. deorum,* Rila, Bulgaria. (Photo: A.J. Richards)
Plate 26. (Below left) *P. parryi,* Colorado, USA.
(Photo: A.J. Richards)
Plate 27. (Below right) *P. elatior* subsp. *meyeri,* Mezovit, Turkey.
(Photo: M. & L. Almond)

Plate 28. (Right) *P. heucherifolia,* Lijiang, Sichuan. (Photo: P. Cribb)
Plate 29. (Below left) *P. palmata,* Juizhaigou, Sichuan. (Photo: P. Cribb)
Plate 30. (Below right) *P. gracilipes,* Nepal. (Photo: J. Templar)

Plate 31. (Top left) *P. deuteronana,* Nepal. (Photo: J. Templar)
Plate 32. (Above, top) *P. boothii* subsp. *autumnalis* in cultivation. (Photo: B. Thompson)
Plate 33. (Above, centre) *P. irregularis,* Annapurna range, Nepal, showing natural variation. (Photo: B. Thompson)
Plate 34. (Left) *P. aureata* subsp. *fimbriata,* Gosainkund, Nepal. (Photo: R. McBeath)
Plate 35. (Above) *P. calderiana* subsp. *calderiana,* Sikkim. (Photo: B. Thompson)

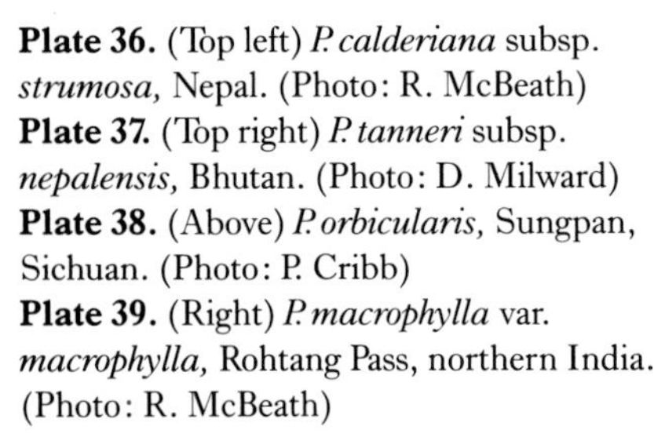

Plate 36. (Top left) *P. calderiana* subsp. *strumosa,* Nepal. (Photo: R. McBeath)
Plate 37. (Top right) *P. tanneri* subsp. *nepalensis,* Bhutan. (Photo: D. Milward)
Plate 38. (Above) *P. orbicularis,* Sungpan, Sichuan. (Photo: P. Cribb)
Plate 39. (Right) *P. macrophylla* var. *macrophylla,* Rohtang Pass, northern India. (Photo: R. McBeath)

Plate 40. (Top left) *P. megalocarpa,* Sikkim. (Photo: R. McBeath)
Plate 41. (Top right) *P. nivalis* var. *nivalis* in cultivation. (Photo: A.J. Richards)
Plate 42. (Below left) *P. nivalis* var. *colorata,* Ala Archa, central Asia. (Photo: C. Grey-Wilson)
Plate 43. (Below right) *P. duthieana* in cultivation. (Photo: A.J. Richards)

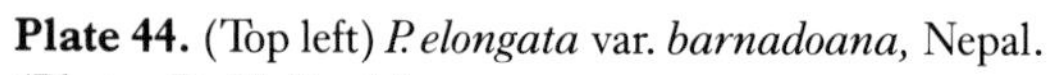

Plate 44. (Top left) *P. elongata* var. *barnadoana,* Nepal.
(Photo: R. McBeath)
Plate 45. (Top right) *P. crassifolia,* Caucasus.
(Photo: M. & L. Almond)
Plate 46. (Above) *P. longipes,* Mezovit, Turkey.
(Photo: M. & L. Almond)
Plate 47. (Right) *P. tschuktschorum* in cultivation.
(Photo: A.J. Richards)

Plate 48. (Right) *P. gambeliana,* Sikkim. (Photo: R. McBeath)
Plate 49. (Far right) *P. amethystina* var. *brevifolia,* Dshesong, Sichuan. (Photo: M. Hirst)
Plate 50. (Below) *P. auriculata,* Turkey. (Photo: M. & L. Almond)
Plate 51. (Right, centre) *P. tibetica,* Nepal. (Photo: C. Grey-Wilson)
Plate 52. (Right, below) *P. glabra,* Sikkim. (Photo: R. McBeath)

Plate 53. (Left) *P. exigua,* Rila, Bulgaria. (Photo: A.J. Richards)
Plate 54. (Below) *P. algida,* Turkey. (Photo: L. & M. Almond)
Plate 55. (Left, centre) *P. concinna,* Nepal. (Photo: R. McBeath)
Plate 56. (Left, below) *P. sharmae,* Nepal. (Photo: C. Grey-Wilson)

Plate 57. (Top left) *P. pulchella,* Lijiang, Yunnan. (Photo: P. Cribb)
Plate 58. (Top right) *P. stenocalyx,* Wolong, Sichuan. (Photo: P. Cribb)
Plate 59. (Left) *P. gemmifera* var. *gemmifera,* Sungpan, Sichuan. (Photo: P. Cribb)
Plate 60. (Above) *P. minutissima,* Rohtang Pass, northern India. (Photo: R. McBeath)

Plate 61. (Top left) *P. tenuiloba,* Sikkim. (Photo: R. McBeath)
Plate 62. (Top right) *P. spathulifolia* in cultivation. (Photo: A.J. Richards)
Plate 63. (Below) *P. muscoides,* Nepal. (Photo: R. McBeath)

Plate 64. (Top left) *P. primulina,* Sikkim. (Photo: R. McBeath)
Plate 65. (Top right) *P. dryadifolia,* Lichiang, Yunnan. (Photo: C. Grey-Wilson)
Plate 66. (Above) *P. pinnatifida,* Lichiang, Yunnan. (Photo: C. Grey-Wilson)
Plate 67. (Right) *P. wigramiana,* Nepal. (Photo: D. Milward)

Plate 68. (Top left) *P. wollastonii,* Barun Khola, Nepal. (Photo: C. Grey-Wilson)
Plate 69. (Top right) *P. soldanelloides,* Sikkim. (Photo: R. McBeath)
Plate 70. (Below) *P. sappharina,* Sikkim. (Photo: R. McBeath)

Plate 71. (Above) *P. albenensis*, Val Noseda, Italy. (Photo: H. Taylor)

Plate 72. (Above) *P. recubariensis*, Mt. Zevola, Italy. (Photo: M. Taylor)

Plate 73. (Left, above), *P. grandis,* Usguli, Caucasus (Photo: D. Milward)

Plate 74. (Right, above), *P. bracteata* in cultivation. (Photo: C. Grey-Wilson)

Plate 75. (Right, below), *P. ovalifolia* in cultivation. (Photo: A. J. Richards)

Plate 76. (Top, left), *P. jonardunii*, Doshong La, south-east Tibet (Photo: A. Chambers)

Plate 77. (Below, left), *P. moupinensis* in cultivation. (Photo: A. J. Richards)

Plate 78. (Right), *P. whitei* in cultivation. (Photo: A. Chambers)

Plate 79. (Below, right), *P. calderiana* (left) and *P. tanneri* (right), Bimbi La, south-east Tibet (Photo: A. Chambers)

Plate 80. (Top, left), *P. brevicula,* Da Xue Shan, Sichuan, China (Photo: D. Rankin)

Plate 81. (Top, right), *P. hongshanensis,* Hong Shan, Yunnan, China. (Photo: D. Rankin)

Plate 82. (Below, left), *P. obtusifolia,* Charang to Lalanti, north-west India (Photo: H & M Taylor).

Plate 83. (Below, right), *P. stuartii,* Nalgan, north-west India (Photo: H & M Taylor)

Plate 84. (Below, left), *P. minor*, white form, Zo La, south-east Tibet (Photo: A. Chambers)

Plate 85. (Below, right), *P. limbata,* Jiuxhaigou, Gansu, China (Photo: D. Milward)

Plate 86. (Top, right), *P. optata*, Gonggan Len, Sichuan. (Photo: H. Jans)

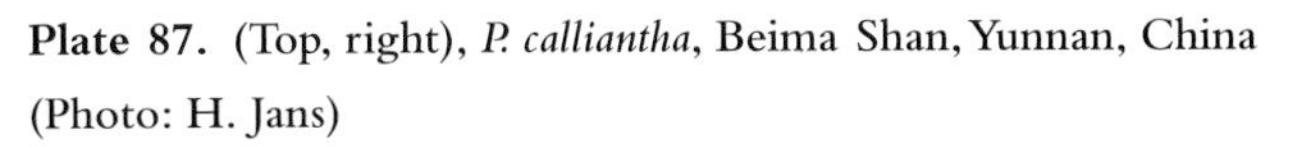

Plate 87. (Top, right), *P. calliantha*, Beima Shan, Yunnan, China (Photo: H. Jans)

Plate 88. (Below), *P. boreiocalliantha*, Tianchi, Zhongdian, Yunnan (Photo: D. Rankin)

Plate 89. (Top, left), *P. falcifolia,* Doshong La, south-east Tibet (Photo: F. Hunt)

Plate 90. (Top, left), *P. baileyana*, Temo La, south-east Tibet (Photo: A. Chambers)

Plate 91. (Below, left), *P. caveana*, Bimbi La, south-east Tibet (Photo: A. Chambers)

Plate 92. (Below, right), *P. ioessa* var. *hopeana*, Ganesh Himal, Nepal (Photo: M. Hirst)

Plate 93. (Right), *P. elliptica*, north-west India (Photo: H & M Taylor)

Plate 94. (Left, centre), *P. fasciculata*, Bi Ta Hai, Zhongdian, Yunnan, China (Photo: A. J. Richards)

Plate 95. (Top, left), *P. zambalensis,* Beima Shan, Yunnan, China (Photo: A. J. Richards)

Plate 96. (Top, right), *P. yunnanensis*, Yulong Shan, Yunnan, China (Photo: A. J. Richards)

Plate 97. (Below, left), *P. rhodochroa* var. *geraldinae*, Poda La, south-east Tibet (Photo: A. Chambers)

Plate 98. (Below, right), *P. nanobella*, Beima Shan, Yunnan, China (Photo: C. Grey-Wilson)

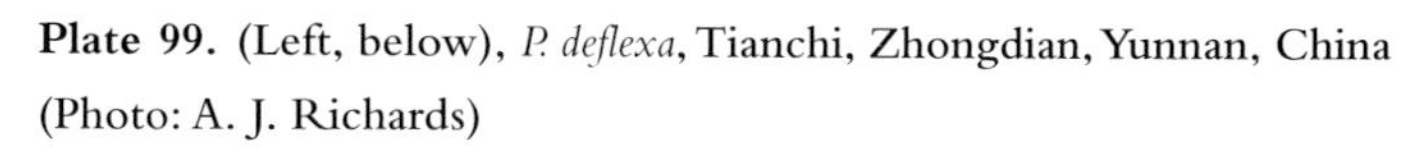

Plate 99. (Left, below), *P. deflexa*, Tianchi, Zhongdian, Yunnan, China (Photo: A. J. Richards)

Plate 100. (Left, centre), *P. apoclita*, Beima Shan, Yunnan, China (Photo: A. J. Richards)

Plate 101. (Top, left), *P. violacea*, Balang Shan, Sichuan, China (Photo: H. J. B. Birks)

Plate 102. (Below, right), *P. bellidifolia*, Nyima La, south-east Tibet (Photo: A. Chambers)

Plate 103. (Top, right), *P. tangutica*, Huanglong Si, Sichuan, China (Photo: H. Jans)

Plate 104. (Below, centre), *P. woodwardii*, Qinghai, China (Photo: H. Jans)

Primula larsenii C.M. Hu, Nordic Botany 10: 399–401 (1990)

DESCRIPTION Another relative of *P. kwangtungensis*, but with the leaf stalk equalling the kidney-shaped, cordate leaf which is hairy throughout and somewhat membranous. The rather small white flowers (to 8 mm in diameter) are homostylous. Chiangmai, Thailand; moist humus-rich ground in mossy forest, 1900–2600 m. Only one of four species of primula native to Thailand.

Primula laevicalyx Hu & Xu, Act. Phytotax. Sin. 26: 309 (1988)

DESCRIPTION A small orbicular-leaved plant related to *P. kweichouensis,* but with a glabrous calyx and flower stalks. Limestone rocks at 1600–2400 m, south Kweichow.

Subgenus **Pinnatae subgenus novum** Type species *P. filchnerae* Knuth.

Plantae graciles, tenues, plerumque monocarpicae. Folia pinnata (vel pinnatifida profunde interdum videtur), revoluta, efarinosa, membranata, glabra vel pilosa. Scapi tenues folia vix superantes.

Section **Pinnatae** Knuth, Bot. Jahrb. Syst. 36: 140 (1905). (Section *Ranunculoides* Chen & Hu, p.max.p.)

DESCRIPTION *Small* hairy or hairless probably deciduous perennials arising from carrot-like stocks, or *annuals*, lacking meal, and with revolute vernation. *Leaves* very thin and membranous, pinnatifid, pinnate or even 2-pinnate, i.e. divided to the mid-rib into lobes like a fern. *Stems* few-flowered in a single umbel, short, weak and wiry, bearing very small linear bracts. Calyx tubular to bell-shaped, usually only 4 mm, but to 10 mm in *P. filchnerae*. *Corolla* rose to purple with a yellow eye, exannulate, heterostylous or homostylous, forming a tube and spreading notched petal lobes, often tiny, but to 25 mm diameter in *P. filchnerae*. *Pollen* (in *P. ranunculoides*) stephanocolpate, resembling that in section Armerina. Capsules, breeding system and chromosomes unknown. Flowering in late winter or early spring.

DISTRIBUTION Eastern China, in the provinces of Chekiang, Anhwei and Kiangsi, i.e in the general lowland area of Nanking and Shanghai where no other primulas occur; *P. filchnerae* occurs in north-central China in the province of Shensi. Habitats vary.

This very little-known group of species from the heavily populated and overcultivated warm temperate regions of eastern China are chiefly remarkable for their highly divided pinnate leaves, resembling those of a potentilla such as silverweed, although much more delicate in construction.

None of the species have ever been in cultivation, and it is difficult from the few scraps of herbarium material to obtain a clear view of their relationships, but these are at best enigmatic. Results from DNA suggest that *P. cicutariifolia* has no close relatives, but is distantly aligned with subgenus *Aleuritia,* its closest relatives being placed in sections Petiolares, Davidii and Proliferae. As the inflorescences rather resemble those of *Auganthus* species, while some species have multicellular hairs, and none have meal, previous classifications had, rather uncertainly, placed the Pinnatae within subgenus *Auganthus*. The pollen type agrees with neither alignment, but, rather, suggests a relationship with section Armerina. Consequently, I do not regard the Pinnatae as sufficiently close to subgenus *Aleuritia* to warrant inclusion there, and I am erecting a new subgenus for this isolated group.

Halda (1992) follows Chen & Hu (1990) in taking *P. filchnerae* out of this section and associating it with *P. sinensis*. As *P. filchnerae* is the type of the section, they needed a new sectional name, Ranunculoides, Chen & Hu (1990). However, I regard *P. filchnerae* as part of this assemblage, so Knuth's taxon stands.

No hybrids are reported.

KEY TO SPECIES

1. Annual; flowers less than 9 mm in diameter, homostylous .... *P. cicutariifolia*
1. Perennial with a persistent tap-root; flowers 10 mm in diameter or more, heterostylous 2

2. Leaves glabrous; corolla about 10 mm in diameter .... *P. merriliana*
2. Leaves hairy, at least below; corolla more than 15 mm in diameter 3

3. Leaves with long hairs above; leaf-lobes deeply dissected .... *P. filchnerae*
3. Leaves glabrous above; leaf-lobes rounded, dentate .... *P. ranunculoides*

Primula cicutariifolia Pax, Jahr.-Bericht Schles. Gesells. 93: 1 (1915)

P. erodioides Schlechter (1924)

DESCRIPTION Annual. Young leaves simple, toothed, hairy; older leaves hairy at first, becoming hairless, with 3–7 pairs of lobes, the bottom pair distant, and a terminal toothed lobe; flowers about 6–8 mm in diameter, homostylous. Limestone rocks near the temple Ling-ying, Hsihu, near Hangchow, Chekiang; and from Anhwei.

Primula filchnerae Knuth, Bot. Jahr. 36: 139 (1905)

DESCRIPTION Perennial with carrot-like tubers. All leaves covered with both long hairs and short glands, 1–2 pinnate with 3–4 pairs of lobes each deeply and sharply lobulate, as is the terminal lobe; corolla purple, about 25 mm in diameter. Between Hsi-ngan and Hsiau-yi, southern slopes of the Tsinling Shan, to the south of Sianfu, Shensi province. Shady bush-covered depressions on very steep slopes of decomposed rocks. (Photo: J. Roy. Hort. Soc. 54: t.6 (1928).)

Primula merrilliana Schlechter, Feddes Rep. 19: 384 (1924)

DESCRIPTION Perennial. Leaves 1–2 pinnate, with up to 8 pairs of sharply and deeply divided lobes, hairless; corolla heterostylous, about 10 mm in diameter, the lobes entire. Another apparent cave dweller from Anhwei.

Primula ranunculoides Chen, Notes Roy. Bot. Gdn. Edinb. 20: 120 (1948)

DESCRIPTION Perennial. Young leaves simple, toothed; older leaves with usually three pairs of coarsely toothed rounded lobes and a terminal lobe, all hairless above, and somewhat glandular-hairy beneath; corolla purplish, heteromorphic, to 20 mm in diameter. This species has leaves resembling *P. cicutariifolia*, but flowers resembling *P. filchnerae*. Despite the name, the leaves look nothing like any buttercup this author knows, but have a striking resemblance to the basal leaves of *Pimpinella saxifraga*, the burnet saxifrage. (Photo: Farrer, English Rock Garden.)

Marshy ground near the pond at Tang Tung Tze Temple, Ying Nu, near Wuling Hsien, east Kiangsi.

Subgenus **Aleuritia** (Duby) Wendelbo, Aarbok Univ. Bergen, Mat.-Nat. 11: 37 (1961).

Type species *P. farinosa* L.

Section **Chartacea** Balf. f., J. Roy. Hort. Soc. 39: 146 (1913)

(Section Petiolares subsection Chartacea (Balf. f.) Smith & Forrest 1928)

Type species *P. chartacea* Franchet

DESCRIPTION Deciduous (?) perennials with revolute vernation, lacking basal bud-scales and meal, and without hairs on the leaf-blades. *Leaves* very thin and *membrane*-like in texture, with rounded blades and long slender stalks, the blades toothed or shortly lobed and with pinnately arranged veins. *Stems* rather slender, about equalling the leaves, usually shortly hairy above, bearing a long-stalked, few-flowered, single umbel with narrow simple, or leaf-like bracts. *Calyx* bell-shaped, usually glandular. *Corolla* blue, pink, rose or purple with a white to orange eye, annulate, heterostylous. Pollen not studied. *Capsule* globose, without valves, covered by a membrane which crumbles at maturity. Chromosome number and breeding behaviour not known. Flowering spring.

DISTRIBUTION Around the watershed boundaries of southern and western Yunnan, and hence including border districts of Vietnam, Burma, Tibet, Sichuan and Kweichow. 'Bamboo thickets, shady rocks, shale bluffs, mossy trunks, pathside banks in warm-temperate monsoon rainforest', 1700–3500 m.

The four species placed in section Chartacea are little known, although three species have been in cultivation. However, they seem to form a natural and rather closely related group. Superficially they resemble various members of section Cortusoides; for instance *P. lacerata* grows intermixed with *P. vaginata* below the Lo La, from which it is readily told only by its fewer larger long-stalked flowers. However, Trift's DNA work (2000) shows that *P. veitchiana* should in fact be placed in subgenus *Aleuritia* in which it appears to have few close relatives, although that study included no representatives of sections Davidii, Petiolares or Crystallophlomis. Despite the superficial resemblance to the Cortusoides, the Chartacea can be immediately distinguished from all possible confusion species by the hairless very thin-textured leaves, and from similar Chinese species belonging to section Cortusoides subsection Geranioides by pinnately, not palmately, arranged leaf-veins.

Although the 'petiolarid' capsule is only known for certain from *P. veitchiana* in this group, it was also observed in field notes by Ward for *P. lacerata*. No hybrids have been recorded. For cultivation, see under *P. lacerata*.

KEY TO SPECIES

1. Corolla lobes cut to more than half; bracts at top of scape rooting to give new plants...............*P. lacerata*
1. Corolla lobes notched and/or shallowly toothed; bracts small, not rooting...2

2. Corolla-lobes both notched and toothed; corolla-tube downy within.................................*P. veitchiana*
2. Corolla-lobes notched, but the lobules rounded; corolla-tube downy to hairy within...........................3

3. Corolla white, not more than 15 mm in diameter...*P. chartacea*
3. Corolla rose, more than 15 mm in diameter...4

4. Calyx very narrow; flower stalks with brown hairs...*P. wenshanensis*
4. Calyx bell-shaped; flower stalks without brown hairs...*P. petelotii*

Primula lacerata Smith, Notes Roy. Bot. Gdn. Edinb. 14: 45 (1923)

DESCRIPTION *Leaf-blades* to 6 × 5 cm, rounded, heart-shaped at the base, bluntly and irregularly toothed or with irregular short lobes, green above, bluish below, with 4–6 pairs of veins; leaf-stalk exceeding blade, narrow, shortly hairy. *Stem* to 18 cm, shortly hairy above, bearing 3–7 flowers on rather long (to 15 mm) shortly brown-hairy stalks from the base of which glandular leaf-like bracts develop markedly at fruiting; these have the capability of rooting and forming plantlets as the fruiting stem collapses (see *P. bracteosa* and *P. griffithii*). *Calyx* 6–7 mm, divided to half-way, the lobes broad, blunt and overlapping at the base, becoming glandular. *Corolla* lavender-blue to bright pink with an orange eye, about 20 mm in diameter, the tube equalling the calyx, long-hairy within; corolla-lobes lacerate, basically divided into two segments, each irregularly and deeply cut. (Photo: Fletcher, Quest for Plants 164, J. Roy. Hort. Soc. 54: 20.)

DISTRIBUTION Apparently disjunct in two limited areas; the closely adjacent Lo La and Nyug La passes, western Pachakshiri, just south of the Tsangpo and east of Tsari, south-east Tibet at about 94° E; and the north-west frontier of Burma adjoining Yunnan, immediately to the west of the

Salween, these two localities being some 500 km apart.

'Dense mixed wet forest' in zones with very heavy winter snow-fall and monsoons, 2500 m in Burma, 2700–3500 m in Tibet. 'In places covers the banks of paths and streams in masses ... strikingly beautiful.' Also 'shale bluffs and mossy trunks'.

P. veitchiana and *P. chartacea* from Yunnan are both closely related, and are possibly conspecific with *P. lacerata*. As understood at present, *P. chartacea* is distinguished by lacking lacerations to the petals, while neither species has the leaf-like fruiting bracts or long corolla-tube hairs of *P. lacerata*.

CULTIVATION Introduced as flown-home living plants by Ludlow and Sherriff from the southern side of the Lo La in 1938. 'For a year or two grew vigorously and produced an abundance of flowers without however ever attaining the size of those of native specimens.' Survived until 1944, but seems to have been lost at Edinburgh soon after. Surprise has been expressed that a species with such a ready method of increase (from pegged-down scape-buds) should have been lost so readily. However, it is likely that all members of this section, coming as they do from extremely wet zones with deep snow cover, will prove very difficult to cultivate, being intolerant of both frost and any dry weather.

Primula chartacea Franchet, Bull. Mus. Hist. Nat. Paris 1: 64 (1895)

DESCRIPTION Differs from *P. lacerata* chiefly by the smaller (to 1.5 cm diameter) white-eyed flowers with notched but otherwise entire petals, the corolla tube only short downy within, and the small narrow bracts which do not form scape-buds. Three sites in the area where the provinces of Yunnan, Sichuan and Kweichow meet, Long-ki, Tchen-fong-chan and Ta Kuan, bamboo thickets and shady rocks, 1800 m. (Fig. Halda: 128.)

Primula veitchiana Petitm., Le Monde de plantes 9: 14 (1907)

P. pirolaefolia Levl. (1915)

DESCRIPTION Differs from *P. lacerata* chiefly by the corolla tube being only shortly downy within, and by the lack of leaf-like bracts with scape-buds. The flower colour is said to be rosy-purple. *P. chartacea* has smaller, notched, not lacerate corolla-lobes. Roots thick and brown, apparently adapted to surface rooting though woodland mould. Yunnan and Sichuan border region, four sites between 1300–2500 m, 'shady places'. Collected by Needham (EN 3149) from Baoxing, Mupine, waterfall at 1300 m in 1991, flowering in March in cultivation. Offered from a Chinese source in 1999. Probably survives in Scotland in 2001, surviving under the humid protection of polythene tunnels, and possibly in Sweden. Very susceptible to damping off. (Fig. Halda: 130.)

Primula petelotii Smith, Notes Roy. Bot. Gdn. Edinb. 16: 226 (1932)

DESCRIPTION Leaf-blades with only a few fine teeth, otherwise entire, oval and with a cuneate base, rugose. Flowers rose in colour, to 20 mm in diameter, with entire but notched corolla-lobes. Vietnam, Mt. Chapa (where two Carolinella-species also grow), 1800 m. This species is less closely related to the other three in the section, and in some sense may be seen as a link with the Davidii. In cultivation with Keith Lever in 2002.

Primula wenshanensis Chen & Hu, Fl. Rep. Pop. Sin. 2: 291 (1990)

DESCRIPTION Apparently similar to *P. veitchiana*, but with a narrowly tubular calyx, and with flower stalks covered with rusty glandular hairs. Wen Shan, Laojun Shan, Yunnan. Wet mixed forest, 2000–2500 m.

Section **Davidii** Balf. f., J. Roy. Hort. Soc. 39: 146 (1913)

(Section Petiolares subsection Davidii (Balf. f.) Craib 1919)

Type species *P. davidii* Franchet

DESCRIPTION Deciduous or less commonly evergreen perennials with lax brown papery *bud scales* and with leaves bearing multicellular hairs (except for *P. odontocalyx*), with revolute vernation, lacking meal except occasionally in *P. drummondiana* and *P. odontocalyx*. *Leaves* usually 'primrose-like', obovate to oblanceolate, rugose, thick and somewhat leathery, or thin and membranous, entire or with small teeth, with a usually short, poorly demarcated or obsolete stalk. *Stem* rather stout, usually shorter than the leaves at flowering, sometimes missing (flowers basal), bearing a single umbel of usually blue or violet flowers; bracts small. *Calyx* bell-shaped with sharp or sometimes rounded and toothed lobes. *Corolla* annulate, rarely exannulate, heterostylous, the corolla-lobes usually notched. *Pollen* globose and 3-syncolpate in *P. drummondiana*. *Capsule* globose or discoid, included within the calyx-tube lacking valves and with an apical membrane crumbling at maturity; seeds 0.75–1 mm, quadrate and reticulate. Chromosome number not known. *P. drummondiana* is slightly self-compatible as a thrum. Flowering October–April.

DISTRIBUTION Of the 17 species, 14 are restricted to the western and central provinces of China, Yunnan, Sichuan, Kweichow and Hupeh. *P. klaveriana* and *P. taliensis* also occur in north-east Burma in the Hpimaw region. *P. drummondiana* is Himalayan, however, occurring from Uttar Pradesh to Sikkim and the Chumbi valley.

Moist or wet rocks, shady thickets and stream-banks, moist shady alpine woods, woodland ravines on sandstone, moist walls of a limestone grotto; 1200–3700 m. Most species seem to be confined to humid sites in warm-temperate zones, often in very summer-wet areas. However, *P. coerulea*, *P. taliensis* and perhaps *P. comata* seem to be true alpines, occuring in exposed situations on rocks from 3000-4000 m.

Regrettably, nearly all the Davidii are very little known and only four species have ever been in cultivation, three very recently. Most of the rest have only been collected on one or a very few occasions, suggesting that they were never very common plants. In view of the widespread deforestation in the regions from which they have been recorded, there must be concern that some have become extinct or are severely threatened. It is noteworthy that only a few species seem to have been recorded during the spate of visits to western China by Western botanists in the 1980s. However, three new species were described by Chen & Hu as recently as 1990.

From the very fragmentary evidence available, it seems that the Davidii include some of the most attractive of all *Primula* species. Morphologically they link between the Chartacea and the Petiolares, all three sections showing the same type of capsule dehiscence. The leaves are generally of a thicker texture and less dissected outline than in the former section, while the latter section lacks multicellular hairs. *P. klaveriana* and relatives approach the Chartacea in leaf texture, while *P. taliensis* and its relatives have a very 'petiolarid-like' aspect. However, most species with their large blue flowers and primrose-like leaves form a distinctive and natural grouping.

DNA studies have so far been restricted to the rather untypical and petiolarid-like *P. taliensis* which groups loosely with members of sections Petiolares and Proliferae in subgenus *Aleuritia*. It is likely that the Chartacea will prove to be relatives of the Davidii, but no study has yet included representatives of both groups. The superficial resemblance that some species have to the western Eurasiatic primrose, *P. vulgaris*, is apparently of no phyletic significance, but seems to be due to convergent adaptation to the temperate woodland habitat.

No hybrids have been recorded in the Davidii.

CULTIVATION Our experience is limited to *P. ovalifolia*, *P. odontocalyx*, *P. davidii*, *P. taliensis* and the Himalayan *P. drummondiana*. Coming from relatively low altitudes these species are not very hardy. Plants kept relatively dry in winter have withstood temperatures to −6°C, but have been killed by harder frosts. They deeply resent cold and wet conditions, or alternate freeze-thaw. Conversely, they also seem intolerant of excessive heat in summer, and shade temperatures of about 30°C, although accompanied by daily spraying and full shade, have led to a basal rot. A related problem arises from the very dense basal inflorescence of *P. drummondiana* which under glass leads to botrytis infections in the crown. However, these rots can be cured, and after total immersion in systemic fungicides followed by meticulous aftercare, even 'stumps' totally defoliated by rot have survived. Another problem proved to be 'whitefly' (aphids), to which the Chinese species seemed to be very attractive; unfortunately, they did not appreciate the use of systemic insecticides.

Given cool, humid conditions away from direct

sun, however, *P. drummondiana* proved a vigorous grower, which appeared regularly at Alpine Garden Society Shows in the UK, although it has now (2001) been lost. It was increased by division, preferably in the spring after flowering, and at least two growers raised seedlings including both pins and thrums from capsules set on the original thrum introduction.

KEY TO SPECIES

1. Flowers borne basally, stem lacking 2
1. Flowers borne together on a stem 5

2. Flowers not exceeding 16 mm in diameter .... *P. drummondiana*
2. Flowers usually exceeding 16 mm in diameter 3

3. Flowers pale pink; corolla tube less than 10 mm .... *P. praeflorens*
3. Flowers purple, blue or rose; corolla tube exceeding 10 mm 4

4. Flowers pale blue or rose .... *P. esquirolii*
4. Flowers purple .... *P. excapa*

5. Plant glabrous, or with unicellular glands only .... *P. odontocalyx*
5. Plant with long multicellular hairs, at least on the leaf-stalk 6

6. Leaf-stalk (petiole) absent or less than 1 cm 7
6. Leaf-stalk exceeding 1 cm 9

7. Calyx exceeding 10 mm; corolla lobes entire .... *P. klaveriana*
7. Calyx less than 10 mm; corolla lobes notched 8

8. Flower stalks exceeding 2 cm .... *P. hylobia*
8. Flower stalks less than 2 cm .... *P. fagosa* (see also *P. davidii*)

9. Flowers usually 2; corolla diameter usually exceeding 3 cm .... *P. coerulea*
9. Flowers usually 3 or more together, corolla diameter less than 3 cm 10

10. Leaf-blade about 4 × as long as wide .... *P. breviscapa*
10. Leaf-blade not more than 2.5 × as long as wide 11

11. Leaf-blade scarcely longer than wide, equalling the stalk .... *P. leptophylla*
11. Leaf-blade at least 1.3 × as long as wide, exceeding the stalk 12

12. Leaves rugose, not varying in shape 13
12. Leaves smooth, the stalk more pronounced in younger leaves 15

13. Corolla about 15 mm in diameter .... *P. crassa*
13. Corolla about 25 mm in diameter 14

14. Leaves glabrous above with marginal teeth of two sizes .... *P. davidii*
14. Leaves shortly hairy above, marginal teeth small and regular .... *P. ovalifolia*

15. Petal-lobes entire, blue .... *P. comata*
15. Petal-lobes notched or toothed, pink or purple, rarely blue 16

16. Petal-lobes with three teeth, pale pink or blue; meal absent .... *P. taliensis*
16. Petal-lobes notched, purple; rosette mealy at first .... *P. tridentifera*

Primula drummondiana Craib, J. Roy. Hort. Soc. 39: 190 (1913)

P. cunninghamii King, Notes Roy. Bot. Gdn. Edinb. 6: 250 (1917)

P. petiolaris var. *stracheyi* Hook. f. (1882) non *P. stracheyi* Hook. f. (1879) = *P. minutissima* Jacq. and *P. reptans* Hook. f.

P. pseudopetiolaris Pax & Hoffm. (1920)

DESCRIPTION *Leaves* obovate, irregularly erose-denticulate, more or less prostrate, to 10 × 4.5 cm, usually smaller at flowering, rather dark green, rugose, sparsely hairy above but more hairy on the margin, somewhat narrowed at the base, but effectively without a stalk, the mid-rib white at the base; bud-scales narrow, brownish, soon dropping off. *Bracts* to 10 × 1 mm. *Flowers* basal, up to 30, produced successively over a long time; flower stalks slender, glandular, occasionally mealy, very short at flowering, but elongating to 2.5 cm in fruit. *Calyx* 5–9 mm, tubular bell-shaped, divided to half-way into narrow and sharp lobes, glandular and occasionally mealy. *Corolla* an intense lilac-blue, or less commonly lilac-pink, with a basal white zone and a small yellow eye, slightly funnel-shaped, to 16 mm in diameter, the tube somewhat exceeding the calyx, to 15 mm; corolla-lobes not overlapping, deeply notched, or rarely entire or with a slight apiculate tooth in a shallow notch. Flowering September–March. (Plate 9.)

DISTRIBUTION Scattered and local throughout the west and central Himalaya. North-west India (Kumaon, Garwhal, Ghorpatta, Naini Tal); Nepal (Marma, Lansung Himal, Modi Khola); Sikkim (Bakkim, Changu, Kanglasa, Sheraothang, Lingtoo to Gnatong, Jelep La); and southernTibet, Chumbi valley.

'Open hillsides or among rhododendrons, often on gravel or turf'; 'wet moss on the sides of damp ravines alongside *P. boothii* and on damp mossy banks almost buried in thick meadow turf along dwarf *Strobilanthes* and *Geranium* spp. on grazed north-facing shady hillsides'; '*Tsuga*/*Abies* rhododendron forest on path edge in shade'; 1700–4300 m. *Primula drummondiana* has a long and chequered taxonomic history. Living specimens somewhat resemble a small stemless *P. denticulata*. In the herbarium, however, the stemless flowers, the occasional presence of meal, and the 'petiolarid capsule' led workers from Hooker to Smith to classify this species with *P. petiolaris*. Only two fragmentary collections were available to Smith and Fletcher, and they failed to connect this species with the rather better known *P. cunninghamii* from Sikkim and the Chumbi valley. Neither *P. cunninghamii* or *P. drummondiana* had by then been in cultivation. Plants were introduced in 1956 from Nepal by Marjorie Brough as '*P. cunninghamii*', but when seen in the early 1970s, plants under this name were the hybrid *P. gracilipes* × *sessilis*.

If the more plentiful gatherings of *P. drummondiana* from India and west Nepal available from the 1950s are compared with *P. cunninghamii,* no distinctions are evident. Smith and Fletcher consider that *P. cunninghamii* lacks multicellular hairs, and is more mealy, but in fact at least some specimens of *P. cunninghamii* clearly do have multicellular hairs, while both taxa vary as to the occurrence of meal.

Once *P. drummondiana* came into cultivation, it was immediately evident that, despite its capsule type, it could not be classified within section Petiolares. In every way, the leaves are extremely similar to most species in the otherwise Chinese section Davidii, while the blue flowers with bifid petals also resemble this group and not the Petiolares. Most other Davidii have flower-stems, this is not so in *P. esquirolii*. None of the other Davidii have meal, but all have the potential to produce meal through 'farinipotent glands', and this character is very variable in *P. drummondiana*. The cultivated strain produced no meal. Thus I suggest that *P. drummondiana* is best placed within the otherwise Chinese section Davidii as a slightly deviant member.

CULTIVATION Introduced by John Templar and Frances Davies in flower from below Landrung, Modi Khola, south of Annapurna, Nepal, 1700 m, November 1978. At least three rosettes and some seed were brought back. John Templar raised several seedlings, and from these the species has had a limited distribution. One of the original plants (a thrum) was sent to me early in 1980, grew well, and I distributed divisions to Eric Watson and Alan Furness, who still grew it in 1992. Furness twice induced it to set seed after artificial self-pollination, and raised a number of seedlings including both pins and thrums. Lost vigour for most growers in the 1990s and had disappeared by 1995. **PC** 1980.

Primula ovalifolia Franchet, Bull. Soc. Bot. Fr. 33: 67 (1886)

P. aequipila Craib (1919)
P. polia Craib (1919)
P. macropoda Craib (1919)
P. limprichtii Pax & Hoffm. (1920)

DESCRIPTION *Leaf-blades* narrowly oval to elliptical, to 16 × 8 cm, smaller at flowering, leathery, entire to distantly, obscurely and bluntly toothed, rounded or retuse at the tip, rounded or heart-shaped at the base, hairless or sparsely hairy above, thickly tawny-hairy on the veins beneath; leaf-stalk very short to half length of blade, thickly tawny-hairy; bud-scales reddish, 2 cm. *Stem* to 18 cm, shorter at flowering, hairy, bearing 2–9 flowers on hairy pedicels to 20 mm; bracts to 7 mm. *Calyx* to 10 mm, narrowly bell-shaped, cut half-way into broad teeth. *Corolla* blue-violet with a broad white eye, to 25 mm in diameter, the tube exceeding the calyx; corolla-lobes deeply notched. Fig. Halda: 136. (Plate 75.)

DISTRIBUTION Apparently widespread in a band through central China from Ou-tchai in east Yunnan, through southern Sichuan (e.g. Moupine, Emei Shan, Nan-chuan Hsien), to western Hupeh.

Moist shady places, vertical cliffs running with water, 1200–2500 m.

VARIATION Subsp. *tardiflora* Hu, Fl. Rep. Pop. Sin. 2: 392 (1990). Generally less hairy, and flowering later, April–May. Emei Shan. Incorrectly identified forms of *P. epilosa* = *P. odontocalyx* were originally placed here.

CULTIVATION Introduced by Edward Needham from the Emei Shan (EN 937, 3071) and Mupine (EN 3141), 1989–91. I grew it for two years and flowered it, but it was weakened by whitefly and insecticide and killed by frost. Best in a frost-free poly-tunnel, and it may survive in these conditions in Scotland, 2001.

Primula crassa Handel-Mazzetti, Anz. Akad. Wiss. Wien 61: 132 (1924)

DESCRIPTION A close relative of *P. ovalifolia*, but with leaves long-hairy above, and with much smaller lilac-blue flowers about 15 mm in diameter. Collected twice at Lololand, Da-liang range, south-west Sichuan. 'Growing on sandstone in the bottom of a gully in a forest of ... oaks and many different trees, together with *Tupistra viridiflora, Rohdea urotepala, Arisaema lobatum, Viola moupinensis, Anemone flaccida, Eutrema yunnanense,* two *Paris* species and other shade plants'; 2600–2800 m.

Primula davidii Franchet, Bull. Soc. Bot. Fr. 33: 66 (1886)

DESCRIPTION Differs from *P. ovalifolia* by the absence of a clearly demarcated leaf-stalk, by the sharp leaf-teeth of two sizes, by the leaves being hairless above and only shortly hairy beneath, and by the large flowers, 4–5 together on a short stem, opening dark violet and fading to a soft mauve with a large white eye, or pinker, up to 30 mm in diameter. This very handsome species had only been collected twice, by David in Moupine, Sichuan; 'moist shady alpine woods', and by Needham from there (EN 3164, humusy boulders and streamsides at 1700 m). In Cornwall, it flowers in March. (Fig. Halda: 132.) I grew it for two years and flowered it, but it lacked vigour, and was viciously attacked by whitefly. May still survive in poly-tunnels. Reintroduced by Chinese sources and flowered by Alan Newton (2002)

Primula fagosa Balf. f. & Craib, Notes Roy. Bot. Gdn. Edinb., 11: 172, 180–183 (1919)

DESCRIPTION Differs from *P. ovalifolia* chiefly by lacking a leaf-stalk, and by the exannulate corolla. Collected once by Farges at Chengkow, eastern Sichuan. The original name was *P. favosa* (meaning honeycombed), but this was miscopied on the manuscript description. It should probably return to the original name.

Primula breviscapa Franchet, Bull. Mus. Hist. Nat. Paris 1: 65 (1895)

DESCRIPTION Bears thin narrowly oval membranous leaf-blades with irregular sharp teeth; the woolly leaf-stalk is well marked, and the blade is narrow, about 4× as long as wide; the violet flowers are about 20 mm in diameter. From the intersection of the provinces of Yunnan, Sichuan and Kweichow; a single collection by Delavay at Tchen-fong-chan; 'moist rocks'.

Primula leptophylla Craib, Notes Roy. Bot. Gdn. Edinb., 11: 174 (1919)

DESCRIPTION Related to *P. breviscapa*, but leaf-blades scarcely longer than wide, rounded, and equalling the narrow stalk, scarcely toothed; the flowers are probably blue. Only known from a single collection by Maire on a plateau at 2500 m; Tse-tchou-pa, east Yunnan.

Primula esquirolii Petitm., Bull. Soc. Sci. Nancy, ser. 3, 8: 16 (1907)

DESCRIPTION A very primrose-like plant, lacking a flower-stem and long leaf-hairs; the calyx (to 7 mm) is much shorter than the narrow corolla-tube (to 18 mm); flowers pale blue to rose. Moist walls of a limestone grotto near Gan-pin, Kweichow, 1300 m.

Primula excapa Chen & Hu, Fl. Rep. Pop. Sin. 2: 293 (1990)

DESCRIPTION A stemless, primrose-like plant, resembling *P. esquirolii,* but with darker coloured purple flowers. Jingdong Shan, Yunnan. Streamsides and wet rocks, 2200–2500 m. Fig. Halda: 134.

Primula klaveriana Forrest, Notes Roy. Bot. Gdn. Edinb. 15: 252 (1927)

DESCRIPTION The only Davidii with homostylous flowers, and with rounded, not divided, corolla-lobes which are blue; the corolla diameter reaches 25 mm; as in *P. hylobia*, the membranous stalkless leaves are also distinctive. On both sides of the frontier between north-east Burma and Yunnan on both sides of the Salween (i.e. divides with the Mekong and the Shweli/N'Maika). Shady thickets and streambanks, 2700–3700 m. Forrest collected this handsome species on no less than 9 occasions, and collected seed, but there is no record that it ever germinated.

Primula hylobia Smith, Notes Roy. Bot. Gdn. Edinb. 15: 251 (1927)

DESCRIPTION Closely related to *P. klaveriana,* and with the same membranous stalkless leaves, but differing in the notched corolla-lobes and the heterostylous flowers. Collected once at Pien-oua, apparently in eastern Yunnan.

Primula odontocalyx (Franchet) Pax, Pflanzenreich 4: 237 (1905)

P. petiolaris Wall. var. *odontocalyx* Franchet (1895)
P. hylophila Balf. f. & Farrer (1917)
P. hupehensis Craib (1917)
P. epilosa Craib (1919)
P. cheniana Fang (1956)
?*P. chienii* Fang (1956)

DESCRIPTION *Leaves* obovate, leathery, slightly mealy narrowed at the base to a very short stalk, lacking long hairs, increasing to 20 cm in summer. *Stem* shorter than the leaves at flowering, lengthening to 20 cm, with 1–10 rich violet-blue, nodding funnel-shaped flowers with a green and white eye 20 to 30 mm in diameter borne on short thick stalks, elongating in fruit; *calyx* robust, cup-shaped, the teeth sometimes toothed. (Fig. Halda: 153 (as *P. moupinensis*) and 154.)

DISTRIBUTION Widespread in Sichuan, Hupeh, Kansu and Shensi, wet rocks and wooded hills, edge of *Abies fabri* forest, flowering in melting snow in April. 1400–2860 m. Introduced into cultivation from the Emei Shan by E. Needham in 1990 (EN 2079) and by Peter Cox from the Mekong Salween divide (BASE 9547).

This species is immediately distinguished as the only species apart from the stemless *P. esquirolii* lacking long hairs. *P. odontocalyx* was classified with the Petiolares rather than the Davidii by Smith & Fletcher (1944), perhaps correctly, presumably because of the absence of long hairs and because most specimens lose their basal bud-scales at an early stage. Now that it has entered cultivation, we can see that it does resemble a blue-flowered petiolarid such as *P. sonchifolia* in many ways, but the leaf-shape and venation is that of the Davidii.

Halda (1992) rightly equates *P. cheniana* Fang with *P. epilosa*, and I am thus including this here, although his figure is not of this species. From Halda's description and figure, I can also see no difference between *P. chienii* Fang and this taxon.

Primula coerulea Forrest, Notes Roy. Bot. Gdn. Edinb. 4: 221 (1908)

DESCRIPTION *Leaves* leathery, covered with long brown hairs below, the blade rounded at the tip and base, with a short thickly hairy stalk. *Stem* short, thickly brown-hairy, bearing one or two very large purplish-blue exannulate flowers with a yellow eye up to 4 cm in diameter; *calyx* long, hairy, up to 13 mm.

DISTRIBUTION The only alpine species known in the section, from 4000 m in the Cang Shan above Dali, Yunnan, growing 'in open exposed situations on rocks in side valleys'. Thought to be rare, and it has not been seen by several expeditions to the Cang Shan during the 1980s and 1990s.

From its description, *P. coerulea* sounds as if it is one of the most beautiful of all primula species, and from its habitat, it may well prove amenable to cultivation, although the only seed brought back (Forrest 6803 in 1913) failed to reach the flowering stage. Its habitat is unlikely to have been destroyed, and this must remain amongst the most sought-after of all species not in cultivation.

Primula taliensis Forrest, Notes Roy. Bot. Gdn. Edinb. 4: 220 (1908)

P. praticola Craib (1919)
P. euosma Craib var. *puralba* Smith (1927)

DESCRIPTION *Leaves* obovate at flowering, forming a compact rosette, later much larger with a rounded blade with a heart-shaped base and a long petiole, covered throughout with long rusty (or white) multicellular hairs, not rugose. *Stem* shorter than the leaves at flowering, longer later, also thickly hairy, bearing 1–12 white, blue or pink flowers of 15–20 mm diameter on long, thick, hairy stalks, the petal-lobes are deeply three-toothed; *calyx* bell-shaped, hairy; sepal-lobes blunt, toothed. (Fig. Halda: 157.)

DISTRIBUTION North-west Burma, near the Yunnan frontier, e.g. Hpimaw; west Yunnan, Cang-Shan above Dali; centred on the divides each side of the Salween. Woodland and open stony pastures, 3000–3700 m.

'A notable feature ... is the marked dimorphism of the leaves. The early ones are almost spathulate in form with a broad winged petiole but these are later replaced by much larger leaves with a distinct quite narrow petiole and a rounded sometimes cordate blade, dentate at the margin. The plant therefore has a quite different appearance at different stages of its development. . . . The flowers are carried on a short scape and vary in shades of pink to bluish-pink, giving it a pleasant but not striking appearance'.

P. taliensis and *P. comata* were classified by Smith and Fletcher (1944) in their subsection Petiolares-Sonchifolia. The leaf-shape and texture and the general appearence of the plant tends to support this placing, as does the marked heterophylly and the three-toothed rather than notched petal-lobes which are unusual for the Davidii. However, no petiolarids have multicellular hairs and consequently I prefer to place these species here.

CULTIVATION Ward (1688) collected plants in 1934 from Hpimaw, but these did not persist. Found in various localities on the western flank of the Cang-Shan by the 1981 Chinese–British expedition. Grown by Ian Scott for several years, obtained from John Mattingley, and probably originating from the CLD expedition from the Cang Shan in 1991, but details not known. Disliked direct sunlight and being divided, and prey to botrytis and aphids, deceased 2001.

Primula comata Fletcher, J. Linn. Soc. Bot. 52: 338 (1942)

DESCRIPTION Differs from its close relation *P. taliensis* chiefly by its deep blue flowers which have entire petal-lobes and a hairy throat. Eastern Yunnan near Chen-Kang Hsien, south of Yunnan-fu, 2800–3200 m. (Fig. Halda: 148.)

Primula praeflorens Chen & Hu, Fl. Rep. Pop. Sin. 2: 293 (1990)

DESCRIPTION An almost stemless species with short (to 9 mm) tubed flowers of a pale pink; petals with a tooth in the notch. Jingdong Shan, Yunnan, 2400 m. Rocks, flowering in the winter.

Primula tridentifera Chen & Hu, Fl. Rep. Pop. Sin. 2: 293 (1990)

DESCRIPTION Distinguished in this group by its overlapping, persistent mealy bud scales and glandular leaves which are mealy when young; sepal-lobes tridentate at the top, as in *P. irregularis*. The rather large purple funnel-shaped flowers are borne on a marked stem, 5–9 together. Several sites in Sichuan and Yunnan, e.g. Ebian Shan, Daguan Shan; wet rocks in forest, 1950–3000 m, flowering May–June.

Section **Petiolares** Pax, Bot. Jahrb. Syst. 10: 21 (1889)

(Section Sonchifolia Balf. f. 1913)
(Section Petiolares-Sonchifolia Craib 1917)
(Subsection Petiolares-Sonchifolia Smith & Forrest 1928)
(Subsection Roylei, Smith & Forrest 1932)
(Subsection Griffithii, Smith & Fletcher 1944)
(Section Craibia Wendelbo 1961b)
Type species *P. petiolaris* Wall.

DESCRIPTION Evergreen or deciduous perennials, often with marked persistent bud-scales, with revolute vernation, often *mealy*, bearing finely toothed, usually narrowly oval, usually stalked rugose leaves, *lacking hairs* but usually with unicellular glands. *Stems* absent, short or rarely exceeding the leaves at flowering, bearing a single umbel of flowers; *bracts* usually small and narrow, occasionally developing and becoming leaf-like after flowering. *Calyx* narrowly bell-shaped to tubular. *Corolla* usually annulate, heterostylous except in *P. hookeri*, blue, violet, purple, red, pink, yellow, cream or white, usually with a white eye surrounded by a yellow zone. *Pollen* globose, 3-syncolpate. *Capsule* globose, included in the calyx tube, lacking valves and with an apical membrane, crumbling at maturity; seeds usually brown, quadrate, 0.7–1.1 mm. Incompatibility total, or up to 5% self-fertile especially in thrums. 2n = 22 (2n = 20 in *P. boothii*). *Flowering* December to May (October).

DISTRIBUTION Chiefly Himalayan, distributed throughout the range except the extreme west, from Kashmir and north-west India (two species) to Yunnan (five species) and Sichuan (three species), showing most diversity in the heavy monsoon regions of the east-central Himalaya from east Nepal to the Tsangpo bend.

Subsection Petiolares, chiefly with pink flowers, subsection Edgeworthii and subsection Sonchifolia with blue or yellow flowers are usually forest plants, mostly occurring from 2500–3500 m. They often grow massed on steep earthy banks above water, although *P. deuteronana, P. aureata* and *P. sonchifolia* occur chiefly above the tree-line. Subsection Griffithii are alpines, occurring in wet alpine meadows, often amongst dwarf shrubs, usually above 3200 m.

There has been much confusion about the correct name for this popular group. Pax's section (1889) was based on the type species *P. petiolaris*, which was then poorly understood and given a wide scope, and three other species. Of the few species then known, he omitted *P. sonchifolia* and *P. griffithii*. However, Pax's diagnosis is quite suitable for our contemporary needs, although he failed to comment on the distinctive 'petiolarid' capsule dehiscence by a crumbling membrane.

Perhaps because Pax (1905) later included two unrelated species, and because he failed to include all known 'petiolarids', later authors felt it necessary to redefine the section, using the clumsy name 'Petiolares-Sonchifolia'. Wendelbo (1961b) later coined a new sectional name Craibia based on his subgenus Craibia (not used here), but all these revisions are redundant and the valid name for this section is undoubtedly Petiolares Pax. (1889).

As yet, only four species have been subject to DNA analysis, but they represent all the subsections except Edgeworthii. *P. petiolaris* and *P. boothii*, both classified in subsection Petiolares, are shown to be closely related, but *P. calderiana* and *P. sonchifolia* are no more related to one another than they are to *P. taliensis* (section Davidii) and members of section Proliferae. This is rather unexpected as all the Petiolarid subsections can be connected by hybridization suggesting that they are in fact quite closely related.

One of the few genuine surprises provided by recent DNA analyses has been the closer relationship of the Petiolares to, not the subsection Agleniana of section Crystallophlomis as predicted (the Agleniana shares the 'petiolarid' capsule), but to the Proliferae. Consequently, it may be necessary to rethink the concept that certain members of subsection Griffithii might be considered 'primitive' and derived from the Agleniana. *P. calderiana* and *P. tanneri* in particular closely resemble members of the 'nivalids' (section Crystallophlomis) and were originally confused with them. Indeed, until the vital capsule character was noted in *P. calderiana*, it was considered to be conspecific with the nivalid *P. obtusifolia*, although with hindsight it does not resemble it very closely. It now seems likely that this close resemblance between the sections has a homophyletic origin, two relatively unconnected groups having adapted to a particular wet alpine environment in similar ways, although they are distantly related.

CULTIVATION For many specialist growers, the 'petiolarids' encapsulate the charm and magic of the whole genus. Dwarf, early flowering, and with a range of jewel-like colours, they originate from remote and magnificent country, yet they are not, in many cases, totally intractable. Temperamental in cultivation, they nevertheless succeed spectacularly with sufficient regularity to inspire hope. In particular, they are soundly perennial, and often present good opportunities for vegetative propagation. Thus, they avoid the spectre of a short-lived monocarpy that bedevils the cultivation of other superb Himalayan primulas (e.g. sections Soldanelloides, Crystallophlomis, Amethystina).

For the petiolarids in general, there are three basic requirements to successful cultivation. Firstly, a cool, humid and rather uniform climate, without excesses of heat or cold; second, regular feeding; and third, freedom from pests and diseases.

All petiolarids detest heat, a dry atmosphere, direct sunlight, and dry roots; any one of these will rapidly lead to death. It has been shown that they are incapable of shutting their stomata (leaf-pores through which they 'breathe') and so they desiccate very rapidly. As a result, they succeed best in summer-cool, humid regions, particularly in the north of the UK.

It follows that they should be grown in total shade, in the coolest part of the garden, and should be regularly sprayed during hot weather. Even this treatment cannot protect plants during very hot spells. Petiolarids often expire as the result of heat alone, in conditions where shade, humidity and watering remain optimal.

Petiolarids vary considerably as to hardiness. In general, the pink-flowered evergreen woodland subsections Petiolares and Edgeworthii are the least hardy. In many parts of the British Isles, only *P. gracilipes, P. petiolaris* and *P. bracteosa* can be considered fully hardy in this group. *P. boothii, P. sessilis* and *P. nana* are the least hardy. However, in parts of northern Scotland with frequent and severe late spring frosts, none of these plants are very reliable.

The deciduous subsections Sonchifolia and Griffithii are much more hardy, and will survive very low temperatures when dormant. However, they too are susceptible to severe frosts once they are in growth.

Petiolarids are heavy feeders. This requirement is best met by a combination of a rich, humus-based (but well-drained) compost, perhaps with the addition of a slow-release fertilizer, or bone-meal; regular foliar feeding when in growth; and frequent disturbance. Given appropriate conditions and times of year (especially April–May and September), all except the subsection Griffithii greatly appreciate regular division (this also stops large clumps rotting, or failing to receive adequate water).

Petiolarids are susceptible to two main ills, vine weevil and virus (p. 23) and, given good cultivation, these are responsible for the majority of failures.

Seed should be collected when the capsule becomes papery and translucent, usually late June or early July. In subsection Petiolares, capsules usually hide themselves deep in the rosettes, under leaves, and these have to be carefully sought out. Seed should be scraped off the receptacle, sown instantly, and kept in a cool, shady place. However, old dried seed will sometimes germinate much later (often as much as three years later) if stored cold. Generally, some seedlings germinate in August, and some the following March. Seedlings should be pricked on at the two-leaf stage, after which they often grow on vigorously, and usually flower the second spring after germination. It should be noted that many hybrids are sterile, and so seed-raising is more suitable for species.

In the open garden, a slightly raised site with a humus-rich, gritty compost in total shade is indicated. Plants often grow well when planted vertically, for instance between peat-blocks. Some species, especially in subsection Sonchifolia, appreciate being cloched in the late winter and early spring as they come into flower.

For pot culture, a plastic pot with a compost basically composed of one-third grit and two-thirds humus is preferred. From April to October the pot should be plunged in the open in total shade (except perhaps for *P. aureata*), but it can be given more light and protection in the winter, and enjoyed in flower under glass in the early spring.

There is a good account of cultivation and propagation in this group by John Dennis in Bull. AGS 64: 390–394. A racier account was written by Gerry Mundey, Bull. AGS 59: 79–86.

HYBRIDIZATION Petiolarids hybridize very readily. *P. griffithii* (subsection Griffithii) is known to hybridize with *P. whitei* in subsection Sonchifolia in cultivation. *P. bhutanica*, in subsection Sonchifolia, has hybridized with *P. nana* (subsection Edgeworthii) and *P. aureata* (subsection Petiolares), while *P. nana* has hybridized with four species in subsection Petiolares. Thus, all the subsections are connected by hybridization, which suggests that their component species are quite closely related, although hybrids are usually sterile. Hybrid swarms between members of subsection Petiolares are found in the wild in east Nepal, while in subsection Griffithii, *P. griffithii*, and subspecies of *P. calderiana* and *P. tanneri* are all interfertile, and at times also form fertile hybrid swarms in the wild.

In cultivation, it is common to find species are represented in collections by a single individual of only one mating type (pin or thrum). Thus, when seed is set, it will usually be hybrid, and these vigorous seedlings may usurp the original, perhaps virused parent. Many clones in cultivation today are hybrid. Although these are generally sterile, they are often offered under the parental name (this situation has improved as I write in 2001). In addition, hybrid clones have on occasion been introduced from the wild, either knowingly (*P. calderiana* × *P. tanneri* 'Wai-Tung'), or as a species (*P. petiolaris* × *P. boothii* 'Redpoll', L. & S. 19856, introduced as *P. petiolaris*).

There have also been a number of intentional crossing programmes, for instance by Randle Cooke and Major and Mrs Knox-Finlay in the 1950s, while in the 1980s, the late Gerry Mundey created a spectacular series of crosses, chiefly using *P. aureata* as one parent, as did John Dennis a few years later. In 2001, most of these clones have now vanished, and growers have recently placed more emphasis on maintaining seed strains and selecting species lines. They have apparently recognized that seed-raised fertile lines are the key to long-term survival for this group in cultivation.

LITERATURE

Smith, W.W. & Fletcher, H.R. (1944). Trans. Roy. Soc. Edinb. 61: 271–313.
Livingstone, D. (1950). Bull. Alp. Gdn. Soc. 18: 211–233.
Cain, R.B. (1962). Bull. Alp. Gdn. Soc. 30: 223–235.
Richards, A.J. (1977). J. Scot. Rock Gdn. Club 15: 1–38.
Richards, A.J. (1986). The Plantsman 7: 217–232.
Mundey, G.R. (1991). Bull. AGS 59: 79–86.
Dennis, J. (1996). Bull. AGS 64: 390–394.
Pearson, J.M. (1999). Bull. AGS 67: 197–199.

KEY TO SPECIES

1. Flowers stemless, or flower stalks exceeding stem 2
1. Flower stem exceeding stalks to individual flowers 23

2. Flowers yellow 3
2. Flowers not yellow 5

3. Leaves cut almost to mid-rib; sepals petal-like .... *P. chionata*
3. Leaves cut to less than half-way; sepals not petal-like 4

4. Plant mealy; corolla-tube glabrous .... *P. aureata*
4. Plant lacking meal; corolla-tube hairy inside .... *P. chionogenes*

5. Plant evergreen; flowers usually pink 6
5. Plant deciduous; flowers rarely pink 13

6. Corolla-lobes pointed, usually four .... *P. sessilis*
6. Corolla-lobes toothed, five 7

7. Corolla-tube hairy inside .... *P. deuteronana*
7. Corolla-tube glabrous inside 8

8. Sepals keeled so that calyx is 5-angled; leaf-veins usually reddish; meal absent .... *P. boothii*
8. Sepals flat, calyx terete; leaf-veins not usually reddish, plant often mealy 9

9. Plant without meal 10
9. At least the sepals mealy 11

10. Sepals pointed, more than 7 mm; flower stalks more than 15 mm .... *P. scapigera*
10. Sepals less than 7 mm; flower stalks less than 10 mm .... *P. petiolaris*

11. Corolla thick, waxy; sepals stiff, spreading, toothed .... *P. irregularis*
11. Corolla texture thinner; sepals erect, not toothed 12

12. Calyx urn-shaped, 8–10 mm .... *P. bracteosa*
12. Calyx not swollen basally, 5–7 mm .... *P. gracilipes*

13. Flowers pale to mid-blue, corolla-lobes toothed or entire 14
13. Flowers rarely blue; if so, corolla-lobes notched 17

14. Corolla-lobes rounded, usually entire; sepals rounded, toothed .... *P. sonchifolia*
14. Corolla-lobes toothed; sepals blunt to sharp 15

15. Corolla exannulate with an open throat; resting bud cabbage-like .... *P. nana**
15. Corolla annulate with a narrow 'eye'; resting-bud egg-like 16

16. Leaves remaining sword-shaped; sepal-lobes blunt and toothed .... *P. whitei*
16. Leaf-blades becoming triangular with a stalk; sepal-lobes sharp and entire .... *P. bhutanica*

17. Flowers pink or white 18
17. Flowers violet or purple 21

18. Flowers not exceeding 12 mm in diameter .... *P. hookeri*
18. Flowers more than 15 mm in diameter 19

19. Leaf-edge wavy, like an oak leaf .... *P. sinuata*
19. Leaf oval 20

20. Corolla-lobes notched; plant often with above-ground stolons .... *P. moupinensis*
20. Corolla-lobes toothed; plant lacking stolons .... *P. nana*

21. Corolla-lobes notched, corolla exceeding 15 mm in diameter 22
21. Corolla-lobes entire or toothed, corolla less than 12 mm in diameter .... *P. hookeri*

22. Corolla-lobes shallowly notched, as wide as long .... *P. pulchra*
22. Corolla-lobes deeply notched, twice as long as wide .... *P. tongolensis*

23. Plant lacking meal 24
23. Plant mealy, at least on calyx 26

24. Bud-scales reddish; leaf-blades orbicular; flowers yellow .... *P. calthifolia*
24. If flowers yellow, then bud-scales not reddish or leaf-blades orbicular 25

25. Corolla diameter not exceeding 12 mm .... *P. bomiensis*
25. Corolla diameter exceeding 15 mm .... *P. tanneri*

26. Flowers yellow 27
26. Flowers blue or purple 29

27. Calyx not exceeding 8.5 mm .... *P. calderiana*
27. Calyx 9 mm or more 28

28. Sepal-lobes very narrow, cut almost to the base, one-veined .... *P. jucunda*
28. Sepal-lobes leaf-like and rounded, pinnately veined .... *P. hilaris*

29. Flowers dark blue; leaf apex sharp .... *P. griffithii*
29. Flowers pink to dark purple, rarely white; if blue, then leaf apex blunt 30

30. Calyx exceeding 9 mm .... *P. laeta*
30. Calyx not exceeding 8.5 mm .... *P. calderiana*

* see also *P. odontocalyx*

Subsection **Petiolares**

Evergreen; leaves erose-denticulate; stems at flowering very short or absent; flowers usually pink (yellow in *P. aureata*), usually annulate (exannulate in *P. boothii* and *P. scapigera*).

Primula petiolaris Wallich in Roxburgh, Fl. India 2: 22 (1824)

P. tridentata Don (1825) p.p.

DESCRIPTION Leaves crowded into a tight crisped rosette and almost stalkless at flowering, to 5 × 1.5 cm, elongating later and developing a long narrow stalk and a spoon-shaped blade, totally lacking meal. *Flowers* stemless and almost stalkless at flowering, up to 30 crowded together, elongating in fruit. *Calyx* to 6 mm, sepal lobes erect, slightly blunt, lacking meal. *Corolla* pink with a mustard yellow eye surrounded by a thin white ring, slightly cup-shaped, to 20 mm in diameter, the tube short, broad, and scarcely exceeding the calyx; corolla lobes rounded, shortly and irregularly toothed, or almost entire. 2n = 22. Flowering April–May in the wild; in cultivation in April, usually slightly later than *P. gracilipes*. (Photo: Bull. AGS 67: 198 as *P. gracilipes*). (Plate 8.)

DISTRIBUTION Nepal and Sikkim; two early records (including the type) from Kumaon. Recorded throughout Nepal from 2100–3800 m; sometimes growing and hybridizing with *P. gracilipes*, but not as common as the latter. Shady, moist banks in the upper forest zone.

Few species have been so misunderstood as *P. petiolaris*. As the earliest described species in the section, it was used as a 'dustbin' during the nineteenth century, most petiolarids being assigned to it. As the section became better understood, most of these were split off, but so few specimens of the type plant existed that they were misinterpreted. Unfortunately, Wallich's type was collected in the summer with a few off-season flowers, so it has summer leaves with long petioles untypical of the usual flowering condition (hence the name of this species, and indeed the section). Furthermore, it was not realized that the flowers of pink petiolarids dry blue. Even as late as 1944, when Nepal was still closed, Smith & Fletcher describe the flowers of this seminal species as 'pale blue'.

The problem was compounded by the introduction in 1949 of a living plant from east Sikkim (Ludlow & Sherriff 19856, now given the cultivar name 'Redpoll'), which Fletcher named *P. petiolaris*. This clone, which is still widespread, has rich bluey-purple flowers and is still regarded as the 'true' petiolaris by many respected authorities, although it is sterile, has 21 chromosomes and apparently represents a hybrid with *P. boothii*.

P. petiolaris is in fact closely related to *P. gracilipes*, and the latter might well be considered a subspecies of it. It differs by the tight, crisped rosette at flowering, the almost stemless, cup-shaped flowers, the tightly clasped, blunter sepal-lobes, and by the total absence of meal. *P. petiolaris* is smaller than the remainder of its relatives, excepting the alpine *P. deuteronana*, the corolla tube of which is full of hairs.

CULTIVATION First introduced during the 1950s. When Nepal was opened in 1951, *P. petiolaris* was certainly collected by Marjorie Brough (1955) and Bowes-Lyon and possibly by others (**FCC** 1964). Introductions continued during the 1970s and 1980s, for instance by Bernard Thompson, George Smith, Millais and John Templar, whose Sikkim gatherings showed this to be a variable species in the wild. Today, it is well-established in cultivation and is offered by several nurserymen. It persists well in suitable conditions, showing a high rate of vegetative multiplication, and it greatly appreciates regular division.

HYBRIDIZATION AND VARIATION Mixed populations, which seem to represent hybrid swarms with *P. gracilipes*, can occur in the wild, and many cultivated clones (e.g. *P. gracilipes* 'minor', 'Linnet', **PC** 1982, 'Tinney's Jewel' (**PC** 1984)) seem to be hybrid and are partially or completely sterile (Photo: Bull. AGS 59: 83). A hybrid is also known with *P. boothii* (see above). Wild populations vary in flower colour, flower size, robustness, and in the form of the rosette, and some of this variation is also seen in cultivation.

Primula gracilipes Craib, Notes Roy. Bot. Gdn. Edinb. 6: 252 (1917)

P. petiolaris Wall. var. *sulphurea* Hook. f. (1882)
P. sulphurea (Hook. f.) Craib (1913)
P. scullyi Craib (1917)
P. nana Watt (1904) p.p. non Wallich

DESCRIPTION *Leaves* forming dense rosettes at flowering, laxer later, mealy when young, obovate and with a short broad usually reddish stalk at flowering, the blade about 6 × 2 cm, elongating to 12 cm later, and developing a long narrow stalk. *Stem* absent; flowers up to 30 crowded together, with short mealy stalks (to 4 cm) at flowering, elongating and recurving in fruit. *Calyx* mealy, to 7 mm, the sepal-lobes erect-spreading and sharp. *Corolla* pink with a green to yellow eye surrounded by a variable white zone, flat-faced, to 30 mm diameter, the tube about twice the length of the calyx and narrower than in *P. petiolaris*, petal-lobes shortly and irregularly acuminate-toothed. 2n = 22. Flowering April to May in the wild, March to early April in cultivation. (Plate 8, 30.)

DISTRIBUTION Himalayas, from central Nepal eastwards through Sikkim, Bhutan, south-east Tibet and Assam, in forests between 2000 and 4700 m, in monsoon zones to the south of the main range. Common, widespread, and often occurring in very large colonies.

P. gracilipes takes an intermediate position between the tighter, dwarfer *P. petiolaris*, and the larger and laxer *P. bracteosa*. All three species have slight but diagnostic differences in the shape of the calyx. *P. gracilipes* also differs from *P. petiolaris* in the flower shape, and in always having meal, at least on the calyx. All forms have at least some meal on young leaves, often forming a delightful contrast with the soft pink flowers, but this meal is usually washed off by rain, and does not persist into the summer.

CULTIVATION First introduced by M. Foster to Kew in 1888 as *P. petiolaris* var. *nana* (Bot. Mag. t.7079B), but did not persist. Reintroduced in 1936 by Ludlow and Sherriff (L & S 1167) as flown-home plants from Bhutan. This introduction still persists ('Sherriff's var.', with good meal and deep rose flowers). There were many subsequent introductions of this portable plant which often grows beside popular Nepalese trails in the 1970s, but the collection of living material in Nepal is now mostly illegal.

The easiest and most persistent of the petiolarids in the garden. Only in the north of Scotland does it prove problematic as it is intolerant of severe late spring frosts.

HYBRIDIZATION AND VARIATION Partially or completely sterile hybrids have been known in cultivation with the following species:

- *P. petiolaris* (p 169).
- *P. sessilis*. This hybrid was often known as *P.* 'Cunninghamii', but was quite different from true *P. cunninghamii* which is synonymous with the Davidii species *P. drummondiana*. This beautiful and vigorous hybrid resembled *P. gracilipes*, but had pointed, often four-petalled flowers of a lilac-pink fading white; origin unknown.
- *P. boothii* ('Sandy'); raised by A. Duguid at Edrom from pin *P. gracilipes* grown with thrum *P. boothii*; 2n = 21.
- *P. irregularis* ('Stonor no.1'); origin unknown, became extinct in about 1976.
- *P. aureata*; a number of seedlings raised by John Dennis of Doncaster from crosses onto *P. gracilipes*, first flowered 1990; these very beautiful plants resemble *P. aureata*, but have very large (to 41 mm diameter) flowers which are usually cream. In early years these plants had a very long flowering season (October to May) in the garden. The best clone has been called 'Netta Dennis' (**AM** 2001) and is palest pink as the flowers open, fading to cream.

P. gracilipes is variable in size, flower colour and presence of meal. Named strains or clones include the original 'Sherriff's var.' (above), still perhaps the best; and 'Tinney's Jewel' (raised by G. Mundey from seed from crosses with a plant named (wrongly) '*P. deuteronana*', which may have been a form of *P. petiolaris*), dwarf, bright pink, and with good meal. 'Linnet' (Jermyn) and 'minor' are *P. petiolaris* hybrids; 'major' was *P. bracteosa*.

- subsp. *sulphurea* (Hook. f.) A.J. Richards (1977). (*P. petiolaris* Wall. var. *sulphurea* Hook. f., Fl. Brit. Indi 3: 493 (1882)). Leaves thickly yellow-mealy on both sides; Kumaon. This little-known form has only been collected once and is not known in cultivation.

Primula sessilis Royle, Notes Roy. Bot. Gdn. Edinb. 6: 256 (1917)

P. petiolaris Wallich var. *nana* Hook. f. (1882) p.p. non *P. nana* Wall.

DESCRIPTION *Leaves* at flowering dark green, lacking meal, with an oval blade and a short but clearly marked and narrow whitish stalk. *Flowers* stemless on short slender stalks, few in number. *Calyx* with very narrow sharp lobes and keeled, to 7 mm, sometimes mealy. *Corolla* pale lilac-pink with a small orange-yellow eye surrounded by a variable and often diffuse white zone, bell-shaped to flat-faced, to 25 mm diameter, but often much smaller, the narrow tube exceeding the calyx; petal-lobes acuminate pointed, not overlapping, often four in number. 2n = 22. Flowering April in cultivation, mid- to late winter in the wild; flowers usually produced singly over a long period. (Photo: Fls Himalaya (suppl.), fig. 309.)

DISTRIBUTION North-west Himalaya; Kulu Valley near Manali east to Gharwal, United Provinces, Punjab, Kashmir and extreme north-west Nepal. Forests from 2500–3500 m.

P. sessilis is a rather plain species which vegetatively resembles a small *P. boothii*. The often four-petalled flowers with a single acuminate tooth are diagnostic. It has only been collected on a few occasions, and is apparently rare, although it is abundant around at least one of the popular hill stations in India.

CULTIVATION. Introduced by Lowndes (1932), Snell (1973), an unknown collector in 1978, McBeath in 1987, by Magnus Ramsay (CC & MR 469) from Himachal Pradesh in 1989 and by Chadwell CC 1470 from Kulu in 1993. Does not usually persist well in cultivation, and apparently not very hardy. The original introduction was quite attractive and persisted until the late 1950s. Ramsay's form from Kulu, which is presently in cultivation at Threave and Branklyn, is also attractive. Growing well at Cluny and Glendoick in 2002.

HYBRIDIZATION AND VARIATION The hybrid with *P. gracilipes* (above) had many of the features of *P. sessilis*, and was a much better garden plant. A white form of the species was grown in the 1950s and 1960s.

Primula deuteronana Craib, Notes Roy. Bot. Gdn. Edinb. 6: 251 (1917)

P. petiolaris var. *nana* Hook. f. (1882) p.p. non *P. nana* Wall.

DESCRIPTION Forming tight stiff dark green crisped and congested rosettes, the young *leaves* sometimes mealy; leaves oblong-spathulate, to 5 cm, with a short broad pinkish or white stalk. *Flowers* stemless and virtually stalkless at flowering, solitary or few. *Calyx* to 8 mm with linear-oblong sepal-lobes, usually slightly mealy. *Corolla* lilac-purple to pale lilac, occasionally white, often streaked darker and paler outside, with a small orange eye, or eye missing, funnel-shaped, to 25 mm diameter, the narrow tube filled with hairs at the mouth and twice the length of the calyx; petal lobes narrow, not overlapping, entire to shortly and bluntly toothed. Flowering May in the wild, slightly earlier in cultivation. (Plates 8, 31.)

DISTRIBUTION Central Nepal and Sikkim. Fairly widespread and occurring in very large populations on open moorland, grassland, rock outcrops and ledges, etc., 3200–4800 m. Confined to wet zones on the south side of the main range usually near the border with Tibet.

This very attractive dwarf species is the only alpine member of the subsection (apart from the yellow-flowered *P. aureata*). In the wild the relatively large crocus-like flowers are borne in ones or twos and hide the tiny rosettes. In flower, the long narrow petals, funnel-like flower and hair-filled flower throat with a small eye are very distinctive. The rosettes resemble *P. petiolaris* (although sometimes with slight meal), but are stiffer and pricklier. They remain very dwarf, showing little if any variation in the size or shape of leaves throughout the year.

CULTIVATION Introduced by Lowndes (1954), Mrs Brough (1956), Bernard Thompson (1979), George Smith (1988) ('Langtang') and Alastair McKelve in the 1990s. A white form has now been in cultivation since 1988 and is now (always) virused. Both colours were offered by a few outlets in 2001. In addition, wild collected seed is occasionally offered in India. Very slow-growing and dwarf in cultivation; probably best grown in a pot in a well-drained compost, plunged outside in full shade in the summer, and taken under glass in a well-lit locality for the winter. When well-grown it can make a stunningly attractive dwarf alpine for the specialist grower.

HYBRIDIZATION No hybrids have been known in cultivation. At Langtang it sometimes grows intermixed with *P. aureata* with which it forms spectacular hybrids (Photo: Bull. AGS 67: 199) and a hybrid clone was offered for sale in 2001.

Primula scapigera (Hook. f.) Craib, Notes Roy. Bot. Gdn. Edinb. 6: 254 (1917)

P. petiolaris var. *scapigera* Hook. f. (1882) p.max.p.

DESCRIPTION *Leaves* smooth, pale green, oblong, lacking meal, to 8 × 2.5 cm at flowering, becoming larger and with a more marked green stalk later, forming a loose rosette. *Flowers* more or less stemless at flowering, but with a short stem in fruit; flower stalks slender, to 5 cm. *Calyx* to 10 mm, with flat long-acuminate sepal-lobes, totally lacking meal. *Corolla* lilac-pink with an orange eye bearing a diffuse white border, flat-faced to slightly funnel-shaped, exannulate, to 33 mm in diameter, the tube narrow and twice the length of the calyx; petal lobes lax, not overlapping, irregularly and often untidily toothed. 2n = 22. Flowering April in cultivation.

DISTRIBUTION Nepal from Annapurna eastwards, Sikkim, and west Bhutan. Apparently uncommon; forests from 2300–3800 m.

One of the five larger species in this subsection which form a short stem when fruiting. *P. scapigera* is easily characterized by its smooth leaves, the total lack of meal, the long narrow corolla tube and the long-acuminate sepals. Although the flowers are often very large, they have a poor substance and the plant characteristically appears untidy in flower. It is perhaps the least satisfactory garden plant in this group.

CULTIVATION First introduced from the Singalelah range in west Sikkim (slopes of Kanchenjunga), where it still grows, in 1876, shown to the RHS by Foster, and figured by Elwes in Garden (1889: 253). Reintroduced in 1934 from Sikkim, possibly by Sherriff. Recent introductions have been from south-east of Ghorapani (Thompson 1979), from east Nepal in the Everest region (Schacht, probably 1978, and Brian Little 1982, including hybrids), from Bakkim, Sikkim (Templar 1979), and from the Thrumseng La Pass, Bhutan (Rushforth 1252).

Although it persisted as a rare plant in cultivation from the 1930s to the 1980s, *P. scapigera* is perhaps the most difficult of its relatives in cultivation and has not been seen in recent years. It seems to be the least hardy, suffering severely from late frosts, and is very susceptible to virus. It is also the least attractive. However, it has given rise to several fine hybrids.

HYBRIDIZATION AND VARIATION Little's collections, chiefly grown by Charles Archbold of Whitley Bay, included a bewildering range of intermediate forms, although some plants were apparently true *P. scapigera*. In the Everest region, it appears that hybrid swarms between *P. scapigera, P. boothii* and *P. irregularis* occur. Most of these plants grew vigorously in the relatively frost-free areas of Whitley Bay, but most had disappointing flowers.

P. scapigera × *P. nana* 'Pandora' (**AM** 1944), with mealy foliage, and large violet flowers with a yellow and white eye was raised by Mrs C.B. Saunders in about 1940. It was a magnificent clone which became virused and no longer survives.

P. scapigera × *P. bracteosa* 'scapeosa' (**AM** 1947) (2n = 22) has foliage identical to *P. scapigera*, but brilliant rose flowers of a good texture, with a narrow white ring and with neat short teeth. It is slightly fertile, and when it seeds it throws scape-buds like *P. bracteosa*. In the 1970s, this was an extremely vigorous, although virused clone, which showed rapid multiplication. In some gardens it was literally grown by the thousand. Between 1980 and 1982 it almost completely disappeared everywhere, presumably as the result of a build-up of virus from an early infection before the clone was spread around the world. However, it still survives in very small quantity (2001). In the mid-1980s, Gerry Mundey raised seedlings from crosses with *P. nana* EN 380 with *P.* × *'scapeosa'*, most of which largely resembled the latter parent.

A white form was raised by Mrs Saunders, but did not persist.

Primula boothii Craib, Notes Roy. Bot. Gdn. Edinb. 6: 249 (1917)

P. petiolaris var. *nana* Hook. f. (1882) p.p. non *P. nana* Wall.

DESCRIPTION *Leaves* rugose, dark olive-green, lacking meal, with a red mid-rib, stalk, and often veins, the blade oval with a markedly narrow stalk, to 6 cm at flowering, the same shape but larger later, forming an open rosette. *Flowers* stemless at flowering, but with a short stem in fruit, borne on short red stalks which elongate later. *Calyx* olive or purple, lacking meal, to 10 cm, the sepal lobes narrow and keeled, giving the calyx an angled cross-section. *Corolla* purple, magenta or lilac with orange spots or an orange zone in the throat and a variable white zone, which is often large and diffuse, but can be absent, flat-faced, to 30 mm diameter, exannulate or annulate, the tube slightly exceeding the calyx; corolla-lobes not overlapping, variable in shape, from nearly entire to deeply lacerate. 2n = 20. Flowering March–April (type plant). (Plate 8, 32.) (Photo: Bull. AGS 61: 25.)

DISTRIBUTION From central Nepal (Annapurna) eastwards through Sikkim, Bhutan and south-east Tibet to Assam. Mossy banks above water among trees, locally abundant, 2200–3300 m.

P. boothii was little-known and poorly understood by Smith and Fletcher (1944), and Fletcher misidentified several collections in the late 1940s and 1950s. Latterly, the true plant became firmly established in cultivation, and its distinctive features, clearly visible on the type, became better understood. However, plants placed under *P. boothii* are quite exceptionally variable, and some recent workers have regarded this species as something of a 'dustbin'. In this account two well-marked variants are described as subspecies, which may help to allay some confusion. The keeled sepals, giving an angled calyx, lack of meal, and red-stalked rugose leaves are common to all forms of this species and, taken together, can be considered diagnostic.

CULTIVATION The true plant was introduced in the 1950s, probably by both Bowes-Lyon and Marjorie Brough, and subsequent plants have arrived from Beer, E.N.A. Morton (1974), Lorraine Brogden (1976), Frances Davies, Templer (1978), George Smith, Thompson (1979), Little (1982), Schilling (1983), Needham (1984) and McBeath (2001). **AM** 1962.

Most of these have initially proved to be vigorous growers, but few have persisted long; they seem to be susceptible to virus and not to be very hardy, at least in cold areas. Subsp. *autumnalis,* and the white form seem to have persisted best, and may be the only clones which survive in 2001. Both have virus.

HYBRIDIZATION Hybrids with *P. irregularis*, and perhaps with *P. scapigera* have been found in the wild by Little, and perhaps by Needham. The wild hybrid with *P. petiolaris* is discussed under that species.

In the 1980s, *P. boothii* proved a popular parent for hybridization, and the following clones were raised by the late G. Mundey:

- *boothii* subsp. *repens* EN 382 × *aureata* 'Tinney's Moonlight'
- *boothii* × *aureata* 'Tinney's Tigger', 'Tinney's Appleblossom' AM 1989 (Bull. AGS 57: 329), 'Tinney's Dairymaid' **PC** 1983, 'Tinney's Pastel'
- *boothii* × *nana* EN 380 'Tinney's Thor'
- *boothii* × *bhutanica* 'Tinney's Icebreaker'
- *P. boothii* × *P. gracilipes* 'Sandy' was raised by A. Duguid.

Of these, 'Tinney's Moonlight', 'Tinney's Appleblossom' and 'Tinney's Dairymaid' survive in 2001.

VARIATION A white form (var. *alba* Hort. PC) was introduced by Tony Schilling (2663) and Frank Cabot from the Kali Gandaki region in 1983, mixed with lilac forms. This persists quite well in cultivation, although it is virused.

- Subsp. *autumnalis* A.J. Richards, Primula: 154 (1993). A distinct invariably autumn-flowering form of *P. boothii* with large deep purple flowers with an orange eye and lacking a white zone to the flower, was first collected by Frances Davies, probably in 1977, from Chitre between Ghorapani and the Kali Gandaki at 2300 m. It has been recollected by Bernard Thompson (1979) and Needham from the Ghorapani area (EN 378; **PC** as 'Annapurna Autumn', 1991). Needham also saw it near Thanti, north-east of Ghorapani. All three collections have been in cultivation, and are almost indistinguishable. It persists quite well in cultivation.
- Subsp. *repens* A.J. Richards, Primula: 154 (1993). This stoloniferous variant of *P. boothii* forms an interesting break in the petiolarids, and is quite distinct from a garden point of view, running around as it does like a strawberry. Morphologically, it is otherwise quite similar to some other forms of the variable *P. boothii*, for instance EN 437 and 518 from Sheopuri. It was first discovered and brought into cultivation by Lorraine Brogdon (1976), from the 'Kali Gandaki', south of Annapurna, and probably from the same area by Needham. It is so distinct, and is apparently restricted to this small area, that it seems to warrant recognition at subspecies rank. Unfortunately, in common with typical *P. boothii* from this region (rather than subspecies *autumnalis*), it is a rather plain plant with unremarkable lilac flowers with pointed tips and annulate throats,

sparsely borne. It is the parent of the spectacular hybrid 'Moonlight' which has not inherited the stoloniferous habit.

The Deorali ridge running northwards towards Annapurna forms the divide between the Kali Gandaki to the west and the Modi Khola to the east. This region, which forms the westernmost extension of the range of *P. boothii* contains several puzzling forms, including Schilling's white form, and subsp. *repens*. In this region, *P. boothii* is apparently undergoing active evolution. Hybridization is not implicated, and as all forms have 2n = 20, it is probable that *P. boothii* is the stock of this radiation. Subsp. *autumnalis* also occurs commonly in at least four stations on this ridge, all lying within about 5 km of Ghorapani. There is an account of both subspecies *autumnalis* and subspecies *repens* in the field by Needham, Bull. AGS 55: 211–217 (1987).

Primula irregularis Craib, Notes Roy. Bot. Gdn. Edinb. 6: 253 (1917)

P. petiolaris var. *nana* Hook. f. (1882) p.p. non *P. nana* Wall.

DESCRIPTION Often a large plant forming stiff somewhat 'cabbagy' rosettes, the young leaves at flowering frequently covered with meal; leaves at flowering obovate, narrowed to the winged stalk, the mid-rib pinkish red lower down, to 15 × 5 mm, later with a more orbicular blade and a narrow stalk. *Flowers* stemless or nearly so at flowering, crowded with as many as 35 in a crown, forming a short thick stem in fruit, the flower-stalks rather long (to 8 cm) and mealy. *Calyx* stiff, bell-shaped, mealy at least on the margin, bluntly and irregularly toothed, to 12 mm. *Corolla* bright pink with a thick waxy texture, with a greenish to orange eye usually but not always surrounded by a clearly demarcated white zone, flat-faced, annulate, to 35 mm in diameter, the broad tube about twice the length of the calyx; petal-lobes with usually regular sharp triangular teeth. 2n = 22. Flowering November to March in the wild and in cultivation. (Plates 8, 33.) (Photo: Bull. AGS 64: 390.)

DISTRIBUTION Scattered throughout Nepal to just inside Bhutan, apparently commonest in the Everest and Kanchenjunga regions, woodland banks, 2500–3700 m.

'On south and east facing slopes forested by *Rhododendron arboreum*, which become quite warm and dry in clear weather, it occurs only by streamsides, and is more plentiful at higher elevations where *Rh. barbatum* and *campanulatum* occur'; '... grows by streamsides and has as its companions *Cardiocrinum* and *Cautleya*, whilst the forest around, a mixture of evergreen oak, *Acer* and *Magnolia*, with an understorey of *Rh. arboreum*, supports a further layer of epiphytic ferns, vacciniums, and orchids such as *Coelogyne corymbosa* and *Pleione humilis*.'

P. irregularis was poorly understood by Smith and Fletcher (1944), but it is now well-known to trekkers in the Everest region, and has been introduced into cultivation on a number of occasions. It has proved to be a well-marked species which is probably closest to *P. bracteosa*, but the thick, waxy corolla with deep regular teeth to the lobes and the stiff mealy bell-shaped calyx are distinctive and constant. It is named for the irregularly toothed calyx teeth, but some of its relatives sometimes develop some teeth there as well. The leaves are similar to those of *P. bracteosa* in spring, and to those of *P. boothii* in summer; thus, unlike either of these species, *P. irregularis* is heterophyllous.

CULTIVATION In cultivation, probably in N. Ireland, by 1962 ('Stonor no.3'), source unknown. Subsequently introduced by Thompson (1974, and possibly 1975, 1977), Templar (1979), Little (1982), Millais (1982), Needham (1984 and other dates?, 351, 437, 538, 584, 692), Rushforth 1081 (1987).

P. irregularis usually proved to be a fast-growing and extremely floriferous grower when first introduced, but the robust low-level forms rapidly lost vigour. Few clones lasted long, although families of vigorous seedlings have been raised. Most forms are apparently not very hardy, and very susceptible to hard winters, but also to heat and a dry atmosphere. In later years a dwarf form collected by George Smith and distributed by John Dennis has proved to be both a vigorous multiplier and much hardier. It resembles *P. gracilipes* in many ways, but is best classified here.

At its best a very lovely plant; a vigorous seedling of this species with over 100 very large flowers gained an **AM** (1981) as *P. 'edgeworthii × irregularis'*; it appeared to be pure *P. irregularis*. The **PC** given to '*P. irregularis*' in 1985 was to a pink form of *P. nana* (= *P. edgeworthii*).

HYBRIDIZATION Little's introductions from the Arun valley included hybrids with both *P. scapigera* and *P. boothii*. A hybrid with *P. gracilipes* ('Stonor no.1') has been known.

Mundey raised three hybrids × 'irregularis EN 380', but that plant is *P. nana*. He also raised a hybrid with *P. bracteosa* (unnamed), and with *P. bhutanica* ('Tinney's Chaffinch') with silvery white foliage and soft violet flowers with a broad inner white zone. None of these persist.

VARIATION On at least two occasions, miniature versions have been introduced, from exposed ridges at about 3300 m in the Everest region, and from 3700 m at Bikbari. The first was called '*P. thompsonii*' and the second '*P. tensingae*', but both seem to have been dwarf *P. irregularis*. Unfortunately, neither seems to have persisted. E. Needham has introduced what seem to be similar plants which have been called '*P. tridentata*', but the type of *P. tridentata* Don is the same as *P. petiolaris*.

A plant otherwise resembling *P. irregularis*, but with little if any meal, and with no white zone to the flower has been in cultivation under the clonal name 'Rankin 131' (or sometimes '161') since at least 1970 (**PC** 1984). It was originally thought to be a hybrid with *P. scapigera,* and has somewhat reduced pollen fertility, but similar plants were found mixed with typical *P. irregularis* in the Dudh Khosi by Bernard Thompson in 1975.

Primula bracteosa Craib, Notes Roy. Bot. Gdn. Edinb. 6: 250 (1917)

P. petiolaris var. *scapigera* Hook. f. (1882) p.p.

DESCRIPTION *Leaves* oblanceolate, rugose, mealy when young, to 10 × 2.5 cm at flowering, forming a loose rosette, with a winged stalk and a pink to brilliant red mid-rib, larger (to 20 cm) but of the same shape in summer. *Flowers* stemless at flowering, stalks mealy, to 4 cm, not crowded with rarely more than 10 in a rosette, but with a short thick stem and leaf-like bracts formed from an apical 'scape-bud' when fruiting; the latter sometimes root, the stem acting as a 'pseudostolon' (see also *P. taliensis* and *P. griffithii*). *Calyx* urn-shaped, mealy, to 10 mm, with sharp entire sepal-lobes. *Corolla* lilac or lilac-purple with a star-shaped greenish eye and a distinct white surround, flat-faced, annulate, to 32 mm in diameter, corolla-tube exceeding the calyx, of medium width; petal-lobes broad, sometimes overlapping, with weak irregular acuminate teeth. Flowering April. (Plate 8.)

DISTRIBUTION Extreme east Nepal, Sikkim, Bhutan and Assam, commonest in central Bhutan. Forests (e.g. of *Abies densa*), 2200–3600 m, often growing in large masses on banks, often above water. Coming chiefly from Bhutan, *P. bracteosa* was known to the early collectors such as Griffith and Cooper, and was collected extensively by Ludlow and Sherriff. It has been correspondingly little known during the 'Nepal years' of the 1950s to 1970s, but now that Bhutan has been regularly visited since the late 1980s, it is more often seen.

In many ways, *P. bracteosa* resembles a giant *P. gracilipes*, although it forms a short stem with characteristic leaf-like bracts with scape buds in fruit. However, until recent years only one clone had persisted in cultivation, so seed was never set and these stems and buds did not appear in cultivation. Although the leaves resemble those of *P. irregularis* in spring, it is not heterophyllous, and the shape of the calyx is diagnostic.

CULTIVATION Introduced in 1937 (L. & S. 3162). This clone with dull lilac flowers persisted remarkably well, but has been seen little of since about 1990 except at Cluny. Rushforth (1244) introduced a much more attractive clone from Bumthang, Bhutan in 1987, with leaves heavily veined with brilliant red, and pinky-purple flowers on shorter stems. This has persisted well and is probably the strain, now propagated from seed, that was being offered by some Scottish sources from 2000. *P. bracteosa* does not produce the masses of flowers of some of its relatives, but it seems relatively immune to virus, and stands heat better than some.

HYBRIDIZATION AND VARIATION Appears from herbarium material to be rather invariable (but see above). Hybrids were known with *P. scapigera* and *P. irregularis* (p.172), and with *P. nana* (*P.* × 'bractworthii', raised by Mrs Saunders at the same time as 'Pandora'). The latter was initially very vigorous, with very large brilliant magenta flowers, but it did not persist. A hybrid with *P. boothii* (× 'bootheosa') has been raised by Jim Jermyn and offered in the trade, but may now have disappeared.

Primula aureata Fletcher, Gard. Illustr. 63: 283 (1941)

DESCRIPTION *Leaves* usually very heavily white-mealy, especially at flowering, with a pink mid-rib, oblanceolate, to 8 × 2.5 cm at flowering, often longer but of the same shape later, forming a loose rosette. *Flowers* stemless at flowering, but with a very short stout red stem in fruit, crowded into the rosette, borne on white-mealy stems up to 5 cm. *Calyx* weakly urn-shaped, white-mealy, to 10 mm, the sepal-lobes sharp, entire. *Corolla* yellow to cream with a very broad orange eye, or a smaller yellow eye, flat-faced, the petals somewhat recurved with age, annulate, to 32 mm in diameter, corolla-tube rather broad, exceeding calyx; corolla-lobes broad, usually overlapping, with short, rounded to lacerate teeth. Flowering April–May. (Plate 9, 34.)

DISTRIBUTION Central Nepal 'to the north of Kathmandu'; towards the heads of two parallel valleys, Langtang and Gosainkund. Steep often vertical crevices or earthy banks, usually overhung, often near rivers or even under waterfalls, locally abundant and frequently growing with *P. deuteronana*, and just overlapping altitudinally with *P. gracilipes*, 3050–4400 m., above the forest zone.

P. aureata is one of the most desirable and beautiful of all primulas. It is the only member of this subsection with yellow-orange flowers, which, nestling in leaves so mealy as often to be completely white, presents a unique aspect which has sometimes been unkindly but aptly compared to a fried egg! Despite its very individual appearance, *P. aureata* is structurally (but not ecologically) very similar to *P. bracteosa*. The number of hybrids it has spawned suggest that genetically it has not diverged far from its relatives.

Gosainkund and Langtang are holy areas to the Nepalese, and consequently seem not to have been visited by a western botanist until 1935, when Lt. Col. F. M. Bailey (of *Meconopsis betonicifolia* fame) brought back seeds to Edinburgh (received 1936). These produced plants (of unrecorded origin) with rather small cream flowers which were identified by Fletcher as *P. edgeworthii* var. *alba*. It was not until 1950 that they were redetermined by Fletcher as '*P. aureata* forma'.

In the meantime, the Royal Botanic Garden Edinburgh had raised a single seedling with larger yellow and orange flowers which first flowered in 1939 (**AM**). According to their records, this had originated in a pan of *Swertia purpurascens* (= *S. ciliata*), (not *S. purpurea* as usually related), sent from the Lloyd Botanic Garden, Darjeeling in 1935, and purporting to have originated in Sikkim. However, A.J.M. Grierson (Bot. Mag. NS 176, t.488) pointed out that with hindsight a more likely explanation is that this plant also originated from Bailey's seed, and that records were confused during propagation.

This seedling proved to be vigorous and beautiful, and so distinct that Fletcher described the species *P. aureata* from this single accession of unknown origin.

The credit for the rediscovery of *P. aureata* in the wild seems to belong to Mrs Desiree Proud (1952). In recent years, Langtang and Gosainkund have become part of trekkers' trails, and many people have been privileged to see this exceptional species in the wild.

CULTIVATION After Bailey's original introductions (above), *P. aureata* was next introduced by S. Bowes-Lyon and Adam Stainton in 1962. This included some plants with purple-tinged petals (below) which were grown at Kew. Subsequent introductions have included those of David Sayers (1974), R. Gibbons (1976), V. Chambers (1977), Templer (1978), Needham (1985) and McKelvie.

Bailey's original introductions, and most of the more recent ones, persisted well in cultivation. The original clones were all pin, and although they occasionally set seed, these only gave rise to pin offspring. Latterly, thrums were introduced as well, and seed was often set in cultivation. Micropropagated plants were also offered, and prices dropped in the late 1980s from astronomical figures to realistic levels as demand has been met. By 2001, most plants of true *P. aureata* were of micropropagated origin. These are a travesty of the original plant, with small, misshapen flowers and distorted, not very mealy leaves and are not worth growing. It seems that they provide a cogent warning as to the potential for genetic damage after micropropagation.

P. aureata is perfectly hardy, for it comes from high areas where it is not covered by snow. Although it has been recorded as growing temporarily even under the water, and commonly under waterfalls, these systems are snow-fed and are dry in the winter, while it always grows in a vertical position, usually under an overhang. Consequently, it strongly dislikes overhead water, especially outside where it rarely succeeds for long. However, it has proved a vigorous grower in pot culture, where it is traditionally and successfully managed 'under the bench' of an alpine house, where it appears to appreciate the relatively dry atmosphere even in summer. However, it strongly resents drying at the root, direct sunlight, or too much heat. Significantly it has been the most successful member of the section in areas such as New Zealand and Australia with relatively warm dry summers.

HYBRIDIZATION Hybrids have occurred in cultivation with the following:

- *P. gracilipes* (p. 170)
- *P. boothii* (p. 173)
- P. × P. × 'scapeosa'; although most of these seedlings resembled P. × 'scapeosa', 'Tinney's Sunset' had large exotically coloured flowers with concentric bands of pink, white and orange
- *P. bhutanica* 'Tinney's Gamble', raised by G.R. Mundey; this remarkable plant was intermediate in form between the parents, having heavily mealy leaves of *P. bhutanica* shape, a deciduous habit, and flowers of a cream overlying ice-blue. Photo: Bull. AGS 59: 81.

In 1962, both Adam Stainton and Simon Bowes-Lyon collected plants from Gosainkund and Langtang respectively with purple edges to the petals. Bowes-Lyon's plant was grown at Kew, where Grierson (Bot. Mag. NS 176, t.511) considered that it was hybrid, probably with *P. scapigera*. Herbarium material shows a massively vigorous plant with a well-developed scape, persistent basal buds (suggesting that it is deciduous), despite Grierson's report to the contrary, and sterile pollen. Stainton considered from field evidence (and his movie film) that purple-edged plants were hybrids with *P. deuteronana*, the only other petiolarid in flower at the same time. Despite later controversy this parentage has now been confirmed by J.M. Pearson (Bull. AGS 67: 197–199). A hybrid clone was collected by McKelvie and is now (2001) offered by Tough nurseries.

VARIATION

- Subsp. *fimbriata* Richards ex Gould, Enum. Fl Nepal 3: 70 (1982) (*P. aureata* 'forma' Hort.). Generally smaller than the type, with more rosettes; corolla cream with a small yellow eye, not exceeding 25 mm in diameter, the lobes sharply and often deeply toothed to lacerate. (Plate 34.)

It has been recognized since 1950 that two distinct forms of *P. aureata* occur in cultivation, and it now appears that both had in fact been introduced by Bailey. *P. aureata* 'forma' had originally been assigned to the superficially somewhat similar but unrelated *P. nana*, which among other differences is deciduous and strongly heterophyllous. Similar plants seem not to have been seen in the wild until Bob Gibbon's visit. Gibbons was quite clear that the two forms were distinct in the wild and did not occur together. It seemed at the time that *P. aureata* type occurred at Langtang, and the 'forma' (subsp. *fimbriata*) at Gosainkund, around the sacred lake.

It now seems that the variation is more related to habitat. All five altitudinally annotated collections of the type plant I have been able to trace occurred from 3050 to 3750 m, while all five collections of subsp. *fimbriata* do not occur below 4200 m. Both subspecies have now been recorded at each site. According to Needham, there may be another habitat difference, for he records subsp. *fimbriata* as occurring in very wet conditions (at flowering), while he states that the type 'always seeks shelter from direct rain'. This certainly matches the behaviour of these plants in cultivation, for subsp. *fimbriata* seemed to be more tolerant of cultivation in the open garden.

LITERATURE. Richards A.J. (1994). The New Plantsman 1: 146–150.

Subsection **Edgeworthii** (Smith & Fletcher) A.J. Richards, J. Scot. Rock Gdn. Club 15: 23 (1977)

Deciduous, forming an open mealy resting bud; strongly heterophyllous, leaves unstalked and scarcely toothed at flowering, markedly stalked and toothed later; flowers of varying colours, exannulate; stems at flowering absent or very short.

Primula nana Wall. in Roxburgh, Fl. Indica 2: 23 (1824) non *P. petiolaris* Wall. var. *nana* Hook. f. (1882)

P. petiolaris Wall. var. *edgeworthii* Hook. f. (1882)
P. pulverulenta Edgeworth (1852 nomen) non Rafin.
P. petiolaris var. *pulverulenta* Hook. f. (1882)
P. edgeworthii (Hook. f.) Pax (1905)
P. winteri Watson (1911)
? *P. saxicola* Craib (1917)

DESCRIPTION *Leaves* at flowering similar to bud scales, the plant flowering as the winter rosette develops, oblong, to 5 × 1.5 cm, grey-green and mealy; summer leaves usually without meal, the blade rounded-triangular, irregularly and often deeply toothed, with a narrow green stalk. *Flowers* borne in dense clusters on short (to 2 cm) mealy stalks, but borne on a short thick stem when fruiting. *Calyx* broadly cylindrical, mealy, to 10 mm, the sepal-lobes rather short and blunt. *Corolla* violet, blue, lilac, pink or white with a cream to orange eye and a variable white border, flat-faced (initially bell-shaped), exannulate, to 35 mm in diameter, corolla tube slightly exceeding calyx, broad; corolla lobes rather broad but not overlapping, entire to lacerate but usually with three short rounded teeth. 2n = 22. Flowering December–March. (Plate 9.)

DISTRIBUTION Western Himalaya, from Himachal Pradesh (Simla) through Uttar Pradesh, Gharwal, Kumaon and Nepal west to Kathmandu. Moist woods, especially near water, 2000–3700 m.

P. nana is another species with a confused taxonomic history, having been known for many years in cultivation as *P. edgeworthii,* and previously as *P. winteri*. Many early authors considered the epithet 'nana' to be confused, as Hooker used it indiscriminately for a variety of species. However, the type of *P. nana* Wall. still exists at Kew ('Gos. Than, 1824'). Smith and Fletcher state that '*P. nana* is based on very imperfect material', but that 'should ever a decision be made in favour of its identity with *P. edgeworthii*, then *P. nana* is the prior name'. It seems that Smith and Fletcher had in fact never seen this type, and had followed the earlier judgements of Craib and Stapf. If they had seen it, I have little doubt that they would have agreed with me that it is the same as the species previously known as *P. edgeworthii*. An earlier confusion arose from the marked seasonal heterophylly in this species, which looks entirely different in summer (type of *P. edgeworthii*) from its spring-flowering condition (type of *P. winteri*).

Although very variable over its wide range, this is a very distinct species, its seasonal behaviour and general appearence resembling no other. In flower the mealy untoothed leaves, persistent bud scales, and exannulate flowers are diagnostic.

Morphologically, *P. nana* forms a rather clear link between subsection Petiolares and subsection Sonchifolia, and it has hybridized with members of both.

CULTIVATION Introduced by seed from the Naini Tal by E.L. Winter, then Commissioner of Kumaon, in 1909 (flowered 1911) (not 1887 as has been stated). It has been in continuous cultivation ever since, thus being the most persistent (although not as often stated the first) petiolarid to be introduced. At the time of the 4th Primula Conference of the RHS in 1928 it was the only species to have been cultivated for some considerable time.

Most subsequent introductions have been from Nepal, by Thompson (1974, 1978), Ghose (1980), Millais (1982), Needham (EN 380 as *P. irregularis*, **PC** 1985).

P. nana grows well from seed, and is initially vigorous, but clones tend not to be long-lived. In my experience it is not very hardy, and certainly resents winter wet, being best cloched outside during the winter. However, in all its forms it is a very beautiful plant which repays every endeavour, and it remains, in its several forms, quite widespread in cultivation and is usually available through the trade. Considered hardy and permanent at Tromso.

VARIATION An extremely variable plant, notably in flower colour, which seems to have a geographical bias. Plants from the west of its range ('British India') seem always to be blue, or lilac-blue in colour. These have been represented in cultivation by strains such as 'Drake's Blue' (a good deep royal blue), and 'Old Lilac', which seems to represent the original introduction (which was said to have been clear blue in the field when introduced). Plants from Nepal all seem to have pink flowers, usually of a soft clear pink with a cream eye. These were often called 'Ghose's variety' from that introduction by seed, but plants so called probably now have a multiple parentage. The original Ghose's variety had very large flowers (often 35 mm in diameter). Collections by, e.g., Thompson have shown Nepalese popul-ations to be very variable in the overall size of the plant, and in flower shape, size and colour, the latter varying from whitish to rose in colour.

The white-flowered form (var. *alba* hort.) was fairly vigorous and had large flowers of a good velvety magnolia. It often came true from seed, although blue seedlings have also arisen from it. I have not seen it in recent years (2001) and it may have been lost.

HYBRIDIZATION Hybrids are known with the following species:

- *P. scapigera* 'Pandora' (p. 172)
- *P. bracteosa* 'bractworthii' (p. 175)
- *P. boothii* 'Thor' (p. 173)
- *P. bhutanica* 'Tantallon'. This beautiful cross, with perfectly formed flowers of the most luminous violet and very mealy foliage was raised by Henry and Margaret Taylor in 1977 and named after their house (**AM** 1983). Unfortunately, this fine clone developed virus, but 'clean' sources still exist in 2001. Michael and Polly Stone raised a large number of seedlings of the same cross, and a number of these have been disseminated by the trade. Some are quite similar to Tantallon, and have sometimes been sold under this name, although none have in fact been given clonal names. Similar crosses were raised at Cluny in 1991, and by Gerry Mundey. (Photo: Bull. AGS 59: 80.)

Primula moupinensis Franchet, Bull. Soc. Bot. Fr. 33: 67 (1886)

P. euosma Craib (1919)
P. hoffmanniana Smith (1926)
?P. prevernalis Chen & Hu (1990)

DESCRIPTION Closely resembling some pink Nepalese forms of *P. nana* in flower, although not later. Best distinguished by the notched rather than toothed ends to the corolla-lobes and also differing by the smaller less cabbagy bud-scales which are shed early, by the calyx which has narrow sharp lobes; and by the leaves which can expand remarkably in summer, often to more than 30 cm, being broadly oval and jaggedly toothed at this stage. Flowers usually a bland pink, sometimes pale lilac-blue. Some forms are strongly stoloniferous, a feature which is never seen in *P. nana*. (Fig. Halda: 153 (below), The Alpine Gardener 69: 506.) (Plate 77.)

DISTRIBUTION From north-east Burma on the Yunnan border, and the Salween and Mekong divides in Yunnan, to south-west, west and central Sichuan. Shady situations by streams, waterfalls, bamboo thickets and moist alpine meadows on the margins of forests, 1300–4700 m.

P. moupinensis from Sichuan was until recently a little known or understood species which has been the subject of much confusion. However, as it occurs at a number of localities which have been well-visited over the last two decades (Wolong, Emei Shan, Baoxing) it has now become a familiar plant. While suggesting that its nearest ally was *P. sonchifolia,* Smith and Fletcher inexplicably placed it in subsection Petiolares, apparently because they considered that it lacks basal bud-scales, and is thus, by inference, evergreen. In fact, it is deciduous, and some specimens do indeed show bud-scales as we can now see in cultivation, although these are small and are lost at an early stage.

Material placed under the more southerly *P. euosma* is inseparable in the herbarium from *P. moupinensis*. The only real distinction Smith and Fletcher make seems to be in stem length, but these specimens merely represent different stages in stem elongation. Curiously, *P. euosma* was classified by them with *P. odontocalyx,* which, being a Davidii species synonymous with *P. epilosa*, is a plant of an entirely different facies. Doubtless Smith and Fletcher were severely hampered in their judgements by an acute shortage of material for these species which are still very poorly represented in herbaria. Some *P. odontocalyx* in cultivation in 2002 had also been named *P. moupinensis*.

P. hoffmanniana was classified by Smith and Fletcher near the Himalayan *P. petiolaris*. However, the fragmentary material cannot be separated from *P. moupinensis*. From the description, particularly with respect to the bilobed petal-lobes which is a condition rare in this group, it is possible that the newly described *P. prevernalis* also falls within this variable species.

A large-flowered form from the Barkam Shan, Sichuan has been separated as subsp. *barkamensis* Hu, Fl. Rep. Pop. Sin. 2: 291.

CULTIVATION *P. moupinensis* was collected in 1987 from the Yulong Shan by Ron McBeath, and in 1991 by Needham from Moupine (Baoxing) (EN 3142). The Needham introduction is stoloniferous as is CD&R 609 from the Erling Shan (1989) and

CD&R 2386 from Wolong (1995). The latter gained a **PC** in 1998. A non-stoloniferous form from the Gonga Shan gained a **PC** under CD&R 2457 in 2001.

P. moupinensis is proving tolerant of relatively warm dry conditions in summer and is hardy (although it prefers cloching in damp winters), and as it is very readily propagated by the runners in stoloniferous forms, it has proliferated remarkably during the 1990s . It is now perhaps the petiolarid most often encountered in cultivation. It is a pretty plant, but unlike its Himalayan relatives, flowers are only borne in twos and threes in the stoloniferous form, so that the effect is rarely striking. However, the non-stoloniferous form, which is not so readily propagated, does produce more flowers. No hybrids have yet been reported.

Primula sinuata Franchet, Bull. Mus. Paris 1: 65 (1895)

P. nemoralis Balf. f (1915)
P. ragotiana Levl. (1915)
P. candidissima Smith & Forrest (1927)
P. plebeia Balf. f. (1916)

DESCRIPTION A very little known plant, which appears to be a relative of *P. moupinensis*, but with leaves of a very distinctive shape, being oval and with a regularly wavy margin, like an oak leaf, and with a well-marked narrow stalk. The calyx resembles that of *P. sonchifolia*; the flowers are rose or white in colour. The taxonomic affinities of this species, which has never been in cultivation, are not clear, and it is not certain that it is deciduous. Banks in damp shaded thickets in north-east Yunnan, 900–3000 m.

Subsection **Sonchifolia** (Smith & Fletcher) Richards, J. Scot. Rock Gdn. Club, 15: 25 (1977)

Deciduous, forming a large closed above-ground resting bud; leaves heterophyllous, toothed at flowering; stems at flowering absent or very short; flowers annulate, blue or yellow.

Primula bhutanica Fletcher, Gardening Illustrated 63: 312 (1941)

DESCRIPTION *Resting bud* rather narrow, acute, chestnut, often multiple; *leaves* heterophyllous, obovate, to 6 × 2 cm at flowering with a broad, indistinct whitish stalk, dusted with meal, enlarging after flowering and forming a triangular, pointed blade and a distinct green stalk. *Flowers* initially stemless, tightly clustered in the opening rosette, shortly stemmed in fruit, with mealy stalks to 2 cm. *Calyx* cylindrical, stiff, mealy, to 7 mm, with erect sharp entire to toothed sepal-lobes. *Corolla* ice-blue to sky-blue with a greeny-yellow eye and an often broad white zone, flat-faced, to 32 mm in diameter, the tube broad and just exceeding the calyx; corolla lobes usually wavy and overlapping, sharply and irregularly toothed, or nearly entire. 2n = 22. Flowering February to April, often through the snow and frozen ground in the wild. (Plate 9).

DISTRIBUTION East Bhutan and west Assam from 91° 30' to 93° E, and a single disjunct area in Tsari, south-east Tibet. Steep banks and streamsides in *Abies* and mixed rhododendron forest, 3000–4300 m.

P. bhutanica is perhaps the finest of the three lovely 'blue primroses' of the eastern Sinohimalaya. These closely related species inhabit different areas. *P. bhutanica* was initially equated with *P. whitei* when discovered by Kingdon Ward in Assam in 1935, and Ludlow and Sherriff in Bhutan in 1936. However, comments by the latter who knew both in the wild led Fletcher to describe *P. bhutanica* as a new species. Sherriff believed that the key distinction between the two was the deeply toothed petals of *P. bhutanica*. The later discovery (L .& S. 12299) of a population with varied types of petal-lobe led him to revise his earlier opinion, and Fletcher followed his advice latterly by including *P. bhutanica* within *P. whitei*.

However, even the type population (L. & S. 1166) has varied petal-lobe toothing, and the other important differences between *P. bhutanica* and *P. whitei* in growth form and calyx morphology which became evident in cultivation can with hindsight also be clearly seen in the herbarium. *P. bhutanica* is not found west of east Bhutan, while *P. whitei* is restricted to central and west Bhutan.

CULTIVATION Introduced as flown-home plants by Ludlow and Sherriff on at least three occasions (1166, 2864, 12021) and by Kingdon Ward (11478). All plants in cultivation probably derive from L & S 2864. Rushforth 1255 (1987) did not survive the 1989 hot summer.

P. bhutanica has proved to be persistent and relatively vigorous when planted out in shaded humid sloping sites in summer-cool areas with good snow cover, notably in Scotland and north Norway, and in a few favoured gardens it is grown in quantity and even self-sows. However, in most areas it is very susceptible to summer heat, which causes it to rot easily, and is best cloched during the winter. When pins and thrums are grown together, it sets seed readily and a number of growers regularly raise batches of vigorous seedlings. It is usually available in the trade, often as the 'Sherriff's var.' strain.

P. bhutanica with its ice-blue toothed and crinkled flowers nestling in tight rosettes of crystalline mealy leaves is one of the most beautiful of all spring flowers. **FCC** 1994.

HYBRIDIZATION Hybrids have been raised with the following:

- *P. boothii* (above)
- *P. irregularis* (above)
- *P. aureata* (above)
- *P. nana* (above)
- *P. whitei*. The plant often known in cultivation as the latter is sterile, and is intermediate in leaf-shape and the form of the calyx between *P. bhutanica* and *P. whitei*. It may have arisen as an unintentional hybrid at Ascreavie, the garden of Major and Mrs Sherriff, where both parents self-sowed. There seems to be only a single vigorous clone involved with flowers of a soft clear blue and rounded, nearly entire petal-lobes. It is nowadays given the clonal name 'Arduaine' (pronounced "Ardunie") from that Argyllshire garden from where it was distributed.(**AM** 2001).

VARIATION Most variation in the wild seems to be confined to the degree of petal toothing. The strain 'Sherriff's var.', which is that usually offered, is a form with very toothed petals and a wide white central zone to the flowers. It is typical of many plants in the wild.

Primula whitei Smith, Rec. Bot. Surv. India 4: 268 (1911)

DESCRIPTION Differs from *P. bhutanica* by resting buds being broader, rounded, and often single; leaves are narrowly oblanceolate, and although they elongate considerably after flowering, they remain essentially the same shape, i.e. not heterophyllous; flower stalks are longer and thinner (to 5 cm); calyx bell-shaped, the sepal-lobes spreading, rounded and always toothed at the tip; corolla cup-shaped, not exceeding 28 mm diameter, usually purple-blue, the white zone reduced or absent, the corolla-lobes entire or with shallow broad rounded teeth, not wavy. Flowering February–April, often through melting snow. (Plate 78.)

DISTRIBUTION West and central Bhutan, from near the Sikkim border to Bumthang, one station on the Tibetan side of the Bhutanese border on the Yu La. Steep shaded banks under rhododendrons, *Abies* and junipers, 3000–4260 m. Apparently common in central Bhutan. Does not overlap with *P. bhutanica*.

First discovered on the Pile La by Sir Claude White in 1905. Closely related to *P. bhutanica* (for discussion see that species), but major structural differences indicate specific rank for these two species.

CULTIVATION Introduced by flown-home plants by Ludlow and Sherriff in 1938, and perhaps later (3053, 3100, 3229, 6621 ?18676). L. & S. 6621 persisted at the Sherriffs' garden, Ascreavie, and perhaps elsewhere until the mid-1970s, but is never seen today (2001), although a hybrid is widespread. Reintroduced by Anne Chambers in 1991, but did not persist. Apparently a less vigorous plant than *P. bhutanica*, and can be less attractive, but the Chambers introduction was of a stunning form.

HYBRIDIZATION Hybrids persist today with *P. bhutanica* (above), and with *P. sonchifolia*.

In the mid 1970s, *P. whitei*, *P. sonchifolia* and *P. bhutanica* grew together in quantity at Ascreavie, where they self-sowed, and all hybrids known in this group probably arose amongst these plantings. The author and Mrs Sherriff agreed that a large vigorous clone with a broad, plate-like structure of emerging leaves and masses of purplish-blue flowers had resulted from hybridization between *P. whitei* and *P. sonchifolia*. Betty Sherriff remarked on the resemblance of this sterile clone to a plate of soup, and it has been known as 'Soup-Plate' ever since. At that time it was already grown by the RBG Edinburgh in quantity. Nowadays it always seems to be virused and has become scarce in 2001. Fig: Bot. Mag. tab. 377.

In 1975 I also noticed a curious plant with small cup-shaped purplish flowers on short stems at Ascreavie which we agreed was probably *P. whitei* × *P. griffithii*. This was also sterile, and did not persist.

Primula sonchifolia Franchet, Bull. Soc. Bot. Fr. 32: 266 (1885)

P. gratissima Forrest (1909)
P. taraxacoides Balf. f. (1915)
P. drymophila Craib (1919)

DESCRIPTION *Resting bud* massive, egg-like, mealy, often multicrowned. *Leaves* to 7 × 2.5 cm at flowering, ovate-lanceolate, mealy, later elongating to 20 cm or more and becoming broadly sinuate down the margins, losing meal. *Flowers* with up to 30 tightly clustered in the opening bud at flowering, stem very short or absent at flowering, short and stout later; flower-stalks short (to 1 cm), stout and mealy. *Calyx* to 7 mm, bell-shaped, mealy, the sepal-lobes suborbicular, toothed. *Corolla* dark blue, ice-blue, lilac, even pinkish, or white, with a star-shaped orange eye; white border absent or broad and conspicuous, slightly cup-shaped, to 30 mm diameter; corolla-tube short, not as broad as *P. bhutanica*; petal-lobes usually not overlapping, not wavy, rounded, entire or fringed with minute teeth. Flowering March–May, as the snow melts. (Plate 9.) (Photos: Bull. AGS 64: 235, 392.)

DISTRIBUTION Widespread in west China, north-east Burma and south-east Tibet in a band from Hpimaw in Burma, through the Salween, Mekong and Yangtse divides to the Cang Shan, Yulong Shan, and Zhondian plateau to Muli, Kulu and Tatsienlu in Sichuan, and Tsarong in Tibet.

High level alpine grassland, scrub and forest on steep slopes, often near melting snow, 3300–4600 m. My experience appears to accord with other observers, in that I found it in two distinct habitats: firstly, in dense shade growing right underneath five metre rhododendrons in leaf-mould (usually under section Taliensia species such as *Rh. aganniphum* and *R. phaeochrysum*), where *P. boreiocalliantha* can be a neighbour; and secondly in the open but on steep north slopes where shallow stream trickles and flushes run over mostly open, but mossy, stony ground. It was very noticeable in both habitats that most plants were too small to flower. Large, multirosetted plants such as are found in favoured gardens seem to be a rare occurrence in nature, and only continuous propagation from seed seems to ensure survival in the wild.

At the end of May, some plants were still in flower at 3700 m, but this is a very early species. 'In many instances I found specimens which had forced their way through the snow. In such cases the surrounding white showed to the greatest advantage the rich blue of the flowers.'

P. sonchifolia was the first known of the 'blue primroses', and is the most widespread, although completely disjunct from its relatives and one of the few petiolarids in China. Although variable, and hence giving rise to several synonyms, it is totally distinct from all its relatives. It has, with its huge bulb-like resting bud, a remarkable structure and growth habit. The summer leaves sometimes become weakly lobed, hence the reference to *Sonchus* (sow-thistles) and *Taraxacum* (dandelions) in its name and synonym.

CULTIVATION Although first discovered on the Cang Shan by Delavay in 1884, and subsequently admired in the field by Forrest, Farrer, Kingdon Ward and Handel-Mazzetti, most attempts at introduction by seed failed. A few plants from Forrest's gatherings were raised at Edinburgh and flowered in 1926, but were lost.

Until recent years, the only successful introductions were made in response to a request by the Royal Parks using the good offices of the Governor of Burma, Sir Charles Innes. In 1929, seed was forwarded in a vacuum flask, and plants flowered in 1931 at Bodnant. In the same year, Forest Ranger Sukve, after a difficult winter journey through deep snow, collected large numbers of dormant buds from the Hpimaw pass. These were packed with ice in bamboo tubes, and transported to London in the refrigerated hold of a P & O liner as a gift to King George V. This introduction has probably persisted to the present day (**FCC** 1962) and has varied in colour from ice-blue and white to a poor lilac. (Bot. Mag. t.9527 (1936)).

In 1982, Bob Mitchell introduced plants from the Cang Shan, to give rise to the 'Dali strain'. These plants had fringed petal-lobes of a rich royal blue and a marked inner white zone. They were exceptionally beautiful. Although similar plants can sometimes be seen in cultivation in 2001, it is likely that most survivors today have a mixed parentage. ARGS brought home plants from Zhongdian and Da Xue Shan in 2000 and Peter Cox introduced material from the Mekong-Salween divide in 1995.

Vegetative increase is slow in this species, which is usually propagated from fresh seed. It usually flowers in a year, when it is worth selecting the best colour forms. In areas with a less reliable snow-cover it is best cloched, although care should be taken that the bud does not become too dry. It is susceptible to both weevil and summer heat which causes basal rot. This is a tricky species which has become no more common or easy in recent years (2001), and is certainly harder to manage than *P. bhutanica*. It is probably fair to say that without the strenuous efforts of John Mattingley of Cluny who has raised many hundreds of seedlings in boxes annually which were donated to less worthy recipients (including myself), *P. sonchifolia* would probably not have persisted as well as it has. Cluny stands nearly 300 m above Loch Tay in Perthshire in cool, humid, forested conditions closely resembling those in the wild. Parents are placed besides streamsides and waterfalls where they are cloched in winter and cross-pollinated. Seedling plant boxes are placed under an open canopy and watered daily when in growth. However, considered hardy and permanent at Tromso in north Norway, and grows well in Glendoick near Perth.

HYBRIDIZATION AND VARIATION

The only known hybrid is with *P. whitei* (p.181). Seedlings can be very variable in flower colour.

A form with very dissected leaves has been separated as subsp. *emeiensis* Hu (1990) (fig. Halda: 162), but similar plants seem to occur in many populations.

Primula hookeri Watt, J. Linn. Soc. Bot. 20: 14 (1882)

P. vernicosa Ward (1916)

DESCRIPTION A very small plant, flowering from dark green narrow non-mealy resting buds as they develop. *Leaves* oblong and nearly entire, to 4 × 1 cm at flowering, becoming longer, broader, white-stalked and deeply toothed in the summer. *Flowers* few, stemless at flowering, but forming a thick whitish stem which elongates rapidly to overtop the leaves in fruit, flowering stalks very short (to 1–2 mm) and thick at flowering, elongating, and becoming even thicker in fruit. *Calyx* 5–8 mm, bell-shaped, dark green or reddish, the sepal-lobes triangular to rounded, entire to toothed. *Corolla* white, cream or violet with a white eye, usually homostyle, cup-shaped, to 10 mm in diameter, usually less, the tube exceeding the calyx; corolla-lobes oblong, not overlapping, truncate to slightly notched. Flowering February–April, often melting a hole in the snow in the wild. (Fig. 16).

Fig. 16. *P. hookeri*

DISTRIBUTION Scattered throughout the Sino-himalaya from central Nepal, through Sikkim, Bhutan, south-east Tibet to northern Burma, Sichuan and Yunnan as far as the Salween–Mekong divide. Apparently thinly distributed, and rarely enountered, but inconspicuous. Mossy forest floors, open hillsides, mosses amongst stones, gravelly avalanche slopes sodden with melting snow, 3300–5000 m '... in the very snow water, amongst slabs of slate ... also on bare earth of open fir forests'.

P. hookeri and *P. vernicosa* were kept apart by Smith and Fletcher (1944) on the basis of the latter being larger with homostyle flowers, and with toothed, veined sepal-lobes. However, all material referred to these species is rather uniform and presents a very distinct facies. I consider differences in size to be merely a matter of vigour, while conspicuous variation in sepal-lobe shape occurs within populations. All the material I have examined has been homostylous.

This inconspicuous plant resembles no other, and the very short thick flower-stalks, and in fruit the long thick stems, are instantly recognizable.

CULTIVATION First introduced by Ward 94 by seed (flowered 1916), and by Ludlow and Sherriff, 3637 in 1938 and 21214 (1949) by air. Latterly introduced in 1961 (Lowndes?), 1973 (Beer). Later introductions may survive in small quantities. Short-lived in cultivation, but sets seed readily (being self-fertile). A small uncharismatic plant, scarcely worth growing.

VARIATION Var. *violacea* (Smith) A.J. Richards (1993). (*P. vernicosa* Ward var. *violacea* Smith, Notes Roy. Bot. Gdn. Edinb. 19: 214 (1937)) has violet-purple flowers. No hybrids have been recorded.

Primula bomiensis Chen & Hu, Acta Phytotaxonomica Sinica 18: 383–4 (1980)

DESCRIPTION Differs from *P. hookeri* by its purple exannulate heterostylous flowers which are borne on a slender stem equal in length to the leaves at flowering; the sepals are acute and entire and the stem and flower stalks do not thicken at fruiting. From woods at 3750 m at Guhsiang, Pome (Bomi), Tibet. There is a figure in the original description, also Halda: 146.

Primula chionata Smith, Notes Roy. Bot. Gdn. Edinb. 15: 81 (1925)

DESCRIPTION Flowering from large narrow resting buds as they develop, bud-scales 1.5 cm, dark red. *Leaves* dark green with a broad white mid-rib, without meal, the blades oval, deeply lacerated, often to the mid-rib towards the base, and even 2-pinnatifid, the narrowly winged petiole pale. *Stems* absent or short at flowering, elongating later; flowers few, borne on long narrow stalks to 6 cm. *Calyx* tube-shaped, long, to 13 mm, often reddish, divided into heavily and multiply veined sharp entire oval petal-like lobes. *Corolla* pale yellow, cream or violet with an orange eye, flat-faced, to 30 mm in diameter, the broad tube scarcely exceeding the calyx; corolla lobes ovate, with a deep notch. (Fig. Halda: 160 (n.b. the sepal characters of the two figures in Halda: 160 seem to have been switched)).

DISTRIBUTION Only known from the southern Pemako side of two passes over the main range above Pe in the Tsangpo valley of south-east Tibet, the Doshong La and Deyang La. Wet grassy alpine slopes and bogs, or amongst boulders, often by melting snow, 4000–4700 m. This is an extremely wet region with a very high snowfall.

Primula chionata (not to be confused with the familar 'nivalid' *P. chionantha*) is a very distinctive species with its lacerated leaves, reminiscent in shape to those of the dog-daisy, *Leucanthemum vulgare*, and its large leaf-like reddish sepals. Yellow and violet (var. *violacea* Smith) colour forms are found in both of the known localities. For distinctions with *P. chionogenes*, see below. *P. chionata* has never been in cultivation.

Primula chionogenes Fletcher, J. Linn. Soc. 52: 337 (1942)

P. chamaethauma Smith var. *chiukiangensis* Chen (1939)

DESCRIPTION Differs from *P. chionata* as follows: bud-scales larger, to 4 × 1.5 cm; leaf-blades rugose and shiny, stiff, deeply and narrrowly toothed, but not lacerate. Sepal-lobes not petal-like, with a single obscure nerve, sharp and toothed. Corolla deep golden yellow with a paler eye and tube, the mouth of the tube hairy; corolla-lobes notched to lacerate. Photo: A Quest of Flowers 173. (Fig. Halda: 160 (as *P. chamaethauma*)). Flowering as the snow melts.

DISTRIBUTION From the south, Pachakshiri, side of three passes over the main range in the Tsari region of south-east Tibet, south of the Tsangpo, to the south west of *P. chionata,* the Chubumba La, Tsari Sama and Lo La. Also, just to the Assam side of the frontier with Tibet on the Poshong La. Open alpine hillsides, especially at the foot of cliffs and avalanche slopes, 3300–3700 m. This is another extremely wet region.

P. chionogenes is a fairly close but distinct relative of *P. chionata*, and they inhabit corresponding niches in neighbouring but different parts of the main Himalayan range in this very remote region. It is a very attractive plant, more so than *P. chionata*, and looks superficially like *P. aureata*, although lacking meal, and deciduous.

CULTIVATION Introduced by air from the Lo La in 1938 (Ludlow & Sherriff 3648); lost at Edinburgh

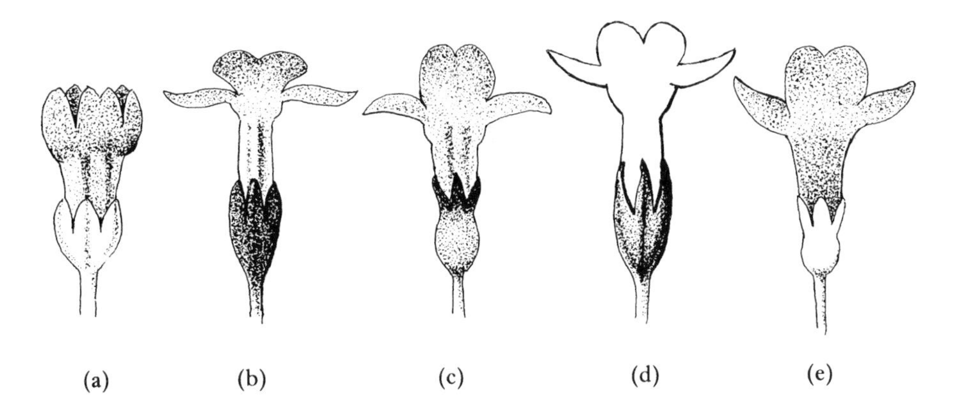

Fig. 17. Corolla and calyx characters of *P. griffithii* (a), *P. calderiana* (b, c), *P. tanneri* (d) and *P. griffithii* × *tanneri* (e)

after about six years, but cultivated elsewhere until about 1955.

Sherriff recorded hybrids with *P. tanneri* on the Chubumba La.

Subsection **Griffithii** Smith & Fletcher, Trans. Roy. Soc. Edinb. 61: 274 (1944)

Deciduous; roots robust thongs; resting buds borne at or below soil surface; leaves not or somewhat heterophyllous, entire to finely crenate-toothed. Stems usually well-developed at flowering, usually equalling leaves. Flowers usually yellow or purple, annulate.

Primula griffithii (Watt) Pax, Bot. Jahrb. 10: 213 (1889)

P. obtusifolia Royle var. *griffithii* Watt (1882)

DESCRIPTION *Roots* black; resting buds sharp, yellow-mealy, bluish; bud scales large, often reddish, to 3× 2 cm. *Leaf-blades* dark bluish-green, mealy when young, oval and sharply pointed, the margins recurved and finely toothed, base cuneate, the stalk winged and whitish; leaf elongating considerably after flowering. *Stem* usually equalling leaves, mealy; flowers up to 20 together, stalks to 4 cm, mealy; bracts small, to 10 × 1 mm at flowering, but becoming leaf-like and much larger in fruit, and capable of forming a plantlet in the same way as in *P. bracteosa* and *P. taliensis*. *Calyx* broadly bell-shaped, short, to 7 mm, blackish and mealy with short broad sharp sepal-lobes. *Corolla* deep clear royal blue with a narrow golden annulus, flat-faced, to 25 mm diameter, the broad tube exceeding the calyx; corolla-lobes rounded, overlapping, notched. Flowering April. (Plate 10.) (Photo: Bull. AGS 67: 393.)

DISTRIBUTION Limited to a small area of west Bhutan, notably above Paro, and the Ha valley; and the neighbouring Chumbi valley, south Tibet. Mossy rocks and peaty turf in rhododendron scrub, and in *Abies* and juniper forest, 3500–3900 m.

P. griffithii is a most beautiful and distinctive species which has been found to vary little. Like its relatives (below) it has the appearence of a 'nivalid' primula (section Crystallophlomis), although with 'petiolarid' capsules. Most plants cultivated under this name are hybrids with *P. tanneri*. Only the true species, a much finer plant, has royal blue flowers, a blackish bell-shaped calyx and sharply pointed leaves. An alternative opinion is held by at least one Scottish grower in 2001, who considered that the wide range of colours he obtains from seed is typical of the species. Herbarium studies of wild material suggest that he is incorrect.

CULTIVATION Introduced only by Sherriff 19610, 19611 as flown-home dormant buds from the Ha La in 1949. The surviving plants proved to be all thrum flowered. These thrived in a few gardens, notably Keillour (**AM** 1953), and Kilbryde, Corbridge. However, vegetative increase was slow, and the only seed set was hybrid. The Kilbryde colony survived a good deal of neglect on a north-facing raised bed in full shade continuously fed by a spring-line, the roots deeply embedded in thick yellow clay. In 1975 and 1976, after hot weather at flowering, most plants in this strong colony fruited well for the first time in 25 years (and incidentally set scape-buds, most of which also rooted). Over 150 seedlings, both pin and thrum, were raised and were distributed widely. Most flowered in the first year, but have only done so occasionally since. The true plant can still be occasionally obtained through the trade, but in recent years most seedlings have once again proved to be hybrid.

HYBRIDIZATION Hybrids were reported with *P. bhutanica* at Bodnant, and a hybrid with *P. whitei* was found at Ascreavie (p. 182). At Keillour both accidental and intentional hybrids were raised with the various forms of *P. tanneri*. The best of these were the rich purple 'Royalty' (× *tanneri tsariensis* 'porrecta') (**AM** 1965), and 'Fan-tail' (probably × *tanneri alba*) which had whitish flowers with a central blue blotch. The latter clone was still in cultivation in 1987, and Mundey raised possibly selfed seedlings of it. Unfortunately most hybrids of *P. griffithii* prove to have flowers of a disagreeable muddy purple, and should they flower, superior forms should be carefully selected.

In about 1993, Ray Fairburn of Allendale, Northumberland, UK raised a very beautiful deep blue hybrid with *P. pulchra*, intermediate in most features but showing the rhizomatous spreading power of the latter. This still survived in 2000, but seems not to have been widely dispersed.

Primula calderiana Balf. f & Cooper, Notes Roy. Bot. Gdn. Edinb. 9: 7 (1915)

P. roylei (Hook. f.) Balf. f. & Smith (1916)
P. roylei Balf. f. & Smith subsp. *calderiana* (Balf. f. & Cooper) Smith & Forrest (1928)
P. roylei Balf. f. & Smith subsp. *dianae* (Balf. f. & Cooper) Smith & Forrest (1928)
P. obtusifolia Royle var. *roylei* Hook. f. (1882) p.p.
P. gammieana King (1916)
P. strumosa Balf. f. & Cooper (1916)

DESCRIPTION *Roots* blackish; resting buds blunt, greenish, often cream-mealy. *Leaf-blades* oblanceolate, dark green, almost entire, to 18 × 4 cm at flowering, elongating further later but not heterophyllous, often mealy when young, cuneate into a short often reddish stalk below. *Stems* mealy, equalling or exceeding leaves at flowering, bearing 2–25 flowers on spreading mealy stalks to 3 cm. *Calyx* bell-shaped, mealy, dark, to 8 mm, cut into blunt oval sepal-lobes. *Corolla* deep purple to cherry red, yellow, or white, usually with an orange annulus, flat-faced, to 28 mm in diameter; corolla-tube mealy outside, about twice the length of the calyx; corolla-lobes scarcely wavy, scarcely overlapping, broadly rounded and usually not notched; scented disagreeably or sweetly to some. Flowering May. (Photo: Riddle of the Tsangpo Gorge: 122.) (Plates 10, 35, 36, 79, Fig.17.)

DISTRIBUTION West Nepal to south-east Tibet as far as the Tsangpo bend, Assam. In moderately wet zones; alpine turf, avalanche slopes, broad wet marshes, and mossy clearings under fir, pine and rhododendron; locally abundant; 3200–4800 m.

P. calderiana has a very confused taxonomic history caused in part by its superficial resemblance to certain 'nivalid' primulas, notably the western Himalayan *P. obtusifolia;* and in part by its variability in flower colour. The earliest epithet to relate to Hooker's original Sikkim plant is var. *roylei* (1882), but part of the material used by Hooker is indeed *P. obtusifolia* from further west. Although Royle's collections were from the western Himalaya, Balfour and Smith had intended that this more easterly petiolarid should be called *P. roylei*, with the epithets *calderiana, gammieana* and *dianae* taking a lesser rank. However, a fluke of publication resulted in the prior publication of *P. calderiana* at specific rank, which in view of the confusion surrounding the name *roylei,* was a fortunate happenstance.

In 1949, Sherriff, on encountering hybrid populations in central Bhutan, noted that *Primula strumosa* is essentially a yellow-flowered version of the purple *P. calderiana*. Nevertheless, perhaps because they essentially inhabit different regions (below), and to some people have a different smell, these species were separated until Richards (1977). Yet, there is no structural or ecological difference between them, their hybrids are fully fertile, and yellow/purple flower colour variation is common in many *Primula* species. Flower colour, alone amongst a host of other distinguishing features, had even sufficiently seduced Smith & Fletcher (1944) to suggest that *P. strumosa* might in fact be conspecific not with *P. calderiana*, but with the yellow *P. nepalensis*, which is in fact the western variant of the otherwise purple *P. tanneri*.

It is noteworthy that in both of the related widespread species *P. calderiana* and *P. tanneri*, it is the western race which is yellow, and the eastern which is purple flowered.

P. calderiana is a very variable species which in some of its forms is a superb plant in the wild, although it very rarely fulfils its potential in the garden. It is only likely to be confused with *P. tanneri*. For distinctions, see under that species.

CULTIVATION First introduced by 1887 (Bot. Mag. t.6956), but apparently soon lost. Reintroduced by Ludlow and Sherriff in 1937 (1754) and on several subsequent occasions. More recent introductions have included those by Lowndes in 1950 (1452), Stainton, Sykes and Williams 1954 (3609), Beer 1973, Millais 1982, the AGS 1983 Sikkim expedition (AGSES 570, 651), KEKE 689, by Anne Chambers from the Nyima La in 1995 and Tony Cox from the Bimbi La in 2000.

Formerly, a few gardens in the Scottish Highlands, notably Keillour, Cluny and Inshriach, grew a range of forms well outside, although most of these I saw were hybrid. In recent years, Anne Chambers' Nyima La seed collection has proved successful for a number of growers and has been offered through the trade. It is a beautiful strain, very white-mealy, and with lustrous dark purple flowers with a blackish eye. In common with many alpine primulas from the Himalaya, the natural conditions of a cool, deep, fertile, wet but well-drained site in summer, combined with relatively dry winter conditions under snow are difficult to provide in the average garden, but I have had good success when open-ground plants were covered with a frame-light from October–March. Two plants have flowered for four successive years in these conditions and have set plenty of viable seed. Subsp. *strumosa* is considered hardy and permanent at Tromso in north Norway, although it is in general less permanent in the garden.

VARIATION

- Subsp. *calderiana*. Flowers purple; flowers disagreeably smelling of bad fish to some. East Nepal eastwards; mostly above 3700 m. (Plate 35.)
- Var. *alba* (Smith) Smith & Fletcher (1944). Flowers white. Often found in company with subsp. *calderiana*, but not with subsp. *strumosa*. A good white form (or hybrid? see below) which flowered freely was introduced by Sherriff in 1949 (19175) and named after its location 'Waitung', **AM** 1964.
- Subsp. *strumosa* (Balf. f. & Cooper) Richards (1976). Flowers yellow; flowers very sweetly scented to some, or less commonly 'fishy'. West Nepal to east Bhutan. (Plate 10, 36.)

Where subsp. *calderiana* and subsp. *strumosa* grow together in the wild, they cross freely to produce a range of intermediate flower colours '... at Waitung, the coloured hybrids, white, powder-blue, violet, cream, yellow and the rest had taken possession'.

HYBRIDIZATION Hybridization is only recorded with *P. tanneri*. This sometimes results in spectacular hybrid swarms in the wild: 'We came to a little grassy hollow and here we found the most extraordinary collection of coloured primulas. There must have been the most awful intermarriage going on. There was *P. calderiana*, quite true and apart. Then there were all shades of colours from mixtures of 3366 (white form of *tsariensis*), of 3367 (blue-violet *tsariensis*), and of 3383 (golden yellow *strumosa* var. *peralata*). I counted seven variations in colour, and all were mixed together.'

However, Sherriff who made these observations in central Bhutan in 1937, also noted that such hybrids only occur very locally, and claimed that they only arose from crosses between what are today recognized as forms of *P. tanneri* (*tsariensis* and *strumosa perlata*). A study of these herbarium specimens clearly indicates that *P. calderiana* was also involved in the hybridization, however.

In the garden, intentional crosses between forms of *P. calderiana* and *P. tanneri* have been made by R.B. Cooke and the Knox-Finlays amongst others. In other gardens, for instance Cluny, self-sowing hybrid swarms arose. These plants were of a wide variety of colours including deep purple, crimson, apricot, orange and cream. Crimson and cream forms (at least) still survive. Most are partially or completely sterile. Most clones called 'calderiana' or 'strumosa' today seem to have been derived from these hybrids.

Primula laeta Smith, Notes Roy. Bot. Gdn. Edinb. 19: 211 (1937)

DESCRIPTION A close relative of *P. calderiana*, but taller and more elegant, very heavily mealy with meal persisting on the underside of the leaves, the calyx narrower and extending to 10 mm, and the corolla very deep plum-red, sometimes lacking a golden annulus. From two neighbouring passes, the Lo La and Tsari Sama in south-east Tibet, high rainfall areas with deep snow cover, 4300–4500 m. This beautiful plant has never been in cultivation. What appears to have been a hybrid swarm between this species and *P. calderiana* was photographed on the nearby Bimbi La by Tony Cox in 2000, 'coarse scree at 4650 m'.

Primula jucunda Smith, Notes Roy. Bot. Gdn. Edinb. 19: 209 (1937)

DESCRIPTION Another close relative of *P. calderiana* (subsp. *strumosa*), but heavily mealy with thick meal persisting on the underside of the leaves, the leaf-blade with a truncate base, so more resembling *P. tanneri* in shape, and with a distinctive calyx 10 mm long, with very narrow lobes cut almost to the base. Despite Smith, the golden flowers are apparently exannulate.

Only known from between Migytun, Mipa and the Bimbi La, east Tsari, south-east Tibet, 3700–5000 m, 50 km west of *P. laeta*.

Primula hilaris Smith, Notes Roy. Bot. Gdn. Edinb. 19: 209 (1937)

DESCRIPTION Another localized relative of *P. calderiana* from the Tsari region, south-east Tibet where active speciation in this group is occurring. Differs from its relatives in particular by the large rounded and pinnately veined lobes to the calyx. The pale yellow flowers are very large, to 40 mm in diameter, and the broad corolla-tube is up to 3× the calyx. Only known from the Kashong La, 4000–5000 m, among rocks on steep open hillsides. This site lies 40 km to the south-west of *P. jucunda*. *P. hilaris* was introduced by Sherriff in 1938 as flown-home plants, but only persisted a short time.

Primula tanneri King, J. Asian Soc. Bengal 55: 227 (1886)

P. nepalensis Smith (1931)
P. tsariensis Smith (1937)
P. strumosa Balf. f. & Cooper var. *peralata* Smith & Fletcher (1944)

DESCRIPTION Differs from *P. calderiana* as follows: roots orange; resting buds small, sharp, lacking meal, as is the whole plant. Leaves heterophyllous, similar to *P. calderiana* at flowering (but lacking meal), later developing a narrowly winged stalk, the blade becoming oval with a truncate base, regularly crenate-toothed. Calyx to 10 mm, the lobes narrow and more or less sharp, lacking meal. Corolla lobes wavy, overlapping, notched; flower unscented. 2n = 22. (Plates 10, 37, 79, Fig. 17.) (Photo: Bull.AGS: 67: 409.)

DISTRIBUTION Very similar to *P. calderiana*, from west Nepal to the Tsangpo bend in south-east Tibet. Alpine meadows, usually amongst melting snow in moderately wet zones, 2500–4900 m, often locally abundant.

The purple-flowered *P. tsariensis* was first detected by Sherriff in 1936, growing with *P. calderiana* at Tsari, Tibet, from which it differed by its lack of meal or scent. Ludlow and Sherriff later collected material from many sites in Bhutan and Tibet, showing it to be a very variable species in stature, flower size and flower colour, white and yellow forms also occurring (e.g. 3366, 3367). Unfortunately, Smith failed to equate this material to the little-known *P. tanneri* from Sikkim and west Bhutan, considering that the leaf-shape was different. However, *P. tanneri* falls comfortably within the wide morphological range of *P. tsariensis* and is the prior name.

Although Sherriff found yellow forms of *P. tsariensis*, Smith never equated these with *P. nepalensis*, which he considered to be dubiously distinct from *P. strumosa*. Confusingly, Smith also described a yellow plant of Sherriff's, growing with and otherwise indistingishable from *P. tsariensis, P. strumosa* var. *perlata*. These plants are all quite clearly yellow forms of *P. tanneri*, for which the earliest available name is *nepalensis*. As for *P. calderiana,* the yellow form tends to be more westerly and the purple more easterly in their distribution. However, on at least two occasions in Bhutan, Sherriff found purple, yellow and white forms mixed and hybridizing, as he had also found for *P. calderiana*.

CULTIVATION Subsp. *tsariensis* was introduced in 1935 by Ward, and later by Ludlow and Sherriff (3367, 17140). They also introduced the magnificent var. *porrecta* (3673), var. *alba* (19835), and subsp. *nepalensis* (21015). Subsp. *tanneri* was originally introduced in 1910 (Cooper?), but did not persist.

In common with the forms of *P. calderiana*, *P. tanneri* requires a cool site in a deep, fertile humus soil. On the whole more tractable than *P. calderiana*, surviving and flowering better away from the Scottish Highlands. A range of forms, some of which are certainly hybrid, can still be seen, and are sometimes offered. Unfortunately, those most commonly met are poor relations of var. *porrecta* and the original, golden-flowered, black-stemmed forms of var. *nepalensis*. In the 1950s and 1960s, gardens such as Keillour had wonderful plantings of both of these. Nowadays (2001) only poor, small-flowered cream versions of var. *nepalensis* seem to have survived, although great swarms of different colours still self-sow at Cluny. Alan Furness seems to have been instrumental in maintaining from seed a good stock of a large-flowered, plum-purple strain of *tsariensis* from seed which is close to the original var. *porrecta*. Considered hardy and permanent in north Norway (Tromso).

VARIATION

- Subsp. *tanneri*. Flowers not exceeding 20 mm in diameter, dull purple; habit slender. Forests and mountain slopes; east Nepal, Sikkim and west Bhutan.
- Subsp. *tsariensis* (Smith) Richards (1976). Flowers to 28 mm diameter, often rich purple; habit robust. Alpine grassland from Chumbi to the Tsangpo bend.
- Var. *porrecta* Smith (1937). This name was given to a magnificently large-flowered and richly purple form of *P. tsariensis* (**AM** 1962).
- Var. *alba* Richards (1976). Flowers white. **AM** 1969.
- Subsp. *nepalensis* (Smith) Richards (1976). Flowers to 28 mm diameter, yellow; stems often blackish; habit various. Alpine grasslands from west Nepal to east Bhutan.

HYBRIDIZATION For hybrids with *P. calderiana*, see above. On the Chubumbu La in 1938, Sherriff found a population of apparent hybrids between *P. tanneri* subsp. *tsariensis* and *P. chiogenes*, with 'pale purplish yellow to a dull yellowish purple' flowers (!).

Primula pulchra Watt, J. Linn. Soc. 20: 3 (1882)

P. chamaethauma Smith (1927)
P. chamaedoron Smith (1937)

DESCRIPTION A *dwarf* plant forming small sharp oval dark green to reddish resting buds. *Leaves* dark green and rather shiny, heterophyllous, at first flowering bluntly rhomboid with a broad and poorly marked pale stalk, and scarcely toothed, soon developing a distinct narrowly oval, blunt to pointed crenately toothed blade to 9 × 3 cm and a narrowly winged whitish stalk. *Flowers* stemless at first flowering, soon developing a pale fleshy stem which may equal the leaves, bearing 1–10 flowers on stalks elongating finally to 3 cm or more. *Calyx* narrowly bell-shaped, to 10 mm but often shorter, lacking meal, with entire lanceolate sharp lobes. *Corolla* violet to rich purple with a small yellow to orange eye, annulate, to 30 mm in diameter, flat-faced or slightly cup-shaped; the tube 1.5× the calyx; corolla-lobes ovate, overlapping, notched. Flowering as the snow melts. (The photo in Flowers of the Himalayas (supplement) is *P. gambeliana*, and the figs. in Halda: 159 as *P. chamaedoron* and 160 as *P. chamaethauma* seem to be of *P. bhutanica* and *P. chionogenes* respectively.) (Plate 10.)

DISTRIBUTION Widespread but scarce and thinly distributed through much of the Himalaya, apparently never common; central Nepal (Langtang) to east Sikkim, north-east Bhutan, south-east Tibet, mostly in the Tsari and Pachakshiri districts, north Assam, and disjunct on the Burma-Tibet frontier at Achung. Wet avalanche slopes and high alpine grassland, thinly vegetated glacial valleys, etc. 3500–5000 m.

P. pulchra is yet another species with a confused taxonomic history. It was originally known by Hooker from Sikkim, where it is evidently scarce and very little material was available to Smith and Fletcher (1944). They placed it in association with the Chinese *P. tongolensis*, a species of uncertain affinity, but admitted that they were not closely related, and that '... *P. pulchra* will ultimately be recognized as a petiolarid ...' After Nepal became accessible in the 1950s, this species was also found there and became better known.

In the meantime, Ward, and Ludlow and Sherriff had found similar plants much further to the east in the 1930s. It seems not to have occurred to Smith and his co-workers to compare these with *P. pulchra*, and they were rather surprisingly classified in subsection Sonchifolia, although they lacked meal or very toothed leaves. Smith described two new species, *P. chamaethauma* and *P. chamaedoron* from this material, but these seem to differ only in robustness and developmental state. *P. chamaedoron* can be regarded as a congested high alpine state of the other. They are identical to *P. pulchra* in every way. Smith regards *P. pulchra* as being exannulate, and *P. chamaethauma* and *P. chamaedoron* annulate, but *P. pulchra* is also annulate.

Now that it is established in cultivation, we can recognize *P. pulchra* as being essentially a dwarf high alpine relative of *P. tanneri*.

CULTIVATION Introduced from the Tsari district and the Lo La as flown-home plants by Sherriff in 1936. It was grown successfully, particularly at Keillour, but also at Edinburgh, Kilbryde and elsewhere. Latterly, good stands at Keillour, identified as both *P. chamaethauma* and *P. chamaedoron*, had been collected by Marjorie Brough from Nepal in 1955–6. These had disappeared by 1965.

P. pulchra was reintroduced by George Smith from Sikkim, probably in 1985. A fragment (thrum) was given to Mike and Polly Stone at Fort Augustus, where it has thrived and has set seed to give rise to both pin and thrum seedlings. This form produces new rosettes from the roots, and is readily propagated. In 2001 it is still intermittently available in the trade, and a number of growers are succeeding with it. This form flowers freely, bearing a few relatively huge purple flowers on its dwarf rosette (**PC** 1991).

HYBRIDIZATION See *P. griffithii* (p. 186).

Primula calthifolia Smith, Notes Roy. Bot. Gdn. Edinb. 15: 300 (1927)

DESCRIPTION A non-mealy relative of *P. tanneri* subsp. *nepalensis*, but with short rounded leaf-blades, looking as the description suggests like those of kingcups, *Caltha*.

The bud-scales and young foliage are reddish and the calyx very short and widely cup-shaped. The petal-lobes of the golden flowers are rounded and entire. Known only from the Burma–Tibet–Assam frontier area around the headwaters of the Mali and Lohit, about 200 km to the south-east of its relatives' nearest sites. Extremely wet slopes at about 4000 m.

Primula tongolensis Franchet, Journ. de Bot. 9: 453 (1895)

P. dielsii Petitm. (1907)
P. gentianoides Smith & Ward (1923)

DESCRIPTION A small non-mealy plant with narrowly spoon-shaped leaves and basally produced violet flowers with deeply notched narrow petals. West Sichuan, 'marshes' and open grassy meadows, 4000–4500 m. This mysterious and little-understood plant has the appearence of a small Oreophlomis species, for instance *P. elliptica*, but it has a 'petiolarid' capsule.

Section **Crystallophlomis** (Rupr.) Federov, Fl. SSSR 18: 143 (1952)

Crystallophlomis Rupr., Bull. Acad. Imp. Sci. St. Petersb. 6: 218 (1863) sin.stat.
Type species *P. nivalis* Pall.
(Section Nivales Pax 1889)
(Section Purpurea Watt 1904)

DESCRIPTION *Plants* deciduous, overwintering as a resting bud, which is often large, mealy and above ground. *Leaves* with revolute vernation, narrowly spear-shaped, decurrent onto the usually sheath-like stalks, entire to minutely toothed, hairless, often fleshy, usually mealy. *Inflorescences* stemmed, forming an umbel or superimposed whorls. *Bracts* small. *Flowers* purple, blue, yellow or white, often mealy, annulate or exannulate, heterostyle or homostyle. *Corolla-lobes* usually entire. *Pollen* oblate, 3-syncolpate. *Capsules* elongate, or rarely rounded, usually exceeding the calyx, usually dehiscing by apical valves. *Seeds* quadrate, usually pale brown and reticulate, somewhat fleshy. Chromosome number 2n = 22. Heterostyle species usually fully self-incompatible. Flowering spring.

DISTRIBUTION Asia, from north-east Turkey and the Urals to Burma and Kamschatka; Alaska.

Species of alpine meadows, rocks and tundra, almost always above the tree-line, typically in very wet regions with deep winter snow, growing in heavy soils saturated by snow-melt.

Although a very widespread section, there is an extraordinary concentration of species in mountains on the borders of Sichuan, Yunnan and Tibet, around the Tsarong, Muli and Mekong–Yangtse divide region. According to Smith and Fletcher (1942) no less than 19 species occur in this limited region, although in this account this number is reduced to 12.

Ruprecht's Crystallophlomis were published without rank at a time when the sectional rank was rarely used. Although Pax's publication at sectional rank used the familiar name Nivales, Federov's combination is validated if it is considered that Ruprecht envisaged a rank and scope equivalent to Pax's later section. Horticulturally, however, these plants have always been called the 'nivalids', and for convenience I shall continue to use this name informally.

Although a very large and widespread group of species which are subdivided into four subsections, the nivalids seem to form a very coherent and natural group, both morphologically and ecologically. As yet, the DNA of only four species, from two subsections, has been examined, and these species form a fairly tightly linked assemblage, apparently sister to a Cordifoliae species, and, less expectedly, to *P. fedtschenkoi*. The DNA evidence also weakly supports the proposition that the nivalids evolved from forerunners of species nowadays classified in the present sections Proliferae and Petiolares. The resemblance to some species in the latter section had already been noted under that heading. Present members of the Proliferae such as *P. poissonii* and *P. secundiflora* also rather resemble nivalids such as *P. obtusifolia*, from which they differ principally by globose capsules.

However, members of section Oreophlomis, which also superficially resemble some nivalids, and the remainder of subgenus *Aleuritia*, are not related to the Crystallophlomis. Consequently my earlier suggestion (1993) that the nivalids take a basal position with respect to subgenus *Aleuritia* appears to be mistaken. Although the American section Parryi superficially resemble the nivalids, and were originally classified there, it is clear from their involute vernation, chromosome number and other features that they are not related. Presumably their resemblance to the nivalids has also arisen in parallel response to similar growing conditions.

CULTIVATION Regrettably, with a few exceptions, the nivalids are amongst the most intransigent of all primulas in cultivation. Although many have been introduced, only *P. chionantha* and *P. macrophylla* have proved at all persistent in garden conditions, although this may also prove to be true for *P. orbicularis*. Most of the remaining species tend to rot in the winter, grow poorly in the summer, are very susceptible to summer heat and drought, and rarely set viable seed.

Doubtless, this intractability can be explained by the ecological niche favoured by this group. Plants which occur in areas with flowing water which are very wet during the short cool growing season, but are relatively dry and protected from climatic extremes under deep snow during the long resting period, respond very poorly to most garden conditions. It is not surprising that the most success has been achieved in gardens in the Scottish Highlands, such as Inshriach, whose conditions approximate most closely to those found in the wild.

In less favoured conditions, the greatest likelihood of success is to be achieved by planting in rich, well-drained but water-retentive conditions in a cool shaded place where the resting buds are kept dry by cloching during the winter. Pot culture seems rarely to be successful.

However, *P. chionantha* and its allies are relatively permanent and vigorous in the open garden in soils which remain moist throughout the summer.

In this section, hybridization seems to be rare and is limited to the *P. chionantha* group which is here treated as one species.

KEY TO SUBSECTIONS

1. Flowers large, few, funnel-shaped, somewhat zygomorphic, usually exannulate; resting buds large, egg-shaped, above ground 2
1. Flowers not exceeding 25 mm in diameter, rotate, flat-faced or lobes reflexed; resting buds at or below ground, not massive 3

2. Flowers usually yellow, exannulate; capsules dehiscing by a membrane ....subs. **Agleniana**
2. Flowers usually pink or blue, if yellow then annulate; capsules valvate ....subs. **Calliantha**

3. Corolla lobes usually narrow, often reflexed, blackish, dark red or yellow; resting bud conspicuous, orbicular ....subs. **Maximowiczii**
3. Corolla lobes not more than 1.5 × as long as wide, not reflexed; resting bud usually not conspicuous subs. ....**Crystallophlomis**

Subsection **Crystallophlomis**

Flowers usually flat-faced, usually annulate, corolla-lobes usually entire; capsules usually exceeding the calyx. Resting buds usually not massive or above-ground.

KEY TO SPECIES

1. Flowers yellow 2
1. Flowers purple, rarely white 9

2. Plant dwarf, to 5 cm; flowers 1–4 together 3
2. Plant usually exceeding 5 cm; flowers usually 4 or more together 4

3. Flowers rarely more than two on a stem; leaves linear ....*P. crocifolia*
3. Flowers two or more together; leaves narrowly spoon-shaped ....*P. cerina*

4. Leaves prostrate or spreading at flowering, blade not more than 2 × as long as wide 5
4. Leaves erect at flowering, the blade at least 2 × as long as wide 7

5. Calyx teeth rounded; bracts ca. 3 cm ....*P. poluninii*
5. Calyx teeth sharp; bracts not exceeding 2 cm 6

6. Corolla-lobes rounded; calyx to 14 mm ....*P. soongii*
6. Corolla-lobes notched; calyx not exceeding 10 mm ....*P. elongata*

7. Calyx narrow, blackish, lined with meal ....*P. duthieana*
7. Calyx not blackish 8

8. Flower stalks not exceeding 15 mm in flower; bracts not exceeding 10 mm ....*P. orbicularis*
8. Flower stalks exceeding 15 mm in flower; bracts exceeding 10 mm ....*P. stuartii*

9. Leaves entire, crenate or shortly toothed 10
9. Leaves with large teeth or pinnatifid 29

10. Largest leaves more than 5 cm wide, rounded at the apex, flat, thin in texture 11
10. All leaves less than 5 cm wide, or if wider, usually keeled and/or with revolute edges and of a thicker texture, obtuse to sharp but not usually rounded at apex 13

11. Flowers annulate, violet-blue 12
11. Flowers exannulate, purple ....*P. obtusifolia*

12. Calyx spreading to patent, cut to base ....*P. youngeriana*
12. Calyx erect, cut to less than half-way ....*P. woonyoungiana*

13. Dwarf plant to 5 cm, flowers 1–3 together, rather pale lilac or blue 14
13. If less than 5 cm or flowers less than 3, then flowers purple 16

14. Corolla-tube very narrow, more than 2× calyx ....*P. minor*
14. Corolla-tube less than 2× calyx 15

15. Leaf margin toothed; corolla concolorous ....*P. diantha*
15. Leaf margin entire; corolla with a white eye ....*P. brevicula*

16. Flowers white, sometimes turning pale pink 17
16. Flowers pink to purple or blue 18

17. Flowers annulate; leaves crenate .... *P. crassifolia*
17. Flowers exannulate; leaves usually entire or nearly so .... *P. chionantha*

18. Flowers pale lilac-pink with a darker purple tube 19
18. Corolla-tube not obviously darker than limb 22

19. Plant with at least some meal, e.g. on stem and calyx 20
19. Plant lacking any meal 21

20. Plant base with sheathing leaves, leek-like .... *P. farreriana*
20. Plant base slender, not leek-like .... *P. limbata*

21. Leaves less than 5 cm, toothed .... *P. optata*
21. Leaves more than 5 cm, entire .... *P. russeola*

22. Corolla annulate; corolla-lobes rather narrow, often pointed .... *P. nivalis*
22. Corolla exannulate; if corolla-lobes narrow, then not pointed 23

23. Flowers 1–3 together; plant lacking meal; corolla-tube scarcely exceeding calyx .... *P. tschutktschorum*
23. Flowers usually more; some meal present; corolla-tube exceeding calyx 24

24. Flower stalks rather thick, usually shorter than calyx; corolla-tube broad 26
24. Flower-stalks slender, longer than calyx; corolla-tube slender 28

25. Homostylous; dwarf arctic plants from the Bering Straits .... *P. eximia*
25. Heterostylous; usually more robust plants from temperate mountains 26

26. Flowering late spring; corolla flat-faced, lobes rounded 27
26. Flowering late summer-early autumn; corolla bell-shaped, lobes squared-off .... *P. hongshanensis*

27. Chinese; calyx-lobes blunt .... *P. chionantha*
27. Turkish; calyx-lobes sharp .... *P. longipes*

28. Leaves decumbent; calyx-lobes rounded or squared off .... *P. megalocarpa*
28. Leaves erect; calyx-lobes sharp .... *P. macrophylla*

29. Leaves pinnate or deeply pinnatifid .... *P. lungchiensis*
29. Leaves with large, regularly spaced teeth 30

30. Leaves ovate-triangular .... *P. hoi*
30. Leaves narrowly oblong .... *P. lactucoides*

Primula chionantha Balf. f. & Forrest, Notes Roy. Bot. Gdn. Edinb. 9: 11 (1915)

P. melanops Smith & Ward (1923)
P. leucochnoa Hand.-Mazz. (1924)
P. sinoplantaginea Balf. f. (1920)
P. sinopurpurea Balf. f. (1918)
P. rigida Balf. f. & Forrest (1920)
P. amabilis Smith & Forrest (1920)
P. nivalis Pall. var. *purpurea* Franch. (1888) non Regel (1874)
P. nivalis Pall. var. *sinensis* Pax (1905)
P. ingens Smith & Forrest (1923)
P. graminifolia Pax & Hoffm. (1920)
?*P. purdomii* Craib (1914)

DESCRIPTION *Bud-scales* reddish. *Leaves* suberect, oblanceolate, but extremely variable in size and shape, to 25 × 6 cm, but sometimes only 5 × 0.6 cm, sharp or blunt, entire to finely toothed, usually revolute, thinly to thickly covered in yellow or white meal, the stalk poorly differentiated. *Stem* about equalling the leaves, rather stout, mealy, bearing 1–3 whorls each with 4–15 patent flowers on ascending stalks to 3 cm. *Calyx* narrowly bell-shaped, to 10 mm, green, reddish, purple or almost blackish, mealy, the lobes oblong and usually rather blunt. *Corolla* white, cream, lilac, purple, with or without a whitish eye, exannulate to weakly annulate, flat-faced, to 30 mm in diameter, often sweetly fragrant; the tube exceeding the calyx, longer in thrums. *Capsule* long, often 2× the calyx. Seeds pale brown. 2n = 22 (also 44 hort.). Flowering May–early June. (Plate 10.)

DISTRIBUTION Widespread in the wetter mountains of western China, throughout much of western Yunnan and western Sichuan; extends into Gansu (T'ao) and east Tibet (*P. purdomii*), south-east Tibet to Pemako, to the west of the Tsangpo bend, with a single isolated and remarkable record much further west near Lhasa.

In my experience a locally common plant of sloping damp humus-rich soils, usually amongst dwarf rhododendrons, and apparently graze-resistant. 3000–5000 m. Unlike most of its relatives not a plant of running water. 'Leaf-mould pasture... the soil here consists chiefly of remains of plants, half-rotten, and under these completely rotten leaves, and especially the leaf-sheaths of the many deep-rooting plants ... and having the bases of their stems enveloped in such ...'

The very complex taxonomic and nomenclatural history of this group begins with Franchet's identification of a Yunnan collection by Delavay as being the same as a Nepalese plant named by Regel *P. nivalis* var. *purpurea*, apparently based on *P. purpurea* Royle from Kashmir. Both of these are now considered as synonymous with the western Himalayan *P. macrophylla*. Pax later considered the Yunnan plant to be different from *P. purpurea*, but used a previously well-known epithet in the genus, *P. sinensis*, when describing it at varietal rank. The first valid publication of this purple-flowered plant at specific rank did not occur until 1918 as *P. sinopurpurea*, a name which conveniently combined the two earlier epithets.

In the meantime, Balfour had described three localized species which he regarded as being variants of his *P. sinopurpurea* which was still awaiting valid publication. *P. chionantha* is a white-flowered plant from the Chungtien plateau; *P. sinoplantaginea*, including *P. graminifolia*, is a dwarf, narrow-leaved variant originally described from high mountains in north-west Yunnan; and *P. brevicula*, based on Franchet's homonym *P. glacialis*, is a dwarf high alpine form from the Cang Shan and elsewhere. Of these, only the lattermost seems to be distinct.

A still earlier publication is Craib's description of a cultivated plant of William Purdom's collecting in northern regions of China (Gansu). It is difficult to see how *P. purdomii* differs from *P. sinopurpurea* except by white rather than yellow meal. Smith and Fletcher maintain that the floral structure is different, the anthers and stigma all being included within the flower, but this is unlikely to prove significant. If further study proves conclusively that *P. purdomii* is definitely synonymous with this group, the species should take this prior name. However, given the present level of knowledge of the group, I hesitate to formalize this change from a name well-known to gardeners.

Of later epithets, the most significant is perhaps *P. melanops* from the Kulu and Muli districts of Sichuan, for which *P. leucochnoa* is a synonym. Smith and Fletcher (1942) emphasize that this plant is distinct amongst Chinese nivalids, quoting the Himalayan *P. macrophylla* as its closest relative. They consider the narrow calyx and capsule, and the white rather than yellow meal, are characteristic. However, *P. melanops* has proved fully interfertile with *P. chionantha* and *P. sinopurpurea* in the garden, to the extent that pure-bred plants can no longer be found. Herbarium material shows it to be sufficiently variable to be united within the broad species concept of *P. chionantha*.

P. ingens is of no significance, being merely a minor variant in meal and flower colour of *P. sinopurpurea*, *P. rigida* cannot be readily distinguished from small *P. sinoplantaginea*, and this is also true of *P. amabilis*, which is said to have toothed leaves, although this is not evident on herbarium material. However, Halda (1992) places *leucops*, *brevicula*, *rigida*, *amabilis* and *glacialis* in synonymy with *P. diantha*, while he keeps *P. graminifolia* and *P. sinoplantaginea* distinct.

In maintaining *P. sinopurpurea*, *P. sinoplantaginea*, *P. melanops*, *P. chionantha* and others at specific rank, Smith and Fletcher did not have the benefit of another 50 years' experience with these plants in the garden. After this passage of time, these plants have effectively become one variable horticultural population which may at times produce variants close to the originals of each, but which more often produce a maze of intermediates. With the benefit of this hindsight, it is now possible to see that the wild collected material is also more variable than was originally perceived, so that these 'species' essentially merge into a seamless interfertile whole. I have chosen to maintain some of the Smith and Fletcher species at subspecific rank, as a recognition of some persisting distinctions, not least ecological, in the wild.

Ironically, the localized *P. chionantha*, the appropriately named 'snow flower', which was originally conceived as a minor variant of *P. sinopurpurea*, is, with the possible exception of *P. purdomii*, the earliest published valid name in the group, and this familiar name should now be used for all these plants, whatever their colour and character. Curiously, Halda (1992), while uniting these two species, chooses the later name *P. sinopurpurea*.

CULTIVATION Another factor linking the synonymous 'species' placed here under *P. chionantha* is that they are effectively the only worthwhile garden plants in the nivalids. Most of the forms are relatively easy garden plants which are moderately vigorous in cool sheltered places in a humus-rich, moisture-retentive, fertile soil, even in a bog garden or shallow pond margin. Although they suffer from many primula pests, notably slugs and vine weevil, they flower readily and set seed freely. They are easily raised from seed, often flowering in their first year. It is often found that white and purple forms come from a single seed packet. They also often multiply to form multicrowned stocks which can be divided, preferably in the autumn.

At its best, well grown and in a good form, this can be a magnificent garden plant, one of the best of all primulas for the open garden.

The plants grown today result from a large number of introductions of the component forms, especially by Forrest and Rock, from 1908 to about 1950.

P. purdomii received an **FCC** on its first appearance in cultivation in 1913, but died out immediately!

HYBRIDIZATION All the varied forms have hybridized freely, and these hybrids are fully interfertile. In the 1970s, C.C. Hollett raised strains of hybrid seedlings with *P. macrophylla* 'Paul Huggins'. These varied in colour from violet through lavender to white.

VARIATION

- Subsp. *chionantha*. Flowers white; plant large and robust, meal yellowish; leaves more than 1.5 cm wide; capsule not more than 2× calyx. Zhongdian plateau, Yunnan.
- Subsp. *sinopurpurea* (Balf. f.) A.J. Richards (1993) (*P. sinopurpurea* Balf. f., Bot. Mag. t.8777 (1918)). As above, but flowers purple. Throughout much of the range, mostly below 4500 m.
- Subsp. *sinoplantaginea* (Balf. f.) A.J. Richards (1993) (*P. sinoplantaginea* Balf. f., Notes Roy. Bot. Gdn. Edinb. 13: 20 (1920)). Flowers purple; plant rather small and semiprostrate; meal yellowish; leaves less than 1 cm wide. Throughout much of the range above 4500 m.
- Subsp. *melanops* (Smith & Ward) A.J. Richards (1993) (*P. melanops* Smith & Ward, Notes Roy. Bot. Gdn. Edinb. 14: 48 (1923)). Flowers purple; plant fairly robust, leaves more than 1.5 cm wide; meal white; calyx narrow; capsule narrow, more than 2× calyx. Sichuan, Muli and Kulu areas at about 5000 m.

Primula longipes Freyn & Sint., Bull. Herb. Boiss. 4: 141 (1896)

P. nivalis Pallas var. *longipes* (Freyn & Sint.) Kusn. (1901)
P. nivalis Pallas var. *farinosa* Koch (1850) non Schrenk (1879)

DESCRIPTION *Leaf-blades* narrowly obovate-elliptic, to 20 × 8 cm, thin in texture, white-mealy beneath, crenate toothed above, entire below, insensibly narrowing into a broad stalk. *Stem* to 45 cm, mealy, carrying one to three whorls of 10–15 flowers on slender mealy stalks which elongate to 6 cm in fruit. *Calyx* bell-shaped, to 10 mm, mealy. *Corolla* violet, purple, mauve or lavender with a white eye, flat-faced and annulate, to 22 mm in diameter; corolla-tube scarcely exceeding the calyx; corolla-lobes rounded, usually entire. *Capsules* more than 2× the calyx. Flowering July–August. (Fig. Halda: 198.) (Plate 46. Fig. 19.)

DISTRIBUTION North-east Turkey; wet north slopes of the Pontus facing the Black Sea from Giresun in the west, eastwards through Gumusane, Trabzon, Rize and Coruh; probably just entering the USSR in west Transcaucasia, Adzharistan in west Georgia.

Damp grassy slopes or ledges, moist crevices, often in running water, 1625–3400 m. Locally common.

Completely disjunct from *P. chionantha* and its Chinese relatives by 5000 km, but as Schwarz (1968) points out, very closely related and should probably be included within that complex. I can find no safe feature which distinguishes them. However, as *P. longipes* is the most westerly of all Asian nivalids, and one of the most accessible, growing by several of the

Fig. 19. *P. longipes*

main Pontus passes, it is at present convenient to maintain *P. longipes* at specific rank.

Schwarz (1968) correctly shows that *P. longipes* and its Caucasian neighbour *P. crassifolia* are only distantly related. Unlike *P. longipes*, *P. crassifolia* has as its closest relatives dwarf forms and relatives of *P. nivalis* from Siberia. Thus, he suggests that the forerunners of this group may have made two distinct western incursions.

CULTIVATION Seed was introduced by E.K. Balls in 1933. This species seems never to have become generally established in Europe, but Corsair (1948) states: 'the requirement of this species, as far as soil is concerned, are easily met, just a heavy loam which can be kept moist during the active season is all that it needs. The drainage of pots must however be good, for excessive moisture at the roots or around the neck of the plant during the dormant period will certainly cause death. As this is a strong-growing primula, mature plants will need rather large pots. Annual repotting after the flowers have withered will be necessary, and a top dressing with a rich compost during the early part of the year will prove beneficial'. Flowered by Pam Eveleigh in Calgary, Canada and Lili-Ann Lindgren in Rosvik, Sweden in 2001. Pam grew it in a 'pseudobog', a ditch 50 cm deep, lined with plastic and filled with a peat-sand mix. Offered in the trade in 2001.

Primula brevicula Balf. f. & Forrest, Notes Roy. Bot. Gdn. Edinb. 9: 150 (1916))

P. glacialis Franch. (1885) non Willden. (1819) nec Ruprecht (1863)
P. leucops Smith & Ward (1924)

DESCRIPTION A very dwarf relative of the *P. chionantha* group, leaves and stems not exceeding 5 cm in the wild, but leaf blade very narrowly oval with a white underside and dark mid-rib, narrowing abruptly into a short but distinct unwinged purple stalk. Flowers usually 1–2 together, pale rather slaty-blue with a distinct broad white annulus. (Plate 80.)

DISTRIBUTION Widespread in south-east Tibet and extreme western China, and recorded in recent years from the Cang Shan, Yulong Shan, Zhongdian district, Beima Shan, Da Xue Shan, Haba Shan, Shu La and Nyima La.

A high alpine, probably always occurring over 4200 m, usually on limestone. Tundra, stabilised scree and thinly grassed slopes between dwarf *Rhododendron, Cassiope* and *Diapensia* species.

In 1993 I was persuaded to reduce this species to subspecific rank under *P. chionantha,* as material collected high on the Cang Shan under this name, perhaps by CLD, grew lush and large in cultivation at the Royal Botanic Garden, Edinburgh. These were presumably environmentally dwarfed forms of *P. chionantha*. Since then the true *P. brevicula* has been collected many times, and several accessions have flowered in cultivation, so that it is much better understood. It is in fact a rather invariable and distinctive little plant which is perhaps most closely related to *P. minor*. The pale blue, white-eyed, annulate flowers seem not to vary significantly (the pink colour in plate 80 is an artefact), so that this species is readily distinguished from dwarf forms of *P. chionantha* subsp. *sinoplantaginea* by the colour and annulate flowers as well as leaf shape when they co-occur, which they do not infrequently, for instance on the Beima Shan.

CULTIVATION Seems never to have been grown until the 1990s when successive introductions of seed by CLD from the Yulong Shan, KGB 118, 376 (Shu La) and ACE (1545, 1689, 1799) from the Beima Shan and Da Xue Shan have been grown. More recently collected by David Rankin (SDR 807, 1576, 1750) and ARGS 407, 508 from Da Zue Shan. Not difficult from seed, flowering after one year if pot-grown and overwintered under glass, but kept cool and humid in growth, but may be difficult to keep alive after that. Has been persuaded to set seed in cultivation, and has been offered commercially by David Rankin and others.

HYBRIDIZATION Fertile hybrids with *P. chionantha* subsp. *sinoplantaginea* were recognized in the field by David Rankin and seed introduced under SDR 1794.

Primula minor Balf. f. & Ward, Notes Roy. Bot. Gdn. Edinb. 9: 29 (1915)

P. atuntzuensis Balf. f. & Forrest (1920)
P. petraea Balf. f. & Forrest (1920)

P. helvenacea Balf. f. & Ward (1915)
P. kiuchangensis Balf. f. & Forrest (1920)

DESCRIPTION A dwarf plant, most closely related to *P. brevicula,* but differing by the long very narrow corolla-tube more than 2× the calyx, the very narrow sepal-lobes and more elliptical and in some forms more toothed leaf-blade which is cream-mealy beneath. Like *P. brevicula* the erect blade is clearly demarcated from the dark narrow stalk with a dark mid-rib below. (Fig. Halda: 203.) (Plate 84.)

DISTRIBUTION The Beima Shan (north-west Yunnan), Da Xue Shan on the Sichuan border, and neighbouring Tsarong, east Tibet, 4000–5000 m, also possibly further to the south-west.

VARIATION *P. kiuchiangensis* seemed to be a relatively low level form from Tsarong with a short leaf-stalk and a crenate blade, while *P. helvenacea* is a small high alpine from 5000 m on the Beima Shan with very long leaf-stalks 4 × the blade. In 1997, Anne Chambers photographed a population at 4450 m on the Zo La, south-east of Shugden Gompa which seems structurally very similar to narrow-leaved forms of *P. minor*, although with white, purple-tubed flowers. This may be best treated as a subspecies of *P. minor*, and would be an extension of range into south-east Tibet.

CULTIVATION Introduced by KGB 330, 363 from the Shu La and 600 from the Beima Shan (1992) and by ACE (as *P. brevicula*) from the latter locality in 1993. Seed from both expeditions germinated well and grew on quite well for some growers, even being offered commercially for a brief period. Alan Furness had a large planting outside in Northumberland which survived for two years. Unfortunately it proved to be shy flowering and disappointing in cultivation. Grown at Glendoick in 2002.

Primula orbicularis Hemsl., Gard. Chron. 3, 39: 191 (1906)

P. reflexa Petitim. (1908)
P. ochracea Pax & Hoffm. (1920)

DESCRIPTION Differing from *P. chionantha* by rather narrow petalled, virtually stalkless yellow flowers borne in single loosely orbicular umbels. The parallel-sided, narrow leaves with strongly revolute margins are held strictly erect in a sheaf in a manner reminiscent of a reed-mace *Typha*. Often a rather tall, slender plant, but dwarf depauperate specimens occur at higher altitudes. The young leaves are covered with a thin white meal below and the capsule is less than 2× the 10 mm calyx. (Plate 38.)

DISTRIBUTION Sichuan (mostly in the north) and south-west Gansu, 3400–3800 m. Wet ground on moorland, often in mineral soils, stream-sides, margins of ponds and ditches, fens and seeps, but not usually in running water or snow-melt and not a high alpine. Tends to replace *P. chionantha* ecologically in this region, although perhaps in somewhat wetter sites.

CULTIVATION Flowered in 1906 from Wilson's seed, and in 1939 from Harry Smith's seed, but did not persist. Reintroduced by Cox in 1990, and collected by Ron McBeath (? 1999) and by SQAE in 2000. Offered by Ron McBeath from 1999–2001. Has grown moderately well in conditions which suit *P. chionantha* and flowered for some growers in 2001. The habitat suggests that it could prove to be as straightforward as *P. chionantha* in cultivation.

Primula soongii Chen & Hu, Fl. Rep. Pop. Sin. 2: 293 (1990)

DESCRIPTION Unlike *P. cerina*, and *P. crocifolia*, a relatively robust yellow-flowered Chinese nivalid. Differs from its other likely confusion species *P. orbicularis* by rounded leaves, very long calyces (to 14 mm), and entire, rounded corolla-lobes. Baoxing Shan, Mupine, Sichuan, 3200–4600 m; alpine wood margins, etc. Flowered by David Rankin from seed from Daochen, Sichuan, in 2002.

Primula hongshanensis Z. Fang, H. Sun & D.W.H. Rankin, Plantsman (in press 2002)

DESCRIPTION A robust species, resembling *P. chionantha* in general habit. *Roots* long and fleshy. *Leaves* 28 × 3 (to 45 × 4) cm, spreading, flat, acuminate, irregularly shortly serrate, mealy white on the under surface. *Flower stem* erect, 50 (to 75) cm, bearing usually two widely separated (by 10 cm) whorls of 2–9 flowers, typically 3 in the first whorl and 4 or 5 in the second. Flower stalks 5 cm, the lower becoming arcuate-erect. *Calyx* pinky-lilac, 12 (to 14) mm, sepal-lobes narrow, acute, 6 (to 8) mm long. *Flowers* heterostyle. *Corolla* bell-shaped, weakly zygomorphic, 30 mm in diameter, amethyst-pink with a broad white-mealy eye, the mouth widely exannulate. Petal-lobes 11 mm wide, square-ended with two shallow notches. *Fruit* 22 mm (about 2× calyx), narrow (6 mm diameter), parallel-sided, truncate, pinkish; seeds dark brown. *Flowering* late July to early August. (Plate 81.)

DISTRIBUTION Hong Shan, north-east of Zhongdian, Yunnan, and across the Sichuan border about 100 km away on Da Xue Shan, so far known from at least six sites.

Growing in sphagnum under mature Taliensia rhododendrons, usually with a canopy of *Abies delavayi*, 4000–4200 m, usually on a north slope.

This remarkable new species is undoubtedly related to *P. chionantha*, near which it often grows, but from which it has become genetically isolated by its late flowering time. When *P. chionantha* is in full flower, *P. hongshanensis* is only just starting into growth. Despite the considerable variability of *P. chionantha, P. hongshanensis* remains distinct in many characters, of which the pinkish-lilac , white-eyed, 'squared-off', bell-shaped flowers, the erect lower fruits which are narrow, parallel-sided and truncate, and the dark-coloured seeds are the most obvious. *P. hongshanensis* was first discovered by Fang Zhendong in July 1995 and has since been studied by the species authors in 1997 and 2000.

No significant variation or evidence of hybridization with *P. chionantha* or other species has yet been noted. Seed collected in 1997 gave rise to seedlings, none of which survived to their second winter. Seed from collections in 2002 has given many robust plants, some of which may bloom in 2002.

Primula macrophylla D. Don, Prodr. Fl. Nepal: 80 (1825) non Koch (1850)

P. nivalis Pall. var. *macrophylla* Pax (1905)
P. purpurea Royle, Illust. Bot. Himal.: 311 (1839)
P. nivalis Pall. var. *purpurea* Franch. (1888)
P. stuartii Wall. var. *purpurea* Watt (1882)
P. stuartii Wall. var. *macrocarpa* (Watt) Pax (1889) non *P. macrocarpa* Maxim. (1868)
P. atroviolacea Jacq. (1844)
P. jaeschkeana Kerner (1871)
P. moorcroftiana Klatt (1868)
P. stuartii Wall. var. *moorcroftiana* Watt (1882)
P. meeboldii Pax (1906)
P. aitchisonii Pax (1905)
P. pulverea Fed. (1952)

DESCRIPTION *Resting buds* small and inconspicuous. *Bud-scales* usually reddish and mealy. *Leaves* narrowly lanceolate, usually erect, rather thin in texture, entire to finely crenulate, usually white (rarely yellow) mealy, especially below. *Stems* slender, mealy above, usually exceeding the leaves, carrying a single umbel of 2–20 somewhat pendulous flowers on slender stalks which are generally longer than the calyx and often elongate further in fruit. *Corolla* rosy-purple, blue, lilac or rarely white, commonly with a very dark eye, or with a yellow eye, annulate, often fragrant, flat-faced, to 23 mm in diameter; tube of varying length; *corolla-lobes* usually entire but sometimes notched. *Capsule* never more than 2× the calyx. 2n = 22. (Photo: Fls Himalaya fig. 865; Halda: 118 seq. bis.) Flowering April in cultivation. (Plates 10, 39.)

DISTRIBUTION From the Tadzhikstan and the Pamir, through the Hindu Kush (Afghanistan) to Chitral (Pakistan), the Karakoram, Kashmir, Ladakh, Garwhal, Hazara, Simla, Kumaon to west Nepal, and again in Sikkim, Bhutan, and neighbouring parts of south-east Tibet. Scattered and disjunct through much of this wide range, due to the limited occurrence of suitable habitats, particularly in drier western and northern areas.

Marshy ground usually by streams or melting snow banks in high, often otherwise dry glacial valleys, 3350–5400 m, often in large colonies. '. . . grows up robustly through the coldest mud, flushed by snow melt water.' There is a good description of this species in the wild in Bull. AGS 63: 175–179.

According to Polunin and to Wendelbo, the meal from the calyx is used for the treatment of eye diseases.

P. macrophylla is very variable thoughout its wide range, and Smith and Fletcher sensibly united six species in their account (1942). In early years it was confused with its relative *P. nivalis*, which occurs to the north of the Tibetan plateau in central Asia, while *P. macrophylla* essentially lies to the south and west of this massif. *P. nivalis* lacks meal and has broad serrated leaves. The other confusion species are the long-fruited *P. megalocarpa*, the yellow-flowered *P. stuartii*, which tends to have more toothed leaves than *P. macrophylla*, and the Chinese *P. chionantha*.

The isolated eastern populations (vars. *macrocarpa* and *ninguida*) of the essentially west Himalayan *P. macrophylla* just overlap with *P. chionantha* geographically. However, they are ecologically quite different, for *P. macrophylla* is limited to areas largely unaffected by the monsoon, relying on the melt of sparse winter snow to provide sufficiently wet conditions in dry zones, while *P. chionantha* occurs in summer-wet regions. This is reflected by the different behaviour of the two groups in the garden.

These two groups (*macrophylla*-agg. and *chionantha*-agg.) present a different general appearance, but each is so variable that it is difficult safely to separate them on the basis of a single character. However, *P. macrophylla* is essentially a more graceful, less robust plant than *P. chionantha*, and typically has a much more open inflorescence which always forms a single umbel.

CULTIVATION In general *P. macrophylla* is a more difficult plant than *P. chionantha*. It comes readily from seed, grows quickly, and flowers within the year. However, it is short-lived, rarely flowering more than twice, and rarely overwinters successfully in the open garden, although it can do so if protected by glass. Fortunately, if several plants are grown together, it sets seed in abundance, and at least one form remains frequent in cultivation, and is often offered in the trade. **AM** 1967.

Possibly first collected under the auspices of B.O. Coventry in 1930 (e.g. a white form s.n.1537 from the Burzil Pass) and then by Ludlow, and Ludlow and Sherriff on several occasions between about 1938 and 1943. Var. *moorcroftiana* was in cultivation in Balblair, Scotland in 1945, probably from these collectors. Len Beer introduced var. *macrocarpa* from western Nepal in 1975.

The most significant introduction was made by a young man, Paul Huggins while on an Oxford University climbing expedition in the Tehri-Garwhal (Rudugaira Gad, Gangotri) in 1952. Seed collected under H78 developed into a delightful slender plant with large semipendulous violet flowers with a broad almost black eye. This is the form which is almost exclusively grown today, and is perhaps the most attractive ever introduced. This is particularly fitting, for later in the same expedition, Huggins died in a mountaineering accident, and this superb plant stands as a fitting memorial to him. I suggest that this strain should be given the name 'Paul Huggins'.

In 1991, Halda introduced Tadzhik material (JJH 918141, 918434, 918632), and Chris Chadwell collected it several times. CC&McK 153 (Nepal 1990) and McK 5 survive in 2001.

VARIATION

- Var. *macrophylla*. Plant relatively robust, white-mealy. Bracts short; calyx about 10 mm, cut to about two-thirds. Corolla lobes entire; capsule not more than 2× calyx. Throughout the range of the species.
- Var. *moorcroftiana* (Klatt) Pax, Bot. Jahrb. 10: 207 (1889) (*P. moorcroftiana* Klatt 1868). A dwarf alpine form with long bracts equalling the corolla and notched corolla-lobes. High localities in Kashmir and surrounding regions. (Photo: Bull. AGS 63: 178).
- Var. *macrocarpa* (Watt) Pax, Bot. Jahrb. 10: 208 (1889). A dwarf plant with yellow meal, and a long calyx, to 15 mm, cut to the base. Corolla lobes notched; fruit very long, to 3 cm. East Nepal, Sikkim, Bhutan and south Tibet. Some of the Tibetan plants from the Tsari region, close to stations for *P. chionantha*, are intermediate between *P. macrophylla* var. *macrophylla* and *P. chionantha* subsp. *sinopurpurea*. These fall between var. *macrophylla* and var. *macrocarpa*, and have been called var. *ninguida* (Smith) Smith & Fletcher (1943). (Photo: Riddle of the Tsangpo Gorge: 107.)
- Var. *pulverea* (Fed.) Halda (1992). (*P. pulverea* Fed., Fl. URSS 18: 727 (1952)). Heavily cream-mealy throughout. East Pamir.

HYBRIDIZATION Hybrids in cultivation have been reported with *P. chionantha*. Var. *moorcroftiana* grows together with *P. stuartii* on the Nalgan Pass above the Baspa Valley, N W India, and hybrids occur quite frequently. (Photo: Rock Garden 27: 141.)

Primula megalocarpa Hara, J. Jap. Bot. 49:133 (1974)

DESCRIPTION A close relative of *P. macrophylla*, resembling var. *moorcroftiana* with the same long bracts and notched corolla lobes, but with broad, short, somewhat decumbent leaves which are markedly crenate-toothed, and with a quite different calyx, the lobes of which are rounded, and squared or even notched at the tip. In common with *P. macrophylla* var. *macrocarpa*, the meal is usually yellow, and the fruits very long. Flowers white, rose or pale lilac. (Photo: Suppl. Fls. Him. t.65, Fig. Halda: 202.) (Plate 40.)

DISTRIBUTION Central and east Nepal, Bhutan and southern Tibet, 3600–4800 m. In similar habitats to *P. macrophylla*, but confined to high rainfall zones. Seed was introduced from the Barun Khola by Ron McBeath in 1991, and by McBeath on at least one later date, still in cultivation in 2001.

Primula poluninii Fletcher, J. Roy. Hort. Soc. 88: 488 (1963)

DESCRIPTION Essentially a softly yellow-flowered form of *P. megalocarpa*, with the same squat toothed leaves, long bracts and rounded calyx lobes, but with rounded corolla lobes and a relatively short fruit. West Nepal, Sisne Himal; wet screes and streamlet margins, 4500–5100 m. (Photo: Fls. Himalaya fig. 869.)

Primula stuartii Wallich in Roxburgh, Fl. Ind. 11: 20 (1824)

DESCRIPTION Another relative of *P. macrophylla*, but with golden flowers and a stout mealy resting bud. The strongly toothed leaves are yellow-mealy below; the mealy bracts are short (to 2 cm), the calyx is greenish-mealy, the tube of the flowers is no more than 2× the calyx, and the corolla-lobes are often toothed, or sometimes entire, but not notched. (Photo: Fls Himalaya fig. 868.) (Plate 83.)

DISTRIBUTION Western and central Himalaya, from Kulu, Garwhal and Simla to Gosainkund north of Kathmandu, apparently scattered and local in wet alpine meadows and stony snow-melt, preferring heavily dunged sites, 4000–5000 m.

CULTIVATION A surprisingly little known plant for one which is distributed through well-frequented regions. However, it has been introduced into cultivation on a number of occasions since 1847, but seems to have persisted for a time only at Inshriach, as with *P. obliqua* and *P. obtusifolia*. In recent years collected from Gosainkund in 1991 (CC & McK 544) and perhaps from beyond Nalgan, N W India by Henry and Margaret Taylor in 2000. Sparingly in cultivation in 2001.

Primula elongata Watt, J. Linn. Soc. Bot. 20: 8 (1882)

P. barnardoana Smith & Ward (1936)

DESCRIPTION A close relative of *P. stuartii* but from the eastern Himalaya, differing chiefly by the sulphur-yellow to orange flowers with a markedly long and narrow corolla-tube, more than 2× the calyx. Also, the resting bud is small and inconspicuous, leaves have small crenate teeth, the corolla-lobes are notched and the capsule is long and narrow, to 3× the calyx. The leaves show a marked heterophylly with age; as they emerge when in early flower the oblong blade is scarcely distinct from the stalk, but later they develop an ovate blade with a heart-shaped base resulting in a very distinct stalk. (Plate 44.)

DISTRIBUTION From extreme eastern Nepal eastwards through Sikkim (Changu, Chola, Zemu), south Tibet (Chumbi) and west and central Bhutan as far as the Rudo La, east of Bumthang. Alpine meadows, cliff ledges, open coniferous forest and rhododendron scrub in very wet zones, 3000–4700 m.

P. elongata takes an intermediate position between the west Himalayan nivalids based around *P. macrophylla* and *P. stuartii*, and the eastern Himalayan section Cordifoliae. Mature forms with rounded leaf-blades were called *P. barnardoana*, and placed in the latter section, for they can look like yellow-flowered forms of *P. rotundifolia*. However, Sherriff claimed that in central Bhutan, *P. elongata* and *P. barnardoana* merged into one another, and a study of herbarium material makes it clear that the two leaf-forms are merely developmental in origin. This species could be readily placed in either section on morphological grounds, but DNA studies show it to be sister to the Crystallophlomis species *P. advena, P.eximia* and *P. tschuktschorum*, rather than *P. rotundifolia*.

Smith & Fletcher (1943) note that some forms can look very like the petiolarid *P. calderiana* subsp. *strumosa* in the field, although the capsule is entirely different.

VARIATION Forma *barnardoana* (Smith & Ward) Richards **comb. et stat. nov**. (*P. barnardoana* Smith & Ward, Notes Roy. Bot. Gdn. Edin. 19: 167 (1936).) Leaf blades orbicular. Distribution of species.

CULTIVATION *P. elongata* has been intermittently in cultivation since 1937 (seed from Sikkim) usually under the name *P. barnardoana*. It was grown from 1940–1943 and in 1950 (resting buds from Bhutan). During the 1970s and 1980s it was introduced by Dr George Smith, and from Ghose's seed collected in Sikkim. It has frequently been flowered in cultivation, is occasionally seen at Shows, and has been intermittently offered in the trade, but does not persist long in cultivation, and rarely sets seed. Still sparsely in cultivation in 2001.

Primula duthieana Balf. f. & Smith, Notes Roy. Bot. Gdn. Edinb. 9: 164 (1916)

P. moorcroftiana Wall. var. *flavida* Smith (1936)

DESCRIPTION A relative of *P. macrophylla* and *P. stuartii*, but having flowers of a soft butter yellow (to creamy-yellow) with a darker yellow eye; leaves with meal absent, or confined to the entire or finely toothed leaf margin below, mid-rib pale, upper leaf-surface shiny, with an irregular pattern; bracts mealy to 3.5 cm long, often equalling the flower, and with a blackish, meal-lined calyx. The corolla-lobes are rounded and entire, and the resting buds are slender and inconspicuous, as in *P. macrophylla*. (Photo: Bull. AGS 54: 242 (1986)) (Plate 43, Fig. 18.)

DISTRIBUTION Baltistan province, bordering Hazara, especially Burzil Pass, Kashmir where it was first discovered in 1893. Discovered four years later in Hazara, south of Gilgit, north Pakistan by Inayat Khan; discovered by Ludlow and Sherriff in the Barai valley, Kishenganga in 1935 and the Nurinar Pass in 1940; now known from four

Fig. 18 *P. duthieana*

localities in west Kashmir. Occurs well to the west of *P. stuartii* and *P. poluninii*. Rivulets and wet scree in dry mountain zones, 3500–5000 m.

CULTIVATION Seems never to have been cultivated until seed was introduced by the Swedish expedition (SEP) to north Pakistan in 1983. Plants flowered for several growers in 1986, but they seem to have been lost soon afterwards.

Primula obtusifolia Royle, Illust. Bot. Himal. Mount.: 311 (1839)

P. traillii Watt ex Balf. f. (1915)

DESCRIPTION Distinguished by broad rounded spathulate very shortly crenate spreading leaf-blades of a rugose texture and rather bluish-grey tone to 10 cm wide, with thin white meal below. Mealy stems bear usually 2–3 upward-facing pale to purplish-blue rounded flat-faced annulate flowers with entire or slightly toothed lobes and a marked white-mealy eye, up to 25 mm in diameter. In well-developed specimens, stems of up to 30 cm can form two or more whorls. Most unusually in this group, the rounded capsule is shorter than the calyx. (Photo: Rock Garden 27: 135.) (Plate 82.)

DISTRIBUTION A rare species from three localized districts in the north-west Himalaya; Kunawar (Rupin pass); Simla, Baspa valley, Haran and Charang passes; Kashmir, Kishtvar, Sharran glaciers. Shady rocks near glaciers, 4000–5300 m.

Despite my comments in 1993, it is clear from photographs and other recent information that this distinctive and attractive species has few close living relatives. Nevertheless, in this section it is perhaps the closest living relative of Proliferae species such as *P. poissonii* and *P. secundiflora*, with which it might conceivably form some sort of evolutionary link.

CULTIVATION Introduced by seed in 1939 by Tsongpen who sent seed to Edinburgh from Baspa. Successful in several places, e.g. Shaw McKenzie's garden in the Black Isle, at Inshriach, and in Oregon. Continuously in cultivation at Inshriach until at least 1980. May have been recollected from the Baspa Valley between Charang and Lalanti in 2000 by Henry and Margaret Taylor and sparingly in cultivation in 2001.

Primula nivalis Pallas, Reise versch. Prov. Russ. Reichs. 3: 723 (1772–3)

P. orientalis Willd. (1819)
P. speciosa Gmel. (1841)
P. regeliana Fed. (1950)
P. turkestanica (Schmidt) White (1916)
P. xanthobasis Fed. (1952)

DESCRIPTION Differs from *P. macrophylla* by usually lacking meal, by the relatively broad, stiffer, often sharply toothed or serrated leaves, and the longer capsule (to 35 mm). The corolla-lobes are entire, narrow and often pointed. 2n = 22. (Photo Halda: 118 seq. bis., Bull. ARGS 49: 177.) (Plates 10, 41, 42.)

DISTRIBUTION Scattered and disjunct on high mountains over a very wide range to the west and north of the Tibetan plateau, from the Alai range at about 67° E 38° N, north-eastwards through the Tien-shan and Ala-Tau, to the mountains of Transbaikalia, the Altai and Lake Ubsa in northern Mongolia (92° E 50° N) and northwards to the Tomsk district of eastern Siberia, and Kamtschatka, a total distance of some 2500 km. Streamsides and wet places resulting from melting snow in dry high alpine areas. It has been recorded in cultivation since 1790, recently by Halda (JJH 918237) but has never persisted for long. Said, howeve,r to be permanent at Tromso, north Norway.

VARIATION The following three taxa all differ from var. *nivalis* by bearing meal. They are usually classified within *P. nivalis* by virtue of their broad serrated leaves and their western or northern geography.

- Var. *colorata* Regel (1874). (*P. turkestanica* (Schmidt) White (1916). Bracts and calyx dark purple. Turkestan.
- Var. *farinosa* Schrenk (1841). Mealy on the leaf edges. Turkestan.
- Subsp. *xanthobasis* (Fed.) Halda (1992). (*P. xanthobasis* Fed. (1952).) Heavily yellow-mealy below leaves. Mongolia, south Siberia.

Primula crassifolia Lehm., Monogr. Gen. Primula: 91 (1817)

P. nivalis Pallas var. *bayernii* Rupr. ex Regel (1874)
P. bayernii Rupr. (1863)

DESCRIPTION *Leaf-blades* elliptic-lanceolate, to 10 × 4 cm, fleshy, the furrowed mid-rib convex on both sides, with irregular blunt teeth, densely white-mealy below, or on the margins only, or occasionally lacking meal. *Stem* robust, to 15 cm, exceeding leaves, with a single umbel of up to 12 spreading flowers on mealy stalks to 3 cm. *Calyx* tubular, mealy, to 8 mm. *Corolla* opening white, turning creamy and often becoming flushed pale pink or flesh-coloured, annulate, flat-faced, to 20 mm in diameter; the tube exceeding the calyx; corolla-lobes rounded, usually entire. *Capsule* more than 2× calyx. Flowering June–July in the wild. (Fig. Halda: 192.) (Plate 45.)

DISTRIBUTION Caucasus; confined to a discrete area of the high central Caucasus; Arkhot range; Ossetien, Zei glacier and Salfidar valley; Kasbek, Mt. Tschanchi. Moraines, snow and glacier melt areas, wet depressions, 2000–3000 m.

One of two westerly nivalids occurring in the Caucasus region, easily distinguished from *P. longipes* by flower colour, and leaf shape and texture. This species is almost always known as *P. bayernii*, but Schwarz (1968) argues convincingly that Lehmann's description, for which no type survives, can only refer to this plant. However, Halda (1992) places the name *P. crassifolia* in synonymy with *P. nivalis* Pallas which does not occur in the Caucasus. *P. crassifolia* had not been in cultivation by 1973, but there have been several recent introductions of seed. However, it seems not to have persisted.

Primula cerina Fletcher, Trans. Bot. Soc. Edinb. 32: 111 (1941)

DESCRIPTION A dwarf non-mealy plant not exceeding 10 cm with spoon-shaped leaves, the blade 2.5 × 1 cm, rounded and toothed. Flowers 2–4, yellow. Capsule scarcely exceeding the calyx. Only known from the Djesi-La south of Tatsienlu, Sichuan, 4400 m. Offered for sale from China in 2001 ('mid-Sichuan') and flowering for at least one UK grower that year.

Primula crocifolia Pax & Hoffm., Feddes Rep. 17: 96 (1920)

DESCRIPTION A dwarf very white-mealy plant not exceeding 10 cm with very narrow (to 3 mm width) linear entire leaves. Flowers 1–2, yellow. Dawo and Schtiala, north-west of Tatsienlu, Sichuan–Tibet border, screes at 4600–4800 m. (Fig. Halda: 194.)

Primula diantha Bur. & Franch., Journ. de Bot. 5: 97 (1891)

DESCRIPTION A tiny relative of *P. chionantha*, not more than 3 cm high, the white-mealy leaves not more than 2 cm, toothed. Flowers two, purple, about 16 mm in diameter. There had only been a single collection from the summit of a pass near Batang, western Sichuan at 4300 m, but recollected from there by the Miehes in about 1995.

In view of its very small size, *P. diantha* has been confused with members of the section Minutissimae, but from the long capsule and rounded entire corolla-lobes, it is clear that it should be placed here. As Halda (1992) suggests, this tiny plant may be part of the *P. chionantha* problem. (Fig. Halda: 194.)

Primula tschuktschorum Kjellman, Nordensk. Veg. Exp. Vetensk. Jagtt. 1: 516 (1882)

P. nivalis Pallas var. *pumila* Ledeb. (1847–9) p.p.
P. pumila (Ledeb.) Pax (1889)
P. pumila (Ledeb.) Pax var. *ledebouriana* Busch (1925) p.p.
P. tschuktschorum Kjellman var. *beringensis* Porsild (1965)
P. beringensis (Porsild) Yurtsev (1975)

DESCRIPTION A *dwarf* plant, to 10 cm, with *leaves* oblong-linear, to 4 × 0.4 cm, the recurved margins entire or slightly crenate, lacking meal, although the resting bud is slightly mealy. *Stem* to 10 cm, shorter at flowering, rather slender, lacking meal, carrying up to 3 flowers on slender stalks to 10 mm. *Calyx* bell shaped, to 7 mm, dark green. *Corolla* usually rose-magenta, heterostylous, exannulate, to 12 mm in diameter; corolla-tube broad and equalling the calyx; corolla lobes rounded and usually entire. Capsule 2× the calyx, cylindrical. 2n = 22. Flowering July in the wild. (Photo: Bull. AGS 65: 95.) (Plates 4, 47.)

DISTRIBUTION Restricted to both sides of the narrowest part of the Bering Straight; Siberia, Anadyr range and Chukchi (Chukotsk) peninsula; St Lawrence and other islands in the Bering Strait, and the Seward Peninsula, Alaska.

'Frost boils and in gravel along small streams; soil saturated during most of the growing season, from sea-level to alpine elevations.' Kelso considers *P. tschuktschorum* to be a rare and possibly threatened species.

The *P. tschuktschorum* group has been very confused taxonomically. There is a recent account by Kelso (1987), who shows that in the Bering area there are two distinct plants. *P. tschuktschorum* correctly refers to rather invariable small heterostyle plants (outbreeders) with a restricted ecological and geographical range. Variable, but often much larger homostyle selfers have a wider ecological and geographical range, and are referred to *P. eximia* Greene.

The situation is further complicated by Federov (1952). In his account, three species are distinguished in this complex from the Siberian shore. Unfortunately, it is not stated which are heterostylous and which homostylous. Federov restricts the name *P. tschuktschorum* to plants with wider leaves (0.5–1.5 cm), stout, 3–10 flowered stems, long, mealy flower-stalks, a short calyx (to 5 mm), a small flower (to 7 mm in diameter) and a corolla tube twice the length of the calyx. Most of these probably fall within Kelso's concept of *P. eximia*.

It is not yet certain which species have been in cultivation. Plants under the name of *P. tschuktschorum* have been rather insignificant, although with have a certain charm. Photos from the wild suggest that they are a travesty compared to the magnificence of forms in the field. They set seed fairly freely, so that most are probably the homostylous *P. eximia*. Although short-lived, they have been maintained sparingly in cultivation since about 1970, usually grown in pots and kept under glass in winter. *P. beringensis* refers to minor variants in which the petal-lobes are divided almost to the base.

Primula eximia Greene, Pittonia 3: 251 (1897)

P. nivalis Pallas var. *pumila* Ledeb. (1847) p.p.
P. tschuktschorum Kjellman var. *pumila* (Ledeb.) Fernald (1928)
P. tschuktschorum Kjellman var. *cairnesiana* Porsild (1965)
P. macounii Greene (1897)
P. arctica Koidz. (1911)
P. pumila (Ledeb.) Pax var. *arctica* (Koidz.) Busch. (1925)
P. tschuktschorum Kjellman var. *arctica* (Koidz.) Fernald (1928)
P. pumila (Ledeb.) Pax var. *ledebouriana* Busch (1925) p.p.
P. tschuktschorum Kjellman subsp. *eximia* (Greene) Porsild (1965)

DESCRIPTION Differs from *P. tschuktschorum* in being at times a more robust and initially mealy plant with up to 10 homostylous magenta flowers up to 15 mm in diameter together in a one-sided umbel, which is sometimes stemless at flowering. The leaves are variable in shape and size, but exceed 4 mm in width, and the corolla tube is 1.5–2× the calyx. 2n = 22. (Photo: Bull AGS 57: 61 (1989) seems to refer to this species.)

DISTRIBUTION The more widespread species, in Alaska and Siberia, occurring to the south, west and east of *P. tschuktschorum,* including the northern Kuriles, Kamtschatka, the Aleutian islands, the Pribilof islands, the Alaskan peninsula and southern and central Alaska.

'Late snowbeds along coastal bluffs and ravines, in the mountains on frost-disturbed areas and in streambeds; from sea-level to alpine elevations, to over 1200 m.'

According to Federov (1952), *P. eximia* is close to Kelso's concept, but the plants are usually robust. Federov separates *P. arctica* Koidz., which is considered to be endemic to Provideniya Bay, Chukchi, and nearby islands, as having few large flowers with short stalks and a short corolla-tube; the leaves are said to be 5–7 mm wide. Thus, it falls between Kelso's definitions of *P. tschuktschorum* and *P. eximia*, although it probably lies within the variability of the latter.

It is curious that the outbreeding *P. tschuktschorum* should be less variable and more ecologically restricted than the inbreeding *P. eximia*. Kelso suggests that *P. eximia* may gain by its reproductive assurance in these extreme environments; most of the variability in this species is expressed between populations, but it also exhibits the considerable plasticity which is typical of inbreeders. *P. eximia* seems to have evolved secondarily from *P. tschuktschorum*.

For cultivation, see *P. tschuktschorum*.

Primula limbata Balf. f. & Forrest, Notes Roy. Bot. Gdn. Edinb. 13: 13 (1920)

P. sinonivalis Balf. f. & Forrest (1920)
P. longipetiolata Pax & Hoffm. (1921)
P. tsiangiae Fang (1956) non *P. tsiangii* Smith

DESCRIPTION Leaves erect, narrowly spear-shaped, but with a rounded tip, smooth, weakly keeled, stiff and leathery, bearing a marginal band of mealy horny teeth quite unlike those of any other Chinese species. Flowers rosy-lilac with a dark eye, 20 mm in diameter, about 7 together, borne one-sidedly on a mealy stalk which about equals the leaves. The capsule is about half as long again as the calyx. (Plate 85.)

DISTRIBUTION The borderlands of Sichuan, Gansu and Qinghai, in the Tatsienlu and Mekong-Salween divide regions, 3700–4300 m. Damp grassy north-facing slopes on limestone. Seen and photographed several times in the 1990s at Juixhaigou, near Songpan, and in 2001 near Jigzhi, but seems not to have been reintroduced in recent years. Flowered at Edinburgh in 1924.

The first of three related species from the Gansu-Sichuan border.

Primula optata Farrer, Notes Roy. Bot. Gdn. Edinb. 9: 187 (1916)

DESCRIPTION A close relative of *P. limbata*, but dwarfer, with glossy serrated leathery leaves which lack meal and a narrow capsule about 2× the calyx; unlike the former the resting bud is inconspicuous. (Fig. Halda: 205.) (Plate 86)

DISTRIBUTION Gansu, Qinghai and their borders with Sichuan, between Juizhaigou and Songpan, near Jigzhi, and Min Shan above Siku, alpine limestone screes, 3900–4600 m.

Related to the other Gansu border species *P. limbata* and *P. farreriana,* with similar flowers, but growing in a distinct habitat and more of a dwarf alpine. Farrer, who knew all three species in the wild, was insistent that they differed although they have very similar inflorescences and occur in the same areas.

Collected by SQBE 545 on the Gonggan Len above Songpan in 2000, and seen by the AGS tour to Qinghai in 2001, near Jigzhi, growing in the same area as *P. limbata* and *P. woodwardii*.

Primula farreriana Balf. f., Notes Roy. Bot. Gdn. Edinb. 9: 167 (1916)

DESCRIPTION A more robust, white-mealy leek-like (the leaf-stalks thus very wide and sheathing) plant than *P. limbata* and *P. optata,* but probably related to them and occurring in a nearby region. Calyx long and purple, to 12 mm; the annulate corolla pale lavender blue with a white eye and a dark purple tube, to 25 mm in diameter, the corolla-lobes deeply notched.

DISTRIBUTION Apparently restricted to shady limestone fissures in the Tatung mountains, Sining, Gansu, 4000–5000 m. A distinctive and handsome species which has never been in cultivation.

Primula russeola Balf. f. & Forrest, Notes Roy. Bot. Gdn. Edinb. 13: 17 (1920)

P. lancifolia Pax & Hoffm. (1921)
P. ionantha Pax & Hoffm. (1921)

DESCRIPTION Leaves rather many, arising from clumps of small below-ground resting buds, spreading, spear-shaped but with a blunt to rounded tip, flat and smooth. Stems exceeding leaves, to 15 cm, bearing 2–6 flowers one-sidedly. Calyx tube-shaped, brownish-purple, the sepal-lobes narrow but blunt. Corolla lilac with a red-purple tube and a broad white eye, or a dark eye, exannulate, flat-faced, to 18 mm in diameter, the tube 1.5× the calyx.

DISTRIBUTION From the borders of Tibet, Yunnan and Sichuan, e.g. Muli, Tsarong, Londre, Beima Shan, Da Xue Shan, Yungning, Batang. Flushes and the edges of snow-melt rills, 4000–4400 m.

This previously little-understood species was collected on a number of occasions in the 1990s from the Beima Shan, Da Xue Shan and Mekong–Salween divide. In the wild it is moderately attractive, but in comparison with many of its relatives a rather understated species.

CULTIVATION Introduced from the Beima Shan by both the KGB (1992) and ACE (1993) expeditions, and possibly by Peter Cox from the Mekong–Salween divide, although not identified at the time. Germinated well and grew vigorously for some growers e.g. Alan Furness who had several good clumps. Proved to be very shy to flower, and has now (2001) largely disappeared from cultivation.

Primula youngeriana Smith, J. Linn. Soc. Bot. 52: 340 (1942)

DESCRIPTION A relative of *P. russeola*, with a similar thin-textured leaf-blade with a rounded tip, but leaves broader, even rounded, and with a remarkable saucer-shaped calyx, the sepal-lobes of which are spreading and cut to the base. The bracts are long, to 4 cm, and the corolla-tube is short, not exceeding the calyx. The white-eyed flowers are a deep blue-violet.

DISTRIBUTION Only known from the Mira La, to the west of Tsela, Kongbo, south-east Tibet, moss under large boulders at 5000 m.

Primula woonyoungiana Fang, Acta Univ. Szechuan 1: 202 (1956)

DESCRIPTION A robust species with overlapping leaf-bases forming leek-like stocks, very broadly ovate deeply crenate leaves, thickly yellow-mealy beneath and large lilac-purple flowers in one or more whorls; corolla to 30 mm in diameter, annulate, darker towards the centre, petal-lobes entire, rounded.

DISTRIBUTION Maowenxian, north-west Sichuan. Stony grassland and rocky slopes, 3800–4600 m. What appears to have been the same species was photographed by Peter Cox from near Londre on the Mekong–Salween divide in 1994.

Primula hoi Fang, Act. Univ. Szechwan 1: 100 (1956)

DESCRIPTION A little-known plant with deeply toothed ovate leaves, yellow-mealy and with purple veins beneath; flower stalks with red glands; flowers pale lilac-blue. Lixian, west Sichuan, meadows, 3500–4800 m.

Primula lactucoides Chen & Hu, Fl. Rep. Pop. Sin. 2: 293 (1990)

DESCRIPTION An extraordinary plant with narrowly oblong leaves with large regular spaced teeth, almost like a dandelion; flowers white. Only dubiously placed in this section but with no other clear relatives. East Tibet, Nangqen Shan, rocks in mixed coniferous forest, 360–4800 m. (Fig. Halda: 197.)

Primula lungchiensis Fang, Act. Univ. Szechuan. 1: 88 (1956)

DESCRIPTION Another extraordinary plant, possibly related to *P. lactucoides*, but with shiny dark green pinnate leaves, and relatively large reddish purple flowers; appears extremely handsome, but little known, and possibly should be placed systematically in a very isolated position. Lixiang, Sichuan, wet meadows and streamsides, 3400–4500 m. (Fig. Halda: 19.)

Subsection **Calliantha** (Pax) Smith & Fletcher

Trans. Roy. Soc. Edinb. 60: 612 (1942)
(Section Calliantha Pax, 1889 p.p.)

Resting bud large, egg-shaped, with massive, usually mealy, scales, above-ground. Calyx tubular; flowers often funnel-shaped, somewhat zygomorphic, exannulate or annulate; corolla-lobes deeply notched; capsule usually included within or equalling calyx, valvate with dry seeds.

KEY TO SPECIES

1. Flowers exannulate, bluish; meal sulphur-green (or absent) .... *P. calliantha*
1. Flowers exannulate or annulate, rose, white or yellow; meal white or cream 2

2. Flowers white or pink 3
2. Flowers yellow, annulate .... *P. mishmiensis*

3. Flowers white or pale pink; meal yellowish .... *P. obliqua*
3. Flowers rose-pink; meal white or absent 4

4. Dwarf plant, flowers annulate, corolla-tube narrow, cylindrical .... *P. bryophila*
4. Plant often robust, flowers exannulate, corolla-tube funnel-shaped .... *P. boreiocalliantha*

Primula calliantha Franchet, Bull. Soc. Bot. Fr. 32: 268 (1885)

P. junior Balf. f.& Forrest (1920)
P. proba Balf. f.& Forrest (1920)

DESCRIPTION *Leaves* arising from a compact spherical mealy resting bud; leaf-blade obovate, bright green, regularly crenate, at first covered with a greenish meal, or without meal. *Stem* to 30 cm but usually much shorter in flower, bearing 3–10 flowers in a single umbel. *Calyx* mealy, to 15 mm, narrowly bell-shaped, blackish. *Corolla* bright dark blue to purple-violet with a large yellow-mealy eye, or eye lacking, to 35 mm in diameter, zygomorphic with the lower three corolla lobes pointing forward and the upper two reflexed; corolla lobes notched to shortly lacerate; corolla-tube inflated above. *Capsule* equalling the calyx. (Fig. Halda: 190–1.) (Plate 87.)

DISTRIBUTION Widespread in north-west Yunnan, well-known on the Cang-Shan, but extending to mountains around the Zhongdian plateau, Fuchuan to the west of the Yangtse bend on the Tum La, Tsanang La and Lusha La, and to the north of it on the Beima Shan. Also in adjoining areas of Burma and Tibet as far as Tsarong. Grassy glades in scrub and *Abies delavayi*, 3500–4000 m.

It is normally stated that this species, and *P. boreiocalliantha*, have annulate flowers. Now that they are well-known in the wild and have flowered in cultivation we can see that they do in fact have wide-mouthed exannulate zygomorphic flowers and are apparently most closely related to the Himalayan *P. obliqua*.

CULTIVATION Plants were raised from Forrest's seed in 1908 and 1925, but they did not persist. Ludlow and Sherriff introduced seed and plants in 1938, but they did not thrive, nor did plants introduced from the Cang Shan in 1982. Reintroduced as resting buds from the Cang Shan in 1990 (CLD 826, 1278) in mistake for *P. sonchifolia* with which it grows. Flowered at Edinburgh in 1991, but soon lost. Reintroduced as seed from the Cang Shan by KGB 811 in 1992 and ACE 2500 in 1993 but did not thrive. ARGS 941 from the Cang Shan in 2000 is the most recent attempt.

VARIATION

- Var. *albiflos* Smith & Forrest (1942); flowers white (Beima Shan).
- Var. *nuda* Farrer (1923); meal lacking except on basal scales (Burma). Such plants tend to have a dark eye to the flower.

Primula boreiocalliantha Balf. f. & Forrest, Notes Roy. Bot. Gdn. Edinb. 13: 4 (1920)

P. propinqua Balf. f. & Forrest, Notes Roy. Bot. Gdn. Edinb. 13: 16 (1920)
P. muliensis Hand.-Mazz., Anz. Akad. Wiss. Wien., Math.-Nat. 9: 116 (1923)
P. coryana Balf. f. & Forrest, Notes Roy. Bot. Gdn. Edinb. 14: 37 (1923)

DESCRIPTION Forms a massive egg-like resting-bud from which arise broadly oval to spear-shaped leaf-blades, narrowing to a winged stalk, white-mealy beneath, to 25 × 8 cm. This often magnificent plant carries a robust *stem* to 40 cm bearing 1–3 umbels of 3–9 huge somewhat zygomorphic bell-shaped exannulate rose *flowers* gold-spangled around the mouth and with notched petal-lobes, up to 40 mm in diameter. *Sepal-lobes* very narrow, acute. In many ways resembles *P. agleniana*, but with reddish flowers. (Fig. Halda: 193.) (Plate 88.)

DISTRIBUTION Widespread at around 4000 m in the region where Tibet, Yunnan and Sichuan meet, from Tsarong through Kulu, Muli to Zhongdian and the Mekong divides. In recent years has been seen frequently at Tianchi Lake, Zhongdian; Beima Shan and Da Xue Shan.

Despite Halda: 193 'limestone rocky grassland', I only saw this species growing underneath the canopy of four metre Taliensia rhododendrons in very dense shade, sometimes accompanied by *P. sonchifolia*.

P. boreiocalliantha is very variable as to leaf-shape. At Tianchi, I only saw populations with nearly isodiametric leaf-blades. Those from less densely shaded sites may have much longer narrower leaves and more closely resemble *P. obliqua* and *P. agleniana* in form, but not flower colour. The flower size and shape is highly distinctive. Closely related to *P. calliantha* but with rose-pink flowers and narrower, acute sepal-lobes.

CULTIVATION Probably not introduced until KGB 59, 747 (1993) and ACE 1172, 1769 (1994). Abundant seed was germinated by many expert growers, all of whom found it very difficult, although briefly offered commercially by Jim Sutherland who may have had the greatest success in northern Scotland. Survived best in deep shade, watered copiously in growth and almost dry in winter. Deeply resented being potted on as it came into growth. These introductions have probably been lost in 2001. Reintroduced by ARGS 464 from Da Xue Shan, ARGS 792 from Tianchi, Zhongdian and ARGS 779 from Hong Shan in 2000.

Massive mature plants were offered for sale from China in 1999 and flowered magnificently before a rapid demise. I initially misidentified some of these as *P. agleniana* and it is possible that the two species are colour forms of the same species. This species was offered again in 2001 under the name *P. veitchiana*.

Primula obliqua Smith, Trans. Bot. Soc. Edinb. 26: 154 (1913)

DESCRIPTION Forms massive bulb-like resting buds swathed in large oval pinkish yellow-mealy scales. *Leaves* spear-shaped, to 20 cm, cream-mealy beneath. *Calyx* long, to 15 mm, the lobes rounded. *Corolla* pendant, cream or flushed rose, somewhat zygomorphic with an oblique exannulate mouth, to 30 mm in diameter, about 5 in the umbel; corolla lobes strongly notched. *Capsule* scarcely exceeding the calyx. 2n = 22. (Photo: Fls. Himalaya Fig. 867, Bull. AGS 53 (1985).)

DISTRIBUTION East Nepal, Sikkim and west Bhutan. Very wet zones, 4000–5000 m. Very wet species-rich slopes, etc., often associated with dwarf rhododendron, cremanthodiums, potentillas, leontopodiums, etc.

This magnificent plant is quite unmistakable by virtue of the shape and colour of its flower, and by the splendid golf ball-like resting buds. Previously classified in subsection Crystallophlomis, it is clearly a relative of *P. calliantha*.

CULTIVATION *P. obliqua* has been introduced on so many occasions in recent years and with such limited success that we despair of its successful culture for any length of time. Only at Inshriach in the very cold climate of the Scottish Cairngorms has any permanent success been achieved. In other areas, both introduced resting buds and seedlings grow fitfully, and sometimes flower, but they rot in hot weather, and are difficult to overwinter successfully.

Primula bryophila Balf. f. & Farrer, Notes Roy. Bot. Gdn. Edinb. 13: 5 (1920)

P. shwelicalliantha Balf. f. & Forrest (1920)
P. tribola Balf. f. & Forrest (1920)

DESCRIPTION Vegetatively close to *P. calliantha*, but smaller, with very dark shiny upper surfaces to the leaves, narrower leaf-blades, and a funnel-shaped corolla limb with an annulate mouth and much more narrow corolla tube, flowers rose-pink. Frontier regions of Burma, Tibet and Yunnan, in the upper basins of the Salween, Shweli and N'Mai Hka; deep moss banks with rhododendrons and diapensia, 4000 m. In 1994, photographed by Peter Cox on the Mekong-Salween divide.

Primula mishmiensis Ward, Ann. Bot. 44: 122 (1930)

DESCRIPTION Vegetatively close to *P. calliantha*, but resembling *P. bryophila* in the narrow-tubed annulate flowers which, distinctively, are a bright buff yellow. Collected once from the Delei valley, Mishmi hills, Assam. Outcrops of rock and steep humus-clad slopes amongst dwarf rhododendron, 3700–4000 m.

Subsection **Agleniana** Smith & Fletcher, Trans. Roy. Soc. Edinb. 60: 623 (1942)

In most regards resembling subsection Calliantha with the resting bud large and bulb-like, leaf-bases broad and sheathing, continuing to form a usually mealy bulb-like base to the plant and the flowers few, large, bell-shaped, pendulous, exannulate. Differs by the flowers usually yellow and calyx cup-shaped with broad blunt lobes; capsule globular, crumbling at maturity, viable seeds moist as in section Petiolares. Seed germinates poorly in cultivation, and may have to be sown fresh, as for the petiolarids. Although members of this subsection are clearly related to other nivalids such as *P. calliantha*, they seem to link with petiolarids in subsection Griffithii, especially in the character of the capsule.

Primula agleniana Balf. f. & Forrest, Notes Roy. Bot. Gdn. Edinb. 13: 3 (1920)

DESCRIPTION A magnificent stately plant arising from a reddish *bulb*-like base; leaf-blades spear-shaped, sharp, serrate, covered with greenish-yellow meal beneath, leaves to 30 cm. *Stems* to 40 cm, carrying 3–8 fragrant flowers pendant on slender stalks to 5 cm. *Flowers* primrose yellow, less commonly ivory, orange yellow or rose with a broad mealy white eye, to 4 cm or more across the bell. (Photo: J. Roy. Hort. Soc. 54: 40 (1929).) (Fig. Halda: 187.)

DISTRIBUTION On the borders of Tibet, Burma and Yunnan; mountains on both sides of the Salween, e.g. Tsarong, Kenichumpo; Assam. Mud-slides, earth slopes and banks on sticky black humus-rich soils based on igneous rocks, 3200–4000 m.

Can closely resemble *P. boreiocalliantha*, which, however, has rose flowers, white meal, and apparently a 'normal' capsule dehiscence. It is not impossible that they represent colour forms of the same species.

Despite copious seed sent home by Forrest, success in cultivation has been slight. However, reports make one wonder how carefully this was tended! At Caerhays, seed 'broadcast under beeches' flowered in 1927, although not surprisingly they didn't persist. The Royal Botanic Garden, Edinburgh appeared also to have treated this superb species in a similarly cavalier fashion, growing it in a rose-bed!

VARIATION

- Var. *alba* Forrest (1923), flowers white, flushed rose. Tsarong, Tibet, and Burma.
- Var. *atrocrocea* Ward (1930), flowers orange-yellow. Delei Valley, Assam.
- var. *thearosa* Ward (1930), flowers bright pink. Upper Burma.

Primula elizabethae Ludlow, Notes Roy. Bot. Gdn. Edinb. 19: 205 (1937)

DESCRIPTION A smaller plant than *P. agleniana*, and lacking meal. Leaves spoon-shaped, the ovate blade 5 × 2.5 cm, exceeded by the long narrow stalk. Flowers 1(–5), primrose-yellow, to 35 mm across the bell. (Photo: Quest of Flowers: 107.) (Fig. Halda: 188.)

South-east Tibet; apparently confined to the very rich and extremely wet passes that lie in Tsari between Pachakshiri and Kongbo, the Tum La, Lo La, Tsari Sama and Chubumba La; open grassy or earth slopes at about 4500 m. Named after Frank Ludlow's mother. Seeds failed to germinate in 1936. Resting buds collected in 1938 never flowered.

Primula falcifolia Ward, Notes Roy. Bot. Gdn. Edinb. 15: 76 (1926)

DESCRIPTION Similar to *P. elizabethae*, differing chiefly in the very narrow almost linear grassy leaf-blades. Flowers daffodil-yellow with a white-mealy eye, to 30 mm in diameter across the bell, contrasting with the red stem and bell-shaped calyx. Endemic to the Doshong La across the main range just west of the Tsangpo bend, about 100 km east of *P. elizabethae*, in south-east Tibet. South-facing steep alpine turf-slopes in a very wet district, 4000–4300 m. Seed collected by Ward in 1924, and by Ludlow and Sherriff in 1938 did not germinate. A resting bud collected on the latter occasion flowered twice at Edinburgh. Photographed by Kenneth Cox, Anne Chambers and party in 1995 (Photo: Riddle of the Tsangpo Gorge: 142, 159; Proceedings 7th Int. Rock Garden Conf.: plate 23.) (Fig. Halda: 189.) (Plate 89.)

KEY TO SPECIES

Leaves spear-shaped, long attenuate onto a short stalk .... *P. agleniana*
Leaves spoon-shaped, blade ending abruptly in a long stalk .... *P. elizabethae*
Leaves linear, grass-like .... *P. falcifolia*

Subsection **Maximowiczii** (Balf. f.) Smith & Fletcher,

Trans. Roy. Soc. Edinb. 60: 616 (1942)
(Section Maximowiczii Balf. f. 1913)

Differs from subsection Crystallophlomis by usually lacking meal, and by the distinctive narrow usually reflexed often dark red to blackish corolla-lobes. Resting buds large, golf-ball shaped, above ground. Several species have flowers in superimposed whorls. Capsules exceeding calyx, dehiscence valvate, seeds dry.

KEY TO SPECIES

1. Flowers black or violet to red in colour 2
1. Flowers at least partly yellow 5

2. Corolla-lobes linear, reflexed, blackish .... *P. tangutica*
2. Corolla-lobes not more than 4 × as long as wide, violet or red to brown 3

3. Corolla dark red; leaves lacking a clear stalk; meal absent .... *P. maximowiczii*
3. Corolla violet or chocolate-colour; leaves with a winged stalk; meal present at least at first 4

4. Corolla violet, strongly annulate; leaf stalk narrow .... *P. woodwardii*
4. Corolla chocolate-coloured, weakly annulate; leaf-stalk broadly winged .... *P. advena* v. *euprepes*

5. Flowers usually in superimposed whorls, 5 or more in a whorl 6
5. Flowers in a single whorl of 2–4 7

6. Plant lacking meal; corolla-lobes strongly reflexed .... *P. szechuanica*
6. Plant mealy at least at first; corolla-lobes patent or slightly reflexed .... *P. advena*

7. Corolla-lobes spreading; base of leaf-blade cuneate .... *P. handeliana*
7. Corolla-lobes reflexed; base of leaf-blade heart-shaped .... *P. tzetsouensis*

Primula maximowiczii Regel, Acta Hort. Petropol. 3: 139 (1874)

P. oreocharis Hance (1875)

DESCRIPTION *Leaf-blades* oblong-elliptic, to 20 × 4 cm, more or less entire, stalk obscure, bright green. The stout *stem* bears 1–3 whorls of dark red to purple (rarely orange) flowers on erect stalks to 4 cm. The *flower* with strongly reflexed lobes is about 15 mm in diameter and annulate; corolla-lobes narrowly oblong, rounded. 2n = 22. (Photo: J. Roy. Hort. Soc. 54: 41 (1929).)

DISTRIBUTION Mountains of north-central China; Chihli, Shensi, Shansi. Rather dry alpine meadows, and shady rocks in fir forests at about 2500 m.

Introduced by Purdom from seeds collected in northern Wei-Chang in 1908 and exhibited in 1910 by Veitch, gaining a Botanical Certificate (**AM** 1913). Still in cultivation in 1942, but lost soon after. Offered by Ron McBeath in 2001, and grows vigorously in a partially shaded bed in pure leaf-mould, over-wintered under glass

Primula tangutica Duthie, Gard. Chron. 38: 42 (1905)

P. silenantha Pax & Hoffm. (1920)

DESCRIPTION Differs chiefly from *P. maximowiczii* by the linear, blackish-red corolla-lobes, and narrower spoon-shaped leaves with a strong grey-purple cast. (Plate 103.)

DISTRIBUTION From the region where Gansu, north Sichuan and Qinghai meet Qingsha Shan, T'ao river, Yellow river, Dayu valley, Juizhaigou to Songpan, Huangshen Guan, Huanglong Si. 2500–3900 m.

CULTIVATION Introduced from Wilson's seed in 1902–3, and later by Purdom, but extinct in cultivation by 1925. Seed and plants were reintroduced by Lord Howick in 1989; still in limited circulation in 2001. Collected on several occasions by SQAE in 2000: 30, 195, 475, 571, 599.

The flowers are very sweetly but somewhat disagreeably scented. A curiosity! Grown in pots, plants have flowered very early, by the end of February. Large plantings are still in flower during late May at Cluny, Perthshire.

Primula woodwardii Balf. f., Notes Roy. Bot. Gdn. Edinb. 9: 61 (1915)

DESCRIPTION Flowers with very narrow slightly reflexed violet corolla lobes, a deeper purple corolla tube, and a very marked 10-lobed annulus. Lacks meal. Leaves with a narrowly winged stalk. (Plate 104.)

DISTRIBUTION Gansu and Qinghai; Min Shan, mountains above Siku, and the Tatung mountains; also on the Qinghai-Sichuan border. Rough alpine turf, 3000–4000 m.

Introduced from seed collected by Purdom (1911) and Fenwick Owen (?1912) and flowered from both collections, but did not persist. Recently photographed by an AGS trip to China led by Harry Jans and John Mitchell at 3980 m on the pass between Sichuan and Qinghai near Jigzhi.

Primula szechuanica Pax, Pflanzenreich Primulaceae: 106 (1905)

P. declinis Balf. f. & Forrest (1920)
P. decurva Balf. f. & Forrest (1920)
P. gagnepainiana Hand.-Mazz. (1924)
P. aemula Balf. f. & Forrest (1915)

DESCRIPTION Similar in structure to *P. maximowiczii*, but with tiers of fragrant *yellow* flowers with longer and broader corolla lobes (to 10 × 3 mm), and toothed leaves with a marked stalk equalling the blade.

DISTRIBUTION Western Sichuan, in the regions of Tatsienlu, Muli, Kulu, etc., and northern Yunnan, Zhongdian plateau. Recently discovered (2000) on the Zo La in south-east Tibet near the Burma border, just north of Zayul, by Tony Cox, a notable extension of range.

CULTIVATION Seeds were collected by Wilson (1906), Purdom (1910) and Forrest (1912 and later). Although the successive Forrest gatherings flowered and were maintained until about 1930, they did not persist. Reintroduced (Cox 5077) in 1989 and probably by ACE 2150 in 1994 (as *P. aemula*, a species lost into synonymy many years previously); good flowering groups have grown at Cluny, but may have disappeared by 2001.

Primula tzetsouensis Petitm., Bull. Herb. Boiss. 8: 366 (1908)

P. yuana Chen (1939)

DESCRIPTION A close relative of *P. szechuanica*, but much more delicate with only 2–4 flowers in the single umbel and differing chiefly by the short oval leaf-blade with a heart-shaped base and a long narrow stalk twice the length of the blade; the short corolla-tube scarcely exceeds the slightly mealy calyx.

DISTRIBUTION Mt. Metigonka, Kiulung, Sikang; Tze-tsoue, near Yargong, west Sichuan. Dry rocky high alpine areas and moist soil in shade, 4000 m.

This very little known plant was classified by Smith & Fletcher (1943) in section Cordifoliae. However, they were clearly unhappy with this analysis, not least because the other species in this section are Himalayan, and none are yellow-flowered. Although comparisons were made with section Sikkimensis, for some reason they did not consider the yellow-flowered Maximowiczii. If they had, it would have become immediately clear that this species is identical with *P. yuana*. Curiously, Halda (1992) agrees independently with this synonomy and classification, but places this species in both sections in duplicate.

Primula handeliana Smith & Forrest, Notes Roy. Bot. Gdn. Edinb. 16: 45 (1928)

DESCRIPTION Very similar to and possibly conspecific with *P. tzetsouensis*, but with spreading rather than deflexed corolla lobes which are longer (7–10 × 3–4 mm), and with cuneate leaf bases. Shensi, Taipei Shan, 3000 m.

Primula advena Smith, Notes Roy. Bot. Gdn. Edinb. 19: 311 (1938)

P. maximowiczii Regel var. *euprepes* Smith (1926)

DESCRIPTION The most distinct of the relatives of *P. szechuanica*, being somewhat mealy, having broad winged but distinct leaf-stalks and, in the type variety, a purple corolla-tube which contrasts strongly with the pale yellow deflexed corolla lobes. Said by Sherriff to be 'the most fragrant primula I have ever seen' (smelt?). (Photo: Riddle of the Tsangpo Gorge: 128.).

DISTRIBUTION From a number of passes in south-east Tibet, principally in the very rich Tsari district, where it occurs from 4000–4600 m in boulder forest and rhododendron scrub. The type variety was photographed by Anne Chambers in Tsari in 1998 and by Tony Cox there in 2000.

P. maximowiczii var. *euprepes* was named from Ludlow and Sherriff's gatherings in Tibet some 700 km south of the range of *P. maximowiczii*. In 'A Quest of Flowers': 204, Fletcher comments that it is probably worthy of specific rank. However, it occurs only slightly to the east of *P. advena*, and appears to be indistinguishable from the latter except in flower colour which is in any case variable in *P. advena*.

VARIATION

- var. *euprepes* (Smith) Richards (1993) (*P. maximowiczii* Regel var. *euprepes* Smith, Notes Roy. Bot. Gdn. Edinb. 15: 79 (1926) **comb. nov**.) Differs from the type by chocolate coloured flowers. Nyima La, east of Tsela, between Kongbo and Pemako, south-east Tibet. Photographed by Anne Chambers on the Nyima La in 1995.
- var. *concolor* Smith (1938) differs from the type by having entirely yellow flowers. Photographed by Anne Chambers on the Zo La in 1997.
- var. *argentata* Smith (1938) is a smaller neater plant with an entirely yellow corolla tube; the edge of the leaf is mealy, giving a neat band of silver teeth. This distinctive variety, which may well be worthy of specific rank has only been collected once from the Du Chu, Pasho, eastern Tibet.

There are photos at Kew of Ludlow and Sherriff 2242 from the Takar La, and the same number cultivated in the Sandeman's garden 'The Laws'. This plant has yellow non-reflexed petals, and is named there var. *concholoba* Smith, which, however, appears never to have been formally described. The type form of *P. advena* was grown from Ludlow and Sherriff seed for several years at Edinburgh.

Section **Cordifoliae** Pax, Bot. Jahrb. Syst. 10: 214 (1889) (Section Rotundifolia Smith & Forrest 1928). Type species *P. rotundifolia* Wall.

DESCRIPTION *Mealy* deciduous plants arising from substantial resting buds at ground level. *Leaves* with involute vernation, the leaf-blades short, broad, rounded at the tip, and well demarcated from the stalk, commonly round and with a heart-shaped base, the stalk often narrow. *Flowers* borne in single umbels, rarely in 2–3 whorls, on a slender stem, bracts small. Flowers violet, reddish, pink, lavender or rarely white, with a pale, usually yellowish eye, annulate, heterostylous. *Pollen* oblate, 3-syncolpate. *Capsules* globose to cylindrical, scarcely exceeding the calyx, dehiscing by apical valves. Seeds quadrate, dry. Chromosome number 2n = 22. Flowering April–May in cultivation.

DISTRIBUTION Eastern Himalaya, from central Nepal to the Tsangpo bend in south-east Tibet, with an undescribed species in northern Burma; typically plants of alpine rocks above the tree-line on the south side of the main range, 3300–6000 m.

There is no doubt that the Cordifoliae, commonly known by the later name Rotundifolia, are closely related to the Crystallophlomis, although as conceived here they seem to form a distinct and natural grouping. DNA studies support this concept, for although *P. rotundifolia* is related to the four Crystallophlomis species studies (two subsections), it appears to be more distinct than any of them. All the species except *P. caveana* have a rounded leaf-blade with a heart-shaped base and a long narrow leaf-stalk which is not found in the nivalids. *P. caveana* has a cuneate base to the leaf-blade, but undoubtedly also belongs here. The remaining six species are very closely related to one another, and it is possible that this group has been 'over-split'. However, these six form an interesting series of 'ecospecies', each varying from the others in geographical area and habitat.

The central Himalayan *P. rotundifolia* is possibly the most primitive, in that it is the most 'nivalid-like' in aspect, and it is also the most robust and inhabits the lowest altitudes (although there are small high alpine forms). Immediately to the east, and at somewhat higher altitudes is found *P. gambeliana*, and this links geographically and morphologically with the high alpines *P. baileyana* of wet zones and *P. littledalei* of much drier sites still further east. *P. baileyana* is perhaps the most specialized species in the series, with its thin wiry stems and stalks, but it has an unexpected counterpart in dry zones of the western Himalaya, *P. ramzanae*.

Previously this was a less coherent group, but in 1993 I transferred the yellow-flowered *P. barnardoana* to section Crystallophlomis within *P. elongata*, while the very little known Chinese species *P. tzetsouensis* had also been placed in the Cordifoliae, but its affinities clearly lie with the nivalid subsection Maximowiczii.

CULTIVATION The Cordifoliae present similar problems in cultivation to the nivalids, and for similar reasons. They tend to be short-lived in cultivation, and only persist when seed is set. The greatest success has been achieved with *P. rotundifolia*, which sets seed regularly, and this germinates well. Consequently, this species has now been continuously although sparingly in cultivation for many years.

Plants require rich, damp, cool and well-drained conditions when in growth, but a nearly dry winter rest, and are probably best managed grown in plastic pots plunged in a shady frame in most areas. They are prone to attack by vine weevil. No hybrids have been reported.

KEY TO SPECIES

1. Base of leaf-blade cuneate .... *P. caveana*
1. Base of leaf-blade heart-shaped 2

2. Plant, except resting bud, lacking meal 3
2. Plant mealy, especially below leaf 4

3. Leaf-blades fleshy, orbicular .... *P. macklinae*
3. Leaf-blades longer than wide, not fleshy .... *P. gambeliana*

4. Corolla-lobes notched 5
4. Corolla-lobes entire or toothed, not notched 6

5. Flowers pinkish-purple, calyx purple .... *P. ramzanae*
5. Flowers lilac, calyx green .... *P. baileyana*

6. Meal white, leaf-veins impressed, conspicuous .... *P. littledalei*
6. Meal cream to yellow, leaf-veins obscure .... *P. rotundifolia*

Primula rotundifolia Wallich, Roxburgh's Fl. India 2: 18 (1824) non Pallas (1776) nomen (= *P. nutans* Georgi)

P. cordifolia Pax (1889) non Rupr. (1863) nec Kit. (1863) nec Schur (1886)

P. cardiophylla Balf. f. & Smith (1916)

P. cordata Balf. f. ex Smith & Forrest (1928) nomen nudum

P. roxburghii Balakr., J. Bombay Nat. Hist. Soc. 67: 63 (1972)

DESCRIPTION *Leaf-blades* more or less orbicular, to 12 × 12 cm, although about 4 × 4 cm at flowering, matt olive-green above, smothered with creamy meal below, slightly concave, coarsely crenate, heart-shaped at the base; the stalk narrow except for the sheathing base, mealy, somewhat exceeding the blade. *Stem* slender to robust, mealy at least above, about 6 cm at flowering, elongating in fruit, carrying 1(–3) whorls of 2–12 flowers borne horizontally on mealy stalks to 2 cm at flowering. *Calyx* bell-shaped, mealy, to 6 mm, divided almost to the base into three-nerved lobes. *Corolla* pinkish-purple with a yellow eye, flat-faced to slightly concave, to 23 mm in diameter; corolla-tube cylindrical, 2–3× the calyx; petal-lobes overlapping crowded and somewhat concave, broadly rounded and entire or slightly crenate. Capsule oblong. (Plate 10.)

DISTRIBUTION Central Himalaya, confined to the wettest zones on the south side of the main range from Gosainkund, Nepal in the west eastwards to the slopes of Kanchenjunga, west Sikkim, commonest in the Everest region.

Exposed rock crevices and boulder scree, 3000–4900 m. Apparently local and rarely plentiful.

P. rotundifolia has a long and complex taxonomic history. It was first named by Wallich (605) from fruiting summer material collected by pilgrims from Gosainkund, then known as Gosain Than (see *P. aureata*). The type at Kew is scant and poor, but quite characteristic of our modern concept of this species. Balakrishnan (1972) was of the opinion that this familiar name must be dropped in deference to Pallas' earlier homonym, but as Smith and Fletcher (1943) point out, it has been long established that Pallas' name has no validity. In any case, if *P. rotundifolia* Wall. was found to be invalid, *P. cardiophylla* Balf. f. & Smith exists as the valid prior synonym (and is so used by Halda, 1992).

More robust forms from Sikkim were for a long time thought to belong to another species, particularly as many have apparently lost their meal. *P. cordifolia* Pax is the original name for these, but this is predated by no less than three earlier homonyms, now placed under *P. elatior* and *P. veris*. *P. cordata* was coined by Balfour to overcome this problem. However, Smith and Fletcher (1943) having seen Schlagintweit's Sikkim specimen on which *P. cordifolia* Pax and *P. cordata* are based were firmly of the opinion that it was the same as *P. cardiophylla* Balf. f. & Smith which is prior to *P. cordata*. They also consider that *P. cardiophylla* falls within the range of plants known as *P. rotundifolia* Wallich. With this I agree and Flora of China (Chen and Hu 1990) has also taken this view.

CULTIVATION First introduced from Sikkim in 1866, and reintroduced from there on a number of occasions. It was not in cultivation in 1928, or in 1943. However, it has been continuously in cultivation certainly since 1960. It is sometimes still seen at shows, and has been offered recently in the trade (2001). Small forms from the Kali Gandhaki have been cultivated under the name of *P. ramzanae*. Reintroduced in 1989 under EMAK 926, in 1991 from Gosainkund (CC&McK 533), in 1992 from Ganesh Himal (CC&McK 1033) and as GOS 60 (1995).

Primula gambeliana Watt, J. Linn. Soc. 20: 3 (1882)

DESCRIPTION A smaller and more delicate relative of *P. rotundifolia*, lacking meal (except on the resting bud), and with leaf-blades which are longer than wide, and much shorter than the long slender stalk. The pale purple corollas have notched lobes, and the capsule is twice as long as the calyx. (Photo: Flowers of the Himalaya (supplement) t.67 (as *P. pulchra*).) (Plate 48.)

DISTRIBUTION From the Nepal–Sikkim border eastwards to 92° E on the Bhutan–Tibet border (Tsona) and Assam. Amongst dwarf rhododendrons and mosses, often in crevices on wet cliffs and amongst boulders, 3600–4500 m.

CULTIVATION *P. gambeliana* is a pretty and delicate little plant which has occasionally been introduced and grown for a few years. It was at Edinburgh from 1930–41, and was in cultivation in 1977, and again in the 1980s, probably from Sikkim seed offered by the firm of Ghose's. It grows and flowers well for a few years in suitable conditions, but rarely sets seed and has not now been seen for nearly two decades (2001).

Primula caveana Smith, Rec. Bot. Surv. India 4: 218 (1911)

P. cana Balf. f. & Cave (1916)
P. younghusbandiana Balf. f. (1922)

DESCRIPTION A dwarf high alpine plant, with plentiful whitish meal, cuneate leaf-bases, strongly dentate leaf-blades and a globular capsule which is shorter than the calyx. Flowers very fragrant and beautiful, to 20 mm in diameter, bland lavender-pink, rarely white. (Photo: Bull. AGS 46: 267; 58: 136.) (Plate 91.)

DISTRIBUTION From eastern Nepal in the Everest region eastwards through Sikkim, Chumbi, Bhutan and southern and south-eastern Tibet as far east as Tsari.

Invariably occurring in high rain-shadow regions away from the direct influence of the monsoon, but with long winter snow-lie. Sheltered, rather dry rock-crevices, 4000–6000 m. Although named for the Himalayan climber and explorer Cave who discovered it in the company of Wright Smith, ironically it sometimes inhabits caves too. This is the highest growing of all primulas, and one of the highest occurring of all higher plants, occurring as it does on the Everest range to nearly 20,000 ft.

Although rather smaller, it has a remarkable resemblance to the completely unrelated *P. marginata* from the Maritime Alps.

CULTIVATION Originally in cultivation in 1909. Flowered, probably from Ludlow and Sherriff's Tsari gatherings, in 1939. This introduction seems not to have persisted. Grown briefly in the 1960s, probably from Ghose's seed, and introduced from the Everest region by Dr George Smith in 1976. Wild collected seed is still sometimes offered, most recently by KEKE 578 (1990). The plant remains intermittently in cultivation, although always very rare.

Growers who have succeeded with it, such as Eric Watson, treated it as a high alpine grown in full light in the alpine house. It is almost certainly very intolerant of overhead damp, requires very cool growing conditions, and a long almost dry winter rest.

Primula baileyana Ward, Notes Roy. Bot. Gdn. Edinb. 15: 82 (1926)

DESCRIPTION Closely related to *P. gambeliana* and *P. littledalei*, differing from the former in being copiously white-mealy, by having orbicular leaf-blades and by the capsule equalling the calyx; and from the latter by notched corolla-lobes, thin wiry leaf-stalks and stems and a 5-veined calyx. The flowers are a delicate lilac, rarely white, with a lemon eye. *P. rotundifolia* is a more robust species with yellowish meal. (Photo: Riddle of the Tsangpo Gorge: 169; Proceedings 7th Int. Rock Garden Conf. plate 22.) (Plate 90)

DISTRIBUTION South-east Tibet; widespread and locally common on most of the passes to the east (main range) and north of Tse, between Pemako and Kongbo; e.g. Nam La, Nambu la. Tse La, Mira La, Tsanang La and Sang La. Larch and rhododendron forest, dry rocks, loose earth of avalanche slopes, etc., in a rich and very wet zone, 4000–5000 m.

CULTIVATION Grown from 1926–1941 from Ward's 1924 seed from the Nambu La. Reintroduced by Ludlow and Sherriff (13268) in 1947. These plants grew well outside for a short time in shady screes and a peat wall, but did not persist long. Seen by Anne Chambers and Kenneth Cox on the Temo La in 1995.

Primula ramzanae Smith & Fletcher, J. Roy. Hort. Soc. 79: 358 (1954)

DESCRIPTION Another delicate relative of *P. gambeliana*, very close to *P. baileyana*, and differing from the latter chiefly by the deep purple calyx and the pinkish-purple flowers; although the leaves are cream-mealy below, the bud-scales and inflorescence lack meal. The corolla lobes are notched. (Fig. Halda: 218. Fls. Himalaya, fig. 307.)

DISTRIBUTION West Nepal, disjunct from all its relatives; Nahure, north-west of the Dhaulagiri massif in a rain-shadow area. Cliffs and scree slopes with abundant surface moisture from snow-melt, 4300–5200 m.

An unexpected discovery by Polunin, Sykes and Williams in 1952, only known from this isolated area. Flowered at Wisley in 1953 and shown at the RHS, but did not persist. Plants grown under this name about 1980 were *P. rotundifolia*.

Primula littledalei Balf. f. & Watt, Notes Roy. Bot. Gdn. Edinb. 9: 179 (1916)

P. consocia Smith (1936)

DESCRIPTION A relative of *P. rotundifolia*, differing by having white meal, conspicuous leaf veins, entire corolla-lobes and a short capsule. *P. baileyana* and *P. ramzanae* are more delicate plants with notched corolla lobes. The flowers are lilac or dark pink with a white or yellow eye.

DISTRIBUTION Widespread in Tibet, from Lhasa, south-eastwards into the range of *P. baileyana* to 94° E, and growing in some of the same localities as the latter, e.g. Nam La, Mira La. Grows in much drier situations than *P. baileyana*, usually in dry moss under a rock overhang, often with Soldanelloides species. 4300–5300 m. It was briefly in cultivation from Ludlow and Sherriff's gatherings from 1938–40. It would probably be best grown as for *P. caveana* (p 215).

Primula macklinae A.J.Richards inedit.

DESCRIPTION Leaves fleshy, lacking meal. Leaf-blade orbicular, to 6 cm in diameter, with a heart-shaped base and a regularly crenate margin. Stalk narrow but firm and expanded at the sheathing base. Stem to 12 cm, lacking meal. Fruiting heads as in *P. rotundifolia*.

DISTRIBUTION Tama Bum, northern Burma; crevices in vertical granite cliffs at 3300 m. Fruiting material of this new species was collected by Kingdon Ward and his wife Jean Macklin on Ward's last expedition in 1953. They note that as the foliage dies down it makes great golden splashes against the dark cliffs. It clearly belongs to section Cordifoliae, and equally clearly is a distinctive new species, but there is no information as to its flowers. It badly requires recollection, at which time a full and formal description should be drawn up. *P. macklinae* will be the easternmost species in the section.

Long after I first published this provisional description, I discovered that Jean Rasmussen, (née Macklin) still lives in England, and I was able to tell her of this belated discovery.

Unfortunately, as I write in 2001, the Burma-Assam (Myamar-Indian-Chinese) border zone remains firmly shut to all visits from outside, so that this new species has not been recollected. This remains one of the least known and botanically richest regions on earth.

Section **Fedtschenkoana** Wendelbo, in Rechinger, Fl. Iranica 9: 7 (1965). Type species *P. fedtschenkoi* Regel. (*P.* sect Calliantha Pax 1889 p.min.p.)

DESCRIPTION *Plants* arising from a divided, fleshy, drought-resistant, tuberous rootstock, winter-green and aestivating. *Leaves* smooth, with revolute vernation. *Bracts* small, not saccate; *flowers* few; *corolla* purple with a yellow eye, annulate, heterostylous, the lobes entire. *Capsule* valvate. *Seeds* angulate, bearing tubercles. Other details as for the only species.

In morphological characteristics this rather isolated species lies between the Crystallophlomis and Oreophlomis, the bracts, entire petals, seeds and few flowers favouring the former, and the capsule and leaf suggesting the latter. Despite the aestivating habit in summer-dry localities so untypical of the former section, DNA studies show clearly that it is indeed sister to the Crystallophlomis and Cordifoliae, but it is not at all closely related to the Oreophlomis.

The underground storage organ, associated with a summer-dormant habit so typical of many plants of the central Asian steppes from which it comes, is unique in *Primula*, and strongly supports the separate sectional status that Wendelbo has given it. There is some doubt as to the correct transliteration of both the sectional and species name. Wendelbo (1965) gives 'fedtschenkoi/ana' and in this follows Federov (1952). However, Smith & Fletcher (1943) give 'fedschenkoi', while Fenderson (1986) consistently followed the first spelling for the section and the second for the species. In this he followed orthographic typology, but common sense would suggest a single spelling.

Primula fedtschenkoi Regel, Tr. Bot. Sada 3: 133 (1874)

DESCRIPTION A medium-sized plant, with narrowly oblanceolate smooth, slightly wavy *leaves* to 9 × 2.5 cm, pale green with a marked whitish midrib, obovate, entire to obscurely crenate dentate, the stalk poorly defined. *Stem* equalling or exceeding leaves, bearing 1–3 horizontally borne flowers on short mealy stalks to 6 mm. *Calyx* slightly mealy, bell-shaped, to 6 mm. *Corolla* flat-faced, deep rose-pink with a darker centre and a purple basal spot, to 18 mm in diameter, with a long narrow tube to 20 mm; pollen 2–3 syncolpate. Flowers heterostylous. Flowering March in cultivation, March–May in the wild. (Plate 6.)

DISTRIBUTION Central Asian USSR, Usbekistan; Samarkand and Bokhara regions. One record from bordering regions of north Afghanistan. 'Mountain slopes, sometimes amongst junipers, and along the banks of streams.' 700–2600 m. Said to grow in 'moist loamy soil', which is no doubt true of these habitats in early spring as the snow melts and the plant flowers. Fortunately growers were provided with the information that these areas bake dry in the summer, the primula disappearing completely. At this stage, the tubers can be lifted and stored dry like the iris or tulips with which it grows.

CULTIVATION Introduced from wild collected seed in about 1985, and subsequently in the possession of a few specialist growers such as Eric Watson. Shown in 1987 and 1988. A number of dormant seedlings were brought to Britain by Henrik Zetterlund in 1991. So far the few plants available have been grown in pots in the alpine house or bulb frame in crock pots using a gritty, free-draining compost. Once growth has started in the autumn they are kept just moist, and watering is increased as plants come into growth. By the end of April, growth has started to die back, and from this point all water is withheld until growth restarts, unaided, in the autumn. This treatment, similar to that used for many difficult bulbs from the same region, seems to be proving successful. However, apparently shy to flower. I have now grown and increased it for ten years (2001) but have only flowered it on two occasions.

Although this is a not unattractive little primula, the main interest to the grower is its curiosity value.

Section **Proliferae** Pax, Bot. Jahrb. Syst. 10: 217 (1889)
(Section Candelabra Balf. f. 1913)
(*Cankrienia* De Vries 1850, sin. stat.)
(Section Cankrienia (De Vriese) Pax 1905)
Type species *P. prolifera* Wall.

DESCRIPTION Usually *robust* perennial or rarely biennial plants, deciduous or less commonly evergreen, the deciduous species forming a multi-crowned series of inconspicuous buds at the soil surface. *Leaves* usually oblanceolate, the stalk poorly demarcated, usually rugose in texture, glabrous, or with single-celled glands, rarely mealy, with revolute vernation. *Stems* often mealy, usually bearing several whorls of flowers in superimposed umbels ('candelabroid'). *Bracts* leafy, to small. *Calyx* usually narrow, ribbed, often mealy. *Corolla* purple, red, pink, orange, yellow or white, usually with a yellow eye, usually flat-faced, annulate or rarely exannulate, heterostylous or homostylous; pollen prolate, 3-colporoidate. *Capsule* usually orbicular, the apex thickened to form a stylopodium, dehiscing by the loss of this cap, or 5 or 10 apical teeth, or by a combination of these, the stylopodium skeleton remaining as a 'cage' around the dehisced apex; seeds irregularly quadrate with honeycombed faces. 2n = 22, 44. Heterostylous species (except *P. pulverulenta*) weakly self-fertile. Flowering early summer.

DISTRIBUTION From east Nepal eastwards through Sikkim, Bhutan, south-east Tibet, Assam and northern Burma to north-east Yunnan and east Sichuan. Outliers occur in Java, Sumatra, Japan and Taiwan. Only *P. prolifera* and the Aleuritia species *P. magellanica,* of all species, occur in the southern hemisphere.

Typically occurring in marshes, ditches, stream and river margins, oxbows, etc., in montane plateaux, 2000–4000 m.

Smith & Fletcher (1941) followed earlier British workers by using Balfour's later name Candelabra in preference to Pax's section Proliferae (1889), believing Pax's section to be heterogenous and poorly diagnosed. Pax himself renamed his section (1905) by recombining De Vriese's earlier epithet Crankrienia of unknown rank at sectional level. On this occasion he included material today classified as ten species placed in this section, and four now classified elsewhere. The type of his section is clearly *P. prolifera*, a characteristic member of this assemblage.

Wendelbo (1961) revived the usage of Pax's original sectional name Proliferae, and as this is the earliest validly published sectional name to include *P. prolifera*, his is probably the most correct option. Over the last 30 years, many gardeners have become familiar with this usage, although this popular group is still widely and informally known as the 'Candelabra' primulas.

Section Proliferae is on the whole a well-marked and 'natural' group, morphologically, genetically and ecologically, and this has been confirmed by two DNA studies. Many of the species have hybridized in gardens, showing their close affinity to one another.

The 3-colporoidate pollen type is unusual in this subgenus (Aleuritia). This caused me to move *P. secundiflora*, which has this pollen type, from the Sikkimensis, where it has no close relatives, to the Proliferae, and this decision has now been strongly supported by the DNA.

It is thought that the Proliferae may represent the most primitive members of Primula alive today, and thus they take a central position with respect to subsequent evolution and geographical migration in the genus (p. 32).

Extant Proliferae show several morphological trends which appear to link with other sections, but only one as yet is confirmed by the DNA. *P. poissonii, P. wilsonii* and *P. secundiflora* appear to be related to the larger petiolarids such as *P. calderiana*, and less strongly, to nivalids such as *P. obtusifolia*.

Although this is not clearly shown by the DNA, it is conceivable that *P. prolifera* may be loosely connected with Sphondylia species such as *P. floribunda* and *P. afghanica*. Also, possibly, fore-runners of *P. prolifera* may have also evolved into members of subgenus *Auganthus*, via Bullatae-like intermediaries. Relatives of the *Auganthus*, notably the Davidii or the Obconicolisteri, may have migrated westwards to form the section Primula.

From this central position in the evolutionary 'web' of *Primula*, many of the sections of *Primula* can be plausibly derived from the Proliferae. Only the curious, involute, five sections of the subgenus *Auriculastrum* seem to stand aside.

Despite the wide distribution of the section, the majority of the Proliferae species are concentrated in the Yunnan/Burma/Assam/Tibet border region, a zone of high monsoon rainfall and deep snow. Of the 23 species, no less than 13 are restricted to this region; two are found in the central Himalaya and two more in Bhutan and south-east Tibet; one species is found in south-east Asia, three in Sichuan and northern Yunnan, and two on islands in north-east Asia. The centre of distribution thus clearly lies around the great parallel gorges of the Salween, Mekong and Yangtse. This area, home today for by far the greatest diversity of primulas, may also represent the original source of the genus, which was derived from a Proliferae-like ancestor.

CULTIVATION Many species in this section are amongst the easiest to grow, and they have made a great impact on our gardens over the last 70 years. Most are soundly perennial and fully hardy, requiring little except a moist nutritious soil which never dries out. Many, including some hybrids, set seed regularly and in favourable conditions they self-sow, even into paths, lawns and shady brick-work, to the extent of becoming invasive. Some species thrive in very wet conditions, even growing semi-submerged in the margins of lakes, streams, etc., but they will tolerate drier, but acidic and humus-rich areas as well.

The chief pest is vine weevil, to which seedlings in particular are very prone, but vigorous adults in suitable conditions are rarely overcome by this problem. However, heat, drought and deep shade, particularly when dry, are anathema to this group, and the site must be carefully chosen, particularly in southern England.

Most of the good garden species are large, robust plants which are too big for the rock garden. They are usually planted in masses amongst rhodo-dendrons and other acid-loving shrubs, or in bog and water gardens where they make extremely effective swathes of colour in May and June. They are usually associated with species in section Sikkimensis, *P. denticulata* and *P. rosea,* and with meconopsis and astilbes, to great effect. Almost all the great British gardens have extensive plantings of this group.

Once established, the candelabra primulas need little maintenance apart from top-dressing with a nutritious mulch in winter, and the division of large clumps, which is best done as they come into growth in the spring.

Some attractive species such as *P. cockburniana* are short-lived, or even biennial, and need to be regularly replaced from seed. Seed generally has a short viability (in contrast with that of section Sikkimensis), but can retain some viability for up to two years. It is best sown fresh in a cool partially shaded frame. Seedlings usually germinate in the spring and grow on well lined out in boxes.

P. prenantha, P. miyabeanum and some geo-graphical races of *P. prolifera* are probably not very hardy, and the first-named is a tiny plant unsuitable for the open garden. Of those species grown today, only *P. serratifolia* has proved to be lacking in vigour, and it is now very rare in cultivation.

HYBRIDIZATION Although hybrids are not often reported in the wild, hybridization has been a major feature of the history of Candelabra primulas in cultivation. In many large gardens where Candelabras self-sow, most plants may be hybrid, and in these conditions every individual may differ from the next, resulting in a rainbow of colour. As many of the hybrids are fertile, backcrossing and multiple hybridization occur; at least one hybrid with four species in its make-up is known. However, some hybrid clones have been selected for their exceptional colour and vigour, and these have been propagated vegetatively. At least one hybrid appears to be true-breeding.

The following species are probably all at least partly interfertile, and many of the hybrid combinations between them have been reported: *P. aurantiaca*, *P. bulleyana*, *P. burmanica*, *P. chungensis*, *P. cockburniana* and *P. pulverulenta*. *P. wilsonii* and *P. poissonii* hybridize with each other and with *P. cockburniana* and *P. secundiflora*, and both cross with *P. prolifera*, as does *P. cockburniana*. Ernst has attempted to cross *P. japonica* with four species, but has only succeeded in producing hybrids with *P. pulverulenta* and *P. burmanica* when the homostyle *P. japonica* is the mother, and the other parent is a thrum.

Ernst, and later Wedderburn, have crossed homostyle species with heterostyle species. This work has shown that the diploid species *P. chungensis* and *P. cockburniana* are probably primary homostyles, while the tetraploid *P. japonica* is a secondary homostyle (p. 59).

KEY TO SPECIES

1. Meal present, at least on stem and calyx 2
1. Meal absent 9

2. Flowers yellow, orange or scarlet-red 3
2. Flowers crimson-red to purple 6

3. Flowers same colour as bud 4
3. Buds red, flowers yellow to orange 5

4. Flowers yellow .... *P. prolifera*
4. Flowers orange-scarlet .... *P. cockburniana*

5. Leaf mid-rib reddish; calyx lobes long and finely pointed .... *P. bulleyana*
5. Leaf mid-rib whitish; calyx lobes short .... *P. chungensis*

6. Flowers bell-shaped, drooping .... *P. secundiflora*
6. Flowers flat-faced, patent 7

7. Flowers red-purple, eye darker .... *P. pulverulenta*
7. Flowers usually dull purple, eye yellow 8

8. Calyx-lobes long and finely pointed .... *P. bulleyana*
8. Calyx-lobes shortly pointed or blunt .... *P. prolifera*

9. Flowers yellow or orange 10
9. Flowers red, purple, blackish, or white 16

10. Corolla not exceeding 10 mm in diameter; calyx red .... *P. prenantha*
10. Corolla exceeding 10 mm in diameter; calyx not usually red 11

11. Corolla-lobes with a darker central stripe .... *P. serratifolia*
11. Corolla-lobes uniform in colour 2

12. Bracts exceeding flower stalk; stem usually dark or blackish 13
12. Bracts scarcely exceeding flower stalk, or if so, stem green 14

13. Stem smooth, without hairs; bracts not leaf-like .... *P. aurantiaca*
13. Stem with short glandular hairs; bracts leaf-like .... *P. mallophylla*

14. Calyx lobes striped and tipped purple .... *P. melanodonta*
14. Calyx-lobes unicoloured 15

15. Corolla-tube 2–3× calyx .... *P. prolifera* (inc. *P. cooperi*)
15. Corolla-tube scarcely exceeding calyx .... *P. polonensis*

16. Leaf smooth, dark bluish-green, entire to finely crenate, mid-rib green 17
16. Leaf bullate, paler, toothed, mid-rib reddish 20

17. Flower-stalk shorter than calyx; flowers often blackish; foliage scented .... *P. wilsonii*
17. Flower stalk at least equalling calyx; flowers red to purple; foliage not scented 18

18. Bracts exceeding flower stalks; calyx-lobes finely drawn-out ....*P. stenodonta*
18. Bracts usually shorter than flower stalks; calyx-lobes shortly pointed ....*P. poissonii*

19. Corolla funnel-shaped, not exceeding 16 mm in diameter ....*P. miyabeanum*
19. Corolla flat-faced, more than 16 mm in diameter 20

20. Leaves semi-prostrate, pale green, jaggedly toothed ....*P. japonica*
20. Leaves erect, mid- to dark green, finely toothed ....*P. burmanica*

Primula prolifera Wallich, Desc. Rare Ind. Pl. 10: 372 (1820)

P. imperialis Jungh. (1840)
P. kuhlii Blume (1844)
P. smithiana Craib (1913)
P. khasiana Balf. f. & Smith (1916)
P. helodoxa Balf. f. (1916)
P. chrysochlora Balf. f. & Ward (1916)
P. sumatrana Merr. (1940)
P. ianthina Balf. f. & Cave (1916)

DESCRIPTION *Evergreen*, lacking meal or with yellow meal on the upper stem and calyx, forming spreading to prostrate rosettes of deep green, rather shiny, roughly rugose shortly toothed oblanceolate to rhomboid *leaves*, to 50 × 10 cm, the thick white stalk being more or less clearly demarcated. *Stems* to 100 cm, usually less, bearing 1–7 whorls each with 3–12 slightly pendant flowers on stalks which are usually very short at flowering but elongate to 3 cm in fruit. *Bracts* varying from linear and shorter than the calyx to large (20 mm) and leaf-like. *Calyx* short, to 5 mm, tubular, 5-angled. *Corolla* pale to golden yellow, or muddy violet, somewhat cup-shaped, to 20 mm in diameter, heterostylous or homostylous, the tube 2–3× the calyx; corolla lobes bluntly rounded, usually shortly toothed or slightly notched. 2n = 22. Pins only 1.5% self-fertile, but thrums 26% self-fertile. Flowering in June in cultivation. (Plate 11.)

DISTRIBUTION Occurs in two very distinct areas, separated by 2500 km: eastern Sinohimalaya, from Sikkim and Chumbi, eastwards through Bhutan to north Assam, extreme northern Burma and just inside its border with Yunnan; and high mountains in north and central Java, and west, central and east Sumatra; the only primula species in south-east Asia south of northern Thailand.

Wet soil along streams and exposed marshy places in montane and elfin forest on mountains peaking above 2650 m, 2000–3500 m.

Bentvelzen (1962) in Flora Malesiana 1 (6): 189–191 has radically changed our perception of this group, which is treated by Smith & Fletcher (1941) as no less than six species. However, within the Himalayan area of its distribution, Smith & Fletcher (1942) had already noted the close resemblance of the two non-mealy species from the Khasia Hills, Assam, *P. prolifera* and *P. khasiana*, with the two mealy species from further north, *P. smithiana* and *P. helodoxa*, and their non-mealy relative *P. chrysochlora*. *P. ianthina*, with dirty violet flowers, has been reported on a few occasions from the Singalila, Sikkim, and is occasionally seen in cultivation. It has yellow meal and seems merely to be a violet form of the neighbouring 'P. smithiana'.

The Indonesian populations are isolated from one another on a series of mountains surrounded by lowland rainforest. Van Steenis, Trop. Natuur 19: 51; 77–84 (1930) showed that these populations vary between each other by a range of characters at least encompassing those of these five Himalayan taxa. For instance, the Indonesian populations vary in robustness, flower size and colour, bract size and shape, and in the presence or absence of meal. The names *P. sumatrana* and *P. kuhlii* had been used to cover some of these south-east Asian variants, but the nature of the variation there is such as to render these species meaningless. It follows that the Himalayan species should also be classified within the same variable species, the prior name for which is *P. prolifera*.

Smith and Fletcher consider that the character of overriding importance which separates the Indonesian populations from those in the Himalaya is the homostyly in the former and heterostyly in the latter. However, ecologically distinct homostyle and heterostyle populations are known in other primulas, e.g. *P. floribunda, P. farinosa* and *P. chungensis*. Bentvelzen points out that marginal isolated populations in many heteromorphic genera tend to be homomorphic, citing *Primula* section Aleuritia in south America as a parallel example (see p. 30).

We must conclude that populations of *P. prolifera* which migrated south down the Malayan peninsula, presumably during the pluvial (= glacial) periods may have been able to do so by virtue of their primary homostyly. Heterostyle populations, as represented today by those in the Himalaya, may have already existed at that time, but would have been less suited to long-distance dispersal, as homostyles can establish a new population from a single seed.

It comes as a relief in the garden, at least for this author, to find the 'yellow' species *P. helodoxa* and *P. smithiana* 'lumped' into *P. prolifera,* for hybridization has long since blurred the margins of whatever once seemed distinctive between these three. For instance, what is usually grown today as 'P. helodoxa' lacks meal.

P. prolifera in the broad sense is readily known from other species by its flowers which are yellow in bud as well as usually in flower, its evergreen habit, and by the lack of coloration in the leaf.

CULTIVATION Forms previously known as 'P. helodoxa' and the smaller 'P. smithiana' are attractive and popular long-lived plants which thrive in suitable conditions. They are fully hardy, which in view of their evergreen habit and altitudinal range is perhaps slightly surprising. 'P. helodoxa' was introduced from Yunnan by Forrest in 1912, and perhaps later. 'P. smithiana' was probably introduced by Ludlow and Sherriff from central Bhutan in 1936, and perhaps again in 1949. 'P. ianthina' was reintroduced by Chadwell from Singalila, Sikkim in 1996 as CC2246.

'P. imperialis' was first introduced from Java in 1889 (**AM** 1902) and was still in cultivation in 1941. There has been no record of it in recent years. It seems unlikely that any of the Assam or Indonesian plants are hardy in British conditions.

HYBRIDIZATION *P. prolifera* only seems to hybridize with *P. wilsonii* and *P. poissonii* in the garden. The resulting hybrids are sterile and have flowers of a disappointing fleshy colour. We have also demonstrated that crosses with *P.cockburniana* and *P.poissonii* are potentially interfertile, but only if thrum plants of *P. prolifera* are used, especially as mothers. For both interspecific and intraspecific crosses, pin *P. prolifera* seems to show greater incompatibility.

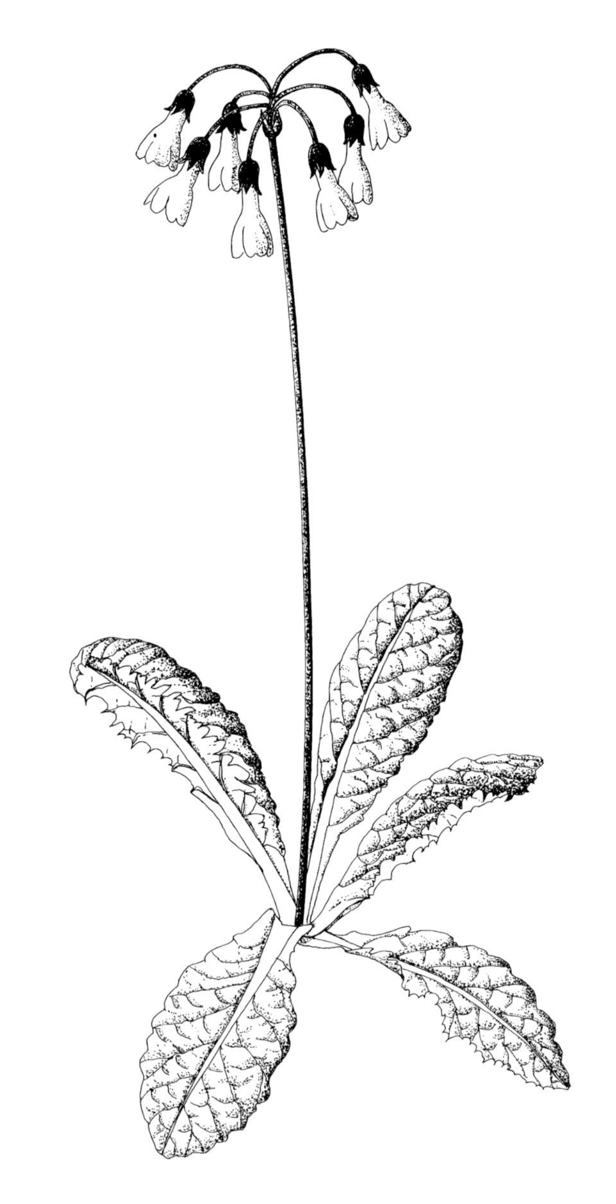

Fig. 20. *P. prenantha*

Primula prenantha Balf. f. & Smith, Notes Roy. Bot. Gdn. Edinb. 9: 191 (1915)

P. brachystoma Smith (1923)
P. microloma Hand.-Mazz.(1924)

DESCRIPTION A *small evergreen* short-lived plant lacking meal, usually only forming single erect rosettes. *Leaves* obovate, rounded to bluntly angled at the tip, finely wrinked-rugose, finely toothed at the margin, the broad green stalk scarcely demarcated. *Stems* exceeding the leaves, usually single, slender, green, to 15 cm, bearing 1 (–2) whorls of 4–8 tiny nodding flowers on slender stalks to 15 mm.

Calyx red, bell-shaped, 5-ridged, to 5 mm, the lobes shortly triangular. *Corolla* brilliant chrome yellow, rarely white, cup-shaped, about 8 mm diameter, *homostylous*, the tube scarcely exceeding the calyx; corolla lobes subquadrangular, slightly notched. Self-fertile. Flowering May. (Plate 12, Fig. 20.)

DISTRIBUTION East Nepal, from the Everest region eastwards through Sikkim, Bhutan, and south-east Tibet to its frontiers with Burma, Assam and Yunnan (var. *microloma*).

Open damp clearings in conifer forest, 2400–3600 m. 'In the wet precipitous margin of a cascade in the lower alpine zone'; 'moist gravel on cliffs'.

This elegant little plant is the most widespread and best known of a small group of three closely related species from the forest zone of the eastern Himalaya and Chinese borderlands. Two of these species are homostylous. DNA studies show that *P. prenantha* is closely allied to *P. prolifera*, so that these too may be 'primary homostyles' (p. 61).

Amongst its relatives, *P. prenantha* is distinguished from *P. melanodonta* by the conspicuously black-striped calyx and heterostylous flowers of the latter, and from *P. polonensis* by being generally smaller, with much smaller flowers with square-ended to notched corolla lobes. In *P. brachystoma* from the Burma/Yunnan frontier some of the larger leaves have bluntly angled rather than rounded ends, but I am including it within the otherwise identical *P. prenantha*.

VARIATION Bigger plants bearing larger flowers with more spreading petal-lobes intermediate with *P. polonensis* occur in south-east Tibet (these were said by Smith & Fletcher to be intermediate with the superficially similar but quite distinct Sikkimensis species *P. morsheadiana*). It may prove more convenient after further research to treat *P. polonensis* as a subspecies of *P. prenantha*.

- var. *microloma* (Hand.-Mazz.) Richards (1993) (*P. microloma* Hand.-Mazz. Anz. Akad. Wiss. Wien 61: 134 (1924).) Flowers white. Mountains of the Salween/Irradwaddy divide on the Burma/Yunnan border.

CULTIVATION Apparently never grown until a plant was brought home to me from Sikkim by John Templar in 1980. This was grown in a crock pot using a gritty peaty compost and was plunged in a shady frame, covered during the winter months. It flowered in 1980 and 1981, setting a small amount of seed on both occasions. A few seedlings were raised and distributed, one of which flowered for me in 1981, but failed to set seed. From a second introduction by the AGSES Sikkim expedition in 1983 (372) I raised one plant to flowering in 1986, which set seed, but this failed to germinate.

This is a tiny delicate species too small for the rough and tumble of the garden, and it may not be very hardy. Although the flowers are very small, they are in proportion, and the brilliant yellow petal colour combines well with the red calyx. I found it a delightful species well worth perservering with. In 1990, a large batch of seedlings were raised to flowering by Edrom nurseries (Kirkpatrick 254), and it is presently (2001) well established in cultivation and regularly offered in seed lists.

Primula polonensis Ward, Ann. Bot. 44: 124 (1930)

DESCRIPTION Very close to *P. prenantha*, and may be best treated as a subspecies of it, but larger in all its parts with stems to 35 cm and homostylous flowers with rounded spreading petal-lobes to 20 mm in diameter. The leaves are only minutely toothed. Assam, Delei valley, 2900 m. 'In a wide rock gulley facing west ... the gulley is open ... and the primulas grow scattered on the rocky plane where little else grows.' Only found once by Kingdon Ward, but grown from 1928 to at least 1940. 'Fine specimens flowered in pots which stood in the cool house with their bases in a water tank' (Edinburgh).

Primula melanodonta Smith, Notes Roy. Bot. Gdn. Edinb. 15: 303 (1927)

DESCRIPTION Similar to *P. polonensis*, but closer in size to *P. prenantha*, and with a distinctive purple-striped calyx with purple teeth, and heterostylous flowers. Seinghku Wang on the Burma/Tibet frontier. Muddy alpine slopes and stream-sides, 3500–4000 m, hence ecologically distinct from its relatives, forming large colonies. Smith and Fletcher compare it with its congener *P. serratifolia*, but this little plant is clearly a *P. prenantha* relative. (Fig. Halda: 171.)

Primula bulleyana Forrest, Notes Roy. Bot. Gdn. Edinb. 4: 231 (1908)

P. beesiana Forrest (1911)

DESCRIPTION Differs from *P. prolifera* by the red mid-rib to the finely toothed oblanceolate deciduous leaves, by the heavily white-mealy stems and calyces, the cup-shaped calyx to 8 mm with 'awl-like' sepal-lobes (the bracts are also awl-shaped), and by the usually red buds which open to deep golden to pale orange flowers (purple in subsp. *beesiana*) and are always heterostylous. 2n = 22. Flowers late May in the garden. (Photo: Bull. AGS 56: 239 (1988).) (Plate 11.)

DISTRIBUTION North-west Yunnan, probably confined to the mountains to the north (Yulong Shan) and south (Yungning) of Lijiang; and northwards into the Muli region of south Sichuan.

Marshy mountain meadows and the sides of ditches and streams, 2500–3300 m. 'Damp places, often in thickets on sandstone as well as on lime.' I found this species locally common on the eastern side of the Yulong Shan, and cannot usefully add to this, except to say that it seems not to be eaten by cattle.

This beautiful and familiar species is distinct in cultivation, where yellow forms are only likely to be confused with *P. chungensis* which has a quite different calyx and lacks the characteristic deep red midrib of *P. bulleyana*, and with *P. aurantiaca* (see under that species). Purple forms (subsp. *beesiana*) differ from *P. burmanica* in being mealy. They differ from other purple-flowered species especially by the characteristic awl-shaped sepals and bracts.

P. beesiana is structurally very similar to *P. bulleyana* and occurs in the same area. In my experience purple-flowered populations (*beesiana*) are more often pure; hybrid populations contain few if any pure *beesiana*. The two are also highly interfertile in the garden, and really only differ in flower colour.

CULTIVATION Easy and vigorous in suitable conditions, often self-sowing with abandon. Introduced by Forrest from the Yulong Shan in 1906 (subsp. *beesiana* in 1908), and disseminated by Arthur Bulley from 'Bees seeds'. Both colour forms have been popular garden plants ever since. ACE 2477, 2478 (1994) sampled hybrid swarms of mixed colours from the Yulong Shan.

HYBRIDIZATION Most garden hybrids have occurred between the subspecies (P. × 'bullesiana') (Janson, 1928, **AM** 1916), and with *P. pulverulenta*, although hybrids with *P. aurantiaca*, *P. chungensis* and *P. burmanica* also probably occur but are more difficult to detect.

Hybrids with subsp. *beesiana* give multicoloured strains with lilac, magenta, scarlet, salmon and orange flowers with a yellow eye and I have seen very similar mixtures in the wild. These were originally given names such as 'Edina' (Edinburgh) and 'Asthore' (Lissadell). It was said that flower colour tended to show maternal inheritance, hybrids with *P. bulleyana* as the mother tending to be yellow or orange, and those with *P. beesiana* as the mother tending to be pink to purple.

With *P. pulverulenta*, hybrids tend to resemble the latter, but have dark pink flowers with a darker centre. P. × 'Ladybird' (**AM** 1915) and P. × 'Inverleith' (**PC** 1912) are named examples, but it is likely that some of the pale-flowered forms of *P. pulverulenta* such as the well-known 'Bartley' strains have some *P. bulleyana* blood.

Primula × 'Inverewe' is a magnificent hybrid, vigorous and with long-lasting flowers of a brilliant scarlet. It is a sterile allotriploid of accidental garden origin and may be a three-way cross between *P.* × *bullesiana* and *P. cockburniana*. *P.* × 'Ravenglass Vermilion' from Muncaster Castle, Cumbria may be of similar parentage, but it is not clear if they had a single origin. It is also reported that Mary Knox-Finlay raised a similar hybrid at Keillour which unexpectedly reappeared at Inverewe.

VARIATION

- Subsp. *beesiana* (Forrest) Richards (1993) (*P. beesiana* Forrest, Gard. Chron. ser.3, 1:242 (1911)). Differs from *P. bulleyana* chiefly by the rose-carmine, yellow-eyed flower with an orange tube; the sepal-lobes are sharp, but not awl-like. For distinctions from *P. pulverulenta* and *P. burmanica*, see under those species. 2n = 22. Yunnan; in the Muli region of Sichuan becomes the dominant form.
- Var. *leucantha* (Balf. f. & Forrest) Fletcher (1941) (*P. leucantha* Balf. f. & Forrest 1920). This white-flowered variety (with a golden eye) is otherwise indistinguishable from *P. bulleyana*. It was found by Forrest in the Muli mountains.

Primula burmanica Balf. f. & Ward, Notes Roy. Bot. Gdn. Edinb. 13: 5 (1920)

DESCRIPTION Essentially a non-mealy purple-flowered *P. bulleyana,* to which it is closely related, although occurring further to the west. The flowers are usually purple to crimson with a greeny-orange eye, the tube also being purple. The leaves are a rather deep dull green with a purple mid-rib. 2n = 22. Completely self-sterile in thrums, but up to 3% self-fertile in pins. Flowering late May–June. (Plate 12.)

DISTRIBUTION From both sides of the Burma-Yunnan frontier to the west of the Salween. Marshy meadows and wet clearings in conifer forests, 2700–3200 m.

Despite its close relationship to *P. bulleyana, P. burmanica* seems distinct in the garden, particularly in flower and leaf colour.

CULTIVATION Introduced by Ward from Burma in 1914, and possibly later by Forrest. This is a vigorous, easy going, garden plant for a rich wet spot, although it rarely self-sows with the abandon of the last species, and it is less commonly found. Large plantings do, however, occur in some gardens. The purple shade of the flower is uncompromising and not to everyone's taste.

HYBRIDIZATION Hybrids have been reported with *P. aurantiaca, P. bulleyana, P. chungensis* and *P. japonica.* In the latter case hybrids were only raised when thrum *P. burmanica* pollen was crossed with *P. japonica.* A triple hybrid was reported in 1931 between *P. burmanica* and *P.* 'Aileen Aroon' which is itself *P. pulverulenta* × *P. cockburniana.* However, my experience with a single thrum clone of this species grown with other candelabras is that it never sets seed, although growing strongly, which suggests that it is not very prone to crossing.

Primula chungensis Balf. f. & Ward, Notes Roy. Bot. Gdn. Edinb. 13: 7 (1920)

DESCRIPTION *Leaves* deciduous, lacking meal, blade elliptical, rounded at the tip, to 30 × 10 cm, tapering to a slender base but without a well-marked stalk, finely but deeply rugose, pale bright olive green with a green to white mid-rib and a green or somewhat reddish stalk, irregularly toothed and somewhat sublobed. *Stems* exceeding leaves, somewhat white-mealy, bearing 2–5 whorls of up to 12 horizontal flowers on somewhat mealy stalks to 2 cm. *Calyx* bell-shaped, short, to 5 mm, strongly white-mealy, cut to one-third into short triangular lobes. *Corolla* deep yellow to orange, usually orange to scarlet in bud, flat-faced and annulate, homostylous or heterostylous, usually homostylous in cultivation, to 20 mm in diameter, the narrow tube 3× the calyx; corolla-lobes broadly obovate, shortly notched. 2n = 22. Usually self-fertile in cultivation. Flowering June. (Plate 11.)

DISTRIBUTION From the Kulu and Muli mountains of south-west Sichuan south to the Zhongdian plateau in north-west Yunnan (where it seems to be rather uncommon) and north-westwards through the Assam border zone to the Temo La just west of the Tsangpo bend near Namche Barwa, south-east Tibet (not in Bhutan as previously reported).

Marshes and wet ground beside streams, etc., in coniferous forest, 2900–3200 m. '... the woodland paths in the picea and abies forest were gay with the maroon *P. calderiana,* a great profusion of the orange-red and orange-yellow *P. chungensis* ... and of the rose, geranium-leaved *P. latisecta.*'

P. chungensis is only likely to be confused with *P. bulleyana* and *P. cockburniana.* The short bell-shaped calyx of *P. chungensis* is quite different from that of *P. bulleyana,* while the latter has a coloured mid-rib to the finely toothed, not sublobate leaf. *P. cockburniana* is a short-lived and much more delicate species with scarlet flowers and regularly and finely toothed leaves, which have a more marked stalk. *P. chungensis* is a less showy plant than most of its relatives.

CULTIVATION Introduced by Ward in 1913, and it has probably been introduced on several subsequent occasions. A good orange form reintroduced by CLD in 1990 and seen in quantity on the Nyima La by Anne Chambers, Kenneth Cox, etc. **AM** 1933.

P. chungensis is less commonly found in cultivation than several other candelabras. However, it is self-fertile and is readily raised from seed, although rarely self-sowing. It appreciates plenty of water in the growing season, but does not relish heavy boggy soils or water-sides. It is best grown in semi-shaded conditions, for instance amongst rhododendrons, in slightly raised but humus-rich sites with moderately good drainage, and here it may form permanent clumps, but elsewhere it may be short-lived.

HYBRIDIZATION The best-known hybrids of *P. chungensis* have been raised from crosses with *P. pulverulenta*, this grex being known as *P.* × *chunglenta*. These are larger, more vigorous plants than *P. chungensis* with bright red flowers which fade to a coral or salmon pink, the eye remaining dark. Hybrids are also known with *P. bulleyana*, *P. burmanica* and *P. cockburniana*. In the latter case the cross is made more easily with *P. cockburniana* as the mother. We have achieved no success in crosses with *P. poissonii* or *P. prolifera*, but it seems that crosses with *P. japonica* are possible with the latter species as the father.

Primula cockburniana Hemsl., J. Linn. Soc. 29: 313 (1893)

P. operculata R. Knuth (1907)

DESCRIPTION A delicate deciduous short-lived, usually biennial plant with a slender stock usually only forming single rosettes. *Leaves* prostrate to ascending, obovate, to 15 × 4 cm, narrowing abruptly to a marked stalk, lacking meal, the mid-rib white, finely and regularly toothed. *Stem* slender, exceeding the leaves, white-mealy, at least at the nodes, bearing 1–3 whorls of 3–8 flowers horizontally on slender mealy stalks to 3 cm. *Calyx* bell-shaped, to 7 mm, sharply lobed to half-way, silvery-mealy. *Corolla* a characteristic orange-scarlet, annulate, homostylous, flat-faced, to 15 mm in diameter; corolla-tube narrowly cylindrical, about 2× the calyx; corolla lobes obovate, not usually notched. 2n = 22. Self-fertile. Flowering June–July. (Plate 11.)

DISTRIBUTION Confined to the mountains to the south, south-west and north of Tatsienlu, south-west Sichuan, extending south as far as Yetsi, to the north of Kulu. Wet alpine meadows, 2900–3200 m.

This is a most delightful plant with a dainty character all of its own. The combination of the delicate stance and flaming flowers set against silver calyces and stems is easily recognized, and renders this amongst amongst the most popular of primulas, despite the need to continuously replenish stocks from the abundant seed. It is only likely to be confused with the more robust, long-lived *P. chungensis,* to which DNA studies show it to be closely related.

While *P. chungensis* is both heterostyle and homostyle, the short-lived *P. cockburniana* is invariably homostyle, so it is likely that *P. cockburniana* evolved from short-lived homostyle forms of the former. Homostyly is frequently seen as an adaptation to a short-lived colonizing life-style in *Primula*.

CULTIVATION Introduced by Ernest Wilson from west of Tatsienlu in 1905, and probably latterly by Rock. It has been in cultivation ever since. Said to have been reintroduced by ARGS 806 from between Zhongdian and Lijiang in 2000, perhaps *P. chungensis*.

Seed sown in trays or boxes in the autumn and kept over winter in the cold-frame will germinate the following spring. Seedlings should be pricked on into pots or trays at the two-leaf stage, probably in late May, and should be kept cool and moist, but in good light. They will have formed robust rosettes by September when they should be planted in their final position. These will give a good display the following summer, and may persist to give a reasonable showing the year after, after which they should be replaced. *P. cockburniana* enjoys a rich, well-drained, humus-rich but loam-based soil in a cool spot with good light. Although it will not tolerate drying out, it enjoys drier conditions than most candelabras, and will not survive bog conditions. It makes the strongest impact grown in groups at the front of the shrub border or rhododendron beds. The vibrant colour does not associate well with many plants, and requires careful placing, but this delightful plant should be grown in any except the smallest gardens.

HYRBIDIZATION. An important parent, giving rise to more perennial hybrids with *P. burmanica, P. chungensis* and *P. pulverulenta*. Crosses with the lattermost were raised at Lissadell early in the century and the grex name is *P.* × 'Lissadell'. These plants included 'Unique' (**AM** 1908), the orange-red 'Aileen Aroon' (**AM** 1920), and tomato-red 'Red Hugh' which has a broad chrome-yellow eye. The latter clone at least survives in some large plantings, is fertile and breeds true. The sterile allotriploid *P.* 'Inverewe' probably has *P. cockburniana* in its ancestry, while other complex hybrids include *P.*

'Excelsior' (**AM** 1913) (*P.* 'Unique' backcrossed to *P.cockburniana*), and *P.* 'Mrs W.R. Lysaght' (*P.* 'Unique' × *P.* 'Mrs R.V. Bartley') which is thus probably a three-way hybrid between *P. cockburniana*, *P. pulverulenta* and *P. bulleyana*.

We have shown that potential hybridization between male *P. cockburniana* and *P. japonica*, *P. poissonii* (especially to a thrum female), and especially to *P. prolifera* (again to a thrum female) can also occur.

Primula aurantiaca Smith & Forrest, Notes Roy. Bot. Gdn. Edinb. 14: 34 (1923)

DESCRIPTION A distinctive species most closely related to *P. chungensis*, but differing by the strong red-purple mid-rib to the darker leaves which have a finely and regularly toothed margin, by the reddish or commonly blackish stems which totally lack meal, long bracts equalling the flower stalk, by the longer (8 mm) narrower purplish calyx and by the corolla tube not exceeding 2× the calyx. The flowers are usually of a characteristic burnt umber colour which contrasts well with the dark stems. 2n = 22. Fully self-sterile in pins, 3% self-fertile in thrums. Flowering in June in cultivation. (Plate 11.)

DISTRIBUTION West Yunnan, near the borders with Burma and Tibet, on the divides between the Mekong and the Yangtse, and the Mekong and the Chienchuan.

Beside streams in wet alpine meadows, 3500 m. '. . . damp spots of meadows, often along rivulets on limestone as well as slate, and is the only one of its section ascending as high as 11,000 feet.'

P. aurantiaca is the only orange-flowered species lacking meal on the inflorescence. Also, at least in the garden, the dark colour to the stem and calyx is very striking, although this may not be constant in the wild. *P. bulleyana* is also distinguished by its long acuminate bracts and sepal-lobes.

CULTIVATION Similar to *P. chungensis*, being neither long-lived, particularly robust, or tolerant of very wet soils, but fairly easy of culture in suitable conditions. Not often seen, although the colour is striking, and this species is very worthwhile. Introduced by Forrest in 1922, and continuously in cultivation since. If true seed is to be gathered, a group of plants should be grown together.

HYBRIDIZATION Hybrids are only certainly reported with *P. burmanica* and *P. bulleyana*, and this species seems not to have been an important parent. However, hybrids may well also occur with *P. chungensis* and *P. cockburniana*, and some of these might be hard to detect.

Primula mallophylla Balf. f., Notes Roy. Bot. Gdn. Edinb. 9: 181 (1916)

DESCRIPTION A relative of *P. aurantiaca*, also completely lacking meal, but with deep yellow or orange flowers, and long leaf-like bracts. The calyx is also long, from 7–14 mm, and diagnostically, this is the only member of the section with a shortly hairy stem. Superficially resembles *P. bulleyana*, with which it has been confused, but lacking meal. Southern and eastern Sichuan; damp meadows and mountain streamsides above 1800 m. This little-known species has never been in cultivation.

Primula serratifolia Franchet, Bull. Soc. Bot. Fr. 32: 267 (1885)

P. japonica Forbes & Hemsley (1889) non Gray (1857)
P. biserrata Forrest (1908)

DESCRIPTION Another non-mealy species related to *P. aurantiaca* and *P. mallophylla*, but smaller with short bracts, hairless stems, deeply and irregularly toothed leaves, a short calyx not more than 7 mm, and distinctive bell-shaped flowers which are normally pale yellow with a central darker bar on each petal-lobe, and only occur in 1 (–2) whorls. (Photo: J. Roy. Hort. Soc. 54: 41 (1928).)

DISTRIBUTION Widespread in north-west Yunnan, including the Cang Shan, Yulong Shan and Mekong divide ranges; just extending into south-east Tibet on the Mekong and Salween divides, and into north-east Burma (Hpimaw and Salween divides). 'Under rhododendrons, at the lateral slopes near the stream, blooming at the alpine spring, but much after the snow has melted'; 3000–4000 m.

A most attractive and individual species with its large, tiger-striped flowers. Unfortunately it is hardly ever seen in cultivation today. Resembles a member of section Sikkinensis

CULTIVATION Introduced from the Cang Shan by Forrest (1905) and probably by Forrest and Rock on subsequent occasions. Reintroduced by ACE 932, 2501 from the Cang Shan in 1994. Survives in a few gardens such as Cluny and Glendoick in 2001.

P. serratifolia is virtually alone in the section as a species which has been assiduously introduced, but has failed to become well established in cultivation. 'Although perfectly hardy, it is not so free a grower as others of this section. It thrives best on a gentle slope in half-shade on the west side of the rock garden in a well-drained position in two parts loam: 1 leaf soil: 1 sand, with some lime rubble added, and is increased by seed and by division after flowering.'

In the wild, *P. serratifolia* is the most alpine member of the section, and it is possible that its intractability results from its choice of habitat, which more resembles that of a nivalid. It is likely that most growers have mistakenly treated it as a typical member of the section. If J. Adamson's instructions of 1928, quoted above, had been followed more often, maybe this extremely attractive and individual species would be more often grown today.

VARIATION

- var. *roseo-tincta* Forrest, Notes Roy. Bot. Gdn. Edinb. 15: 254 (1927). Flowers purple in bud, pale yellow suffused with deep pink, lacking the central stripe. N E Burma.

- var. *unicolor* Forrest ibid. 255. Flowers soft yellow, lacking the central stripe. N E Burma.

Primula cooperi Balf. f., Notes Roy. Bot. Gdn. Edinb. 9: 158 (1915)

DESCRIPTION A close relative of *P. serratifolia*, differing in the uniformly yellow corolla, the short corolla-tube which does not exceed the calyx, and the marked leaf-stalk.

Geographically very distinct, apparently only collected once, above Toong in Sikkim, sandy streamsides, 3300 m.

P. cooperi has never been in cultivation. An **AM** given to a plant of this name in 1919 seems to relate to *P. prolifera*. *P. cooperi* is something of a mystery, as it has never been recollected from a well-visited area. The single collection seems distinct from neighbouring forms of *P. prolifera*, having aromatic leaves which are deeply and jaggedly toothed with long slender stalks, and a longer narrower calyx with a correspondingly shorter corolla-tube. However, *P. cooperi* may, if rediscovered, finally rest within the *P. prolifera* complex.

Primula pulverulenta Duthie, Gard. Chron. ser. 3, 38: 259 (1905)

P. shihmienensis Fang (1956)

DESCRIPTION The biggest candelabra, and one of the most robust of all primulas, forming large multicrowned deciduous clumps. *Leaves* oblanceolate, rounded, to 30 × 8 cm, irregularly toothed, finely rugose; the mid-rib is whitish-green and the winged stalk is poorly demarcated. *Stem* to 1 m, white-mealy, with up to 8 whorls of 3–10 flowers borne horizontally on white-mealy stalks to 2 cm. *Calyx* to 8 mm, white-mealy chiefly within, cut to half-way into narrow sharp sepal-lobes. *Corolla* usually carmine-red with a darker eye, flat-faced, to 30 mm in diameter; corolla tube 2× calyx; corolla-lobes broad and deeply notched. 2n = 22. Completely self-sterile. Flowering mid-May. (Plate 12.)

DISTRIBUTION Western Sichuan about Tatsienlu, the same area as the orange-flowered *P. chungensis* to which it is probably closely related. Marshy sites and streamsides, often in semi-shade, above 2000 m.

P. pulverulenta is only likely to be confused with *P. bulleyana* subsp. *beesiana*, which has a yellow eye to the flower and a different leaf-shape; those of *P. pulverulenta* are broadest near the tip. All other red- or purple-flowered species lack meal on the stem and calyx.

VARIATION None recorded in the wild, but a variety of colour forms have arisen in cultivation; many, perhaps all, are probably hybrid, chiefly with *P. bulleyana* and *P. chungensis*:

- 'Mrs R.V. Bartley', white, sterile.
- 'Lapworth forms' pink.
- 'Hidcote strain' rose with a yellow eye (**AM** 1911).
- 'Bartley strain', raised by Huw Dalrymple, various shades of pink and rose with pale or dark eyes (**AM** 1924 as 'Lady Thursby').

CULTIVATION Introduced by Wilson in 1905, since when it has been an easy-going, robust and popular species which is found as large plantings in most important gardens. It is very long-lived in rich wet loam soils, and stands periodic flooding at pond margins, etc., well. In these conditions it self-sows, often profusely. Usually the earliest candelabra to flower in the garden.

HYBRIDIZATION A most important parent, especially with its relative and congener *P. chungensis*. Hybrids are also known with *P. bulleyana*, *P. burmanica*, *P. chungensis* and *P. cockburniana*. With *P. japonica*, Ernst was only able to obtain hybrid seed by using thrum *P. pulverulenta* as a male parent.

Primula japonica A. Gray, Mem. Amer. Acad., new ser. 6: 400 (1857)

DESCRIPTION A moderately *robust*, deciduous species lacking meal with rather prostrate broadly obovate *leaves* of a characteristic pale green, jaggedly and irregularly toothed, with a bright red mid-rib most obvious in the broad and poorly marked stalk. *Stems* exceeding leaves, to 45 cm, lacking meal, stout, green or tinged red or purple, bearing 1–6 whorls of 3–10 flowers on stout horizontally borne stalks to 2 cm. *Calyx* green to purple, usually reddish-green, white-mealy inside only, to 8 mm, with narrowly drawn-out tips. *Corolla* rather waxy, white, pink, purple or usually deep cherry red with an orange or concolorous eye, flat-faced, to 20 mm in diameter; homostylous; the cylindrical tube 2–3× the calyx; corolla lobes squared off and rounded at the base, often overlapping. 2n = 44. Self-fertile. Flowering late May–June. (Plate 12.)

DISTRIBUTION Japan; scattered through Hokkaido, Honshu, Shikoku and Kyushu. Records from Taiwan probably refer to the next species. Boggy places by mountain streams. 'Swamp by the side of a river in dense hardwood shade growing . . . with its toes in the running water or as near as it could get to it ... shade ... reduced to dappled cover at flowering time.' Said by Stace (1999) to be naturalized in the UK, but I have not seen this and would predict that *P. bulleyana* is the more likely candidate.

P. japonica is most likely to be confused with *P. burmanica*, the only other garden species lacking meal (except inside the calyx) and with red-purple flowers. From *P. burmanica* it is easily distinguished by the broad squat coarsely toothed pale leaves which hardly narrow to the broad stalk.

P. japonica is clearly an example of a secondary homostyle. Whereas *P. cockburniana* and some forms of *P. chungensis* and *P. prolifera* are diploid, and the latter two are sometimes variably heterostyle, *P. japonica* is tetraploid and always homostyle. Ernst (1955) showed that whereas *P. cockburniana* and *P. chungensis* were able to hybridize freely with *P. pulverulenta* in all types of cross, *P. japonica* would only cross with *P. pulverulenta* and *P. burmanica* when used as a female parent to thrum pollen. Thus, it is suggested, the female control of the long homostyle is of the pin type, having been derived from heterostyle recombinants, unlike *P. cockburniana* and *P. chungensis* which are primary homostyles (see p. 61).

It seems likely that during a former period when Japan was closer to the Asian mainland, and cool wet conditions prevailed in the lowlands, northern tetraploid homostyles from the mainland colonized Japan, while related diploid homostyles colonized Taiwan. Here they have been able to survive in the mountains, while relatives on the mainland were only able to survive later warm dry episodes in the mountains of western China. Tetraploid homostyles are typical island colonizers, as they can establish from a single self-fertile seed.

VARIATION Usually with red-purple flowers in the wild, although white forms have been recorded. Variable in colour in the garden, the best-known colour strains being:

- 'Postford White'. A very good vigorous large-flowered and clear white with an orange eye.
- 'Millers' Crimson'. A good dark red with a concolorous eye.
- 'Valley Red'. Raised at Harrogate, nearly scarlet, usually with an orange eye. Similar to the hybrid 'Red Hugh' in colour, but lacking meal.

CULTIVATION The first attempt at introduction by Robert Fortune from gardens near Yedo failed (1861). Successfully introduced in 1870 from both Hong Kong and Yokohama and flowered in 1871. It has been in cultivation in the west since then, and many large gardens have substantial plantings.

One of the easiest primulas to grow, perennial,

although not often long-lived, self-sowing and easily raised from seed which is produced in abundance. *P. japonica* thrives in partial shade or full light in any moist fertile soil which never dries out, where it forms modest clumps. It tolerates a substantial clay fraction in the soil, and moderate levels of waterlogging, although it does not tolerate extremely boggy conditions as well as *P. bulleyana* or *P. pulverulenta*. It is reputedly not tolerant of too much lime.

HYBRIDIZATION Not as promiscuous as some species, being self-fertilizing, and the triploid hybrids are sterile, so no backcrossing occurs. It is said that *japonica* characters tend to be 'recessive' in hybrids, often appearing as colour streaks in the flower. Hybridization has been recorded with homostyle *P. cockburniana* and *P. chungensis*, and with thrum *P. pulverulenta* and *P. burmanica*, with *P. japonica* always acting as the mother, probably as a result of endosperm/embryo imbalance (see p. 107). *P.* 'Rowallen Rose' is a named clone of the hybrid with *P. pulverulenta*.

Primula poissonii Franchet, Bull. Soc. Bot. Fr. 33: 67 (1886)

P. planiflora Hand.-Mazz. (1936)

DESCRIPTION *Leaves evergreen, smooth,* not aromatic, spreading and somewhat involute, slightly dark bluish-green with an obscure mid-rib of the same colour, oblanceolate, the margin finely toothed, lacking a marked stalk. *Stems* green, to 45 cm, bearing 2–6 whorls of between 3–9 flowers on short (1 cm) spreading green stalks. *Calyx* cup-shaped, green often with reddish stripes, with blunt short sepal-lobes. *Corolla* velvety plum-purple with a golden eye (rarely white), heterostylous, flat-faced, to 30 mm diameter, the tube up to 3× the calyx; corolla-lobes broad, deeply notched and sometimes toothed. *Capsule* ovoid, equalling or exceeding the calyx. 2n = 22. About 2% self-fertile in pins, 10% self-fertile in thrums. Flowering June. (Plate 12.)

DISTRIBUTION Widespread in the mountains of north-west Yunnan and south-west Sichuan, in well collected localities such as the Cang Shan, Yulong Shan, Zhongdian plateau, Muli and Kulu.

'In enormous masses, it colours the meadows red over large stretches, and these meadows are of quite a characteristic nature. The subsoil is probably always alluvial gravel which fills depressions and valley bottoms or forms soft alluvial cones, and this is covered with a layer of black earth which is hardly more than one or a few feet in depth. Samples of this earth, collected, one over limestone, the other over sandstone ... were found to be practically free of lime, containing only (0.03%) calcium carbonate.' I found this species to occur commonly both on the lower slopes of the Cang Shan, and throughout much of the Yulong Shan and Zhongdian plateau. It is characteristic of rather species-poor wet meadows and seems to be graze-resistant.

One of a group of four related evergreen Proliferae species which may be allied to *P. obtusifolia* (section Crystallophlomis), having short-stalked purplish flowers, an elongate capsule and smooth leaves. DNA shows it to be closely related to *P. wilsonii*. Amongst these species it is identified by its flat-faced flowers, short sepals lacking meal and non-aromatic foliage.

CULTIVATION Introduced by Delavay to Paris in 1882–3, and sent from there to Kew in 1890. It has been in cultivation since, although there have almost certainly been later introductions by Forrest and Rock. A new introduction (CLD 486) flowered in 1992 and was a handsome plant with cherry-red flowers, while also introduced by ACE 1946, 2030 (1994), and by David Rankin (SDR 1732) in 1999/2000.

This is a fairly easy-going species which is long-lived and can be multiplied by division in spring, or by seed if several are grown together. It enjoys a cool and humus-rich soil which is fairly well drained, but never dries out, and it will tolerate partial shade.

HYBRIDIZATION Crosses readily with *P. prolifera*, but chiefly with *P. poissonii* as the pin mother or *P. prolifera* as the thrum mother. Crosses also with *P. cockburniana*, chiefly as a thrum male parent, and perhaps with *P. chungensis*. Freely inter-fertile with its relative *P. wilsonii* and these hybrids were offered by David Rankin in 2001. Hybrids with *P. secundiflora* (*P.* × *dschungdienensis* Hand.-Mazz.) were found on the Zhongdian plateau at 3350 m with both parents. and were rediscovered by David Rankin in 2001.

Primula wilsonii Dunn, Gard. Chron. ser.3, 31:413 (1902) emend. Smith & Fletcher, Trans. Bot. Soc. Edinb. 33: 178–81

P. anisodora Balf. f. & Forrest (1916)
P. angustidens (Franch.) Pax (1905) p.p.
P. glycosma Petitm. (1908)
P. oblanceolata Balf. f. (1914)

DESCRIPTION Differs from *P. poissonii* by the greener, aromatic leaves smelling somewhat of aniseed, the virtually stalkless smaller cup-shaped flowers not exceeding 15 mm in diameter, the entire corolla-lobes and the capsule markedly exceeding the capsule. On the whole a taller plant with stems reaching 90 cm. The flowers vary in colour from red to black with a golden to green annulus which is often markedly 10-lobed. 2n = 22. Pins 6–8% self-fertile; thrums 2–5% self-fertile (compare *P. poissonii*). Flowering June.

DISTRIBUTION Mountains of southern, western and north-western Yunnan and south-west Sichuan; widespread, but in general occurring rather further north than *P. poissonii,* and always at a higher altitude.

'Loves springy places in and along thickets of *Philadelphus, Lonicera,* willows and others, both on limestone and slate.' At about 3700 m.

Smith and Fletcher already pointed out that *P. wilsonii* and *P. anisodora* only differ in flower colour and minor details of flower structure, so I propose to unite them, as they are otherwise indistinguishable in the garden.

In general a rather leggy plant of less charm than *P. poissonii,* which is only likely to be of interest to the collector, although forms (var. *anisodora*) with blackish flowers are certainly curious.

VARIATION Forms originally placed under *P. oblanceolata* have long leaves with large teeth, but probably only represent late-season phenotypes.

- Var. *anisodora* (Balf. f. & Forrest) Richards (1993). (*P. anisodora* Balf. f. & Forrest, Notes Roy. Bot. Gdn. Edinb. 9: 147 (1916).) Flowers deep purple to black with a green, scarcely lobed annulus. Sichuan and northern Yunnan.

CULTIVATION Probably introduced several times as both varieties by Forrest and Rock; var. *anisodora* is known to have been introduced by Forrest in 1918. Both varieties are still occasionally met in cultivation, where they are easy-going in a rich moist loam which never dries out, tolerating very wet soils in the summer. They have a tendency to be short-lived, but establish well from seed.

HYBRIDIZATION Crosses with *P. prolifera* have been well-known, with a flower colour variously described as 'salmon' and 'crushed strawberry'. They have been given the grex name *P.* × *anisodoxa.* Smith and Fletcher report that the original F1 hybrid was chocolate in colour, but subsequent backcrosses resulted in a range of magenta shades. However, another report suggests that the hybrid was sterile. Crosses freely with *P. poissonii.*

Primula miyabeana (Ito) Ito & Kawakami, Miyabe Festschrift, 1 (1911)

P. japonica A. Gray var. *miyabeanum* Ito (1880)

DESCRIPTION A diploid homostyle relative of *P. prolifera* from Taiwan (Formosa), but with the calyx not more than 6 mm, the meal within the calyx yellow, and the purple corolla funnel-shaped, the corolla-lobes being notched and toothed. 2n=22. Probably self-fertile.

DISTRIBUTION Taiwan; Mount Morrison. Shady sites in mountain forest at 2300 m.

The colonization of Taiwan by *P. miyabeana* presumably occurred in a similar way to that of *P. japonica* in Japan. However, DNA studies suggest that it is more closely related to *P. poissonii* than *P. japonica.* It is unexpected that this homostylous species is diploid, although other diploid secondary homostyles are known (p. 61).

The original description had 'miyabeanum' and this is followed by Smith & Fletcher. Fenderson (1986) has 'miyabeana' without comment. This would appear to be the correct form.

CULTIVATION Introduced by W.R. Price (of *Lilium formosanum* var. *pricei* and *Pleione bulbocodioides* var. *pricei* fame) in 1913. It was said by H.D. McLaren of Bodnant to be not worth growing, and it seems to have disappeared by 1940. Reintroduced on at least two occasions during the 1990s. I raised seedlings which proved to be very slow growing and eventually died without flowering. Seems to be difficult, but flowered in at least one Scottish garden where it was said to be disappointing.

Primula stenodonta Balf. f. in Smith & Fletcher, Trans. Bot. Soc. Edinb. 33: 120 (1941)

P. japonica A. Gray var. *angustidens* Franch.(1886) p.p.
P. angustidens (Franch.) Pax (1905) p.p.
P. poissonii Franch. subsp. *angustidens* (Franch.) Pax emend. Smith & Forrest (1928)
P. wilsonii Dunn (1902) non sensu Smith & Fletcher (1941) p.p.

DESCRIPTION Apparently a small relative of *P. poissonii*, differing by long drawn-out tips to the calyx teeth, long bracts which exceed the flower-stalks and smaller flowers (to 15 mm diameter). Only known from two early collections in north-east Yunnan, well away from its relatives and other members of the section.

P. angustidens (Franchet) and *P. wilsonii* Dunn are both heterotypic, including material of *P. wilsonii* and *P. stenodonta*. *P. wilsonii* is the prior name at specific rank, and has been emended, so that *P. angustidens* is dubiously considered by Smith and Fletcher (1941) to be synonymous with it. If lectotypified, it could prove a more correct name for this species if it should ever be re-encountered.

Primula secundiflora Franchet, Bull. Soc. Bot. Fr. 32: 267 (1885)

P. vittata Bur. & Franch. (1891)

DESCRIPTION Forms long-lived *evergreen* rosettes of smooth bright green ascending oblanceolate leaves with a crenate margin arising from a poorly marked short winged stalk, the mid-rib green and obscure, to 20 × 3 cm at flowering (usually smaller). *Leaves* are said to be yellow-mealy when young in the wild but this seems never to be seen in cultivation. *Stems* to 90 cm, usually shorter, green, somewhat slender, bearing 1(–2) drooping whorls of 4–20 flowers on slender white-mealy stalks to 2 cm at flowering, becoming erect and elongating to 5 cm in fruit. *Calyx* narrowly bell-shaped, to 10 mm, with 10 stripes, alternating blackish-purple and silver-mealy, divided to half-way into sharp teeth. *Corolla* a brilliant dark crimson, bell-shaped, exannulate, heterostylous, to 2.5 cm long and in diameter, the lobes overlapping, rounded to square ended. *Capsule* elongate, 1.5 times the calyx. Seeds quadrate, rough and vesicular. 2n = 22. 3.4% self-fertile in pins, 0.7% self-fertile in thrums. Flowering June. (Photos: Bull. AGS 56: 226 (1988), 'A Quest of Flowers' 178.) (Plate 13.)

DISTRIBUTION Very widespread in north-west Yunnan and south-west Sichuan, occurring abundantly in such well-visited localities as the Yulong Shan, Beima Shan, Zhongdian plateau, and the mountains around Kulu and Muli. Just extends into south-east Tibet.

Alpine and subalpine regions; 'swampy places on limestone ground and clay-slate; . . . deep humus of depressions and moory edges of clumps of rhododendrons'. Typically occurs in huge populations intermixed with *P. sikkimensis* beside streams, rivulets, flushes and soaks. No intermediates ever occur. Higher up, extends to moraine and scree zones near glaciers where it can be very dwarf and relatively large-flowered. 3200–4300 m.

Originally placed by Franchet and the Edinburgh workers from Balfour (1913) onwards in section Sikkimensis. My lengthy arguments (1993) that *P. secundiflora* should definitely be classified in Proliferae have now been conclusively confirmed by DNA studies and will not be repeated here. In the Proliferae, apparently related to *P. prolifera* and *P. prenantha* rather than *P. oissonii* and *P. wilsonii*.

In section Proliferae, *P. secundiflora* is exceptional in its drooping bell-shaped exannulate flowers, long capsule and large seeds. The beautifully marked calyx is instantly diagnostic.

VARIATION Exceptionally variable in size. Plants from low-level marshy sites are robust, and were originally separated as *P. vittata*. High alpines from wet screes are relatively tiny, often only 10 cm in the field. There is some suggestion that these characters are at least partially fixed, as cultivated strains also seem to differ in vigour and potential size.

CULTIVATION First introduced by Wilson (**AM** 1905), and in cultivation since then, although collected on several subsequent occasions by Forrest, Rock, etc.

Requires a fertile, humus-rich, moist but well-drained location which never dries out, to give of its best, and in the south of England at least is probably best in a position which offers partial shade. When suited, long-lived, vigorous, and self-sows with abandon, for instance amongst the pavement cracks on my terrace. Long-lived and easily divided vegetatively at any time of year. Fully hardy and resistant to winter wet, but may be intolerant of waterlogging which causes roots to die back. Susceptible to vine weevil. This easy, stunning species is seen less often than it deserves.

No hybrids are known in the garden. Hybrids with *P. poissonii* have been seen in the wild.

Primula section **Sikkimensis** Balf. f., J.Roy. Hort. Soc. 39: 159 (1913). Type species: *P. sikkimensis* Hooker

DESCRIPTION Delicate to very robust *deciduous* perennials with revolute vernation, forming an inconspicuous multicrowned series of resting buds at the soil surface. *Leaf-blades* rounded and often with a heart-shaped base, rugose, lacking hairs or meal, with small regular often crenate teeth; leaf-stalks long, narrow. *Stems* exceeding the leaves with a single pendant whorl of flowers on long, often mealy stalks. *Bracts* spear-shaped, somewhat leaf-like but usually shorter than the flower stalks. *Calyx* typically bell-shaped and often mealy, especially within, the sepal-lobes short and blunt. *Corolla* white, cream, yellow, pink, purple or violet, almost always with a heavily mealy eye and face, bell-shaped, pendant, exannulate, heterostylous (except for *P. morsheadiana*), the lobes entire; *pollen* oblate, 3-syncolpate (except for *P. morsheadiana*). *Capsule* elongate, exceeding the calyx, opening by 5 apical valves; seeds large, usually smooth, quadrate to ovoid, with a long viability. 2n = 22. Flowering late spring to late summer. With the exception of thrum *P. alpicola*, and the homostylous *P. morsheadiana*, fully self-incompatible.

DISTRIBUTION Concentrated in the east Himalaya, but occurring from central Nepal eastwards to the Chinese borderlands, extending to north-west Burma and Gansu. Mostly found on the wetter, monsoon influenced side of the main range. Bogs, streamsides, wet alpine meadows, moraines, 2900–5200 m.

Characteristics which unite the members of this section are the nodding, bell-shaped flowers, meal on the flower face, short, often cordate leaf-blades with a long narrow stalk, and large smooth seeds. Individually, some of these features can be found in other sections, but together they occur only in the Sikkimensis. The group is also very coherent in biological characteristics such as the number and form of the chromosomes, the breeding behaviour, the type of seed and capsule, and the pollen, while several species are capable of hybridization, and often the hybrids are fertile, indicating a close relationship between the parents. Section Sikkimensis forms a very natural group, but its affinities outside the section are less than obvious.

Like section Proliferae, many Sikkimensis are robust, deciduous bog plants of the eastern Sinohimalaya which are vigorous garden plants, and it is tempting to suppose, as I did in 1993, that the sections are related and show orthogenetic links. However, the primitive cladistic analysis I undertook then (p. 39) did not support this view, and evidence from the DNA has since shown that the sections are homoplasic, belonging to quite separate evolutionary branches of the genus. Unexpectedly, the nearest relatives of the Sikkimensis are in fact to be found not in the Proliferae, but in the Yunnanensis. Both analyses so far undertaken show weaker links with members of the Muscarioides, Soldanelloides, Denticulatae, Capitatae and Minutissimae. These latter sections possess what are often thought to be derivative characteristics. It is difficult to avoid the conclusion, however tentative, that the Sikkimensis represent an plesiomorphic condition with respect to the later evolution of those sections of the genus which follow hereafter in this account. From where the Sikkimensis themselves were derived, evolutionarily, is far less clear, and I assume that most links with early developments in *Primula* have become extinct long since.

The one exception is *P. morsheadiana* which forms an obvious morphological connection between the Proliferae species *P. prenantha*, with which it shares the pollen type and homostyly, and the Sikkimensis species *P. reticulata*. Possibly, the Sikkimensis evolved from primitive heterostyle Proliferae related to *P. prenantha*, for a clear morphological series exists today from *P. prenantha* through *P. polonensis*, to *P. morsheadiana* and *P. reticulata*. Perhaps, if the DNA of some of these species was sampled (and so far of these species only *P. prenantha* has been examined) a closer evolutionary link between the Sikkimensis and Proliferae would emerge.

CULTIVATION Effectively, we can divide the section into two main groups in the garden:
a) large robust and vigorous long-lived perennials for the bog garden, water margin, etc. (*P. florindae, P. sikkimensis, P. alpicola*);
b) smaller, often short-lived plants for choicer, less waterlogged habitats, which need regular replacement from seed.

Species vary from the very easy, even invasive, to the delicate, tricky and short-lived, and are best dealt with individually.

Constant characteristics of all species are the long-lived seed which may retain its viability for five years or more, and a requirement for rich moisture-retaining soils in humid locations.

On the whole, Sikkimensis species are not very vulnerable to pests or diseases, although the smaller species may suffer from vine weevil.

Although of less overall importance than section Proliferae, section Sikkimensis has contributed significantly to the modern garden, and includes some of the most generally grown of all species.

HYBRIDIZATION Garden hybrids are not so pervasive as in section Proliferae, but the five Tibetan species *P. florindae, P. sikkimensis, P. alpicola, P. ioessa* and *P. waltonii* probably all interbreed to a limited extent in the garden, and may do so when they meet in the wild as well. Hybrids are often characterized by colours such as orange and pink which do not occur in the species.

KEY TO SPECIES

1. Base of leaf-blade attenuate onto stalk, stalk winged to base 2
1. Base of leaf-blade heart-shaped, rounded or cuneate, stalk not winged to base 3

2. Calyx 5 mm long; flowers homostylous .... *P. morsheadiana*
2. Calyx more than 6 mm long; flowers heterostylous .... *P. sikkimensis*

3. Base of leaf-blade rounded or cuneate; blade usually 2–3× as long as wide 4
3. Base of leaf-blade heart-shaped; blade less than 2× as long as wide 6

4. Leaf-blade dark green, smooth with a wide whitish mid-rib 5
4. Leaf-blade rather olive-green with a close-set rugose bullation .... *P. alpicola*

5. Flowers lilac-blue or white, cowbell-shaped .... *P. ioessa*
5. Flowers deep pink, lampshade-shaped .... *P. waltonii*

6. Plant large; leaves usually exceeding 20 cm; flowers more than 6 .... *P. florindae*
6. Leaves less than 20 cm; flowers usually less than 6 together 7

7. Flower-stalks wiry, pink, exceeding 4 cm .... *P. chumbiensis*
7. Flower-stalks not pink, less than 4 cm 8

8. Leaf-blade not more than 1.5× as long as wide; calyx angled in section .... *P. firmipes*
8. Leaf-blade 1.5× as long as wide or more; calyx round in section .... *P. reticulata*

Primula sikkimensis Hooker f., Bot. Mag. t.4597 (1851)

P. penduliflora Kern ex Stein (1881)
P. microdonta Franchet ex Petitm. (1907)
P. pseudosikkimensis Forrest (1923)
P. pudibunda Smith (1913)

DESCRIPTION A medium-sized to robust long-lived perennial. *Leaf-blades* oblanceolate to elliptical, to 40 × 7 cm, often much smaller, rounded at the tip, attenuate to the stalk at the base, often shining-rugose and dark green; stalk and mid-rib greenish, stalk poorly marked, or well-marked and narrow, but shorter than the blade. *Stem* to 90 cm, often much shorter, stout, green, cream to yellow-mealy above, bearing 1(–2) umbels of 20 or more pendant flowers on narrow mealy stalks to 10 cm. *Calyx* narrowly bell-shaped, to 12 mm, heavily mealy, 5-nerved, cut to half-way into sharp, somewhat recurved sepal-lobes. *Corolla* sweetly fragrant, sulphur-yellow, cream or rarely ivory, to 3 cm long and in diameter, the tube exceeding the calyx; corolla-lobes entire or shallowly notched. *Capsule* usually just exceeding calyx. Seeds 2 mm. 2n = 22. 0.5% self-fertile in pins, completely self-sterile in thrums. Flowering June (Photo: Bull. AGS 56: 228 (1988) (subsp. *pseudosikkimensis*); 57: 353 (1989) (habitat photo). (Plate 13.)

DISTRIBUTION One of the most widespread and common of all primulas, occurring in local abundance in many suitable habitats from west-central Nepal through Sikkim, Bhutan, south-east Tibet, Assam and northern Burma to western Yunnan and Sichuan. One of the surprises of the AGS expeditions to Gansu and Qinghai, culminating in SQAE 684 (2000) was the discovery of this species in the Zhiqin valley far into the dry zones north of Tibet, much further to the north-west than had previously been expected. Naturalized on Snowdon in Wales, UK.

Wet alpine meadows and stream-sides, usually in glacial valleys, ascending to near the bare rock or snow-line and descending into wet glades in the forest zone. Commonly associates with *P. secundiflora* in masses. 'Decidely wet and cold localities enable (*P. sikkimensis*) to descend from higher altitudes. In springs gushing over limestone boulders and filled with aquatic mosses . . . it is more common in the subalpine zone, preferring rivulets by springs, and on humose places I saw it still on one of the highest spots reached ... at 15,600 ft.' 'Inhabiting the high bleak moraines although ... at a somewhat lower altitude colonizing fine moist screes.' 2900–5200 m. I found it to be a very common and locally dominant plant in north-west Yunnan, but agree that it is usually associated with limestone.

VARIATION Not surprisingly for such a widespread and catholic species, *P. sikkimensis* is very variable in the wild, varying in stature by a factor of at least 10, and also in leaf-shape, the relative and absolute size of flowers, and flower colour. Some of these differences seem to be lost after cultivation, but some of the following entities have survived in the garden:

- Var. *lorifolia* Smith, Notes Roy. Bot. Gdn. Edinb. 19: 313 (1938). A form with very narrow entire leaves from eastern Tibet. Only collected once and possibly a local mutant.
- Var. *pudibunda* (Smith) Smith & Fletcher, Trans. Bot. Soc. Edinb. 33: 454 (1943). Slender dwarf plants with small yellow flowers from high localities throughout the range. Such plants are grown today, but are less attractive than var. *pseudosikkimensis*.
- Var. *pseudosikkimensis* (Forrest) Richards (1993). (*P. pseudosikkimensis* Forrest, Notes Roy. Bot. Gdn. Edinb, 14: 52 (1923); *P. sikkimensis* subsp. *pseudosikkimensis* (Forrest) Smith & Forrest, Notes Roy. Bot. Gdn. Edinb. 16: 39 (1928).) Very dwarf and rigid with disproportionately large yellow flowers. High alpine screes, Yulong Shan, Yunnan. Said to be very distinct in the wild (Bull. AGS 56: 228), but to lose its distinctive characters in cultivation (Smith & Fletcher 1943). Probably best at varietal rank for the present.

CULTIVATION Var. *sikkimensis* was first introduced from Sikkim by Hooker in 1849, and it may have been in cultivation ever since, although there have been many later introductions, some in recent years. Var. *pseudosikkimensis* was introduced by Forrest.

Var. *sikkimensis* is a vigorous, long-lived plant for a fertile, moist, humus-rich soil, where it often self-sows, and it withstands a degree of waterlogging especially in the summer. Although quite popular, it has a similar effect, but a lesser impact, than *P. florindae* which is more often seen.

The other varieties are much smaller and less vigorous plants which require choicer sites with better drainage and less competition, although they should not be allowed to dry out. Var. *pudibunda* is in my experience rather plain.

HYBRIDIZATION I have raised plants from seed with orange flowers, and have also seen plants similar to *P. sikkimensis* but with pink flowers with a mealy white face. These are probably hybrids with *P. waltonii*, or possibly with *P. alpicola* var. *violacea*. Where *P. florindae* and *P. sikkimensis* are grown together, plants with intermediate foliage characteristics sometimes occur.

Primula morsheadiana Ward, Notes Roy. Bot. Gdn. Edinb. 15: 70 (1925)

DESCRIPTION Very close to *P. sikkimensis* var. *pudibunda*, and similarly fragrant and with mealy flowers, but with sharp irregular leaf-teeth, and somewhat annulate homostylous flowers, the calyx only 5 mm. Pollen 3-colporoidate, as in section Proliferae and possibly linking with *P. prenantha* and *P. polonensis* of that section (p. 223). 2n = 22.

DISTRIBUTION On several very wet passes in Tsari, south-east Tibet. 'Rocky hill-slopes near water'; 3200–3900 m. Said by Smith & Fletcher (1943) never to have been in cultivation, but as Bruun (1930) reports a chromosome count, it was presumably briefly in cultivation from Ward (1924).

Primula alpicola (Smith) Stapf, Bot. Mag. t.9276 (1932)

P. microdonta Franchet ex Petitm. var. *alpicola* Smith (1926)

DESCRIPTION Similar to *P. sikkimensis*, but leaf-blades very distinctive, being olive-green and narrowly oval but with a *rounded* base, unwinged stalks and with a very *close-set* rugosity. The flowers are sweetly fragrant and most commonly have a single umbel in cultivation, but have been found with up to 4 superimposed whorls in the wild; they are broadly funnel-shaped to *saucer-shaped* rather than bell-shaped, and can be white, yellow, cream flushed pink, rose, claret, purple or violet, although smothered with white or yellow meal on the face, while the corolla-lobes are always *notched*. Seeds 1.5 mm, brown. 2n = 22. Nearly totally self-sterile in pins, but 25% self-fertile in thrums. Flowering June. (Plate 13.)

DISTRIBUTION South-east Tibet, chiefly in the Tsari region of the Tsangpo basin where it appears widely distributed and locally abundant on primula-rich valleys and passes in the wet zones. Four records from west-central Bhutan, 300 km to the west; these yellow-flowered Bhutanese plants connect morphologically with *P. reticulata*, but the stalk is shorter than the leaf blade which is scarcely heart-shaped at the base.

Wet alpine meadows, especially stream banks, and open wet areas in conifer forest, often sub-dominant and forming masses of colour. 3600–4600 m.

Originally described as a variety of *P. microdonta*, the type of which is a Chinese form of *P. sikkimensis*. Although *P. alpicola* was given specific rank soon afterwards, the name *P. microdonta* persisted for this plant in cultivation for many years afterwards. Ward, the original discoverer, and Ludlow and Sherriff describe how this species nearly always occurs in multi-hued hordes, a wide variety of beautiful colour forms occurring together. In the 1990s, a number of parties have been able to visit the Tsari valley and confirm these earlier reports. It seems not to be certain which of the colour forms is most correctly equated with the type, each of the three main colour forms having been given a varietal name. In view of the original confusion with the yellow *P. sikkimensis*, I am taking yellow to be the type colour here.

P. alpicola is instantly recognized by the flower shape, reminiscent of a 'Chinese coolies hat'. The close-set reticulation of the olive-green oval leaf-blades is also distinctive.

VARIATION

- Var. *alpicola* (= var. *luna* (Stapf) Smith & Fletcher 1943). Flowers yellow.
- Var. *alba* Smith, Trans. Bot. Soc. Edinb. 33: 437 (1943). Flowers white.
- Var. *violacea* (Stapf) Smith & Fletcher, Notes Roy. Bot. Gdn. Edinb. 19: 214 (1937). Flowers

pink, rose, purple or violet with a white-mealy face.

CULTIVATION First introduced by Ward (1924), and on at least two later occasions by Ludlow and Sherriff.

Easy and long-lived in cool humid spots in fertile and moist but not heavily waterlogged soils, self-sowing when suited. Large clumps are best divided before flowering in spring. Deeply resents excessive heat and drying out at the roots, and rather susceptible to vine-weevil. A species of intermediate robustness and vigour, falling between the larger forms of *P. sikkimensis* and *P. ioessa*. Some small-flowered varieties are around, but if good forms are selected, this is amongst the most lovely of all garden primulas, and is justly popular, especially in Scotland.

HYBRIDIZATION Hybrids with *P. florindae* were reported in the field by Ward, and wild plants of *P. florindae* may also be introgressed by purple *P. alpicola*, for some were collected with flowers of a reddish amber. These two species cross freely in the garden, giving a wide range of vegetative types, and flower colours including reddish and brownish shades not found in either parent. Seems to cross less frequently with *P. sikkimensis* in the garden.

Primula waltonii Watt ex Balf. f., Notes Roy. Bot. Gdn. Edinb. 9: 57 (1915)

?*P. prionotes* Balf. f. & Watt (1915)
?*P. waltonii* subsp. *prionotes* (Balf. f. & Watt) Smith & Forrest (1928)
P. vinosa Stapf (1932)

DESCRIPTION A medium-sized plant with oblanceolate to elliptical crenate to serrately toothed *leaf-blades,* about 15 × 3 cm, cuneate below, matt dull slightly bluish green above with a marked whitish mid-rib and narrowly winged stalk, shorter than or equalling the blade. *Stem* to 50 cm in cultivation carrying a single umbel of 7–30 pendant flowers on wiry cream-mealy stalks to 7 cm. *Calyx* bell-shaped, mealy but often also purplish, to 10 mm. *Corolla* scented of fruit-drops, strawberry pink to wine-red with a cream-mealy face and an abruptly demarcated red eye, rarely cream or white at Lhasa, lampshade-shaped, to 20 mm in diameter; corolla-lobes entire or shallowly notched. *Capsule* just exceeding calyx; seeds not exceeding 1.5 mm, brown. 2n = 22. Fully self-sterile. Flowering June. (Plate 13.)

DISTRIBUTION Tibet; Lhasa, and in widely scattered localities to the south-west towards Sikkim in the Singalila area, and to the south-east towards Bhutan, where it occurs in the Sakden region, and in the Tsangpo gorge region. Grows in flood pastures beside rivers in relatively dry rain-shadow regions. Grows as high as 5800 m in central Tibet.

Primula waltonii was first collected from Lhasa. It has distinctive leaves, which are, however, almost identical to those of *P. ioessa,* with which it is undoubtedly closely associated. *P. prionotes* is a dwarf high level plant with narrow corollas from the area north of Sikkim, while *P. vinosa* from further to the south-east has a more open corolla. In uniting the three, Smith & Fletcher (1943) note that the distinctive banding of the meal on the face of the corolla, so that the eye is free, is common to all. Curiously, they separate *P. ioessa* as having a wider corolla, but as these species are seen in gardens, *P. waltonii* has a distinctively wide, lampshade-shaped corolla, while that of *P. ioessa* is the shape of a cowbell. It may be that *P. prionotes* lies between *P. ioessa and P. waltonii*. Possibly, all three as well as '*P. hopeana*' should be treated within the compass of *P. waltonii*.

As grown in gardens, *P. waltonii* is a taller, leggier and less elegant plant than *P. ioessa* with flowers usually of a characteristic and not altogether attractive crushed strawberry hue, whereas those of *P. ioessa* are lilac-blue. However, field collections seem to encompass other plants much closer to *P. ioessa*. Nevertheless, the mealy band on the flower face does seem to be characteristic. Most plants called *P. waltonii* in gardens in recent years appear to have been hybrids, mostly with *P. sikkimensis*.

CULTIVATION First introduced from the Nambu La in the Tsangpo region ('vinosa' types) by Ward in 1924, and at about the same time from Gyantse, between Sikkim and Lhasa ('prionotes' types). Ludlow and Sherriff introduced seed and flown-home plants from Bhutan in 1934. By 1983 the true plant probably no longer survived in British gardens, although hybrids certainly did. At least one seed collection from the AGSES expedition to Sikkim in that year (572), determined merely as '*P.*

section Sikkimensis' proved to be *P. waltonii*, a new record for that state.

These seedlings grew strongly in a shady humid humus-rich site beside a pond but with fairly good drainage. They first flowered in 1985, and flowered well for two subsequent years, setting some seed, after which they started to 'go back'. This seems to have been the last introduction. Pure plants exist in cultivation in 2001 only at Cluny.

HYBRIDIZATION Apparently promiscuous in the past, most seed proving hybrid with *P. sikkimensis* and *P. florindae*. It probably also crosses with *P. ioessa*, and possibly with *P. alpicola*. Hybrids with the first two species show little signs of *waltonii* parentage apart from reddish flowers. However, hybrids survive which much more closely resemble *P. waltonii*, although usually with narrow flowers of a muddy purple and leaves more like *P. sikkimensis*. Often called '*P. waltonii* or '*waltonii* hybrids' in gardens, they seem to be complex hybrids involving *P. sikkimensis* and *P. ioessa*.

Primula ioessa Smith, Notes Roy. Bot. Gdn. Edinb. 19: 216 (1937)

P. hopeana Balf. f. & Cooper (1917)

DESCRIPTION Differs from *P. waltonii*, at least in the garden, by being smaller and neater (stems to 15 cm) with relatively large cowbell-shaped flowers which are usually lilac-blue or white in colour (also pinkish in the field), and which have a mealy eye. (Photo: Proceedings 7th Int. Rock Garden Conf.: plate 28.) (Plates 13, 92.)

DISTRIBUTION Commonest in very wet primula-rich passes in the Tsari district of south-east Tibet, but also recorded in Bhutan and east Nepal. Very wet alpine meadows, 3600–4300 m, often growing in masses.

This most delightful little plant of refined charm is pronounced 'yo-essa'. The least closely related of the four species examined by DNA (*P. florindae, P. firmipes* and *P.* 'waltonii' were the others). Although distinct in the garden, it fills a narrow morphological gap between 'prionotes' forms of *P. waltonii* and *P. hopeana*. All three taxa share the same leaf morphology, with a narrowly oblong-oval crenate leaf-blade which is smooth, flat, dark green and has a broad white mid-vein. The white forms (var. *subpinnatifida*) of *P. ioessa* are very similar to *P. hopeana*. Smith & Fletcher (1943) inexplicably transferred var. *hopeana*, based on Balfour and Cooper's *P. hopeana*, from their previous treatment as a synonym of *P. ioessa* v. *subpinnatifida* (1937) to a variety of *P. sikkimensis*. In my view their earlier treatment was preferable.

Reputedly v. *subpinnatifida* is distinguished from v. *hopeana* by its purple-stained calyx, more deeply toothed leaves and less narrow corolla. It is best separated from 'prionotes' forms of *P. waltonii*, which come from a quite different part of Tibet, by the mealy eye. However, Ludlow and Sherriff had the greatest difficulty separating *P. ioessa, P. waltonii* and *P. hopeana* in the field, and they should all perhaps be united under *P. waltonii*. I am compromising by keeping *P. ioessa* but losing *P. hopeana*. If *P. ioessa* is lost, the prior epithet at varietal and subspecific rank for *P. ioessa* is *subpinnatifida*.

VARIATION In the wild, said to vary in flower colour from pale pink through mauve to violet, but in cultivation usually lilac-blue.

- Var. *subpinnatifida* (Smith) Smith & Fletcher, Trans. Bot. Soc. Edinb. 33: 445 (1943) (*P. sikkimensis* Hooker subsp. *subpinnatifida* Smith (1936). Flowers white, leaves jaggedly toothed. South-east Tibet. **AM** 1949.
- Var. *hopeana* (Balf. f. & Cooper) Richards **comb. nov**. (*P. hopeana* Balf. f. & Cooper, Trans. Bot. Soc. Edinburgh, 27: 236, 1917). Similar to v. *subpinnatifida* but with crenate teeth, and with a narrower ivory corolla. Merges into v. *subpinnatifida*. East Nepal (Ganesh Himal), Bhutan and south-east Tibet.

CULTIVATION Introduced in 1938 by Ludlow, Sherriff and Taylor. Since then it has remained in cultivation, and seeds and plants are occasionally offered still, but it remains uncommon. **AM** 1957. Var. *hopeana* was first introduced from Bhutan in 1915 by Cooper, and again by Ludlow and Sherriff, and Ward.

Best grown in a humid, partially shaded and sheltered location in a well-drained but moisture-retentive soil. Short-lived, rarely flowering for more than three seasons, and thus demanding regular replacement from seed. Well worth every effort.

Primula chumbiensis Smith, Trans. Bot. Soc. Edinb. 26: 118 (1912)

DESCRIPTION A small to medium-sized plant with a short *elliptical* rugose rather leathery leaf-blade with a rounded tip and base, and a *long* narrow discrete *pinkish* stalk about twice the length of the blade. *Stem* pinkish, to 25 cm, bearing up to 7 pendant flowers on relatively long (4 cm) creamy-mealy wiry stalks. *Calyx* tubular, about 8 mm, mealy. *Corolla* ivory-cream, narrowly bell-shaped, to 25 mm long. Capsule equalling the calyx. (Fig. 21).

DISTRIBUTION Restricted to the Chumbi valley, between Sikkim and Bhutan, and neighbouring regions of north-west Bhutan (Mem La, Thimbu Chu). High alpine rocks and scree, but carried down to alluvial flats by rivers, where it is more robust; 3800–5300 m.

This delightful, delicate species was scarcely known to Smith and Fletcher, for it was not introduced until 1949, and their description is misleading. Despite their comment it is closely related to neither *P. sikkimensis* or *P. reticulata*, but in structure comes closest to *P. firmipes* which however has ovate leaf-blades and an angular bell-shaped calyx. The small, spoon-shaped leaves and disproportionately large inflorescence with delicate hanging moonlit flowers is most distinctive.

CULTIVATION Introduced from Bhutan by Ludlow and Sherriff in 1949. A rather difficult species which seems to require very cool and humid conditions in a rich, well-drained soil. This, like *P. kingii*, is a species which only the Sherriffs really succeeded with, although some success was also achieved in gardens such as Keillour, Branklyn, Cluny, Edrom and Kilbryde where difficult Asiatic species flourished. Extinct in cultivation by 1990.

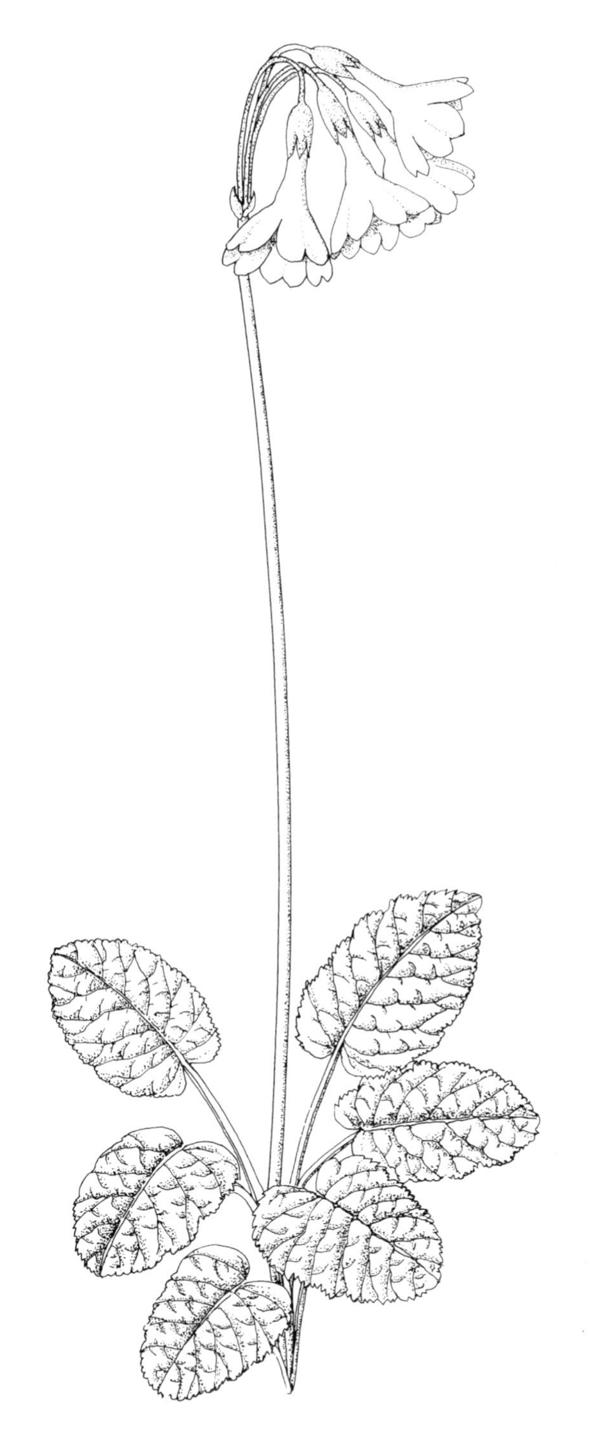

Fig. 21. *P. chumbiensis*

Primula florindae Ward, Notes Roy. Bot. Gdn. Edinb. 15: 84 (1926)

DESCRIPTION A *massive* plant, the largest primula. Deciduous leaves raise from a large stock with deep red thongy *roots*. *Leaf-blade* ovate, *heart-shaped* at the base, to 20 × 15 cm; stalk robust, narrowly winged, often reddish, to 40 cm. Stem to 1.5 m, but usually shorter, robust, bearing an often substantial umbel of up to 80 pendant flowers (very occasionally with 2 whorls), the flower stalks cream-mealy, wiry, to 10 cm. *Calyx* bell-shaped, cream-mealy, to 10 mm with sharp slightly recurved sepal-lobes. *Corolla* fragrant, sulphur-yellow, to 2.5 cm long, 2 cm in diameter, bell-shaped; corolla-lobes rounded, entire, pointed, or slightly toothed but not notched. Capsule 2× the calyx; seeds 2 mm, fawn. 2n = 22. Almost completely self-sterile. Flowering late June–August. (Plate 13.)

DISTRIBUTION South-east Tibet, Tsangpo basin, from Tsari to the Pachakshiri. Locally abundant at riversides and islands, very wet rivulets and forest bogs, at about 4000 m, often growing with *P. alpicola*.

Another of Kingdon Ward's magnificent discoveries from south-east Tibet, this is a huge and stately plant when well-suited, which can be as high as a man in flower. Could only be confused with *P. sikkimensis*, which has a quite different leaf-shape. Almost the only primula flowering in gardens as late as August.

P. florindae has become well established in parts of the Scottish Highlands in fens and by riversides far from gardens, where seeds have been carried by flood water.

CULTIVATION Introduced by Ward in 1924 (**FCC** 1926), and probably later by Ludlow and Sherriff. Grows well in any rich moist soil, usually self-sowing even into cracks in paving, etc. In very wet situations such as the edges of ponds and streams it reaches its full potential; in relatively dry situations it is a much smaller plant. Very tolerant of waterlogging. One of the most significant garden primulas, making a great impact in wet semi-wild situations and big enough to influence large landscapes. Not on the whole a plant for the small garden, but extremely popular in larger ones.

HYBRIDIZATION For crosses with *P. alpicola* and *P. sikkimensis* see pages 236 and 237. Strains with chestnut to orange flowers are often seen in gardens, and even in wild Scottish locations, and are probably introgressed with the former. Plants with pink flowers ('Rasp Red') are occasionally seen; these are probably crosses with *P. waltonii*.

Primula firmipes Balf. f. & Forrest, Notes Roy. Bot. Gdn. Edinb. 13: 10 (1920)

P. flexilipes Balf. f. & Forrest (1920)
P. firmipes subsp. *flexilipes* (Balf. f. & Forrest) Smith & Forrest (1928)
P. deleiensis Ward (1930)
P. erythra Fletcher (1943)
P. subansirica G.D. Pal (1985)

DESCRIPTION Another delicate species, differing from *P. chumbiensis* by the oval leaf-blade, to 7 × 5 cm, with a heart-shaped base, and the angled bell-shaped calyx. The flowers seem to be a soft yellow, rarely red. Seeds 1.5 mm. 2n = 22. (Fig. Halda: 179.) According to DNA studies, closely allied to *P. florindae*.

DISTRIBUTION From Tsari, south-east Tibet to the frontiers between Tibet, Yunnan and Burma, and just into Assam. 'Wet alpine meadows, by streams and on the margins of thickets, 3000–4500 m.' Should perhaps be considered as a geographically distinct subspecies of *P. reticulata*.

VARIATION

- Var. *erythra* (Fletcher) Richards (1993) (*P. erythra* Fletcher, Trans. Bot. Soc. Edinb. 33: 440–1 (1943); *P. rubra* Ward 1930 non Gmelin 1775). Flowers maroon red; meal apparently absent; leaves finely scabrid. Delei Valley, Assam, with *P. firmipes*.

CULTIVATION Introduced by Forrest in 1924, but probably extinct in culture, where it was generally known as *P. flexilipes*, by 1940. 'Requires a well-drained position in half-shade in light rich soil with plenty of grit round the collar.' Apparently in cultivation by Tromso Botanic Garden in 2000, origin unknown, and with Ian Christie in 2002.

Primula reticulata Wall. in Roxburgh, Fl. India 2: 21 (1824)

P. altissima G. Don (1825)
P. didyma Smith (1931)

DESCRIPTION Dubiously distinct from *P. firmipes*, distinguished chiefly by the narrower, oblong leaf-blade of a thinner texture and the smaller seeds of 1 mm. *P. alpicola* has a leaf-blade longer than the stalk without a heart-shaped base, and usually has more flared flowers, but intermediates occur in Bhutan. 2n = 22. Fully self-sterile. Flowering May. (Fig. 22).

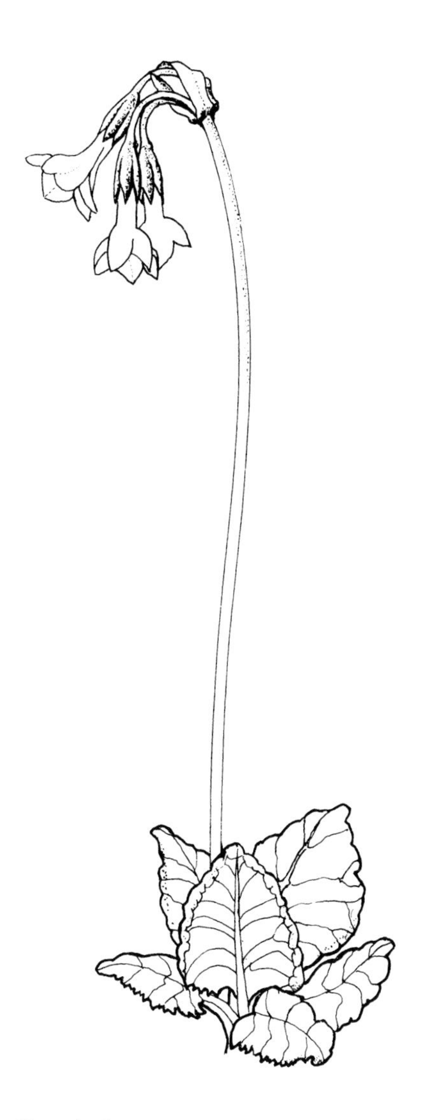

Fig. 22. *P. reticulata*

DISTRIBUTION Central Nepal (Gosainkunde) to Sikkim, just entering Tibet and Bhutan in the Chumbi area. Alpine meadows, 3300–5000 m.

For distinctions from *P. firmipes* and *P. alpicola* see p.236. *P. chumbiensis* is a much more distinguished plant with larger paler flowers on longer stalks with a tubular calyx and distinctive firm spoon-shaped leaves.

VARIATION Extremely variable in size; high altitude forms remain dwarf in cultivation, and are the smallest Sikkimensis, but forms from lower altitudes are quite as robust as *P. firmipes*.

- Var. *didyma* (Smith) Richards (1993). (*P. didyma* Smith, Notes Roy. Bot. Gdn. Edinb. 16: 228 (1931). Flowers purple or blue (Nepal).

CULTIVATION Introduced from Chumbi in 1886, and has been intermittently in cultivation since, usually from Sikkim seed. Seed collected there by Ghose's seed firm under the name *P. sappharina* in 1981 and 1982 grew well in pots plunged in a shady frame and flowered in 1982 and 1983, but then died without setting seed. Also AGSES 65, 220 (1983). Probably short-lived. These were dwarf forms from high altitude, and of no great merit.

Section **Oreophlomis** (Ruprecht) Federov, Fl. SSSR 18: 182 (1952).

Oreophlomis Ruprecht, Bull. Acad. Imp. Sci. St. Petersb. 6: 218 (1863) sin. stat.
(Section Auriculatae Pax 1889 p.p.)
(Section Farinosae Pax subsection Auriculatae (Pax) Smith & Fletcher 1943)
(Section Rosea Watt 1904 p.p.)
Type species *P. auriculata* Lam.

DESCRIPTION *Plants* perennial, small to moderate-sized, arising from a rather stout rhizome, deciduous, overwintering as a clump of resting buds at the soil surface, or creeping, the bud-scales conspicuous, lacking meal and usually sharp and reddish. *Leaves* smooth in texture, regularly and sharply toothed, usually blunt, often heterophyllous, hairless, usually lacking meal, with revolute vernation. *Inflorescences* stemmed, although sometimes apparently stemless at flowering, bearing 1 (–4) whorls of up to 20 flowers in an umbel with long flower stalks, or in a tight subcapitate head; bracts conspicuous, pouch-like. *Calyx* narrow, often angled, usually lacking meal. *Corolla* frequently bright rose-pink with a yellow eye, also violet, purple, yellow and white, flat-faced with a long tube, exannulate or weakly annulate, heterostylous, the corolla-lobes usually notched; *pollen* oblate, 3–4 syncolpate. *Capsules* globose to ovoid, usually included within the calyx, opening by five short apical valves; seeds rather small, dark, pointed at both ends. 2n = 22, 44. Chromosome size variable. Self-sterile to strongly self-fertile. *Flowering* spring (chiefly April).

DISTRIBUTION Eastern Turkey, Iraq, Caucasus, Iran, Afghanistan, Pakistan, Kashmir, north-west India and Soviet Central Asia.

Wet alpine meadows, often growing in rivulets, stream and lake-sides arising from snow-melt in summer-dry areas, 1400–5000 m.

There has been much confusion about the most suitable, and correct, classification of plants that lie morphologically between section Crystallophlomis and section Aleuritia. Smith & Fletcher (1943) placed them all within Pax's section Farinosae, the classical members of which, grouped around *P. farinosa*, are here known by the earlier name Aleuritia. Within the 'Farinosae', they delimited no less than 8 subsections, two of which usually lack any meal and have saccate ('pouched') bracts. These subsections, Sibirica and Auriculatae, were also cytologically distinct, having x = 11.

Schwarz (1968, 1972) showed that the 'Sibirica' (section Armerina) and 'Auriculatae' (section Oreophlomis) can indeed be very clearly distinguished, by using the reliable characters of pollen type and overwintering bud. Section Armerina, remarkably, has stephanocolpate pollen similar to that in section Primula, and forms small spherical unstabilized resting buds anew at the end of the often disintegrating rhizome. In contrast, these features in section Oreophlomis do not differ from those in the Aleuritia. The seed morphology of the Oreophlomis is however very distinctive, as are the chromosomes which are of a highly 'derived' type. Federov (1952) resurrects Ruprecht's Oreophlomis for these plants, which although published without rank, predates Pax's Auriculatae and can be taken to have the equivalent at that time of sectional rank; it shares with the Auriculatae the type species *P. auriculata*.

Of the species which Smith & Fletcher placed in subsection 'Auriculatae'. *P. sertulum* (= *P. obsessa*) is now placed in section Denticulata, and *P. efarinosa* in a solitary position following the Aleuritia. Another isolated species, the Japanese *P. macrocarpa* with 2n = 16, has been placed, with considerable misgivings, in association with section Glabra. Also, *P. oxygraphidifolia*, classified by Smith & Fletcher within subsection 'Sibirica', has been added to the Oreophlomis.

This reclassification of certain species has been geographically predictive, so that the Oreophlomis, once thought to stretch from Turkey to Japan, are now essentially restricted to summer-dry regions of west-central Asia. They form a geographically distinct and related group, at least three species of which are capable of hybridization. However, DNA studies show that they are formed of two sister clades, one composed of *P. auriculata* and *P. luteola*, while the other containing *P. clarkei* and *P. elliptica* is more related to some Asian Aleuritia. We need a more complete survey before sectional boundaries are reviewed again

P. auriculata and *P. luteola* are unusual in being polyploid heterostyles. The chromosomes, although twice the number of those of relatives, share the same 'derived' type of morphology. These species

KEY TO SPECIES

1. Plant creeping; flowers stemless, or stems not exceeding 5 cm 2
1. Plant tufted; stems usually exceeding 5 cm 3

2. Leaf-blades orbicular, heart-shaped at base .... *P. clarkei*
2. Leaf-blades oblong at least at flowering, truncate to cuneate at base .... *P. warshenewskiana*

3. Flowers yellow .... *P. luteola*
3. Flowers pink to violet 4

4. Flowers violet; leaf-blades elliptical and narrowly stalked at flowering 5
4. Flowers pink to purple; leaf-blades oblong and with winged poorly marked stalks at flowering 6

5. Flowers exceeding 15 mm in diameter, exannulate .... *P. elliptica*
5. Flowers not exceeding 15 mm in diameter, annulate .... *P. flexuosa*

6. Flowers solitary, not exceeding 10 mm in diameter; leaf-blades orbicular .... *P. oxygraphidifolia*
6. Flowers two or more together, exceeding 10 mm in diameter; leaf-blades ovate or oblong 7

7. Flowers lilac to purple, including dull pink, not exceeding 20 mm in diameter .... *P. auriculata*
7. Flowers brilliant rose-pink, exceeding 20 mm in diameter .... *P. rosea*

can be considered as derivative within the Oreophlomis, and closely related to each other as shown by the DNA.

It seems useful to consider that the Oreophlomis (x = 11) may represent an ancestral condition with respect to the Aleuritia (x = 9), Glabra, Pulchella and Souliei (x = 8). It could also be suggested that the Denticulata evolved from Oreophlomis-like predecessors.

CULTIVATION All the species except *P. flexuosa* and *P oxygraphidifolia* are quite well known in cultivation. Despite their close relationship and common habitat, they have disparate requirements, which are best dealt with separately.

HYBRIDIZATION No hybrids seem to be known in the wild, but all three possible hybrids between *P. rosea, P. clarkei and P. warshenewskiana* have been recorded in cultivation.

Primula auriculata Lam., Tab. Encycl. Meth. Bot. 1: 429 (1792)

P. longifolia Curtis (1797)
P. glacialis Adam ex Rupr. (1863) non Willd. ex Roemer & Schultes (1819) (= *P. algida* Adams) nec *P. glacialis* Franchet (1885) (= *P. chionantha* Balf. f. & Forrest)
P. pycnorhiza Ledeb. (1847–9)
P. tournefortii Rupr. (1863)
P. olgae Regel (1874)
P. archibaldii Schwarz (1970) nom. nud.
P. dealbata Schwarz (1970) nom. nud. non Englemann (1863) (= *P. incana* Jones)
P. auriculata var. *bornmuelleri* Hausskn. ex Bornmueller (1905) non *P. bornmuelleri* Pax (1909) (= *Dionysia bornmuelleri* (Pax) Clay
P. auriculata var. *calva* Hausskn. & Bornmueller ex Bornmueller (1905)
P. auriculata var. *caucasica* Ledeb. (1847–9)

DESCRIPTION A small to medium-sized plant. *Leaves* extremely variable, from squatly ovate without a distinct stalk to narrowly lanceolate with a long stalk, entire to deeply serrate, mid-rib and stalk green. *Stem* very variable, short and stout, scarcely exceeding the leaves, to long and narrow, occasionally mealy at the top, bearing a spherical umbel of many flowers or a tight head of 3-many flowers. *Bracts* exceeding the flower stalks. *Calyx* 3–9 mm, bell-shaped to cylindrical, the sepal-lobes oblong or triangular, sometimes mealy. *Corolla* lilac to deep reddish-purple, usually with a narrow yellow or greenish eye fading to white, usually weakly annulate, heterostylous, flat-faced, to 15 (–20) mm in diameter, usually smaller; *corolla tube* 2–3× the calyx; corolla-lobes deeply notched. *Capsule* equalling to slightly exceeding the calyx. 2n = 44 (originally reported as '*P. algida*' by Bruun, a species now known to have 2n = 18. (Plates 14, 50.)

DISTRIBUTION From Eastern Turkey to the Transcaucasus and Caucasus, N Iraq, Elburz in northern Iran and scattered eastwards to the mountains of northern and eastern Afghanistan to the Pamir and Tien Shan in Soviet central Asia.

Wet alpine meadows and streamsides above the tree-line, often flowering near melting snow, commonly associated with *P. capitellata*. 1250–4000 m.

P. auriculata is an extremely variable species scattered over a wide range of some 3000 km. It has been known for over two centuries and yet has been rather seldom collected in its remote habitats. Consequently, it has one of the most complex and muddled taxonomic histories of any primula. The type probably originated in Iran, and similar plants seem to be found in Turkey. However, variable but distinct morphological forms seem to occur in the Caucasus, the Pamir, and elsewhere in Iran. At least nine epithets have been used for these at the ranks of species, subspecies, variety and forma. I reduced these to four geographical forms at subspecific rank in an attempt to reduce chaos to order, but it may be found at times that plants from a given district do not neatly fall into these groupings.

P. auriculata is distinguished from its relatives by a combination of its usually short, poorly demarcated leaf-stalk, the flower stem which exceeds the leaves, and the usually rather tight, capitate or spherical head of somewhat annulate flowers. Unlike its relatives it is occasionally somewhat mealy about the inflorescence, although this seems to be uncommon. The only other Oreophlomis which is slightly mealy is the closely related yellow-flowered *P. luteola*, which shares with *P. auriculata* a tetraploid chromosome count.

VARIATION An extremely variable species within and between regions; the flowers vary in colour, and occasional white forms are also known.

- Subsp. *auriculata* (?*P. auriculata* var. *bornmuelleri* Hausskn. ex Bornm. (1905)). A relatively robust race with oblong leaves and spherical heads on stout stems, the flower-stalks about equalling the calyx. Eastern Turkey, Iraq and the Elburz, Iran.
- Subsp. *pycnorhiza* (Ledeb.) Wendelbo in Reichb. f., Fl. Iranica, Primulaceae: 10 (1965) (*P. pycnorhiza* Ledeb. (1847–9); ? *P. auriculata* var. *caucasica* Ledeb, 1847–9; *P. auriculata* var. *glacialis* (Adams) Boiss (1875); *P. dealbata* Schwarz (1970). A dwarf squat form with prostrate obovate deeply serrate leaves and large orbicular heads, the flower-stalks exceeding the calyx. Caucasus. This seems to be the form generally in cultivation. '*P. dealbata*' is a heavily mealy form.
- Subsp. *tournefortii* (Rupr.) Richards, (1993) (*P. tournefortii* Ruprecht, Bull. Acad. Sci. St. Petersb. 6: 228 (1863); *P. auriculata* var. *tournefortii* (Rupr.) Kusn. (1901); *P. auriculata* var. *calva* Hausskn. & Bornm. ex Bornm. (1905); *P. archibaldii* Schwarz (1970). A delicate form with narrow entire leaves with narrow stalks, a slender stem and a few-flowered capitate head, the flower stalks shorter than the calyx. North Iran and Transcaucasia.
- Subsp. *olgae* (Regel) Richards (1993). (*P. olgae* Regel, Tr. Bot. Sada 3, 1: 151 (1874); *P. auriculata* var. *calva* Hausskn. & Bornm. ex Turkev. (1923) non ex Bornm. (1905). Similar to subsp. *tournefortii*, but smaller, to 15 cm, with short leaves (to 10 cm) and a very long corolla tube. Pamirs and Tien Shan.

CULTIVATION First introduced into France in 1784, and imported into England in about 1794 when it was illustrated as *P. longifolia* Curtis. It is quite an easy plant to grow, so that it is curious how scarce it has been in cultivation, perhaps because relatively unattractive forms had been introduced. At the Botanic Garden on the Col de Lautaret, French Alps, it has escaped and has sown in hundreds down a flushed slope. This is a coarse form of a poor lilac colour. In the 1980s an attractive dwarf form with globular heads of a bright pink, probably subsp. *pycnorhiza*, was increasingly grown, and this is a very worthwhile plant for a rich well-drained location in good light, where it is soundly perennial. Introduced again in 1990 as B & H 60. No hybrids are reported.

Primula luteola Rupr., Bull. Acad. St. Petersb. 6: 233 (1863)

P. auriculata Lam. var. *luteola* (Rupr.) Regel (1868)

DESCRIPTION Related to tall robust forms of *P. auriculata* subsp. *auriculata*, but flowers *yellow*, *exannulate*, somewhat funnel-shaped, and borne in a loose umbel of up to 25 flowers (occasionally 2 superimposed umbels are seen). The calyx is mealy and the erect lanceolate leaves are sharply and regularly *double*-toothed. 2n = 44. Heterostylous; pins and thrums both 3% self-fertile. Flowering May. (Plate 1.)

DISTRIBUTION A local endemic from Daghestan, north-east Caucasus, where the best known locality is the pass between Kidero and Kituri. Wet meadows, springs and flushes in the alpine zone, 1400–3000 m.

P. luteola is a most distinctive plant with its yellow flowers. However, there is no doubt that it is closely related to *P. auriculata* which occurs slightly to the south in the Caucasus, although the flowers and leaves have a slightly different structure. As both species are tetraploids (2n = 44) and have very similar chromosomes, they almost certainly share a common ancestry.

CULTIVATION Introduced by Ruprecht, probably at the time of its discovery, flowering in 1867 in Leningrad, from where seed was sent to Britain. This may have been the only introduction.

P. luteola comes fairly readily from seed, growing well in well-drained sites which never dry out, in sun or partial shade, and flowering usually in its second summer. Plants can be maintained by division, but are not very long-lived, usually going back after about 5 years. Seed is regularly set. This is a most attractive species, obtainable through the trade, which is seen comparatively seldom. No hybrids are known, although it may prove to be interfertile with *P. auriculata*.

Primula elliptica Royle, Ill. Bot. Himal. 311 (1839)

P. spathulacea Jacq. ex Duby (1844)

DESCRIPTION Similar to *P. auriculata*, but never

mealy and with a distinct, long, narrowly winged whitish leaf-stalk, an *elliptical* blade, and a loose, somewhat *one-sided* umbel of 2–7 *violet*, blue or purple, slightly funnel-shaped *exannulate* flowers with a golden eye. *Capsule* subglobose, not exceeding the calyx. 2n = 22. Flowers May in the garden, July–August in the field, later than *P. rosea*. (Photo: Fls. Himalaya, fig. 859. (Plate 93))

DISTRIBUTION North-west Himalaya, from north Pakistan (Gilgit and Hazara) through Kashmir to north-west India (Uttar Pradesh and Himachal Pradesh, Garwhal). Despite reports to the contrary, I can find no indication that it enters Nepal or Tibet.

'Moist hilly slopes and near melting snow, 3300–4880 m'.

Within the Oreophlomis, the flower colour and spoon-shaped leaves are distinctive.

CULTIVATION First introduced prior to 1886, and intermittently in cultivation since. It was available for Bruun's cytological analysis (about 1930), perhaps from Prem Kohli who introduced it, and seed was introduced again from Kashmir in 1975 (CHP & W 143) and since mostly from Himalch Pradesh e.g. CC & MR 428, CC & McK 490, 735. It is occasionally available today.

Limited experience suggests that this is one of the less amenable members of the section in cultivation, as it is short-lived, rarely sets seed, and offers little opportunity for vegetative propagation. It probably succeeds best in cool, well-drained but moisture-retaining media with winter cover. Every effort should be made to raise a batch of seedlings and cross-pollinate, as this is a delightful species which should be seen far more frequently. No hybrids have been recorded.

Primula flexuosa Turkewicz, Bot. Mat. Gerb. Fl. Bot. Sada 2, 4: 15 (1921)

DESCRIPTION Related to *P. elliptica*, but differing in the more deeply and irregularly toothed leaves and smaller (10–15 mm in diameter) annulate rose (violet?) flowers. The whole plant is rough with non-sticky glands. Pialandvun Pass, Shugnan, Gorno-Badakhshan (near Bokhara, central Asian USSR), and from Tadzhikstan, rock edges at 3200 m and grassy mountain slopes. This little-known species was not in cultivation until introduced in 1991 by Halda (JJH 918135). (Fig. Halda: 231.).

Primula rosea Royle, Illustr. Bot. Himal. Mtn. 1: 311 (1836)

P. elegans Duby (1843)

DESCRIPTION Similar to some forms of *P. auriculata*, but forming loose umbels of much larger (to 30 mm in diameter) flowers of a pale to bright rose-pink with a yellow eye; the stem is almost absent at first, although it elongates later. Meal always missing, flowers exannulate. 2n = 22. 44% self-fertile in pins, 26% in thrums. Flowering April (–May), (May–June in the wild). (Plate 14.)

DISTRIBUTION North-west and west Himalaya, from east Afghanistan through northern Pakistan and Kashmir to Garwhal.

'Fairly common and gregarious in alpine pastures, meadows, by melting snow from 2600–4300 m, where boggy or peaty conditions prevail.'

This superb garden plant is justly one of the most popular of all primulas in cultivation. Although somewhat variable it is instantly recognizable, being more robust than most of its relatives, and with relatively much bigger flowers of a finer colour than *P. auriculata*. Characteristically the flowers open as soon as the stem bursts through the ground, set amongst the reddish bud scales before the leaves expand, while those of *P. auriculata* are set on a stem and are arranged in a head from the beginning.

VARIATION

- Var. *elegans* (Duby) Hook. f., Fl. Br. India 3: 489 (1882) (*P. elegans* Duby 1843). Delicate, with flowers opening on top of a long slender stem, thus intermediate with *P. auriculata*. Kashmir.

In cultivation, a number of named strains have arisen. The best of these is 'grandiflora', which is compact with very large flowers of a brilliant rose. 'Splendens' is a tall large-flowered deep pink, while 'Micia Visser de Geer' (**AGM** 1969), sometimes known as 'Delight', is dwarf at first with deep almost carmine flowers. There is also a (not outstanding) white form 'alba'.

CULTIVATION First introduced from Gulmarg in 1879 (Aitchison) and continuously in cultivation since then. Amongst others, Chris Chadwell has reintroduced this from Kashmir and Himachal Pradesh, while the seed firm of Ghose supplied seed of wild origin from around Gulmarg for many years. Although subject to the attentions of vine-weevil, *P. rosea* is only really resentful of drying out, and is easy and vigorous in a rich wet soil, even clay. It is a popular subject for pond-sides, etc., where it tolerates waterlogging and combines well with calthas and *P. denticulata*. When suited, it self-sows regularly, but is not really robust enough for the wild garden. *P. rosea* is strongly heterophyllous, so that although it forms a neat and attractive plant at flowering, it can develop long strap-like leaves to 25 cm in summer, and care should be taken that these do not smother small surrounding plants.

P. rosea is readily propagated by division, especially as it comes into growth.

HYBRIDIZATION A hybrid is known with *P. clarkei* (*P.* × 'Peter Kleine', **PC** 1972). This hybrid was raised in the USA in about 1966 by Peter Kleine, and was originally called 'Kleinii' and, informally, 'Rose Clarke'. It resembles a robust *P. clarkei,* although bearing flower stems, and some initial controversy arose over its identity, until the summer leaves were seen to be 'intermediate' between the parents (in fact they resemble a rather more compact *P. rosea* at this stage). Photo: Bull. AGS 39: 90 (1971). It seems to be quite easy, is self-fertile (a character apparently originating with *P. rosea*), and backcrosses readily to *P. rosea*, some of the offspring being white.

Primula warshenewskiana Fedtsch., Trav. Mus. Bot. Acad. St. Petersb. 1: 149 (1902)

P. radicata Balf. f. & Smith (1916)
P. rhodantha Balf. f. & Smith (1916)
P. rosiflora Balf. f. & Smith (1916)
P. harrissii Watt (1915)
P. rosea Royle var. *harrissii* (Watt) Smith & Fletcher (1943)

DESCRIPTION In effect a very *dwarf* and *creeping* relative of *P. rosea,* stemless at first, and not exceeding 5 cm at flowering, usually shorter; rosettes only 2 cm in diameter, and flowers 1–6 together, each about 10 mm in diameter; flowers bright *pink*, paler in the centre, *annulate*. The short oblong leaves are entire and lack a stalk at flowering but are strongly and irregularly toothed and develop a marked stalk later in the season. (Plate 14.)

DISTRIBUTION From a limited but politically complex area in the Hindu Kush/Pamir massif. North-east Afghanistan and the Wakhun corridor, north Pakistan (especially Chitral), and Tadzhikstan (Russian Turkestan). 'Streams and moist places, 1500–2700 m'; 'humid meadows near springs and brooks'.

Although totally distinct from *P. rosea* in the garden, *P. warshenewskiana* possibly intergrades with it in east Afghanistan and Chitral, although usually occurring at lower altitudes (surprisingly as it is the dwarfer plant). '*P. harrissii*' has been equated with both species, and may represent intermediate forms, as may subsp. *rhodantha* (below). Diagnostically, *P. warshenewskiana* has annulate corollas.

VARIATION

- Subsp. *rhodantha* (Balf. f. & Smith) Wendelbo, Act. Univ. Bergen Mat.-Nat. 1: 7 (1957) (*P. rhodantha* Balf. f. & Smith 1915; *P. rosea* subsp. *rhodantha* (Balf. f. & Smith) Smith & Forrest (1928), *P. harrissii* Watt. Attenuate forms with a slender stem to 15 cm and narrowly lanceolate, toothed leaves, approaching small forms of *P. rosea*, but with strongly annulate flowers.

CULTIVATION Seems to have been first introduced by expeditions to Afghanistan in the 1960s, possibly by Furse, and has been in cultivation since, although there have also been recent introductions from Pakistan.

Best grown unprotected in a well-drained, gritty, humus-rich site in partial shade, such as a trough or raised bed. Also suitable for pot cultivation in a gritty mix in a shady plunge. Grows rapidly initially, but seems to run out of nutrient and requires frequent division and propagation if it is to be maintained. Very shallow rooted, and will not tolerate drying out. Not in my experience an easy plant, but one which remains freely available in the trade. It rarely sets seed and seems to be fully self-sterile. **AM** 1963.

HYBRIDIZATION

A hybrid is known with *P. clarkei* (*P.* × 'Johanna', **AM** 1986). This quite outstanding plant was raised by Henrik Zetterlund of Gothenburg as the result of hand-pollination onto *P. warshenewskiana* under glass, in about 1980. Photo: Bull. AGS 51: 334; 54: 353. It is named after Henrik's daughter. The details of the raising are important as this distinctive plant resembles neither of its parents, but rather *P. rosea*. So far it has proved easy and vigorous in the open ground, or in pots, and increases rapidly. It seems to be sterile.

Primula clarkei Watt, J. Linn. Soc. Bot. 20: 4 (1882)

DESCRIPTION A totally distinct species, forming *creeping* rhizomatous mats of very small leaves with an *orbicular* blade, about 1.5 cm across with a finely crenate margin and a *heart-shaped* base; the stalk is narrow although slightly winged, reddish and about 3 cm; unlike related species no rosette is formed. *Stem* usually obsolete and flowers borne singly, but some forms have a short stem to 5 cm; flower stalks wiry and reddish, to 5 cm. *Corolla* rose-pink, becoming whitish in the centre and with an orange eye, flat-faced, *exannulate*, to 18 mm in diameter, usually smaller, the tube 2× the calyx, and the corolla-lobes deeply notched, so that the flower seems almost 10-petalled. *Capsule* globose, not exceeding the calyx. Apparently fully self-sterile. Flowering April. (Plate 14.)

DISTRIBUTION Extremely localized in the wild, and only known from damp rock faces at Poshiana, ('Poosiana') in the Poonch Hate on the south slope of the Pir Pangal range near the pass of this name in Kashmir (2100 m) where it was first collected by Charles Baron Clarke in 1876. The sole known locality today lies within Pakistan-controlled Kashmir, a hotly disputed territory which is dangerous to visit.

This extraordinary little plant with its violet-like leaves has not surprisingly had a very chequered history with respect to its classification, having been placed in sections Auganthus, Cordifoliae, Petiolares and Aleuritia. However, it is clearly correctly placed here, not least as a result of the readiness with which it crosses with related species. It is unmistakable.

CULTIVATION Introduced by Prem Nath Kohli of the Kashmir Forest Service in 1933 on the express instructions of B.O. Coventry, although his superior in the Service Amin Chand took the credit, and an RHS Gold Medal. Thomas Hay of the Royal Parks in London was probably the first recipient in the UK. Kohli later established the well-known seed firm of P. Kohli & Son of Srinagar. Collected also by Frank Ludlow in 1937. **AM** 1939.

It is remarkable that this delightful little plant should still be in cultivation, and obtainable from the trade at times, for it is undoubtedly difficult. It should be grown in similar conditions to *P. warshenewskiana*, but is less tractable, and only very regular propagation ensures its survival. We probably owe its continued existence to dedicated nurserymen in favoured (humid and summer-cool) conditions, notably at Inshriach. It seems to favour a similar regime to that for *P. reptans*, and is about as difficult. It rarely if ever sets seed in cultivation.

HYBRIDIZATION See under *P. rosea* and *P. warshenewskiana*.

Primula oxygraphidifolia Smith & Ward, Notes Roy. Bot. Gdn. Edinb. 14: 50 (1923)

DESCRIPTION A very small plant somewhat resembling *P. clarkei*, but rosette-forming and not creeping, with similar non-mealy spoon-shaped leaves of only about 1 cm, the orbicular blades of which have characteristic 'turned down' margins; flowers solitary in the rosette, pinkish, about 10 mm in diameter; pollen 3-syncolpate. Mountains near Muli, south-west Sichuan; open moist pastures by streams, mossy crevices of limestone cliffs, 4000–5000 m. Fig. Halda: 275.

I have transferred this little-known Chinese alpine from the 'Sibirica' (Armerina) to the Oreophlomis on the basis of its pollen type and Oreophlomis-like resting buds.

Section **Armerina** Lindley,

Edward's Bot. Reg. 32: t. 31 (1846) emend.
Schwarz, Wiss. Zeit. Fried.-Schill. Univ.
Jena, Mat.-Nat. 17: 4 (1968)
(*Armerina* Lindl., Bot. Reg. 31 (1846) sin. stat.)
(Sect.Farinosae Pax subsect. Sibiricae Bruun (1932) nom. nud.)
(Sect. Farinosae Pax subsect. Sibirica (sic) Smith & Fletcher (1944))
(Sect. Aleuritia Duby series Sibiricae Federov (1952) stat. invalid.)
Type species *P. involucrata* Wall.

DESCRIPTION Small to medium-sized *glabrous* perennials, usually *lacking* meal except sometimes on the stem, forming slender rosettes of often spoon-shaped, delicate, *smooth, mostly entire* deciduous leaves often with long narrow stalks showing *involute or revolute* vernation, arising from small, usually *rootless spherical resting buds. Stems* slender, usually exceeding the leaves, with often long *saccate* (pouched) or gibbous-based bracts, bearing a single umbel (except *P. conspersa*) of relatively few flowers on long stalks. *Corolla* white, pink, rose, purple or lilac with a yellow eye, annulate or exannulate, heterostylous or homostylous, the tube usually markedly exceeding the calyx; pollen subspherical, 3–6 stephanocolpate, or 3-colporoidate. *Capsule* oblong, usually exceeding the calyx, opening apically by 5 valves; seeds smooth, rather small, 0.5–1 mm, rounded or somewhat angled. x = 10, 11 (except *P. egaliksensis*). Chromosome morphology uniform. Heterostylous species about 5% self-fertile. Flowering April–May.

DISTRIBUTION Circum-arctic, and further south in the mountains of America, China, Tibet, and Siberia, centred on central Asia.

Arctic and alpine tundra beyond or above the tree-line, typically growing on rather bare wet areas by streams and rivulets formed from snow-melt.

These small plants from harsh localities have a superficial resemblance to those members of section Aleuritia which lack meal. However, Schwarz (1968) showed that important features such as the pollen type and nature of the overwintering bud are very distinct, fully warranting sectional rank for this group. Also, the chromosome number(s) and the nature of the saccate bracts make it clear that any supposed relationship to the Aleuritia (= Farinosae) is entirely superficial.

In fact DNA studies show that although they belong to the same clade as the Aleuritia, they seem not be closely related to any investigated members of this or any other sections. This isolated position is supported by the recent surprising observation by Tass Kelso that *P. involucrata* has involute vernation, and this also proves to be true of other Asian species *P. tibetica*, *P. pamirica* and *P. fasciculata*. However, the circumboreal *P. nutans*, the north American *P. egalikensis* and the Chinese relatives of *P. gemmifera* are revolute. A number of unusual features, notably the resting bud and bract structure otherwise link these species, and the position of both involute and revolute species within the Aleuritia DNA clade, which is otherwise revolute, strongly argues that revolute vernation is plesiomorphic and involute vernation apomorphic within these related species. This is the only section within which are classified both revolute and involute species. It is very likely that the section was originally formed from a revolute clade, but that one or more lines became hybridogenous and involute after hybridization with an involute (e.g. section Amethystina) male parent (p. 34).

The recent finding from the DNA that *P. zambalensis* is sister to *P. nutans* has caused me to include the three species related to *P. gemmifera* into this section. For most morphological characters, this merger has been satisfyingly predictive, but it seems that the Gemmifera have tricolporoidate pollen. It also now seems likely that this section contains species with both x= 10 and x = 11, so that several apomorphic character states appear to have arisen within this otherwise distinct section.

This group has traditionally been known as the Sibirica or Sibiricae (the latter is probably correct), being based on *P. sibirica* Jacq., an extraordinarily widespread species for which *P. nutans* is the correct name. In fact, this group name Sibiricae seems never to have been validated at any legal rank and many authors, including Smith & Fletcher (1944) and Wendelbo (1961) have classified them within, or as a subsection of the 'Farinosae' (= Aleuritia). Schwarz (1968) pointed out that Lindley's group *Armerina*, validly published, but without rank, has as its type *P. involucrata*, which undoubtedly belongs to this group. It is reasonable to interpret the rank as sectional, so this becomes the correct name.

Apart from the Aleuritia, this is the only section of Primula reported to have more than one base chromosome number. Schwarz's colleague, Lepper, reports in Schwarz (1968) that three species have 2n = 22, including *P. involucrata* and *P. 'yargongensis'*, previously reported as having 2n = 44 and 20 respectively. In addition, Bruun (1932) reports 2n = 22 for *P. nutans*, but *P. egaliksensis* has 2n = 36 and possibly 40. This leaves reports by Bruun of 2n = 20 for *P. tibetica* and 2n = 18 for *P. fasciculata*, both of which Schwarz doubts. In view of the history of the cytology of *P. algida*, reported under *P. auriculata*, I believe that Smith's identification of the source material, rather than Bruun's technique, may have been responsible for the apparent unreliability of Bruun's findings in this area. However, *P. zambalensis*, which I am also uniting with this group, also has a report of 2n = 20.

On the basis of the pollen type and other characters, I have removed *P. oxygraphidifolia* to section Oreophlomis and *P. urticifolia* to section Yunnanensis. *P. walshii*, placed here in section Minutissimae in accordance with tradition, has some affinities with the Armerina. I have added its relative *P. pumilio* to this section.

CULTIVATION Most of the 14 species are relatively little known, and only one, *P. involucrata* in its various forms, has a long history in cultivation. However, *P. fasciculata, P. zambalensis* and *P. pamirica* have recently become quite popular amongst specialist growers. *P. involucrata* can be a good-tempered plant which grows well from seed and is best grown in a cool, humid, well-drained location, although it is rarely long-lived. I have also grown *P. nutans* and *P. tibetica*, which proved to be fairly straightforward in pots placed in a shady plunge, but they were not long-lived and failed to set seed. A number of other species have been grown particularly by Schwarz at Jena, but none seems to have persisted in cultivation. No hybrids are known in the section.

KEY TO SPECIES

1. Flowers 8 mm in diameter or less, usually whitish 2
1. Flowers more than 10 mm in diameter 5

2. Flowers homostylous; bracts not strongly saccate; arctic .... *P. egaliksensis*
2. Flowers heterostylous; bracts saccate at base; central Asian or Himalayan 3

3. Flower stalks less than 5 mm in length .... *P. pumilio*
3. Flower stalks more than 5 mm in length 4

4. Flower stalks less than 2 cm; calyx more than 4 mm .... *P. iljinskii*
4. Flower stalks more than 2 cm; calyx less than 4 mm .... *P. knorringiana*

5. Flowers not usually more than 3 together, often single, immersed in foliage 6
5. Flowers usually 4 or more together; if fewer then borne well above foliage 7

6. Flowers crinkly, waxy; leaves with distinct narrow stalk .... *P. fasciculata*
6. Flowers flat-faced; leaf-stalk obscure .... *P. tibetica*
6. Flowers flat-faced; leaf-stalk distinct but not narrow .... *P. gemmifera*

7. Stems mealy; bracts swollen at base but not saccate 8
7. Stems without meal; bracts often noticeably saccate at base 10

8. Flowers in more than one whorl .... *P. conspersa*
8. Flowers in a single whorl 9

9. Flowers bluish, zygomorphic, exannulate .... *P. zambalensis*
9. Flowers pink to purple, rotate, annulate .... *P. gemmifera*

10. Flowers bright rose with golden central spots, more than 20 mm in diameter .... *P. chrysostoma*
10. Flowers lilac, pink or white with a continuous gold centre, usually less than 20 mm in diameter 11

11. Flowers nodding, one-sided, weakly zygomorphic .... *P. involucrata*
11. Flowers patent to erect, not held to one side, rotate 12

12. Flowers lacking blackish glands on calyx, white .... *P valentinae.*
12. Flowers usually with blackish glands on calyx, lilac, pink or rarely white 13

13. Flowers 1–4 together, flower stalks exceeding 5 mm .... *P. nutans*
13. Flowers usually more than 4 together, flower-stalks 5 mm or less .... *P. pamirica*

Plants with x = 11, stephanocolpate pollen and revolute vernation.

Primula nutans Georgi, Bemerk. Reise Russ. Reich. 1: 200 (1775) non Delavay (1889) = *P. flaccida* Balakr.

P. integrifolia Oeder (1767) non L.
P. rotundifolia Pallas (1776) nomen. non Wallich
P. sibirica Jacq. (1778)
P. finmarchica Jacq. (1778)
P. finno-marchica Georgi (1802)
P. norvegica Retz. (1795)
P. intermedia Ledeb. (1815) non Sims (1809) nec Portenschlag (1814) nec Busch (1925)

DESCRIPTION A delicate and *insubstantial* plant with annual rhizomes and a weak rosette of 2–4 fleshy strongly *spoon*-shaped leaves with *revolute* vernation, the blade almost *orbicular*, about 2–3 cm in diameter, abruptly narrowed to a narrowly winged stalk. *Stem* to 15 cm bearing 1–4 suberect flowers on slender stalks to 3 cm, exceeding the lanceolate bracts with *auriculate* bases. *Calyx* narrowly bell-shaped, sometimes with black stemless glands. *Corolla* whitish to pale pink with a pale yellow annulus, funnel-shaped, heterostylous, to 16 mm in diameter, usually smaller, the corolla-lobes slightly notched. *Pollen* 6-stephanocolpate. *Capsule* exceeding the calyx. Seeds ovoid. 2n = 22. Pins fully self-sterile, thrum behaviour not known. Flowering May. (Fig. Halda: 274.) (Fig. 24.)

DISTRIBUTION This is the most widespread species in the genus, occurring as it does around much of the Arctic, and into the mountains of central Asia.

Arctic Europe in four areas: the northern arc of the Gulf of Bothnia; Norway north of 70° N; and around the Varanger Fjord to Murmansk; and the north-western arm of the White Sea. Stretches from there across scattered localities in northern Siberia as far as Kamtschatka, in Alaska inland in the Seward Peninsula, and far north-western Canada in south-west Yukon. Further south in Asia it extends from the Siberian shore southwards to the Tarbatatgai, the northern Altai, the mountains south-east of Lake Baikal and the mountains of northern Mongolia. It is disjunct further south in the mountains of Gansu, China, and in the north-west Himalaya in Ladakh, Lahul, Chitral and Baltistan.

In arctic regions, a plant of 'moist meadows, grassy mounds and river valleys near the sea', usually somewhat saline; also 'sandy, gritty deposits of soft soil wet from melting ice'. In the mountains on glacial outwash gravels and moraines. 'Sedgy rocks and soggy alpine swards, drying out by September when the plant becomes dormant.' Grows to 4500 m.

For a remote and still little-known species from frozen arctic shores and mountain wastes of central Asia, *Primula nutans* has a very complex taxonomic history, some of the earliest and most familiar names in the genus having been applied to it. It has most often been known as *P. sibirica,* but there are in fact no less than three earlier names than this, although only one, *P. nutans* is valid. This change of name from *P. sibirica* to *P. nutans* has caused distress to many gardeners, for the superb Soldanelloides species now known as *P. flaccida* was for generations known as *P. nutans*.

Jacquin originally separated the European plant as *P. finmarchica* from the Siberian one (*P. sibirica*, for which *P. nutans* is prior), and this treatment is followed by Federov (1952). However, the latter author notes that the two species merge in west Siberia, and Schwarz unites them under *P. nutans*. Kelso (1987) considers *P. nutans* to be an 'ancient' species. She considers that its propensity for vegetative propagation may have allowed it to persist through difficult arctic conditions in its many refugia.

P. nutans is easily recognized by its simple few spoon-shaped leaves and few pale flowers. According to the DNA, it is closely related to *P. zambalensis*.

VARIATION

- Subsp. *nutans*. (*P. sibirica* Jacq. var. *kashmirana* Hook. f. (1880)). Leaves small, the blade equalling the stalk, both to 2.5 cm. Flower stalks at flowering to 1.2 cm. Corolla to 12 mm in diameter, the tube 2× the calyx. Asia, north America.
- Subsp. *finmarchica* (Jacq.) A. & D. Love, Bot. Notiser 114: 54 (1961) (*P. finmarchica* Jacq., Misc. Austr. 1: 160 (1778); *P. sibirica* subsp. *finmarchica* (Jacq.) Hulten (1948), *P. nutans* var. *jokalae* Hort.). Leaves larger, the stalk often exceeding the blade. Flower stalks at flowering

Fig. 24. *P. nutans*

1.5 cm or more. Corolla to 16 mm in diameter, the tube equalling the calyx. Northern Europe and north-west USSR.

CULTIVATION First grown as early as 1798, and intermittently since, usually from European stock. It is really only a botanical curiosity, with little garden value, but good stocks have been maintained in the Alpine House at Kew and elsewhere. I found it came well from seed and grew and flowered for six years in a pot kept in a cool plunge and covered in winter. In 1991, I received an introduction from the mountains near Lake Baikal (Little and Bishop).

Plants with x = 11, stephanocolpate pollen and involute vernation

Primula involucrata Wallich, Cat., Num. List 7107 (1828/32) non Sweet (1839) = *P. boveana*

P. involucrata Duby ex De Candolle (1844)
P. munroi Lindley (1847)
P. traillii Wilson (1897) non Watt (1882)
P. yargongensis Petitm. (1908)
P. wardii Balf. f. (1915)

DESCRIPTION *Leaves* spoon-shaped, involute, the blade shortly *elliptical,* to 4 × 2.5 cm, entire and with a shortly cuneate base; the petiole about twice as long, narrow, green. *Stem* to 30 cm, usually shorter in flower, bearing a spreading umbel of 3–10 flowers on stalks about equalling the calyx; *bracts longer* than the stalks, to 18 mm. *Calyx* bell-shaped, to 8 mm, 5-ribbed, with short triangular sepal-lobes. *Corolla* white, pink or pale purple with a golden annulus, faintly zygomorphic, flat-faced, to 20 mm in diameter, heterostylous, the tube 2× the calyx; corolla-lobes somewhat concave, overlapping, broadly notched or square-ended. *Capsule* exceeding calyx; seeds ovoid. 2n = 22 (?20, ? 44). Pins 7% self-fertile, thrums 3% self-fertile. Flowering May. (Plate 14.)

DISTRIBUTION One of the most widespread of Sinohimalayan primulas, occurring from Hazara, N. Pakistan through Kashmir, north-west India, Nepal, south Tibet, Sikkim, Bhutan to west Yunnan, south-west Sichuan and the Burma frontier, a distance of nearly 3000 km. Locally common in moist meadows near streams in the alpine zone, usually in dry rainshadow zones, 2740–5000 m.

There was some doubt as to whether Wallich's name was validly published, but these catalogue names have been recognized in the Flora of China (Chen & Hu, 1990).

It has been recognized for many years that the more commonly dark flowered plants *P. yargongensis* and *P. wardii* from the eastern Himalaya and China are structurally identical to the pale western *P. involucrata*, and are equally good tempered in gardens. However, before Schwarz (1968) discovery that both western and eastern plants had 2n = 22, the fusion of these species was impeded by Bruun's (1932) statement that *P. involucrata* had 2n = 44, and *P. yargongensis* 2n = 20. It now seems likely that both these counts were made on incorrectly identified material.

P. involucrata is the most robust member of the section, and has relatively much longer bracts than all except *P. knorringiana*. Some forms of *P. auriculata* can look similar, but that species has a short capsule and a robust rooted stock with conspicuous resting buds. *P. zambalensis* has non-saccate bracts and mealy stems.

VARIATION Most of the variation exhibited is in flower colour; as this shows a rough correspondence with geography, it seems useful to describe two subspecies:

- Subsp. *involucrata*. Flowers whitish or pale pink. Western Himalaya.
- Subsp. *yargongensis* (Petitm.) Smith & Forrest (1928) (*P. yargongensis* Petitm., Bull. Herb Boiss. 8: 366 (1908), *P. wardii* Balf. f. (1915)). Flowers deep pink or purple. Eastern Himalaya and west China.

However, it should be noted that plum-purple forms can occur in north-west India.

CULTIVATION Introduced by Munro in 1845 (subsp. *involucrata*) and by Wilson in 1903 (subsp. *yargongensis*), the latter usually being grown as P. 'wardii' in gardens. Doubtless there have been many introductions of both since, for instance CC & MR 370 from Rohtang, CC & McK 517, McK 52 (Baspa Valley) and MECC 87 from the western Himalaya, and KGB 225, ACE 1868 from Yunnan in 1993 and 1994. Sets seed readily, this remaining viable for at least a year. When suited it flowers within a year, and is soundly perennial, flowering freely. It can be multiplied by careful division of the small rosettes as they appear in April. This is a charming little plant which does not make an enormous impact, but is very suitable for a moist but well-drained position where it is not overwhelmed by coarser plants. Said by Schwarz not to tolerate acidic soils.

Primula knorringiana Federov, Fl. USSR 18: 726 (1952)

DESCRIPTION Closely related to *P. involucrata*, differing chiefly by the much smaller white flowers with a golden annulus, to 7 mm in diameter, the leaves rather more spoon-shaped. Flowers similar to *P. iljinskii*, but plant more robust reaching 40 cm in fruit. Endemic to the Tien-Shan, Russian central Asia, from the Ala-Tau, above Tekes valley. Wet alpine pastures. (Fig. Halda: 273, photo Halda: 118 seq.)

Primula pamirica Federov, Fl. URSS 18: 724 (1952)

P. tibetica Wendelbo (1958) et auct. plur. non Watt

DESCRIPTION Superficially resembles *P. nutans*, but a more substantial plant with more leaves which are involute in vernation, so that it may be more closely related to *P. involucrata*, and with more flowers on a stouter stem, with semi-prostrate smooth rather fleshy spathulate leaves with a distinct stalk, stems exceeding the leaves from the start, and with small (to 12 mm in diameter) and more numerous lilac-pink to pale violet flowers. Tends to have scattered blackish glands on the calyx. (Plate 14.)

DISTRIBUTION Central Asia; Tien Shan, Tadzhikstan; Pamir-Alai; and north Pakistan (Chitral, Kashgar). Wet alpine meadows, springs and marshes in dry zones, to 5200 m.

CULTIVATION Presently (2001) in limited cultivation and offered in the trade, having been introduced by Bohme and Zaprajagajow from Badchu, Pamir, and by Halda (JJH 918597, and later collections. (Photo Halda: 118 seq.)

Primula valentinae Federov, Bot. Mater. Gerb. Bot. Inst. Komarova Akad. Nauk SSSR 1: 258 (1964)

DESCRIPTION Very close to *P. pamirica*, and possibly only a form of it, but flowers white, and with pairs of saccate bracts fused at the base to form a cup-like structure; unlike *P. pamirica* and *P. nutans*, the calyx always lacks black glands or hairs. Only known from the shores of Lake Ranghul in the south-east Soviet Pamir at 3790 m. (Fig. Halda: 278.)

Primula iljinskii Federov, Fl. USSR 18: 726 (1952)

P. sibirica Jacq. var. *parviflora* Regel. nom. nud.

DESCRIPTION A tiny flimsy plant with white (or pink?) flowers less than 5 mm in diameter. It also differs from *P. nutans* by cuneate leaf bases and wiry stems. 2n = 22. Russian central Asia in the Pamir-Alai and Tadzhikstan, and neighbouring west Tibet. Soggy ground around springs in the alpine and juniper zones, 2500–5100 m. Cultivated by Schwarz in the 1960s, reintroduced by Halda in 1991 (JJH 918513). (Fig. Halda: 273.) Plants under this name offered by Ron McBeath in 2001 were *P. pamirica*.

Primula chrysostoma Schwarz, Wiss. Zeit. Fried.-Schill. Univ. Jena, Mat.-Nat. 17; 325 (1968)

DESCRIPTION Markedly heterophyllous, the early rosette being composed of short, stiff, fleshy, spoon-shaped leaves, later leaves being limp, thin and wavy, and much longer, to 18 cm. The stem is very thin and stiff and bears *large rose flowers* with golden central pentagonal spots, to 23 mm in diameter; the calyx is cylindrical and 5-angled, but swollen at the base. 2n = 22.

DISTRIBUTION Wakhan corridor, east Afghanistan, wet grassy and sedgy meadows, 2900–3500 m, from Quazi-Deh eastwards.

This fine species was discovered by H. Roemer in 1964 and introduced into cultivation at Jena. Although Schwarz gives detailed cultural notes, it seems not to have survived in cultivation. Included within *P. nutans* by Halda (1992).

Plants with x = 9 and 10, stephanosyncolpate pollen and revolute vernation

Primula egaliksensis Wormsk. in Hornem., Fl. Danica 9: t.1511 (1816)

P. sibirica Hook. f. (1838) p.p. non Jacq. = *P. nutans* Georgi.
P. sibirica Jacq. var. *minor* Duby (1844)
P. sibirica Jacq. var. *arctica* Fernald (1926) non Pax
P. borealis Gray (1878) p.p. non Duby (1843)
P. stricta Hornem. var. *groenlandica* Warming (1887)
P. groenlandica (Warming) Balfour (1913)

DESCRIPTION A shortly but persistently rhizomatous relative of *P. nutans*, but even smaller and with lavender or white *homostylous* flowers not exceeding 8 mm in diameter, and very slender pointed bracts with a shortly saccate but not auriculate base. Leaf vernation revolute. The pollen is of a type unique in the genus, best called 5-stephanosyncolpate, which is apparently intermediate between the stephanocolpate pollen of one parent and the 3-syncolpate pollen of the other. *Capsule* elongate and cylindrical, reminscent of a small *Dodecatheon*. 2n = 36, 40. Self-fertile. (Fig. Halda: 271.)

DISTRIBUTION Largely fills the circum-arctic gap left by its putative parent *P. nutans*. Northern Iceland, around Myrvaten; west Greenland, 5 localities in the interiors of the Tunungdliarfik and Igaliko Fjords at about 61° N; eastern north America, Newfoundland, Labrador and northern Quebec between 51° and 60° N, and north-west of Hudson Bay between 61° and 64° N; central arctic Canada; western north America in the Graham River district of northern British Columbia, with two localities further south, the neighbouring coast of southern Alaska, northern Alaska (avoiding the Seward Peninsula where *P. nutans* grows), Chuchki, and isolated stations in South Park, Colorado and north-west Wyoming.

'Wet meadows, edges of creeks, wet peaty limestone barrens.' Grows at sea-level and near the sea in northern regions, but becoming alpine, to 3300 m, in Colorado, where it grows with *P. incana* in flat open rather calcareous sedgy flushes.

P. egaliksensis has been shown by Kelso (1991)

to be the allotetraploid derivative of species placed in different sections. The pollen type, chromosome number and morphology all suggest that it has arisen from hybrids between *P. nutans* (2n = 22) and *P. mistassinica* (2n = 18) which have doubled the number of chromosomes and have become homostylous. This tends to be confirmed by the mitochondrial DNA (maternally inherited) which places this morphological Armerina as a close sister to the Aleuritia *P. mistassinica* which must therefore have been the female parent to the original hybrid cross.

Siberian plants of *P. egalikensis* have 2n = 40 as predicted, but plants from Alaska, Greenland and Colorado have apparently lost two pairs of chromosomes, having 2n = 36. The isolated localities in the Rocky Mountains suggest that *P. egaliksensis* arose during an interglacial period and during glacial periods had a wider distributiion from which the southern stations are now relictic (as is also the case for *P. incana* which grows with it in Colorado).

P. egaliksensis is often found in the arctic together with the superficially similar but unrelated *P. stricta*. The latter species always has violet-coloured flowers, and the leaves when well developed are toothed and sometimes mealy. However, when both species are poorly developed, as is often the case in their arctic wastes, they are easily confused, and are best distinguished by their very different fruits.

P. egaliksensis also has a violet-flowered form (var. *violacea* Fernald 1928), for which *P. groenlandica* (Warming) Balf. f. (1913), and other 'groenlandica' combinations are synonymous.

CULTIVATION This little species has no garden value, but is sometimes grown in Botanic Gardens, as for instance on the 'arctic bench' in the Alpine House at Kew.

Plants with x = 10, stephanocolpate pollen and involute vernation

Primula tibetica Watt, J. Linn. Soc. Bot. 10: 6 (1882) non auct. plur. = *P. pamirica* Federov

Primula tanupoda Balf. f. & Smith (1915)

Fig. 23. *P. tibetica*

DESCRIPTION A dwarfer, squatter plant than *P. involucrata* with obovate involute leaves scarcely differentiated into a stalk, at first flowering deep in the rosette, although the stalk elongates to exceed the leaves later; bracts short, the non-saccate part scarcely 1 mm; calyx with darker ridges; corolla brilliant carmine pink with an orange-yellow eye, sometimes paler. Capsule to 3× calyx. 2n = 20?. Flowering May in cultivation. (Photo: Riddle Tsangpo Gorge: 113). (Plate 51, fig. 23.)

DISTRIBUTION From Uttar Pradesh eastwards through Nepal, west and south Tibet to Sikkim and west Bhutan. Confined to regions near to the main range, but invariably in rainshadow districts with a 'Tibetan' climate.

Alpine meadows, especially by runnels and streamsides, often locally abundant; also near snow melt and glaciers in high gravelly tundra. 3000–6000 m. Grows at a higher altitude than any other primula apart from *P. caveana*, being particularly common in the region of Everest base camp, but dropping in glacial valleys to quite low levels.

A most attractive and distinctive species in the wild, especially at high levels, where it forms vivid carmine mats which superficially resemble *P. integrifolia* from Europe and *P. angustifolia* from America. Unfortunately it rarely reproduces this glory in cultivation.

CULTIVATION First introduced by Cooper (1915) from Bhutan, and still in cultivation at Wisley in 1928. There were probably subsequent introductions, although it was not apparently being grown in 1977. Reintroduced by Bernard Thompson from below Everest base-camp at 5500 m in 1981, and again by Ron McBeath from the

Marsyandi region of central Nepal in 1984. These plants persisted during the 1980s, but had disappeared by 1993.

P. tibetica is not a particularly difficult plant grown in a gritty peaty mix in a pot plunged in a shady frame, or in a shady trough, provided that it is not allowed to get too hot, or to dry out. In these conditions however it tends to become rather drawn. It allows for modest increase by vegetative division. Unfortunately, it sets seed rarely if at all in cultivation, and seems to be relatively short-lived, so that it is difficult to establish permanently.

Primula fasciculata, Balf. f. & Ward, Notes Roy. Bot. Gdn. Edinb. 9: 16 (1915)

P. reginella Balf. f. (1916)

DESCRIPTION Forms semi-prostrate mats of small (to 4 cm) narrow, spathulate, deciduous, green leaves with *involute* vernation. Flowers usually borne *singly*, or 2–3 on a short wiry scape with very narrow bracts which lack auricles (appendages). *Calyx* about 5 mm long, sepal-lobes narrow and blunt. *Corolla* about 12 mm in diameter, waxy, not flat-faced but crinkled, bright rose-pink with a golden annulus, the corolla-lobes deeply bifid. '2n = 18', but identity doubted. (Fig. Halda: 272.) (Plate 94.)

DISTRIBUTION Gansu, south-west Sichuan, Yunnan including the Zhongdian plateau and east Tibet. Rather open dwarf grassy or sedgy peat-rich seeps with water at soil surface, including trackways and animal paths, 3500–4000 m. In the locality I saw it in 1995 it was accompanied by *P. involucrata*, but no hybrids were evident.

Scarcely known in 1993, this most attractive dwarf is now very well understood and seems to have few close relatives, although it may be related to *P. tibetica* from further west. The relatively large, solitary, crinkled, waxy, pink flowers are distinctive and render this species unmistakable and quite desirable.

CULTIVATION Originally cultivated from Farrer (1915) and Forrest (1918). Reintroduced by CLD 345 (1991), KGB 97 (1993) from the east side of the Zhongdian plateau *en route* to Geza. Jim Sutherland played an important part in the initial dispersal of this species in cultivation, where it is now well established and offered by several commercial outlets. Best grown as for *P. clarkei*, so that it requires repropagation and new compost every year, but is extremely easily propagated by division and this is best done as it comes into growth in the spring. This tiny plant is easily lost in the garden but is excellent in a cool humid partially shaded frame, covered in winter when it is dormant. It makes an excellent show plant, but fails to flower if not propagated annually.

Plants with x = 10, tricolporoidate pollen and revolute vernation

Primula gemmifera Batalin, Act. Hort. Petropol. 11: 491 (1891)

P. helmsleyi Petitm. (1909)
P. licentii Smith & Forrest (1928)
P. monantha Smith & Forrest (1923)
P. carnosula Balf. f. & Forrest (1920)

DESCRIPTION Plants producing basal buds so that a characteristic jointed short rhizomatous stock is formed; this breaks up to overwinter by unrooted segments. *Leaves* lacking meal, smooth, entire, rather fleshy, oblanceolate, to 7 cm, with revolute vernation. *Stem* robust, elongating to up to 30 cm in fruit, *white-mealy* at the top, bearing 3–10 flowers on long (to 35 mm) suberect stalks; *bracts* lanceolate, swollen at the base. *Calyx* 5–10 mm, bell-shaped, purplish, slightly mealy, divided to half-way. Corolla annulate, heterostylous, pinkish to purple, rotate, 15–25 mm in diameter, the tube 2–3× the calyx; pollen 3-colporoidate. Capsule oblong, exceeding the calyx. (Plate 59.)

DISTRIBUTION North Yunnan, west Sichuan, east Tibet, Gansu and west Shensi. Peaty turf and silty stream margins, screes and rocks, steep and not very damp pasture, 3000–4200 m.

P. gemmifera and its allies were classified by Smith & Fletcher in a subsection Gemmifera of the 'Farinosae'. In the first edition of the present book (1993), I noted their distinctive mode of vegetative reproduction and overwintering, the 3-colporoidate pollen, and the chromosome count of 2n = 20 for *P. zambalensis* (under the name *P. chrysopa*). I concluded that they had no close allies and possibly deserved sectional status.

Since then, DNA evidence has shown that *P. zambalensis* (under the name *P. gemmifera*) is sister to *P. nutans*, providing a very strong indication that the previously 'homeless' 'Gemmifera' should be classified within the Armerina. There are several indicators to support this move. For instance, the 'Gemmifera' have an overall appearence (especially the leaves) strongly reminiscent of the Armerina, they possess the same unrooted fragmented resting buds, and have saccate, or at least gibbous-based, bracts. However, the pollen type differs between the two groups, and some meal is present in the 'Gemmifera' (although not on the leaves).

VARIATION

- Var. *gemmifera*. Inflorescence mealy, calyx 5–10 mm, flowers annulate, 3–10 per scape, corolla 15–25 mm in diameter, pink or purple. Widespread in northern China.
- Var. *licentii* Smith & Fletcher, Trans. Roy. Soc. Edinb. 61: 38 (1943) (*P. licentii* Smith & Forrest). Meal absent, calyx 4 mm, corolla 10 mm in diameter. Shensi.
- Var. *monantha* Smith & Fletcher, loc. cit. (*P. monantha* Smith & Forrest). Very dwarf, flowers solitary, exannulate. North-west Yunnan on the Mekong-Yangtse divide.

CULTIVATION Introduced on a number of occasions between 1914 and 1934 as var. *gemmifera*, but these did not persist. In recent years probably introduced from the Wolong Shan, where it is frequent, and by CLD 280, 442, 452, 507, KGB 521, and SQAE 317, 515, 767 from a variety of sites from Gansu and northern Sichuan to west of Dechen. None of these introductions seems to have persisted. Those still found under this name in cultivation are *P. zambalensis*.

Primula zambalensis Petitm., Bull. Herb. Poissier 8: 365 (1908)

P. chrysopa Balf. f & Forrest (1920)
P. rupestris Pax & Hoffm (1920) non Balf. f. & Farrer (1917)
P. gemmifera var. *amoena* Chen (1939)
P. gemmifera var. *rupestris* (Pax & Hoffm.) Smith & Fletcher 1943
P. gemmifera var. *zambalensis* (Petitm.) Smith & Fletcher (1943)

DESCRIPTION Differs from *P. gemmifera* as follows: flowers lilac-blue to sky-blue, somewhat zygomorphic, exannulate; corolla-tube less than 2× calyx. 2n = 20. (Plate 95.)

DISTRIBUTION As yet incompletely known, as previously confused with *P. gemmifera* in the herbarium, but well known in recent years from the Beima Shan and Da Xue Shan, and also occurring towards the northern and eastern limits of the Zhongdian plateau.

Fine damp open earthy screes, mostly above 4000 m. Particularly abundant and conspicuous on roadside banks and workings beside the Beima Shan road. Gives the impression of being a rapid colonizer of open ground and a poor competitor.

Originally considered distinct by early growers using the later synonym *P. chrysopa* , but sunk into *P. gemmifera* by Smith and Fletcher, perhaps because it is difficult to separate from *P. gemmifera* in the herbarium. I followed this treatment in 1993. However, when I was able to observe them in the field the different colour and structure of the flower of *P. zambalensis* is immediately evident, and the ecology of the two taxa also seems to be different. Consequently, my immediate reaction was that they should be separated at specific rank. This is also supported by the apparently much easier culture of *P. zambalensis*.

CULTIVATION Introduced on a number of occasions as *P. gemmifera* var. *zambalensis* and *P. chrysopa* between 1914 and 1934 and persisting in cultivation (usually as *P. chrysopa*) at least until 1943. Was grown successfully outside by Cooke at Kilbryde, Corbridge, from where colour photos still exist (1932). These show a good group grown in a cool north-facing scree bed.

In 1992, Keith Lever offered for sale abundant and attractive flowering material as *P. involucrata*, which this taxon can resemble, particularly in its zygomorphic, exannulate flowers. However, the mealy stems, blue flowers and non-saccate bracts seemed wrong for that species, and an examination of the pollen confirmed that these plants, probably raised from seed collected by George Smith and Pete Boardman, were in fact *P. zambalensis*. Since then introduced by ACE 1375, 1427, 1541, 1867 from the

Beima Shan. Presently well-established in cultivation, setting seed, and easily propagated vegetatively as it comes into growth so that it has become obtainable commercially. Usually grown plunged in a cool frame kept covered and nearly dry in winter, but groups have been established in north-facing uncovered rich screes, although plants are not very permanent. Often seen on the show bench.

Primula conspersa Balf. f. & Purdom, Notes Roy. Bot. Gdn. Edinb. 9: 14 (1915)

DESCRIPTION Vegetatively and structurally similar to *P. gemmifera*, to which it is undoubtedly closely related, but with a thin elongate stem bearing two or three whorls of lilac flowers 10–15 mm in diameter. Pollen 3-colporoidate. North China; Gansu, from Minchow to the Minshan range, and seen in recent years in the Dayu Valley (SQAE 193). Moist alpine meadows and 'hillside woodland', 2400–3000 m. Collected by Purdom in 1911 and flowered by Veitch. Still in cultivation in 1943. (Fig. Halda: 262.)

Doubtless the means of vegetative spread enabled this species to be maintained in cultivation for some years.

Affinities obscure

Primula pumilio Maxim., Bull. Acad. St. Petersb. 27: 498 (1881)

P. pygmaeorum Balf. f. & Smith (1920)

DESCRIPTION A tiny tufted non-mealy plant with 1–9 stemless pink, fading white, exannulate flowers about 6 mm in diameter immersed in the rosette of green spoon-shaped leaves to 15 mm. A high alpine from the mountains of south Tibet and the Nepal and Bhutan borderlands, from the Arun valley and Chumbi east to Tsona, 4000–4600 m.

DNA studies show that that although *P. pumilio* occurs in the same clade as *P. nutans*, it is not very closely allied to it, but has no other obvious close relatives amongst those species studied.

In cultivation in 1991 from seed collected by J. Grimshaw in 1989. DNA samples were taken in 2000 from a plant at Gothenburg Botanic Garden under Dickore 9496.

A tiny, insignificant plant scarcely worth growing. (Fig. Halda: 276.)

Section **Glabra** (Smith & Fletcher) Richards (1993)

(Section Farinosae Pax subsection Glabra Smith & Fletcher, Trans. Roy. Soc. Edinb. 61: 46 (1943)).
Type species *P. glabra* Klatt.

DESCRIPTION Small deciduous plants lacking meal or hairs, with spoon-shaped *leaves* showing revolute vernation, probably related to section Armerina, but with rooted resting buds; *bracts* saccate at the base or non-saccate; *flowering* heads tight, few-flowered, the flower stalks usually shorter than the calyx; and with the annulate short, broad corolla tube not exceeding the short (to 5 mm) bell-shaped calyx; *flowers* small, not exceeding 10 mm in diameter, heterostylous, or homostylous in *P. macrocarpa*, pollen 3-syncolpate; capsule usually short; $x = 8$.

DISTRIBUTION Eastern Nepal, Sikkim, Bhutan, south-east Tibet, northern Burma, Yunnan, Sichuan, and Rikuchu, Japan.

Wet alpine turf often overlying acidic substrata, 4000–5000 m (somewhat lower in Japan).

The Glabra are a little-known and rather insignificant group which have usually been dismissed as an outlier of the Aleuritia. However, they possess a number of significant features, notably the absence of meal, the short broad corolla tubes, the sub-capitate flower heads, the often subsaccate bracts, the bell-shaped calyx and the chromosome number $x = 8$ which make it clear that they are not closely related to the Aleuritia. Further, their acidic turfy habitat is very untypical of the latter section which is characteristically found in open calcareous ground. Rather, it seems likely that the Glabra may have arisen from the same stock as the Armerina and Oreophlomis, although they now have a different chromosome number. As yet we have no information from the DNA.

In comparison with the *P. glabra* group, the Japanese tetraploid homostyle *P. macrocarpa* takes an isolated position both geographically and morphologically, being more robust than the other species, and bearing a long capsule. *P. macrocarpa* was placed by Smith & Fletcher in their subsection 'Auriculatae', i.e. the Oreophlomis. Instead, I am placing it here, but with some hesitation. However, the pollen type, base chromosome number, short saccate floral tube, bell-shaped calyx and small flowers are as for the rest of the Glabra.

It is possible that *P. efarinosa*, which I have placed in association with the Aleuritia, and *P. sertulum*, classified here in the Denticulata, but with some doubt, could be classified in the Glabra. As yet, we do not know the chromosome number or have any DNA information for these species.

CULTIVATION *P. glabra* has been introduced into cultivation on a number of occasions, and *P. macrocarpa* has also been introduced. They have proved short-lived plants of little charm, scarcely worth the effort to keep them in cultivation, although *P. gesnestieriana* might be worth growing. No hybrids have been reported.

Primula glabra Klatt, Linnaea 37: 500 (1872)

P. kongoboensis Ward (1926)
P. pseudoglabra Hand.-Mazz. (1926)

DESCRIPTION Distinguished by the toothed margin to the short (to 3 cm) smooth leaves, the long spindly stem bearing up to 10 flowers in a tight cluster and the small awl-shaped non-saccate bracts. The tiny flowers are usually grey-slate, shading darker to the dirty violet eye. 2n = 16. (Photo: Bull. AGS 52: 246.) (Plate 52, Fig. 25.)

Fig. 25. *P. glabra*

DISTRIBUTION East Nepal, Sikkim, Bhutan and south-east Tibet eastwards to the Pachakshiri, and again in northern Sichuan. Open peaty turf, 3600–5000 m, locally frequent.

Subsp. *glabra* probably first introduced by Cooper in 1904, and subsequently introduced amongst others by Ludlow and Sherriff, Thompson, Millais, by AGSES 433, 487, and by KEKE 794 . A plant strictly of curiosity value only. It is easy to raise in a small pan plunged in a cool spot outside, but is scarcely worth the effort to obtain the seed required to keep it going. The tiny flowers, about 5 mm in diameter, are of a strange colour, seen in no other primula.

KEY TO SPECIES

1. Flowers 1–4; flower-stalk equalling or exceeding the calyx 2
1. Flowers 3–10; flower-stalk shorter than calyx .... *P. glabra*

2. Flowers white; Japanese .... *P. macrocarpa*
2. Flowers purple; south-east Tibet .... *P. genestieriana*

VARIATION

- Subsp. *kongoboensis* (Ward) Halda (1992). (*P. kongboensis* Ward, Notes Roy. Bot. Gdn. Edinb. 15: 72 (1926)). A close relative of *P. glabra*, but with scabrid, less toothed leaves and distinctive, large oval saccate bracts. Snowy hollows from 4700–5000 m on two passes near Tsela, Kongbo on the Tsangpo, south-east Tibet.
- Subsp. *pseudoglabra* (Hand.-Mazz.) Halda (1992). (*P. pseudoglabra* Hand.-Mazz., Acta Hort. Gothoburg. 2: 104 (1926).) Also differs from subsp. *glabra* by the larger blunt bracts, subsaccate at the base and the less toothed leaves, but flowers deep pink, 7 mm in diameter. Snowy hollows, 4800–5000 m on Dongrergo, and 3875 m, Deng Zhanzwa pass towards Huanglong Si, near Songpan, north Sichuan. Recently collected by KGB 381 (Shu La) in 1993 and SQAE 611 (2000) and now better understood. Disjunct, seems to be distinct, and perhaps better treated as a full species.

Primula genestieriana Hand.-Mazz., Anz. Akad. Wiss. Wien Math.-Nat. 59: 250 (1922)

P. doshongensis Smith (1926)

A relative of *P. glabra*, but with only 1–3 flowers on longer stalks which equal or exceed the calyx; bracts small, awl-shaped; corolla purple, about 10 mm in diameter. 2n =16. Acidic alpine turf at about 4000 m on the borders of Yunnan, Burma and Tibet, extending to the west of the Tsangpo bend on several very wet primula-rich passes in Tsari. Photographed on the Doshong La by Tony Cox in 2000; (also photo by Kenneth Cox on the Bimbi La as *P. glabra*: Riddle of Tsangpo Gorge: 99). Briefly in cultivation in the 1920s from Ward.

Primula macrocarpa Maxim., Bull. Acad. St. Petersb. 12: 68 (1868) non Tanaka (1874) = *P. cuneifolia* subsp. *hakusanensis*

P. hayaschinei Petitm. (1907)
P. nipponica Pax (1905) non Yatabe (1890)

DESCRIPTION *Leaves* ovate, serrate, pale green, prostrate, to 3 × 1 cm. *Stem* to 8 cm, bearing 1–4 small white flowers on stalks to 10 mm. *Bracts* non-saccate, sharp and narrow, to 5 mm. *Calyx* bell-shaped, to 5 mm. *Corolla* to 8 mm in diameter, the short broad tube not exceeding the calyx, homostylous. *Capsule* oblong, disproportionately large and markedly exserted from the calyx. 2n = 32. Presumably self-fertile.

DISTRIBUTION Only known from high on Mt. Hayachine, Rikuchu, Honshu, Japan.

Although *P. macrocarpa* is horticulturally insignificant, the occurrence of this homostyle tetraploid on the top of a Japanese mountain far from its apparent relatives is interesting. Although *P. macrocarpa* superficially resembles a small flowered form of *P. nipponica* from the same general area, the latter has involute vernation and a quite different chromosome number, so this similarity has presumably arisen by convergent evolution.

It must be presumed that *P. macrocarpa* is relictic from Armerina/Glabra forerunners which may once have had a wider distribution on the eastern Asian seaboard, possibly colonizing its isolated fastness by long-distance dispersal.

Section **Yunnanensis** Balf. f., J. Roy. Hort. Soc. 39: 154 (1913)

(Section Farinosae Pax subsection Yunnanensis (Balf. f.) Smith & Fletcher (1944).)
Section Souliei Balf. f. (1928)
Type species *P. yunnanensis* Franchet

DESCRIPTION Dwarf short-lived but usually perennial plants densely covered with *yellow meal*, usually not creeping, deciduous, overwintering as an above-ground conspicuous mealy resting bud. *Leaves* ovate, glabrous, smooth, very mealy beneath, strongly crenate-toothed to subpinnatifid, spoon-shaped with a usually short winged or long narrow stalk and revolute vernation. *Stems* slender, often flowering in the developing rosette at first, later bearing a single umbel of few (1–8) relatively large often semipendant usually *bell-shaped* flowers one-sidedly, the *bracts* large, often *leaf-like*, exceeding the rather long stalks, or much smaller, not pouched or swollen at the base. *Calyx* bell-shaped, very mealy within. *Corolla* lilac, rose or purple with a yellow eye, exannulate, or less commonly annulate, heterostylous, to 25 mm in diameter, with a long tube usually more than 2× the calyx and bifid petal-lobes so that the flower can appear 10-petalled; pollen 3-colp(or)(oid)ate. *Capsule* globose, usually shorter than the calyx, or oblong and equalling the calyx, dehiscing by short apical teeth and rather 'nivalid-like' in aspect, seeds small and round. (2n = 16, 2n = 22?). Chromosomes large, uniform and metacentric. Flowering May–July in the wild.

DISTRIBUTION East Bhutan, south-east Tibet, Gansu, Kweichow, Sichuan, Yunnan, and Upper Burma. Crevices in limestone cliffs and also grassy rock ledges, boulder screes, mossy cliffs and rocks in forest, usually on limestone, 2000–5000 m. It is noteworthy that six of the species, related to the widespread *P. florida*, are confined to the mountains around Tatsienlu in western Sichuan.

In 1993, I followed previous authors in separating the sections Yunnanensis and Souliei, although nearly all of the species included in both these sections are essentially limestone chasmophytes from western China with a very similar morphological appearence. The Souliei were supposed to have membranous, scabrid leaves, oblong capsules and small bracts, while the Yunnanensis should have globose capsules and large leaf-like bracts, while the single chromosome count for *P. yunnanensis* was 2n = 22 and that for the only Souliei for which this was known, *P. rupicola*, 2n = 16.

Since 1993, I have travelled in western China, where I encountered *P. yunnanensis*, *P. rupicola*, *P. florida* and *P. membranifolia*. In recent years I have also been able to cultivate *P. souliei*, so that I now understand some members of these sections much better than previously. I am now firmly of the opinion that they should be classified within the one section, and that characters by which the sections are supposed to differ are essentially trivial. After I had reached this conclusion, it was further supported by the DNA which showed *P. yunnanensis* and the Souliei species *P. membranifolia* to be sisters and closely related. Consequently, I have united these sections for which Yunnanensis is the prior name.

As yet it is unclear as to whether both the base numbers x = 8 and x = 11 both occur in this section, but there are as yet only single counts of each, and the possibility of misidentification of at least one of the subjects exists (see p. 249).

The essential features which link the Yunnanensis and which are not found in, e.g., the Aleuritia or Pulchella are the deeply toothed to lacerate spoon-shaped leaves, pendant flowers on long stalks, bell-shaped flowers and large bracts. Not all these features are found in all species, but they all have at least one or two of them. As far as is known the pollen is never syncolpate and the base chromosome number is never x = 9.

CULTIVATION Eleven of the 14 species listed here have been in cultivation, mostly introduced between 1915 and 1920. None entered general cultivation, mostly being restricted to the Royal Botanic Gardens, Edinburgh, where they mostly failed to set seed, but proved in some cases very persistent, lasting for 20 years or more. In recent years, at least five species have been reintroduced. These have proved straightforward to raise from seed, usually flowering after a year, but then typically died without setting seed.

These plants should probably be best treated as high alpines, grown in pots in a gritty compost, under glass and almost dry in the winter, and plunged outside in a cool well-watered site in summer.

They are mostly beautiful little alpine plants with disproportionately large, well-formed flowers of dazzling colours and with attractive mealy foliage, which would repay every effort. No hybrids have been reported.

KEY TO SPECIES

1. Meal absent; leaves dissected to ⅔ or more .... *P. urticifolia*
1. If leaves deeply dissected, then very mealy below 2

2. Plant bearing conspicuous runners (stolons) .... *P. clutterbuckii*
2. Runners absent 3

3. Flower stalks equalling or exceeding the stem, or stem apparently missing 4
3. Flower stalks shorter than the stem, stem usually exceeding leaves 5

4. Calyx exceeding 7 mm .... *P. kialensis*
4. Calyx 5 mm or less .... *P. membranifolia*

5. Flowers 10 mm or less in diameter, homostylous .... *P. homogama*
5. Flowers larger, heterostylous 6

6. Leaf-blades entire to shortly crenate 7
6. Leaf-blades sharply toothed or more deeply lacerate 8

7. Leaves to 10 cm; flower stalks to 10 mm .... *P. umbrella*
7. Leaves not exceeding 3.5 mm; flower stalks not exceeding 5 mm .... *P. yunnanensis*

8. Corolla bright rose-pink with a cream eye, flat-faced; plant forming mats and clumps .... *P. rupicola*
8. If corolla pink, then usually not with a marked eye; rosettes 1–few together 9

9. Corolla blue, bell-shaped; calyx deep purple, baggy .... *P. aliciae*
9. Corolla pink, purple or lilac-pink; calyx not loosely baggy 10

10. Leaf-stalk exceeding blade, narrow; flowers drooping 11
10. Leaf-stalk shorter than blade or indistinct; flowers erect to drooping 12

11. Stem not exceeding 5 cm .... *P. brevis*
11. Stem exceeding 5 cm .... *P. souliei*

12. Leaf-stalk broad and sheathing at base; plant thickly yellow-mealy 13
12. Leaf-stalk narrow, non-sheathing; meal cream 14

13. Flowers pendant; flower-stalks wiry, to 18 mm .... *P. nutaniflora*
13. Flowers patent to suberect; flower stalks not exceeding 10 mm .... *P. xanthopa*

14. Flower stalks not exceeding 10 mm .... *P. florida*
14. Flower stalks more than 11 mm .... *P. laciniata*

Primula yunnanensis Franchet, Bull. Soc. Bot. Fr. 32: 269 (1885)

P. kichanensis Franchet ex Petitm. (1907)
P. calcicola Balf. f. & Forrest (1920)
P. fragilis Balf. f & Ward (1915)

DESCRIPTION An insubstantial, rather frail little plant, often with only one small rosette and apparently short-lived or monocarpic. Leaves to 3.5 cm, stem to 10 cm., bearing 1–5 relatively huge flowers to 20 mm diameter on short stalks. Calyx 4–9 mm; corolla flat-faced, to 25 mm in diameter, pink to lilac, the tube 2–3× the calyx. 2n = 22. Flowers late May–early June. (Fig. Halda: 269.) (Plate 96)

DISTRIBUTION Yunnan; Cang Shan, Yulong Shan, Zhongdian, Haba Shan and other north-western ranges; Muli, Sichuan, and both sides of the Sichuan/Tibet frontier; Upper Burma.

Limestone cliffs, large boulders, rocks by river banks, etc., essentially chasmophytic, 2800–5000 m. Widespread and frequent in suitable sites. Frequently occurs in the company of *P. rupicola*.

CULTIVATION Introduced by Forrest in 1908 and subsequently, but did not persist. Reintroduced by CLD 181 from the Zhongdian plataeau, Yunnan in 1990, and by Cox 701 from there in the same year. ACE material originated from the Haba Shan. Flowered for a number of growers and some seed set. Still persisted in cultivation in 2000. Some of the material, for instance collected by ACE from the Gan Ho Ba, Yulong Shan, was originally collected as *P. bella*.

VARIATION

- Subsp. *socialis* (Chen & Hu) Halda (1992) (*P. socialis* Chen & Hu, Fl. Rep. Pop. Sin. 2: 295 (1990). Flowers borne singly. West Yunnan.

Primula umbrella Forrest, Notes Roy. Bot. Gdn. Edinb. 9: 51 (1915)

P. maikhaensis Balf. f. & Forrest (1920)

DESCRIPTION Very close to *P. yunnanensis*, but more robust plant, with leaves to 10 cm, roughly equalling the stem which bears usually 3–4 flowers on stalks of about 10 mm; calyx to 8 mm; corolla about 20 mm in diameter, the tube not more than 2× the calyx. North-west Yunnan, divides each side of the Salween. Dry limestone cliffs, 3000–3700 m. Introduced by Forrest in 1908 and described from cultivated plants.

Primula kialensis Franchet, Jour. de Bot. 9: 450 (1895)

P. scopulorum Balf. f. & Farrer (1917)

DESCRIPTION A relative of *P. yunnanensis*, with leaves to 4.5 cm, but with the stem equalling the flower-stalks, so that the flowers stalks are much longer than in the previous species, or even appear to be basal. Flowers 1–8, calyx to 10 mm, corolla to 25 mm in diameter, the tube more than 2× the calyx. Sichuan; Tatsienlu, well-known from around the gates of the old city. Gansu; Satani mountains and Siku. Limestone rocks, 2000–4000 m. Introduced in 1915 and 1936 by Farrer and Smith respectively. (Fig. Halda: 268.)

- Subsp. *brevituba* Hu, Fl. Rep. Pop. Sin. 2: 295 (1990). Corolla tube scarcely exceeding calyx; leaf margin apex with triangular teeth. South-west Sichuan.

Primula membranifolia Franchet, Bull. Soc. Bot. Fr. 33: 68 (1886)

P. longituba Forrest (1908)

DESCRIPTION Usually single rosettes formed of thinly white-mealy crenately toothed spathulate leaf-blades with winged stalks, a small calyx to 4 mm and 1–5 relatively huge exannulate, flat-faced flowers borne on a short stem with mealy stalks of about 10 mm, pink to violet-rose with a yellow eye, to 20 mm in diameter and with the cylindrical tube 2.5–4× the calyx of 4–5 mm. Pollen 4-colporoidate. (Fig. Halda: 270.)

DISTRIBUTION Yunnan, Cang Shan above Dali, mossy crevices in limestone cliffs with a northern exposure, usually near waterfalls, 2500–3700 m. Forms substantial colonies, but only the largest rosettes (perhaps 10%) flower.

I found this species at least twice in the lower reaches of the Cang Shan in 1995. It very much has the aspect of a small, pink-flowered petiolarid such as *P. nana*, and at the time I considered it to be a non-stoloniferous form of *P. moupinensis*. Pam Eveleigh has since flowered similar plants from this area (ARGS 941), showing them to have valvate capsules, and it is clear that *P. membranifolia* is their correct name. This is a misleading misnomer as the leaves are in fact rather thick and fleshy in texture. These plants do not have the appearence of a Yunnanensis species at all, but DNA studies place them in close juxtaposition with *P. yunnanensis*. Although occurring in a quite separate region, they seem to be difficult to separate from *P. kialensis* except by virtue of the shorter calyx.

CULTIVATION Introduced by Forrest in 1908 and flowered at Edinburgh in 1912. Currently (2001) in limited circulation from seed collected by ARGS 941 in 2000, and possibly earlier by CLD (1990).

Primula nutaniflora Hemsl., J. Linn. Soc. Bot. 29: 313 (1892)

P. fargesii Franchet (1895)

DESCRIPTION Similar to *P. yunnanensis*, but with *bell*-shaped pendant lilac or rose flowers on slender stalks to 18 mm, giving it the superficial appearence of a small member of section Soldanelloides. However, the deeply toothed leaves are yellow-mealy and without hairs, and the bracts large and cup-shaped. Kweichow, and adjoining districts of east Yunnan and Sichuan. Damp limestone rocks, 1200–2500 m. (Fig. Halda: 269.)

Primula florida Balf. f. & Forrest, Notes Roy. Bot. Gdn. Edinb. 9: 16 (1915)

P. incisa Franchet (1886) non Lam. (1778) = *P. integrifolia* L.
P. blinii Lev. (1915)
P. oresbia Balf. f. (1915)
P. pectinata Balf. f. & Forrest (1920)
P. asperulata Balakr. (1972)
P. longipinnatifida Chen (1939)

DESCRIPTION Plant white to yellow-mealy below, or non-mealy, the *leaves* to 10 cm, the blade oblong, to 3 cm, deeply toothed to *incised*, the stalk well-marked, slender, virtually unwinged, exceeding the blade. *Stem* exceeding the leaves at flowering, elongating greatly in fruit, slender, slightly mealy at the top, bearing 2–10 drooping flowers on pendant wiry stalks elongating to 8 mm in fruit; bracts mealy, to 8 mm. *Calyx* to 6 mm, narrowly bell-shaped, 5-ribbed, mealy within, divided to half-way. *Corolla* amethyst-pink to pale lilac-purple, or sometimes white, usually lacking a white eye, bell-shaped, to 20 mm in diameter, the tube exceeding 2× the calyx; corolla-lobes deeply notched, the lobules rounded. *Pollen* 3-(col)porate. *Capsule* cylindrical, but short. Flowers in July in the wild. (Fig. Halda: 279, 280 (as *P. blinii*).)

DISTRIBUTION Widespread in western Sichuan, extending southwards into Yunnan. Well-known from the Muli, Kulu and Minya Konka ranges.

Limestone or sandstone rocks in upper level forests, cliff ledges and stony slopes and meadows, 3200–4500 m.

Originally, this species was most commonly known as *P. florida,* not least in cultivation, but was considered to be distinct from *P. incisa*, being a more robust, *P. souliei*-like plant with less dissected leaves. Smith and Fletcher showed these leaf-forms to be part of a continuum, and united the two species. Later, it was found that the prior name *P. incisa* Franchet was a later homonym for *P. incisa* Lam., which caused Balakrishnan to coin the new name *P. asperulata*. However, Smith and Forrest's revision provided no less than four epithets which could replace *P. incisa,* of which the prior is in fact either *P. blinii* or the original familiar name *P. florida,* which were both published in the same year. I have chosen to use the epithet 'florida', but in fact most material has entered cultivation labelled 'blinii'.

VARIATION A variable plant. *P. blinii* refers to very mealy forms, while *P. pectinata* was used for non-mealy forms with very dissected leaves. The type of *P. incisa* is similar, while *P. florida* referred to large plants with toothed leaves. These forms grade into one another, and probably do not merit recognition.

CULTIVATION Introduced by Forrest (1915), persisting at Edinburgh until 1939. Cooke also grew this species outside in a cool north-facing raised scree bed at Kilbryde, from where there still exists an early colour photo (F28389). Has been quite frequently seen in cultivation in recent years, often in very dissected leaf-forms as 'blinii', having originated from ACE (Da Xue Shan) and probably from CLD. I acquired a plant from Glendoick in 1993 which may have originated from seed collected by Kenneth Cox. ARGS 405 (2000) from the Da Zue Shan flowered for a number of growers as *P.* 'aff. bella'. Easy to flower, but short-lived.

Primula laciniata Pax & Hoffm., Feddes Rep. Nov. Sp. 17: 98 (1920)

DESCRIPTION Closely related to *P. florida* (*P. incisa*-forms), but with *longer*, more pendulous flower-stalks, to 40 mm, becoming erect in fruit, the pinkish-mauve flower *white-eyed*, and the capsule exceeding the calyx. Said to have the jointed disintegrating rhizome of *P. gemmifera*, but this is not evident in herbarium material. Only known from between Tatsienlu and Dawo, west Sichuan, spring-fed flushes at 3900 m. Introduced by Harry Smith in 1934, persisting for a few years, but not fruiting. (Fig. Halda: 263.)

Although closely related to *P. florida*, and originally placed in *P. incisa*, Smith and Fletcher later associated this species with *P. gemmifera*, which is certainly mistaken.

Primula brevis A.J.Richards, Primula ed. 1: 247 (1993)

P. humilis Pax & Hoffm., Feddes Rep. Nov. Sp. 17: 94 (1921) non Steudel, Nomencl. Bot. ed. 2, 2: 395 (1841) = *P. primulina* (Sprengel) Hara.
P. souliei Franchet subsp. *humilis* (Pax & Hoffm.) Smith & Forrest (1928)
?*P. tenuipes* Chen & Hu (1990)

DESCRIPTION Dubiously distinct from *P. florida*, differing by the stems not exceeding the leaves, and by the deeply toothed but scarcely pinnate leaf blades, heavily white- or cream-mealy. Sichuan, around Dawo, to the north-west of Tatsienlu. Granite and limestone rocks, 4400–4800 m. (Fig. Halda: 281 (as *P. humilis*).)

This species has invariably been known as *P. humilis* Pax & Hoffm., but this is a later homonym for *P. humilis* Steudel and a new name is needed. I cannot see from the description how the recently described *P. tenuipes* differs from this species.

Primula souliei Franchet, Journ. de Bot. 9: 450 (1895)

DESCRIPTION Another relative of *P. florida*, differing chiefly by the *purple-violet annulate* corolla, longer flower-stalks (to 15 mm) giving a looser inflorescence, longer, more baggy calyx (to 8 mm), and shortly ovate leaf-blades. Pollen 3-colporoidate. Sichuan; around Tatsienlu, Tchito, Lat Sa, Yulong-Hsi; cliffs at 4000–4200 m. (Fig. Halda: 283.)

I grew and flowered this species in the mid-1990s from seed collected by Edward Needham from the Pitiao Valley, Wolong Shan. Reintroduced by David Rankin in 2001 as SDR 1653, 1758 under the name *P. bella*.

- Subsp. *legendrei* (Bonati) Smith & Forrest, Notes Roy. Bot. Gdn. Edinb. 16: 41 (1928). (*P. legendrei* Bonati (1913), *P. parvula* Pax & Hoffm. (1921).) Flower stalks to 25 mm, corolla exannulate.

Primula xanthopa Balf. f. & Cooper, Notes Roy. Bot. Gdn. Edinb. 9: 204 (1916)

DESCRIPTION Related to *P. florida* and *P. souliei*, but with deeply incised leaves which are very heavily golden-mealy, especially below, and geographically disjunct. Bracts very unequal, to 2 mm in width; corolla deep pink with a yellow eye. (Fig. Halda: 284.)

Only known from the Donga La, east Bhutan, mossy rocks on the floor of fir forest, 3600–3800 m.. Plants and seed collected by Hicks (LSH 21230) in 1949, survived for at least twelve years (**PC** 1950), notably at Branklyn.

Primula rupicola Balf. f. & Forrest, Notes Roy. Bot. Gdn. Edinb. 9: 41 (1915)

DESCRIPTION In the wild a much longer-lived plant than most of the previous species, forming considerable tufts and mats, cream-mealy below. Otherwise most obviously distinguished by the *bright rose, cream-eyed* nearly flat-faced annulate flower, by the longer (7–12 mm) calyx, and the narrowly spear-shaped, *serrate* leaves. Pollen 3–4 colpor(oid)ate. 2n = 16. (Plate 14).

DISTRIBUTION North-west Yunnan; East and north side of the Yulong Shan, east side of Zhongdian plateau, Labo Shan and Yungling and north-east of the Yangtse bend. Cliff ledges and river banks, usually on limestone rocks above water, 3000–4000 m.

CULTIVATION Flowered in 1921 from Forrest's seed, and persisted at Edinburgh until 1938. Reintroduced as CLD 180 from the Bi Ta Hai forest, Zhongdian, shaded cliff on river bank, 3360 m, growing with *P. yunnanensis*. I saw it there in 1995. Flowered at Edinburgh and Kew in 1990. Cox 5078 (1991) was also this. Also collected by ACE, but not under this name, probably as *P. yunnanensis* or *P. bella*. Rather longer-lived than most of its relatives, it has persisted in cultivation in 2001 in small quantity, for instance with Henry and Margaret Taylor, but is not usually correctly named. A most attractive plant of real merit.

- Var. *albicolor*, Smith & Fletcher, Trans. Bot. Soc. Edinb. 33: 468 (1943). Meal white, flowers exannulate. South-west Sichuan in the Muli district. Ledges of limestone cliffs at 4300 m.

Primula aliciae Taylor ex Smith, J. Linn. Soc. 52: 336 (1942)

DESCRIPTION Leaves similar to *P. rupicola* and *P. xanthopa*, lanceolate and serrate with the same poorly marked winged leaf-stalk, yellow-mealy below. *Stems* mealy, bearing 2–6 semipendant flowers on very short stalks. *Calyx* 8–10 mm., slightly baggy. *Corolla* a beautiful luminous lavender-blue with a white-mealy eye, reminiscent of section Soldanelloides, widely bell-shaped, to 20 mm in diameter.

DISTRIBUTION Originally described from a single very rich valley above Tripe, on the wet southern slopes of the mountain Namcha Barwa just north of the Doshong La, Pemako, south-east Tibet. Grassy rock ledges amongst *Rhododendron lepidotum*. Found by Sir George Taylor, and named for his wife, seed of this very beautiful dwarf species collected by him flowered for Randall Cooke at Kilbryde in 1940 (a good colour transparency still exists). Seed was set for Cooke, but the species was lost by 1953. It was seen by Tony Cox, western end of Senguti plain, Tsari, 3800 m in 2000. This seems to be a new locality, although not far from the type station.

Primula homogama Chen & Hu, Fl. Rep. Pop. Sin. 2: 295 (1990)

DESCRIPTION Flowers purple, lacking a golden eye, and homostylous, only to 10 mm in diameter. Leaves similar to *P. brevis*. Emei Shan and Jingang Shan, Sichuan, damp shaded places, 2200–3000 m.

Primula urticifolia Maxim., Bull. AScad. St. Petersb. 27: 497 (1881)

DESCRIPTION An extraordinary little plant with non-mealy pinnatisect leaves with narrow blunt lobes, suggest not so much a primula, or indeed a nettle, as a small valerian. Flowers rose-pink, exannulate, to 15 mm in diameter; pollen 3-colporate. Gansu, Ta-tung and Si-ning ranges, limestone cliffs, 3000–4700 m. Collected by Farrer in 1915, flowering in 1918. (Fig. Halda: 277.)

Placed by Smith and Fletcher in subsection 'Sibiricae', but the lobed leaves, exannulate flowers, non-pouched bracts, pollen morphology and capsule type, as well as the general appearence rather suggest the Yunnanensis. In this section it is unusual in lacking meal, but it otherwise fits here quite well.

Primula clutterbuckii Ward, Ann. Bot. 44: 122 (1930)

DESCRIPTION A dwarf creeping plant, producing flowering rosettes at the end of long stolons. Leaves jaggedly toothed, with a long stalk, thickly white-mealy beneath. Flowers 1–2 together, deep purple, to 20 mm in diameter, almost as large as the rosette, homostylous. Assam, Delei valley, Mishmi hills, shady crevices in gneiss or granite, 3600–4000 m. (Fig. Halda: 242.)

Introduced by Ward in 1928, flowering in 1934 at Edinburgh. A mysterious plant, the stolons suggesting the section Minutissimae, and apparently related to *P. rimicola*, but the large exannulate bell-shaped flowers, large baggy calyx (to 10 mm), long flower-stalks (to 9 mm) and dentate leaf-shape strongly suggest the Yunnanensis as originally suggested by Ward.

Section **Aleuritia** Duby,

Bot. Gall. ed.2, 1: 384 (1828) emend. Schott, Sippen d. Oesterr. Prim.: 10 (1851)

(Section Farinosae Pax (1889) et auct. plur. post. p.p.)

Type species *P. farinosa* L.

DESCRIPTION Small to medium-sized *usually mealy* perennial plants, usually not creeping, deciduous, overwintering by an above-ground mealy resting bud. *Leaves* lanceolate to spoon-shaped, glabrous, smooth to rugose, the stalk usually winged, often obscure, the blades entire to finely crenulate, usually rounded at the tip, with revolute vernation. *Stems* usually exceeding leaves at flowering, bearing a single umbel of flowers on stalks which usually exceed the calyx and usually small bracts which are often somewhat swollen (but usually not saccate) at the base. *Calyx* cylindrical, not angled. *Corolla* flat-faced, purple, lilac, pink or white with a yellow annulus, rarely exannulate, heterostylous or homostylous, with a narrow tube usually exceeding the calyx, the corolla-lobes deeply bifid, the corolla often appearing 10-lobed; *pollen* 3–5 syncolpate, or in three species 3-colporoidate, spherical to oblate. *Capsules* usually elongate and cylindrical, usually exceeding the calyx and dehiscing by 5 apical valves. *Seeds* rather small, rounded, often spherical and smooth. x = 9, heterostylous species diploid, homostylous species normally polyploid, chromosomes uniform in size. Heterostylous species often fully self-sterile. Flowering May–June (often April in cultivation).

DISTRIBUTION Almost throughout the range of

the genus, circum-arctic and in all the major mountain systems of Europe, north America, greater Caucasus, Siberia and central Asia, but absent from the central and eastern Sinohimalaya. The only primula in south America.

Characteristically plants of spring-fed, often calcareous marls by flushes, stream-sides, etc., although occurring in other damp open habitats. Often occur in assemblages with *Gentiana* spp., *Pinguicula* spp. and *Carex* spp. throughout their range.

The section Aleuritia was originally based by Duby on three species, including the type species *P. farinosa*, and *P. halleri*, and this is the correct name for whichever section contains *P. farinosa*. Pax's later and more familiar name Farinosae was usually taken also to include members of some or all of the sections Armerina, Oreophlomis, Yunnanensis, Glabra, Pulchella and Souliei which are excluded from it in the present treatment (Smith & Fletcher, 1944, Wendelbo, 1961b). This vast assemblage (Smith & Fletcher list 82 species in their Farinosae) is clearly heterogenous, and the DNA confirms this. It includes plants with the base chromosome numbers x = 11, 10, 9 and 8; all the pollen types known in the genus; species with and without meal; and varies in many other features as discussed under those sections.

The cytologist Bruun was of the opinion that evidence from the chromosomes, pollen and morphology strongly suggested that the Farinosae should be split into a number of sections. Although later authors largely ignored these proposals, Smith & Fletcher (1944) did subdivide the Farinosae into eight subsections.

Of their 11-chromosome subsections I have followed Wendelbo (1961) in establishing the Auriculatae as section Oreophlomis, Schwarz (1971) in establishing Smith and Fletcher's Sibirica as section Armerina, and Bruun (1932) in recognizing Balfour's section Yunnanensis. Bruun's 'Stenocalyces', and subsection Inayatii, both with x = 8, have been included with some other species with 3–4 colporoidate or colporate pollen in a section Pulchella; while the subsection Glabra, also with x = 8, but with 3-syncolpate pollen is also established here as a section. Consequently, only 27 of the original 82 species now remain within the Aleuritia. In the present treatment, the Aleuritia are differentiated amongst their relatives by the base chromosome number x = 9; abundant farina, which is most usually white, at least on the resting buds and inflorescences: the corolla tube which is usually at least 2× the calyx; the oblong capsule which exceeds the calyx; and, except for three species, syncolpate pollen.

Under this definition, the section appears morphologically and ecologically to be a natural assemblage. However, the DNA shows that whereas all 19 species investigated fall within a single major clade, the group is nevertheless paraphyletic. In particular, the Asiatic species *P. algida*, *P. daraliaca*, *P. longiscapa* are allied more with the two Oreophlomis species *P. elliptica* and *P. clarkei* than with the remainder of this large assemblage. Like them they have colporoidate pollen and smooth leaves which distinguishes them from the rest of the Aleuritia. They are found only in the greater Caucasus region and Siberia, from which the rest of the section is completely absent. It is tempting to unite these three species with the Oreophlomis, but the latter section has x = 11 rather than x = 9, and no Oreophlomis species have meal. Consequently, on morphological grounds, I have decided that this *P. algida* group should remain in the Aleuritia, but classified within a new subsection. Possibly forerunners of the Oreophlomis were involved in their parentage.

Rather surprisingly, the European, American and eastern Asian species also fall into two distinct subclades. One (subclade I) is based on the diploids *P. farinosa* and the American *P. mistassinica*, and includes the polyploid homostyles *P. incana*, *P. laurentiana*, *P. magellanica*, *P. stricta* and the Japanese *P. yuparensis*. The hypothetical female parent of the intersectional alloploid *P. egaliksensis*, classified in the Armerina, is also located here. The other subclade (II) is based on the eastern Asian diploid *P. modesta*, and includes the localized American diploids *P. alcalina* and *P. specuicola*, the tetraploid *P. borealis*, and it seems, intriguingly, the central Asian *P. capitellata* (there is a possibility of misidentification here). Thus, it seems possible that the forerunners of the Aleuritia invaded north America twice, once westwards from Europe (subclade I), and once eastwards from Asia (subclade II).

Nevertheless, remarkably, section Aleuritia, the most widespread section of the genus and native to four continents, is not represented in the main Sinohimalayan region, the heartland of *Primula*, where it is replaced by the sections Pulchella and Yunnanensis with different pollen types and base chromosome numbers. This strongly suggests that the Aleuritia are a highly derived group which have proved remarkably successful in migrating through most of the mountain regions of the northern hemisphere.

The Aleuritia display a spectacular polyploid complex, all the diploid species being heterostyle, and all the polyploids apart from *P. borealis* homostyle. Species are known at the diploid (2n = 18), tetraploid (2n = 36), hexaploid (2n = 54), octoploid (2n = 72), and 14-ploid (2n = 126) levels. Diploid and tetraploid species have 3-syncolpate pollen, hexaploids and octoploids have 4-syncolpate pollen, and the 14-ploid *P. stricta* has 5-syncolpate pollen.

There is a distinct tendency for polyploids to occur at higher latitudes (in both hemispheres), and the highest polyploids, the octoploids *P. laurentiana*, *P. scandinavica* and *P. magellanica* and the 14-ploid *P. stricta* do not occur south of latitude 60° N or north of latitude 50° S. It seems likely that the self-fertile homostyles have proved to be more efficient long-distance dispersers than heterostyles, and that polyploidy has helped the homostyles to be 'buffered' against the deleterious effects of selfing (p. 61). Doubtless, the tendency to homostyly which this group has shown has been instrumental in its spread. Selfing will have also been beneficial in high arctic habitats where pollinators are scarce.

CULTIVATION Seed loses its viability slowly and germination is usually still good after at least two years if the seed is stored at 4°C. Seedlings respond to well-drained but moisture-retentive conditions in a nutritious neutral to slightly acidic soil and seem to do best in well-lit but rather cool conditions. Although some species appreciate overhead protection for their winter resting buds, this is not necessary for many. All species are fully hardy. Young plants usually flower in a year, and in good conditions will form a robust floriferous plant in their second year. After this they commonly die, most species tending to be short-lived. It is rare for a plant to flower for more than four seasons, with the notable exception of *P. frondosa*.

This is not the condition in the wild, for studies on *P. farinosa* and *P. scotica* show that many individuals survive for 10 years or more, although they flower much less regularly than in the garden. Garden plants probably exhaust themselves by flowering regularly in rich conditions.

Most species are relatively little affected by garden pests or diseases, although some are susceptible to winter damp.

Although propagation by division after flowering is possible, this is usually not worthwhile for such short-lived plants, and every effort should be made to cross-pollinate heterostylous species, saving and sowing the seed. Homostylous species will normally set seed automatically, but if crosses are made artificially between individuals, the offspring are frequently more vigorous (Richards 2002).

Most members of the section are rather small plants, which, although suitable for the raised bed, small rock garden or trough, rarely make a sufficient impact unless planted in groups. Although individually charming, most have a marked family resemblance. For garden purposes, *P. frondosa* is by far the most satisfactory plant, and only the keenest collector will feel the need to attempt to grow many of its very similar relatives. Only a few, such as *P. scotica*, *P. modesta*, *P. magellanica* and *P. halleri*, have sufficiently distinct personalities to warrant their separate culture.

HYBRIDIZATION Hybridization is unknown in the wild. In recent years we raised *P. farinosa* × *P. scotica* hybrids for experimental purposes (Arnold & Richards, 1998). Wedderburn (1988) undertook an extensive crossing programme between eight species, more fully reported on page 59. Some of Fran Wedderburn's hybrid seed germinated well, although it was noteworthy that the sparse seed resulting from illegitimate-type crosses did not germinate. She raised seedlings of the following crosses:

P. modesta × *P. laurentiana*
P. modesta × *P. halleri*
P. frondosa × *P. laurentiana*
P. halleri × *P. laurentiana*

These seedlings were not grown on, but it should be noted that some potential for raising garden hybrids exists within the section.

Ernst (1955) raised a few seedlings from crosses between *P. halleri* and the Oreophlomis species *P. rosea*, but these died in infancy.

LITERATURE

Hultgaard U-M. (1990)
Hultgaard U-M. (1993)
Mazer S.J. & Hultgaard U-M. (1993)
Tremayne M. & Richards A.J. (2000)

KEY TO SPECIES

1. Flowers white, American 2
1. Flowers pink, blue or purple 3

2. Calyx more than 6 mm; flowers homostyle .... *P. magellanica*
2. Calyx 4–6 mm; flowers heterostyle .... *P. alcalina*
2. Calyx 4 mm or less; flowers heterostyle .... *P. anvilensis*

3. Flower stalks very short or absent, not exceeding 3 mm at first flower; plants of central Asia 4
3. Flower stalks usually more than 3 mm; not native to central Asia 5

4. Flower-stalks absent; flowers pink; leaves pointed; bracts ovate .... *P. capitellata*
4. Flower-stalks less than 3 mm; flowers pink; leaves rounded; bracts narrow .... *P. schlagintweitiana*
4. Flower stalks less than 6 mm; flowers violet; leaves rounded; bracts narrow .... *P. baldschuanica*

5. Meal completely absent, even from calyx and underside of leaf; leaf-edge smooth, petiole very narrow (Bulgaria) .... *P. exigua*
5. If meal apparently absent, then leaf-edge crenate and petiole wider 6

6. Flowers heterostyle (mouth with either stigma or anthers but not both) 7
6. Flowers homostyle (mouth of flower with both anthers and stigma, dissect and use a lens) 13

7. Flower-stalks usually exceeding 1 cm; leaves jaggedly toothed. Colorado River .... *P. specuicola*
7. Flower-stalks usually less than 1 cm; leaves not deeply toothed 8

8. Calyx usually less than 4 mm; plants rather squat; petiole usually distinct, narrow (Pacific Rim) 9
8. Calyx usually more than 4mm; plants more elegant, petiole rather indistinct, winged 11

9. Meal white, often thin; capsule not more than 1.5× the calyx .... *P. borealis*
9. Meal yellowish, usually thick below the leaf; capsule more than 1.5× the calyx 10

10. Fruit-stalks elongating to 10 mm or more; fruits more than 2.5× the calyx .... *P. sachalinensis*
10. Fruit-stalks not elongating; fruits less than 2× calyx .... *P. modesta*

11. Meal below leaf usually absent, if present thin, yellowish (America) .... *P. mistassinica*
11. Leaves white-mealy below (Europe) 12

12. Young leaves heavily mealy above; sepal-lobes divided to one-half, blunt .... *P. farinosa*
12. All leaves without meal above; sepal-lobes divided to one-third, sharp .... *P. frondosa*

13. Corolla-tube more than 2 cm in length; calyx more than 10 mm .... *P. halleri*
13. Corolla-tube less than 1 cm; calyx less than 8 mm 14

14. Flowers less than 8 mm in diameter, stiffly erect, purple or blue 15
14. Flowers usually more than 8 mm in diameter, erect to patent, usually pink 17

15. Flowers deep violet to intense red-purple (Scotland) .... *P. scotica*
15. Flowers rather pale lavender to lilac-blue (America and Arctic) 16

16. Scarcely mealy; capsule narrow and at least 1.5× calyx .... *P. stricta*
16. Heavily white-mealy; capsule ovate, scarcely exceeding calyx .... *P. incana*

17. Flower stalks shorter than calyx, flowers capitate (South America) .... *P. magellanica*
17. Flower-stalks exceeding the calyx, at least in fruit 18

18. Flowers lilac (-pink), corolla-tube scarcely exceeding calyx (America) .... *P. laurentiana*
18. Flowers purple, corolla-tube 1.5–2× calyx (Scandinavia) .... *P. scandinavica*
18. Flowers purple, corolla tube at least 2× calyx (Japan) .... *P. yuparensis*

Subsection **Aleuritia**

Outer leaves spreading to erect, usually more than 3× as long as wide, usually somewhat bullate. Pollen parasyncolpate. Absent from the Greater Caucasus and Siberia (except the Bering Coast).

Primula farinosa L., Sp. Pl. 143 (1753) BIRD'S-EYE PRIMROSE

P. nivalis Turcz. (1841) non Pallas (1776)
Aleuritia farinosa (L.) Spach (1840)
Androsace farinosa (L.) Sprengel (1815)

DESCRIPTION *Leaves* oblanceolate to ovate, to 10 × 2 cm, usually with a narrower stalk, entire to slightly crenate-toothed, rather smooth, slightly mealy and grey-green above, white or cream with meal beneath. *Stems* slightly mealy, somewhat exceeding leaves, occasionally to 30 cm, or rarely stemless. *Flowers* 5–30 forming a more or less flat-topped umbel, the stalks to 10 mm, equalling the bracts which are swollen at the base but not saccate. *Calyx* mealy, to 6 mm, often purple-tipped, the blunt sepal-lobes divided to half-way. *Corolla* lilac, pink or rarely white, to 15 mm in diameter, heterostylous; corolla-tube only slightly exceeding the calyx; pollen 3-syncolpate. *Capsule* exceeding the calyx. 2n = 18 (one unconfirmed report for 2n = 36 in Gotland) Almost completely self-sterile. Flowering May. (Plate 15.)

DISTRIBUTION England; from south Lancashire and west Yorkshire to northern Cumbria and one site in south Northumberland, introduced into Derbyshire; formerly in the Edinburgh region of Scotland; Denmark (nearly extinct); Sweden to 64° N; Finnish archipelago; Baltic states to 60° N; Montes Universales, Spain and Pyrenees; Alps extending north into France (Jura, Vosges) and Germany; Tatra.

Considerable doubt and controversy exists concerning the Asiatic range of this species. Federov (1952) considers it to be largely absent from western and central Siberia, but suggests that it occurs from the east of the Altai through Mongolia and north Sinkiang to eastern Siberia and Kamtschatka. He notes that problems exist with related species through much of this range, but that the Kamtschatka plant in particular is indistinguishable from European specimens, while *P. sachalinense* from the Pacific islands grades into his *P. farinosa* var. *xanthophylla* from the Irkutsk region. In contrast, Schwarz (1968) rejects all Asiatic records of *P. farinosa* as belonging to other species, notably *P. serrata*, *P. longiscapa* and *P. sachalinensis*. DNA studies show that *P. longiscapa*, which outwardly resembles *P. farinosa*, is in fact a relative of *P. algida* and only distantly related to *P. farinosa*. It is quite likely that this finding will also apply to the other eastern Asian taxa which so closely resemble *P. farinosa* morphologically. Until more molecular evidence is to hand, I am following Schwarz's scheme, although with some reservations.

Typically a plant of rather open, marly, calcareous spring-fed ground, but also sometimes in drier calcareous grassland, locally common. Usually a montane to alpine plant, reaching 2900 m, but at sea-level in the Baltic and on the Durham coastline.

Primula farinosa, the familiar bird's-eye of northern England, takes a central position in the confusing complex of closely related species which occurs through much of northern Eurasia and America. Distinctions will be noted under accounts of relatives, but it should be noted that some populations of *P. farinosa* are very variable and may include individuals which can be scarcely separated from those of geographically remote relatives. Typically, *P. farinosa* has leaves white-mealy on both sides, a relatively short corolla-tube, erect non-saccate bracts, a non-creeping habit and hetero-stylous flowers.

In recent years, *P. farinosa* and its relatives have played central roles in experimental work on reproductive biology by three teams. Our own work (Tremayne & Richards 2000) has shown that outcrossing species such as heterostylous *P. farinosa* may benefit from poor reproductive assurance by setting fewer seeds per capsule which are however larger and fitter than seed resulting from fecund capsules. In homostylous species which set more seed per capsule than heterostylous species, this large seed number per capsule does not disadvantage the seedlings as is the case for heterostylous species. This may be because the homostylous species produce fewer flowers so that the overall burden to the plant is lower.

VARIATION

Most of the named varieties in, for instance, Smith & Fletcher (1943) are trivial, and fall within the range of variability of many populations. The eastern Asian varieties with yellow meal, var.

chrysophylla Trautv. & Mey and var. *xanthophylla* Smith & Fletcher, are here placed under *P.sachalinensis*, while non-mealy Siberian varieties included under var. *denudata* Koch non Pancic are here placed under *P. serrata* and *P. longiscapa*.

- Var. *albiflora* Pax (1905). Flowers white. Occurs sporadically, such as in Upper Teesdale, England.

- Var. *nana* E.S. Arnold & A.J. Richards **var. nova**. Typo differt in scapo nullo, pedicellis basi fixis. Type gathering: Cronkley Fell, Teesdale, James Backhouse jr, 1852 **BM** (a single gathering). Protologue material at **K** (two specimens). *P. farinosa* v. *nana* was subsequently recorded on Cronkley Fell on several occasions (Arnold 1999), and the rather remote population beside the Black Arc at 550 m persists to the present (grid reference NY 846277). Here, approximately 1000 plants occur of which about 90% are scapeless (v. *nana*). This population is grazed by sheep and rabbits. Plants from the scapeless population, including those with stems, are more nearly homostylous with less herkogamy than the typically distylous scaped plants. They are protected within a National Nature Reserve.

CULTIVATION Easily grown from seed, and flowering over several seasons when grown in pots plunged in cool frames covered in winter (and protected by netting from blackbirds). Appreciates regular repotting in spring. Neither so vigorous nor so long-lived as *P. frondosa*, which for garden purposes is almost indistinguishable, and the better plant. Unfortunately, var. *nana* has proved to be difficult to grow, and almost impossible to flower, in cultivation.

LITERATURE

Arnold, E.A. (1999)
Arnold, E.A. & Richards, A.J. (1998)
Baker, K., Richards, A.J. & Tremayne, M.A. (1994).

Primula exigua Velenovsky, Abh. Boehm. Ges. Wiss. 7: 38 (1886)

P. farinosa ssp. *exigua* (Velen.) Hayek, Prodr. Fl. Penins. Balcan. 2: 25 (1928)

DESCRIPTION Differs from *P. farinosa* particularly by completely *lacking* meal. Also, a much more *spindly* plant, with stems very slender and wiry, up to 6 × leaves in length, bearing 6 flowers or fewer, the flowers not usually exceeding 10 mm in diameter, and the corolla-tube not exceeding the calyx. The green leaves are markedly *spoon*-shaped, the blade being without teeth and very rounded, and the stalk narrow, unwinged below and exceeding the blade. 2n = 18. Flowering July in the wild. (Plate 53.)

DISTRIBUTION Confined to the Vitosha, Pirin, Rila and Rhodope ranges of south-west Bulgaria as far as the Greek border but not crossing it. Does not overlap with *P. farinosa* or *P. frondosa*.

Locally abundant in wet flushes and streamsides usually in acidic areas, growing in association with *P. deorum* in the Rila, and often nothing else. 1200–2800 m.

Most accounts treat this rather unattractive little plant as a subspecies of *P. farinosa*. This was also my intention until I encountered large populations in several parts of the Bulgarian mountains in 1992 (and again in 2001). In fact it is quite distinct from *P. farinosa*. The lack of meal, spindly shape and spoon-shaped leaves even suggest that it might be related to the Armerina. However the chromosome count and pollen type confirm that it should be classified here. The acidic habitat is distinctive and untypical for the section.

Invariable in the wild. No hybrids reported. Unlikely to be of garden value.

Primula frondosa Janka, Osterr. Bot. Zeit. 23: 204 (1873)

DESCRIPTION Very similar to *P. farinosa*, but more *robust* and more often *multi-rosetted*, the leaves sharply toothed when young and markedly *crenate-toothed* when mature, rather more rugose in texture, darker, duller green and *never* mealy above. Bracts not swollen at the base. Calyx more bell-shaped, with *sharp* sepal-lobes about *one-third* the length of the calyx. Pollen 3-syncolpate. Apparently always heterostylous in cultivation, but homostylous forms are said to occur in the wild. The ecology and cytology of these is not known. 2n = 18. Thrums fully self-sterile, but pins 10% self-fertile, this differing from *P. farinosa*. (Plate 15, 16 as *P. algida*.)

DISTRIBUTION Only known from the central part of the Stara Planina, north-east Bulgaria.

Rock crevices, steep rocky slopes, usually on rocks of an acidic reaction, often in light woodland, never in closed turf or flushes, thus ecologically quite distinct from *P. farinosa*, which does not occur in Bulgaria. 900–2000 m.

It is often stated that widespread, variable species make the better garden plants, as they are more likely to produce forms amenable to garden conditions. However, this highly localized species, little-known in the wild, is an excellent garden plant, one of the most popular and widely grown of all primulas. The contrast with *P. farinosa*, widespread and familiar in the wild, but short-lived and rarely encountered in the garden, is striking. Probably the distinctive habitat preference of this species has preadapted it to garden conditions. However, according to the DNA it is closely related to *P. farinosa*.

VARIATION Little variation is known in cultivation, but the following variety has been described in the wild:

- Var. *jordanovii* D. Peev, Izv. Bot, Inst. Sofia 20: 131 (1970). Corolla-lobes narrow, Y-shaped; calyx hairy. Limestone rocks.

CULTIVATION Easy and vigorous in any good well-drained soil in good light. Sets seed well if pins and thrums are grown together, sometimes self-sowing. Rapidly multiplies, and clumps should be divided after flowering if vigour and good flowering is to be maintained. It should be noted that most plants in cultivation under the names *P. daraliaca*, *P. algida* and *P. scandinavica*, and some called *P. farinosa*, are in fact this species. **AM** 1974.

Primula halleri Gmel., Onomatalog. Bot. Compl. 7: 407 (1775)

P. longiflora Allioni, Fl. Pedem. 1: 92 (1785)
Aleuritia longiflora Opiz (1838)

DESCRIPTION A more robust plant than *P. farinosa* with stiffer more erect *leaves* to 8 × 3 cm, the *stem* much stouter, elongating to 15–30 cm in fruit, the *stalks* usually shorter than the calyx but erect and elongating in fruit, bearing a usually one-sided inflorescence of up to 20 slightly nodding flowers (usually 3–8). *Calyx* cylindrical, 5-ribbed, the narrow oblong sepal-lobes divided to two-thirds, to 12 mm. *Corolla* lilac to violet with a reddish tube, to 20 mm in diameter, usually homostylous, with a notably long cylindrical tube to 3 cm, long-exserted from the calyx. *Pollen* 3–4 parasyncolpate (Hultgaard 1990, contradicting Spanowsky 1962). 2n = 36. Self-fertile (however, it is said that heterostylous forms are found in Bulgaria; the cytology and ecology of these is unknown). (Plate 15.)

DISTRIBUTION Alps; main area throughout the eastern Alps eastwards from the Engadine and Bergamasque to the High Tauern, but excluding the eastern Low Tauern. The northern limit in the west is the Inn valley, but eastwards its distribution includes all of the main range. To the south all the main eastern ranges are included. There are two other disjunct areas to the west; in central Switzerland between the Matterhorn and the Tessin; and in the French and Italian Cottian Alps around Monte Viso, to the south-east of Briancon.

Elsewhere in the Tatra, several parts of the Romanian and Russian Carpathians, several mountain systems in Yugoslavia and Albania, and in the Rila and Pirin, Bulgaria, to the Greek border. Reports from Turkish Armenia bordering on the Caucasus seem to be incorrect.

Rather dry, somewhat open calcareous grassland usually dominated by coarse fescues and *Carex sempervirens*, 1500–2700 m.

Primula halleri is a distinctive species, familiar to visitors to the eastern Alps where it is often abundant within its characteristic habitat. It is a bigger plant than the relatives of *P. farinosa*, and the very long ruby corolla-tubes are distinctive. DNA studies show it to be closely related to *P. farinosa*, from which it probably evolved as a polyploid homostyle during the glacial periods in the Alps. Unrelated to *P. algida* with which it was aligned in the earlier edition.

CULTIVATION Grows well from seed, often flowering within a year. Although it will grow for a short time in most fertile well-drained sites in good light, we have found it to be most permanent in wet humus-rich locations, growing with *P. rosea*, *P. denticulata* and 'candelabras'. In these conditions, different from its wild locations, it forms robust multi-rosetted clumps and will flower freely for a decade or more. It sets seed freely, and is easily multiplied by division after flowering.

Primula scotica Hooker, Fl. Lond. 4, t.133 (1821)

P. farinosa L. subsp. *scotica* (Hooker) Smith & Forrest (1928)
P. farinosa L. var. *pygmaea* Pax (1905) non Gaudin

DESCRIPTION A *dwarf, blue-grey* plant suffused with whitish meal forming compact rosettes of nearly stalkless leaves; almost *stemless* at first flowering, the stem elongating to 7 cm later, and bearing 1–4(–6) sweetly scented *violet to intense red-purple* white-eyed flowers to 8 mm in diameter on *suberect* stalks to 5 mm in a rather tight head; bracts saccate at the base; *calyx* 4–5 mm; *pollen* 4-syncolpate; flowers *homostylous*, and possibly also pin flowered, the stigma somewhat 5-lobed; capsule 1 to 1.5× the calyx. 2n = 54. Self-fertile. Flowering June–July. (Photo: Primulas of Europe and America, plates 52, 53; Primulas of the British Isles plate 11) (Plate 15).

DISTRIBUTION Endemic to northern Scotland, one of very few British endemic plants. North coast of Scotland from Cape Wrath, Sutherland, to Dunbeath, east Caithness; Orkney, most of the larger islands, but missing from the north-eastern islands of Stronsay, Sanday and Shapinsay.

Always within 1.5 km from the sea; sand-dune turf, limestone turf and cliff-top grassland where wind-blown sand accretes. Typical of exposed, open, heavily sheep-grazed sites with reasonably good drainage which do not dry out. 0–150 m.

Although it is frequently stated that *P. scotica* is a short-lived plant, Bullard *et al.* (J. Ecol., 75: 589–602, 1987) show that many wild plants live in excess of 20 years. They demonstrate two distinct cohorts of long-lived, vigorous and relatively free-flowering plants, and of short-lived, poor flowering plants. They suggest that the latter arise as a result of selfing, and show inbreeding depression. These are more likely to arise in years when flowering and cross-pollination is poor. Michelle Tremayne (Tremayne & Richards 1997) has confirmed this at least in part, showing that seedlings arising from artificial crosses germinate, grow, survive and flower better when reintroduced into the wild than those arising from selfs. These effects are much more important after one year than those resulting from different seed sizes. Performance is also strongly correlated with mild winters. Many populations are small in number, and although a few very large populations survive, the species is threatened in many of its sites, particularly after prolonged hard weather.

P. scotica is a most delightful and charming little plant. A hexaploid homostyle, its maternal origins presumably lie with heterostylous *P. farinosa* with which the DNA shows it to be closely related. Possibly, during an interglacial episode, an octoploid race, similar to *P. scandinavica*, crossed with a tetraploid mother in the *P. farinosa* complex to give rise to these hexaploid plants which subsequently became isolated in northern Scotland. Arnold & Richards (1998) raised pin tetraploid hybrids between *P. scotica* and *P. farinosa* from which they deduced that at least some *P. scotica* still possessed four or five (out of a possible six) pin rather than homostyle chromosomes. Consequently, a few pin seedlings may segregate out amongst *P. scotica* progeny and probable pin plants have been detected in the wild. These may require an insect visit for seed to set and so may be reproductively unsuccessful and selected against during periods of bad weather.

CULTIVATION Seed is readily set in cultivation, and germinates well for at least a year after collection. Most plants will flower a year after germination, but in cultivation they rarely flower for more than two years. This is an excellent subject for a pan, kept plunged and partially shaded in summer, a cool trough or a raised bed, grown in a gritty but water-retentive compost. Best grown in groups, increasing the chance of cross-pollination and subsequent vigour.

LITERATURE.

Arnold, E.A. & Richards, A.J. (1998)
Bullard, E.R, Shearer, H.D.H, Day, J.D. & Crawford, R.M.M. (1987)
Ennos, R.A., Cowie, N.R., Legg, C.J. & Sydes, C. (1999)
Glover, B.J. & Abbott, R.J. 1995. Tremayne, M.A. & Richards, A.J. (1997)

Primula scandinavica (Bruun) Bruun, Svensk Bot. Tidskr. 32: 249–260 (1938)

P. scotica Hooker var. *scandinavica* Bruun (1932)

DESCRIPTION A taller plant than *P. scotica*, particularly at first flowering, and intermediate in many features with *P. farinosa*. Flower *stalks* erect but longer than in *P. scotica* (to 10 mm); *calyx* also longer (5–7mm); *flowers* usually of a dull purple, less commonly bright red-purple, often small but up to 15 mm in diameter, 5–10 commonly borne together on a stem. *Stigma* globose. *Leaves* in summer bear a well-marked stalk to half the length of the leaf. Pollen 4-syncolpate. 2n = 72. Homostylous and self-fertile. Flowering two weeks before *P. scotica* when grown together. (Plate 15.)

DISTRIBUTION Norway; two areas, from 59° N to 63° N, away from coastal ranges, and again from 66° N to 70° N, on both coastal and inland ranges, including the Lofoten islands. A few sites in Sweden near the Norwegian border, but to 17° E in Vasterbotten.

Ecologically quite distinct from *P. scotica, P. scandinavica* is an arctic-montane species of alpine grasslands and broken ground on limestones and schists, altitudinal limits not known. Does not overlap with *P. farinosa*, always occurring on higher, drier ground to the west. Overlaps with *P. stricta* in both the main Norwegian areas, although in general more westerly in distribution (map in Hultgaard 1993).

DNA studies suggest that the octoploid *P. scandinavica* is not maternally as closely related to *P. farinosa* as is *P. scotica*. Possibly it originally arose from alloploid hybrids to which *P. farinosa* supplied paternal genomes to a less related maternal line. Hultgaard (1993) suggests that its origins should be sought in the arctic and that it may have dispersed to Scandinavia in a circumpolar fashion. However, her suggestion that the American *P. laurentiana* may be its closest relative is not borne out by the DNA.

CULTIVATION Very rarely grown. In recent years we have raised and flowered many plants for experimental purposes, originated from Bodo in 1994 and have supplied seed to the exchanges. It proved rather more vigorous and permanent than *P. scotica*, but less attractive, and not as showy as better forms of *P. farinosa*. Tremayne & Richards (2000) found that seedlings born of heavy seeds performed best, but that because these seedlings were stronger, they produced more, but disadvantageously light, seeds than did weaker seedlings born of light seeds. Seed weight effects thus persisted over three generations.

Primula stricta Hornem., Fl. Dan. 8 (24) t. 1385 (1810)

P. hornemanniana Lehm. (1817) p.p.
P. glabrescens Nylander (1859)
P. mistassinica Gray (1878) p.p. non Michx.
P. borealis Gray (1878) p.p. non Duby (1843)
P. sibirica Jacq. var. *arctica* Fernald (1926) non Pax

DESCRIPTION A *tiny* reduced relative of *P. farinosa* with 1–3 (–8) pale lilac flowers up to 8 mm in diameter together on short erect stalks which elongate in fruit; *bracts* awl-shaped, to 10 mm, saccate at the base; *calyx* 4–6 mm; *leaves* usually entire, but slightly toothed when developed, rather smooth. *Pollen* 5-syncolpate, uniquely in the genus. This species is rather mealy when protected from rain in cultivation, but in the wild often appears to be nearly without meal. 2n = 88–136 (Hultgaard 1990), the highest counts in the genus. Homostylous and self-fertile. (Fig. 26.)

DISTRIBUTION Scandinavia; central mountain spine around Norwegian/Swedish border, occupying two main centres in the Norwegian mountains as does *P. scandinavica*, but generally lying more to the east, from 62° N to 70° N and nowhere near the coast. Unlike *P. scandinavica*, also scattered eastwards through arctic Finland south to Kuusamo and eastwards to the Russian Kola peninsula; Novaya Zemlya. Northern coast of Iceland; coastal areas of east and west Greenland north of 64° N; much of arctic Canada including Labrador and the whole of Hudson Bay. Records from Alaska and the Yukon west of the Mackenzie basin are referable to *P. incana, P. anvilensis* or *P. borealis*.

Coastal regions including meadows, marshes, dunes, beach ridges, cliffs, etc., more rarely inland along rivers, to 750 m.

Sometimes found with *P. nutans* in Scandinavia, and with *P. egaliksensis* in Iceland, and Canada, and often confused with them, these all being tiny reduced plants adapted to high arctic conditions. Both of the Armerina species lack meal, but this can be difficult to detect on *P. stricta*. Best distinguished by lacking the long narrow leaf-stalk of the Armerina species, and from *P. nutans* by its homostylous flowers. Closely related to its probable parent *P. incana* which tends to be bigger, is more mealy, and has flat-tipped bracts. Also overlaps with the more robust, darker-flowered *P. scandinavica* in north-

Fig. 26. *P. stricta*

central Norway.

The pollen type (5-syncolpate) is otherwise known in the genus only in *P. egaliksensis*. However, it is clearly derived from the 4-syncolpate pollen of *P. incana* and *P. laurentiana* and is quite distinct from the stephanocolopate pollen of the other Armerina species.

The approximately 10–15-ploid *P. stricta* was first diagnosed as a 14-ploid (2n = 126) by Bruun (1930). Modern techniques make the accurate counting of high chromosome numbers more possible, and Hultgaard's discovery of a wide range of aneuploid numbers is typical of high polyploids which can tolerate considerable fluctuations in gene dosage through accidental chromosome loss, and more rarely, gain. Possibly this species started life as a 14-ploid, but it may originally have been 16-ploid.

Not very closely allied to the remainder of the *P. farinosa* clan according to the DNA, suggesting that several species may have been involved in its maternal parentage. Possibly dispersed across the arctic ice to Europe from America according to Hultgaard (1993).

CULTIVATION Grows readily from seed in a pan plunged in a cool place and protected from winter damp, flowering in a year, and setting seed, but rarely persisting for another season. At Kew in the 'arctic' chilled bench in the alpine house, robust plants several years old have resulted. Although of considerable botanical interest, the species has virtually no horticultural merit. Curiously, and alone amongst its relatives, Tremayne & Richards (2000) found that seedlings born of light seeds did better than those from heavy seeds, possibly because their growth rate was more steady and uniform.

Primula mistassinica Michaux, Fl. Bor.-Amer. 1: 121 (1803)

P. pusilla Goldie (1822)
P. hornemanniana Hooker (1838) p.p. non Lehm. (1817) = *P. stricta*
P. maccalliana Wiegand (1900)
P. intercedens Fernald (1900)

DESCRIPTION A delicate but variable species, sometimes mealy when young but adult plants usually *without meal*, or with a trace of yellow meal. *Stalk* 5–15 cm, slender, bearing 1–5 flowers on arcuate slender flower stalks to 2 cm, the awl-shaped bracts with a flattened and not noticeably swollen base. *Calyx* 3–5 mm, greenish, *flowers* lavender-blue or white, heterostylous, 8–15 mm in diameter, tube 1.5–2× calyx. *Capsule* (diagnostically amongst American species) 1.5× the length of the calyx. 2n = 18. The earliest of its relatives to flower in cultivation, in early April, summer in the wild. (Plate 16.)

DISTRIBUTION Right across boreal forest regions of Canada, south to the Great Lakes and north to Hudson Bay, eastwards to Newfoundland and westwards to isolated stations in the Yukon; east Alaska; Maine, New York, Michigan, Minnesota, Illinois, Vermont and Wisconsin in the USA.

'Open meadows and riverbanks, lakeshores, and around hot springs, in the southern part of its range on cool wet north-facing slopes and cliff faces; calcareous substrates.' Sea-level to 1500 m.

P. mistassinica is essentially the American counterpart of *P. farinosa*, with a comparable range of location and morphological variability, and occurring in similar habitats. Indeed, it is not possible to separate some forms of *P. mistassinica* from some forms of *P. farinosa* morphologically, and the two species should perhaps be merged. However, in view of the very different geographical distributions of the two complexes it is convenient to treat them separately. DNA studies show them to be related but distinct, and also show that *P. mistassinica* is related to the polyploid homostyles *P.*

incana and *P. laurentiana* which probably evolved from the forerunners of *P. mistassinica*.

VARIATION Kelso (1991) considers that variation within populations is such as to render the following varieties meaningless; however, they are frequently cited in the horticultural literature, and are therefore worth repeating here.

- Var. *mistassinica*. Rather delicate and spindly; nearly lacking meal except beneath the leaf; seeds smooth. Much of the range, but absent from the Great Lakes, eastern seaboard and USA.
- Var. *intercedens* (Fernald) Boivin, Natur. Can. 93: 644 (1966) (*P. intercedens* Fernald (1928)). yellow-mealy, especially below the leaves; seeds reticulate and papillose. Great Lakes region.
- Var. *novaboracensis* Fernald, Rhodora 30: 91 (1928). Flowers concolorous, lacking orange eye, not exceeding 10 mm in diameter; leaves broadly obovate. Northern USA, eastern seaboard of Canada.

CULTIVATION Vigorous, but short-lived in a cool, well-drained situation, but not commonly met. Not self-fertile and not so attractive as *P. laurentiana*.

Primula anvilensis Kelso, Systematic Botany 12: 9–13 (1987)

P. parvifolia Fernald (1928) non Duby (1844) = *P. borealis*

DESCRIPTION A close relative of *P. mistassinica*, but differing by the *white* flowers, not exceeding 8 mm in diameter and the scarcely exserted corolla tube. 2n = 18. Heterostylous. 'Frost boils, late snow-beds, creek banks and gravel bars with calcareous substrates.' Bering Strait region of Alaska. Very common on the Seward Peninsula, extending to the Noatak River region in the north and southwards into the mountains. The relatively unrelated *P. borealis* can occur with *P. anvilensis,* although it is more typical of saline habitats. It has larger flowers with a longer tube and bracts swollen at the base. Fig. Halda: 238. In cultivation in the UK in 1990.

Primula incana M.E. Jones, Proc. Calif. Acad. Sci. 5: 706 (1895)

P. dealbata Engelm. (1863) inedit. non Schwarz (1970) = *P. auriculata* Lam.
P. americana Rydb. (1901)
P. farinosa L. var. *incana* (Jones) Fernald (1907)

DESCRIPTION A close relative of *P. stricta*; the homostylous lavender-blue erect *flowers*, 4–8 mm in diameter, on stiff stalks equalling the bracts, are smaller flowered than in *P. laurentiana* and *P. mistassinica*. *Calyx* 4–10 mm, usually shorter than the flat-ended bracts with a swollen base, to 10 mm. *Pollen* 4-syncolpate. Differs from *P. stricta* principally by the ovate capsule only equalling or slightly exceeding the calyx, and by being much more mealy. 2n = 54. (A report of 2n = 72 from Colorado is probably mistaken.) (Plate 16.)

DISTRIBUTION Western America, from eastern Alaska (not coastal) southwards through the Yukon and Canadian Rockies to the Colorado Rockies and Saskatchewan, keeping chiefly to the drier eastern side of the ranges; two isolated stations on the south-west and south-east corners of Hudson Bay. Scarcely overlaps with the other American Aleuritia, keeping further to the west.

Open wet calcareous conditions. 'Alkaline clay soil in river flood plains and moist open meadows', 0–3500 m. Grows in bare wet marshy areas with *P. egaliksensis* in South Park, Colorado.

P. dealbata Engelm. is the earliest name for this species, but this was invalidly published. In cultivation, most likely to be confused with the octoploid *P. laurentiana* from further east which also has 4-syncolpate pollen, but larger flowers and longer fruit stalks. The arctic *P. stricta* is less mealy and has longer, curved fruits.

Occasionally cultivated, and charming with its small bluish flowers set against whitish foliage, but short-lived.

Primula laurentiana Fernald, Rhodora 30: 68–72 (1928)

P. farinosa L. var. *macropoda* Fernald (1907)
P. mistassinica Michx. var. *macropoda* (Fernald) Boivin (1966)

DESCRIPTION Closely related to *P. incana*, and likewise heavily mealy, but more robust, differing chiefly by the *larger* (10 to 16 mm in diameter) flowers, flower-stalks which elongate in fruit, broader, more toothed leaves, and bracts which are *inrolled*. Flowers homostylous, self-fertile; pollen 4-syncolpate. 2n = 72. The latest of this group to flower in cultivation, in June. (Plate 16)

DISTRIBUTION Eastern north America, from north-east Maine through the Gaspe peninsula of Quebec to west Newfoundland, Labrador and the eastern Hudson Bay.

Usually confined to open damp places on limestone, often by rivers, 0–300 m.

According to DNA studies, closely related to *P. incana*, both species probably having been derived from *P. mistassinica*.

CULTIVATION Rather commonly met in cultivation at present, but short-lived although setting seed freely and persisting and flowering quite well in well-drained sites which do not dry out in summer. A robust, attractive plant, the best of the American Aleuritia for the open garden. As I write in 2002 I have had a plant flower in a trough for four successive years.

Primula magellanica Lehm., Monogr. Prim. 62 (1817)

P. farinosa L. var. *magellanica* (Lehm.) Hooker (1847)
P. decipiens Duby (1844) non Stein (1905) = *P. hirsuta*
P. comberi Smith (1941)

DESCRIPTION The only south American *Primula*, morphologically close to the north American *P. laurentiana*, with the same chromosome number and breeding system, but with usually *larger* often *whitish* (or lilac or purple) flowers, to 20 mm in diameter in a *subcapitate* head, and usually *broader* leaves arising from a notably large resting bud. 2n = 72. Homostylous and self-fertile (possibly also heterostylous?). Flora of Tierra del Fuego, D.M. Moore (1982), p.125, figs. 95 a-c. (Plate 16.)

DISTRIBUTION Tierra del Fuego, Patagonia on the main cordillera north to 43° S; Falkland Islands (Malvinas).

Wet ground by streams and flushes, often on acidic peaty ground, 0–2000 m.

Although it seems remarkable that a primula species should occur in the subantarctic regions of South America, some 10,000 km south of its nearest relations, this is in fact a disjunctional pattern rather commonly found in plants.

It is generally considered that such 'bipolar disjuncts' were enabled to migrate south from the northern hemisphere down the American mountain chains during glacial epochs. During those times, tropical montane regions had much cooler wetter climates than today, while mountain ranges stood further above sea-level. As such migrations were rather recent events, it is not surprising to find that southern species such as *P. magellanica* have differentiated morphologically relatively little from their northern counterparts. However, the DNA shows that *P. magellanica* today is in fact not very closely allied to any contemporary species, although it is part of the same alliance as *P. mistassinica, P. incana* and *P. laurentiana*, from which it must ultimately have been derived.

It is noteworthy that it has been a homostylous, self-fertile strain that has been able to undertake this remarkable journey, as new disjunct populations can arise (perhaps as a result of transport by birds) from a single seed.

VARIATION The South American primulas are variable both within and between localities, and various accounts describe between one and three different species. As there are essentially three different ecogeographical populations, which show some consistent morphological differences, I have recombined these at subspecific rank:

- Subsp. *magellanica*. Relatively delicate plants; bracts awl-shaped; corolla-tube exceeding the calyx; flowers white to purple. Lowland areas of Tierra del Fuego and the Magellan Straits.
- Subsp. *comberi* (Smith) Richards (1993) (*P. comberi* Smith, Trans. Bot. Soc. Edinb. 33: 112 (1941). Delicate plants; bracts subulate; corolla-tube 2× the calyx; flowers lilac. High altitudes (1700–2000 m) in the southern Andes.
- Subsp. *decipiens* (Duby) Richards (1993). (*P. decipiens* Duby, Mem. Soc. Phys. d'Hist. Nat. Geneve 10 : 46 (1844). Often robust plants; bracts lanceolate; corolla-tube equalling the calyx, or shorter; flowers usually white or cream, occasionally purple. Falkland (Malvinas) Islands.

CULTIVATION Has been intermittently in cultivation since about 1910, usually as subsp. *decipiens* (**PC** 1980). This is a vigorous and moderately attractive plant, somewhat resembling a small white *P. denticulata*. It does well in a cool, well-drained position, for instance in a trough or raised bed in a peaty, gritty compost, but seems rarely to flower for more than two or three seasons before dying, although it sets seed freely. Subsp. *comberi* had probably not been in cultivation in recent years, but seed of all three subspecies was collected by Peter Erskine in 2000 and these plants are growing on as I write early in 2002.

Primula yuparensis Takeda, Notes Roy. Bot. Gdn. Edinb. 8: 94 (1913)

P. modesta Bisset & Moore subsp. *yuparensis* (Takeda) Smith & Forrest (1928)
P. sorachiana Miyabe & Tatew. (1933)

DESCRIPTION The only Asian relative of *P. farinosa* and *P. mistassinica* and morphologically very similar to the latter, but with abundant *white* meal and *purple* (occasionally white), white-eyed, relatively large (to 15 mm in diameter), *homostylous*, self-fertile flowers. Tetraploid. Often confused with the widespread Japanese complex of *P. modesta* which has spoon-shaped leaves of a different shape, yellow meal, and a shorter calyx (not exceeding 5 mm). 2n = 36. (Fig. Halda: 261.)

DISTRIBUTION Only known from Mt. Yubari, Hokkaido, Japan.

Chiefly in alpine areas, but '*P. sorachiana*' (var. *sorachiana* (Miyable & Tatewaki) Halda (1992)) refers to low-level plants with more flowers per stalk from the same mountain.

DNA studies suggest that this Japanese endemic is relict from an earlier incursion of the *P. farinosa*/*mistassinica* alliance into the western Pacific, presumably from north America. The relatively unrelated *P. modesta* group, assumed to be of central Asian origin, now predominates in this region.

CULTIVATION I have grown var. *sorachiana* in a trough for five years. Unlike most of this section it clumps up well and can be propagated vegetatively from cuttings. It flowers freely, is dwarf (to 3 cm), and makes a good garden plant.

Primula capitellata Boiss., Diag. Ser. 1, 7: 64 (1846)

DESCRIPTION Distinguished by the *stalkless* flowers (becoming very shortly stalked in fruit), so that the small lilac to mauve flowers form a tight capitate head, like a little *P. denticulata*; leaves with a pointed tip; corolla tube to 3× calyx; bracts *saccate* at the base, ovate; *calyx* only 4 mm; capsule *not* exceeding the calyx. Pollen 3-syncolpate. Heterostylous. (Fig. Halda: 241; Flora of Pakistan 157: fig. 6.)

DISTRIBUTION From the Elburz, north Iran, eastwards and southwards to much of the Iranian and Afghan mountains, Kurram and Chitral, Pakistan. Wet alpine meadows, near snow-melt, 2700–4900 m.

The most widespread of three closely related central Asian species which are apparently related to the *P. modesta* complex from the Pacific region. Often found in the wild with *P. auriculata*, and sometimes with *P. algida*, but quite distinct with mealy leaves and small capitate heads. The many expeditions to Iran and Afghanistan in the 1960s reported this to be an abundant species in suitable habitats.

Introduced on several occasions since 1925, but impermanent. **PC** 1968.

Primula baldschuanica B. Fedstch., Conspect. Fl. Turkest. 5: 6 (1913)

DESCRIPTION Differs from *P. capitellata* by having *rounded* leaves, very short but distinct flower-stalks (to 6 mm, usually shorter) and larger *violet* flowers (9–15 mm in diameter). Tadzhikstan, eastern Bokhara (Zeravschan), east Afghanistan, on the slopes of river valleys, 700–2800 m. (Fig. Halda: 239.)

Primula schlagintweitiana Pax, Pflanzenreich 22 (4): 91 (1905)

DESCRIPTION Differs from *P. capitellata* by having rounded leaves; by the very short flower-stalks (absent in the latter) to 3 mm, the linear-lanceolate bracts swollen but *not* saccate at the base;

calyx 5–6 mm; the corolla tube not exceeding 2× the calyx. Often without meal. (Fig. Flora of Pakistan 157: fig. 4.)

DISTRIBUTION Northern Pakistan (Gilgit, Baltistan), Sanskar (Pensi La, 4400 m), Kashmir (Suru Valley) and north-west India (Himalch Pradesh, Uttar Pradesh). Wet meadows, 1700–5200 m. Easily confused with *P. atrodentata* with which it often grows.

CULTIVATION Collected by Chris Chadwell (CC 282) in 1987, and probably by SEP in 1983.

Primula modesta Bisset & Moore, Journ. Bot. 16: 134 (1878)

P. farinosa L. subsp. *modesta* (Bisset & Moore) Pax (1905)
P. matsumurae Petitm. (1907)
P. ajanensis Busch (1926)
P. fauriae Franch. (1886)

DESCRIPTION This complex from the north-west Pacific is distinguished chiefly by the *spoon*-shaped leaves with narrow petioles which exceed the rounded blade and which are *yellow*-mealy at least below, and by the calyx being usually *shorter* (rarely exceeding 5 mm). In general the plants have a different appearence from most of the relatives of *P. farinosa*, being rather squat and dumpy, and the flowers clear pink. Pollen 3–4 syncolpate. 2n = 18. Heterostylous. Thrums fully self-sterile; pins up to 5% self-fertile. (Plate 15.)

DISTRIBUTION Mountains through much of Japan, on all four principal islands, descending to sea-level in the north. Extends through the Kurile islands where it grades into *P. sachalinensis* which is distinguished by longer fruits, and with the tetraploid and mostly American *P. borealis* which extends down the Aleutians. Also in a few stations on the Korean mainland and neighbouring Siberia. Usually on wet open rather base-rich sites.

DNA shows *P. modesta* to be related to both the central Asian *P. capitellata* and the American species *P. borealis, P. alcalina* and *P. specuicola*. It seems likely that this group colonized the Pacific rim from central Asia.

VARIATION This, the principal member of the Aleuritia in Japan, is a locally common and very variable species with a wide range of distribution and habitat. There has been much discussion about the taxonomic limits and status of variants; the following arrangement is nowadays most usually employed:

- Var. *modesta*. Leaves lanceolate, gradually narrowed to the stalk, the margins scarcely inrolled; flowers 10–15 mm in diameter; flower-stalks about 10 mm. All four main Japanese islands. **AM** 1982.
- Var. *fauriae* (Franchet) Takeda, Notes Roy. Bot. Gdn. Edinb. 8: 88 (1913). Leaves ovate, the margins strongly inrolled, abruptly narrowed to the stalk; flowers 7–8 mm in diameter; flower-stalks up to 20 mm. Northern Honshu, Hokkaido and the Kuriles. 'Leucantha', flowers white, **AM** 1980 (but was this the same as 'fauriae alba'? see below).
- Var. *matsumurae* (Petitm.) Takeda, Fl. Japan: 720 (1965). A squat robust plant with oblanceolate leaves gradually narrowed to the base; stalk indistinct; flowers 15–20 mm in diameter; flower-stalks 10–15 mm; calyx to 8 mm. Rebun island and Teshio province, Hokkaido; Korea and the Vladivostok region. A white-flowered form which generally comes true from seed has been popular in cultivation. This is usually known as '*P.* modesta fauriae alba', but it is a squat, robust, large-flowered plant which is probably a form of var. *matsumurae*, possibly from Rebun where seed has been collected on several occasions. **PC** 1974.

A rather unstable semi-double flowered form has developed in cultivation.

CULTIVATION Plants have been frequently grown under all three varietal names, although they are less popular in 2002 than formerly. These plants, although nearly always *P. modesta*, usually have the wrong varietal names. Var. *fauriae* is a rather squinny and is unlikely to make a good garden plant; most plants so-named were probably var. *matsumurae*. Smaller, more delicate plants were also popular and can be referred to var. *modesta*.

When grown in groups outside, seed is often set, and this germinates well, flowering within a year. Not long-lived, but vigorous, free-flowering, attractively dwarf and very suitable for well-drained reasonably cool troughs, raised beds, etc. Does not need covering in winter. After *P. frondosa*, possibly the best garden plant in the section, although *P. yuparensis* has tended to replace it in my affections.

Primula sachalinensis Nakai, Bot. Mag. Tokyo 46: 61 (1932)

P. farinosa L. var. *chrysophylla* Trautv. & Mey (1856)
P. farinosa L. var. *xanthophylla* Smith & Fletcher (1944)

DESCRIPTION Very close to *P. modesta*, but in typical forms distinguished by the heavily yellow-mealy leaves which are rather more robust, have a more distinct stalk, and are more rhomboidal in shape, by the long capsule, often 3× the calyx, the elongating fruiting stalks and the saccate base to the bracts. From far eastern Siberia, Kamtschatka, and Sakhalin island. Wooded rocks, and a 'mud-volcano'. Responsible for most far-eastern records of *P. farinosa*, from which it is disjunct by nearly half the world. Southwards, grades into *P. modesta* var. *matsumurae* in the Kuriles, which is largely distinguished by shorter fruits.

Primula borealis Duby, Mem. Soc. Phys. d'Hist. Nat. Geneve 10: 31 (1843)

P. parvifolia Duby (1844) ('parviflora' (sic) Fenderson 1986)
P. hornemanniana Hook. (1838) p.p. non Lehm. (1817) = *P. stricta*
P. sibirica Jacq. var. *borealis* (Duby) Kurtz (1894)
P. chamissonis Busch (1926)
P. tenuis Small (1898)

DESCRIPTION Differs from its American and eastern Asian relatives by the following combination of characters: leaves elliptical, only slightly *white-mealy*; *large* usually *lavender*, but violet to rosy or white *heterostylous* flowers up to 15 mm in diameter (frequently much smaller), borne on stalks to 8 mm; calyx *short*, about 3(–5) mm; bracts to 5 mm, awl-shaped, *swollen* at the base; capsule 1.5× calyx. Pollen 3-syncolpate. 2n = 36. (Fig. Halda: 240.)

DISTRIBUTION Coastal western and northern Alaska, (excluding all but the tip of the Seward Peninsula) and the northern shore of the Canadian arctic east to the Mackenzie river delta; inland records are *P. mistassinica*. Aleutian and Pribilov islands. Also in north-east Siberia west to the Chuchka peninsula. Chiefly on the shores of the Arctic Ocean. Salt marshes and estuarine marshes; sand-dunes.

A characteristically squat, short-stemmed plant with relatively large flowers, closely resembling the diploid and mostly Japanese *P. modesta* var. *matsumurae*, which is however usually more mealy and has yellow meal. It merges imperceptibly into the latter in the southern Aleutians/ Kuriles.

Of Siberian relatives which mostly lack meal in subsection Algida, *P. serrata* differs by its toothed leaves and very short bracts. The others are more robust plants with stout scapes. In north America, sympatric confusion species are *P. anvilensis* and *P. nutans*. Wild material is often very small and is best distinguished by the bracts which are swollen at the base (flat in *anvilensis*, long-saccate in *nutans*). *P. mistassinica* occurs in similar areas but is an inland plant, usually lacking meal.

It is likely that the diploid *P. modesta* was a parent to the allotetraploid *P. borealis* to which the DNA shows it to be closely related. *P. borealis* is the only example of a polyploid heterostylous species in the Aleuritia.

Attractive but impermanent in cultivation.

VARIATION Extremely variable in the wild, both in size and in mealiness. Exposed dune plants are often very small (less than 2 cm) and have been called *P. tenuis*. Robust mealy plants from saline marshes have been called *P. chamissonis*, but both are probably just environmental modifications not worthy of formal recognition. In all forms, young plants are mealy, but this wears thin with age.

Primula specuicola Rydb., Bull. Torrey Bot. Club 40: 461 emend. Vogelmann, Rhodora 62: 36 (1960)

P. hunnewellii Fernald (1934)

DESCRIPTION A distinct and disjunct very white-mealy plant, with *large* (to 16 mm in diameter) lavender to dark violet heterostylous flowers borne on stalks which *lengthen* to more than 1 cm in fruit; the corolla-tube is twice the length of the calyx; capsule *shorter* than the calyx which has sharp and narrow sepal-lobes; the leaves are *jaggedly* toothed. In growth in the winter, flowering by the end of February in cultivation, and aestivating in late summer. 2n = 18. Heterostylous.

DISTRIBUTION South-eastern Utah, near Bluff City, and northern Arizona, North Rim, Grand Canyon. Limestone grottos and crevices on seepage lines of carbonate canyon walls along the Colorado river and its tributaries, on usually shady cliffs in 'hanging garden' communities, 2000–2500 m.

Rather surprisingly, the DNA shows this isolated plant to be closely related to the 'Pacific Rim' group of *P. modesta* and *P. borealis*.

This very local endemic is a most delightful species which is currently in limited cultivation. Short-lived, it only thrives in alpine house culture, abhorring overhead watering. However, it must not be allowed to become too dry, except when resting in summer.

Primula alcalina Cholewa & Henderson, Brittonia 36: 59 (1984)

DESCRIPTION Plant white-mealy when young, becoming green. Flowers *white*, heterostylous, with short erect flower stalks, shorter than the bracts which have a flattened base. Corolla-lobes triangular, deeply and broadly bifurcate. 2n = 18. A recently described little plant from wet alkaline meadow flats in north-east Idaho, west of the Lemhi Range, 2000 m. Previously occurred in Montana near Monida. Another unexpected relative of *P. modesta* according to the DNA. (Fig. Halda: 237.)

Subsection **Algida** A.J. Richards **subsectio nova**

Subsection Aleuritia differt in foliis subprostratis haud 3-plo longioribus quam latioribus, laevibus. Pollen colporoidatus.
Outer leaves usually prostrate, often less than 3× as long as wide, smooth in texture. Pollen colporoidate. Greater Caucasus and Siberia only.

Primula algida Adams, Beitrage Naturkunde 1: 46 (1805)

P. farinosa L. var. *caucasica* Koch (1843)
P. caucasica Koch (1850)
P. farinosa L. var. *armena* Koch (1843)
P. farinosa L. var. *multiflora* Koch (1850)
P. farinosa L. var. *pauciflora* Koch (1850)
P. farinosa L. var. *luteo-farinosa* (Rupr.) Regel (1874)
P. luteo-farinosa Rupr. (1863)
P. auriculata Lam. var. *sibirica* Ledeb. (1847–9)
P. longifolia Marsch. (1808)
P. bungeana Mey (1849)
P. hookeri Freyn & Sintenis (1896) non Watt (1882)

DESCRIPTION Leaves *smooth*, lightly mealy at first to (usually) *non-mealy*, obovate with a widely-winged and poorly marked stalk, finely toothed, blunt, the outer prostrate. *Stems* usually exceeding leaves, slightly mealy. *Bracts* are not swollen at the base, and enlarge and often *reflex* in fruit, while the flower stalks elongate markedly in fruit, but stay erect. Calyx *long, tubular*, to 10 mm, with purplish blunt narrowly oblong sepal-lobes cut to over half the calyx length. Corolla tube *not* exceeding the calyx; corolla *large*, to 16 mm in diameter, varying in colour from violet to lilac-pink; the capsule does not exceed the calyx. Pollen 3-colporoidate. 2n = 18. Heterostylous. (Plate 54.)

DISTRIBUTION From the eastern Pontic ranges of north-east Turkey and north Iraq through the Caucasus and cis- and Trans-Caucasus to the Elburz (northern Iran). (Has also been recorded from much further east including the Altai, Pamir, Alatau, Tien Shan, Afghanistan, as far as northern Mongolia but all this central and eastern Asian material which lacks meal and has been called var. *sibirica* (Ledeb.) Pax (1905) probably refers to *P. longiscapa*.) The figure and description of Pamir (Chitral) material of *P. algida* in Nasir (1984) is not convincing, and Pakistan material may also refer to *P. longiscapa*, or another undescribed species.

Wet alpine meadows and rock ledges, above 2000 m.

KEY TO SPECIES

1. Flowers usually more than 10 together in a tight head; stem robust, exceeding leaves; meal absent 2
1. Flowers usually less than 10 in a laxer head; stem less robust; meal usually present at least on young leaves 4

2. Bracts ovate with a saccate base, spreading ....*P. fistulosa*
2. Bracts linear 3

3. Bracts 2–3 mm; calyx 3–4 mm, leaves serrate ....*P. serrata/pinnata*
3. Bracts 5–6 mm, calyx 4–5 mm, leaves subentire ....*P. longiscapa*

4. Calyx 5 mm; corolla bright pinkish-red ....*P. daraliaca*
4. Calyx 7–8 mm; corolla lilac to pink ....*P. algida*

DNA studies have shown that the west Asian Aleuritia species with colporoidate pollen *P. algida* and *P. daraliaca* and the east Siberian group based around *P. longiscapa* are not closely related to the remaining Aleuritia, and I have separated them here as a new distinct subsection.

VARIATION Resting buds and scapes are usually lightly mealy, but this can be white or yellow. Mature leaves usually lack meal. Eastern plants completely lacking meal are probably *P. longiscapa*.

CULTIVATION Cultivated intermittently since 1886, and still sometimes offered. Usually short-lived and impermanent.

Primula daraliaca Rupr., Bull. Acad. St. Petersb. 6: 236 (1863)

P. farinifolia Rupr. (1863)
P. zeylamica Char. & Kap. (1951)

DESCRIPTION A close relative of *P. algida*, with similar leaves, and 3-colporoidate pollen, but with a much *shorter calyx*, to 5 mm, the corolla tube at least one and a half times the calyx, and the flower usually a *bright pinkish red;* shorter, less reflexed bracts, and flower stalks which are more slender and slightly nodding, giving a *very open head* of flowers. Capsule twice the length of the calyx. 2n = 18.

DISTRIBUTION Central and eastern Caucasus (Ciscaucasus and Daghestan).

Moist shaded rocks in forested ravines; 300–900 (–?2200) m.

P. daraliaca is frequently confused with *P. frondosa*, and less commonly *P. algida*, in cultivation, but has quite different flowers from either; the leaves also differ markedly from those of *P. frondosa*. Although plants and seed are often offered under this name, the true plant is rarely seen. However, seed collected in the Caucasus by M. Davlianidze and M. Bokezia was grown in Zurich for the DNA study. Has also been collected recently by Vojtek Holubec. A close relative of *P. algida* and occurring in the same regions, but grows at much lower altitudes and quite distinct.

VARIATION

- Subsp. *daraliaca*. Flowers 10 mm or more in diameter; calyx 5 mm; leaves to 8 × 3 cm. Daryal ravine, east of Mt. Kasbek, north-central Caucasus, 300–900 m.
- Subsp. *farinifolia* (Rupr.) Smith & Fletcher (1943) (var. *farinifolia* (Rupr.) Kusn. (1901). Flowers 3–6 mm diameter; calyx 3 mm; leaves to 13 × 3 cm, usually more mealy beneath.

P. ossetica Kusn., Fl. Cauc. Crit. 4: 112 (1901). Has only been collected once from alpine meadows on Mt. Kariukhokh, Ossetia, Ciscaucasus. It seems to be close to *P. daraliaca*, but occurs at a much higher altitude, and is said to have rather large, very deeply dissected flowers of a luminous violet. Until it is better known its status must remain obscure.

Primula longiscapa Ledeb., Mem. Acad. Sci. St. Petersb. 5: 520 (1815)

P. farinosa L. var. *denudata* Koch (1837) p.p.
P. farinosa L. var. *longiscapa* (Ledeb.) Pax (1889)

P. altaica Lehm. (1817) non Turcz. (1856) p.p. = *P. serrata* nec Pax (1905) = *P. elatior*
P. intermedia Busch (1925) non Sims (1809) (= *P. serrata* Georgi) nec *P.* × *intermedia* Portenschl. (1814)

DESCRIPTION A close relative of *P. algida,* but occurring further east and always *lacking meal*, and with a *long and stout* stem to 30 cm in fruit bearing a rather dense, *many-flowered* inflorescence; bracts linear; capsule 2× the calyx. 2n = 18. Heterostylous. From Soviet Transylvania eastwards through western Siberia and the Altai to eastern Siberia and north-west Mongolia. Possibly also in the Pamir and Chitral. Shores of rivers and lakes, wet meadows and saline hollows in steppic areas. I am currently growing this species from seed collected from the Alma Ata south of Lake Baikal by John Grimshaw. It has proved perennial in an uncovered trough and has flowered for two seasons. (Fig. Halda: 252.)

Primula fistulosa Turkev., Fl. Ross. Asiat. 2: 23 (1923)

DESCRIPTION A close relative of *P. longiscapa*, likewise without meal, but easily distinguished by the ovate, saccate bracts, and the very robust, stout stem which is swollen at the nodes. Far eastern Siberia, Manchuria and north-east Mongolia, further east than *P. longiscapa*, but overlapping with *P. serrata*. Wet meadows and river valleys. (Fig. Halda: 246.)

Primula serrata Georgi, Bemerk. Reise Russ. Reichs 1: 200 (1775)

P. gigantea Jacq. (1778)
P. davurica Spreng. (1804)
P. exalata Lehm. (1884)
P. lepida Duby (1844)
P. undulata Fisch. (1824)
P. intermedia Sims (1809) non Busch (1925) = *P. longiscapa* Ledeb.
P. farinosa L. var. *denudata* Koch (1837) p.p.
P. farinosa L. var. *gymnophylla* Trautv. & Mey (1856)
P. farinosa var. *glabrata* Maak (1871)

DESCRIPTION A relative of *P. longiscapa* and *P. algida*, differing from the latter by the sharply, even spinosely toothed leaves, the calyx of only 3–4 mm, and the total lack of meal. The bracts are only 2–3 mm, and adhere to the flower stalk. East Siberia and northern Mongolia, mostly to the west of *P. fistulosa* and to the east of *P. longiscapa*. Wet meadows in the taiga. Probably responsible for some of the most easterly records of *P. farinosa* (see the discussion under that species). Usually known by its inappropriate synonym *P. gigantea* (this species is no larger than its relatives).

Primula pinnata M. Popov & Federov, Fl. URSS, 18: 725 (1952)

DESCRIPTION A close relative of *P. serrata*, but with leaves still more deeply cut, and very much smaller, to 8 cm with not more than 10 flowers per stem. Probably best regarded as a subspecies of *P. serrata*. Shores of Lake Baikal near Sarma; wet *Kobresia* flushes.

Section **Pulchella** (Smith & Fletcher) Richards (1993)

(Section Farinosae Pax subsection Pulchella Smith & Fletcher, Trans. Bot. Soc. Edinb. 61: 40 (1943) sin. diag. lat.).
(Section Nivales Pax sens. Smith & Forrest (1928) p. min. p.).
Type species *P. pulchella* Franchet.

DESCRIPTION Similar to section Aleuritia, but with leaves usually *long, narrow* and spear-shaped, commonly thickly cream to yellow-mealy below and dark green, shiny and *without meal* above, the entire to finely toothed margins often turned down at the margin. *Bracts* swollen to pouched at the base. *Flowers* rather few, often rather *large* and with *long stalks*, flat-faced, frequently *dark blue* or purple with a golden eye, less commonly pink or yellow, *exannulate*, or annulate, heterostylous in all species, usually with a long cylindrical corolla-tube 2–3× the calyx; pollen 3–4 *colporoidate*. *Capsule* usually *cylindrical,* 2–3× the calyx, dehiscing by short apical teeth and rather 'nivalid-like' in aspect. x = 8. Flowering May–June.

DISTRIBUTION Sinohimalaya, from Pakistan to Gansu. Chiefly plants of turfy rock ledges in alpine zones, frequently on limestone. Ecologically quite distinct from the Aleuritia which are typical of open spring-fed calcareous marls, and geographically quite distinct from the Aleuritia, replacing the Aleuritia in the Sinohimalaya, the two sections only overlapping in north-west Pakistan.

Primula pulchella was originally associated with the nivalids (section Crystallophlomis), and the spear-shaped leaves, relatively large mealy resting buds and capsule type are reminiscent of this section. However, the flowers, although exannulate, have more in common with those of the Aleuritia, and to a lesser extent those of the Yunnanensis.

As Smith and Fletcher admitted, *P. pulchella* is clearly closely related to a group of Himalayan species, *P. sharmae, P. jaffreyana, P. hazarica, P. assamica* and *P. flava* which have always been associated with 'section Farinosae' (Aleuritia). (*P. fernaldiana* and *P. fangii* also seem to belong here). However, this group fitted uneasily into the Aleuritia, morphologically, geographically and ecologically. Unfortunately, the chromosome number is unknown for any of these, but in common with *P. pulchella* they all have 3- or more commonly 4-colporoidate (or even 4-porate) pollen, a type not found in the main Aleuritia subsection.

Once this group of five Himalayan species is recognized as being related to *P. pulchella*, it can be seen that a number of other species of uncertain affinity can be readily associated with it. Foremost amongst these is the enigmatic *P. inayatii*. Bruun showed this species to have x = 8, and considered that it was only distantly related to the Aleuritia. Smith and Fletcher accordingly placed it in its own subsection within the Farinosae (Aleuritia). However, it easily falls within the *P. pulchella* alliance, differing only in its short globose capsule.

The concept that the *P. pulchella* alliance contains plants with x = 8 and colporoidate pollen allows the consideration of other mystery plants.

First are a set of five species, placed by Smith and Forrest (1928) in the 'Farinosae', but which Bruun showed to have x = 8, and informally termed the 'Stenocalyces'. However, an examination of the pollen and general morphology of these shows that this is a heterogenous group. *P. stenocalyx* itself has 4-colpor(oid)ate pollen, and morphologically seems to fall between *P. pulchella* and the Yunnanensis. I agree with Smith and Fletcher that it is close to *P. jaffreyana*, and it seems to be rather typical of the 'Pulchella'.

P. blandula is more problematic, being much more 'Farinosae-like' in aspect, although with purple flowers. However, it also has x = 8 and 3-colporoidate pollen, and ecologically resembles the Pulchella, where I am tentatively placing it.

To summarize, the Pulchella comprise a group of Sinohimalayan alpine species formerly placed in the 'Farinosae'. In common with the Yunnanensis they have x = 8 and 3- or 4-colporoidate pollen. They differ from the Yunnanensis, however, in leaf shape, by having flat-faced corolla limbs, subtubular calyces and usually pouched bracts. In these features, they more resemble the Aleuritia, which, however, have x = 9 and usually 3-syncolpate pollen, and differ by other features as listed in the description. The DNA shows that *P. pulchella* and *P. concinna* are in fact only distantly related to *P. yunnanensis*, being somewhat more closely allied to the *P. farinosa* group of the Aleuritia, from which they remain, nevertheless, very distinct.

CULTIVATION A number of species were briefly in cultivation towards the beginning of last century, and several Chinese species have become intermittently available in the 1990s. In general plants seem fairly easy to raise to flowering from seed in a year, but tend not to set seed or to persist and so are easily lost. Best grown in a pot, protected from excesses of moisture and cold in winter, and from hot dry conditions in summer.

No hybrids have been reported.

KEY TO SPECIES

1. Plant dwarf, cushion-forming, flowers pink, immersed in cushion .... *P. concinna*
1. Plant tufted, flowers exserted, usually blue, purple or yellow 2

2. Flowers yellow 3
2. Flowers blue or purple 4

3. Leaf-blades orbicular, deeply toothed .... *P. qinghaiensis*
3. Leaf-blade spoon-shaped, shallowly toothed .... *P. flava*
3. Leaf blade narrowly spear-shaped, crenately toothed .... *P. pulchella* ssp. *prattii*

4. Leaves very narrow, grass-like, rarely exceeding 1 cm in width, abundant .... *P. inayatii*
4. Leaves not grass-like, usually exceeding 1 cm in width, fewer 5

5. Calyx cylindrical, teeth blackish, sinuses white-mealy ('striped') .... *P. stenocalyx*
5. Calyx more or less uniform in colour 6

6. Stem usually exceeding 10 cm; flower-stalks usually exceeding calyx 7
6. Stem less than 10 cm; flower stalks shorter than calyx (except *P. hazarica*) 8

7. Leaves sharp, regularly toothed; flowers blue, tube 2× calyx .... *P. pulchella*
7. Leaves blunt, irregularly toothed; flowers mauve or purple, tube 2–3× calyx .... *P. jaffreyana*
7. Leaf tip rounded, regularly toothed; flowers blue-purple, tube 3× calyx .... *P. fernaldiana*
7. Leaf tip rounded, entire to crenate; flowers rose-pink, tube 2× calyx .... *P. fangii*

8. Calyx less than 5 mm; flowers purple, annulate .... *P. blandula*
8. Calyx more than 5 mm; flowers usually blue or pink, usually exannulate 9

9. Flowers stalks greatly exceeding calyx .... *P. hazarica*
9. Flower stalks usually shorter than calyx, at least in flower 10

10. Flowers blue (to purple) .... *P. sharmae*
10. Flowers mauve *11*

11. Chinese; corolla-tube about 1.5× calyx; stalks 6mm .... *P. pulchelloides*
11. Himalayan; corolla-tube scarcely exceeding calyx; stalks 4mm .... *P. assamica*

Primula pulchella Franchet, Bull. Soc. Bot. Fr. 35: 429 (1885)

P. stuartii Franchet (1885) non Wall.
P. prattii Helmsley (1893)
P. compsantha Balf. f. & Forrest (1915)
P. sulphurea Pax & Hoffm. (1921) non Craib = *P. gracilipes*

DESCRIPTION *Resting buds* large, acute, yellow-mealy, above ground. *Leaves* spreading, narrowly spear-shaped, crenate to shortly serrate, to 20 × 2 cm, thickly covered with yellow meal beneath, dark rather blue-green with paler veins above, the margins notably revolute. *Stems* equalling leaves, mealy, bearing 2–15 flowers on stalks to 2 cm in a lax umbel. *Bracts* linear, not saccate or swollen at base, about equalling calyx. *Calyx* cylindrical, 6–10 mm. *Flowers* deep blue with a yellow eye, or yellow, flat-faced, 15–20 mm in diameter, corolla-tube about 2× calyx. *Fruit* cylindrical, 2–3× calyx. Pollen (3)–4 colporoidate. (Fig. Halda: 267.) (Plate 57.)

DISTRIBUTION North-west Yunnan and south-west Sichuan, including well-known localities such as the Gan Ho Ba in the Yulong Shan, and the Zhongdian plataeau, extending into Tibet. Subsp. *prattii* occurs further north in Sichuan. Rather dry open grassy alpine meadows on limestone, 2000–4500 m, gregarious and often in large quantities.

CULTIVATION First introduced in 1908 and subsequently by Forrest, Ward and Rock, but had disappeared from cultivation by 1940. Introduced by Chengdu 1536 from 4200 m on the Balang Shan in about 1992, grown at the Royal Botanic Gardens Edinburgh in 1994 and appearing on the show-bench about then, but apparently did not persist. Surprisingly not collected by the CLD, KGB, ACE or SQAE expeditions which visited localities where this species is common. However, ARGS in 2000 made a collection from the Gan Ho Ba (935) while their 257 and 258 might have been this or the next species.

VARIATION

- Subsp. *prattii* (Helmsley) Halda (1992) (*P. prattii* Helmsley, J. Linn. Soc. Bot. 29: 314 (1893)). Flowers *yellow*, usually less robust. Especially in the mountains around Tatsienlu. Introduced by Forrest, flowering in 1920, but soon lost. Little understood and should perhaps be recognized at specific rank. Compare *P. flava*.

Primula pulchelloides Ward, Notes Roy. Bot. Gdn. Edinb. 9: 38 (1915)

DESCRIPTION Differs from *P. pulchella* as follows: leaf-blades shorter and relatively broader, to 8 × 2 cm, less acute and more spathulate, less thickly mealy. Stems to 8 cm, bearing up to 8 pinkish-lilac flowers to 14 mm in diameter; calyx to 7 mm; corolla-tube less than 2× calyx.

DISTRIBUTION Poorly understood, but from the southern edge of the Zhongdian plateau, Yunnan, north-east to Be Ta Hai and San Ba. Apparently the same taxon appears again in Gansu (Tao He valley and Kaba) and Qinghai, Zhiqin valley. Rather damp, mossy sites, roadside bluffs, etc., often partially shaded, 2600–3700 m.

This species has usually been treated as a synonym of *P. pulchella*, as in Richards (1993). However, I was able to see both typical *P. pulchella* and this taxon in several sites in 1995, and I was impressed by how distinct *P. pulchelloides* was. It has flowers of a quite different colour (this difference is lost in the herbarium), leaves of a different shape, and is smaller in most of its parts. It is also ecologically distinct, and seems to extend much further to the north than *P. pulchella*.

CULTIVATION Offered by Keith Lever in 1999 (source unknown). Flowered the following year and died without setting seed. A quite pretty little plant, but less than sensational.

Primula fernaldiana Smith, Trans. Bot. Soc. Edinb. 33: 115 (1941)

DESCRIPTION Another relative of *P. pulchella* with blue-purple flowers, differing by the longer corolla-tube (to 3× the calyx), shorter calyx (5–6 mm) and more spathulate leaves with a rounded apex. Only known from Muti Konka, east of Yalung, south-west Sichuan, 4000 m. Briefly in cultivation from Rock's seed in 1934.

Primula fangii Chen & Hu, Fl. Rep. Pop. Sin. 2: 294 (1990)

DESCRIPTION Close to *P. fernaldiana*, but distinguished by the long flower stalks (to 3 cm), the long barrel-shaped capsule (to 11 mm) and the rose-red flowers. Several subalpine localities in west Sichuan; 2700–3100 m.

Primula flava Maxim., Bull. Acad. St. Petersb. 27: 497 (1881)

P. citrina Balf. f. & Purdom (1915)

DESCRIPTION In many ways characteristic of the section, but flowers *yellow*, with a very long tube 3–4× the calyx, heterostylous. Leaves spoon-shaped, or the blade even orbicular, shallowly toothed. Pollen 3-colporoidate. West Gansu, north-west China and east Tibet; 'dry powdery calcareous silt in overhung grottos and sunless crevices of limestone cliffs, 2700–4500 m'. *P. citrina* was described from robust low-altitude plants which superficially resemble some species in section Crystallophlomis. Probably related to *P. pulchella* subsp. *prattii* which also has yellow flowers, but the latter has *yellow* (not cream) meal, narrower leaves and a longer calyx. Briefly in cultivation from 1914–16 from seed collected by Purdom and Farrer. Collected by SQAE 340 near Maya, Gansu in 2000 at 2900 m. (Fig. Halda: 247.)

Primula qinghaiensis Chen & Hu, Fl. Rep. Pop. Sin. 2: 294 (1990)

DESCRIPTION Closely related to *P. flava* and possibly conspecific, but more robust and with very deeply and jaggedly toothed orbicular leaf blades which have the shape of many Cortusoides species; flowers yellow. Qinghai (between Gansu and northern Tibet, one of the few primulas from this remote region), Nan Shan; damp shaded rocks, 3900–4300 m. (Fig. Halda: 256.)

Primula jaffreyana King, J. Asiatic Soc. Bengal 55: 229 (1886)

P. lhasaense Balf. f. & Smith (1915)
P. tayloriana Fletcher (1949)
P. knuthiana Pax (1905)

DESCRIPTION The irregularly toothed *narrowly oblong* leaves are white-mealy below and greyish-green above. A *leggy* plant with stems to 30 cm, long flower stalks (to 25 mm) and *annulate* flowers which are violet to *mauve-purple* and about 15 mm in diameter; the corolla-tube is at least 2× the somewhat bell-shaped calyx of about 6 mm. Pollen 3-colporoidate. 2n = 16. (Fig. Halda: 251.)

DISTRIBUTION Tibet, from the Chumbi valley northwards to Lhasa, and eastwards to the Tsangpo gorges and Pemakochung. Occurs again disjunct much further to the north in north-central China from central Sichuan northwards; one of the few primulas occurring in Shensi, Tai-pei Shan and Hua-ton Shan.

A plant of rather dry habitats, even when growing in predominantly wet zones. 'Dry evergreen oak forests, dry roadside banks, sandy or rubbly banks, grass covered rock faces in ravines', 2700–3000 m in N China, 3200–5300 m in the Himalyas.

When viewing material collected from Wolong in 1998, it became clear that plants referable to *P. knuthiana* were indistinguishable from the Himalayan *P. jaffreyana* of which abundant material was at that time being sent from south-east Tibet by the Cox Expeditions, the Miehe's and others.

The Himalayan *Primula tayloriana* is said to differ from *P. jaffreyana* by its even larger exannulate flowers, and in some ways is intermediate between *P. jaffreyana* and *P. sharmae*. It grows within the range of *P. jaffreyana* which was also well known to its collectors, Ludlow and Elliott. However, after a close and prolonged examination of many specimens in the herbarium I can find no reliable distinction between them, and I am reluctantly reducing *P. tayloriana* to synonymy.

For distinctions from *P. pulchella*, see under *P. sharmae*.

CULTIVATION Grown by Veitch in 1912 from Purdom's seed. Smith and Fletcher give no further account of it in cultivation, but apparently supplied a plant to Bruun in about 1930 for a chromosome count. Introduced by Ludlow and Sherriff in 1938, and as *P. tayloriana* in 1947, and still in cultivation in the 1950s. Plants collected by Templer in 1981 and exhibited under this name were *P. sharmae*. Introduced by Dr Miehe from Chimphu, Tibet, in 1998 and grown on by Brian Burrow. Seed collected by Pete Boardman was raised and offered by Keith Lever in 2000. Flowered for up to two years, but tended to be short-lived and not hugely exciting. Also encountered by Anne Chambers and others from the Tsari region in 1995 and 1997.

Primula sharmae Fletcher, Trans. Bot. Soc. Edinb. 33: 119 (1941)

DESCRIPTION *Leaves* white- or cream-mealy below, sharply and often regularly toothed to subentire, to 6 × 1.2 cm. *Stems* to 10 cm, shorter in flower, bearing 3–8 flowers on short stalks to 7 mm. *Calyx* 5–10 mm, with long narrow sepal-lobes, cut to well over half-way. *Corolla* deep blue to purple, heterostylous, *exannulate*, with a pale 'eye', somewhat funnel-shaped, up to 20 mm in diameter, the maroon tube 2–3× the calyx; corolla-lobes deeply notched. *Pollen* 3-colporoidate. *Capsule* equalling the calyx. Thrums completely self-sterile, pins not tested. (Fig. Halda: 258.) (Plate 56.)

DISTRIBUTION West and central Nepal. Alpine meadows, steep grassy banks and rock ledges, 2500–5000 m.

A fine species, closely related to *P. jaffreyana* and differing chiefly by the shorter flower stalks and exannulate flowers.

The Himalayan *P. jaffreyana* and *P. sharmae* are closely related to the Chinese *P. pulchella*, which has yellow meal and a capsule which exceeds the more bell-shaped calyx. However, in south-east Tibet, forms of *P. jaffreyana* occur which merge imperceptibly into *P. pulchella*.

CULTIVATION First introduced by Dhwoj in 1927. Often encountered in recent years within the Nepalese trekking districts and has been introduced on several occasions in the 1970s and 1980s. Occasionally has been offered. Grows well from seed, flowering in a year, but rarely persists for more than two flowering seasons. Requires winter protection if grown outside in a cool trough or raised bed; suitable for pot culture in a shady frame.

Primula assamica Fletcher, Trans. Bot. Soc. Edinb. 33: 107 (1941)

DESCRIPTION A dwarf relative of *P. sharmae*, with only 2–6 exannulate lilac, white-eyed flowers to 20 mm in diameter borne on short stalks to 4 mm. The corolla-tube scarcely exceeds the narrowly egg-shaped calyx of 7 mm, and teh suberect leaf-blades are bluntly lanceolate.

Orka La, Bhutan/Assam frontier, steep slopes and cliffs, 4000–4600 m. and elsewhere in east Bhutan.

Introduced as seed by the Miehes from east Bhutan and flowered by Brian Burrow in 2002.

Primula hazarica Duthie, Ann. Bot. Gdn. Calcutta 9: 49 (1901)

DESCRIPTION Another close relative of *P. sharmae* and *P. jaffreyana*, but with longer flower-stalks, pinker flowers and broader, more spoon-shaped leaves than the former; differing from the latter chiefly by the exannulate flowers and shortly toothed leaves. Pakistan and adjoining north Kashmir; Hazara, Kaghan and Siran valleys, Swat. Wet vertical cliffs, 3300–4300 m. Introduced by Ludlow and Sherriff in 1935, flowering after three years. Seems not to have been grown again until offered in the Scottish Rock Garden Club seed list in 1994. Seed germinated well, but grew on very slowly and I lost all the seedlings before they flowered.

Primula stenocalyx Maxim., Bull. Acad. St. Petersb. 27: 498 (1881)

P. loczii Kanitz (1891)
P. leptopoda Bur. & Franchet (1891)
P. cognata Duthie (1906)
P. biondiana Petitm. (1907)
P. dealbata Farrer (1915) inedit. non Engelm. (1863)
= *P. incana* nec Schwarz (1970) = *P. auriculata*
P. kanseana Pax & Hoffm. (1921)

DESCRIPTION Best distinguished by the *narrowly cylindrical striped* calyx, with dark, narrow but rounded teeth cut to over half-way, interspersed with white-mealy grooves. Larger forms can resemble *P. jaffreyana*, although with a different calyx, differing chiefly by the *broader, daisy*-shaped leaves which are scarcely toothed. Pollen 4–5 colporoidate. 2n = 16. (Photo: Bull. AGS 60: 60 (1992).) (Plates 15, 58.)

DISTRIBUTION Widespread in the mountains of northern China; Gansu, northern and central Sichuan and extending into north Tibet. 'Dry crumbling soil on warm sunny banks or on limestone rocks, 2700–4300 m.'.

'*P.* fortunae' (sic) of cultivation, a mysterious plant with rounded, heavily white-mealy leaves and blue flowers, might well be this. A supposedly tender species, it had been grown under this name at Edinburgh for many years, and was certainly still in cultivation in 1980.

VARIATION An extremely variable plant in both stature and meal, low-altitude forms being 15 cm and lacking meal, while high-altitude forms are heavily white-mealy and as small as 1 cm; however, both forms can occur together.

CULTIVATION Introduced by Wilson (1904), Farrer (1915), and also in cultivation in 1936, but not apparently persisting for long. *P. stenocalyx* was reintroduced in 1990 from the Wolong Shan (Cox 701) and proved an amenable and attractive little plant in cultivation, although short-lived. Collected by SQAE 174, 598 from Gansu and Sichuan. A collection from near Baima, Qinghai (856) is particularly interesting as it seems to be intermediate with *P. pulchelloides*.

Primula concinna Watt, J.Linn. Soc. 20: 5 (1882)

P. farinosa L. var. *concinna* (Watt) Pax (1905)

DESCRIPTION A very *dwarf* tufted to cushion-forming cream-mealy plant, with oblong, deeply crenate to prickly-toothed leaves about 1.5 × 0.7 cm, rather reminiscent of *P. allionii* in habit. Flowers pinkish or whitish, deeper pink towards the centre with a yellow eye, annulate, to 12 mm in diameter, corolla tube not exceeding the bowl-shaped mealy calyx, more or less immersed in the cushion. Flower-stalks of about 6 mm exceed the stem. (Plate 55.)

DISTRIBUTION East Nepal, Sikkim, west Bhutan and Chumbi, south Tibet. A high alpine from very open sites by moraines in the region of glaciers, often in the company of *P. caveana*. 4000–5700 m.

A totally distinct species which the recent DNA studies have placed close to *P. pulchella*. This has resolved considerable uncertainties as to the allegiances of this delightful species, placed by Richards (1993) with considerable misgivings in section Aleuritia, but also compared there with the 'Gemmifera' and the 'Souliei', whereas more recent experience had suggested it might be placed in the Minutissimae. The indication that it should be regarded as a condensed high-alpine relative of *P. pulchella* is geographically coherent and seems satisfactory at present, although we still need information as to the chromosome number and pollen type for this enigmatic plant. Nevertheless, one would not readily classify unidentified material of this species amongst the Pulchella. Superficially it seems more to resemble Minutissimae such as *P. stirtoniana* or *P. rubicunda*.

CULTIVATION First flowered from seed provided by Darjeeling collectors in 1912. Frequently encountered these days by trekkers in the Everest and Kanchenjunga regions. Reintroduced by George Smith in 1976 and by Ron McBeath in 2000–2001. Survived for a few years grown as a high alpine in alpine house conditions for a few specialist growers, but apparently difficult, probably intolerant of heat, and did not persist.

Primula inayatii Duthie, Ann. Bot. Gard. Calcutta 9: 49 (1901)

DESCRIPTION Mat-forming. *Leaves numerous, very narrow*, strap-shaped, to 20 × 3 cm, but not usually more than 0.8 cm wide, dark green and shiny above, brilliantly and thickly *golden-mealy* beneath, minutely serrulate. *Stems* to 13 cm, *reddish* and lacking meal, rather stout, bearing up to *40* flowers on rather untidy long and slender (to 20 mm) stalks giving a somewhat 'mop-headed' appearance; *bracts* to 12 mm, not pouched or thickened. *Calyx* cup-shaped, mealy about 5 mm. *Corolla* blue-purple with a golden eye, exannulate, heterostylous, flat-faced, to 16 mm in diameter, the tube 2× the calyx; *pollen* 3-colporoidate. *Capsule globose,* included within the short calyx. 2n = 16. Flowering June (April in cultivation). (Photo: Bull. AGS 47: 327.) (Plate 16.)

DISTRIBUTION Northern Pakistan, including the Gilgit and Hazara districts and around Uri, west Kashmir (scarce). In dripping water on cliffs, 800–1900 m.

A distinctive plant, closely related to no other, the golden-backed grass-like leaves giving it a very individual appearence. However, the chromosome number, pollen type and general structure make it clear that it belongs to this section, despite long arguments in earlier literature; only the capsule type is untypical of the Pulchella. Named for the discoverer Inayat Khan, a local collector.

CULTIVATION First introduced to Glasnevin from Kashmir, flowering in 1913. Despite an absence of evidence of later introductions, it was still sparsely in cultivation in the Royal Botanic Garden Edinburgh in the 1990s, but I have not heard of it in recent years (2002), As might be expected from a plant coming from such low altitudes, it is not hardy, but thrives in a cool shady glasshouse protected from frost, and kept almost dry in winter and watered copiously when in growth. In these conditions it is long-lived and occasionally seed is offered.

Primula blandula Smith, Notes Roy. Bot. Gdn. Edinb.15: 299 (1927)

DESCRIPTION A little-known species with a short bell-shaped calyx with narrow sharp sepal lobes cut to over half-way, pouched bracts, and with dentate leaves which are white-mealy below; flowers bright purple, 15 mm in diameter, annulate. Pollen 3-colporoidate. 2n = 16. Collected once by Ward in 1926 at Seinghku Wang, on the Assam/Tibet/Burma frontier; cliff ledges, gravelly, stony or turfy slopes on limestone or granite, 3700–4300 m. Said by Smith and Fletcher not to have been in cultivation, but they sent Bruun plants from the type gathering KW 6911, from which the chromosome count was made.

Section **Minutissimae** Pax,

Bot. Jahr. Syst. 10: 212 (1889)
(Section Tenellae Pax, loc. cit. p. max. p.)
(Section Bella Balf. f. (1913)).
Type species *P. minutissima* Jacq.

DESCRIPTION *Dwarf*, deciduous *mat- or cushion-*forming perennial plants, less commonly as single rosettes, rhizomatous or commonly *stoloniferous*, overwintering by small resting buds at ground level, often *mealy*, not hairy except sometimes in the mouth of the flower, with revolute vernation. Leaves *very small*, entire to (usually) toothed, often deeply so or even lacerate, rarely exceeding 1 cm, often oblong with a poorly marked stalk, often rugose. *Flowers* often *single* and stemless, or virtually stalkless and 1–3 together on a short stem; bracts small, not pouched or swollen at the base. *Calyx* small, cylindrical to bell-shaped, often angled. *Corolla* blue, violet, rose or rarely white, often with a broad white to yellow eye, commonly annulate and flat-faced, the narrow cylindrical tubes usually exceeding the calyx and sometimes filled with hairs, heterostylous or homostylous, the corolla-lobes *bifid*; *pollen* 3–4 colporoidate in two species (but 3-syncolpate in *P. minutissima*). *Capsule* narrowly cylindrical, dehiscing by longitudinal valves, seeds to 1 mm, angular, brownish, covered in small blisters. 2n = 22 (*P. reptans* only). Apparently fully self-sterile when heterostylous. Flowering June–August, during the monsoon.

DISTRIBUTION Sinohimalaya, from Pakistan and Kashmir through the whole Himalayan range to Burma, Yunnan and Sichuan; most diverse in the eastern Himalaya. Typically high alpines from moist mossy pockets in stony barrens, chiefly in rather dry rain-shadow zones, rarely dropping below 4000 m.

With 24 species recognized here, the Minutissimae is one of the larger sections of Primula, but most of the species are very little known. It is formed by a mixed collection of very dwarf high alpines, which have become morphologically reduced to the extent that they present relatively few diagnostic characters. Consequently, the section probably represents a number of evolutionary lines which have adapted to this extreme habitat convergently, rather than a natural grouping. This concept tends to be confirmed by the DNA of the two species tested so far (*P. reptans* and *P. minutissima*). These are associated with the Aleuritia subgenus clade, but are not closely related to one another, or to any other species, although *P. minutissima* does link weakly to the Denticulata, Muscarioides and Soldanelloides.

Within the Minutissimae, species seem to be related to several different sections, and may represent high alpine developments of each of these. For instance, *P. rimicola, P. rhodochroa* and *P. walshii* with scabrid leaves and usually single rosettes may be related to the Yunnanensis.
P. tenella and *P. moschophora* may be related to the Soldanelloides, especially to *P. jigmediana*, and to a lesser extent with *P. sappharina* and *P. soldanelloides* itself. *P. triloba* links to the Dryadifolia, and the aspect presented by the relatives of *P. bella* and *P. primulina* with 'pom-pom' –filled corolla-tubes suggests that they may also be Dryadifolia relatives, although there is as yet no evidence to confirm this.

Nevertheless, there is a related group of seven species, centred around *P. stirtoniana,* and also including *P. waddellii, P. tenuiloba, P. spathulifolia, P. annulata, P. rubicunda* and *P. candicans,* which takes a central, 'typical' position within the section. These are cushion-forming plants. To this 'core', the western species *P. reptans,* and the small-flowered homostylous cushions *P. muscoides, P. praetermissa* and *P. subularia*, take a more peripheral stance. Some species, centred around *P. minutissima* itself and probably including the *P. stirtoniana* group may have been derived from the Denticulata, as is suggested by both the DNA and syncolpate pollen of *P. minutissima,* but in general the relationships of most species are still far from certain. As yet we only know the chromosome count of one species, and the pollen type of only three.

There is a most informative set of comparative drawings of the Minutissimae in Halda: 297.

CULTIVATION Of the 24 species placed here, at least ten species have been introduced into cultivation, but only *P. reptans, P. minutissima* and *P. primulina* have proved to be at all permanent. The greatest successes have been achieved in the eastern Scottish Highlands, particularly at Jack Drake's, and at Schachen Botanical Garden in the Alps, suggesting that cool summers and a prolonged winter rest under snow are necessary to ensure survival. Plants tend to be shallow-rooted, and are thus very susceptible to drying out, and to disturbance by birds, etc; at the same time they rot easily, and require a very free-draining compost, and a dryish winter rest. As single clones are nearly always grown, seed is rarely set, although vegetative propagation is in most cases very easy. Plants seem to exhaust nutrient very quickly, and travel in search of new resource, after the manner of many dwarf campanulas. This makes them difficult to manage in pots.

For most growers, the best recipe is probably to grow plants in a gritty compost in a plastic pot top-dressed with fragments of coal (see *P. reptans*), plunged in a cool, north-facing frame, kept almost dry in winter, but frequently misted with an automatic system in summer. Plants should be repotted at least annually. Other problems are compounded by the susceptibility of these plants to aphids.

No hybrids have been reported.

KEY TO SPECIES

1. Tube of flower filled with hairs, often forming a distinctive 'pom-pom' at the mouth 2
1. Corolla-tube hairless or sparsely hairy 9

2. Hairy 'pom-pom' at mouth of flower purple in colour .... *P. nanobella*
2. 'Pom-pom' white or yellow in colour, or corolla-tube hairs less dense 3

3. Hairs in corolla-tube diffuse, not forming an impenetrable 'pom-pom' in mouth 4
3. Hairs in corolla-tube forming a dense impenetrable 'pom-pom' in mouth 7

4. Corolla-lobes very narrow, Y-shaped, outline skeletal 5
4. Corolla-lobes shallowly bifid, but outline not skeletal or Y-shaped 6

5. Corolla pink; leaves crenate .... *P. waddellii*
5. Corolla pale bluish; leaves dissected to mid-rib .... *P. tenuiloba*

6. Leaves with 3 lobes, stolons absent .... *P. triloba*
6. Leaves with (5) 7–11 lobes (3–5 each side), stolons often present .... *P. tenella*

7. Stolons ('runners') usually present; leaves white-mealy below .... *P. moschophora*
7. Stolons absent; meal, if present below leaf, yellowish 8

8. Yellow meal below leaves, or missing, leaves smooth; flowers 1–3, exceeding 15 mm in diameter .... *P. bella*
8. Leaves not mealy, leaves rough; flowers 2–6, less than 12 mm in diameter .... *P. primulina*

9. Flowers not exceeding 9 mm in diameter, tube-shaped, homostylous 10
9. Flowers exceeding 9 mm in diameter, usually flat-faced, heterostylous 11

10. Flowers purple; leaves linear, acute, entire .... *P. subularia*
10. Flowers blue-purple; leaves mostly entire, rounded at tip .... *P. praetermissa*
10. Flowers pale pink; leaves rounded, finely toothed to dissected .... *P. muscoides*
10. Flowers violet; leaves rounded with coarse teeth .... *P. annulata*

11. Rosettes single or few; flowers to 20 mm in diameter, calyx exceeding 6 mm 12
11. Rosettes single to many, usually mat or cushion-forming, flowers not exceeding 15 mm in diameter, calyx not exceeding 6 mm 13

12. Leaves entire or nearly so; flowers solitary, basal .... *P. spathulifolia*
12. Leaves toothed; flowers 1–2 on stem with bracts .... *P. candicans*

13. Leaves more than 4× as long as wide, acute .... *P. minutissima*
13. Leaves less than 4× as long as wide 14

14. Flowers bright pink, less than 10 mm in diameter; leaves rough to touch .... *P. walshii*
14. Flowers usually more than 10 mm in diameter; leaves smooth 15

15. Rosettes solitary or forming small clumps; leaves mealy, at least beneath 16
15. Mat or cushion-forming; leaves without meal 17

16. Leaves sharp, saw-edged (to entire), meal white .... *P. rhodochroa*
16. Leaves rounded, spoon-shaped, meal yellow .... *P. rimicola*

17. Flowers violet, or bluish with a white eye 18
17. Flowers carmine to red-purple, eye inconspicuous 19

18. Flowers violet; leaves not exceeding 1 cm ......*P. reptans*
18. Flowers (rather pale) blue; leaves 1–3 cm ......*P. stirtoniana*

19. Calyx 3–4 mm, cut to less than half ......*P. glandulifera*
19. Calyx 5 mm, cut to more than half ......*P. rubicunda*

Primula minutissima Jacq., Mem. Soc. Phys. D'Hist. Nat. Genev. 10: 1 (1843)

P. saundersiana Royle ex Hook. f. (1882)
P. stracheyi Hook. f. (1879) p.p.
P. heydei Watt (1882)

DESCRIPTION A *mat*-forming cream-*mealy* plant, forming both rhizomes and short stolons. *Leaves* spear-shaped, narrow, acute, to 10 × 2 mm, with rather short, sharp regularly spaced teeth. *Stem* absent, very short or ('P. heydei') elongating in fruit, bearing 1–3 stemless flowers. *Calyx* tubular, to 3 mm. *Corolla* pink to purple with a yellow eye, exannulate, to 12 mm in diameter. *Pollen* 3–4 colporoidate. *Capsule* equalling the corolla. Flowers April in cultivation. (Photo: Bull. AGS 50: 223.) (Plate 60.)

DISTRIBUTION The Tibetan borderland districts of Pakistan and north-west India; Zanskar, Suru, Rupshu and Baltistan. Occurs as far south as the Rohtang Pass, where, unlike *P. reptans*, it is very scarce, and then increasingly common northwards around the Baralacha La (Rupshu) and Pensi La and around Padam (Zanskar).

Mossy and turfy ledges and north-facing open grassland in areas cool and misty in summer, but with little snow cover and dry for much of the year, including banks of irrigation channels, 3500–5000 m.

CULTIVATION In cultivation in 1886. In recent years, *P. minutissima* was in cultivation, apparently continuously, from at least 1978 until 1995, but I have not seen it recently (2002). These introductions apparently originate from visits by Barry Starling to the Rohtang Pass, and possibly also by David Riley to the Nanda Dewi in that year. Margaret and Henry Taylor and parties have also frequently visited it on the Rohtang in the 1990s. I found that it grew quite well during cool damp summer weather, but disliked heat, and was very difficult to coax into growth in the spring.

However, some growers seemed to manage it quite successfully, although it rarely flowered freely. Chadwell 934 (1991) was growing well at Cluny in 1992 and CC 1949 from Spiti was dispersed by Chadwell in 1996.

Primula glandulifera Balf. f. & Smith, Notes Roy. Bot. Gdn. Edinb. 9: 20 (1915–16)

DESCRIPTION Differs from *P. minutissima* in lacking meal, being covered with short glands, and with broader elliptical leaves to 2 cm; the cup-shaped calyx is 5 mm, and up to 4 flowers are borne together. Collected by Duthie from above the village of Napalcha, Kutti valley, Byans, and above Dudh-pani, Kumaon, 4300 m. Recently recorded from west Nepal. (Fig. Halda: 290.)

Primula stirtoniana Watt, J. Linn. Soc. 20: 15 (1882)

DESCRIPTION Another *non*-mealy plant but with *spoon*-shaped leaves, only some of which tend to be lobed, often forming large *cushion*-like clumps. Flowers 1–5, almost without stalks, lavender blue to 'grape purple' with a white eye, to 15 mm in diameter, the corolla-lobe divisions rounded; corolla *exannulate*, glabrous; calyx bell-shaped, to 7 mm. (Photo: 'A Quest of Flowers' p.52. Fig. Halda: 294.) (Plate 18, Fig. 27.)

Fig 27. *P. stirtoniana*

DISTRIBUTION From Annapurna, central Nepal, to Sikkim, south-west Tibet and to central Bhutan, where it is locally abundant.

'Sheer cliff faces' and mossy rock ledges 4200–4700 m.

CULTIVATION Ludlow and Sherriff attempted an introduction in 1934, apparently unsuccessfully. Introduced from Annapurna by Ron McBeath in 1983. Flowered for a number of growers, but short-lived, and had apparently disappeared by 1991.

Primula rubicunda Fletcher, Trans. Bot. Soc. Edinb. 35: 192 (1949)

DESCRIPTION Forms a geographical and morphological link between *P. stirtoniana* and *P. annulata,* forming a stem and with annulate flowers like the latter, but with much larger pinkish-red heterostylous flowers about 15 mm in diameter borne 1–3 per stem. Leaf-blades orbicular, finely toothed. Described from Nambu La, within the Tsangpo bend, south-east Tibet, rock-faces and earth banks, 4500 m. Photographed by Anne Chambers on the nearby Zo La in 1997.

Primula annulata Balf. f. & Ward, Notes Roy. Bot. Gdn. Edinb. 9: 6 (1915)

DESCRIPTION Similar to *P. stirtoniana,* but the solitary violet homostylous flowers of only 8 mm in diameter are borne on a short stem, and have a prominent lobed annulus. Yunnan, border with Tibet, a limestone peak near Dechen, 4700 m. (Fig. Halda: 289.)

Primula waddellii Balf. f. & Smith, Notes Roy. Bot. Gdn. Edinb. 9: 56 (1915)

DESCRIPTION Effectively without meal, *cushion-forming* but differing from *P. stirtoniana* and *P. tenuiloba* by the *thick* spoon-shaped *crenate* leaves, the calyx to 5 mm and by the corolla-tube containing *cottony hairs.* The reddish-purple corolla lobes are much narrower and more spaced at the base than in *P. stirtoniana,* giving a skeletal flower with the appearence of *P. minima.* (Photo 'A Quest of Flowers' p.316. Fig. Halda: 296.) North-west and central Bhutan and neighbouring south Tibet, peaty turf and rock cracks, 4000–5000 m.

Primula tenuiloba (Hook. f.) Pax, Bot. Jahrb. 10: 204 (1889)

P. muscoides Hook. f. var. *tenuiloba* Hook. f. (1882)
P. indobella Balf. f. & Smith (1915)

DESCRIPTION Similar to *P. waddellii,* with the same skeletal flower shape and sometimes forming cushions, but with *blue-violet* or white flowers which have scattered long white hairs *all over* although concentrated at the mouth, and by the leaves which are dissected to the mid-rib. Central Nepal to Sikkim, west and central Bhutan and south-east Tibet, east to Tsari. Rocky hillsides and moss-covered boulders, 4100–5400 m, this being one of the highest occurring of all primulas. (Photo: Fls. Himalaya (suppl.) fig. 313; Halda: 295.) (Plate 61.)

Primula spathulifolia Craib, J. Roy. Hort. Soc. 39: 190 (1913)

P. minutissima Jacq. var. *spathulata* Hook. f. (1882)
P. melichlora Balf. f. & Smith (1915)

DESCRIPTION Rosettes usually solitary or in small clumps, mealy, and with the leaves oblong, nearly entire; flowers stemless, the stalks to 10 mm, flowers glabrous, violet-purple with a white or yellow eye, to 20 mm in diameter; calyx 5–7 mm. East Nepal and east Sikkim in the Lachung Valley region, 3000–4300 m. Collected by George Smith and briefly in cultivation in the late 1970s, and again by EMAK in 1991 (flowered June 1992). Somewhat resembles a dwarf *P. scotica.* (Plate 62.)

Primula candicans Smith, Trans. Bot. Soc. Edinb. 35: 190 (1949)

DESCRIPTION A heavily cream-mealy relative of *P. spathulifolia,* but leaves with bigger teeth and bearing a short 1–2 flowered stem like *P. annulata* and *P. rubicunda,* the calyx to 8 mm, and the violet-mauve, white-eyed exannulate heterostylous flower to 20 mm in diameter. Despite comments by Smith, possibly not distinct from *P. spathulifolia,* differing chiefly by the flower(s) borne on a stem. Only known from the Sobhe La, Pome, south-east Tibet, abundant on rock-faces at 3850 m. (Fig. Halda: 289.)

Primula reptans Hook. f., J. Linn. Soc. 20: 14 (1882)

P. stracheyi Hook. f. p.p.

DESCRIPTION A *minute, creeping*, almost moss-like plant, rooting all along the stems and rapidly covering the ground by relatively stout at or below-ground *stolons*; leaf-blades rounded, *tiny*, to 1 cm but usually less, deeply *incised* with rounded lobules, bright green, lacking meal. *Stem* missing, or to 3 mm, bearing a single flower, stalk 3 mm, both usually slightly white-mealy; *calyx* 3 mm, green, cup-shaped. *Corolla* brilliant violet-purple to midnight blue with a white eye, relatively huge, to 15 mm in diameter, the exannulate eye and throat sparsely hairy. Pollen 3–4 colporoidate. 2n = 22. Flowers June–July in cultivation. (Photo Bull. AGS 56: 77.) (Plate 18.)

DISTRIBUTION Widespread in the North-west Himalaya, from Pakistan (Hazara), through Kashmir, north-west India (Kumaon, Simla) to west-central Nepal. Common on the Rohtang Pass where most people have encountered it in recent years.

Amongst moss on rocks and other steep places in damp sheltered localities in relatively dry zones, usually where the snow lies longest, 4000–5000 m.

This relatively familiar species is quite unmistakable. The flowers are reminiscent of *P. juliae*, although rather more blue and even more intense in tone. They appear to have nothing to do with the minute mats of dissected apple-green foliage.

CULTIVATION First introduced by P.N. Kohli as 'broad masses' (i.e. vegetatively) through the Kashmir Forest Department on behalf of the Maharajah of Kashmir and sent to the London Parks Department as a gift to the King in December 1927. Later collected on behalf of Sherriff by Tsongpen Lepcha from the Baspa valley in 1939, and it is probably this collection which survives today. Seed was later collected by Chadwell in Kashmir in 1985 (CC & MR 129). This is an extremely tricky species which has only remained in cultivation through its extreme propensity for vegetative propagation, and the ability of a few gardens to grow it well. It is extremely shallow-rooted, and unless continuously humid conditions are provided when in growth, it rapidly dies. Equally, a less than perfectly drained compost causes it to rot, and it must be kept on the dry side in winter. It rapidly runs out of resource, and requires repotting frequently, at least annually. Even so, it is difficult to produce a plant in a pot without a 'hole' in it. It is occasionally offered, and is well worth every care and attention.

At the Bavarian alpine garden at Schachen, it was observed that it grew best where coal fragments had been spilt, and some growers successfully top-dress it with fragments of coal. These may reduce the frequency of fungal attack, and certainly reduce the likelihood of this tiny plant being submerged by mosses and liverworts.

We grew it successfully for some time in a plastic pot stood in a mist propagation area, but although it was removed in winter we tended to lose it during this season. One grower grows it successfully in a plastic greenhouse, where it is frequently very hot, but high levels of humidity are invariably maintained. Warm spells during winter tend to bring it into growth with disastrous consequences, and gardens which have succeeded with this beautiful plant over a long period have reliably cold winters with frequent snow-lie. It rarely if ever sets seed, perhaps because only a pin clone is usually grown, but it is so easily propagated that this is unimportant. However, Margaret and Henry Taylor introduced a thrum strain to accompany the pin in about 1995, and this caused seed to set. Chadwell notes that in the wild, seed has rarely matured in the snow-hollows it tends to frequent when snow reappears in the autumn, so seed capsules may overwinter. **AM** 1981.

Primula muscoides Hook. f., J. Linn. Soc. 20: 15 (1882)

DESCRIPTION Somewhat similar to *P. reptans*, but tending to form 'dense cushions of pallid moss-green foliage sparsely dotted with *minute, lilac-pink* flowers', these being *homostylous* and *tube-shaped*, and sometimes violet or white; has yellow-mealy flower-stalks and sharp leaf-lobes. Central Nepal (Langtang) and Sikkim to Bhutan and south-east Tibet east to Pachakshiri. Amongst clumps of moss on scree, 4200–5300 m. This tiny plant is presumably self-fertile. In the wild on the top of the Goecha La, Sikkim, it was likened to *Dionysia curviflora*. Briefly in cultivation from George Smith's introduction in the late 1970s. A second attempted introduction (AGSES 612) in 1983 seems not to have yielded any plants. Recollected again in 1991 (EMAK, 930). (Photo: Fls.Himalaya (suppl.), fig.305. Fig. Halda: 291.) (Plate 63.)

Primula subularia Smith, Notes Roy. Bot. Gdn. Edinb. 19: 204 (1937)

DESCRIPTION A mat-forming non-mealy plant probably related to *P. muscoides* but distinguished by its *linear entire* leaves with *sharp* ends; flowers solitary, rose-purple, exannulate, homostylous, to 8 mm in diameter. Endemic to the Lo La and the nearby Tsari Sama, south-east Tibet, where *P. rhodochroa* v. *geraldinae* is also found, on very wet mossy boulders, 4500–4800 m. (Fig. Halda: 294.)

Primula praetermissa Smith, Trans. Bot. Soc. Edinb. 33: 117 (1941)

DESCRIPTION Very close to *P. subularia*, but the *entire* leaves are broader and blunt and the homostylous blue-purple flowers are *tube-shaped*, only 5 mm in diameter. Lusha La, above Tsela, Pemako, south-east Tibet, in a very wet zone, growing amongst *P. genestieriana*. Sodden gravelly soil beside snow-fed streams. An insignificant plant, not noticed by Ludlow who collected it accidentally. Grows near to its much more spectacular relative *P. rhodochroa*.

Primula rimicola Smith, Trans. Bot. Soc. Edinb. 33: 118 (1941)

DESCRIPTION Not cushion-forming, but with solitary rosettes. Links with *P. clutterbuckii* in section Yunnanensis, with similar *membranous* spoon-shaped leaves to 3 cm, but not stoloniferous and leaves less jaggedly toothed, thickly yellow-*mealy* beneath, and with solitary purplish-pink flat-faced exannulate flowers with a white to yellow eye to 15 mm in diameter borne on a very short, yellow-mealy stem; calyx cup-shaped, 6–7 mm.

Only known from the very rich Kashong La, south of Tsari, in a very wet zone of south-east Tibet, sheltered crevices in cliffs near the lake at 5000 m.

Coming from a very wet region, *P. rimicola* is, like its relative *P. rhodochroa*, ecologically as well as morphologically unusual for the Minutissimae, but the flat-faced flowers argue against a relationship with the Yunnanensis, within which, however, it might be better placed.

Primula rhodochroa Smith, Notes Roy. Bot. Gdn. Edinb. 15: 75 (1926)

DESCRIPTION Forms individuals or small clumps of little rather *narrow*, acute and usually *serrate* to entire-leaved heavily white-mealy rosettes from which arise very short *mealy* stems bearing 1–4 usually *disproportionately large* purplish-pink, cherry red or white annulate flowers with an orange eye, to 15 mm in diameter. Probably related to *P. rimicola*, but with different leaves and annulate flowers. South-east Tibet in the wet Tsari and Pachakshiri districts; wet moss on boulders or rock faces, 4000–5000 m. (Fig. Halda: 257.) (Plate 97.)

- Var. *geraldinae* (Smith) Chen & Hu (1990) (*P. geraldinae* Smith, Trans. Bot. Soc. Edinb. 33: 116 (1941). Very close to *P. rhodochroa*, but with more or less entire, yellow-mealy leaves and larger, lilac to wine-red flowers, to 20 mm in diameter, larger than the rosette. Originally known from the two very rich and wet neighbouring passes in the Pachakshiri, south-east Tibet, the Lo La and Chubumbu La, where it accompanies several other spectacular endemics such as its relative *P. subularia*, *P. chionogenes*, *P. laeta* and *P. elizabethae*. In 1997 photographed by Anne Chambers on the neighbouring Poda La. Wet moss on almost inaccessible cliff faces, 3800–4600 m.
- Var. *meiotera* Smith & Fletcher, J. Linn. Soc. Bot. 52: 339 (1942). Flowers small, bluish, not exceeding 6 mm in diameter.

Primula walshii Craib, J. Roy. Hort. Soc. 39: 187 (1913)

P. petrocharis Pax & Hoffm. (1920)
P. hsiungiana Fang (1956)

DESCRIPTION With solitary rosettes, but lacking meal, and with scabrid leaves, stems and calyces, which are otherwise typical of some Yunnanensis. This little plant with its rose-pink flat-faced flowers not much more than 8 mm in diameter and short stems (to 2 cm) has the aspect of the Oreophlomis *P. warshenewskiana* or the Armerina *P. pumilio*, with which it grows in Chumbi, but the scabridity, tough oblong leaves and exannulate flowers suggest otherwise. Calyx tubular, to 5 mm. (Fig. Halda: 296.)

DISTRIBUTION Sikkim on the Goecha La, Bhutan, neighbouring Chumbi in south Tibet. Found on most of the high dry passes on the road east from Lhasa to south-east Tibet, e.g. Yarto Tra La and Cha La, and through to Si-kang, west Sichuan, dry sparsely vegetated slopes, 4000–5000 m.

Introduced from China in 1936 by Harry Smith, but not persisting. The introduction from Sikkim in 1983 (AGSES 611) seemed not to yield any seedlings.

P. walshii rests uneasily in the Minutissimae, but until we have more information on its chromosomes and pollen, it is perhaps best left here. Its synonym *P. hsiungiana* was originally placed in section Glabra.

Primula tenella King ex Hook. f., Fl. British India 3: 492 (1882)

P. flagellaris Smith (1913)

DESCRIPTION Forms loose white-*mealy* mats of rosettes with small (to 1.5 cm) obovate to spoon-shaped leaves with 3–5 large triangular teeth each side; in some forms markedly *stoloniferous* in late summer, the strawberry-like runners forming small rooting rosettes at the tip. Flowers 1–(2) on a short mealy stem, with or without bracts. Calyx broadly tubular, to 8 mm. Corolla flat-faced, annulate, to 25 mm in diameter and so disproportionately *huge*, blue-violet with a large white eye, the tube finely hairy inside, heterostylous. (Photo: A Quest of Flowers: 134, Halda: 295.)

DISTRIBUTION North-east Sikkim, Chumbi, south Tibet, and west Bhutan, to 90° E. Mossy cliff faces and cracks in rocks, 4000–5000 m.

Unlike many of its relatives, does not form cushions, although some forms spread by spectacular spidery runners. In many ways, links with the relatives of *P. bella*, although with a less hairy throat, and like them in some ways intermediate with small members of section Soldanelloides.

VARIATION

- Var. *flagellaris* (Smith) Richards (1993). (*P. flagellaris* Smith, Rec. Bot. Surv. India 4: 219 (1913). Strongly stoloniferous, bracts usually absent. Fig. Halda: 290. This variety was maintained at specific rank by Smith & Fletcher (1942). They state that *P. flagellaris* is a 'very close ally', and 'closely linked in general aspect' to *P. tenella*; noting that the only important distingishing character is the stolons in the former. However, they also state that *P. tenella* can produce short stolons. Introduced as *P. flagellaris* by Ludlow and Sherriff (3052) in 1939, but did not persist. However, stated by Halda (1992) to be 'again in cultivation'.

Primula moschophora Balf. f. & Forrest, Notes Roy. Bot. Gdn. Edinb. 9: 186 (1916)

P. bella Franchet subsp. *moschophora* Smith & Forrest (1928)

DESCRIPTION Very similar to *P. tenella*, and similarly with stoloniferous and non-stolon-forming variants, but approaching *P. primulina* and *P. bella* with its white pom-pom filling the corolla-tube, and similarly with a small pair of bracts. In effect, *P. bella* with runners, but white-mealy. Both sides of the Yunnan/Burma border. Moist stony pasture at 3700 m.

Primula primulina (Sprengel) Hara, J. Jap. Bot. 37: 99 (1962)

Androsace primulina Sprengel (1827)
P. pusilla Wall. (1824) non Goldie (1822) = *P. mistassinica* Michx.
P. humilis Steudel (1841) non Pax & Hoffm. = *P. brevis* Richards

DESCRIPTION Rosettes usually solitary, or a few together in a small tuft, very shallowly rooted; leaves scabrid, suberect, *non-mealy*, rather pale green and slightly rugose, very narrowly oblanceolate to broadly and bluntly linear, with regular, even, crowded coarse teeth, to 3 × 0.5 cm. *Stem* slender, slightly mealy, to 8 cm, bearing a pair of bracts and with 2–4 stalkless flowers. *Calyx* bell-shaped, to 4 mm. *Corolla* lilac-blue to pinky-violet, usually with a white eye and a very *conspicuous 'pompom' of cottony white hairs in the throat*, heterostylous, flat-faced, to 12 mm diameter, the corolla-lobes deeply bifid. (Photo: Bull. AGS 52: 246. Fig. Halda: 288.) (Plate 64.)

DISTRIBUTION From central Nepal (Langtang, where it is locally abundant) eastwards through Sikkim to east Bhutan and just into Tibet, east to Tsona, 92° E. There is a single record from Kumaon. Common and widespread, probably the commonest member of the section.

Damp shaded rocky crevices, under boulders, etc., usually in moss, 4000–5000 m.

Despite its wide range, *P. primulina* is a remarkably invariable species. It takes a central position amongst the relatives of *P. bella*, which have at times been given sectional and subsectional rank. These plants differ from most other members of section Minutissimae in being rather larger (although still very small) with a more marked stem, and by lacking obvious means of vegetative reproduction, so that they do not form large mats or cushions. As a result they can look superficially like small members of section Soldanelloides to which they may well be related.

Nevertheless, it is difficult to treat the 'Bella' as a section or subsection separate from the Minutissimae, as *P. tenella* and *P. moschophora* form obvious intermediates between the two groups. The hairy corolla throat of the Bella is also seen in some more typical Minutissimae such as *P. reptans*, and not all typical Minutissimae invariably form large mats or cushions.

CULTIVATION First introduced in 1886. Has been intermittently in cultivation ever since. Unlike most members of this large section, *P. primulina* is frequently met with on the 'trekking trails' of Nepal and Sikkim and there have been several introductions, for instance by AGSES 432 in Sikkim (1983) and KEKE 653 in 1990. Material from Gosainkund collected by Alastair McKelvie (CC & McK 534) flowered for several growers, and collected again by Chadwell (CC 2687) from east Nepal. Ron McBeath also collected seed in east Nepal in 2000 and 2001.

Most introductions are short-lived, flowering well for two seasons in a shady trough covered in winter, or in a pan plunged in a shady frame, kept wet in summer and almost dry in winter. Seed is rarely set, although success has been achieved by poking a bristle into the narrow tube through the pom-pom at the throat. Occasionally offered, especially by Inshriach who have perhaps achieved the greatest success with this pretty and delicate little species. Although relatively easy to grow, it readily dries out and lacks the propensity for vegetative propagation of its relatives. In cold climates, the flowers tend to be frosted.

Primula occlusa Smith, Trans. Bot. Soc. Edinb. 33: 263 (1942)

DESCRIPTION Very close to *P. primulina*, but with more rounded, serrate leaf-blades and usually single long-tubed flowers to 15 mm in diameter. South-east Tibet; Chera La, Mago (near the Bhutan border at 92° E), the nearby Orka La, and the Le La, Tsari. Grassy ledges or banks, about 5000 m. Seed collected in 1934 did not apparently thrive.

Primula bella Franchet, Bull. Soc. Bot. Fr. 32: 268 (1885)

DESCRIPTION The Chinese and east Tibetan counterpart of *P. primulina*, similarly widespread and with the same *white* pom-pom in the flower, but very variable, with or without *yellow meal*, and varying markedly in size, number of flowers and stem length, but generally with more *deeply incised* and smoother leaves and fewer *larger* flowers, at least 20 mm in diameter. (Figs. Halda: 286.)

DISTRIBUTION Widespread in western Yunnan, south-west Sichuan, upper Burma and across the Yunnan and Sichuan borders into Tibet.

Rock faces and damp shaded corners amongst moss, often near streams, mountain summits, bare patches of sandy soil, snowy depressions and peaty soil on limestone or granite. 4000–5300 m.

VARIATION

- Subsp. *bella*. Yellow-mealy with a long stem, spear-shaped leaves and narrow bracts. Throughout much of the range; well-known on the Cang Shan near Dali.
- Subsp. *cyclostegia* (Hand.-Mazz.) Smith & Forrest, Notes Roy. Bot. Gdn. Edinb. 16: 15 (1928) (*P. cyclostegia* Hand.-Mazz. (1920)). Robust mealy plants with orbicular bracts and leaf-blades. Zhongdian plateau, Yunnan.
- Subsp. *sciophila* (Balf. f. & Ward) Smith & Forrest loc. cit. (*P. sciophila* Balf. f. & Ward (1915)). One-flowered mealy plants with narrow sepal-lobes and orbicular, shallowly toothed leaves. Upper Burma.
- Subsp. *bonatiana* (Petitm.) Smith loc. cit. (*P. bonatiana* Petitm. (1907); *P. stragulata* Balf. f. & Forrest (1920)). A non-mealy form with a short stem and long corolla-tube. South-east Tibet on the Yunnan border. Probably collected by CLD 716.
- Subsp. *coryphaea* (Balf. f. & Ward) Smith & Forrest loc. cit. (*P. coryphaea* Balf. f. & Ward (1915)). Possibly the same as subsp. *bonatiana*, but with narrower sepal-lobes. Upper Burma on granite.

CULTIVATION Subsp. *bella* was collected by Forrest from the Cang-Shan in 1908 and on several subsequent occasions, but it did not persist. It was reintroduced from there in 1990 (CLD 783) and seen there by ACE (1994). Also collected from the Da Xue Shan (KGB 120) and Cang Shan (KBG 822). However, a number of seed collections made under this name in the 1990s proved to be various Yunnanensis species. Out of flower, this mistake is very easily made.

Primula nanobella Balf. f. & Forrest, Notes Roy. Bot. Gdn. Edinb. 9: 31 (1915)

P. bella subsp. *nanobella* (Balf. f. & Forrest) Smith & Forrest (1928)
P. barbatula Smith (1937)

DESCRIPTION A *dwarf mat-forming* high alpine *non-mealy* relative of *P. primulina* and *P. bella*, but the pom-pom in the pink to violet (usually amethyst) flowers of 8–15 mm diameter is *purple, and surrounded by a darker ring;* leaves orbicular, less than 1 cm. The flowers are borne singly just above the foliage. (Fig. Halda: 285.) (Plate 98.)

DISTRIBUTION Yunnan, from the Yulong Shan north-westwards, through Zhongdian to the Beima Shan where it is locally common, and into south-east Tibet, on very wet passes in the monsoon belt; Kashong La and Chubumba La, Tsari, Zo La, and further east on the Tum La, near the Lo La, Pachakshiri. Mossy rocks and tundra, 4200–5000 m, often growing with *Diapensia purpurea*.

I encountered this very beautiful high alpine on the Beima Shan, and was immediately convinced that it was very distinct from *P. bella*, having a quite different aspect strongly reminiscent of dwarf relatives of *P. dryadifolia*. The mat-forming habit and purple-centred flowers are diagnostic. In finding the correct name for this plant, it was immediately clear that the Tibetan *P. barbatula* did not differ from *P. nanobella* in any important feature.

CULTIVATION Introduced in 1992 by KGB 56 from above Napa Hai, Zhongdian, 524 from the Xi Shan and 646, 716 from the Beima Shan; and in 1994 by ACE 1325, 2145 from Tianchi Lake, Zhongdian, and the Beima Shan respectively. David Rankin collected SDR 1855 in 1999/2000 which he offered for sale in 2001. Also, ARGS 774 was collected from the Hong Shan in 2000. Has yet to become firmly established, although it should be easy to propagate if it settles down in cultivation.

Primula triloba Balf. f. & Forrest, Notes Roy. Bot. Gdn. Edinb. 13: 21 (1920)

DESCRIPTION Links *P. muscoides* with *P. bella* and with *P. mystrophylla* (section Dryadifolia). A non-mealy cushion-forming plant unique in the genus in having *trilobed* leaves. The one-flowered stems do not exceed 5 mm, and the rose, cream-eyed flower, up to 15 mm in diameter, resembles that of *P. bella*, although the pom-pom in the tube is only poorly developed. South-east Tibet on the Yunnan border, Tsarong region; peaty pasture, screes and cliff-ledges, 4600–5000 m. (Fig. Halda: 302.)

Placed by Smith & Fletcher (1944) in section Dryadifolia, but with the note that it should be transferred to the Minutissimae. In fact it links with

P. mystrophylla and *P. tsongpenii* in the former section, and forms a rather clear phyletic link between the two groups.

Section **Denticulata** Watt,

J. Roy. Hort. Soc. 29: 297 (1904) p.p. emend. Balf. f. J. Roy. Hort. Soc. 39: 155 (1913). Type species *P. denticulata* J.E. Smith

DESCRIPTION Medium to *robust* perennial, deciduous or less commonly evergreen, clump-forming plants overwintering by large at- or above-ground buds often furnished with large leathery *bud-scales*; roots penetrating and thongy. *Leaves* usually obovate with a poorly marked winged stalk, rugose, entire to denticulate, covered with a fine pubescence of single-celled, or multicellular hairs, less commonly glabrous, often mealy when young, with revolute vernation. *Stems* often robust, usually equalling to exceeding leaves except when young, bearing a usually compact, often spherical, many-flowered head of erect, *stalkless* to short-stalked flowers; bracts small, not pouched or leafy. *Calyx* cylindrical, often mealy, often with darker sepal-lobes which are narrow and divided to at least half-way. *Corolla* violet, blue, lavender, lilac, pink or white, usually with a golden eye, flat-faced and with a narrow tube, rather small, exannulate or annulate, heterostylous, the lobes deeply notched; pollen 3-syncolpate, possibly also 3-porate. *Capsule* subglobose, not exceeding the calyx, dehiscing by five short apical teeth; *seeds* small, about 0.5 mm, often angular, covered with blisters. 2n = ?16, 22, 44. Varies from fully self-sterile to highly self-fertile. Flowering March–May in the garden.

DISTRIBUTION Sinohimalaya, from Afghanistan in the west continuously to Burma and Sichuan in the east, mostly confined to wetter districts, or in wet sites in dry valleys, often abundant and conspicuous. Forest clearings, alpine meadows and streamsides. 1300–5300 m.

Wendelbo (1961b) considered that the remaining four sections of the genus, Denticulata, Capitatae, Muscarioides and Soldanelloides, are closely related to one another and can be immediately distinguished by their hairy leaves and capitate inflorescences. This relationship tends to be confirmed by the DNA. Only one typical member of section Denticulata (2n = 22) has been examined as yet, and this is sister to the enigmatic stoloniferous *P. erratica* (2n = 16) which is now transferred to this section. Other more distantly related members of this subclade are indeed Soldanelloides, Muscarioides and Capitatae species, and, less expectedly, *P. minutissima* and three Armerina species.

All four sections under discussion have 3-syncolpate pollen. The chromosome numbers are very informative. Of these four sections, the Denticulata with x = 11 should be considered to be the least derived cytologically, and the Capitatae with x = 9 the most derived, while the Soldanelloides and Muscarioides with x = 10 take an intermediate position.

Thus, it is not possible to agree with Smith & Fletcher (1946) that the Denticulata are derived from the 'Farinosae' (= Aleuritia) (x = 9) with the Glabra (x = 8) taking a linking position. Rather, when searching for a precursor to the Denticulata and its derived relatives, we must rather look for x = 11 members of the subgenus with 3-syncolpate pollen. The Crystallophlomis best answer this description, and among the Denticulata species, *P. cachemiriana* in particular has a 'nivalid'-like aspect vegetatively.

The Denticulata nevertheless form a quite well-marked section centred around *P. denticulata* itself, the very familiar 'drum-stick' primula. The tight spherical flower-heads and obovate wrinkled leaves give a distinctive facies to most of this section., although *P. sertulum*, *P. efarinosa*, *P. erratica* and *P. caldaria* take more peripheral positions.

Despite their chromosome number, the Capitatae are also undoubtedly closely related to the Denticulata, and *P. glomerata* links between these sections. The former section can only be safely diagnosed from the Denticulata by the discoid flower-head with reflexed marginal flowers.

CULTIVATION In temperate climates, *P. denticulata* is one of the easiest and most widespread species in cultivation. It thrives particularly on heavy fertile soils and seems indifferent to lime in the soil. It is extremely hardy, surviving prolonged winter cold, as in Scandinavia, and is only intolerant of summer desiccation, suffering particularly on light dry soils. It is one of the few primulas which flourish in a 'normal garden soil', and as such it is a regular component of most small gardens, especially in the north of England and in Scotland and Ireland. *P. denticulata* seems relatively immune from most of the pests and diseases which affect primulas, although repeated division can lead to a loss of vigour, perhaps due to a build-up of virus. It occasionally suffers from a basal rot after hot weather, and can be invaded by vine weevil.

P. erythrocarpa, P. pseudodenticulata and P. cachemiriana are much less well-known in cultivation but also appear to be robust and easy-going garden plants. Only the last-named is sufficiently distinct from *P. denticulata* to warrant cultivation. *P. atrodentata* is a much smaller and less vigorous plant which is intolerant of summer heat and seems prone to root-rot. The true plant is now very uncommon. The evergreen *P. erosa* is a charming little plant from low altitudes which is not hardy.

KEY TO SPECIES

1. Plants producing abundant leafy stolons (runners); capsule globose....2
1. Stolons absent; capsule usually narrow....4

2. Plant lacking meal; leaves deeply toothed....*P. pseudodenticulata*
2. Plant mealy; leaves shortly crenate....3

3. Flowers white, about 7 mm in diameter, nearly stalkless....*P. caldaria*
3. Flowers pinkish, more than 8 mm in diameter, stalks more than 3 mm....*P. erratica*

4. Plant covered with red-brown hairs....*P. denticuloides*
4. If plant hairy, hairs whitish....5

5. Plant partially evergreen or deciduous; persistent bud-scales missing (look below leaves)....6
5. Plant completely deciduous; bud-scales persisting until flowering....9

6. Flowering head flat; corolla-tube more than 2× the calyx....7
6. Flowering head subglobose; corolla tube not more than 2× the calyx....8

7. Evergreen; leaves deeply and irregularly toothed; calyx teeth green....*P. erosa*
7. Deciduous; leaves shortly crenate; calyx teeth tipped black....*P. atrodentata*

8. Leaf hairs multicellular (use lens)....*P. erythrocarpa*
8. Leaf hairs absent....*P. pseudodenticulata*

9. Flowers with stalks of at least 6 mm....10
9. Flower stalks virtually absent....11

10. Whole plant lacking meal....*P. efarinosa*
10. Mealy inside calyx only....*P. sertulum*
10. Lower stalks and outside of calyx mealy....*P. fanginensis*

11. Leaves smooth, nearly entire, very mealy above when young....*P. cachemiriana*
11. Leaves bullate, denticulate, usually lacking meal above....*P. denticulata*

Primula denticulata J.E.Smith, Exot. Bot. 2: 109 (1805) non Wight (1853) = *P. elliptica* Royle. DRUMSTICK PRIMULA

P. adenophora Blatter (1934)
P. aequalis Craib (1918)
P. harsukhii Craib (1919)
P. hoffmeisteri Klotzsch (1862)
P. paucifolia (Hook. f.) Watt (1918)
P. platycrana Craib (1918)
P. telemachica Klatt (1868)
P. alta Balf. f. & Forrest (1915)
P. limnoica Craib (1919)
P. cyanocephala Balf. f. (1920)
P. sinodenticulata Balf. f. & Forrest (1920)

DESCRIPTION Extremely variable in size in the wild, but in cultivation usually *robust, deciduous*, with large persistent leathery *bud-scales* outside the rosette; *leaves* sparsely *hairy* with single-celled hairs, mostly on the veins, and sparsely *mealy* below when young, tough and leathery, elongating to 30 cm or more in fruit; stalk usually red at the base. *Stem* stout, usually mealy above at first; *inflorescence spherical* when mature, to 8 cm in diameter, the flowers stalkless, or nearly so. *Calyx* to 10 mm, mealy, sometimes faintly striped purple. *Corolla* usually lilac to lavender with a yellowish eye in the wild, varying to deep purple, blue, red, pink or white in cultivation, to 20 mm in diameter in small heads, usually smaller, the tube to 2× the calyx. 2n = 22. Pins about 15% self-fertile, thrums totally self-sterile. (Plate 17.)

DISTRIBUTION Throughout the Sinohimalaya, encompassing the whole range of the section; east Afghanistan in the Hindu Kush, northern Pakistan, Kashmir through northern India and Nepal, Sikkim and Bhutan to south-east Tibet, northern Burma, Yunnan, Sichuan and Guizhou, thus spanning some 3000 km.

Abundant in a wide variety of wet open places, the commonest Himalayan primula; 1500–4500 m. 'Within its lower altitudes I have seen miles of country, from March to May or June, literally rendered blue with its lovely heads of flowers.'

This familiar garden plant takes a central position in the section. For differences from related species, see under the latter.

VARIATION Varies enormously in stature in the wild, by a factor of at least 10, not only with altitude, but also within populations. 'It is not uncommon, amid a mass of plants arising to as much as a foot in height, to find dwarf states, perfect in every detail and in full flower, the whole plant not exceeding one and a half inches in height.' Such dwarf forms may have very few, disproportionately large flowers in a flattish head, and may then superficially resemble less familiar species in other sections. The obovate wrinkled leaves with external leathery bud-scales should always reveal their true identity. Otherwise remarkably uniform in the wild within the Himalaya, but in China another form occurs:

- Subsp. *sinodenticulata* (Balf. f. & Forrest) Smith & Forrest (1928) (*P. sinodenticulata* Balf. f. & Forrest, Notes Roy. Bot. Gdn. Edinb. 13: 19 (1920); *P. alta* Balf. f. & Forrest (1915); *P. limnoica* Craib, 1919; *P. cyanocephala* Balf. f. (1920)). Stem at flowering disproportionately long, to 6 × the leaves. Burma and China. Chinese material in extreme forms is very leggy, to an extent never seen in the Himalaya. However, many intermediates and typical *P. denticulata* also occur in these areas.

In cultivation, variation is seen mostly in flower colour, which now varies to a spectacular extent. These colour forms were originally raised from a pink mutant seedling raised by Robert Leslie of Carlisle in about 1920. From this plant, John Stourmouth's nursery at Kirkbride developed the startling range of reds and brilliant purples which are seen today. White forms, which are also occasionally seen in the wild, are commonplace in the garden, and a visit to any UK Garden Centre (and doubtless those of many other temperate countries) will allow a selection of purple, blue, red and pink forms to be acquired. Some of these are propagated vegetatively, but few have been given varietal or clonal names, perhaps because clones tend to become weaker with time, and new, often self-sown, seedlings are arising continuously. Strains offered by seedsmen today usually contain a variety of flower colours. Thus, such named varieties as 'Bressingham Beauty', 'Glenroy Crimson', 'Inshriach Crimson' and 'Snowball' are no longer very relevant.

However, in this species, more than any other, local strains seem to have become associated with particular areas. For instance, in my own town of Hexham many small front gardens are full of a rather small-flowered plant with tight spherical heads of a very good powder blue, and I have rarely seen such plants elsewhere.

Consequently, I intend to mention further only two horticultural varieties. 'Robinson's Red' has presumably been selected by Martin's Nest Nursery. This clone is dwarf, slow-growing, and has small tight spherical heads of a brilliant deep carmine. It is a distinctive and attractive plant much more suited for the rock garden than most. 'Karryann', with its leaves edged with cream, is perhaps the only variegated primula.

CULTIVATION First introduced by Royle in 1838 and continuously in cultivation since, although there have doubtless been many subsequent introductions. For further notes on this easy and vigorous species, consult the sectional account.

Primula denticuloides Y. Nasir, Flora of Pakistan 157: 30–32 (1984)

DESCRIPTION Similar to a small and leggy form of *P. denticulata*, but with the leaves covered throughout with relatively thick, often *rusty, multicellular hairs*, and lacking meal; the small heads have only 5–7 flowers and are borne on long stems several times longer than the small leaves. Only known from the Kurram valley, by the Khyber Pass on the Pakistan side of the Afghan frontier. Superficially resembles the Aleuritia species *P. capitellata* from the same region, and *P. baldschuanica*, but these are mealy species lacking hairs.

Primula pseudodenticulata Pax, Pflanzenreich Primulaceae 91 (1905)

P. polyphylla Franchet (1908)
P. stolonifera Balf. f. (1915)

DESCRIPTION Similar to a small form of *P. denticulata*, but usually *without* persistent bud scales and sometimes *stoloniferous;* leaves usually lacking meal or hairs, deeply *toothed;* flowers annulate, rose to lavender, the tube scarcely exceeding the calyx. Yunnan (including the east) and Sichuan, open wet places, 1600–4000 m. A variety, var. *monticola* Hand.-Mazz., Symb. Sin. 7: 744 (1936), has persistent yellow-mealy bud-scales, and thus in some sense is intermediate with *P. denticulata* subsp. *alta*. It usually occurs at higher altitudes than var. *pseudodenticulata*.

Primula cachemiriana Munro, The Garden, 16: 535 (1879)

DESCRIPTION Strikingly different from *P. denticulata* in the winter and early spring, forming narrow, sharp, yellow-mealy resting buds resembling those of members of section Crystallophlomis, which expand to form narrow smooth leaves, lacking hairs, thickly covered with yellow meal and strongly recurved at the margin; at this stage the foliage resembles that of *P. chionantha*. At flowering the leaves are still smooth and yellow-mealy and almost without teeth. In summer, however, the leaves much more closely resemble those of *P. denticulata*, as do the inflorescences earlier. (Plate 17.)

DISTRIBUTION Kashmir; Gulmarg, edges of streams amongst alpine meadows at about 3700 m. Other distribution unknown, possibly elsewhere in the western Himalaya.

P. cachemiriana was originally described from a garden introduction which mentions the narrow leaves with very heavy yellow meal. Plants under this name, or as *P. denticulata* var. *cachemiriana* Hook. f. (1882), are still sometimes seen in gardens today, but most are essentially very mealy *P. denticulata*. Smith and Fletcher were familiar with this latter plant in cultivation, and considered that such plants were hybrid. Although they accept that very mealy plants do occur in the western Himalaya, they follow earlier authors in subsuming these under *P. denticulata*, perhaps because they were only familiar with the hybrid.

This hybridity is also suggested by a remarkable chromosome count of the cultivated plant by Bruun (2n = 52), a count which is on the face of it very difficult to explain. However, the published figure suggests that this plant may have had many B chromosomes, and that it was in fact a tetraploid (2n = 44); possibly therefore the plant of Bruun and of Smith and Fletcher is a true breeding allotetraploid hybrid between *P. denticulata* and *P. cachemiriana*.

CULTIVATION In 1979, Miss K.M. Firby of Corbridge, Northumberland collected a plant from Gulmarg which I have grown ever since and have given limited distribution. I have little doubt that this represents Munro's original plant. Although the flowering heads resemble *P. denticulata*, it is so different in every other way that I maintain it at specific rank. In a garden where *P. denticulata* self-sows freely, it has remained quite distinct, with no indication of hybridization. Also successfully introduced by P. Kohli & Co. in 1985, according to Chadwell, probably from above Khelanmarg above Gulmarg, Kashmir at more than 3500 m (K29 and K30).

In cultivation, *P. cachemiriana* is a distinctive and valuable plant which should be grown more often. However, it is less vigorous than *P. denticulata* and in recent years I have come close to losing it. It appears to link with section Crystallophlomis, and thus might be regarded as the most primitive member of the section.

Primula erythrocarpa Craib, Notes Roy. Bot. Gdn. Edinb. 10: 206 (1918)

P. laxiuscula Smith (1949)

DESCRIPTION Very similar to *P. denticulata*, but *lacking* basal bud-scales and meal and with white *multicellular* hairs on the leaves above; sometimes semi-evergreen, although deciduous in the garden. Flowers annulate or exannulate with a yellow eye, the tube 2× the calyx. 2n = 22. Both pins and thrums fully self-sterile, thus differing from *P. denticulata*.

DISTRIBUTION Western and central Bhutan, just extending into Tibet and Assam. Wet places in forest clearings, 1500–3000 m.

In many ways, as a low-level forest plant *P. erythrocarpa* is the eastern counterpart of *P. erosa*, and it falls between *P. erosa* and *P. denticulata* in many features. It also resembles the glabrous, short-tubed *P. pseudodenticulata* from still further east. It is a more robust plant than *P. erosa*, much more resembling *P. denticulata*, but the semi-evergreen habit and leaf characters favour the former. *P. atrodentata* is a much smaller, high-altitude plant, the flowers of which have a white eye. *P. laxiuscula* in many ways falls between *P. erythrocarpa* and *P. atrodentata*, but the long white hairs and absence of bud scales suggests that it is a dwarf few-flowered alpine form of the former.

CULTIVATION Introduced by Cooper in 1914, and persisted in cultivation for at least 30 years. As its distinctions from *P. denticulata* are more of botanical than horticultural merit it did not become widely grown.

Reintroduced from the Paro region by an expedition from the Royal Botanic Garden, Edinburgh in 1980. These plants, unlike *P. erosa*, are unexpectedly completely hardy, and make vigorous and attractive garden plants which are, however, superficially very like lilac forms of *P. denticulata*, but rather more leggy.

Primula atrodentata Smith, Rec. Bot. Surv. India 4: 217 (1911)

P. orestora Craib & Cooper (1918)

DESCRIPTION A *compact deciduous* plant, *lacking* basal bud-scales, white-mealy at first, and *scabrid* throughout with unicellular hairs. *Stems* slender, usually shorter than the leaves at flowering and not exceeding 15 cm even in fruit, bearing a usually *flat* tightly packed head of usually blue-violet, *white-eyed*, annulate to exannulate stalkless flowers, the long narrow tube 2 –3× the bell-shaped calyx which has *blackish* sepal-lobes. Pins about 20% self-fertile; thrums about 60% self-fertile: one of the most self-fertile of heterostylous species. (Photo: Riddle of the Tsangpo Gorge: 84.) (Plate 17.)

DISTRIBUTION Widespread through much of the Himalaya from Kumaon in the west, through much of Nepal, Sikkim and Bhutan to Assam and in south-east Tibet east to Tsari.

Stony and grassy sites above the tree-line, usually well-drained but in summer-wet regions, locally abundant so that 'cows and yaks are fond of grazing on it'; 3000–5300 m.

A distinctive little plant, more likely to be confused with Aleuritia species such as *P. schlagintweitiana* or Pulchella species than other Denticulata, but with stalkless flowers and scabrid leaves. Best distinguished from dwarf alpine states of *P. denticulata* by the absence of bud-scales outside the stock. The most high-alpine member of the section.

CULTIVATION Introduced by Ward in 1925, and by many other collectors on subsequent occasions, e.g. CC & McK 159 (1990). Still occasionally seen, mostly in Botanic Gardens, but offered in the trade by Keith Lever and others around the year 2000. Slow-growing and not particularly easy, resenting summer heat and rotting readily, requiring good drainage.

Primula erosa (Duby) Wallich ex Regel, Bot. Zeitung 11: 333 (1853)

P. erosa Wallich (1828) nomen nudum
P. denticulata J.E. Smith var. *erosa* Duby (1844)

DESCRIPTION A *squat* little *evergreen* plant, *lacking* basal bud scales or meal on the leaves and with *prostrate* very *oblong* rugose nearly *glabrous* leaves, which can, however, have multicellular hairs on the *irregularly* toothed margin. Stems slender, sometimes mealy, about equalling the leaves, bearing a *flat*-topped head of rather few (to 20) exannulate stalked flowers of a luminous *violet* with a yellow eye; corolla-tube 2× calyx. *P. erosa* has a particularly long flowering period, of some two months. (Plate 17.)

DISTRIBUTION Western Himalaya, apparently scarce, chiefly recorded from Kumaon, but also from Dalhousie and Lahul, Himalch Pradesh and Uttar Pradesh; also very scattered in Nepal east to Annapurna. There is a very dubious record from Bhutan, probably referable to *P. erythrocarpa*.

Wet soils in forest gaps, 1300–3000 m, sometimes growing with *P. sessilis* and *P. floribunda*.

This delicate little species has suffered a chequered history and has been poorly understood, perhaps because it has been found so infrequently. At times it has been said to have very long flower stalks, up to 20 mm, but this seems to have resulted from an early confusion with the very different alpine species *P. elliptica*. In the 1970s, this confusion was perpetrated by material introduced by the late Len Beer under the name *P. erosa* which was in fact *P. elliptica*. *P. erosa* has short flower-stalks, unusually in this section in which the flowers are normally stalkless. However, it is unlikely to be mistaken for anything except a small Denticulata, although it has a superficial resemblance to the unrelated and stemless *P. drummondiana*.

Unfortunately, the Bot. Mag. plate 6916 (1887) is *P. glomerata*.

Within the Denticulata, *P. erosa* is most likely to be confused with the more easterly *P. erythrocarpa*, which is, however, a much more robust plant with more hairy leaves.

CULTIVATION Although *P. erosa* is said to have been not uncommon in cultivation in the 1890s, these plants are likely to have been *P. glomerata*. Regel (1853) correctly states that *P. erosa* is tender, but it is not clear whether this was based on evidence from cultivation in France.

Introduced by Bernard Thompson from the Modi Khola, Nepal in 1974 and again in 1978. These plants were collected at 3000 m and at 2800 m, and proved to be relatively hardy, but they succumbed to the very hard winters of 1979 and 1982 respectively. Until then they thrived in the same shady humid well-drained conditions as were provided for petiolarid primulas. Correctly named wild collected seed from Nepal was offered by the AGS in 1990. A charming little plant, very distinct and well worth growing, which should, however, be protected from severe frost.

Primula sertulum Franchet, Journ. de Bot. 9: 451 (1895)

P. obsessa Smith (1943)

DESCRIPTION A little-known and rather mysterious plant apparently closely related to *P. efarinosa*, *P. erratica* and *P. caldaria*, but lacking stolons and with somewhat persistent basal bud-scales. However, it is very like a small form of *P. denticulata* except for the stalked (to 2 cm) flowers and the leaves which are covered with glands rather than unicellular hairs. Pollen 3-syncolpate. Capsule globose. The chromosome count reported for this species refers to *P. erratica*. Two sites in east Sichuan, 2500–3000 m.

Smith and Fletcher placed this species, and *P. obsessa*, which seems merely to be a dwarf high-level form from the same locality, in section Oreophlomis. It has some affinities with this section, but lacks the characteristic pouched bracts, and the leaf-shape and form is typical of the Denticulata. The similar *P. efarinosa* has a quite different pollen type. Grown in 1992 from Cox 5108, but not heard of in recent years.

Primula fangingensis Chen & Hu, Fl. Rep. Pop. Sin. 2: 294 (1990)

DESCRIPTION This newly described species is apparently a close relative of *P. sertulum*, and may be synonymous with it. In the meantime I am placing it here rather than in section Oreophlomis where it was placed by Halda (1992). From *P. sertulum*, *P. fangingensis* may best be distinguished by shorter, mealy flower stalks. Jiangkou Shan, Jingding Shan, Kweichow, damp subalpine areas, 2100–3300 m.

Primula caldaria Smith & Forrest, Notes Roy. Bot. Gdn. Edinb. 14: 35 (1923)

DESCRIPTION A rather *robust* plant, producing *abundant leafy mealy stolons*, the narrowly spear-shaped leaves being white-mealy beneath, and with small (to 7 mm in diameter) *white* flowers *clustered in* *a tight head*, the tube 1.5× the calyx. Heterostylous; pollen 3-syncolpate. Capsule globose. 2n = 16.

DISTRIBUTION Yunnan, hot springs (hence the name) on the Mekong-Salween divide; in a second site on the Mekong it is associated with calcareous springs, 2700–4000 m. Introduced by Forrest (1921) and Ward (1922); still in cultivation in 1943, persisting by its stoloniferous habit.

Primula erratica Smith, Proc. Linn. Soc. Lond. 153: 120 (1940)

DESCRIPTION Closely related to *P. caldaria*, with the same stoloniferous habit, white meal and globose capsule, but with *lilac-pink* flowers, 8–15 mm in diameter and longer flower-stalks giving a much looser head. Heterostylous, pollen 3-syncolpate, 2n = 16.

DISTRIBUTION Southern Gansu (near Siku), western Shensi (Ta P'ae Shan), northern Sichuan (near Tatsienlu). Also apparently much further south by the Yangtse near Benzilan in Yunnan. Calcareous spring in hot dry zones and 'grassy downs', 2700–3000 m.

CULTIVATION Introduced by Farrer in 1914 and still in cultivation in 1943. Reintroduced as a living plant by ACE 702 in 1994 and persisting well by vegetative spread in 2002. Neither very hardy nor tolerant of winter wet, this plant tolerates the hot dry conditions of an alpine house in summer very well and is extremely vigorous, persistently self-rooting into the sand plunge.

ACE 702 was introduced as *P. caldaria*, which the original habitat and locality would certainly suggest is the correct name. However, the description is closer to that of *P. erratica* which is reputed to grow much further north and in a different habitat. Possibly they are ecological and geographical variants of the same species. The DNA proves this species to be sister to *P. denticulata*, so I am placing it here after several previous misalliances.

Primula efarinosa Pax, Pflanzenreich Primulaceae 79 (1905)

DESCRIPTION A mysterious plant of uncertain affinity, resembling a small member of section Denticulata such as *P. erosa* or *P. sertulum*, with the same obovate, rugose, erose-denticulate leaves and globose capsule, but with the leaves hairless, the bracts pouched at the base and the flower stalks to 12 mm. Pollen 3-porate, uniquely in the genus. 2n = 16. Central China; west Hubei, Fang Hsien, moist grassy places, 2300–3300 m. Flowered at Edinburgh, 1914–15, and apparently in cultivation before 1938 when Bruun reported its chromosome number. This enigmatic species was inauspiciously classified within the 'Auriculatae' (= Oreophlomis) by Smith and Fletcher, together with its look-alike species *P. sertulum*. If correctly reported, the pollen, chromosome number and general appearance show that this species has nothing to do with the Oreophlomis. The pollen and chromosome number may also preclude a relationship with the Denticulata, where Balfour had understandably placed this species. However, the two preceding species also have 2n = 16, and the DNA shows *P. erratica* nevertheless to be a close relative of *P. denticulata*, so I am placing all three species in this section pro tem, until more evidence is available.

Section **Capitatae** Pax,
Bot. Jahrb. Syst. 10: 192 (1889)
(Section Sphaerocephala Balfour 1913).
Type species *P. capitata* Hook. f.

DESCRIPTION Differing from the Denticulata in the following characters: plants tufted but scarcely clump-forming, *deciduous*, or largely so, *lacking* basal bud-scales; leaves often suberect (although largely prostrate in some forms), pale green, usually without any reddish colour, mealy, often very heavily so, or lacking meal, narrowly oblong to somewhat spoon-shaped, the margin strongly and irregularly *crisped*-dentate. Flowers arranged at the end of a long rather slender stalk into a tight *disc*-like head, in which all open flowers are spreading to reflexed around the edge, and central flowers often *fail to develop*, or sometimes subglobose; the whole head is often strongly mealy, flowers blue to deep purple. Pollen 3-syncolpate, flowers heterostylous. Capsule usually elliptical, but not exceeding the calyx. 2n = 18. Flowering May–September in cultivation; usually late and after the monsoon in the wild.

DISTRIBUTION From central Nepal eastwards through Sikkim, south and south-east Tibet, Bhutan, northern Burma to Yunnan as far as the Yulong Shan.

In a variety of alpine habitats above the tree-line, usually well-drained and with low levels of competition in rather wet districts; 3300–5000 m.

A small and distinctive section of only two species. The main feature which distinguishes the Capitatae from the Denticulata is the flattened discoid head of usually stalkless flowers. Richards (1993) treated this section as monotypic, placing the intermediate *P. glomerata* in section Denticulata. In this I was heavily influenced by an early chromosome count by Bruun of 2n = 44 for *P. glomerata* (as its synonym *P. crispa*), apparently based on x = 11 as in section Denticulata, rather than x = 9 as in section Capitatae. Since then I have discovered that Kress, Phyton 10: 225 (1963) reported 2n = 18 for authentic *P. glomerata*, the same number as for the many reports for *P. capitata*. It seems likely that Bruun's material was wrongly identified, and was probably a polyploid member of section Denticulata. This reclassification is also supported by the DNA, which places *P. glomerata* and *P. capitata* as sisters, although fairly closely related to *P. denticulata* despite the differing chromosome number. It seems likely that the Capitatae have evolved from forerunners of the Denticulata via intermediates resembling the linking *P. glomerata*. This evolution has involved the loss of two chromosomes.

CULTIVATION All are relatively easy-going garden plants in a well-drained but moisture-retentive situation where they are in good light, but do not get too hot or dry out. They grow well from seed, flowering after a year, but are short-lived, rarely performing well for more than three seasons, and so they need regular replenishment from seed. If *P. capitata* is grown in groups, as is frequently the case, this is freely set. No hybrids have been reported.

Primula capitata Hook. f., Bot. Mag. t.4550 (1850)

P. craibeana Balf. f. & Smith (1916)
P. crispata Balf. f. & Smith (1916)
P. lacteocapitata Balf. f. & Smith (1916)
P. mooreana Balf. f. & Smith (1916)
P. sphaerocephala Balf. f. & Forrest (1915)
P. pseudocapitata Ward (1916)

DESCRIPTION As for the section. Differs from *P. glomerata* by often being heavily mealy, by the head which is held horizontally, and by the usually closed, sterile, central florets. 2n = 18. (Plate 17.)

DISTRIBUTION From east Nepal in the Everest region eastwards through Sikkim, south and south-east Tibet, Bhutan, northern Burma to Yunnan as far as the Yulong Shan.

In a variety of alpine habitats above the tree-line, usually well-drained and with low levels of competition in rather wet districts; 3300–5000 m.

P. capitata is a well-marked but very variable species, showing several geographical races.

Typically, the flowering head is notably discoid, so that the marginal flowers in the head are spreading or even reflexed, while the central florets are also spreading, but do not mature, so that only an outer ring of fertile flowers is formed. This feature, when well developed, is quite distinct from the usually globose head of the Denticulata, but some of the races of *P. capitata* do form more of a subglobose head, in which most flowers mature, and these heads closely resemble those of *P. glomerata*.

Several vegetative features, notably the leaf with a strongly crisped margin, otherwise serve to separate *P.capitata* and *P. glomerata* from the Denticulata.

VARIATION

- Subsp. *capitata*. Leaves narrowly oblong, blunt to sharp at the tip, thickly white-mealy below; head strongly discoid, the bracts forming an apical tuft, corolla with spreading lobes. East Nepal, Sikkim, Chumbi and Bhutan.
- Subsp. *craibeana* (Balf. f. & Smith) Smith & Forrest, Notes Roy. Bot. Gdn. Edinb. 16: 18 (1928) (*P. craibeana* Balf. f. & Smith (1916). Leaves narrowly spoon-shaped, yellow-mealy below; head globose, bracts small. Sikkim and Chumbi, south Tibet.
- Subsp. *crispata* (Balf. f. & Smith) Smith & Forrest loc.cit. (*P. crispata* Balf. f. & Smith (1916). Leaves lacking all meal, robust; head discoid, corolla with spreading lobes. Sikkim, Bhutan, south-east Tibet and north-west Burma.

This subspecies has been frequently confused with *P. glomerata,* partly because both are robust plants largely without meal, and partly because the name is confusing close to the common synonym '*P. crispa*' of *P. glomerata.* The vertically held globose head of the latter immediately separates it.

- Subsp. *lacteocapitata* (Balf. f. & Smith) Smith & Forrest loc.cit. (*P. lacteocapitata* Balf. f. & Smith (1916). Leaves cream-mealy below, narrow, sharply pointed, the stalk reddish; head globose, bracts small. Sikkim and south Tibet.
- Subsp. *mooreana* (Balf. f. & Smith) Smith & Forrest loc.cit. (*P. mooreana* Balf. f. & Smith (1916). Robust with rounded ends to the leaves which are up to 3 cm in width and are thinly white-mealy below; heads discoid with the flowers stalked, bracts large forming a marked ruff or crown. Sikkim.
- subsp. *sphaerocephala* (Balf. f. & Forrest) Smith & Forrest loc. cit. (*P. sphaerocephala* Balf. f. & Forrest (1915); *P. pseudocapitata* Ward (1916)). Leaves lacking all meal, very similar to subsp. *crispata,* but less robust, the head globose and with the corolla funnel-shaped. Widespread in Yunnan, extending west over the Tibet border.

CULTIVATION Introduced by Hooker from Sikkim in 1849, and has probably been in cultivation since, although there have been many subsequent introductions.

Currently, subspecies *capitata, crispata, mooreana* and *sphaerocephala* are all probably grown, although after many generations they are now less distinct, and hybridization between the races has probably occurred. Subsp. *mooreana* is the most robust grower, and is probably the most significant garden plant, not least because of its late flowering; it is frequently at its best in September. There is a very good form of subsp. *capitata,* L & S 17507, collected from Bhutan in 1949, in which the brilliant deep violet heads contrast well with the very white leaves. This has a long flowering season. The Chinese subsp. *sphaerocephala* tends to be the earliest to flower, often at the end of May.

Primula glomerata Pax, Pflanzenreich Primulaceae 92 (1905)

P. crispa Balf. f. & Smith (1916)

DESCRIPTION *Leaves* many, semi-deciduous, erect, bright green, occasionally faintly white-mealy below at first, glandular but not hairy, rather narrowly oblanceolate with a distinctly narrowed often reddish stalk, irregularly and sharply crisped-toothed, finely rugose, to 15 × 3 cm, usually much smaller. *Stems* long and rather slender, exceeding leaves, bearing a *tight rather flattened, somewhat disc-shaped* head which is held *vertically,* in the same plane as the stem; flowers many, stemless, erect to spreading, all opening. *Calyx* slightly mealy. Corolla *bright deep violet,* usually with a dark eye, more or less exannulate, heterostylous, to 10 mm in diameter, the tube 1–2× the calyx. *Capsule* elliptical, but not exceeding the calyx. 2n = 18. Flowering in April in cultivation, but late, often after the monsoon in September in the wild. (Plate 17.)

DISTRIBUTION Central and eastern Nepal, Sikkim, and Chumbi, southern Tibet. Banks and light shade in wet areas, 3300–5700 m.

P. glomerata definitely has links between the Denticulata and the Capitatae. In most of its foliage characters it favours *P. capitata,* although all the forms of the latter species are fully deciduous, and have more meal than in *P. glomerata.* The manner in which the stem bends at right angles at the very top, so that the discoid head is held vertically, is very distinctive.

P. glomerata has frequently been known by its synonym *P. crispa,* as recently as the AGSES expedition to Sikkim in 1983. This has led to confusion with the very similar *P. capitata* subsp. *crispata* (q.v.), formerly known as *P. crispata,* which also largely lacks meal and is best distinguished by its horizontally held discoid heads.

CULTIVATION Flowered in cultivation in 1887 from Sikkim seed, but did not survive. Reintroduced from Nepal in about 1936. A more recent introduction from there in 1978 (BMW 36) survived for some years, and was augmented by AGSES 407 from Sikkim in 1983. By 1991, scarcely surviving, if at all. Has more recently been introduced on several occasions, e.g. by KEKE, and by Chadwell, and offered by several commercial sources in 2002.

AGSES 407 grew well plunged in a pot in a shady frame, flowering after a year, and for four subsequent years, but it showed only a very limited capacity for vegetative propagation, and never set seed. This species seems to be quite easy, but is regrettably rather short-lived.

Section **Muscarioides** Balf. f., J. Roy. Hort. Soc. 39: 151 (1913). Type species *P. muscarioides* Hemsley

DESCRIPTION Perennial, but short-lived, or occasionally biennial medium-sized (occasionally robust) *deciduous* plants, overwintering by tiny green at- or below-ground resting buds without bud-scales, forming individual rosettes or small tufts; roots fibrous and rather shallow. *Leaves* prostrate to erect, usually oblanceolate to obovate with a rounded apex, characteristically *pale green and rather fragile, hairy often throughout with soft multicellular hairs*, usually lacking meal, entire to deeply toothed or even pinnatifid, with revolute vernation; stalks usually broadly winged and poorly demarcated. *Stems* usually exceeding leaves, often mealy above, with small non-pouched bracts and bearing a *spike* of many, or a capitate head of rather few rather small stalkless or short-stalked usually *deflexed* flowers. *Calyx* usually blackish or purple, rarely red, often mealy, bell-shaped but unequal, the *two upper teeth markedly longer than the bottom three*, so that the deflexed calyces overlap in a regular pattern reminiscent of a tiled roof. *Corolla* usually sweetly fragrant, purple, violet, blue, lavender or lilac, rarely white, exannulate, heterostyle or homostyle, with a long narrow often mealy tube much exceeding the calyx, and much smaller spreading lobes which are usually notched; pollen 3-syncolpate. *Capsule* ellipsoidal to globose, equalling to slightly exceeding the calyx, dehiscing by five apical valves; *seed* small, usually brownish, about 0.5 mm. 2n = 20, 40. Flowering during the monsoon in the wild, May–July in cultivation.

DISTRIBUTION From Sikkim eastwards through Bhutan (but only one Himalayan species), south-east Tibet, Assam, northern Burma, Yunnan, Sichuan to Gansu and Shensi, most diverse in western Yunnan and neighbouring areas of Tibet.

Typically plants of grassy rock-ledges on limestone cliffs in high rainfall areas; less commonly in stony alpine meadows, stabilized screes, edges of rivulets, etc., 2500–5300 m.

The Muscarioides are very closely allied to the section Soldanelloides. Both sections have x = 10, a chromosome number otherwise almost unknown in *Primula,* uniformly 3-syncolpate pollen, and soft pale hairy leaves with multicellular hairs. Further, at least one hybrid is reported between species classified in different sections. Furthermore, the DNA has shown that whereas *P. bellidifolia* and *P. muscarioides* are sister and linked to the Soldanelloid *P. reidii*, the Muscarioid *P. vialii* is less closely related to these, but is sister to *P. flaccida* which is intermediate between the sections morphologically. A very good case can be made to unite the sections, but the resultant group of 37 species would be very unwieldy and until the DNA of more species is known I am keeping them apart. However, I have decided to transfer *P. flaccida* and its little-known relatives *P. spicata* and *P. siamensis* from the Soldanelloides, where they have traditionally been placed, to the Muscarioides.

Typically, the Muscarioides have many (10–50 or more) flowers tightly clustered in an imbricated head or spike; the flowers have very long narrow tubes, so that the corolla lobes, which sometimes form a flattish face to the flower, are rarely more than a quarter of its length; and the ellipsoidal capsules at least equal the calyx.

In contrast, the Soldanelloides usually have fewer, less tightly imbricated flowers, in which the corolla-lobes which form a bell or cup are usually at least as long as the tube, while the globose capsules are usually included within the calyx. Moreover, the Soldanelloides are chiefly high alpines from the Himalaya, while the Muscarioides are mostly alpines from lower levels in China. The species within the Muscarioides can be informally divided into those species, based around the widespread *P. muscarioides* itself, which have many flowers arranged into a tight spike; those, based around *P. bellidifolia*, which have a relatively few-flowered capitate inflorescence; and the large-flowered *P. flaccida* alliance. With the exception of a few species, notably *P. vialii*, the Muscarioides species appear to be very closely related to one another. They share a very similar general appearence and differ from one another by few, possibly trivial, characters. Once these species are better known in the wild, and their DNA studied, it is possible that a number of species around *P. muscarioides* should be lumped together, as should those around *P. bellidifolia*.

The relationship between polyploidy and homostyly has been carefully studied in 15 of the species (Tremayne & Richards 1993). There are 12 heterostylous species; unusually in this genus, no less than four of these are or can be tetraploid. There are two tetraploid secondary homostyles, *P. concholoba* and *P. watsonii*. *P. bellidifolia* has perhaps the most varied mating systems in the whole genus, for it appears that diploid heterostyles, diploid homostyles, tetraploid heterostyles and tetraploid homostyles all occur and can all be found in both subspecies and at various altitudes.

In the diploids *P. vialii* and *P. pinnatifida*, thrum individuals are strongly heteromorphic for one chromosome type, homologues of which are heavily inverted with respect to each other (Bruun, 1932). It seems quite probable that the inverted segment carries the supergene responsible for the heteromorphy, in a manner analogous to that of sex chromosomes, so this is protected from recombination. This may explain why several species in this group have been able to maintain polyploid heterostyles.

Of the homostyles, the long-tubed *P. watsonii* in particular shows great variation in style length and separation of anthers from the stigma, so that some individuals are probably self-pollinating, but others, although self-fertile, will only set seed after an insect visit (Tremayne & Richards 1993).

CULTIVATION Most members of the section seem to be relatively easy to cultivate. Seed generally germinates readily in April. If seedlings are pricked out at the one-leaf stage into a fertile, well-drained but moisture-retentive compost in small pots or boxes and grown on in a partially shaded and humid frame, they will have formed flowering-size plants by the autumn, when they will die back. At this stage, they should be kept almost dry during the winter; this is usually best achieved by keeping the plunge material wet, but by not watering the pots. Growth will restart during the following April, and once top-growth is well-established, plants will take all the water they can be given. They can then be transferred to their final position, where they will flower in late May and June. A reasonably well-drained, fertile, sheltered location in fairly good light is indicated.

Although 13 of the 20 species in the section have been in cultivation, only seven are probably grown today, two from recent introductions. Except for the spectacular *P. vialii* and *P. flaccida*, none are commonly met. Doubtless, two factors have contributed to this scarcity.

Firstly, most members of the section are regrettably short-lived. Indeed such species as *P. muscarioides*, *P. bellidifolia* and *P. concholoba* are best treated as biennials, although if they are protected from excess moisture in the winter they will sometimes flower a second, and rarely a third year. *P. vialii* and *P. flaccida* are exceptional, in that robust plants will often flower for four or five years without protection, although plants are often less vigorous after the second year of flowering.

Secondly, it has to be said that, for all their charm, most members of this section have a rather insignificant flowering display. Only the dedicated specialist is likely to undertake the labour-intensive programme necessary to maintain these species, and one suspects that several are kept going largely as a result of the efforts of a few leading Botanical Gardens. Once again, the spectacular *P. vialii*, which is commonly met as a major feature of parks and recreation areas, forms the exception.

It should be noted that species of this section are usually displayed in mass plantings, partly because the display is thus rendered less insignificant, and partly because this technique is more likely to result in the production of viable seed so necessary for future cultivation.

With the exception of *P. vialii* × *P. flaccida* (q.v.), no hybrids seem to have been reported.

LITERATURE. Tremayne, M.A., & Richards, A.J. (1993).

KEY TO SPECIES

1. Calyx bright red; stem commonly exceeding 20 cm and flowers more than 30 .... *P. vialii*
1. Calyx purple to green, often mealy; stem rarely exceeding 20 cm; flowers fewer than 30 2

2. Corolla of largest flower more than 15 mm in diameter; face of flower mealy 3
2. Corolla less than 15 mm in diameter; face of flower usually lacking meal 5

3. Flowers in a tight spike with overlapping calyces; corolla-tube more than 4 mm wide .... *P. flaccida*
3. Flowers in a lax, distant spike; corolla-tube less than 4 mm wide 4

4. Leaves serrate, irregularly toothed (Yunnan) .... *P. spicata*
4. Leaves nearly entire (Thailand) .... *P. siamensis*

5. Corolla tube broad, not exceeding the calyx; flowers homostylous .... *P. concholoba*
5. Corolla tube less than 2 mm in diameter, at least 2× calyx; flowers usually heterostylous 6

6. Corolla-tube blackish-purple, lobes erect; flowers homostylous .... *P. watsonii*
6. Corolla-tube usually paler, lobes spreading; flowers heterostylous 7

7. Stem hairy, without meal 8
7. Stem glabrous, usually mealy at least at top 9

8. Flowering heads capitate, calyces with long black hairs .... *P. euchaites*
8. Flowering heads cylindrical, calyces glabrous .... *P. deflexa*

9. Flowering heads tightly cylindrical; flowers usually more than 15 10
9. Flowering heads tightly capitate; flowers less than 15 15
9. Flowering heads loosely cylindrical; flowers less than 15 .... *P. inopinata*

10. Flowers more than 8 mm in diameter 11
10. Flowers less than 8 mm in diameter 13

11. Corolla-tube longer than the corolla diameter; leaves lacking obvious stalk .... *P. cernua*
11. Corolla-tube less than corolla diameter; leaves narrowing to stalk 12

12. Corolla-lobes entire; meal whitish .... *P. pinnatifida*
12. Corolla-lobes notched; meal yellowish .... *P. mairei*

13. Leaves shiny above, nearly glabrous; flower-stalks exceeding leaves .... *P. muscarioides*
13. Leaves matt above, hairy; flower stalks about equalling leaves 14

14. Flowers 10–12 mm long; leaves scabrid with rough hairs .... *P. violacea*
14. Flowers 7 mm long; leaves softly hairy .... *P. apoclita*

15. Meal absent; corolla-lobes narrow, sharp .... *P. gracilenta*
15. Meal present, at least on stem; corolla-lobes blunt to rounded, sometimes notched 16

16. Leaves prostrate, rounded, not more than 1.5 × as long as wide .... *P. bellidifolia*
16. Leaves usually erect, narrower 17

17. Corolla-lobes deeply notched, lacking meal (Gansu) .... *P. aerinantha*

17. Corolla-lobes entire, mealy on face (Shaanxi) .... *P. giraldiana*

Primula muscarioides Hemsley, Kew Bull. 8: 319 (1907)

P. tsarongensis Balf. f. & Forrest (1920)
P. giraldiana Balf. f. (1913) non Pax

DESCRIPTION *Leaves* oblong to elliptical, to 20 × 5 cm, usually much smaller, shiny mid-green and almost glabrous above, the margin crenately toothed. *Stem* exceeding leaves, usually glabrous, slightly white-mealy at the top. *Flowers* many, forming a short spike, highly reflexed so that the bottommost are held almost vertically. *Calyx* purplish, usually without meal or hairs, to 5 mm, the upper lobes usually 2–3 toothed. *Corolla* purple-blue, the tube about 8 mm, very narrow, the somewhat spreading corolla-lobes about 2 × 2 mm. Heterostylous. 2n = 40. (Plate 18.)

DISTRIBUTION Fairly widespread in the border

zone between south-east Tibet, north-west Yunnan and south-west Sichuan, extending east to Muli and Beima Shan.

'A swamp plant growing amongst willows along streams down to 3350 m', but also said to grow in 'moist alpine meadows'.

Amongst the species with many deflexed flowers in a spike, *P. muscarioides* is diagnosed by its spreading corolla lobes, crenately toothed leaves, and shiny, almost glabrous leaves. For distinctions with the closely related *P. cernua*, see there. *P. deflexa* is best distinguished by having a hairy stem and completely non-mealy stems. *P. apoclita* also looks superficially similar, but has much more hairy leaves and smaller flowers.

VARIATION Some gatherings from the Chienchuan/Mekong divide in Yunnan have much more dissected leaves, which approach those of *P. pinnatifida* in shape. One gathering by Rock from Sichuan has leaves lightly mealy below. A white-flowered form arose in cultivation but has not been seen recently.

CULTIVATION First introduced by Forrest in 1905. There were many subsequent gatherings by Forrest, Rock and Ward, and some of these may have led to later introductions. However, it has persisted in cultivation without definite introduction since at least 1935, and is still quite frequently met with and offered. Not a difficult plant to grow, but only usually flowering for one or two seasons.

Primula cernua Franchet, Bull. Soc. Bot. Fr. 32: 271 (1885)

DESCRIPTION A tall robust plant when well grown, the cream-mealy stem to 40 cm, closely related to *P. muscarioides*, and chiefly distinguished from it by the relatively large and spreading corolla-lobes giving a *cup-shaped* limb to the long-tubed violet flower *8–10* mm in diameter, the flowers being somewhat pendant (but not strongly deflexed) and very numerous, crowded into a spike up to 4 cm long; unlike *P. muscarioides,* the stalk to the oblanceolate to obovate, entire to serrate leaves is almost *missing*. Heterostylous. 2n = 20. (Fig. Halda: 316.) (Plate 18.)

DISTRIBUTION From the Yunnan-Sichuan borderlands, including Chienchuan, Muli and Kulu.

'Rather bare soil in relatively dry pine forests' on sandstone, 2500–4000 m.

P. cernua seems to stand very close to the tetraploid *P. muscarioides*, and may represent a diploid parent of it. However, it occurs further to the north-east in a drier climate, and seems to be ecologically quite distinct.

CULTIVATION Introduced by Forrest in 1918, **AM** 1928, but thought to be lost by 1942. Reintroduced in 1987, possibly by Martyn Rix, and established by Cluny Gardens. A magnificent stand was exhibited by Jim Jermyn (Edrom Nurseries) at the 1990 International Garden Festival at Gateshead. Still quite regularly seen in cultivation and offered in 2002.

Primula deflexa Duthie, Gard. Chron. ser. III, 39: 229 (1906)

P. conica Balf. f. & Forrest (1916)

DESCRIPTION Similar to *P. muscarioides,* but with the stem markedly *hairy* and lacking meal, the *leaves hairy* on the mid-rib and veins, and the flowers usually *longer*, to 15 mm, blue-purple, mid-blue, or white with a bluish eye. Heterostylous. 2n = 40. (Photo: Bull. AGS 64: 233.) (Plate 99.)

DISTRIBUTION Primarily in north-west Yunnan, locally common in many sites around the Zhongdian plateau, where it has become very familiar in recent years; less common on the northern and eastern flanks of the Yulong Shan and extending to the east side of the Beima Shan. Extends over the Sichuan border via the Da Xue Shan and possibly further to the north. Generally to the south of *P. muscarioides* and the south-west of *P. cernua*.

Marshy sites, streamsides, wet pathsides, etc., often with *P. chionantha*, 3300–4300 m.

CULTIVATION Introduced, probably by Wilson, in 1905, and probably latterly by Forrest and Rock. **AM** 1916. Reintroduced at least by KGB 759 in 1992 and ACE 2263, 2283 in 1994 from Tianchi Lake, Zhongdian and commonly grown in the late 1990s, probably persisting in 2002. ARGS 921 from 99 Dragons was perhaps the most recent accession. Similar plants collected in north Sichuan by SQAE 487 in 2000 were probably *P. violacea*.

Primula apoclita Balf. f. & Forrest, Notes Roy. Bot. Gdn. Edinb. 12: 3 (1920)

P. lepta Balf. f. & Forrest (1920)

DESCRIPTION Another close relative of *P. muscarioides*, but less robust, and with *matt*, not shiny leaves which are *softly hairy* throughout. The stem is *shorter*, scarcely exceeding the leaves, and not exceeding 16 cm, and is strongly *yellow*-mealy above, as is the calyx, the lobes of which have hairy margins. Corolla-tube about 7 *mm*, purplish-blue. Heterostylous. 2n = 40. (Plate 100.)

DISTRIBUTION The wetter parts of the Yunnan-Sichuan borderlands, centred around the Beima Shan, Haba Shan and Da Xue Shan, but extending further east in Sichuan to Litang. It is possible to consider *P. muscarioides, P. cernua, P. deflexa, P. apoclita* and even *P. violacea* as geographically and ecologically distinct but overlapping parts of a single polymorphic species-group. The smaller, and smaller-flowered *P. apoclita* is perhaps the most alpine of this assemblage.

'Moist stony alpine pastures', 4000–4700 m. Also in gaps amongst dwarf shrubs, usually on limestone.

P. lepta referred to even smaller plants with nearly entire leaves. They seem to refer to 'high alpine snow valley (forms) on lime ground'. On the Beima Shan, it can closely resemble *P. watsonii* and although I saw both species there, I was confused by the identity of a few plants. These species were fused in Flora of China. It is necessary sometimes to establish whether flowers are heterostylous (*P. apoclita*) or homostylous (*P. watsonii*), a fiddly job with such tiny flowers, particularly as the style length in the latter varies so much. Some intermediates might be hybrids.

CULTIVATION Introduced by Forrest in 1922, and maintained in cultivation for some years. Said in 1928 to be 'a poor thing with small purplish flowers of little value'. Introduced by ACE 2124 , and KGB 567 from the Beima Shan was also probably this.

Primula violacea Smith & Ward, Notes Roy. Bot. Gdn. Edinb. 14: 54 (1923)

DESCRIPTION Close to *P. apoclita*, but with *longer* (10–12 mm) darker (*deep violet*) tubes to the more deflexed flowers which have smaller (about 2 mm) corolla-lobes; diagnostically, the leaves are *rough* (scabrid) rather than softly hairy. Presumably heterostyle, but five specimens examined were all thrum flowered. (Plate 101.)

DISTRIBUTION Sichuan, in the Kulu area and to the west of it. Recently found by John and Hilary Birks on the Balang Shan during an AGS Tour in 2001, and SQAE 487 from the Gonggan Len in 2000 may also have been this. Alpine boulders among scrub, 4000–4300 m. Probably occurs further to the north-east than any of its relatives.

Primula watsonii Dunn, Notes Roy. Bot. Gdn. Edinb. 5: 63 (1911)

P. cyanantha Balf. f. & Forrest (1920)
P. vialii Franchet (1891) p.p. non sens. Delavay

DESCRIPTION Closely related to *P. apoclita* in particular. Distinguished by the *blackish-purple* corolla which is *tube-like* throughout, the corolla lobes being very short and held erect. *Homostylous*, and self-fertile, but with considerable variation in style length (see sectional account). 2n = 40.

DISTRIBUTION From the common borders of Tibet, Yunnan, Sichuan and Burma, from Tsarong to Tatsien-lu and Seinghku Wang. Grows in exposed, well-drained alpine moorland on limestone at about 4350 m on the Beima Shan, in gaps between dwarf shrubs.

CULTIVATION Introduced by Watson in 1908, and by Forrest in 1918, apparently grown quite widely under the name *P. cyanantha* and still in cultivation in 1942. Reintroduced by Lancaster (1010) in 1981, and still in cultivation in 1992. Reintroduced again in 1994 (ACE 1402).

Primula pinnatifida Franchet, Bull. Soc. Bot. Fr. 32: 271 (1885)

DESCRIPTION More distinctive and attractive than most of its relatives, distinguished chiefly by the narrowly lobed hairy leaves, *often cut almost to the mid-rib*, a *white*-mealy stem, and a *flared*, shallowly bowl-shaped corolla-limb about 10 mm in diameter, wider than the tube is long; corolla-lobes entire, deep blue to *amethyst-pink*. Heterostylous. 2n = 20 with a pair of heteromorphic chromosomes in the thrum (see p.308). (Photo: Bull. AGS 56: 228.) (Plates 19, 66.)

DISTRIBUTION Widespread in north-west Yunnan, and well known from many stations on the Yulong Shan in particular, but extending to the Kulu and Muli regions of Sichuan.

'(Deep) soil in snow cauldrons on slate or limestone, descend(ing) into dense subalpine fir forests (3500?) 4000–5000 m.' In 1987 found growing on the Yulong Shan at 4250 m in a 'small shattered cirque of giant boulders and moraine' in a 'flower garden to savour for many years with patches of yellow, blue, purple and red set amongst a bleak rock landscape with snow patches and drifting mist'. Here its companions included *P. secundiflora, P. sikkimensis* var. *pseudosikkimensis, P. chionantha* and *P. dryadifolia*.

VARIATION Although *P. muscarioides* is less alpine in character and more typical of wetter regions to the west of the main distribution of *P. pinnatifida,* confusing intermediates occur. These may represent hybrids, or possibly morphologically and ecologically intermediate populations. Tiny high alpine forms have been called var. *nana* inedit., while forms with very narrow, doubly serrate leaf segments have been called var. *sectilis* inedit.

CULTIVATION Originally introduced by Forrest in 1908. Still in cultivation in 1929 (an early Dufay colour slide of a magnificent plant from R.B. Cooke's garden labelled 'seed from Forrest's garden' is in my possession), but apparently lost soon afterwards. Reintroduced in 1987, and 1991 (CLD 1092) from the Yulong Shan. I have found that in pot culture it enjoys good light and the high humidity provided by mist culture when in growth, but needs to be kept almost dry in winter. Not seen much in cultivation after about 1998.

Primula mairei Levl., Le Monde de Plantes 17: 2 (1915)

P. cephalantha Balf. f. (1915)

DESCRIPTION Closely related to *P. pinnatifida*, but coming from much further east, and with *yellow-mealy* stems and calyces, and *notched* corolla-lobes. Heterostylous. Very little known from two sites in north-east Yunnan in alpine meadows, 3200–3300 m. Included within *P. pinnatifida* by Flora of China and Halda (1992).

Primula inopinata Fletcher, J. Linn. Soc. 52: 339 (1942)

DESCRIPTION Also apparently related to *P. pinnatifida*, but with flowers arranged in a *loose* raceme rather than a tight imbricated spike; corolla-lobes *notched*. Heterostylous. Only known from cultivated material originating from seed collected on the Zhongdian plateau, Yunnan in 1937 as *P. aromatica* (section Monocarpicae) and possibly a variant of another more widespread species such as *P. deflexa* as it has not been rediscovered. Not recognized by Flora of China. (Fig. Halda: 319.)

Primula concholoba Stapf & Sealy, Bot. Mag. t.9289 (1932)

DESCRIPTION Immediately distinguished from all its relatives by the *short* tube to the soft blue to purple mealy flowers which is no longer than the calyx; the corolla-lobes are rounded and usually unnotched, forming a *subglobose*, cowbell-shaped limb scarcely open at the mouth; inflorescence few-flowered (rarely more than 10), capitate; leaves pale green and softly hairy with large irregular teeth. *Homostylous* and self-fertile. 2n = 40.

DISTRIBUTION From the Seinghku and Delei valleys close to the frontiers of Assam, Burma and Tibet; and on two passes on the main range north of the Pemako district and east of Tsela, south-east Tibet, 300 km to the north-west.

Steep grassy slopes and on cliff ledges, amongst dwarf rhododendrons and junipers in very wet districts, about 4000 m.

This is a quite unmistakable little species which although rather spindly, has a quiet charm. Curiously, most reports in the field and from early cultivation refer to the flowers being purple or violet, but today cultivated plants seem uniformly to be a soft blue in colour.

CULTIVATION There appears to have only been a

single introduction, by Ward from the Seinghku Wang in 1926. It has proved one of the more amenable species in cultivation, and is quite frequently met with today; seed and plants are often offered from specialist sources. Although very short-lived, seed sets well and it is easy to raise in a moist but well-drained site.

Primula bellidifolia King, Fl. Brit. India 3: 486 (1882)

P. menziesiana Balf. f. & Smith (1916)
P. adenantha Balf. f. & Cooper (1920)
P. micropetala Balf. f. & Cooper (1920)
P. atricapilla Balf. f. & Cooper (1920)
P. hyacinthina Smith (1936)

DESCRIPTION A species with *few-flowered* capitate heads, distinguished by the distinctive rosette of *prostrate*, daisy-like leaves (as the name suggests), which are matt, shortly hairy, dull green, and have a *rounded, nearly entire blade*; in some forms these leaves are white-mealy beneath. Stem mealy above, glabrous, the mauve, blue or violet flowers with rounded, usually slightly notched corolla-lobes. Flowers heterostylous or homostylous. 2n = 20, 40. (Plate 102.)

DISTRIBUTION The only Himalayan member of the section, occurring from East Nepal through Sikkim, Chumbi, west and central Bhutan to south-east Tibet east to Tse (94° E).

Commonly on cliff ledges under overhangs, but also at higher altitudes in thinly grassed open sites with good drainage in high rainfall areas, 3200–5000 m.

VARIATION *P. bellidifolia* is one of very few primula species which occurs at two 'ploidy levels, and has heterostyle and homostyle races. In the context of the rest of the genus, it is most unexpected that there is no apparent relationship between ploidy and mating system.

- Subsp. *hyacinthina* (Smith) Richards (1993). (*P. hyacinthina* Smith, Notes Roy. Bot. Gdn. Edinb. 19: 170 (1936)) differs chiefly in being white-mealy beneath the leaves, uniquely in this section. It is very strongly fragrant, but does not otherwise significantly differ from
- Subsp.*bellidifolia*, and the amount of meal on the leaf can vary in both subspecies. Smith & Fletcher (1942) have already suggested that they may warrant no more than varietal status. However, subsp. *hyacinthina* is somewhat geographically distinct, coming from the eastern end of the species range, in the Tsari district of south-east Tibet, and so I am suggesting subspecific rank for it. In both subspecies, diploids, tetraploids, heterostyles and homostyles all occur, and there is no apparent altitudinal differentiation between subspecies.
- David Rankin flowered in 2002 a mysterious plant close to subsp. *hyacinthina*, mealy below leaves but with toothed leaves and originating from Daochen, Sichuan. This should probably be recognised as a distinct subspecies.

CULTIVATION Introduced from Bhutan by Cooper in 1915 (**AM** 1928), and latterly by Ludlow and Sherriff. Still met with occasionally as both subspecies, and seed and plants are intermittently offered, but not as commonly seen as *P. concholoba* or *P. muscarioides*. Resentful of winter wet, and best overwintered in a frame, or with the plants cloched, and very short-lived. Not very attractive in flower, but with attractive foliage.

REFERENCE. Tremayne M.A., Richards A.J. 1993.

Primula aerinantha Balf. f. & Purdom, Notes Roy. Bot. Gdn. Edinb. 9: 146 (1916)

DESCRIPTION A rather robust species, the stems, white-mealy above, reaching 30 cm and bearing a small capitate head of 3–15 flowers; flowers lavender blue, the tube 8 mm and the shallowly bowl-shaped non-mealy limb to 10 mm in diameter; corolla-lobes diagnostically *deeply notched*. Leaves pale green, sparsely hairy and crenate-dentate. Heterostylous. Fig. Halda: 315.

Only known from the mountain Lien Hwa (Lotus mountain) in west Gansu, limestone rocks in a big gully and neighbouring alpine meadows, 3000–4000 m. Introduced by Purdom and Farrer in 1914, but the resultant plants failed to set seed.

Primula giraldiana Pax, Pflanzenreich Primulaceae 92 (1905)

DESCRIPTION Closely resembles *P. aerinantha*, but the blue-violet corolla lobes are entire and rounded, not notched, and are mealy within. Heterostylous. Only known from Taipa Shan, Shaanxi and has never been cultivated. *P. aerinantha* and *P. giraldiana* represent two related northern outposts of the section, presumably relictic from colder periods when relatives were more widespread in the intervening lowlands.

Primula gracilenta Dunn, Notes Roy. Bot. Gdn. Edinb. 5: 62 (1911)

DESCRIPTION Similar to *P. aerinantha* and *P. giraldiana*, but the capitate heads borne on non-mealy stems to 20 cm have 7–15 deep bluish-purple non-mealy flowers with *narrowly acute* entire corolla-lobes. Heterostylous.

Confined to the borderlands of Sichuan, Yunnan and Tibet to the west of Yungling and Yungning. Recorded in earlier years from localities which are now well-known such as Zhongdian and the Yulong Shan. It seems to be uncommon there, but one record from near Zhongdian was made in 1995 by the Miehes. Limestone cliff ledges and neighbouring limestone slopes, 3500–4000 m. Introduced in 1912 and 1932, but soon lost on both occasions.

Primula euchaites Smith, Notes Roy. Bot. Gdn. Edinb. 15: 301 (1927)

DESCRIPTION Another close relative of *P. aerinantha*, *P. giraldiana* and *P. gracilenta*, but smaller, the stems to only 8 cm and chiefly distinguished by the *long black hairs* on the calyces and bracts; the violet flowers, 5–8 together, have rounded, *shallowly notched* corolla-lobes and the plant lacks meal. Heterostylous.

Only known from the Seingkhu Wang, Burma/Tibet frontier on the grassy ledges of limestone cliffs where it grows with *P. concholoba*, which is superficially similar but has quite different flowers.

Primula flaccida Balakr., J. Bombay Nat. Hist. Soc. 67: 63 (1972)

P. nutans Delavay (1886) non Georgi (1775)
P. penduliflora Franchet (1908)

DESCRIPTION A *robust* plant with narrowly elliptical finely toothed sparsely hairy leaves to 20 cm. *Stems* to 50 cm, usually shorter, mealy above, bearing a *compact* somewhat *pyramidal* white-mealy spike of 5–20 pendant lavender-blue mealy-faced flowers which expand from a rather broad short tube into a shallowly bell-shaped limb 20–25 mm in diameter; corolla-lobes entire or shallowly notched; the dark green to purplish calyces overlap in a manner typical of this section. 2n = 20. Thrums fully self-sterile; pins 1% self-fertile. (Plate 19.)

DISTRIBUTION West and north-west Yunnan, and just into south-west Sichuan, also disjunct in eastern Yunnan. Formerly in many sites around Dali lake, but not apparently seen in this now intensively cultivated area in recent years and may now be rare and threatened (see also *P. vialii*).

'Open pine forests and rocky pastures'; 'stone-strewn but earthy slopes rich in herbs on diabasic soil', 2700–3700 m.

This familiar and beautiful species has been usually known as *P. nutans* in cultivation, but it was shown by Schwarz that this is the correct name for what had been usually called *P. sibirica*. Unfortunately, perhaps, this appropriate name (nutans = nodding) for an elegant plant has been replaced by the rather infelicitous 'flaccida'.

As discussed under the sectional heading, this species, together with *P. spicata* and *P. siamensis*, takes an intermediate position between the sections Muscarioides and Soldanelloides. They have been traditionally classified within Soldanelloides, perhaps because of the large flowers, but this is an otherwise Himalayan section. The Chinese location, ease of cultivation, spike-like inflorescence of overlapping calyces, and ability to hybridize with *P. vialii* all suggested a Muscarioides affinity, and the close relationship with the Muscarioid *P. vialii* has since been confirmed by the DNA. Consequently, I have moved them to this section.

CULTIVATION Introduced by Forrest in 1914, and has been well established in cultivation ever since. If groups of plants are grown together, seed is readily set, and in favourable conditions plants self-sow. Easily the most amenable member of the section, growing well in a rich peaty soil in shelter and partial shade, as amongst dwarf rhododendrons, etc., and not requiring winter protection. Too robust to be suitable for pot culture. Will flower in a year from seed, and will then flower for two to six seasons. Original reports suggested that it was monocarpic, but this is certainly not so today, and it may be that more perennial forms have been selected in cultivation. One of the most outstanding garden primulas. Remarkably, it seems not to have been refound in the 'modern era' and in common with species from agricultural altitudes in this region, it may be very rare in the wild now.

Primula spicata Franchet, Bull. Soc. Bot. Fr. 32: 269 (1885)

P. delicata Forrest (1908) non Petitm. (1908) = *P. malacoides*
P. delicatula Dunn (1917)

DESCRIPTION Differs from *P. flaccida* by its less robust habit (leaves to 8 cm, serrate and some at least obviously stalked), and its *lax, one-sided* spike of funnel-shaped *blue* flowers with a white-mealy face, the narrower tube at least 2× the short mealy calyx. Confined to the Dali region of west Yunnan. Stony meadows and cliff ledges, 3000–3700 m. Introduced by Forrest in 1908 and later (**AM** 1918). Failed to set seed in cultivation, and soon lost. Apparently a beautiful species which may prove to be amenable in cultivation, and every effort should be made to reintroduce it. Rediscovered on the Cang Shan by Harry Jans in 1998. (Fig. Halda: 333.)

Primula siamensis Craib, Kew Bull. Misc. Inform. 8: (1922)

DESCRIPTION Similar to *P. spicata,* with the same lax one-sided spike of funnel-shaped flowers, but with nearly *entire* leaves, and with pale violet corolla-lobes which are always entire. Thailand; upper Meping Valley north of Chiangmai, limestone crevices, 1700–2000 m. This area, close to the Burmese border, is within the 'Golden Triangle' controlled by opium barons, and access is consequently difficult and perhaps dangerous. Introduced in 1921 and 1932, but short-lived in cultivation, and failed to set seed. Very likely not hardy. One of only three primulas native to Thailand.

Primula vialii Franchet p.p., Extr. Proces-Verbaux Seances Soc. Philom. Paris 3: 148 (1891) emend. Smith & Fletcher, Trans. Bot. Soc. Edinb. 33: 290–292 (1942)

P. littoniana Forrest (1908)

DESCRIPTION A quite unmistakable and often robust plant, the erect spear-shaped leaves with the margins markedly recurved and softly hairy to 30 cm. *Stems* rather stout, glabrous, mealy above, to 60 cm, bearing a distinctive *cylindrical* (at first narrowly pyramidal) bottle-brush-like spike of *very many* (often in excess of 100) crowded flowers, the spike to 20 cm. *Calyces brilliant scarlet-red,* corollas blue-violet, so that the spike has a red apex as in a red-hot poker (*Kniphofia*). *Corolla-lobes* narrow, acute, undivided. Heterostylous, both pins and thrums almost totally self-sterile. 2n = 20, the thrums with a pair of heteromorphic chromosomes. Flowering in cultivation June and July (to August in the wild), the leaves usually appearing during the last week of May, later than any other primula species. (Plate 18.)

DISTRIBUTION Formerly widespread and scattered throughout much of north-west Yunnan and south-west Sichuan, including sites around Lijiang and the Yulong Shan (where it was always local), Zhongdian, Muli, Kulu, and Yungning. Seems never to have been rediscovered in the 'modern era', although it occurred in areas which are now intensively botanized. Most sites may now be intensively cultivated, and *P. vialii,* like *P. flaccida,* may have become rare and threatened. Every effort should be made to relocate and conserve these fine species in the wild.

'Damp meadows in masses (but) enters the most varied thickets, even the dense and dwarf evergreen bush of prickly oaks ... and dry stony meadows.' 2850–3350 m.

With its blue and red spires of flowers, this extraordinary species presents an aspect unique in *Primula,* and one seen in no other plant. It is compelling, curiously attractive, and deservedly popular in cultivation. Nevertheless, it has suffered a tortuous taxonomic history. This arose due to the failure of the discoverer, Pere Delavay, to mention the most conspicuous feature of this species, its brilliantly red-topped spikes. These fade in the herbarium, and consequently Franchet also included material belonging to *P. watsonii* in the original description and citations. Pax (1905) did not see Delavay's original specimens, and following Franchet he further confused the situation by also including material of *P. gracilenta* in his description, while his figure is considered to be of *P. deflexa*. By 1906, *P. vialii* had become a very confused name not clearly associated with this distinctive plant.

Consequently, when Forrest found this conspicous species growing abundantly in that year, he naturally concluded with some surprise that it was new and described it after the local British Consul as *P. littoniana*. Garden material, particularly in robust forms, remained under this name for many years, although Smith and Fletcher showed that Delavay's material can clearly and unambiguously be assigned to the species in question, and so *P. vialii* is the prior and correct name. The original orthography is *P. viali*, but this must be corrected according to the Code.

CULTIVATION Introduced by Forrest in 1906 and subsequently, and certainly one of the finest of his many introductions. Since then its popularity has ensured its continued survival. It was originally considered a rather tricky species to grow and constant renewal from seed may have fostered the selection of more amenable strains. Today it is freely available, and is often offered by non-specialist sources.

Typically, it is grown in groups in the shelter of shrubs such as rhododendrons, but in good light, in a humus-rich, fertile and moist but well-drained soil. It germinates well in the spring from seed which remains viable for at least two years, and seedlings can be pricked out and grown on in deep trays in a sheltered and cool place, to be overwintered in a covered frame. Plants should be placed in their final position as they come into growth, and most will flower the same summer. Although some losses may occur during the winter, these are minimized in an open humusy soil and it is not usually necessary to cover the winter crowns, which disappear completely for 7 months. Plants are usually best in their second flowering year, but in a suitable place they may persist for some seasons. I have had plants flower for nine successive seasons in a peat bed top-dressed with leaf-mould.

If pins and thrums are grown together, seed is usually set in abundance, and when well suited this species sometimes self-sows.

HYBRIDIZATION In a mass planting of *P. vialii* and *P. flaccida* at Ascreavie in 1976, I noted with great surprise intermediates which basically resembled *P. flaccida,* but which bore darker and more numerous flowers in a more pyramidal spike, the pale grey calyces of which were strongly tinted with a reddish purple. Betty Sherriff said that such plants of self-sown origin had been appearing for some years, and she was quite sure that they were hybrids. They had already been reported to R.B. Cain (1963) by Major George Sherriff where they were called *P.* × *vaniana*, a name I have been unable to trace elsewhere. Similar presumptive hybrids have since been observed in other Scottish gardens (Cluny and Tantallon).

Section **Soldanelloides** Pax,

Bot. Jahrb. Syst. 10: 186 (1889).

Type species *P. soldanelloides* Watt.

DESCRIPTION Closely allied to section Muscarioides, and differing in the following particulars: stems not always exceeding the leaves, bearing *1–few flowers*; calyx zygomorphically subequal, but the flowers are rarely so crowded that the calyces overlap like roof-tiles; corolla often *white*, the tube usually *shorter than the corolla-lobes* and scarcely exceeding the calyx, the corolla-lobes suberect and thus usually forming a *bell-shape* or even a cowbell-shape, rarely flat-faced; capsule globose, included within the calyx. Flowers hetero-stylous, except for *P. sherriffae*. 2n = 20. Almost completely self-sterile. Flowering May–June in cultivation, during the monsoon in the wild.

DISTRIBUTION From Kashmir (one species) and northern India through Nepal, Sikkim, Bhutan, Assam, northern Burma to south-east Tibet. Centred on Bhutan and south-east Tibet and thus primarily east Himalayan, in contrast with section Muscarioides which is primarily Chinese with only one Himalayan species.

All except *P. sherriffae* are high alpines from moraines, boulder fields, cliff ledges and rocky tundra in the Himalaya, usually above the zone of continuous vegetational cover and typically in wet areas with snow cover for about 6 months and a heavy monsoon while in growth, 3700–5700 m. Remarkably, *P. sherriffae* is from limestone cliffs in warm temperate forest zones at about 1700 m in south-east Bhutan and Assam, habitats which become dust-dry in the winter and spring, when this species is dormant.

It seems likely that the Soldanelloides section originated with the Muscarioides in China and migrated westwards into the Himalaya, becoming adapted to the high alpine habitat as the Himalayas rose higher and became glaciated. Presumably the lowland cliff species *P. sherriffae* was isolated in locally suitable habitats, free from competition from forest trees, after glacial epochs when the alpine species would have been more widespread at a lower altitude. The DNA of only one species, *P. reidii,* has yet been studied. Unexpectedly, this species proves to be more closely allied to the small-flowered Muscarioides species *P. muscarioides* and *P. bellidifolia* than to *P. flaccida*. Consequently, the large-flowered Muscarioides *P. spicata* and *P. flaccida*, more usually classified as Soldanelloides, may not represent the link between the sections as originally thought.

Otherwise the section can be roughly divided into two groups. In one group, loosely based around *P. reidii,* plants typical of crevices and sheltered places under boulders form small tufts composed of very hairy nearly entire leaves, and have very few large, lampshade-shaped flowers.

In the other group, based around *P. soldanelloides* itself, plants may creep and form small mats or individual rosettes of narrow, often dissected leaves which are less hairy, while the flowers are much smaller, and narrower in form. Typically these are plants of stony wastes and tundra at great altitudes. In the latter group, a few species, notably *P. jigmediana,* and to a lesser extent *P. fea, P. flabellifera* and *P. sappharina*, resemble some Minutissimae. However, this resemblance is probably of a secondary, parallel origin resulting from adaptation to the high alpine stony habitat, rather than the result of a direct phyletic link.

With their long dormancy as a tiny bud, frequently small size, and few conspicuous strongly scented flowers, the Soldanelloides can be regarded as extreme specialists to the sheltered high alpine habitat, where they attract scarce flower visitors such as migrant moths, butterflies and bees. Many are of quite exceptional beauty, outstanding even with this genus of lovely flowers, typically forming few large strongly scented hanging bells of mealy blue or white flowers.

For some reason the spelling Soldanelloides used by Pax in 1889 was changed by him to Soldanelloideae in 1905, and the latter has been used by most subsequent authors, but not by the more recent reviews Wendelbo (1961) or Fenderson (1986). The initial spelling is correct, not least because the latter form is not permissible at sectional level by the Code.

CULTIVATION Of the 18 species, no less than 16 have been flowered in cultivation, but it is probable that as I write in 2002, only five survive, and of these only one is commonly grown. These statistics emphasise several points. Firstly, the desirability of most of the species is such as to encourage exceptional efforts on the part of collectors who attempted to introduce them to cultivation from their remote and inaccessible habitats.

Secondly, they are in the main the most maddeningly difficult of all primulas in cultivation. Species which emerge from under snow in an almost dry dormant state to encounter immediately a torrential and almost continuous monsoon, while growing in a water culture supported by a largely 'soilless' medium of stones and grit, might well prove to be difficult in cultivation! When these conditions are associated with a naturally short-lived life-cycle, offering few opportunities for vegetative increase, and a requirement for cross-pollination if seed is to be set, the difficulties are compounded.

Thirdly, it is surely no accident that the only species to have become strongly established in cultivation, *P. reidii*, is the westernmost, occurring beyond the reach of the more severe effects of the monsoon. Although a high alpine, it grows in more moderate soils and climates than the majority of its relatives.

Clearly, if we are to meet sustained success in the cultivation of these lovely plants, every effort should be made to provide highly specialized conditions. Pot culture, using an extremely gritty medium, is indicated. As soon as (but not before) growth starts late in spring, plants should be regularly irrigated, as for instance by a mist or sprinkler system, while being regularly fed by dilute liquid feeds. A number of seedlings should be grown together, and artificially cross-pollinated to ensure seed-set. As foliage dies down in autumn, water should be gradually withheld until the only water reaching the resting bud comes from the damp plunge within which the clay pot is immersed. It has been suggested that the winter resting bud is not very hardy (ironically in these high alpines, which however are protected by snow in the wild), and protection from severe frost is also recommended.

Raising seedlings seems much less problematical. Seed sown in a gritty compost in a clay pot and plunged outside in a frame in February or March will usually germinate well in late April or May. Seedlings grow on well when plunged in a cool humid spot where they are not allowed to dry out and are given occasional dilute liquid feeds. Both seedlings and adult plants are susceptible to aphids and slugs. Conventional treatments, in the former case a standard systemic insecticide given at half-strength, will usually guard against these. Seedlings can usually be pricked out into individual pots by August, and dried off as the foliage dies back. It is in the next season that the problems generally start!

HYBRIDIZATION Hybrids were raised between *P. reidii* and its close relative *P. wigramiana,* and perhaps more surprisingly with *P. wollastonii* by R.B. Cooke in the 1950s. The latter cross was repeated in about 1990 by Peter Burnett. These proved to be relatively vigorous, but there is no record that they set seed.

In contrast, a hybrid strain between *P. reidii* and *P. eburnea* which was raised during the 1950s, possibly by Miss Nic Alaisdair of Yorkshire, proved to be fertile, giving rise to a range of attractive hybrid types of varying flower colour. Such plants seem to have been grown, and were sometimes offered, until at least 1980, but have not been heard of recently.

LITERATURE. Cain R.B. (1963). Bull. AGS 31: 18–47.

KEY TO SPECIES

1. Small usually creeping plants; leaves not exceeding 2 cm, usually divided to half-way or more 2
1. Plant tufted, rarely creeping; largest leaves usually exceeding 2 cm, entire or divided less than half-way 6

2. Flowers white; corolla-lobes entire or notched .... *P. soldanelloides*
2. Flowers bluish; corolla-lobes entire to fringed 3

3. Corolla flat-faced, annulate .... *P. jigmediana*
3. Corolla bell-shaped, exannulate 4

4. Leaf blade fan-shaped, widest at apex .... *P. flabellifera*
4. Leaf blade widest near the middle 5

5. Corolla to 10 mm long; corolla-lobes entire .... *P. fea*
5. Corolla 4–7 mm long; corolla-lobes notched .... *P. sappharina*

6. Corolla-tube more than 2 cm, very narrow .... *P. sherriffae*
6. Corolla-tube less than 1 cm, short and broad 7

7. Corolla tubular, parallel-sided, more than 3× as long as broad 8
7. Corolla bell-shaped, usually wider at mouth, less than 3× as long as broad 9

8. Leaves with long white hairs beneath; corolla-lobes shortly toothed .... *P. siphonantha*
8. Leaves shortly hairy beneath; corolla-lobes with long narrow teeth .... *P. cawdoriana*

9. Flowers usually borne singly, parabolic, to 40 mm in diameter .... *P. klattii*
9. Flowers usually 2 or more together, bell-shaped, less than 30 mm in diameter 10

10. Stem hairy 11
10. Stem without hairs 12

11. Calyx and corolla without hairs .... *P. umbratilis*
11. Calyx, corolla and stem with long hairs .... *P. buryana*

12. Leaves lacking multicellular hairs, but sticky-glandular .... *P. eburnea*
12. Leaves softly hairy, not sticky 13

13. Corolla-lobes fringed, flowers pendant; calyx lobes toothed .... *P. wattii*
13. Corolla-lobes toothed or notched, flowers patent to pendant; calyx lobes usually entire 14

14. Meal absent; leaves shallowly lobed .... *P. chasmophila*
14. Meal present at least on upper stem and calyx; leaves entire to toothed 15

15. Flowers violet, funnel-shaped; leaves oblong .... *P. sandemaniana*
15. Flowers white or pale blue, bell-shaped; leaves oval 16

16. Plant creeping; flowers pendant, blue .... *P. wollastonii*
16. Plant tufted; flowers patent, white or blue 17

17. Leaves stalked; corolla-lobes notched .... *P. reidii*
17. Leaves without stalks; corolla-lobes toothed .... *P. wigramiana*

Primula reidii Duthie, Rep. Saharanpur Bot. Gard. (1885): 30 (1886)

DESCRIPTION *Leaves* oblong, to 20 × 3 cm, pale green, very hairy throughout, rounded at the tip and crenately to acutely toothed, the winged stalk poorly demarcated and almost equalling the blade. *Stems glabrous,* white-mealy above, somewhat exceeding the leaves, bearing a head of (1) 3–10 sessile declined flowers. *Calyx* broadly bell-shaped, green, or purplish in blue varieties, hairy at the margin, to 9 mm. *Corolla* white or ivory (usually pale to mid-blue in var. *williamsii*), often mealy outside, the tube about equalling the calyx and abruptly expanding into a bell-shaped limb about 20 mm in diameter, the corolla-lobes broadly rounded and notched. 2n = 20. (Plate 19.)

DISTRIBUTION North-west Himalaya from Kashmir through Himachal Pradesh and Uttar Pradesh to west-central Nepal, including Garwhal, Kumaon and Kulu.

Cliff crevices and wet rock-ledges, often near streams and waterfalls, usually in shade, 3200–4800 m.

The westernmost member of the section, growing at considerable altitudes for this far north. It is noteworthy that in these relatively summer-dry regions this species chooses humid localities, usually near running water. Unlike its relatives from wetter regions to the east, it usually roots into a humus-rich soil. Chadwell made the interesting observation that on the Rohtang Pass, Kulu, he had on several occasions passed by the site where he eventually discovered this species. It can come into growth very late in the wild, flowering in late summer, so that it is easily missed.

Most closely related to *P. wigramiana* and *P. eburnea* from further east in Nepal.

VARIATION

- Var. *williamsii* Ludlow, J. Roy. Hort. Soc. 80: 428 (1955). A more robust plant, larger in all its parts, commonly with 5–8 flowers in a head, the flowers 18–22 mm in diameter and commonly pale blue, or blue with a white centre, although white ('f. *alba*') and purple forms also occur. West-central Nepal.

Said to be easier in cultivation than var. *reidii.* However most strains now produce both blue- and white-flowered forms and a variety of sizes of plant, and are probably hybrids of the two varieties. It has to be said that poor cultivation of white 'var. williamsii' readily produces plants indistinguishable from var. *reidii!* The only real distinction in the wild seems to be that blue forms are only found in the east of its range.

CULTIVATION Introduced at Kew from seeds taken from Duthie's type herbarium specimen in 1883, and has probably been in cultivation continuously since, although there have been later introductions, i.e. by Sherriff in 1941, by Stainton, Sykes and Williams in 1952 and by Chadwell 1471 in 1996. Var. *williamsii* was introduced in 1952 by Stainton, Sykes and Williams (1770) and subsequently under a number of SSW and PSW numbers. More recently brought back by Jurasek 54 and Pavelka 374 from Nepal.

A very beautiful but rather temperamental plant, obtainable through the trade, which appears to favour some gardens (or growers?!) at the expense of others. Usually grown in a pot in a compost containing a good admixture of leaf-mould and grit in a frame or alpine house, kept almost dry in winter, and watered regularly in summer. Dislikes heat, and probably best plunged in a cool north-facing frame in summer; very susceptible to aphids. Seed sets well after cross-pollination between pins and thrums, and this germinates very readily. In some gardens, it can also thrive in troughs or raised beds where it may even self-sow. In these conditions, survival can be aided by winter cloching, but in some gardens even this precaution seems to be unnecessary. Such success has been met with in such disparate conditions as Cornwall and the Scottish Highlands, and it may be that mild winters, or reliable snow cover, help to protect the winter buds from extreme cold. **FCC** 1965.

HYBRIDIZATION Hybrids have been raised with *P. wigramiana*, *P. wollastonii* and *P. eburnea* (see sectional account), but none seem to survive today.

Primula wigramiana Smith, Notes Roy. Bot. Gdn. Edinb. 18: 182 (1934)

DESCRIPTION Closely related to *P. reidii*. Differs by the *obovate* leaves which lack a defined stalk, by the longer stem, which is usually at least 2× the leaves, and by the more open invariably pure white flowers (to 25 mm in diameter) the lobes of which are *irregularly toothed* rather than notched at the tip. Flowering late July in the wild. (Photo: Bull. AGS 57: 356 (1989), Fls. Himalaya fig.80.) (Plate 67.)

DISTRIBUTION Central Nepal in the Annapurna region. Steep grassy banks and fine stabilized screes, 3600–5700 m. 'Prefers a moist but not very wet, heavy brown soil, either amongst grass or in such dwarf shrubs as *Potentilla arbuscula*, *Rhododendron lepidotum* and *Spiraea*.' Sometimes in company with *P. buryana* which invariably chooses a quite different, scree, habitat.

Possibly best treated as a subspecies of *P. reidii*, but ecologically and geographically distinct, and the tall heads of large pure white flowers give this species a distinctive aspect.

CULTIVATION Introduced from Sherkathan (5200 m) by Sharma in 1931 (**AM** 1934). Reintroduced by Lowndes (1035) in 1950, and by Stainton, Sykes and Williams (8634) in 1954. Did not set seed so freely as *P. reidii*, and despite repeated reintroductions, now lost. However, it was persuaded to set seed at Bodnant, Kilbryde, Inshriach, Keillour and Branklyn for some years. Coming from a relatively dry area it ought to be one of the more amenable species in cultivation, but may be bedevilled by its apparent infertility. However, grown alongside *P. reidii*, I have found this species fiendishly difficult, much more so than its neighbour which is long-lived and flowers regularly.

Primula eburnea Balf. f. & Cooper, Notes Roy. Bot. Gdn. Edinb. 9: 166 (1916)

P. harroviana Balf. f. & Cooper (1918)

DESCRIPTION Closely related to *P. reidii* and *P. wigramiana*, but generally smaller than either, with slightly more numerous and smaller, more funnel-shaped ivory flowers not more than 10 mm across. Diagnostically, the leaves have *no multicellular hairs*, although they are strongly glandular. Stems glabrous and mealy. (Photo: 'A Quest of Flowers': 36. Bot. Mag. t. 8901.)

DISTRIBUTION Several sites on both sides of the main range where it forms the border between Bhutan and Tibet from 90°–92° E, e.g. Narim Thang, Cha La.

Crevices, or peaty or stony substrates under cliff or rock overhangs 'sheltered from the wind and rain but open to the sun'; very localized, but occasionally found in masses, 4300–4800 m.

'The gem of the whole of the eastern Himalaya' (Sherriff). *P. eburnea* does indeed seem to be a most beautiful little plant, very like *P. reidii*, but more delicate and with more globular heads of flowers.

CULTIVATION First introduced by Cooper in 1915 (**AM** 1919 as *P. harroviana*), and again as flown-home plants by Ludlow and Sherriff (21329) in 1949 (another AM, this time as *P. eburnea* in 1950!) Maintained from seed for some years at Kilbryde, Keillour and at Inshriach (Jack Drake's) from where the plant was regularly offered well into the 1970s, but it has now disappeared.

Primula buryana Balf. f., Kew Bull. Misc. Inform. 4: 151 (1922)

DESCRIPTION Similar to the last three species, with funnel-shaped flowers as in *P. eburnea*, but with the flowers virtually *stalkless* and held horizontally and the leaves still smaller, not exceeding 5 cm, and immediately distinguished by the leaves, stems and calyces being covered with long *shaggy white hairs*;

corolla white or (var. *purpurea*) faintly lilac, softly pubescent. 2n = 20. (Photo: Fls. Himalaya, fig. 66.). (Plate 19.)

DISTRIBUTION Central and eastern Nepal, from Dolpo, west of Annapurna and Gosainkund eastwards to the Everest region, just extending into neighbouring regions of Tibet. Mostly confined to relatively dry, rainshadow regions (but see var. *purpurea*).

'Shady earth, rock banks and rock crevices amongst boulders'; 'damp shale and in short turf by a small brook'. 3300–5000 m. Inhabits usually higher and more scree-like habitats than *P. wigramiana*.

P. buryana, another very beautiful little plant, was discovered earlier than most Nepalese species by virtue of the 1922 Everest expedition which entered the then 'forbidden kingdom' from the northern, Tibetan side. Dr Wollaston discovered this species on the western flanks of the mountain within Nepal.

VARIATION

- Var. *purpurea* Fletcher, J. Linn. Soc. Bot. 52: 323 (1941). Flowers faintly lilac (sometimes darker or bluish) with a white eye, only 1–3 together, and more open, even flat-faced. (Photo: Fls. Himalaya (suppl.) fig. 63). Central Nepal in the Gosainkund region, in very wet areas on peaty banks. The two varieties are never found together, and var. *purpurea* is ecologically and morphologically distinct and should perhaps be treated at specific rank.

CULTIVATION First flowered in 1931 from seeds collected by Dhwoj. There have been several subsequent introductions by Lowndes (1029) in 1950, and by Stainton, Sykes and Williams (SSW 4537, 4655, 8513) in 1954 and 1955. The latter collectors also flew home dormant plants. Reintroduced by Chadwell (CC & McK 144, 146) from Dhaulagiri ice-falls in 1990. This germinated and grew in large numbers; some growers such as Mike Northway flowered and sold it by the hundred. Little if any seed was set, despite persistent attempts at cross-fertilization between pins and thrums, and very few plants flowered a second time.

Primula umbratilis Balf. f. & Cooper, Notes Roy. Bot. Gdn. Edinb. 13: 22 (1920)

P. metria Balf. f. & Cooper (1920)

DESCRIPTION Very closely allied to the four foregoing species, but diagnostically with a *hairy* (but not shaggy) *non-mealy* stem, but with the calyx (apart from its minutely ciliate margin) and corolla *glabrous*. Flowers funnel-shaped, commonly *pale purple to violet-blue*, but also white (var. *alba*). Leaves usually with short lobes and less flat than in the preceding. (Photos: 'A Quest of Flowers: 154, 357.)

DISTRIBUTION North central Bhutan, to the south of the main range in the Black Mountain region, near to Bumthang, Maruthang and Pangotang.

Ledges of sheer and often inaccessible cliffs, 3700–4500 m.

Sherriff graphically describes how dormant and totally desiccated plants, in which the only sign of life was a tiny green heart to the bud, were taken from dust dry cliffs in late May. If thoroughly soaked, these could be in flower within a fortnight, as were plants on the ledges immediately after the arrival of the monsoon.

VARIATION

- Var. *alba* Fletcher, J. Linn. Soc. Bot. 52; 332 (1941). Flowers white. Said to be easier and more vigorous in cultivation than var. *umbratilis*, so that some growers considered that it merited specific status. There seem to be no other important differences between the colour forms, although they do not occur mixed.

CULTIVATION Introduced by Cooper (4787), flowering in 1918. Reintroduced on several occasions by Ludlow, Sherriff and associates in 1937 and 1949, both as seed and flown-home resting buds of purple and white forms. Of these the purple LSH 19128 and the white 19832 were the most successful. **AM** 1941. Failed to set seed except at Keillour, and had apparently disappeared by 1963.

Primula klattii Balakr., J. Bombay Nat. Hist. Soc. 67: 63 (1970)

P. uniflora Klatt (1872) non Gmelin (1805) = *P. vulgaris*

DESCRIPTION A shortly creeping plant producing

small tufts of hairy, *incised* leaves to 2× 1 cm. Stem wiry, to 9 cm, bearing *1–2 disproportionately huge* saucer- to cup-shaped nodding pale blue flowers, stained red at the base, to 40 mm in diameter. (Photos: 'A Quest of Flowers': 154, Fls. Himalaya (suppl.) fig. 66. Fig. Halda: 328.)

DISTRIBUTION Nepal east of Mt. Everest, Sikkim, Chumbi and Bhutan east to Chendebi. High level alpine grassland in very wet regions, 3800–5000 m.

An unmistakable species in flower, the single or paired flowers larger than the leaves and resembling those of a small poppy. Vegetatively it is close to *P. wollastonii*. This species has generally been known as *P. uniflora* Klatt, but this familiar name had unfortunately been already taken by Gmelin in 1805.

CULTIVATION First flowered in cultivation in 1911 from Smith & Cave's gathering in Sikkim. Reintroduced by Ludlow & Sherriff from Bhutan in 1937 and 1949, and by George Smith from the Barun Valley, Nepal in 1976. None of these introductions seem to have set seed or to have lasted more than a few years in cultivation.

Primula wollastonii Balf. f., Kew Bull. Misc. Inform. 4: 152 (1922)

DESCRIPTION A *rhizomatously creeping* plant forming *small flattened rosettes* of prostrate, rounded, pale green, hairy, entire to slightly crenate leaves to 5 × 2.5 cm, these sometimes white-mealy beneath. Stems white-mealy, to 25 cm, bearing 2–8 pendant sky blue to purple-mealy flowers. Corolla thimble-shaped, to 25 mm in length, not spreading and even sometimes somewhat *constricted* at the mouth, the lobes rounded and entire, *white-mealy* within. 2n = 20. (Photo: J. Scot. Rock Gdn. Club 21: 404, Fls. Himalaya fig. 83, Bull. AGS 47: 320–2.) (Plate 68.)

DISTRIBUTION Central and eastern Nepal on the main range from the Shiar and Langtang valleys to the Lumbasamba Himal just east of Everest, and in neighbouring areas of Tibet.

'Mossy cliff faces and steep gritty earth banks among small shrubs of berberis, cotoneaster, potentilla and dwarf rhododendrons', often associated with *P. concinna* and *P. primulina*. 3600–5500 m. 'The whole colony drips with water.'

The blue-mealy cloche-shaped flowers of this species are beautiful, but in cultivation tend to be stuck on the end of a stem which is ridiculously long for the leaves or flowers; the stems often become unattractively twisted or bent.

VARIATION It is said that forms from the Nepal side of the Everest region are smaller flowered and more mealy than the original collections from the Tibetan side, which approach *P. klattii*.

CULTIVATION Introduced by Dhwoj from Khumbu, Everest, in 1930, possibly remaining in cultivation for 30 years. Reintroduced by Poluinin in 1949, by George Smith from the Upper Barun valley in 1976, and by Ron McBeath from the same locality in 1981 and 1991 (EMAK). **AM** 1984.

Unlike most of its relatives, *P. wollastonii* is readily propagated from daughter rosettes which appear from roots growing near the soil surface. These are easily detached, and if treated as cuttings, grow on well.

P. wollastonii has been reported as thriving in an unprotected peat-bed, surviving winter temperatures down to –15°C, but is usually grown in a pot with winter protection. One soil recipe was formed of a mixture of lime-free loam, old leaf mould and chopped sphagnum moss. I have found that it is shy to flower, the main rosette being weakened by its propensity for producing offsets, so that it rarely achieves the size required for flowering. Flowering stems tend to be leggy and distorted in cultivation, and at least part of this problem may result from pot rotation, which is to be discouraged; plants are best fed heavily, and grown cool, but in maximum light.

Still occasionally seen in 2002, but not often flowered.

Primula wattii King, J. Linn. Soc. Bot. 20: 10 (1882)

DESCRIPTION A rather small species with slightly *lobed* and somewhat crisped long-hairy obovate leaves with an *indistinct stalk*, to 10 cm, and with glabrous, non-mealy stems to 18 cm. The compact often *semiglobose* head of 5–10 pale violet, white-eyed pendant flowers resembles that of a small *P. reidii* var. *williamsii*, but diagnostically the corolla-lobes are *fringed*, and the calyx lobes are themselves toothed. (Photo: Bull. AGS 31: 36. Fig. Halda: 334.)

DISTRIBUTION High up on the wet south side of the main divide from east Sikkim eastwards to the Burma border, including Bhutan, Arunchal Pradesh and just extending north into Tibet. 'Steep banks and ridges', 4300–4900 m. Apparently local and scarce, and has only been collected about 10 times.

CULTIVATION First flowered in 1912 from Cooper's Sikkim seed, and again in 1949 (Ludlow and Sherriff) and 1951 (Ghose) (**PC** 1951). Generally regarded as short-lived and rarely setting seed, but offered by Jack Drakes for more than a decade, and self-sowing for a time in Majorie Brough's Hertfordshire garden, so apparently not impossible given the correct conditions. Has not been seen in cultivation for some 20 years.

Primula sandemaniana Smith, Notes Roy. Bot. Gdn. Edinb. 19: 314 (1938)

DESCRIPTION Closely related to *P. wattii* and *P. chasmophila*, but with a *mealy* stem, and with very beautiful fewer (3–5), larger and more widely open (to 30 mm in diameter) blue-purple flowers, the corolla-lobes *notched*, but not fringed. The hairy leaves are flatter, less crisped or lobed and more oval in shape than *P. wattii*. (Photo: Bull. AGS 31: 26.)

DISTRIBUTION Only known from Migyitun, Tsari, south-east Tibet. 'Moss covered boulders at the edge of fir forest'; 'streamsides', 3500–4000 m.

Only found by the 1936 and 1938 Ludlow and Sherriff expeditions, introduced by both, and named from flowering material in cultivation. Apparently difficult, and only survived in cultivation for about five years.

Primula chasmophila Balf. f., Bot. Mag. t.8791 (1919)

DESCRIPTION Closely related to *P. wattii*, with similar lobulate leaves which are, however, finely hairy only and *truncate* at the base, giving rise to a well-defined and narrow *stalk*. Also related to *P. sandemaniana*, but totally lacking meal, with more lobulate and crisped leaves, and with deep violet flowers with crimson veins about 20 mm in diameter. (Photo: Bull. AGS 31: 25; 'A Quest of Flowers': 139. Fig. Halda: 324.)

DISTRIBUTION Central Bhutan, like *P. umbratilis* endemic to the Black Mountain area, but occurring only around the holy mountain of Dushinggang ('fir mountain'). High-level crevices and ledges amongst grass, 5000–5300 m, locally common.

Collected by Cooper (1915) and by Ludlow and Sherriff (1937) and successfully introduced on both occasions, but only surviving for a few years in cultivation.

Primula cawdoriana Ward, Notes Roy. Bot. Gdn. Edinb. 15: 87, 96 (1926)

DESCRIPTION Forms compact rosettes of semi-prostrate, velvety, somewhat crisped and lobulate oblong leaves to 5 cm, occasionally multiplying from root buds as in *P. wollastonii*. Scapes slender, erect, exceeding leaves, somewhat mealy, bearing a compact head of 3–8 *downward-pointing* blue to pale mauve broadly *tubular* flowers with a large whitish eye to 30 mm in length, the corolla-lobes deeply cut into *2–3 narrow segments* which are themselves sometimes somewhat *lacerate*. (Photo: Riddle of the Tsangpo Gorge: 25, Fig. Halda: 324.) (Plate 19.)

DISTRIBUTION South-east Tibet in the very wet and rich Tsari region, where it appears to be widespread, and east to the Doshong La and Deyang La, Pemakochung. 'Grassy banks and bare black soil ... in rhododendron/fir forests', 'rocky places especially on cliff ledges', 4000–4700 m.

This beautiful species is only likely to be confused with *P. siphonantha* from further to the south-east, which has not been in cultivation. The downward-pointing broadly cylindrical and lacerate flowers are otherwise distinctive, and unique in the genus. It was named for the Earl of Cawdor, a descendent of the Thane of Cawdor who sided with the King of Norway in opposition to Duncan in the Scottish Play. The latter Cawdor accompanied Ward on his 1924 expedition to solve the 'Riddle of the Tsangpo Gorges', although they did not make easy companions.

CULTIVATION Introduced by Ward (**AM** 1926), at least twice by Ludlow and Sherriff, and more recently by members of Kenneth Cox's excursions

(1997 and possibly other years). It has been in cultivation ever since, and is still occasionally offered. Several, including pins and thrums, must be grown together for seed to set, and it requires winter cover, but in some gardens it has been known to thrive in a well-drained but water-retentive spot in the open garden. However, it is more usually grown in a pot plunged in a north-facing frame. Relatively long-lived (I have had a specimen flower for five successive years, often as late as September) and can be vegetatively propagated if offsets are produced during a cool period in the early summer.

It is pleasantly unexpected that this high alpine from a very high rainfall zone should have proved relatively amenable in cultivation when so many of its relatives have not.

Primula siphonantha Smith, Notes Roy. Bot. Gdn. Edinb. 15: 303 (1927)

DESCRIPTION Differs from *P. cawdoriana* by the leaves with long white hairs covering the midrib beneath and by the shorter flowers (to 17 mm), the corolla lobes which are only shortly toothed. Seingkhu valley on the Burma/Tibet frontier, exposed earthy slopes and under boulders, 3500–3800 m. Has not been in cultivation.

Primula sherriffae Smith, New Flora and Silva 18: 130 (1936)

P. ludlowii Smith (1936)

DESCRIPTION *Leaves* forming a pale green, softly hairy somewhat flattened rosette of narrowly obovate usually entire leaves to 17 cm. *Stem* shorter than the leaves, or (var. *ludlowii*) sometimes absent, glabrous, sometimes slightly mealy, bearing 1–6 stalkless flowers horizontally. *Corolla* pale violet to lavender-blue, with an *extraordinarily long and slender cylindrical tube*, usually about 50 × 2 mm, abruptly expanded at the end into a flat to slightly cup-shaped limb about 25 mm in diameter, the corolla-lobes orbicular and nearly entire. Homostylous, both the extremely long style and the anthers borne shortly inside the mouth. Apparently self-fertile and frequently setting seed. (Plate 19.)

DISTRIBUTION Only known from two disjunct sites; about 26 km north of Diwangiri on the road to Chungkar, south-east Bhutan, on a cliff immediately to the east of the road, 1700 m; near the summit of Sirhoi Kashong, Mishmi Hills, Arunchal Pradesh, where it was so thickly plastered that 'it loomed out of the mist like the white cliffs of Dover'.

Vertical cliffs, growing in pure living moss, which is very wet when flowering occurs during the monsoon and is bone-dry when the plant is dormant in winter (but when *P. filipes* flowers in the same Bhutanese locality).

While marching through subtropical zones of east Bhutan on the way to south-east Tibet in 1934, Ludlow and Sherriff came across a cliff by the side of the road. On this they spotted a new yellow variety of *Lilium nepalense* (var. *concolor*). In order to reach this, Sherriff climbed a tree, which proved to be a very beautiful new species *Lucilia grandifolia*. In doing so, he also found what were considered to be two new species of primula. The most striking was *P. sherriffae*, which was named for George Sherriff's mother. Growing with it were a few depauperate individuals which were basically similar, but much smaller, the leaves only to 3 cm and the solitary, stemless cylindrical corolla tubes 18 mm in length, the limb 12 mm in diameter. These plants were also thought to differ by having a non-mealy and hairy corolla-tube, and so were called *P. ludlowii*.

The coincidence of finding two new very closely related primula species at a single site is so great, and unlikely, that the status of the depauperate *P. ludlowii* deserves close examination. Now that we have the benefit of many years' cultivation of *P. sherriffae*, we know that solitary, and sometimes stemless flowers can be produced, and that the flowers of *P. sherriffae* are often without much, if any, meal. Also, the flower is (invariably?) downy especially at the mouth of the flower, as is described for *P. ludlowii*, but not for *P. sherriffae*. Thus, after a close examination of herbarium material, I have come to the reluctant conclusion that *P. ludlowii* is no more than a depauperate form of *P. sherriffae*, which I am maintaining at varietal rank for the time being.

P. sherriffae is one of the most remarkable, and beautiful, of all primula species, and in this genus the long, jasmine-like corolla-tubes are unique. Presumably, these have evolved to restrict flower-visitors to long-tongued (e.g. sphingid) moths.

It may be that this overspecialization for flower

visitors favoured the evolution of homostylous self-fertility, the only example of this mechanism in the section. The chromosome number of *P. sherriffae* is unknown; it would be interesting to know if it was tetraploid.

VARIATION

- Var. *ludlowii* (Smith) Richards (1993). (*P. ludlowii* Smith, Notes Roy. Bot. Gdn. Edinb. 19: 172 (1936)). Dwarf, stemless and one-flowered. (Fig. Halda: 329.)

CULTIVATION Introduced as seed and dormant plants from Bhutan in 1934 and 1936 (**AM** 1936). Distinctly tender, although it has survived winters outside in Cornwall. Usually grown in a shady, humid and frost-free glasshouse, copiously watered in growth, but almost dry in winter; short-lived, but sets seed regularly, and this was relatively easily raised. Formerly widespread, but in recent years it seems to have lost vigour, perhaps as a result of continued selfing. Until recently, the main stock was maintained by the Royal Botanic Garden, Edinburgh, who had in excess of 20 plants in 1985. This stock was lost in a dry spell in 1990. Seed was retrieved from a seed bank where it has been stored in 1980, and good germination took place in 1992. Not heard of in recent years (2002) but seed should still be in the bank. Neither of the sites for this highly threatened and remarkable species are accessible; it is vital that it should be maintained in cultivation.

Primula soldanelloides Watt, J. Linn. Soc. Bot. 20: 10 (1882)

DESCRIPTION A *tiny creeping* plant with *glabrous*, non-mealy, *deeply divided* spoon-shaped leaves to 1.5 cm; the growth habit strongly resembles members of section Minutissimae such as *P. reptans*. Stem to 4 cm carrying a single disproportionately large crystalline white nodding bell-shaped somewhat zygomorphic flower to 15 mm in diameter; this does somewhat resemble that of a white-flowered *Soldanella*, although the corolla lobes are entire or deeply notched, not fringed. (Photos: 'A Quest of Flowers': 60; Fl. Himalaya (suppl.) 312. Fig. Halda: 332.) (Plate 69.)

DISTRIBUTION From central Nepal eastwards to the Me La on the border between east Bhutan and Tibet, including Sikkim and Chumbi, apparently scarce and scattered.

Rock ledges and cliff faces growing in wet moss, 4300–5000 m.

It is ironic that the type and eponymous species of the section is both relatively little known, and untypical of most of the other species classified with it. In common with the following four species it shares many of the features of section Minutissimae, especially the creeping habit, and tiny divided glabrous leaves. However, the bell-shaped exannulate flowers with entire corolla-lobes are typical of this section.

Introduced from Bhutan in 1949 (LSH 19420, 21197), but apparently very difficult and has never been flowered in cultivation.

Primula sappharina Hook. f. & Thoms, Fl. Brit. India 3: 492 (1882)

DESCRIPTION Similar in growth habit to *P. soldanelloides*, but the leaves have some hairs above, and the wiry scapes of some 4 cm have 1–4 tiny *blue-violet* funnel-shaped flowers only 5 mm long with notched corolla-lobes. (Fig. Halda: 330.) (Plate 70.)

DISTRIBUTION Sikkim, Chumbi and Bhutan, in very wet alpine zones on the south side of the main divide on mossy rocks, 4000–5000 m.

First introduced in 1949 by Ludlow, Sherriff and Hicks (16576), and grew for 3–4 years for the Rentons at Branklyn, but apparently very difficult and never flowered. Collected by AGSES (1983), but seems not to have grown in cultivation. Seed offered by Ghose in 1981–82 proved to be *P. reticulata*.

Primula fea Ward, Notes Roy. Bot. Gdn. Edinb. 15: 302 (1927)

DESCRIPTION Close to *P. sappharina*, but with leaves hairier above, and the usually single bluish-mauve bell is longer (to 10 mm) and has *entire* corolla-lobes. Only known from mossy crevices in granite cliffs at 4700–5000 m on the border between Burma and Tibet (Sengkhu pass). (Fig. Halda: 325.)

Primula flabellifera Smith, Notes Roy. Bot. Gdn. Edinb. 19: 169 (1936)

DESCRIPTION Another close relative of *P. fea* and *P. sappharina,* but with a very distinctive fan-shaped leaf, the broad deeply toothed apex being bluntly rounded or even cut across shear. Flowers 2–4, corolla violet, to 10 mm, the lobes entire. Only known from two passes in the Tsari distrinct of south-east Tibet; mossy boulders in very wet alpine zones, 4700–5000 m. (Fig. Halda: 326.)

Primula jigmediana Smith, Notes Roy. Bot. Gdn. Edinb. 19: 171 (1936)

DESCRIPTION A curious plant, which in many ways is intermediate between sections Minutissimae, Dryadifolia and Soldanelloides, having single annulate *flat-faced* flowers, lilac-blue with a reddish eye, about 10–12 mm in diameter, the corolla-lobes deeply notched, borne on wiry stems of 3 cm; the rosettes of bluntly toothed hairless leaves are only about 2 cm across, so the flower appears disproportionately large. (Fig. Halda: 328.)

DISTRIBUTION Only known from wet rocks on the Me La, central Bhutan, near the Tibet border at 4700 m. Introduced in 1949 (LSH 20681, 21187), but did not thrive.

P. tsongpenii (Dryadifolia) looks similar but with a white 'pom-pom' in the eye of the flower. Several Minutissimae species seem to be related, but those with singly borne rosettes are all heavily mealy. Nevertheless, possibly best placed in that section. Named for Ludlow and Sherriff's good friend, the Maharajah of Bhutan.

Glossary

acaulescent stemless
actinomorphic radially symmetrical
acuminate with a narrow, sharp, drawn-out tip
aestivation becoming dormant in summer
allergenic causing allergic reactions in humans
annulate with a ring-like constriction at the mouth of the corolla
anther that part of the stamen containing the pollen
apomorphic of a character state which is not ancestral but which has evolved subsequent to the origin of the group under discussion
articulated hairs with 'joints', i.e. multicellular
auriculate of bracts with appendages at the base
base chromosome number the lowest common denominator in the chromosome numbers of a group of related plants see p. 30
bract organ subtending an inflorescence, often leafy
bullate of a leaf surface which is reticulate and honeycombed in three dimensions
calyx the whorl of the flower, outside the corolla, forming sepal-lobes, most usually smaller than the corolla and green
candelabroid inflorescence with superimposed whorls of flowers
capitate forming a tight head-like structure
chasmophyte a plant which lives on cliffs
chiasma structure formed between homologous chromosomes at meiosis which allows recombination to occur
chromosome structures found within the nucleus on which the genetic material (DNA) occurs. The number of chromosomes is typical for a species
ciliate marginal hairs, like eye-lashes
circumscissile see **operculate**
clade a branch of a cladogram representing a monophyletic group of organisms
cladistics a method of classification which employs phylogenetic relationships deduced by e.g. resemblances in the DNA as the main source of evidence
cladogram a branching diagram representing the relationships between organisms based on evidence of taxonomic distance (e.g. through resemblances in the DNA) from which phylogenetic inferences can be drawn
cline gradual variation in a genetic feature over distance, for instance frequency of flower colour
clone genetically identical individuals which arise by asexual reproduction, e.g. division
colpae see p. 31
colporae, colporate see p. 31
conduplicate (of leaf vernation) when the leaf margins are folded together adaxially
corolla the inner, coloured whorl of the flower, forming petal-lobes
corolla limb the radiating, distal portion of the corolla, including the petal-lobes
crenate regular rounded tooothing
crenulate smaller regular rounded toothing
cuneate where the leaf lamina narrows obliquely to the stalk
cuticle the outer 'skin' of a plant cell
cytology the study of chromosomes
dehiscence the means by which a capsule, for instance, opens to shed its seeds
diploid with two sets of chromosomes (twice the base number), see p. 30
elliptical narrowly oval
endemic distributionally restricted to a localized area
erose an irregular especially margin or border as if nibbled by an animal
exannulate without an annulus to the flower
exine the outer siliceous wall of a pollen grain

flavonoid pigments, often giving yellow or purple colours
glabrous smooth, lacking hairs
glandular bearing unicellular glands which secrete a sticky substance
glaucous blue-green, 'the colour of Athene's eyes'
glycoprotein a protein associated with a sugar moiety
Gondwanaland the southern continent before the break up of the continents by continental drift
heterophylly bearing two quite distinct types of leaf
heterostyly where plants have either 'pin' or 'thrum' type flowers
heterozygote where an individual possesses two different alleles for a gene, e.g. *Ss*
hexaploid with six sets of chromosomes (six times the base number, see p. 30)
homostyly where plants have only one flower type, with anthers and stigma at the same level
homozygote where an individual possesses only one allele for a gene, e.g. *ss*
hydrophyte water plant
illegitimate where a cross occurs between flowers of the same heterostylous morph
imbricate tightly overlapping in a scale or catkin-like arrangement
inflorescence the flowers and associated organs which occur together on one stem
introgression where hybridization and repeated backcrossing causes the variability of one of the parental species to be increased
inversion where a segment of one homologous chromosome is inverted with respect to the other in such a way that recombination within the inverted segment is restricted
involucre where bracts lie together to form a cup or ruff-like structure
involute (of leaf vernation), inrolled adaxially, see p. 33
IUCN International Union for the Conservation of Nature
keeled folded to form a ridge like a house roof or the bottom of a boat
lanceolate spear-shaped
Laurasia the northern continent before the break-up of the continents by continental drift
legitimate where a cross occurs between flowers of different heterostyly morphs (pin and thrum)
marcescent of persistent dead foliage or bud scales which do not rot
meal the white or yellow crystalline pigments (technically known as farina) typical of many *Primula* species, and composed of flavone (white), hydroxyflavones, dihydroxyflavones such as primetin and trihydroxyflavones such as pulveruletin which are mostly yellow (Harborne, 1968).
meiosis the process of pairing and segregation of chromosomes prior to the sexual process, during which unlinked alleles are sorted by segregation, and linked alleles are recombined by chiasmata
membranous covered by a thin, usually transparent membrane
metacentric of a chromosome, where the centromere takes a central position, often thought to be a primitive condition
micropile the channel in the ovule down which the pollen tube gains access in order to effect fertilization
monocarpic flowering once, then dying
monophyletic plants which share a single evolutionary origin
morph an individual manifestation of a gene, as for instance a 'pin morph' or a 'thrum morph' (plant)
oblate wider than long, flattened at the pole, see p. 31
oblique neither vertical nor horizontal to an axis, thus slanting
obovate egg-shaped, but with blunt ends
octoploid with eight sets of chromosomes (eight times the base number, see p. 30)
operators parts of genes which cause that gene to be expressed
operculate opening as a lid, for instance like a teapot, cut in a circle, so also circumscissile
orbicular rounded and more or less isodiametric
ovate egg-shaped
ovule organ which, after fertilization, develops into a seed
palaeoendemic localized species of ancient origin, representing taxa that were formerly more widespread
palmate with veins radiating from a common point, like fingers from a hand
papillae specialized cells on the stigma which receive pollen grains
papillose covered with small projections
petal lobes segments of the corolla limb, commonly thought of as petals
phyletic see phylogenetic

phylogenetic a classification which attempts to describe evolutionary relationships
pin morph in which the style is long, so that the stigma appears at the mouth of the corolla, and the anthers are inserted in the corolla tube
pinnate with veins or lobes arranged in opposite pairs from a mid-rib, like a feather
pinnatifid where pinnately arranged lobes are not divided as far as the mid-rib
plesiomorphic of a character state, the origin of which predates the group under discussion and so is ancestral to it
polyphyletic a group of plants which have more than one evolutionary stem
polyploid with more than two sets of chromosomes
prolate longer than wide, as in pollen, see p. 31
pubescent shortly and softly hairy
raceme arrangement of flowers in a lax spike
recessive of an allele of a gene which is not expressed in the heterozygous condition, i.e. where *s* is recessive to *S*; genotype *Ss*, phenotype *S*
recombination where segments of chromosomes are swapped at meiosis by the formation of chiasmata
reticulate finely honeycombed, see also **bullate**
revolute (of leaf vernation) rolled back longitudinally, see p. 33
rhizome more or less horizontal root-like stem, at or below surface of soil
rugose three-dimensionally reticulate, see also **bullate**
saccate of bracts, forming a small pouch at the base
scabrid rough, due to short unicellular hairs
sepal-lobes segments of the calyx, commonly thought of as sepals
serrate saw-edged
sister part of the same final clade on the cladogram and thus the most closely related of taxa examined, perhaps inseparable
stalk narrow base to the leaf, or pedicel to the individual flower
stem common stalk (scape) to the flowers of an inflorescence
stephanocolpate pollen with more than four (commonly six) longitudinal grooves which do not meet, see p. 31
stoloniferous bearing slender stems which creep on the soil surface
syncolpate pollen with longitudinal grooves which fuse at the apex (pole), see p. 31
tetraploid with four sets of chromosomes, four times the base number, see p. 30
thrum morph in which the style is short, so that the stigma is included in the corolla tube, and the anthers are positioned at the mouth of the flower
tribe taxonomic rank between genus and family
tristyly heterostylous condition where flowers may have one of three stigma positions, not found in *Primula*
tubercles peg-like extrusions
valvate (of a capsule) opening apically by (five) triangular teeth
vernation (of young leaves) longitudinal alignment, see p. 30
Wallace line hypothetical line running between the islands of south-east Asia which separates Asian and Australasian biogeographical elements
zygomorphic bilaterally rather than radially symmetrical

References

Al Wadi, H. & Richards, A.J. (1992). Palynological variation in *Primula* L. subgenus *Sphondylia* (Duby) Rupr., and its relationship with *Dionysia* Fenzl. *New Phytologist* 121: 303–310.

Al Wadi, H. & Richards, A.J. (1993). Primary homostyly in *Primula* L. subgenus *Sphondylia* (Duby) Rupr. and the evolution of distyly in *Primula*. *New Phytologist* 124: 329–338.

Anderberg, A.A. & El-Ghazaly, G. (2000). Pollen morphology in *Primula* section Carolinella (Primulaceae) and its taxonomic implications. *Nordic Journal of Botany* 20: 5–14.

Anderberg, A.A., Stahl, B. & Kallersjo, M. (1998). Phylogenetic relationships in the Primulales inferred from rbcL sequence data. *Pl. Syst. Evol.* 211: 93–102.

Anderberg, A.A., Trift, I. & Kallersjo, M. (2000). Phylogeny of *Cyclamen* L. (Primulaceae): Evidence from morphology and sequence data from the internal transcribed spacers of nuclear ribosomal DNA. *Pl. Syst. Evol.* 220: 147–160.

Arnold, E.A. (1999). Investigation of a scapeless form of *Primula farinosa*, and related studies. PhD thesis, University of Newcastle, UK.

Arnold, E.A. & Richards, A.J. (1998). On the occurrence of unilateral incompatibility in *Primula* section Aleuritia Duby and the origin of *Primula scotica* Hook. *Bot. J. Linn. Soc.* 128: 359–368.

Baker, K., Richards,A.J. & Tremayne, M. (1994). Fitness constraints on flower number, seed number and seed size in the dimorphic species *Primula farinosa* and *Armeria maritima*. *New Phytol.* 128: 563–570.

Balakrishnan, N.P. (1970). Nomenclatural notes on some flowering plants. II. *J. Bombay Nat. Hist. Soc.* 67: 62–32.

Bentvelzen, P.A.J. (1962). Primulaceae. In: C.G.G. van Steenis, ed. *Flora Malesiana*. Ser. 1, 6: 173–192. Wolters Nordhof, Groningen.

Boyd, M., Silvertown, J. & Tucker, C. (1990). Population ecology of heterostyle and homostyle *Primula vulgaris*: growth, survival and reproduction in field populations. *J. Ecol.*, 78: 799–813.

Bruun, H.G. (1930). The cytology of the genus *Primula*. *Svensk Bot. Tidskr.* 24

Bruun, H.G. (1932). Cytological studies in *Primula*. *Symb. Bot. Upsala,* 1: 1–239.

Bullard, E.R., Shearer, H.D.H., Day, J.D. & Crawford, R.M.M.(1987). Survival and flowering of *Primula scotica* Hook. *J. Ecol.* 75: 589–602.

Cahalan, C. & Gliddon, C. (1985). Genetic neighbourhood sizes in *Primula vulgaris*. *Heredity* 54: 65–70.

Cain, R.B. (1965). The genus *Primula*. *Bull. AGS* 35: 128–171.

Charlesworth, B. & Charlesworth, D. (1979). The maintenance and breakdown of distyly. *Amer. Nat.* 114: 499–513.

Charlesworth, D. & Charlesworth, B. (1979). A model for the evolution of distyly. *Amer. Nat.* 114: 467–498.

Chen, F.H. & Hu, C.M. (1990). Primulaceae. In: *Flora Republicae Popularis Sinicae*, 59 (2). Science Press, Beijing.

Chittenden, R.J. (1928). Notes on species crosses in *Primula, Godetia, Nemophila* and *Phacelia*. *J. Gen.* 19: 285–314.

Crosby, J.L. (1949). Selection of an unfavourable gene-complex. *Evolution* 3: 212–230.

Curtis, J. & Curtis, C.F. (1985). Homostyle primroses revisited. 1. Variation in time and space. *Heredity* 54: 227–234.

Darwin, C. (1877). *The different forms of flowers on plants of the same species.* John Murray, London.

De Winton, D. & Haldane, J.B.S. (1935). The genetics of *Primula sinensis*. III. Linkage in the diploid. *J. Gen.* 31: 67–100.

Dowrick, V.P.J. (1956). Heterostyly and homostyly in *Primula obconica*. *Heredity* 10: 219–236.

Eisikowitch, D. & Woodell, S.R.J. (1975). The effect of water on pollen germination in two species of *Primula*. *Evolution* 28: 692–694.

Ennos, R.A., Cowie, N.R., Legg & C.J, Sydes, C. (1999). Which measures of genetic variation are relevant to plant conservation? A case study of *Primula scotica*. In: *The role of genetics in conserving small populations*, ed. Tew, T.E. *et al.*, 73–79. Peterborough, JNCC.

Ernst, A. (1933, 1936). Weitere untersuchungen zur phananalyse, zum fertilitats-problem und zur genetik heterostyler primeln. 1. *Primula viscosa*. II. *Primula hortensis* Wettst. *Arch. Julius Klaus-stiftung Vererbungsf.* 8: 1–215; 11: 1–280.

Ernst, A. (1953). "Basic numbers" und polyploidie und ihre bedeutung fur das heterostylie-problem. *Arch. Julius Klaus-stiftung Vererbungsf.* 28: 1–159.

Ernst, A. (1955). Self-fertility in monomorphic primulas. *Genetica* 27: 391–448.

Fang, W.P. (1956). Primulas collected from Szechwan in recent expeditions. *Acta Univ. Szechwan* 1: 61–125. (n.b., this article is not availible in the UK).

Federov, A.A. (1952). *Primula*. In: Komarov, V.L. *et al.* eds., *Flora SSSR*, 18: 85–155, 53—535 (in translation by N. Landau). *Izd. Akad. Nauk. SSSR*, Moscow & Leningrad.

Fenderson, G.M. (1986). *A Synoptic Guide to the Genus Primula*. Allen Press, Lawrence, Kansas.

Fletcher, H.R. (1975). *A quest of flowers*. 387 pp. University of Edinburgh Press, Edinburgh.

Ganders, F.R. (1974). Disassortative pollination in the distylous plant *Jepsonia heterandra*. *Can. J. Bot.* 54: 2401–2406.

Ganders, F.R. (1979). The biology of heterostyly. *N.Z.J.Bot.*17: 607–635.

Glover, B.J. & Abbott, R.J. (1995). Low genetic diversity in the Scottish endemic *Primula scotica*. Hook. *New Phytol.* 129: 147–153.

Gould, S. (1982). Primulaceae. In: Hara, H., Chater, A.O. & Williams, L.H.J. eds., *An enumeration of the flowering plants of Nepal* 3: 61–75. British Museum (Nat. Hist.) London.

Halda, J.J. (1992). *The genus Primula in cultivation and in the wild*. 364 pp. Tethys books, Denver, Col.

Handel-Mazzetti, H. von (1929). The natural habitats of Chinese Primulas. *J. Roy. Hort. Soc.* 54: 51–62 (Report of the fourth Primula Conference, 1928).

Harbourne, J.S. (1968). Comparative biochemistry of the flavonoids-VII. Correlations between flavonoid pigmentation and systematics in the family Primulaceae. *Phytochemistry* 7: 1215–1230.

Hildebrand, F. (1863). *De la variation des animaux et des plantes à l'état domestique*. C. Reinwald, Paris.

Holmgren N.H. & Kelso, S. (2001). *Primula cusickiana* and its varieties. *Brittonia* 53: 154–156.

Hu, C.M. (1990). A new species of *Primula* from Thailand with critical notes on the section Carolinella. *Nord. J. Bot.* 10: 399–401.

Hultgaard U-M. 1990. Polyploidy and differentiation in north American species of *Primula* section Aleuritia. *Sommerfeltia* 11: 117–135.

Hultgaard U-M. 1993. *Primula scandinavica* and *P. stricta* – patterns of distribution, variation, reproductive strategies and migration. *Opera Botanica* 121: 35–43.

Kelso, S. (1987a). *Primula tschuktschorum* and *Primula eximia* (Primulaceae, section Crystallophlomis): a distylous species and its homostylous derivative from the Bering Strait region, Alaska. *Brittonia* 39: 63–72.

Kelso, S. (1987b). *Primula anvilensis* (Primulaceae): a new species from northwestern Alaska. *Syst. Bot.* 12: 9–13.

Kelso, S. (1991a). Taxonomy and biogeography of *Primula* sect. Cuneifolia (Primulaceae) in north America. *Madrono* 38: 37–44.

Kelso, S. (1991b). Taxonomy of *Primula* sects. Aleuritia and Armerina in north America. *Rhodora* 93: 67–99.

Kelso, S. (1992). The genus *Primula* as a model for evolution in the Alaskan flora. *Arctic & Alpine Res.* 24: 82–87.

Kurian, V. & Richards, A.J. (1997). A new recombinant in the heteromorphy 'S' supergene in *Primula*. *Heredity* 78: 383–390.

Lamond, J. (1978). *Primula*. In: P.H.Davis, ed.,

Flora of Turkey and the East Aegean Islands 6: 112–120. University of Edinburgh Press, Edinburgh.

Lewis. D. & Jones D.A. (1992). The genetics of heterostyly, in *Evolution and Function of Heterostyly* 129–150 (ed. S.C.H. Barrett). Springer-Verlag, Berlin.

Lloyd, D.G. & Webb, C.J. (1992). The evolution of heterostyly, in *Evolution and Function of Heterostyly* 151–178 (ed. S.C.H. Barrett). Springer-Verlag, Berlin.

Lunn, J. (1991). Wild primulas of western America. *Bull. Amer. Rock Gdn. Soc.* 49: 125–131.

Marsden-Jones, E.M. & Turrill, W.B. (1944). Experiments on colour and heterostyly in the primrose, *Primula vulgaris* Huds. *New Phytol.* 43: 130–134.

Mast, A., Kelso, S., Richards, A.J., Lang, D.J., Feller, D.M.S. & Conti, E. (2001). Phylogenetic relationships in *Primula* L. and related genera (Primulaceae) based on noncoding chloroplast DNA. *Int. J. Plant Sci.* 162: 1381–1400.

Mather, K. (1950). The genetical architecture of heterostyly in *Primula sinensis*. *Evolution* 4: 340–352.

Mather, K. & De Winton, D. (1941). Adaptation and counteradaptation of the breeding system in *Primula*. *Ann. Bot.* II 5: 297–311.

Mattson, O. (1983). The significance of exine oils in the initial interaction between pollen and stigma in *Armeria maritima*. In: Mulcahy, D.L. & Ottaviano, E. eds., *Pollen biology and applications for plant breeding*, pp. 257–267. Elsevier, New York.

Mazer, S.J. & Hultgaard, U-M. (1993). Variation and covariation among floral traits within and among four species of northern European *Primula* (Primulaceae). *Amer. J. Bot.* 80: 474–485.

McKee, J. & Richards, A.J. (1998). The effect of temperature on reproduction in five *Primula* species. *Annals of Botany* 82: 359–374.

Miller, J., Litvak, M. & Kelso, S. (1994). Comparative reproductive biology of two alpine primrose species. *Arctic and Alpine Research* 26: 297–303.

Nasir, Y. (1984). Primulaceae. In: Nasir, Y. & Ali, S. eds., *Flora of Pakistan* 157: 1–103. Pakistan Agricultural research council, Islamabad.

Ohwi, J. (1965). *Primula*, in *Flora of Japan* pp: 719–721 (in translation by Ohwi, J., Meyer, F. & Walker, E.). Smithsonian Institute, Washington.

Oogaki, K., Taril, T. and Hara, K. (1992). *An invitation to the world of Japanese Primulas*. Publ. Matsumoto Sakurasoh Primula Club, Matsumoto Nagano, Japan.

Piper, J. & Charlesworth, B. (1986). The evolution of distyly in *Primula vulgaris*. *Bot. J. Linn. Soc.* 29: 123–137.

Piper, J., Charlesworth, B. & Charlesworth, D. (1986). Breeding system evolution in *Primula vulgaris* and the role of reproductive assurance. *Heredity* 56: 207–217.

Polunin, O. & Stainton, A. (1984). *Flowers of the Himalaya*. 580 pp. Oxford University Press, Oxford.

Richards, A.J. (1977). An account of *Primula* section Petiolares in cultivation. *J. Scot. Rock Gdn. Club* 15: 177–214.

Richards, A.J. (1988). Petiolarid Primulas. *Plantsman* 7: 217–232.

Richards, A.J. (1989). *Primulas of the British Isles*. 24 pp. Shire, Prices Risborough.

Richards, A.J. (1993). *Primula*. 299 pp. B.T. Batsford, London.

Richards, A.J. (1997). *Plant Breeding Systems*. 2nd ed. 529 pp. Chapman Hall, London & New York.

Richards, A.J. (1998). Lethal linkage and its role in the evolution of plant breeding systems. In: S.J. Owens and P.J. Rudall (eds.) *Reproductive Biology*. pp 71–83. Royal Botanic Gardens, Kew.

Richards, A.J. (2002). Pin and thrum flowers in *Primula*; crosses, seed-setting and vigour. *7th International Rock Garden Conference Report, Edinburgh*, 2001.

Richards, A.J. & Mitchell, J. (1990). The control of incompatibility in distylous *Pulmonaria affinis* Jordan (Boraginaceae). *Bot. J. Linn. Soc.* 104: 369–380.

Robinson, M.A. (1990). *Primulas. The Complete Guide*. 271 pp. Crowood Press, Swindon.

Rosvik, A. (1969). Investigations on petal epidermis and its bearing on taxonomy in Primulaceae. *Aarb. Univ. Bergen, Mat.-Nat.* 1968 (3): 1–32.

Schwarz, O. (1964). Primulas on the edge of the desert. *Bull. AGS* 32: 283–290.

Schwarz, O. (1968). Beitrage zur kenntnis der gattung *Primula*. *Wiss. Z. Friedrich Schiller-Univ. Jena, Mat. Nat. Reihe* 17: 307–332.

Shivanna, K.R., Heslop-Harrison, J. & Heslop-Harrison, Y. (1983). Heterostyly in *Primula* 3. Pollen water economy: a factor in the intramorph incompatibility response. *Protoplasma* 117: 175–184.

Smith, G.F., Burrow, B. & Lowe, D.B. (1984). *Primulas of Europe and North America*. 251 pp. Alpine Garden Society, Woking.

Smith, W.W. & Fletcher, H.R. (1941). The genus *Primula*: section Candelabra. *Trans. Bot. Soc. Edinb*. 33: 122–181.

Smith, W.W. & Fletcher, H.R. (1942a). The genus Primula, sections Amethystina, Minutissima, Bella, Muscarioides. *Trans. Bot. Soc. Edinb*. 33: 209–194.

Smith, W.W. & Fletcher, H.R. (1942b). The section Soldanelloideae (sic) of the genus *Primula*. *J. Linn. Soc. Bot*. 52: 321–335.

Smith, W.W. & Fletcher, H.R. (1942c). The genus *Primula,* section Nivales. *Trans. Roy. Soc. Edinb*. 60: 563–627.

Smith, W.W. & Fletcher, H.R. (1943a). The genus *Primula*: section Farinosae. *Trans. Roy. Soc. Edinb*. 61: 1–69.

Smith, W.W. & Fletcher, H.R. (1943b). The genus *Primula*: sections Sikkimensis, Souliei and Rotundifolia. *Trans. Bot. Soc. Edinb*. 33: 431–487.

Smith, W.W. & Fletcher, H.R. (1944a). The genus *Primula*: section Petiolares. *Trans. Roy. Soc. Edinb*. 61: 271–314.

Smith, W.W. & Fletcher, H.R. (1944b). The genus *Primula:* sections Cortusoides, Malvacea, Pycnoloba, Dryadifolia, Capitatae. *Trans. Bot. Soc. Edinb*. 34: 55–158.

Smith, W.W. & Fletcher, H.R. (1946). The genus *Primula:* sections Obconica, Sinenses, Reinii, Pinnatae, Malacoides, Bullatae, Carolinella, Grandis and Denticulata. *Trans. Roy. Soc. Edinb*. 61: 415–478.

Smith, W.W. & Fletcher, H.R. (1948a). The genus *Primula*: section Vernales. *Trans. Bot. Soc. Edinb*. 34: 402–468.

Smith, W.W. & Fletcher, H.R. (1948b). The genus *Primula*: sections Cuneifolia, Floribundae, Parryi, and Auricula. *Trans. Roy. Soc. Edinb*. 61: 631–686.

Spanowsky, W. (1962). Die bedeutung der pollen morphologie fur die taxonomie der Primulaceae-Primuloideae. *Feddes rep. spec. nov. reg. veg*. 65: 149–213.

Stainton, A. (1988). Supplement to the Flowers of the Himalaya. 87 pp. Oxford University Press, Bombay, Delhi, Calcutta, Madras.

Tremayne, M.A. & Richards, A.J. (1993). Homostyly and herkogamous variation in *Primula* L. section Muscarioides Balf. f. *Evolutionary trends in plants* 7: 67–72.

Tremayne, M.A. & Richards, A.J. (1997). The effects of breeding system and seed weight on plant fitness in *Primula scotica* Hooker. In: *The role of genetics in conserving small populations,* ed. Tew, T.E. *et al.*, 133–142. Peterborough, JNCC.

Tremayne, M. & Richards, A.J. (2000). Seed weight and seed number affect subsequent fitness in outcrossing and selfing *Primula* species. *New Phytol*. 148: 127–142.

Trift, I. (2001). *Phylogenetic relationships within non-monophyletic Primulaceae*. Postgraduate thesis, Department of Botany, University of Stockholm, Sweden.

Trift, I., Kallersjo, M. & Anderberg, A.A. (2001). The monophyly of *Primula* (Primulaceae) evaluated by analysis of sequences from the chloroplast gene *rbc*L. Unpublished MS.

Valentine, D.H. & Lamond, J. (1978). The taxonomy and nomenclature of *Primula amoena*. *Notes Roy. Bot. Gdn. Edinb*. 36: 39–42.

Watson, J.W. (ed.) (1967). *Pictorial Dictionary of the cultivated species of Primula*. 2nd Ed. American Primrose, Primula and Auricula Society Quarterly 25 (3).

Webster, M.A. & Grant, C.J. (1990). The inheritance of calyx morph variants in *Primula vulgaris* (Huds.). *Heredity* 64: 121–124.

Wedderburn, F.M. (1988). A comparison of heteromorphic incompatibilities in Primula. Ph. D. thesis, University of Newcastle upon Tyne, UK.

Wedderburn, F.M. & Richards, A.J. (1990). Variation in within-morph incompatibility inhibition sites in heteromorphic *Primula* L. *New Phytol*. 116: 149–162.

Wedderburn, F.M. & Richards, A.J. (1992). Secondary homostyly in Primula L. section Aleuritia Duby. *New Phytol*. 121: 649–655.

Wendelbo, P. (1961a). Studies in Primulaceae. I. A monograph of the genus *Dionysia*. *Aarb. Univ. Bergen, Mat.-Nat*. 1: 1961 (3): 1–83.

Wendelbo, P. (1961b). Studies in Primulaceae. II. An account of *Primula* subgenus *Sphondylia* with a review of the subdivisions of the genus. *Aarb.*

Univ. Bergen, Mat.-Nat. (1961) (11): 1–49.
Wendelbo, P. (1961c). Studies in Primulaceae. III. On the genera related to *Primula* with special reference to their pollen morphology. *Aarb. Univ. Bergen, Mat.-Nat.* 1961 (19): 1–31.
Wolf, P.G. & Sinclair, R.B. (1997). Highly differentiated populations of the narrow endemic plant Maguire primrose (*Primula maguirei*). *Conservation Biology* 11: 375–381.
Woodell, S.R.J. (1960). Studies in British Primulas. VII, VIII. Development of seed from reciprocal crosses between *P. vulgaris* Huds. and *P. veris* L., *P. vulgaris* and *P. elatior* (L.) Hill and *P. veris* and *P. elatior*. *New Phytol.* 59: 302–322.

Measurements Conversion Table

m	ft
50	164
100	328
200	656
300	984
400	1312
500	1640
600	1969
700	2297
800	2625
900	2953
1000	3281
1500	4921
2000	6562
2500	8202
3000	9843
3500	11,483
4000	13,123
4500	14,764
5000	16,404

Conversion Formulae

	multiply by
mm to inches	0.0394
cm to inches	0.3937
m to feet	3.281
m to yards	1.094
km to miles	0.6214
km^2 to square miles	0.3861

Index of Plant Names

Page numbers in bold refer to the main entry for a species. The species entries that do not have bold page references are synonyms.